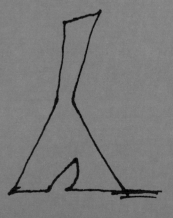

More of a visual jackdaw than a compulsive collector, I acquire stuff. Things which catch my eye. Ammonites in Morocco, votive offerings in Sicily, paper cuts in Hong Kong, glass pens in Tokyo. That sort of thing. I'm intrigued by useless information such as that eight per cent of the population is left-handed, that giraffes only sleep five minutes every twenty-four hours, that Italians kiss twice, the Swiss three times. I enjoy encountering incongruities – a sign announcing '*Blue Movies in Full Colour*'.

Like *Wunderkammern*, those eighteenth-century glass-fronted cabinets which displayed curios, this book is a collection of shards. In an unmarked field it is easy to wander …

Most books written on visual matters are authored by those who analyse rather than experience. Many are hard work and littered with academic jargon – autistic tendencies, cognitive expectancy, formative causation. They are concerned with the mechanics rather than the thoughts, with the match rather than the fire.

This book attempts to open windows to glimpse views rather than dissect the pictures on the wall. To look at things from unlikely angles. References to sources are occasionally provided to keep you going. The book has no thesis, is neither a whodunnit nor a how-to-do-it, has no beginning, middle or end. It's a journey without a destination.

Alan Fletcher

Michel de Montaigne

'I quote others only the better to express myself.'

'What is the use of a book … without pictures or conversations?' asked Alice

CHRESTOMATHY   Anthology of passages compiled to help those engaged in learning a language.

'A book is a product of another self to the one we display in our habits, in Society, in our vices.' *Marcel Proust*

This is a publication of conversations with New York City cab drivers. The blurb states: 'Forget that ashram! Fire your shrink! You can get all the spiritual healing, chakra alignment, and relationship counselling you need right here – real advice from the fellows in the front seat.'

a history lesson

ENGLAND, THAT WAS CALLED BRITANNIA. THEN THE JEWISH TRIBES CAME IN AND THEY WERE YIDDISH AND THEY USED A LOT OF "ISH" SO THEY CALLED THEM BRITISH.

Risa Mickenberg. *Taxi Driver Wisdom*. Chronicle Books (San Francisco 1996)

Thomas Mann   'We are no more than God's curiosity about himself.'

We are made of stardust.

The history of the universe is engraved within us. We are children of the stars from the very first moment of the Big Bang whence we came.

The universe is 12 billion years old, give or take a few million years. The world, a tiny satellite to a marginal star on the edge of this universe, is 4.5 billion years old. After an eternity of boiling gas and molten material the elements coalesced into earth, air, water. Life began in this primordial soup about 3.5 billion years ago. One billion years after that cellular organisms appeared and the next five-sixths of life belongs to them. 500 million years ago amphibians crawled onto land.

The southern hemisphere was occupied by Gondwana, a landmass which comprised Australia, Antarctica, Africa, India and South America. Adrift elsewhere were bits and pieces of North America, Europe and Asia.

About 270 million years ago [another source says 200] all the pieces stuck together to form one huge supercontinent. This is called Pangaea, and was surrounded by a vast ocean called Panthalassa. After more millions and millions of years Pangaea imperceptibly began to float apart at the rate of an inch a year – until all the pieces ended up where they are today.

75 million years ago an asteroid crashed into the world and lofted dust and debris which blocked out sunlight. This drastically altered the climate, destroyed plant life and killed off 95 per cent of all living species – including the dinosaurs. The upside was that a very few mammals – previously dinosaur fodder – managed to survive. Without these ancestral forebears we would not be here.

Such global cataclysms have happened several times since life began, although not always due to asteroids. A catastrophic volcanic eruption took place in Sumatra some 75,000 years ago. This showered ashes all over the world severely affecting temperatures and ocean levels, and decimated the burgeoning human race which became reduced to a few thousand.

In consequence astronomers on a mountain in Arizona are calculating where and when the next object from outer space is likely to crash into us. This is *Project Spacewatch*, although for the life of me, so to speak, I can't imagine what they're going to do once it's on the way. The current prediction is that it's bound to happen within the next 100 years. The International Astronomical Union reckon it's going to be on Saturday 21 September 2030 – you'd better put that in your diary.

Anyway, after more millions of years, some of the small mammals mentioned ended up as gorillas. Eight million years ago the common forebear of humans and chimps twigged off that evolutionary line. And early man diverged from chimps about 350,000 generations ago. Indeed we are more closely related to chimps than chimps are to gorillas, mice to rats, or turkeys to chickens.

Indigenous peoples – Oriental, African, Caucasian – were defined 50,000 years ago. Civilizations, agriculture and systematic religions appeared within the last 10,000 years, industry within the last 500 and man set foot on the moon on 21 July 1969.

A brief synopsis, but adequate to raise the question: Are we pawns of destiny or wildly improbable flukes?

The five kingdoms of life: Bacteria, Protista, Fungi, Plants and Animals.

Oliver Sachs [about a remote island in Micronesia]: 'The sense of deep time brings a deep peace with it, a detachment from the timescale, the urgencies, of daily life. Seeing these volcanic islands and coral atolls, and wandering, above all, through this cycad forest on Rota, has given me an intimate feeling of the antiquity of the earth, and the slow, continuous processes by which different forms of life evolve and come into being ... I feel part of a larger, calmer identity; I feel a profound sense of being at home, sort of companionship with the earth.'[1]

James Lovelock: 'The planet is not inanimate. It is a living organism. The earth, its rocks, oceans, atmosphere and all living things are one great organism. A coherent holistic system of life, self-regulating, self-changing.'

W.N.P. Barbellion: 'I take a jealous pride in my Simian ancestry. I like to think that I was once a magnificent hairy fellow living in the trees and that my frame has come down through geological time via sea jelly and worms and Amphioxus, Fish, Dinosaurs, and Apes. Who would exchange these for the pallid couple in the Garden of Eden?'

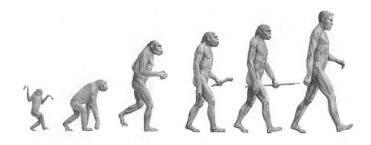

1. Oliver Sachs. *The Island of the Colour-blind*. Picador (London 1996)   **Illustration.** BSP/Science Photo Library

Note. When Russian astronaut Yuri Gagarin orbited the earth on 12 April 1961 he became the first human to physically see planet earth. The object illustrated opposite, the size of a not-so-old English penny, is where we're at. On this tiny disc, or on the reverse side, is where you were born, grew up, fell in love, breathe, eat, see sunsets, play, work, dream and die. Indeed it's where you are now while looking at this page. I wouldn't be surprised if we are really no more than a twinkle in God's eye.

Out of Africa

Originally there were three – possibly more – species of early man.

Homo Habilis (handyman) who could make crude tools and was more than ape and yet not man. He was followed by *Homo Erectus* (upright man) who was the first to walk the earth and was our distant ancestor. A recent find indicates that a few could still have been around some 50,000 years ago which according to *Newsweek* is 'like finding a family of *Neanderthals* living in 1996'. Anyway that left the world to *Homo Sapiens* (thinkers), as we label ourselves, and our cousins the *Neanderthals*.

Neanderthals were a rough crowd. As an anthropologist suggested : 'if an early man sat next to you on a train you'd change seats but if it was a *Neanderthal* you'd change trains.' Not that they were stupid. They even anticipated afterlife by burying their dead in a foetal position – an imaginative leap of some magnitude since they had no evidence to support the idea. *Neanderthals* became extinct around 30,000 years ago.

There are two principal theories as to where we come from and how we developed into who we are :

The *'Out of Africa'* hypothesis, based on gene reading, claims that everyone in the world outside Africa is descended from a group of about a hundred individuals.[1] This group of *Homo Sapiens* made its way out of Africa into the Middle East roughly 100,000 years ago – although some say much earlier – and slowly spread out, reaching Australia 45,000 years later and America, via Alaska, in the last Ice Age some 15,000 years ago. By 1000 AD they reached the outermost islands of the Pacific and Indian Oceans. Only a handful of remote mid-Atlantic islands, including St Helena and the Azores, remained uninhabited until recent times.

The *'Candelabra'* hypothesis holds that *Homo Erectus* migrated from Africa at various times and evolved separately into Caucasians, Asians, Aborigines and Africans. One piece of evidence cited is stone tools found in the bleak end of Siberia which are claimed to be two million years old. If this is true, then it would put the *'Out of Africa'* hypothesis in deep trouble.

Either way, as physiologist Jared Diamond has pointed out: 'History unfolded differently on different continents because of differences among continental environments, not because of biological differences among people.'[2]

The colourful character pictured opposite is a citizen of Papua New Guinea. These ancient peoples, who live in the inaccessible highlands of an island six times the size of Britain, were only discovered in the 1930s. They have travelled from the Stone Age to the Space Age in less than 70 years.

There is more genetic variation in almost any single African tribe than in all the rest of the world put together. The explanation is that Africa is where early humans evolved over the past million to a million and a half years. Plenty of time for genetic variations to develop. Whereas the rest of the world has only been populated during the last 100,000 years.

Photograph. Malcolm Kirk   1. Steve Jones. *The Language of Genes.* HarperCollins (London 1993)   2. Jared Diamond. *Guns, Germs and Steel.* Jonathan Cape (London 1998)

Once upon a time Adam and Eve lived in Africa but in the anthropological story they never met. Today their closest living relatives are the Khoisan peoples also known as Bushmen or Hottentots; they live in the Kalahari Desert. The Khoisan have inherited more of Adam's genes than any other ethnic group, a scientifically verifiable fact since the Y chromosome is only inherited by sons from fathers.

Similarly DNA mitochondria is only passed down by the mother and the result of a gene analysis covering Australian Aborigines, Danish housewives and Patagonian Indians also suggests that every single living person is descended from one African Eve. Furthermore it is also highly probable that you, the reader, share with your neighbour an ancestor who lived within the last 500 years.[1]

OETZI TO MARIE MOSELY

OETZI, or 'The Iceman', who died aged around fifty is 5,000 years old. He was discovered beneath the ice in the Alps in the 1980s. MARIE MOSELY, who lives in Bournemouth in the south of England, has inherited more of OETZI's genes than anyone else. The last link in a 200-generation line leading back to an ancestor who lived 1,000 years before Stonehenge was built.

OETZI was found frozen along with his quiver of arrows and copper axe. He suffered from chilblains and arthritis, and had seventy tattoos. These pinpoint the locations used by the acupuncturist today. [SEE P329]. After OETZI's discovery ten women contacted Innsbruck University asking for donations of his frozen sperm. They were refused. Perhaps unfortunately, because MARIE MOSELY says she's decided not to have children. Not that it matters really, because as J.B.S. Haldane remarked, he would happily lay down his life for eight of his cousins since they collectively possessed more of his genes than he did.

In the 1990s archaeologists found an ancient skeleton in Somerset which they christened CHEDDAR MAN as he comes from the same place as the cheese. He is 4,000 years older than OETZI. Lord Bath called up the researchers after the discovery – which was on his estate – to ask if they could do a test to see if he was a descendant. He wasn't, but his butler was. A local history teacher is also a direct descendant and his wife predictably remarked that he likes his steaks rare. That aside, imagine the personal resonance of discovering a relative so far back in the roster of humankind. Somerset must be a nice place. The family has been hanging around there for thousands and thousands of years.

Palaeontologists, fossil experts, inform us that 99 per cent of all the species which have lived on earth since the world began are now extinct. Obviously we too are an endangered species, and MARIE ain't helping.

I usually carry a notebook, particularly when travelling. These are some of the ancestral types I've noted around the world in terminals, tea-rooms, cafés, pubs, bars, hotel lobbies, conferences, planes, trains and beaches.

1. Richard Dawkins. *River Out of Eden*. Weidenfeld & Nicolson (London 1995)

> **a human is
> an arboreal animal
> which makes
> itself at home in
> genealogical trees.**
>
> [Ambrose Bierce]

The Atavar:

The shuffling of genes
in each new generation
can sometimes throw
up an echo of our
ancient heritage. One
extreme – only fifty have
been recorded since
medieval times – are
those born covered with
a thick coat of hair like
a chimp. This is an
engraving of one such
unfortunate: the
Russian Andrien
Jeftichew.

A similar atavistic
visitation was Caesar's
war horse, and
Alexander the Great's
some 200 years before
that. Both steeds had
toes instead of hooves.
Even today horses still
retain remnants of
ancient toes.

Although we share 99.6 per cent of our make-up with chimps, for most people the differences obscure the similarities. Chimps live in a non-stop orgy of indiscriminate copulation (several times an hour) and one might assume that nothing else crossed their minds. However (in between) they reason, plan, trade, work, fight and play, are affectionate, bear grudges. They indulge in cannibalism, have a social hierarchy, exercise proprietorial rights and have an incest taboo.* They live in small groups and dislike strangers, although that doesn't inhibit them getting a leg over when given the chance. One of nature's ploys, occasional sexual transgression helps avoid genetic stagnation.

Politicians know *esprit de corps* can be engendered by fuelling inbuilt hostility towards minorities and strangers. People everywhere are similarly disposed. Allocating each other unfavourable features helps exaggerate the differences. Colour of skin, shape of nose, eating habits, social mores, religious belief. The list is as thick as it is long. It's all in our blueprint. As someone mischievously commented, those with brown hair owe it to their monkey ancestors who could hide from predators among the coconuts.

Hostility hardwiring, combined with ignorance, stupidity, intolerance and politics, produces bigotry. One tribe against another. Jew versus Muslim, Protestant versus Catholic, Serb versus Croat. However, we no longer live in isolated groups and strategies for survival must change – so must we.

During 1940 Saul Steinberg graduated as *Dottore in Architettura* in Milan. On his diploma awarded by Victor Emmanuel III, King of Italy, King of Albania and (thanks to Mussolini) Emperor of Ethiopia, was written: *Saul Steinberg, di razza Ebraica*. '… although I was a *Dottore* I could be boycotted from practising, since I am a Jew. The beauty for me is that this diploma was given by the King: but he is no longer King of Italy. He is no more King of Albania. He is not even the Emperor of Ethiopia. And I am no architect. The only thing that remains is *razza Ebraica*!' Steinberg left for the United States via Portugal, with a passport which he had doctored with his own rubber stamp.[1]

Statistics in 1996 revealed that in that year there were 41 armed conflicts spanning five continents. Soldiers outnumbered doctors and educators by six to one. Fewer than 12 national and sovereign governments were in power because a majority of voters put them there. And only seven of these recognized and guaranteed ethnic rights, cultural plurality, freedom of action and speech.

We have too high an opinion of ourselves. We align ourselves with the angels instead of the primates.

---

* Taboo is probably the only Tongan word (I'm not sure about tattoo) to have entered English. However, few would guess the number of incest taboos listed in The Church of England's *Table of Kindred and Affinity*. They appear in the *Book of Common Prayer*. I know because I passed the time trying to fathom them out at a funeral … 'wife's daughter's daughter, son's daughter's husband'. God knows how chimps figured all this out.

1. Robert Hughes. *Nothing if not Critical*. Penguin (London 1992)

'Man did not weave the web of life, he is merely a strand in it. Whatever he does to the web, he does to himself.'
Chief Seattle, Amerindian

'Why the toil, yearning, honesty, aesthetics, exaltation, love, hate, deceit, brilliance, hubris, humility, shame, and stupidity that collectively define our species?'
Edward O. Wilson

'... all behaviour is an interaction between nature and nurture, whose contributors are as inseparable as the length and width of a rectangle in determining its area.'
Steven Pinker

One of a hundred flags designed to represent the world – displayed in the Polish Pavilion at the Expo Seville in 1990.

At first
Senseless as beasts
I gave men sense
Possessed them of mind ...
In the beginning, seeing,
they saw amiss,
and hearing, heard not,
but like phantoms huddled
In dreams, the perplexed
story of their days
Confounded.

Aeschylus. *Prometheus Bound*

Umberto Eco   'By means of the sign man frees himself from the here and now for abstraction.'

Quantum Leap

The term was coined by physicist Niels Bohr in 1913 to describe how the electrons which zip around in atoms can instantaneously switch from one orbit to another without physically passing between the two.

'How many "faces" lie hidden, waiting for the time when curious eyes will find them in their secret places. In the heart of a leaf or the bark of a tree. In a frozen pond or the turning sea. In the twist of a chair or the look of a key or the shrivelled skin of an elephant's knee.'

Irwin Dermer

'Beasts abstract not,' wrote John Locke. Although not altogether correct, he highlighted the fact that man's use of symbols to make sense of the world distinguishes him from roughly a million species and the other hundred and ninety-two different kinds of ape and monkey.

Symbols are the instruments which convert raw intelligence into culture. Without them, explained Lewis Mumford, 'man's life would be one of immediate appetites, immediate sensations, limited to a past shorter than his own lifetime, at the mercy of a future he could never anticipate, never prepare for. In such a world, out of hearing would be out of reach, and out of sight would be out of mind.'

Whether it all happened by a slow dawning consciousness, or through a series of spontaneous mental sparks which ignited a dormant imagination, at some point the mindless became mindful. Perhaps blankly gazing into a fire someone, somewhere, sometime, suddenly saw a face in the flickering flames. At that moment matter became mind and man stepped through the looking glass.

Being conscious of self, man was able to invent languages to communicate thoughts, work his environment, create concepts to express ideas, and images to identify the supernatural forces which surrounded him.

Seeing God in a tree he could summon him forth in a totem pole.

Joyce Kilmer: 'Poems are made by fools like me, But only God can make a tree.'

Man invented things by imposing a shape on nature.

(Moulding, Weaving, Carving, Building, Painting)

'Art is I ... science is we.' *Claude Bernard*

'Science is spectrum analysis; art is photosynthesis.' *Karl Kraus*

Man discovered things by revealing the pattern of nature.

(Cutting, Splitting, Skinning, Crushing, Heating)

'The first real civilization of Europe came into being in the Aegean around 2000 BC. First in Crete, in the culture known as Minoan, and then in mainland Greece, in the settlements termed Mycenaean, places are seen, with sophisticated products of skilled craftsmen, and numerous other indications of a complex and highly organized society which we term a civilization.' *Colin Renfrew*

Henry Ford: 'History is bunk!'

'The concept of culture leapt fully armed from the head of Johann Gottfried Herder in the mid-eighteenth century, and has been embroiled in battles ever since. Kultur, for Herder, is the life-blood of a people, the flow of moral energy that holds society intact. Zivilisation, by contrast, is the veneer of manners, law and technical know-how. Nations may share a civilization; but they will always be distinct in their culture, since culture defines what they are.' *Roger Scruton*

Goethe: 'He who cannot draw on three thousand years is living from hand to mouth.'

MOONSHINE

Will Burtin: 'With the first step by which the first man made the first human footprint on the surface of the moon, mankind became conscious of a new era in its evolution. It is difficult to think of an equally momentous event in human history which so convincingly demonstrated what man can accomplish when he has a plan by which he designs the organisation, materials, power resources and a multitude of devices that can transport his functioning body from its earth home to a far-away point in universal space and back.
The significance of this epochal event was further magnified by a sophisticated communication technology which – at the instant it occurred – encircled the earth with the images and sounds of man's first advance into a new future.
Regardless of age, nationality, social class or political system, all people watching television screens saw themselves and felt like this first man. Television turned his individual feelings and observations into an earthwide mass communication experience.'

The spectacular 20,000-year-old cave paintings at Lascaux were discovered in 1940. After the war anthropologist Abbé Breuil petitioned UNESCO for funds to study them but was turned down on the grounds that they were fraudulent. Cartoonists are responsible for our picture of 'early man as a cow-browed, club-wielding lout, hunkered beside a fire looking dazed and immensely stupid'.[1] However, besides bludgeoning each other, rape and cannibalism, Stone Age peoples also placed flowers in graves, wore ornaments, carved figures, made music, painted pictures, and had a notion of time and season by tracking the stars. The differences between primitive and civilized are marginal. Certainly we have acquired more social graces and made breathtaking scientific and technological advances. On his way to the moon Buzz Aldrin exclaimed, 'Got the earth right out our front window,' thus becoming the first human to articulate our capability to literally cut loose from our roots. The process is accelerating. The computer is fast becoming an extension of the brain, electronics of the imagination, chemicals of the body. Pharmaceutical farming envisages asexual cows feeding on engineered grass under the shade of clonal trees. Soon we will end up unable to distinguish between the synthetic and the real stuff. Come to think of it, the other day I had a soya bacon sandwich and couldn't tell the difference. However, life is not a technological ladder, it's more of a cultural wheel. So, what we have gained in some respects we have lost in others. At religious festivals in India devout believers walk safely (at least most of them) across white hot coals. I find that incredible. A Lapp can telepathically communicate over a vast distance to another Lapp, walk a few hundred miles, and then meet them under a particular tree. I find that mystifying. The African bushman points to a specific point on the horizon and says – 'there are zebras'. We look – and see nothing. I find that rather sad.

Arabian oryx which were returned to Oman after eight generations in captivity could still navigate across the desert to find water over a hundred miles away.

1. Guy Davenport. *Geography of the Imagination*. Pan Books (London 1984) **Photograph.** Buzz Aldrin's bootprint on the moon

Gilbert Islander

'It is true the white man can fly;

he can speak across the ocean ...

but he has no songs like ours,

no poets to equal the island singers.'

Two million years ago our ancestors were not men, but by one million years ago they were. By then they had discovered how to make fire, fashion tools and create images.

400,000-year-old wooden spears have been unearthed in Germany. They are two metres long, weighted like javelins with the centre of gravity one third away from the point. Each was carved from a spruce tree and the tip from the base where the wood is hardest. The spears demonstrate planning, skill and an understanding of technology and the potential of materials.

Some 100,000 years later a group of hunters in southern France left behind 60 pieces of colour pigment in their refuse. This pigment could only have been produced by firing and so was deliberately made to colour something. 60,000 years ago, in Iraq, a man was buried with spring flowers: yarrow, cornflowers, St Barnaby's thistle, groundsel, grape hyacinths, woody horsetail and mallow.[1] All with medicinal values, so perhaps he was a shaman. In Swaziland, a child's skeleton, buried 50,000 years ago, was found with a decorated pendant seashell. In north Australia there are rock paintings which are 44,000 years old. In Indo-China a neolithic instrument of ten stones, shaped and chipped, renders a musical scale when given a good bang.

30,000 years ago during the last Ice Age, bounded in the north by Arctic ice sheets and in the south by alpine glaciers, was a cold windy tundra stretching from western Europe to eastern Siberia. An inhospitable and hostile region populated by woolly mammoths, sabre-toothed tigers, bison, reindeer and humans. These early forebears had the same physique, brain capacity and intelligence as we have today. They built huts of skin and mammoth bones, made fire, hunted and gathered, buried the dead, wore ornaments, sculpted clay, engraved bones.

Art, and its association with magic, was probably in the hands of shamans. Little remains, nomadic societies travelled light carrying unguessed technologies in their heads and putting art on their perishable goods and weapons of wood and bone.

The earliest known engraving[2] is at least 135,000 years old, possibly twice as old as that. Scholars can't agree. It's an animal bone scratched with 70 lines of arcs, bands and chevrons. Whether for decorative reasons, to record something, some mystical rite, or to pass the time of day, doesn't matter. Like the other examples mentioned – it was done to communicate, express or record something: a thought, a feeling, a moment, an idea.

The world has always been subject to sequences of night and day, rising and setting of the sun, phases of the moon, the cycle of seasons. All have direct bearing on the quality of life. An animal rib scratched with markings made about 12,000 years ago, at the end of the Ice Age, records the movements of the sun and moon. It demonstrates that early man had an intimate knowledge of the solar system far surpassing anything previously imagined.

In 1879 an archaeologist took his daughter to a cave in Altamira (Spain). Scratching at the floor in the hope of turning up a relic she glanced up and suddenly saw spectacular bison and horses pulsating in the lantern light.

Archaeologists are often accused of looking down rather than up at the skies. This, the first known discovery of cave art, was dismissed just as those at Lascaux were some sixty years later. Prehistorians insisted that primitive man was incapable of such creativity.

'The Bible says, "In the beginning was the word", but that is simply not true. In the beginning, tens of millennia before the Bible, there were pictures. And the people who produced them were prepared to risk their lives by travelling many kilometres underground into great chasms of mysterious darkness just to paint imaginary animals on the walls of caves. That's how important making art was to them. We will never know exactly why. But we can sense that magic and wonder provide this art with its true underpinnings. That it probably had a religious purpose. The cleverer we get, the more "civilised" we become, the more we seem to hunger for that old sense of mystery that must have brimmed up in us when we looked out across our extraordinary world and understood none of it.'

Waldemar Januszczak
[*The Guardian*, 3 December 1998]

1. Richard Leakey. *Origins Reconsidered.* Doubleday (New York 1992)   2. Guy Davenport. *The Geography of the Imagination.* Picador (London 1984)

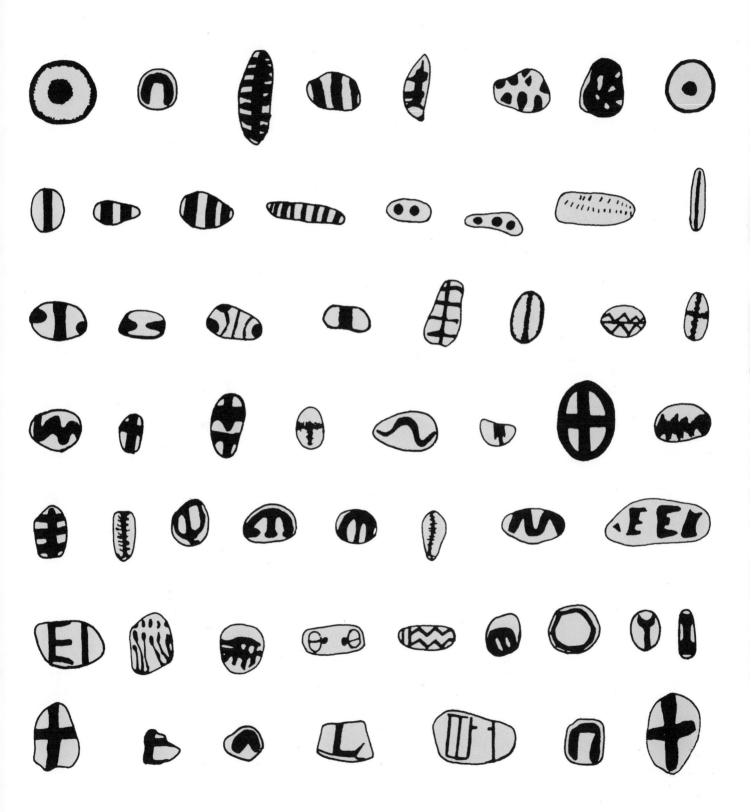

CIVILIZATION

'Western civilization? I think it would be a good idea.'
Attributed to *Mahatma Gandhi*

'Man is a singular creature … he is not a figure in the landscape –
he is a shaper of the landscape. In body and in mind he is the
explorer of nature, the ubiquitous animal who did not find but has
made his home in every continent.' *Jacob Bronowski*

'The lines of
communication
between the
conscious and
unconscious zones
of the human psyche
have all been cut,
and we have split
in two.'

Joseph Campbell

'All pasts are like
poems; one can
derive a thousand
things, but not live
in them.'

John Fowles

'… human thought
and emotion have
a universality that
transcends time
and converts the
different stages of
history into theaters
that provide lessons
for modern players.'

Stephen Jay Gould

'Darwinian man,
though well behaved,
is really just
a monkey shaved!'

W.S. Gilbert

IS ONLY

'Culture is everything you don't have to do … cuisine is culture, but
eating is not; fashion is, but clothing isn't.' *Brian Eno*

'When I hear the word culture, I reach for my Browning.'
Attributed* to *Hermann Goering*

'Cultures are maps of meaning through which the world is made
intelligible.' *Peter Jackson*

Culture is something you grow tomatoes or viruses in.

* According to the *Oxford Dictionary of Quotations* first said by Hanns Johst

CHAOS

'Those newly arriving Ice Age Americans, trekking in from Siberia across the Bering land bridge, would have faced the most appalling conditions between 17,000 and 10,000 years ago. It was then that the Wisconsin glaciers, all at once, went into their ferocious meltdown, forcing a 350-foot rise in global sea levels amid scenes of unprecedented climatic and geological turmoil. For *seven thousand years of human experience*, earthquakes, volcanic eruptions and immense floods, interspersed with eerie periods of peace, must have dominated the day-to-day lives of the New World peoples. Perhaps this is why so many of their myths speak with such conviction of fire and floods and times of darkness and of the creation and destruction of Suns ... The myths of the New World are not in this respect isolated from those of the Old.'[1] Australian aborigines still tell stories of landscapes that have been lost under the sea for 8,000 years.

Henry Ford said history was bunk. He was wrong. Indifference to the past reduces human experience to a life span rather than one of thousands of years.

'The past is a foreign country; they do things differently there.'

L.P. Hartley
(The Go-Between)

'... yesterday a drop of semen, tomorrow a handful of spice or ashes.'

Marcus Aurelius
(Meditations)

'I've found the link between apes and civilized men – it's us.'

Konrad Lorenz

TAKING A REST

1 . Graham Hancock. *Fingerprints of the Gods*. Heinemann (London 1995)

'the other side of yesterday'

In the Library of Congress is a map dated 1513, originally owned by Piri Re'is, a Turkish admiral. A copy of copies, it goes back to ancient Greece.[1] History credits Magellan with the discovery of the Pacific in 1520, but this map shows *both* sides of South America. The implication is obvious.

There seems little doubt that Columbus was preceded by St Brendan of Ireland and the Viking Leif Ericsson. A stone engraved with Scandinavian runes was discovered in Minnesota in 1898. The translation[2] reads:

8 Swedes and 22 Norwegians on exploration journey from Vinland westward. We had camp by two rocky islets one day's journey north from this stone. We were out and fished one day. After we came home found 10 men red with blood and dead. AVM save from evil. Have 10 men by the sea to look after our ships 14 days' journey from this island. Year 1362.

To me it seems unlikely that weary travellers on the edge of the world, under constant attack by hostile natives, would sit down to carve a message. I also suppose the national references are the translator's identification for different Scandinavian tribes. Still, the reference does appear in several respectable publications.

What is known is that after 1408 the Vikings abruptly disappeared from Greenland possibly because they found a more congenial life in North America. One far-fetched notion concerns lacrosse, a kind of game long popular with the indigenous peoples across North America. Lacrosse is uncannily like a game played by the Vikings, so similar indeed that an anthropologist reckons the probability of independent origin small. Then there were a tribe of Inuits living high above the Arctic Circle in a place so remote that its inhabitants were not known until early in the last century. Many of the tribe not only looked European but were found to be carrying European genes.

Peoples have been sailing between continents for millennia. How else did the green stone from the Alps used to make tools by the ancient inhabitants of Malta 6,000 years ago get there? Among the wilder shores of archaeology speculative theories include finding ancient fragments of Japanese pottery in Ecuador, early Hebrew inscriptions in Tennessee, and Celtic scripts in New Hampshire. One expert even believes Tennessee was settled by pygmies. Another, more predictably, reckons humans arrived from outer space and the Garden of Eden was California. They then crossed over to France and vanquished the Neanderthals. Mind you, this expert also believes in Atlantis, Lemuria and crystal power.

However, improbable scenarios can't be casually dismissed. Take the island of Madagascar off South Africa. Sometime in the distant past, it was settled by peoples who sailed west from Borneo.[3] In the middle of Wales there is a small group of women whose genes are more related to the peoples of Papua New Guinea, than anyone else in the British Isles.[4] Then there are the aborigines of the Andaman Islands (between India and Thailand) who are closely related to African pygmies and Hottentots. Descendants of an ancient migratory peoples 'Out of Africa'. [SEE P7]. And the American Mandan tribe, with one of the most elaborate cultures of the Great Plains, have myths uncannily similar to those of the Welsh.

The Micronesian islands in the Pacific, with primitive palm-tree cultures, were once home to long disappeared civilizations[5] who built the giant basalt ruins in Kosrae, the ancient terraces in Palau, the five-ton faces of Babeldaop, the immense stones in Tinian. Ruins so old that local mythology refers to them as from 'the other side of yesterday'.

'The world begins to feel very small,' wrote Samuel Butler in 1859 during his voyage from England to New Zealand, 'when one finds one can get half round it in three months.' While just over a hundred years later, in 1969 the Pope removed St Christopher, patron saint of travellers, from the Church calendar. The very same year man took off and walked on the moon. Presumably the Pope acted to discourage anyone attempting to visit heaven.

Then there are fellow travellers. Eugene Schieffelin, a wealthy German emigrant to America, had the odd idea of introducing all the birds mentioned in the writings of Shakespeare into the New World. Most species failed but forty pairs of starlings he released in Central Park during 1890 are now the most abundant bird species in America. And one of its greatest pests.

Finally there are the wipe-offs: 'On New Zealand, the laughing owl is extinct. So are the New Zealand quail, the North Island bush wren, and the New Zealand grayling. On Jamaica, two species of macaw as well as the Jamaican iguana are extinct. On Cuba, three species of rodent and ... the Cuban yellow bat. Christmas Island ... no longer harbors the bulldog rat or Captain Maclear's rat or the Christmas Island musk shrew ... The Falkland Islands once supported the warrah ... The Japanese wolf is extinct. The Tasmanian emu is extinct. Two species of Puerto Rican agouti are extinct. Hawaii alone has lost more bird species than were lost from all the continents on Earth ... the Samoan wood rail is extinct ... the Macquarie Island parakeet ... the Tristan gallinule ... the Cape Verde giant skink ... the Wake Island rail ... the Guadalupe flicker ... the São Thomé grosbeak ... the Auckland Island merganser ... the Iwo Jima rail ... the Ryukyu kingfisher ... the Lord Howe Island pigeon is extinct, as are the Lord Howe Island white-eye, the Lord Howe Island fantail, and the Lord Howe Island flycatcher ... On the islands of the northern Atlantic, between Norway and Newfoundland, the great auk ... '[6]

A litany not without its tragi-comic moments. In 1857 naturalist Gerard Kreff on an expedition in the Australian outback caught two rare bandicoots. Desperately hungry, he ate them. They were, he later discovered, the last pair.

1 . Graham Hancock. *Fingerprints of the Gods*. Heinemann (London 1995)   2 . Stephen Williams. *Fantastic Archaeology*. University of Pennsylvania Press (Philadelphia 1991)   3 . Jared Diamond. *Guns, Germs and Steel*. Jonathan Cape (London 1997)

Ireland – as seen from Wales

4. Steve Jones. *In the Blood*. Harper Collins (London 1996) 5. Oliver Sachs. *The Island of the Colour-Blind*. Picador (London 1996) 6. David Quammen. *The Song of the Dodo*. Hutchinson (London 1996)

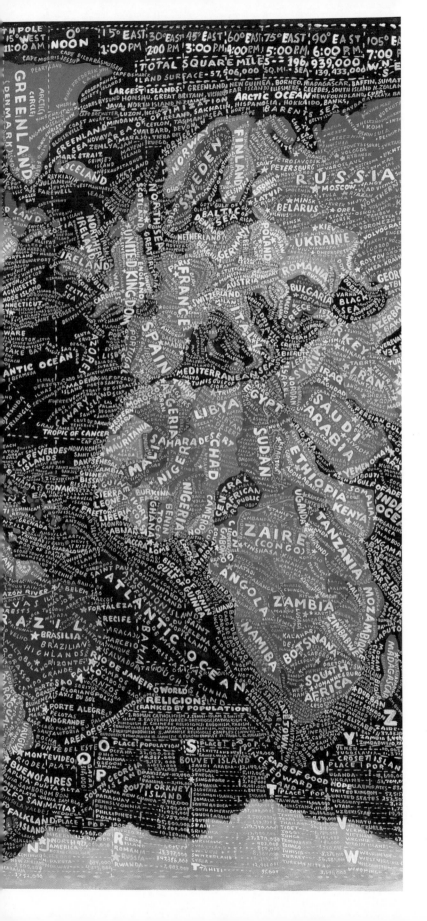

Prester John (c.1175) : ' … In our domains live elephants, dromedaries, camels, hippopotami, crocodiles, *metagallinari, cametennus, tinsirete,* panthers, onagers, red and white lions, white bears and blackbirds, mute cicadas, gryphos, tigers, jackals, hyenas, wild oxen, centaurs, wild men, horned men, fauns, and women of the same species, pygmies, men with dogs' heads, giants forty cubits tall, monocles, cyclops, a bird called the phoenix, and almost every kind of animal that lives beneath the vault of the heavens … In one of our provinces the river known as Indus flows … This river, whose source is in Paradise, winds its way along various branches through the entire province and in it are found natural stones, emeralds, sapphires, carbuncles, topazes, chrysolytes, onyx, beryl, amethyst, sardonics, and many other precious stones … '[1]

Doctor Dee (1527–1608) : 'Our navigators and cosmographers have traced the outlines of Atlantis, or the New World, where have been found the crocodile that lives for a thousand years and the quail that has the falling sickness: certain provinces or domains there we have named Norumbega, Nova Francia and Mocosa, in which latter part of the world has been found the horse that weeps and sighs like a man. There also is the agopithecus, an ape-like goat whose voice is very like a man's but not articulate, sounding as if one did speak hastily with indignation or sorrow. Africa is underneath my hand, and within it Barbarie where live the lions that couple backwards and the panthers that have the odour of the sweetest spices. In Numida, not so far distant, live men with the tails and heads of dogs, as well as the infamous yena that inhabit the tombs of the dead and eat only corpses. In Libya dwells the monoceros that feasts upon poison, and can make itself into male or female as it wishes; there are people here called Astomii, who live very long and neither eat nor drink but feed upon air and the smell of fruits. In Selenetide there are women who lay eggs and hatch them, from which come children fifty times greater than those which are generally born, and the far-off Land of the Negroes is inhabited by the basilisk that kills at a look, the hydrus of two heads, and the salamander of perfect coldness … and I find myself suddenly aloft in the yellow land of Samotra and on a wonderful path to Monacabo, Capasiasa, Taprobana, Bacornara and Birae. Then can I see the men whose bodies shine at night, and the phoenix tree which blooms for an hundred years and imparts an odour more perfumed than musk or civet or ambergris. On this far-off shore I view the wonders of the world beneath the stars, and see before me the creature that is born twice, crying out upon the top of a mountain and saying, "I am the white of the black, and the red of the white, and the yellow of the sun, I tell truth and lie not" … at which I started and awakened, for I was in a dream of my own devising.'[2] **[SEE** P470**].**

1. Umberto Eco. *Serendipities.* Weidenfeld & Nicolson (London 1999)   2. Peter Ackroyd. *The House of Doctor Dee.* Penguin (London 1994)   **Map.** Paula Scher

Werner Karl Heisenberg   'Every tool carries with it the spirit by which it has been created.'

An *Acheulian* hand axe

Some primitive tools in Ethiopia are reckoned to be two and a half million years old. With new discoveries dates shift, pushing early man back further in time than thought possible. The dates in this section are probably already out of date.

A hand axe discovered in the Olduvai Gorge in Kenya is over a million and a half years old. As a metaphor for the first thing made by man, it prefigures the whole world of making and shaping. No earlier artefact exists on earth. All art and technology began when early man chipped an oval stone flint with symmetrical precision to produce a point and extremely sharp edges. The prosaic name given to these exquisite objects is the *Acheulian* hand axe. In a world where tools might have been the most important things made, their qualities were sometimes brought to a perfection far beyond the needs of practicality. Craft, symmetry and elegance speak of pride in creation, pleasure in contemplation, prestige in possession. There are three factors which set this particular artefact apart from other prehistoric tools. Firstly, it does not reflect the natural shapes of stones nor is it the result of natural fractures. There is nothing accidental about the design. Secondly, the design seems to be the result of a shared aesthetic as these tools are found all over Africa, the Middle East and Southern Europe. A vast distance at the time. Thirdly, they were made with a painstaking refinement which far exceeds practical requirements. They are 'the first real evidence of style'.[1]

1. Lyall Watson. *The Lightning Bird*. Simon & Schuster (New York 1983)

'The obsidian flake

and the silicon chip

are struck by the light

of the same campfire

that has passed from

hand to hand since the

human mind began.'

George Dyson

Longmans Dictionary: 'Tool, machine, implement, instrument, appliance, utensil, device and gadget all mean "piece of equipment for doing work". A tool (the word first appeared in King Alfred's translation of *De Consolatione Philosophiae* (c. 883) is typically small and hand-held, performs a physical task (e.g. culling, scraping, banging or moulding), and can be powered: a hammer is a tool but so is an electric drill. A machine is typically larger and more elaborate than a tool, consisting of several parts that transmit forces, and need not be powered or perform a physical task: a crane is a machine, but so are lawn mowers and cash registers. An implement is usually a simple tool, particularly one used for agriculture: a rake or a spade is an implement. An instrument is either a delicate tool for skilled precision work, or a measuring device: a scalpel and a thermometer are instruments. An appliance is usually an item of domestic or office equipment powered from the mains: vacuum cleaners and liquidisers are appliances. A utensil is portable, and is usually in practice a domestic container: a saucepan is a utensil. A device is usually a piece of mechanical equipment ingeniously contrived for a stated purpose ("an improved steering device"). A gadget is a small, often novel and electronic device that may form part of a piece of machinery (fire engine covered with gadgets).'

Museo Guatelli di Ozzano Taro, Parma, Italy. 'Guatelli, the son of a peasant, and a self-taught elementary school teacher, has all his life collected agricultural and artisans' tools from all over the north of Italy, particularly Emilia. In doing so Guatelli, like a modern Noah, has filled his Ark with all those objects doomed to disappear, swallowed up by oblivion, through the ignorance of a superficial affluence that wants to forget the hardships and poverty of the past. In reality the museum praises poverty, not for itself, but because it can generate an immense amount of patience and dedication – a minimal elegance. A surprising metamorphosis of objects of the past, worn out and unusable, that are transformed into something else. Guatelli tells his story by filling the white-washed walls of the family barn, like leaves of an enormous book, with hundreds of objects showing the minute differences between these artefacts, due to necessity or differences in soils, culture or climate. The walls that he has composed with such originality are, unknown to him, an example of poetic "writing", a kind of anthropology as told by a brilliant and refined naïve personality.' *Enzo Ragazzini*

Enzo Ragazzini also took the photograph of the Guatelli Museum shown overleaf.

And here's a useful tool. An ELLIPSE CURVE IN PERSPECTIVE. A combination of ellipse curves and radii points.

This ingenious apple peeler is typical of the labour-saving contrivances invented by Shakers.

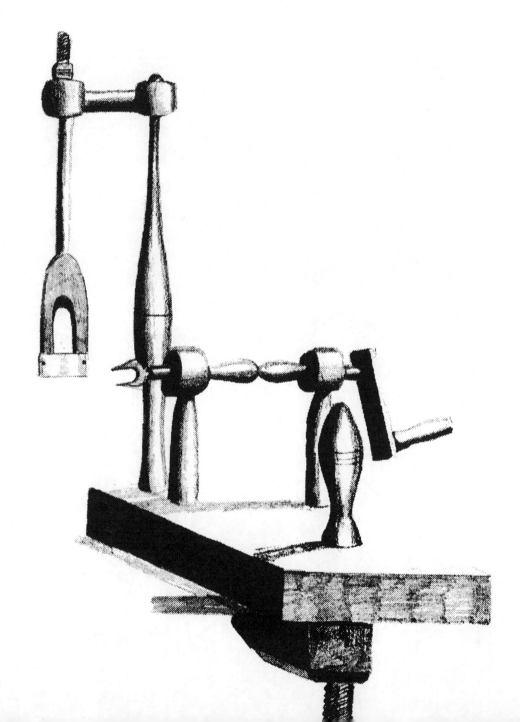

from
how
to cut
paper
to
where
did
I leave
the
scissors

Paul Klee's studio was once described as an alchemist's lair, stuffed with the materials and instruments that he made and kept about him – home-made brushes, whittled reed pens, dental picks and razor blades fastened to improvised handles, gesso-caked cups and bent bits of wire to scrape, incise and abrade the compounded surfaces of his paintings.

'Computers are to design as microwaves are to cooking.' Milton Glaser

'An artifact is an object suitable for attaining some end that a person intends to be used for attaining that end. The mixture of mechanics and psychology makes artifacts a strange category. Artifacts can't be defined by their shape or their constitution, only by what they can do and by what someone, somewhere, wants them to do.'[1]

'We make tools, and as we evolved our tools made us.' Steven Pinker

The tools designed by Marc Isambard Brunel to make ships' blocks are often cited as the first instance of mechanical mass production. Priority might be given to clockmakers, or locksmiths, but the Royal Dockyard in Portsmouth was the first large enterprise. Ships' blocks are wheels encased in a wood housing, threaded with a rope, and used as pulleys to lift weights and furl sails. The introduction of these tool-made blocks replaced 110 skilled workers with ten unskilled men within a few months.

'Technology is best defined as the production of the superfluous.' Ortega Y Gasset

In 1867 Karl Marx made much of the 500 different kinds of hammer produced in Birmingham, each adapted to fulfil a specific task. He also neatly defined machines as 'knowledge objectified'. Machines had become an extension of man. Previously we shaped tools, thereafter they shaped us. A profound change which meant that instead of wondering how to breed a better horse there were those, like Henry Ford, imagining a world without the horse.

'The camera is an instrument that teaches people how to see without a camera.' Dorothea Lange

My infrequent acquaintance with factories has left me with an impression of unpleasant smells, dimness and dirt. However, the last I visited was a mystical experience – unsurprisingly it was in Japan. The factory makes zippers for the world. The tour of the factory was undertaken on a driverless electronic golf cart which scudded along some pre-ordained route through one incredibly vast shed after another. Each populated not with people but with thousands upon thousands of chattering automatic machines in dense neat ordered lines. Occasionally I spotted a human in an impeccably clean bright blue overall doing a repair job. There is a possibility that if you bought a pair of trousers in the late 1980s or shortly thereafter, I actually saw your fly zipper being made. Check to see if it's stamped YKK. Calculate when you bought it, allow a year for distribution, garment incorporation, retail distribution and purchase. Yours aren't stamped YKK? I'm surprised, check your neighbour's.

'If we can't fix it – it ain't broke!' American garage sign

We are fast reaching a point where technology will create a store of available solutions to supply instant solutions for all problems. The problem of the problem will have been transferred from how can I cut paper, to one of where did I leave the scissors.

'Technology is the name we have for stuff that doesn't work yet.' Daniel Hillis

---

1. Steven Pinker. *How the Mind Works*. Penguin (London 1998)

NET

'A gill net is a net anchored slightly above the ocean floor. It looks somewhat like a badminton net. Groundfish become caught in it and, trying to force their way through headfirst, end up being strangled at the gills. The nets are marked by buoys, and the fisherman has only to haul them up every day and remove the fish. But sometimes the nets detach from their moorings. As they drift around the ocean, they continue to catch fish until they become so weighted down that they sink to the ocean floor, where various creatures feast on the catch. When enough has been eaten, the net begins to float again, and the process continues, helped by the fact that, in the twentieth century, the gill net became almost invisible when hemp twine was replaced first by nylon and then by monofilament. Since monofilament is fairly indestructible, it is estimated that a modern "ghost net" may continue to fish on its own for as long as five years.' [1]

This is an extract from a remarkable book by Felipe Fernández-Armesto subtitled *A history and a guide for the perplexed* which has been described as a high-spirited vacation in a realm of dangerous ideas. 'Polynesian navigators literally felt their way. "Stop staring at the sail and steer by the feel of the wind on your cheeks," was a traditional navigator's advice ... According to a European observer, "the most sensitive balance was a man's testicles". They could correct a few degrees' variation in the wind by checking against the long-range swells ... Caroline Islanders interviewed in modern times knew the currents over an area nearly 2,000 miles broad. Above all, they judged their latitude by the sun and monitored their exact course by the stars ... whose movements were remembered by means of rhythmic chants ... accurately enough, according to a Spanish visitor of 1774, to find the harbour of their choice at night.' [2]

'THERE IS A UTOPIAN DREAM THAT THE COMING OF THE NET WILL BRING POSITIVE SOCIAL CHANGES. I HAVE MY DOUBTS ABOUT THAT. IT IS GOING TO BRING GREAT SOCIAL CHANGES, BUT THEY WON'T ALL BE POSITIVE. AT THE SAME TIME, IF I HAVE A POSITIVE FEELING ABOUT WHAT'S HAPPENING WITH DIGITAL TECHNOLOGY AND THE REVOLUTION THAT IT BRINGS, IT IS BECAUSE NETIFICATION, COMPUTERIZATION, AND DIGITALIZATION ALL INCREASE CHOICES. THAT IS ABOUT ALL THAT TECHNOLOGY GIVES, BUT THAT IS A VERY LARGE THING. FOR EXAMPLE, A PERSON BORN NOW WHO IS INTERESTED IN THE ARTS CAN PAINT, SCULPT, MAKE FILMS AND MAKE MUSIC IN MANY DIFFERENT SPHERES. TWO CENTURIES AGO, THERE WERE FEWER CHOICES. EACH TIME THE MEDIA REINVENT THEMSELVES, THEY EXPAND THE NUMBER OF CHOICES WITHOUT EXCLUDING ANY OF THE PREVIOUS ONES. ON THIS SIMPLE LEVEL, THE NET AND THE LITERARY SPACE — THE THINKING SPACE THAT IT CREATES — WILL ALLOW A WHOLE NEW SPACE FOR THE ARTS. IT IS ALSO A SPACE THAT WILL ALLOW NEW KINDS OF POLITICAL AND SOCIAL STRUCTURES, AND IT WILL ALLOW THEM AS A NET GAIN.' KEVIN KELLY [1990s] [3]

1. Mark Kurlansky. *Cod.* Vintage (London 1999) 2. Felipe Fernández-Armesto. *Truth.* Bantam Press (London 1997) 3. John Brockman (ed.). *Digerati.* Orion (London 1997)

WORKING

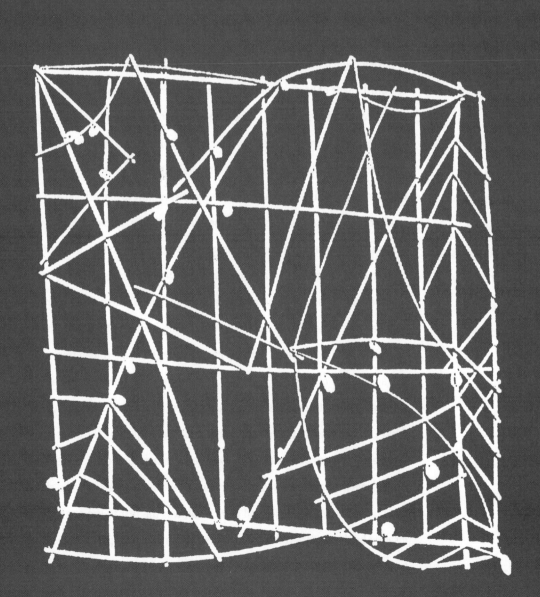

Fishermen in the remoter Pacific have intricate knotted nets which also serve as string maps to navigate the seas by trade winds and sea currents. The map illustrated here was made by fishermen of the Marshall Islands. The shells represent atolls and the sticks of bamboo currents and winds. An example of the ancient knowledge which enabled the Micronesians and Polynesians, a thousand years ago, to sail across the immensities of the Pacific Ocean, in journeys comparable to interplanetary travel. Similarly in the mythology of the Toba people in South America an intricate fragile net stretches across the skies with its knots representing the constellation of the Pleiades. [SEE P.95].

The Lunar Society of Birmingham was founded by Erasmus Darwin in the 1760s, the group of self-styled 'Lunaticks' formed a nucleus for the industrialization of Britain, and between them had a hand in the origin of almost every mechanism used in the technologies of today. Among the members were Josiah Wedgwood (pottery), William Small (taught Thomas Jefferson), James Watt (steam engines), Joseph Priestley (oxygen), Benjamin Franklin (electricity), James Keir (chemist). Erasmus (grandfather of Charles) was physician, poet, and inventor of a speaking-machine, an artificial bird with flapping wings, a sun-operated device for opening cucumber-frames, a horizontal windmill to grind colours, pumps, steam turbines, canal lifts, internal combustion engines, a compressed-air-powered ornithopter, a hydrogen-oxygen rocket motor and a water closet that flushed when the door was opened to leave. He was also obsessed with the vision of a steam-driven 'fiery chariot' to replace the horse-drawn post-chaise. The society only met during the full moon as the ride home late at night was less dangerous. Philosopher Ludwig Wittgenstein designed a house, fixtures and fittings, and the door handle illustrated opposite, for his sister. He also worked on a sewing machine and an airplane propeller. The Chinese designer Lu Pan, who was around some 2,500 years ago, is said to have designed the saw, drill, shovel, plane, hook, lock and ladder. His wife is given credit for inventing the umbrella. The brush made of hair is attributed to General Meng T'ien, builder of the Great Wall (c. 210 BC) and Chai Lun is credited with inventing paper (107 AD). The Chinese also came up with the compass, gunpowder, canal lock gates, cast iron, efficient animal harnesses, kites, type, porcelain, printing, sternpost rudders and wheelbarrows. Papermaking techniques were acquired by Islam when an Arab army defeated a Chinese army at a battle in Central Asia in 751 AD. Papermakers were among the prisoners of war, and they were brought to Samarkand and set to work. The Greek Daedalus also claims credit for the saw and drill, as well as the axe, plumb line, carpenter's glue, and making life-like automata. [SEE P113]. The Lesbian Rule is an antique lead instrument, used by masons to take the contour of an existing form to create a mould to form an identical shape. At Islamic courts the brushes used to render royal signatures were composed of 24 donkey hairs. Gainsborough sometimes worked on his larger paintings with a six-foot brush made from a fishing rod. The traditional quill pen was made from one of the first four wing feathers of a goose. The rumour that László Moholy-Nagy designed the Parker 51 fountain pen is not true. Pentel is a brand name coined from pen and pastel. A good-quality ball-point pen has a write-out of between 2.5 and 3.5 kilometres. The boomerang was perfected by Aborigines as a digging tool, cutting instrument, for bird scaring, ritual dances, attack and defence. Author Anthony Trollope (employee of the Post Office) was inventor of the pillar box. Charles Babbage invented the great analytical engine (forefather of the computer), the speedometer, cowcatcher and life expectancy tables. During the 1940s movie star Hedy Lamarr and composer George Antheil invented and patented a system to prevent the jamming of radio signals. [1] The typewriter was patented in 1868 by Christopher Latham Sholes and Mark Twain was the first to use one to write a book. The Lebanese Loop is a gadget inserted by thieves into cashpoint machines. When you unsuspectingly insert your credit card it gobbles it up. Sometime later the thief dextrously retrieves the loop with your credit card.

'I see this strange tool, my brain, that sees itself and calls itself a tool and tries to find in itself a thing not a tool that it is a tool for!'

John Fowles

1. *The Guardian*, 20 January 2000

Door handle. Design, Ludwig Wittgenstein

the QWERTY factor

The first patent for a typewriter was granted to William Burt of Detroit in the 1860s. The QWERTY keyboard, so called for the six letters in the left top row, was designed so that people had to type slowly. To ensure this the commonest letters were scattered on the left side to confound the majority of right-handers [SEE P460]. This machiavellian strategy was to avoid adjacent keys jamming when struck in quick succession. In addition salesmen could also acquire fluency in typing the letters TYPEWRITER as these occur in the top row of the keyboard. In 1888 a star pupil of the Shorthand and Typewriter Institute in Cincinnati entered a widely publicized contest and won on a typewriter with a QWERTY keyboard – thereby QWERTY became so entrenched in the public mind that it is still the layout of today's computer keyboard.[1] Recently – over 100 years later – watching a documentary on the 1939-45 war I noticed that the famous German encrypter – the ENIGMA machine – had the first six letters as QWERTZ. Hmmm.

The Boston Post (1865):'Well-informed people know it is impossible to transmit the voice over wires and that were it possible to do so, the thing would be of no practical value.' Despite this prediction the telephone imperiously forced its way into our lives with a bell. Telephone codes in the United States were selected on the opposite principle to that of the typewriter keyboard. They were selected to encourage speed. When area codes were introduced large cities were given low numbers because they took less time to dial. New York City was ②①② and although logically New Jersey should be ②①③ the two could easily be misdialled, so ②①③ was given to Los Angeles. And ③①② to Chicago.[2]

We assume that technological progress develops along logical functional engineering paths. It doesn't. Factors outside utility or purpose can influence results. For instance aeronautical engineers have calculated that an aircraft with one wing swept back and the other swept forward, would be a better configuration for flight than conventional bilateral wings. I can imagine the enthusiasm with which passengers would greet that proposal.

   1. Jared Diamond. *Guns, Germs and Steel*. Jonathan Cape (London 1997)   2. Douglas Hofstadter. *Metamagical Themas*. Penguin Books (London 1986)

As his most famous statement had it, Klee took a line for a walk. It snaked, looped, wandered off, and turned back on itself as it made its fitful journey through the worlds of his invention. A line can run dead straight, be wildly crooked, nervously wobbly, make sensuous curves or aggressive angles. It can meander, wander, track or trace. Be a scribble, doodle, scratch, hatched, dashed, dribbled or trickled. It can be precise or fuzzy, hard or soft, firm or gentle, thin or thick. It can be smudged, smeared, erased – or just fade away. You can push a line, drag it, manipulate and manoeuvre it, make it delineate, accentuate, attenuate, emphasize. A line may be imperious or modest, authoritative or servile, brutal or seductive, passive or active, weak or strong, thick or thin. A line is born, and dies, in a point.

The pencil developed from wrapping up lumps of *plumbago* (graphite) which were used to mark sheep. Incidentally *plumbago* was also a cure for urinary disorders. The best *plumbago* came from the north of England and was exported to Europe. Nowadays the pencil is a multinational affair. The lead is combined with graphite from Mexico and Sri Lanka, mixed with Mississippi mud. The eraser is a blend of Italian pumice and South American rubber. The shaft is cedar from California or discarded polystyrene cups.

Pencil connoisseurs favour the Eberhard Faber Mongol, insanely painted with 13 coats of yellow and with a potential of 45,000 words per pencil.[3] Other favourites are the Berol Mirado No. 2, Faber's Castell Velvet and the Faber Blackwing – 'half the pressure, twice the speed'. The comment on this page was pencilled with my favourite – the Staedtler Mars Lumograph EE.

By the way I'm told that one claimant to the invention of the pencil lies in Dublin's Jewish Cemetery. His tombstone declares him to be Barnaby Pencil Cohen.

Overleaf :

The Biro ballpoint pen posed the first real threat, then the fibre tip, then the rollerball, and now electronics. The simple pencil is now an endangered species. So, for posterity, I made a *Technological Graveyard.* It hangs in my studio.

No ban on pencils for Iraq

The UN yesterday denied it has banned the export of pencils to Iraq because their graphite lead could be put to military use. It said pencils are entering Iraq under a UN-authorised programme. *AP, Baghdad*

3. Henry Petroski, *The Pencil: A History*, Faber & Faber (London 1991) **Quotation.** Frank N. Furter (*The Rocky Horror Picture Show*, 1975)

"THE ELEPHANT'S TRUNK IS SIX FEET LONG AND ONE FOOT THICK AND CONTAINS SIXTY THOUSAND MUSCLES. ELEPHANTS CAN USE THEIR TRUNKS TO UPROOT TREES, STACK TIMBER, OR CAREFULLY PLACE HUGE LOGS IN POSITION WHEN RECRUITED TO BUILD BRIDGES. AN ELEPHANT CAN CURL ITS TRUNK AROUND A PENCIL AND DRAW CHARACTERS ON LETTER-SIZE PAPER. WITH THE TWO MUSCULAR EXTENSIONS AT THE TIP, IT CAN REMOVE A THORN, PICK UP A PIN OR A DIME, UNCORK A BOTTLE, SLIDE THE BOLT OFF A CAGE DOOR AND HIDE IT ON A LEDGE, OR GRIP A CUP SO FIRMLY, WITHOUT BREAKING IT, THAT ONLY ANOTHER ELEPHANT CAN PULL IT AWAY.

Steven Pinker. The Language Instinct. Penguin Books (London 1995)

BLINDFOLDED ELEPHANT TO ASCERTAIN THE SHAPE AND TEXTURE OF OBJECTS. IN THE WILD, ELEPHANTS USE THEIR TRUNKS TO PULL UP THEIR CLUMPS OF GRASS AND KNOCK THEM AGAINST THEIR KNEES TO OUT OFF THE DIRT, AND TO SHAKE POWDER THEIR BODIES TREES, AND THEY USE THEIR TRUNKS WITH GROUND AS THEY WALK, TO PROBE THE PIT TRAPS, AND TO DIG WELLS AND AVOIDING WATER FROM THEM. ELEPHANTS SIPHON WALK UNDERWATER ON THE CAN BEDS OF DEEP RIVERS OR SWIM LIKE SUBMARINES FOR MILES, USING THEIR TRUNKS AS SNORKELS. THEY COMMUNICATE THROUGH THEIR TRUNKS BY TRUMPETING, HUMMING, ROARING, PIPING, PURRING, RUMBLING, AND MAKING A CRUMPLING-METAL SOUND BY RAPPING THE TRUNK AGAINST THE GROUND. THE TRUNK IS LINED WITH CHEMO-RECEPTORS THAT ALLOW THE ELEPHANT TO SMELL A PYTHON HIDDEN IN THE GRASS OR FOOD A MILE AWAY. ELEPHANTS ARE THE ONLY LIVING ANIMALS THAT POSSESS THIS EXTRAORDINARY ORGAN."

INHIBITION IS A NAIL IN THE HEAD

Arthur Koestler   'Creativity is the defeat of habit by originality.'

Some attributes of creativity:

Challenging assumptions

Being receptive to new ideas

Recognizing similarities or differences

Making unlikely connections

Taking risks

Building on ideas to make better ideas

Looking at things in new ways

Taking advantage of the unexpected

Taking chances

Every discovery

by definition

is unpredictable.

If it were predictable

it would not be

a discovery.

Creativity exposes

unpredictable things

to be discovered.

Ambrose Bierce, a journalist in San Francisco in the 1880s, described creativity, in the prose style of his time, as *'that particular disposition of the intellectual faculties which enables one to write poetry like Hector Stuart and prose like Loring Pickering; to draw like Carl Browne and paint like Mr Swan; to model like the immortal designer of the Cogswell statue or the Lotta fountain; to speak like the great O'Donnell …'* parodying a commonly held view that creativity is something some are born with and others are not. Actually it could be that everybody has creative potential but that some seem able to access this more easily than others.

The barrier is inhibition – not wanting *'to make a fool of oneself'.*

No one seems to know where creativity comes from or how it works. *'I have thought about the nature of this creative process',* wrote scientist William Beck, *'and have reached a somewhat aberrant conclusion. I don't understand it and I don't think anyone else does either.'* Certainly those who try to pin it down only come up with unintelligible answers to what is probably an unanswerable question. Poet A.E. Housman said he could no more define poetry than a terrier could define a rat. And somebody else, although I can't recollect who, lucidly explained it as *'a leap across a chasm not bridgeable by reason'.* For those who find that inadequate I can only recommend the Fortune Cookie message which declares : *'The answer you seek is in an envelope.'*

However, when it comes down to where creativity operates, things get clearer. I think Arthur Koestler got it right when he said it was in *'the absurd, the useful and the beautiful'.*[1] *Humour* makes us laugh. *Discovery* makes us understand. *Art* makes us marvel.

A leap across a chasm

1. Arthur Koestler. *The Act of Creation.* Hutchinson (London 1964)

creative alchemy

Creativity is a compulsive human urge which demands more than ritual actions or routine responses, and is only valid when one is **trading beyond experience**.

The word 'Creativity' is frequently appropriated to enhance the mediocre or justify the mundane. That ceaseless and frenetic activity – easy to mistake for purposeful action – which without anything new to say only produces noise and aggregate. No new thoughts, no magic moments, just more patchwork and fingerpainting. An activity in which **process becomes product**.

'I have nothing to say and I'm saying it,' declared John Cage.

The true creative act is something else. It produces something which never existed before. Whether of small consequence or amazing significance, it's usually generated by a spontaneous insight. A glimpse of the blindingly obvious ignited by the heat off the wires caused by short-circuiting thoughts. **Insight is unreasoning.**

Of course what appears to be a spontaneous thought may well have been a long time cooking in the unconscious. Furthermore, despite an apparent 'moment of truth', one is often unsure as to whether one has actually 'seen the light' or been hoodwinked. But if you still feel warm inside on the next day it's like having turned lead into gold. Now for a secret. With practice, *chutzpah* and a lot of luck, insights can sometimes be generated. The trick is to focus the mind to **create a combustion** between intuition and experience.

George Nelson put it another way: 'What the creative act means', he wrote, 'is the ... sudden realization that one has taken a lot of disconnected pieces and **found, not done,** a way of putting them together.' It was put in yet another way by Bernard Shaw, who in his late 80s was interviewed by a reporter who remarked that over the years a great many interesting things must have happened to him. 'No,' replied Shaw, 'Interesting things never happen to me. **I happen to them**.' While Paul Klee said that he knew when a picture was finished, as that was when **he stopped looking at it, and it started looking back.**

Consilient (kǫusi·liĕnt), a. 1867. [– mod.L. *consiliens, -ent-* 'jumping together' (cf. RESILIENT), after concurrent.] 'Jumping together', concurrent, accordant. Hence **Consilience**, the fact of 'jumping together'; coincidence, concurrence : said of inductions.

British Patent No. 14,204 (1884): A formula for making gold from wheat. Cut a straw into fine square nips, put them in cold water, keep at a steady 59 degrees F. for ten hours, strain the liquid into a china dish, leave it to stand for 24 hours at a temperature of 60 degrees F. The surface skim is pure gold.

The word had originated in an articulated verbal insight, but this evaporated at once, leaving in its wake only a wordless essence, a fragrance of eternity, a quiver of the arrow in the blue.

Arthur Koestler

Scientist
Jacob Bronowski

'A man brings together two facets of reality and by discovering a likeness between them, suddenly makes them one.'

Writer
Arthur Koestler

'... any mental occurrence simultaneously associated with two habitually incompatible contexts.'

Biologist
Lyall Watson

'... that moment of insight becomes the creative act as a joining of two previously incompatible ideas.'

Surrealist
Comte de Lautréamont

'... the association of two, or more, apparently alien elements on a plane alien to both is the most potent ignition of poetry.'

Designer
Bruce Mau

'I'm interested in the moment when two objects collide and generate a third. The third object is where the interesting work is.'

Writer
William Plomer

'... to perceive the relations between thoughts, or things, or forms of expression that may seem utterly different, and to be able to combine them ...'

Architect
Rem Koolhaas

'... perceiving analogies and other relations between apparently incongruous ideas or forming unexpected, striking or ludicrous combinations of them.'

Mathematician
Jacques Hadamard

'... invention or discovery takes place by combining ideas.'

'The unlike is joined together, and from differences results
the most beautiful harmony.'

Philosopher
Heraclitus

'The more distant and distinct the relationship between the two realities
that are brought together, the more powerful the image.'

Poet
Pierre Reverdy

'... where the imaginative and the functional fuse and
finally become indistinguishable.'

Designer
Milton Glaser

'... apparently unrelated things become interesting
when we start fitting them together ...'

Mathematician
John Kouwenhoven

'Only the spirit has the power of unanimously embracing
contradictory aspects and fusing them into one.'

Artist
Amédée Ozenfant

'New discoveries in science and mathematics often consist
of a synthesis between theories or concepts which
have hitherto been regarded as unconnected.'

Psychiatrist
Anthony Storr

'... creativity seems to be something which links things together ...
within a new whole, which didn't exist before.'

Biochemist
Rupert Sheldrake

'You can take two substances, put them together,
and produce something powerfully different (table salt),
sometimes even explosive (nitroglycerine).'

Writer
Diane Ackerman

'... QUALITIES LIKE

QUIVERINESS AND VULNERABILITY

COME TO MIND

WHEN I THINK OF CREATIVITY...

CREATIVITY REQUIRES

A SENSE OF SMELL,

A PALATE TO TASTE THE SCENTS

THAT MAKE BRILLIANCE.

ALL LIFE FEEDS

UPON THE RANDOM.

CREATIVITY IS THE HAUTE CUISINE.'

DOUGLAS HOFSTADTER

Christopher Frayling: '... at the beginning of the nineteenth century, the verb "to create" was confined to descriptions of the book of Genesis. God did the creating: human beings did their best with what they were given. But with the romantic period, and the emphasis on individual genius, artists started describing themselves as "creative artists". Hence William Blake in *Jerusalem*, "I will not reason and compare; my business is to create"; and William Wordsworth in one of his sonnets, "creative art demands the service of a mind and heart; though sensitive yet heroically fashioned". Creativity meant flying without a net; risking all; challenging the gods; using different parts of the brain to the reasoner (today, we'd say right side equals creativity; left side equals reasoning); and being arty.'

Andrés Segovia: 'It is not so hard to be original, what *is* hard, is to be original with continuity.'

John Fowles: 'The creative person's simplest purpose is to describe the outer world; his next is to express his feelings about that outer world, and his last is to express his feelings about himself.'

Ralph Caplan: '... one of the hallmarks of a creative person is the ability to tolerate ambiguity, dissonance, inconsistency, things out of place. But one of the rules of a well-run corporation is that surprise be minimized. Yet if this rule were applied to the creative process, nothing worth reading would get written, nothing worth seeing would get painted, nothing worth living with and using would ever get designed.'

Martin Gardner: 'The sudden hunch, the creative leap of the mind that "sees" in a flash how to solve a problem in a simple way, is something quite different from general intelligence.'

Maggie Smith (on acting): 'The way it ends so totally, with nothing to put on the wall or in the bookcase. Just a lot of yesterdays, and then you have to start out all over again.'

Jean Giono: 'When he reached the place he was aiming for, he began making holes in the ground with his rod, putting an acorn in each and then covering it up again. He was planting oak trees. I asked him if the land was his. He said it wasn't. Did he know who the owner was? No, he didn't. He thought it must be common land, or perhaps it belonged to people who weren't interested in it. He wasn't interested in who they were. And so, with great care, he planted his hundred acorns.'

Albert Einstein: 'Creating a new theory is not like destroying an old barn and erecting a skyscraper in its place. It is rather like climbing a mountain and gaining new and wider views.'

Robert Grudin: 'The ways of creativity are infinite: the ways of formal learning are numbered. Restless, curious, playful, contriving, the innovative mind feeds on challenge and makes its home in the province of mystery.'

Gert Dumbar: 'I want to link creativity with something known as *serendipity*, which means to find something that you haven't been looking for but which changes everything that went before and comes after. The English word *serendipity* was coined by Horace Walpole, who used it for the first time in 1754 in a letter. Walpole described the adventures of the Three Persian Princes of Serendip. "By chance and shrewdness they discovered things which they were not looking for. They looked for one thing and found another. They were very surprised about this themselves." That is creativity ...'

Emilio Ambasz: 'It is not hunger, but love and fear, and sometimes wonder, that make us create ... to give poetic form to the pragmatic.'

Oliver Sachs: 'Creativity ... involves the power to originate, to break away from existing ways of looking at things, to move freely in the realm of the imagination, to create and re-create worlds fully in one's mind – while supervising all this with a critical inner eye. Creativity has to do with inner life – with the flow of new ideas and strong feelings.'

Georgia O'Keeffe: 'To create one's own world in any of the arts takes courage.'

Saul Steinberg: 'The life of the creative man is led, directed and controlled by boredom. Avoiding boredom is one of our most important purposes. It is also one of the most difficult, because the amusement always has to be newer and on a higher level. So we are on a kind of spiral. The higher you go, the narrower the circle. As you go ahead the field of choice becomes more meagre ...'

Marty Neumeier: 'The history of invention can be seen as a series of marriages of incompatible ideas, or at least ideas that previously had not been introduced. The matchmaker in most of these marriages is the unconscious mind.'

Francisco Varela: 'Creativity, common sense and love do come together in one fundamental sense. The three of them happen when you reach the point of awareness where you let go of something and let something else emerge.'

Arthur Koestler: 'The prerequisite of originality is the art of forgetting, at the proper moment, what we know.'

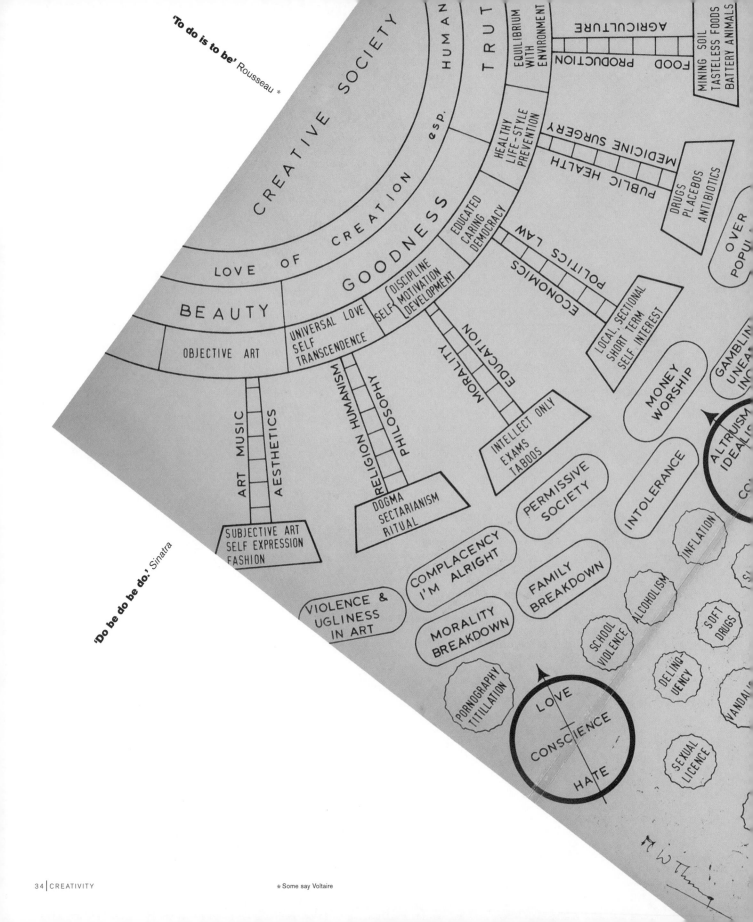

'To do is to be' Rousseau *

'Do be do be do.' Sinatra

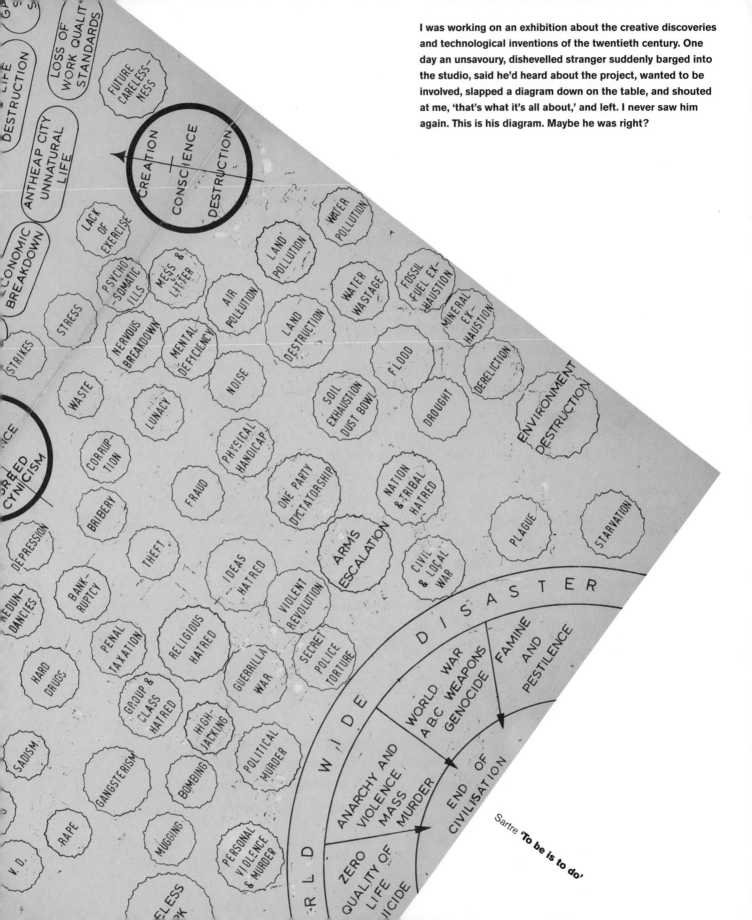

I was working on an exhibition about the creative discoveries and technological inventions of the twentieth century. One day an unsavoury, dishevelled stranger suddenly barged into the studio, said he'd heard about the project, wanted to be involved, slapped a diagram down on the table, and shouted at me, 'that's what it's all about,' and left. I never saw him again. This is his diagram. Maybe he was right?

Sartre 'To be is to do'

Opening speech by Brian Eno at The Turner Prize Awards in 1995.

The Turner prize is justly celebrated for raising all sorts of questions in the public mind about art and its place in our lives. Unfortunately, however, the intellectual climate surrounding the fine arts is so vaporous and self-satisfied that few of these questions are ever actually addressed, let alone answered.

Why is it that all of us here – presumably members of the arts community – probably know more about the currents of thought in contemporary science than those in contemporary art? Why have the sciences yielded great explainers like Richard Dawkins and Stephen Gould, while the arts routinely produce some of the loosest thinking and worst writing known to history? Why has the art world been unable to articulate any kind of useful paradigm for what it is doing now? I'm not saying that artists should have to 'explain' their work, or that writers exist to explain it for them, but that there could and should be a comprehensive public discussion about what art does for us, what is being learned from it, what it might enable us to do or think or feel that we couldn't before. Most of the public criticism of the arts is really an attempt to ask exactly such questions, and, instead of just priding ourselves on creating controversy by raising them, trying to answer a few might not be such a bad idea. The sciences rose to this challenge, and the book sales those authors enjoy indicate a surprising public appetite for complex issues, the result of which has been a broadening social dialogue about the power and beauty and limits of science. There's been almost no equivalent in the arts. The making of new culture is, given our performance in the fine and popular arts, just about our only growth industry aside from heritage cream teas and land-mines, but the lack of a clear connection between all that creative activity and the intellectual life of the society leaves the whole project poorly understood, poorly supported and poorly exploited.

If we're going to expect people to help fund the arts, whether through taxation or lotteries, then surely we owe them an attempt at an explanation of what value we think the arts might be to them … And if I had another two minutes of your time I'd have a go.

 Brian Eno. *A Year with Swollen Appendices*. Faber & Faber (London 1995)

Beware
of artists—
they mix with
all classes
of society
and are
therefore most
dangerous

Queen Victoria

Art is
what
you can
get
away
with

Marshall McLuhan

Art is pattern informed by sensibility

Sir Herbert Read

Art,
like morality,
consists
in drawing
the line
somewhere

G.K. Chesterton

Professor Gilbert J. Rose, a clinical psychiatrist at Yale, has a theory about the artistically creative mind. I came across an account of this speculation in an essay by John Fowles, who described it as follows:

'In simple terms, his proposition was that some children retain a particularly rich memory of the passage from extreme infancy, when the identity of the baby is merged with that of the mother, to the arrival of the first awareness of separate identity and the simultaneous first dawn of what will become the adult sense of reality – that is, they are deeply marked by the passage from a unified magical world to a discrete "realist" one. What seemingly stamps itself indelibly on this kind of infant psyche is a pleasure in the fluid, polymorphic nature of the sensuous impression, visual, tactile, auditory, and the rest, that he receives; and so profoundly that he cannot, even when the detail of this intensely auto-erotic experience has retreated into the unconscious, refrain from tampering with reality – from trying to recover, in other words, the early oneness with his mother that granted this ability to make the world mysteriously and deliciously change meaning and appearance. He was once a magician with a wand; and given the right other predisposing and environmental factors, he will one day devote his life to trying to regain the unity and the power by re-creating adult versions of the experience: he will be an artist. Moreover, since every child goes through some variation of the same experience, this also explains one major attraction of art for the audience. The artist is simply someone who does the journey back on behalf of the less conditioned and less technically endowed.'[1]

John Fowles added a footnote to this piece: '*Sensitive female readers may not be too happy about the pronoun used in this paragraph, but the theory helps to explain why all through more recent human history, men have seemed better adapted – or more driven – to individual artistic expression than women. Professor Rose points out that the chances of being conditioned by this primal erotic experience are (if one accepts Freudian theory) massively loaded towards the son ...*' Actually I don't see why girls would have differing memories than the boys as described by Professor Rose, but I thought it sufficiently controversial to merit an airing.

1. John Fowles. *Wormholes*. Vintage (London 1999)

Humour is the enemy of **AUTHORITY.**

Milton Glaser	**'Wit is insight.'**
Aristotle	**'Wit is educated insolence.'**
Friedrich Nietzsche	**'A joke is an epitaph on an emotion.'**
Surrealist proverb	**'When reason is away, smiles will play.'**
Mark Twain	**'Humour is like a frog; if you dissect it, it dies.'**
Henri Bergson	**'Laughter appears to stand in need of an echo.'**
Milan Kundera	**'Laughter … the most democratic of all facial aspects.'**
Mel Calman	**'Jokes join up the invisible dots between two subjects.'**
Gelett Burgess	**'To appreciate nonsense requires a serious interest in life.'**
Ludwig Wittgenstein	**'A serious work in philosophy could be written entirely of jokes.'**
Marcel Duchamp	**'… when the serious is tinted with humour, it makes a nicer colour.'**
Edward de Bono	**'Humour reveals a whole different universe of information processing.'**
Dorothy Parker	**'Wit has a truth to it, wisecracking is simply callisthenics with words.'**
Thomas Carlyle	**'True humour … issues not in laughter, but in still smiles, which lie far deeper.'**
Noël Coward	**'Wit ought to be a glorious treat, like caviar; never spread it around like marmalade.'**
Rich Saul Wurman	**'Consider the doorway as a metaphor for information, humour a passageway to understanding.'**
Paul Rand	**'The frame of mind that looks at humour as trivial and flighty mistakes the shadow for the substance.'**

The Humours: In the Middle Ages humours referred to blood, phlegm, choler and melancholy. The perfect man was a cocktail of all four in equal parts. If someone had more of one humour than another then they were unbalanced, irregular, capricious. In other words eccentric. Edward Lear would qualify as one such eccentric. 'I see life as basically tragic and futile,' he complained, 'and the only thing that matters is making little jokes.' So he did. His drawings, limericks and rhymes are full of comicalities like *The Dong with the Luminous Nose* and *The Pobble who had no Toes*. The natural world also has a sense of humour. Consider the elephant which, as far as I know, is the only animal with a flexible nose and four knees. And humankind which are the only animals that can smile. Actually I've just read that behavourists reckon that, in their own fashion, chimpanzees can smile. Since chimps and humans are cousins perhaps they can, but perhaps what we think of as their smile is really our grimace. 'Laughter disarms and opens the way for instinct,' said Saul Steinberg, 'It is like hiccups or yawns. When you try to repress a yawn, it comes out of your ears.' In 1964 Steinberg took a trip with Saul Bellow to Murchison Falls in East Africa. At one point they both found themselves sitting in a very small wooden boat surrounded by hundreds of very large crocodiles. They were terrified, Steinberg recalled, at the thought of the comical obituaries. The library in *The Name of the Rose* contains a seditious volume by an Egyptian alchemist, who 'attributes the creation of the world to divine laughter'. An unnerving thought matched by an equally frightening conjecture posed by another writer, Robert Graves, who innocently asked whether the height of silent humour might be to cause an unknown change in the earth's climate? Wit and creativity go hand in hand. 'Wit is the sudden marriage of ideas which before their union were not perceived to have any relation,' wrote Mark Twain using a beautifully sustained metaphor.

a corner for the fool

Aristophanes said the brain of the sage has a corner for the fool, Freud related humour to creativity, Arthur Koestler gave the jester equal billing with the scientist and the artist, and Peter Ustinov explained that comedy is simply a funny way of being serious. In an endeavour to explain this unlikely connection, introspective psychologists resort to comical knee-slappers like 'conceptual thinking is a necessary pre-requisite for the experience of humour based on a violation of cognitive expectancies', and unwittingly prove that trying to define humour is one of the definitions of humour! Victor Borge suggests it is the shortest distance between two people; Jonathan Miller describes it as 'vague, runaway stuff that hisses around the fissures and crevices of the mind, like some sort of loose psychic gas …' A pragmatic view: the refusal of circumstances to conform to expectations. This aspect of the unlikely can be further refined by the difference between the comic who opens funny doors and the comedian who opens doors funny. Whereas one merely tickles the ribs, the other conveys a vivid new perception. A sudden switch from one way of looking at something to another. The Polish-Irish-Jewish joke which catches you off balance. Charlie Chaplin eating the sole of his shoe. Getting led down the garden path before being yanked into the bushes. Although Nietzsche said something frightfully stern about humour being an escape from serious thought, he allowed that wit makes connections no one thought of in quite the same way before. Wit exposes a likeness in things that are different and a difference in things that are alike. Wit makes sense out of nonsense. *How come we laugh when tickled by others but not when we tickle ourselves? One scientist has suggested that it's a throwback to primeval times when, grasped by a predator, we instinctively squirmed to escape and automatically released our inner tensions by nervous laughter. Doesn't sound funny to me.*

This is Jean Robert. He stands 2 metres high in his socks.

What's the difference between a nitwit, a dimwit, a halfwit, and a witless twit? Not much I guess but I understand that nitwit is an early American expression concocted from the Dutch '*Ik niet weer*' ['I don't know']. No doubt a common complaint among the first Dutch settlers who nevertheless shrewdly bought an island from the Indians for $50 which they then called Stuyvesant and ended up being called Manhattan. **[SEE** P442].

wit¹, *n.* **1.** humour, facetiousness, drollery, funniness, wittiness, cleverness, piquancy, quickness; jocularity, waggishness.

2. badinage, persiflage, repartee, quip, wisecrack, saying, sarcasm; irony, satire, burlesque, parody, caricature, travesty; witticism, Atticism, bon mot, jest, jocosity, joke; pun, wordplay, play on words, spoonerism, double entendre; raillery, banter, joshing; buffoonery, playfulness.

3. humorist, lampoonist, parodist; jokester, joker, comic, comedian, comedienne, slapstick artist, *Fr.* *farceur*, droll fellow, funny person, *Both Inf.* card, character; wag, reparteeist, banterer, *Inf.* wisecracker, punster, zany, madcap, *U.S. Inf.* cutup, antic; mummer, mimer, mimic.

4. intelligence, brains, braininess, *U.S. Sl.* smarts; sagacity, sageness, wisdom, sapience, sapiency; acumen, discernment, perspicacity, penetration; perception, percipience, insight; astuteness, shrewdness, savvy, keenness, long-headedness, hard-headedness, common sense; ingenuity, cleverness, aptness, quickness; brilliance, acuity, sharpness.

wit², to wit, namely, *Latin.* *videlicet,* viz.; that is to say, that is, *Latin. id est,* i.e.; specifically, explicitly, scilicet; for example, for instance, as a case in point, as an illustration.

Samuel Butler

As all feats of activity are the [more] admired the nearer they come to danger, so is all speacularor wit the nearer it comes to nonsense.

This shadow picture of a motorbike owes its presence to an ingenious arrangement of 848 knives, spoons and forks, and of course to the innovative genius of Shigeo Fukuda, who not only thought it up in his head in the first place, but also meticulously stuck each piece of cutlery into position.

Julian Schnabel   'I work with things left over from other things.'

Ceri Richards

Sir Laurence Olivier

Graham Sutherland

Frank Leavis

Julian Trevelyan

Sir John Pope-Hennessy

Creative addition always yields more than the prosaic sum of the parts. By addition I mean putting salient factors together to arrive at an answer: on his march to the Alps, Hannibal crossed the river at Arles by persuading his elephants to stick their trunks up like snorkels. In Japan it's so crowded that they grow cucumbers vertically, in Kuwait I've seen dhows with thin rigid wooden flags so as to catch the slightest puff of any wind. A recent best-selling book was called *101 Uses for a Dead Cat*. Rodin claimed that he never invented anything new but only discovered things. Beethoven produced new compositions within an established medium and a firm tradition. Frank Lloyd Wright exploited existing building materials to make dramatic volumes and spaces. Picasso conjured up the head of a bull from an old bicycle seat and handlebars. Henry Ford organized new procedures and techniques of mass production. He didn't invent or patent a single machine, tool or process. He only used what was to hand.

Il Dolce fa Niente, the painting by William Holman Hunt, portrays the body of his mistress and the face of his wife. It hangs in the drawing room of Old Battersea House in London.

Exotic Eve, by Gauguin, has the head of his mother, copied from a photograph taken in her younger days, and the sinuous body from a temple sculpture at Borobudur in India.[1]

A face used on a poster for The National Portrait Gallery in London plays a similar game. The segments extracted from portraits in the collection, are montaged to create a royal person. Most people recognize him. More fool them because it isn't who they think they thought it was. The six segments are from portraits of Ceri Richards, Sir Laurence Olivier, Frank Leavis, Graham Sutherland, Julian Trevelyan and Sir John Pope-Hennessy.

1. Robert Hughes. *Nothing if not Critical*. Alfred A. Knopf (New York 1990)

MAN RAY

Man Ray (Man of Light) made an art out of cobbling things together. In 1921 the American painter, sculptor, film-maker and photographer, born Emmanuel Radnitzky [SEE P497] in 1890 but known since he was 15 as Man Ray, set sail from New York for Le Havre and reached Paris on 14 July. At his first exhibition he met Erik Satie, who gave him the idea for the celebrated iron studded with nails. In the same year he met Alice Prin, *Kiki de Montparnasse*, whose back, superimposed with the two holes of a violin, he photographed in homage to the nudes of his favourite artist and called *Le Violon d'Ingres*. In 1922 he created his first *Rayograph* – a cameraless print – for which he is best remembered today. His portraits included Duchamp with a star-shaped tonsure shaved into the hair on the back of his head, Jean Cocteau, Gertrude Stein, James Joyce, Ernest Hemingway, Aldous Huxley, Max Ernst, Pablo Picasso, Le Corbusier, Igor Stravinsky, André Derain, Wallis Windsor and Henri Matisse. When he went to photograph Matisse he forgot the lens. Taking his spectacles apart, he taped the two bits of glass together and fixed them to the camera. The result was an impressionistic shot which so delighted him that for a while he did everything out of focus. When he arrived to photograph the Marquise de Casati he forgot to take his lights and had to resort to a long exposure but accidentally kicked the camera and depicted the Marquise with two pairs of eyes. Suddenly Man Ray was credited with being a new visionary who could 'capture people's souls'. Then he caused a series of dark-room fiascos by accidentally switching on the light: the resulting *Rayographs* and *Solarisations* led to Man Ray being pronounced an Alchemist. Other tricks included layering pictures with gels and gauze to striking effect; introducing extraneous props like tribal effigies or Brancusi's sculptures for no reason other than that they looked right or wrong. Aged 81, by then in a wheelchair, Man Ray attended the first major exhibition of his work. 'If this had only happened forty years ago,' he was heard to mutter, 'I might well have been encouraged.' As Douglas Hofstadter pointed out, invention is sometimes more like falling off a log than like sawing one in two.

I came across this typographic improvisation rubber-stamped on wine cartons from a French vineyard.

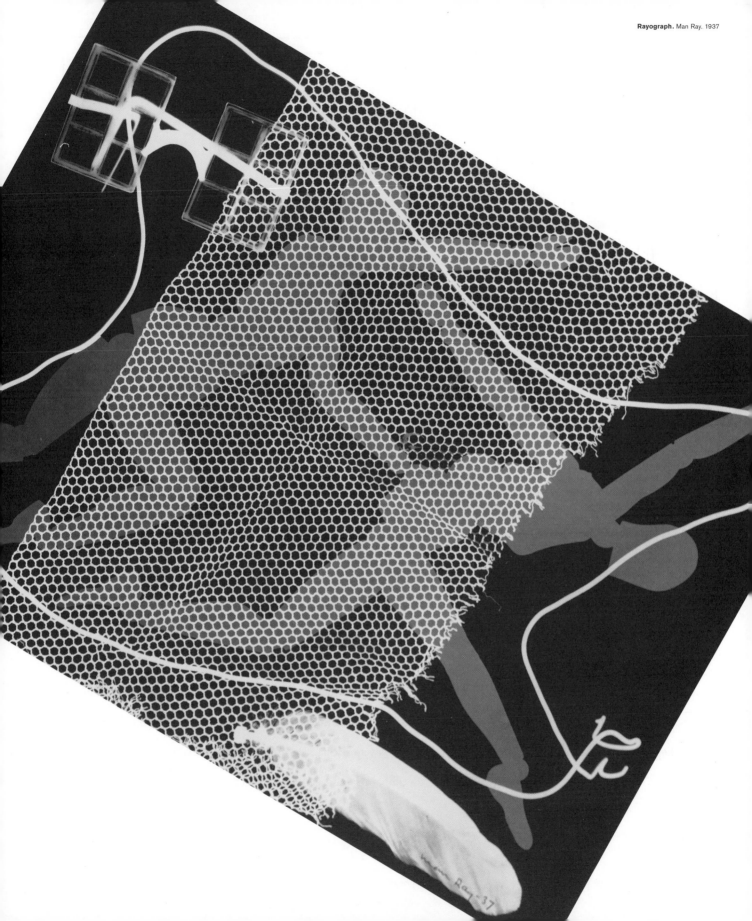

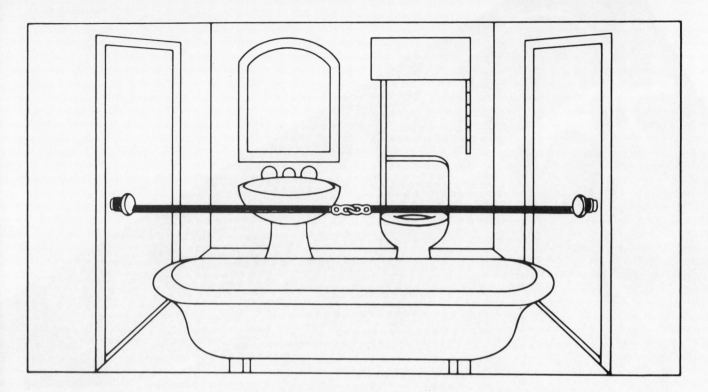

Object and circumstance Until the Berlin Wall came down the veteran traveller visiting Eastern Europe always included a squash ball in his suitcase. In most hotels showers were few and far between, although usually compensated for by ancient bathtubs of sensational dimensions. The snag was an inevitable lack of bath plugs, hence the squash ball. At the other extreme, one bathroom I encountered in a melancholy hotel in Ljubljana was so small that the bidet was installed in the diminutive shower stall. However, the best bathroom innovation must be the contraption described by Ralph Caplan in his book *By Design*: 'An ingenious example of the product-situation cycle could be found in the Quebec waterfront hotel called L'Hotel Louis XIV, lamentably destroyed by fire a few years ago. At the Louis XIV, the term "private bath" meant what it means in many European hotels: the bath is yours but not yours alone, for it is also the private bath of the guest on the other side of the bathroom. This creates a problem. If the bathroom has no inside locks, you have no privacy. But if the doors can be locked from the inside, one forgetful guest can lock the other out indefinitely and almost surely will. Well, there were no locks inside the bathrooms of the Louis XIV, but tied to each doorknob was a three-and-a-half-foot length of leather thong to which a hook was attached. When you were in the bathroom you simply linked the two hooks together, holding both doors shut. There was no way to get back into your own room without at the same time unlocking the door for the other guest.' 'It was memorable,' the author records, 'as the total integration of object and circumstance.'[1]

   1. Ralph Caplan. *By Design.* St Martin's Press (New York 1982)   **Illustration.** Milton Glaser

According to Egyptian mythology the eye of Horus symbolically represented the sun. The design was modelled on the marks which appear on a falcon's face – appropriate for Horus the falcon-headed God. Anyway it was destroyed (probably in an eclipse) by Seth, the wicked god of darkness. Thoth, the good god who also invented writing, used ancient Egyptian mathematical fractions to put it back together again. The hieroglyph also incorporates the geometric progression commonly referred to as the Fibonacci series. For some odd reason they add up to 63/64. A scholarly wit attributes the missing 1/64 to the god's commission.

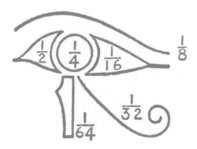

Improvisation is a crude form of innovation. This drawing of Milan Cathedral intimates rather than imitates. A collation of lines which imply flying buttresses, finials, clerestories, crockets, dripstones, acroteria, mullions, quoins, spandrels, and other architectural refinements.

Electric perfume: Salvador Dalí was approached to design the pack of a new perfume for a large American cosmetic company. He agreed on condition that he had a free hand. An apprehensive board of directors accepted. Months later, on the day of the presentation, a nervous reception committee met Dalí at the airport. They were even more worried when they saw that he wasn't carrying anything. Although questioned he gave nothing away. Dalí took his place in the conference hall. When the press photographers surged forward snapping away with their flashes he stood up, took a dead flash bulb, tapped it sharply on the table to flatten the hot bulbous end, sat it upright, and dramatically intoned into the microphones, 'Ladies and gentlemen, I give the world a new perfume – *Electric*.'

Mae West Sofa: Salvador Dalí collaborated with Edward James on the design and manufacture of the famous sofa. When a guest burnt a hole in the bright pink upholstery they resolved the problem by embroidering a caterpillar over the hole. A solution much the same as that adopted by Louise Bourgeois, who in her younger days had stitched fig leaves over male figures on antique tapestries for her parents' wealthy American clients.

A Marvel Comic: After his death, the ashes of Mark Gruenwald the editor of *Marvel Comics* were blended with the ink to print a special edition.

Adrian Searle: art critic, reviewing an exhibition at the Whitechapel Art Gallery. '... Peter Doig is an omnivorous scavenger and borrower: from other people's paintings, from movies, from newspaper and magazine photographs, and, of course, from memories and incidents in his own life. Post-impressionism and Polke, Munch and Monet, Hopper and Seurat collide with family snapshots, memories of growing up in Canada, images grabbed with the video recorder pause button, and moments embellished and re-invented on the canvas. Some of the images might even come from song lyrics. It is difficult to write about Doig's paintings without falling back on inventories, detailing the diversity of material that gets fed into them ...'

The WOBO: On a visit to the West Indies beer baron Alfred Heineken, disturbed by shanty towns surrounded by discarded bottles, had a thought. Use bottles as bricks. He commissioned Dutch architect John Habrakan to design the first mass-production container with secondary use – the WOBO. 100,000 WOBOs (acronym for *World Bottle*) were chuntered out with a plan of a simple dwelling printed on the label. The bottle was rectangular with a short neck to fit into the base of its neighbour, the sides were moulded with projections to aid bonding. They built a prototype bottle house but it was not well received by those who saw bottles as bottles, and houses as houses. Rumour has it 60,000 WOBOs are still stashed away in a Rotterdam warehouse.

Christopher Cockerell. Inventor: One day, back in the early 1950s, a former aeronautical engineer for Marconi living in a caravan in Norfolk took a can of cat food, a coffee tin and a vacuum cleaner and carried out one of those feats of experimental imagination that earned him a place in history. Christopher Cockerell had invented the hovercraft.

Masks of Aeschylus: Ancient Greek theatrical masks were instruments. The interior cavities created resonances for the voice which could trigger a state of ecstasy in both actor and audience. Vitruvius writing on amphitheatres: 'due to suitably placed reflecting walls, the voice is supported and strengthened when two identical soundwaves, arriving at the same point at the same time, combine to produce the sum of its effects.' He also mentioned sound reflectors of ceramic built into the rows of seats.

McDonalds: In the early days the McDonald brothers streamlined food production with dispensers to pump out a precise dollop of ketchup or mustard, and revolving trays so up to twenty-four buns could be speedily dressed. They also introduced specialization so that one person did nothing but cook hamburgers, another make shakes, another dress buns, and so on. They were also one of the first to have food prepared so that customers could be served immediately.

Palimpsests: Parchment was expensive and ancient manuscripts were often scrubbed clean by monks to be re-used for Latin texts. Others were cut up and used to strengthen the bindings of new manuscripts. At art school I was wrapping up a parcel, and finding a piece of card with an indifferent drawing in a drawer – cut it up. I later discovered it was a McKnight Kauffer. I feel ashamed whenever I think about it.

Philately: Rowland Hill suggested to the Postmaster-General that he should sell a small piece of paper with a design on one side and gum arabic on the other which a sender could lick and stick on an envelope. They thought he was out of his mind.

Bats, turds and rats: In the First World War the Royal Navy trained sea lions to track German submarines. It didn't work. Once at sea the creatures took off. During the Second World War the Americans developed the Bat Bomb. The project called for two million bats to have tiny incendiary devices attached to their legs. The intention was to drop them at night over Japanese cities, where they would home into the eaves of the wood buildings. In the morning timers would ignite the devices and create firestorms. Roosevelt cancelled the scheme in favour of the atom bomb. Whilst the Americans were busy working on bats, Misha Black, a British product designer, was busy designing an explosive device which could be dropped on roads without being noticed. At the time there was plenty of horse-drawn traffic. Horse droppings were the answer. Then there was the rat bomb. This was intended to be hidden by the underground forces in the coal bunkers of German industry. When it hit the furnace – bang.

RATS, EXPLOSIVE.

On the Moscow front in 1941 the Russians introduced a secret weapon — dogs trained to forage for food beneath trucks. They were strapped up with explosives and an upright hinged stick which was a detonator.

**'Something old
something new
something borrowed
and a touch of blue.'**

**A radiant sun
cut out of the
cylindrical lid
of an oil drum
is a favourite
subject among
the naïve
artists of Haiti.
I have this one
hanging right
next to my
front door so
when leaving
each morning
it will remind
me that
less is more.**

Novelist Sir Walter Scott thought of a smart turn of phrase while out hunting. Frightened of forgetting, he shot a crow, whittled a quill from a feather and jotted down a note in its blood on his sleeve. This anecdote may seem dubiously related to design yet recycling, often for a comically different purpose, occupies a central place in the creative process.

Recycling is often a testimony to human ingenuity. In the Third World they make bracelets from electrical cable, musical instruments from gasoline drums, and convert gutted television sets into birdcages. In Morocco I've noticed pots made out of old tyres in the shape of *amphoras*, in Turkey welded Coca Cola cans making chimneys for hovels, in the south of Italy gates cobbled up from perforated metal panels originally used as aircraft landing strips. I used to spend my summers at a fishing village in Puglia where they sold two-foot-high pisspots (the old ladies wore long skirts) which I used for plants. Dangerously close, now I come to think about it, to lamps made out of Chianti bottles.

⋙→

However, recycling is not necessarily just making do.

Coco Chanel took a shine to photographer Horst, handed him a small lump of soft clay, told him to clutch it tightly in his hand, then had it cast in metal as his personal cigarette lighter. The French sculptor César made a chair out of industrial packaging. Simon Rodia built Watts Towers in Los Angeles out of debris (70,000 bits of coloured glass, pottery shards, clam shells, broken bathroom tiles). On his delivery route postman Ferdinand Cheval spent 33 years picking up odd stones and fossils to build his *Palais Idéal* in Hauterives, now listed as a historic monument. Raymond Isidore built and decorated his house near Chartres all over (outside and inside) with mosaics made from discarded fragments. And Justo Gallego, former Trappist monk, spent years building a cathedral out of abandoned rubbish in a small town near Madrid. Then there is the spectacular visionary *Rock Garden* of Road Inspector Nek Shand in Chandigarh, India. An extraordinary kingdom of magical sculptures and structures created from recycled urban waste.

Nature's technologies can be recycled, as can culture and commerce. Swiss inventor George De Mestral, intrigued at the tenacity of burrs sticking to his clothes and his dog after walking up mountains, looked at their structure under a microscope and came up with *Velcro*.

Velours (velvet) plus **cro**ché (hooked) = **Velcro**

By the way, the ultimate style of footwear for the really dedicated environmentalist is a shoe made of recycled metal, car tyres, coffee bags and disposable nappies. It's called the *Dejashoe* (*déjà vu*?). It probably smells like it.

'Eels have been put to work testing water quality in Japan. Five years ago they discovered that eels react to slight variations in water quality. Harmful substances cause an eel's heartbeat to slow down, or rapidly rise. A machine is now being marketed that utilizes this unique sensitivity. An eel is inserted into an acrylic tube in the machine. As the water flows through the tube, electrodes monitor the eel's heart rate, and any changes are relayed to a technician. Eels selected for this job are from especially clean waters and are replaced monthly to maintain accuracy.'
The Daily Yomiuri

'… originality houses many rooms, and the views from the windows are all different.'
Guy Davenport

'Matisse renovates rather than innovates.'
Guillaume Apollinaire

'I neglected nothing.'
Nicolas Poussin

'I do not seek – I find.'
Pablo Picasso

Elmer McCurdy, the Oklahoma outlaw, was a bandit of extravagant ineptitude. When he blew a safe, he used so much nitroglycerine that 4,000 silver dollars melted and fused to the safe. When he held up a train, it was the wrong one. On a tip-off the sheriff turned up to arrest him on a farm where Elmer was working for Charlie, a Red Indian with a glass eye. Elmer came out shooting, but like all his recorded actions, this was not a good idea. Elmer's embalmed body lay unclaimed in the funeral parlour, slowly mummifying in the prairie air. The mortician's son would put roller skates on him and take him for a spin. Eventually he was sold to a freak show, an enterprise which developed into producing cheap lurid movies. Elmer appeared among the skeletons and weird props in the blood-curdling scary scenes. At one point he lost an arm as the showman's son sawed it off to goose Bea, his secretary. Elmer was then sold in a job-lot to the Hollywood Wax Museum. The owner, Spoony Singh, a Sikh who used to be a Canadian lumberjack, was so taken aback by his appearance that he sold him on to the operators of a carnival ghost train who painted him in fluorescent Day-Glo colours and hung him up in the tunnel to terrify the passengers. A set dresser, working on location with *The Six Million Dollar Man*, took a ride and saw him glowing in the dark, his remaining arm modestly covering his crotch. A closer inspection revealed he still had the remnants of his genitals and wasn't made of *papier mâché*. The dresser notified the authorities. After hearing Elmer's history the coroner decreed that the cadaver should be buried under six feet of concrete. But before this could be carried out a posse of Oklahomans arrived to claim his corpse. Ranchers on horses clinking with silver, a black hearse, and lots of white lilies. They buried him on Boot Hill with the other outlaws – alongside Charlie Pearse, eternally misspelled on his gravestone as 'Desparado.'[1]

1. Abridged from a review by Nancy Banks Smith **Illustration.** Recycling emblem designed by William J. Lloyd

THE SORCERER IS A PREHISTORIC CAVE PAINTING (15,000 BC) OF A SHAMAN. PART HUMAN, PART ANIMAL, PART SPIRIT – A **CHIMERA**. THE HIND LEGS ARE HUMAN, THE TAIL PROBABLY BELONGS TO A WOLF, THE BODY A SKIN FROM A FOUR-LEGGED ANIMAL; THE FACE, MADE TO RESEMBLE A BIRD SURMOUNTED WITH ANTLERS, GAZES DIRECTLY INTO THE EYES OF THE ONLOOKER.[1] IN GREEK MYTHOLOGY THE **CHIMERA** WAS A FIRE-BREATHING MONSTER WITH A LION'S HEAD, A GOAT'S BODY AND A SERPENT'S TAIL. THE **EGYPTIAN SPHINX** IS A LION WITH THE HEAD OF A MAN, THE **GREEK SPHINX** HAS A WOMAN'S HEAD, BREASTS AND THE BODY AND FEET OF A LION. THE **ORIENTAL PHOENIX** HAS A FRONT LIKE A GOOSE, REAR LIKE A TORTOISE, HEAD OF A SNAKE AND BEAK OF A CHICKEN. THE **CHINESE DRAGON** IS EQUALLY FANCIFUL. THE VERSION ILLUSTRATED BELOW IS COMPOSED USING EYES FROM A TOMATO CAN WRAPPER, EARS OF HOTEL STICKERS, TEETH OF AN INDEX CARD, A FIERY TONGUE OF TRANSIT LABELS, AND ODD ITEMS INCLUDING MY FIRST MOTOR VEHICLE LICENCE. THE CHARACTERS FROM A **MENAGERIE** SPORTING THEMSELVES OPPOSITE RELY ON EMPTY CIGARETTE

Jorge Luis Borges also composed a menagerie of 120 fantastic, legendary and mythological creatures in his *Book of Imaginary Beings*.

PACKS, CORES OF TOILET ROLLS, CORKS FROM WINE BOTTLES, SCREW TOPS FROM PLASTIC CONTAINERS, AND OTHER BITS OF CONSUMER SOCIETY DETRITUS. ALL DISGUISED BY PAPIER MÁCHÉ AND CRUDE POSTER COLOURS. INVENTING IMAGINARY CREATURES IS FUN BUT CREATING LIVING BREATHING ONES SEEMS CREEPY. AT LEAST THAT'S WHAT I FEEL ABOUT THE PATENTED **ONCOMOUSE** WHICH HAS GENES RELIED UPON TO CAUSE CANCER SO THAT RESEARCHERS CAN DEVELOP TUMOURS. BY THE WAY **DOLLY**, THE WORLD'S FIRST CLONED SHEEP, WAS FIRST SHORN IN SPRING 1997 AND THE WOOLLY JUMPER PRESENTED TO THE SCIENCE MUSEUM IN LONDON. SHE WAS NAMED AFTER DOLLY PARTON AS HER CELLS WERE EXTRACTED FROM MAMMARY TISSUE. [SEE P8] ACTUALLY THERE'S NOTHING NEW IN DESIGNING PLANTS AND ANIMALS. IT'S ONLY THROUGH HUMAN INTERVENTION THAT WE HAVE CAULIFLOWERS, BROCCOLI, CABBAGES AND BRUSSELS SPROUTS. AND THAT THE **WOLF** WAS BRED INTO GREYHOUNDS, PEKINESE, BULLDOGS, ROTTWEILERS, BEAGLES, BLOODHOUNDS AND CHIHUAHUAS TO MENTION A HANDFUL. CRUFTS DOG SHOW EVEN CATEGORIZES THEM INTO: TOY GROUP (POODLES ETC), WORKING (BOXERS ETC), UTILITY, TERRIER, HOUND AND GUNDOGS.

1. Chris Stringer & Robin McKie. *African Exodus.* Jonathan Cape (London 1996)

AGIP TRADEMARK

Illustration. William McCaffrey

USELESS INFORMATION All breeds have altered, either by accident or on purpose. The Bolognese are said to have dwarfed their spaniels by immersing them daily in *eau-de-vie* and bashing in their noses. A book published in 1570 only recognized seventeen dogs: Terar, Harier, Bloudhound, Gasehunde, Tumber, Stealer, Setter, Wappe, Turnspit, and others. The Cruft's show of 1890 had 220 classes. The champion of the 1998 Westminster Kennel Club Dog Show, America's premier event, was Fairwood Frolic, a Norwich terrier. She was selected from a group that included a malamute, a toy poodle, a long-haired dachshund and an Old English sheepdog. Previous winners have come from breeds as extreme as the pug (whose eyes are sometimes furtively pressed back into their sockets by their owners).

Steve Jones. *Almost Like a Whale.* Anchor (London 2000)

EVERY BREED RECOGNIZED BY THE AMERICAN KENNEL CLUB FROM THE SMALLEST TO THE LARGEST

MAKING DO. HEAD-SMASHED-IN is a cliff in Alberta where buffalo were stampeded to death. Dressed in pelts the Blackfoots lured buffalo towards the edge of the precipice, and then created a panic – the animals jumped – and provided dinner. It was an ancient ploy. In the Saône-et-Loire region of France there are remains of 100,000 horses similarly stampeded to death by Neolithic man. A different order of innovation was a medieval culinary conceit which put a fresh egg into the cavity of a pigeon, which was then put into a goose, the goose into a piglet, the piglet into a lamb and the lamb into an ox. The whole was then spit roasted. When ready, a swordsman clove it in half to magically release a chick, newly hatched by the warmth of its housing.[1] Until someone puts a zip in an egg that's hard to follow. A similar concept is echoed in the folk song about an old lady who swallowed a fly, who swallowed a spider to catch the fly, a bird to catch the spider, a cat to catch the bird, and so on. Each verse gets longer except the last: 'There was an old lady who swallowed a horse. She died of course.' In California the current wheeze is to buy a meal from a 'greasy spoon', put it on the engine of your automobile, and drive home. By the time you arrive it's cooked. The less fastidious put their meal in a plastic bag and pop it in the washing machine with the laundry. Marinetti, *agent provocateur* of modern art, proposed an ideal meal which was an orchestration of cutlery, glasses, china, colours, foods, flavours and aromas in unlikely combinations such as chocolate and spinach, hare in vanilla sauce, nougat and mortadella. Certain dishes were passed under the nose to stimulate appetite or evoke an association – a love affair, or a journey to the exotic East. Courses were accompanied by fragrances to provoke the senses, poetry to enhance the flavour, music and flashing coloured lights to create ambience. Presentation on the plate was important and recipes accompanied by detailed drawings and captions to show the precise layout.[2] Marinetti died in 1944 shortly after swearing allegiance to Mussolini's doomed Republic of Salo. The glass in the illustration contains a lethal cocktail (called Fire in the Mouth) invented by Futurist engineer Barosi.

1. Prue Leith. *Royal Society of Arts Journal* (London, August 1986)   2. Marinetti. *The Futurist Cookbook.* Trefoil Publications (London 1989)

pizza

Photograph. Franco Fontana. *Paesaggio* 1985

Paul Klee

'Colour is the place where our brain and the universe meet.'

The Great Eskimo Vocabulary Hoax

This was a scientific paper which debunked the myth that the Inuit (Eskimo) have a hundred or more words for snow – actually they have no more than the English do for rain. A similar misconception was propagated by William Gladstone, who thought Homer was colour blind[1] because of his meagre use of colour words. Some ethnologists extended his conclusion to include the entire Greek population of that time. They were both wrong.

Names for colours enter language slowly. The ancient Greeks had no word for **blue** and even in the Middle Ages there was still no English word for **orange**. Chaucer referred to it as 'bitwixe **yelow** and **reed**'. **Orange** has always suffered an identity crisis. [SEE P92]. Today, although we can differentiate millions of shades, our vocabulary still only has about thirty colour words.

Colour words are acquired by cultures in a strict sequence according to anthropologists who analysed 98 widely differing languages.

All languages have **black** and **white**.
If there are three words, the third is **red**.
If there are four, then it is **green** or **yellow**.
If five then whichever didn't make four, **yellow** or **green**.
If six, it is **blue**.
If seven, it is **brown**.
If eight or more, then **purple**, **pink**, **orange**
and **grey** are added in any order.[2]

However, it's not quite this neat. An African desert tribe has no word for **green**, but six for **red**. Italian has three words for **blue : celeste**, **azzurro** and **blu**. Swahili doesn't have any, so coined **bulu** from English. Creek and Natchez Indians use the same name for **yellow** and **green**, as do the Highland Scots for **blue** and **green**. French has two words for **brown : brun** and **marron**, but there isn't one in Chinese, Japanese, Welsh, or (less surprisingly) Inuit. These, despite the hoax, do have at least seven words for **white**.

And a primitive tribe in the New Guinea Highlands still speak a **black** and **white** language and distinguish colours in terms of brightness.

1. Joseph Chilton Pearce. *The Crack in the Cosmic Egg.* Washington Square Press (New York 1971)   2. Martin Gardner. *Order and Surprise.* Oxford University Press (Oxford 1984)

ONE ALBINO DOESN'T A SUMMER MAKE

BLACK

IN ANGLO-SAXON **BLACK** IS **BLAECE**

WHITE

contra_diction_ means the same as **gain**_saying_

AND **WHITE** IS **BLAC**, THUS **BLANCH**, **BLANK**, **BLEAK**.

On the film set of *Bonnie Prince Charlie*, producer Alexander Korda took aesthetic exception to Scotland. 'I hate it. All that purple stuff, vat's it called? Feather? Then all this green and orange and the blue sky. It makes me sick. It looks like a biscuit tin. And vat are those tings with spikes? Fizzles?' He was obviously overwrought.

Associations with colour are emotive, irrational and deep-seated. There is an old advertising story about making up three packs of a detergent in different colours to test market reactions. One was done in yellow, one in blue, and one in yellow and blue. A panel of housewives were asked to try them out. They judged the powder in the yellow pack as corrosive, the blue one as too mild, the yellow and blue just right. Actually the packs all contained the same stuff.[1]

Colour colours our lives. Dr Max Luscher diagnosed personality disorders through colour associations, and his application of the principles to marketing is thought by some to be mildly sinister. Broadly speaking, his conclusions are that dark blue appeals to people motivated by security – a popular house-colour among financial institutions. Blue-green is associated with constancy and is often used on packaging for intimate products like toiletries. Orange-red seems to be related to activity and is a common choice for those who market leisure and pleasure. As a corporate colour bright yellow is associated with modernity. Not surprisingly, combinations of yellow and red are the corporate colours of Kodak and Shell.

Not that Henry Ford seemed to give a toss – remarking you could have his cars in any colour you liked as long as it was black. He had his reasons – only black enamel dried quickly enough to be used on the conveyor belt. However, he also had fixations, believing that 'machine' blue and 'eggshell' white were beneficial for 'order and morale'. Five thousand men continuously painted in the vast Ford plant in Detroit. Every month they used eleven thousand gallons of both colours. They are still the company colours.[2]

When I was designing an identity for a classy hotel group in the Far East, it was suggested that each manager should have a say in the choice of colour for each hotel because of local cultural preferences. The scenario went like this: the hotel in Hong Kong didn't want blue as it symbolizes death and requested 'Chinese' red. To avoid debate on the precise shade I cut a corner off the red menu of the *China Garden* restaurant behind the hotel. A sample of the saffron orange material worn by Buddhist priests provided the specification for the hotel in Bangkok. The manager in Singapore was keen on the same maroon as his tie (but declined to provide a swatch). San Francisco wanted the same red as the Stars and Stripes. The daughter of the hotel owner in Malaysia suggested a delicate salmon pink.

Not my inclination, but as she was going to marry the chief executive I thought it ungracious to quibble.

A character in a George Eliot novel explains that colours deeply penetrate her like scent, and author Dorothy Parker went for reds. She painted her living room in nine shades of red: pink, vermilion, scarlet, crimson, maroon, raspberry, rose, russet and magenta.[3] Pianist Glenn Gould's favourite colour was battleship grey (he committed suicide), and Matisse more subtly is said to have loved 'the delicate transparent pinks of baked shrimp shells'.

Green has always been considered restful. Pliny wrote that 'emerald delights the eye without fatiguing it'. Nero peered through an emerald while enjoying lions devouring Christians. In the Middle Ages engravers gazed into a green beryl to rest their eyes, and since the seventeenth century theatres have had a green room so actors could relax from the footlight glare. Green was Oscar Wilde's colour – decadent, provocative. He told his followers in the Aesthetic Movement to always wear green carnations supplied by his florist, Goodyears: 'They grow them there.' Then of course there was the Emerald City in *The Wizard of Oz* whose citizens saw everything in beautiful shades of green.

Psychologist Nicholas Humphries: 'As I look around the room I'm working in, man-made colour shouts back at me from every surface – books, cushions, a rug on the floor, a coffee-cup, a box of staples – bright blues, reds, yellows, greens. There is as much colour here as in any tropical forest. Yet while almost every colour in the forest would be meaningful, here in my study almost nothing is. Colour anarchy has taken over.'[4]

colour prejudice

1. Vance Packard. *The Hidden Persuaders*. Penguin (Harmondsworth 1981)   2 & 3. Alexander Theroux. *The Primary Colours*. Picador (London 1995)   4. Daniel Dennett. *Consciousness Explained*. Penguin (London 1993)

Genetic anthropology confirms that variations between races are trivial compared to variations between individuals within a race. Of course there are social differences and a sense of collective identity held by differing groups of people. Similarly there are many differences between individuals within those groups. But the overwhelming evidence is that everybody is very similar to everyone else. The colour of one's skin is an environmental effect, a biological response to lack of, or subjection to, fierce sun. African Bushmen and Australian Aborigines are as far apart genealogically as any two peoples on earth – yet both have dark skins. If the Queen had come from Timbuctoo she might have looked like this … [SEE P8].

In 1947 Bugsy Siegel was terminated by fellow Mafiosi. 'The Operation was losing money', Tom Wolfe recorded, 'at a rate that rather gloriously refuted all the recorded odds of gaming science.'

THE FLAMINGO In 1945 mobster Bugsy Siegel arrived in Las Vegas, at that time no more than a patch in the desert, with several million dollars to put up a hotel and casino. He called it **The Flamingo**. An iridescent name which, wrote Tom Wolfe,[1] burst upon the scene with 'all the new electrochemical pastels of the Florida littoral. Tangerine, broiling magenta, livid pink, incarnadine, fuschia demure, Congo ruby, methyl green, viridian, aquamarine, phenosafranine, incandescent orange, scarlet-fever purple, cyanic blue, tessellated bronze, hospital-fruit-basket orange.' Colourful prose which captures the principle in the fixing of names to colours – that of association.

Describing a colour in terms of something else has a long history. Homer wrote of 'wine-dark' seas, Romans called a particular blue from overseas, ultramarine, and a dye produced by a whelk, purple (*Porphyra*). Take a herd of cows, feed them mango leaves, make a purée of the earth on which they've urinated day after day for months. Dry, refine, and you've got Indian yellow. Mummy (now unavailable) was a brown produced from grinding up Egyptian corpses [SEE P60]. *Caput mortuum* was a purplish-brown made of decomposed brains. Puce is named after the supposed hue of a flea's belly (Latin *pulex*), and the blue of jeans (*bleu de Gênes*) after a shade once associated with the city of Genoa. The dye magenta was invented in 1859 and named to commemorate the Battle of Magenta which occurred the same year. Crimson is derived from the Sanscrit word for the bug which produced the dye – a *krmi*. Like many colour names turquoise is a semi-precious stone and although there is a proposal to call it grue – a combo of green and blue – I doubt it will catch on.

Some old colour terms referred to material rather than colour. In the tenth century *purpura*, or purple, was the name of an expensive silk. In the eleventh century a scarlet was a fine woven cloth which was generally an undyed white, or coloured black, blue or green.

1. Tom Wolfe. *The Kandy-Kolored Tangerine-Flake Streamline Baby.* Farrar Straus (New York 1965)

A sign of refinement among the English middle class in the 1930s was to describe outfits in terms of fruit. 'Lemon', 'crushed rasberry' and 'burnt apricot' were particular favourites. The phrasing was important. A two-piece should not be 'lemon' but 'in lemon'. 'In a nice lemon' was even more tasteful. Calling anything a mineral, fungus or building material was unthinkable but fashion eventually came round to anthracite, mould and putty. In the 1950s Joyce Grenfell bought a length of tweed which, she wrote to a best friend, was 'a lovely mud colour'. She could have said taupe or grège. The launch of a new computer offers a choice of tangerine or blueberry and although such associations seem silly it is impossible to convey the sensation of a colour without relating it to something else.

To be more precise you have to resort to an agreed system and give the colour a number. There are several such systems. How would you fancy a tie in Pantone 537? Alvin Lustig, a distinguished American graphic designer who went blind some years before his premature death, had memorized the number references of the Pantone colour system so that he could still work, and specify the hues and shades in his mind's eye.

Paul Auster wrote a detective story[2] populated with colourful people. The private detective is Blue who learned the tricks of the trade from Brown. White is a client who hires Blue to watch Black who lives on Orange Street. To pass the time while trailing suspects, Blue recalls cases he's worked on in the past: the obsessions of Gold, the Gray case – who'd changed his name to Green – the Redman affair, and an encounter he once had with a hooker called Violet. The names Auster picked for his protagonists weren't arbitary, they echo associations. For instance White is good, Black is bad, Gold is dodgy. Colours used as code names also occur in the movies, *The Taking of Pelham 123* and *Reservoir Dogs* come to mind.

2. Paul Auster. *The New York Trilogy*. Penguin (Harmondsworth 1990)

Rose madder was made from the juice of a plant brought back from Palestine by Crusaders. This was so precious that the price was fixed by the French authorities and it was first known as *La garance* (guarantee). *Massachusetts* is a tribal word for 'the blue mountains'. Malaria used to be rife in East Anglia which is why the Canaries (Norwich City football team) wear yellow jerseys – a relic of the endemic jaundice which killed King James I, Oliver Cromwell and Sir Walter Raleigh. The precise hues of Phoenician purple and *perse* have long been forgotten as have: – *Quercitron* (or *flavin*): a yellow dye from the bark of an oak. *Celadon*: a pale fusty green. *Fulvous*: a dull tawny yellow. *Luteous*: a deep orange. *Carthamin*: a red from the safflower. *Kermes*: a bright red made by tiny bugs. *Sinoper*: a red pigment. *Almagra*: a deep red ochre. *Rubescent*: a reddening. *Turnsole*: a violet/purple. *Smalt*: a deep blue. *Tenebrous*: dark, obscure, gloomy. *Lapis lazuli*: a bright blue. *Murrey*: a medieval word for the colour of mulberry. *Puniceus*: an orange colour derived from a wax used by painters in ancient Greece.

'Darkened yellow beside full or bright clear orange, is perhaps something of the most repulsive that can be seen.'

AEMILIUS MULLER

'I think God's silly because he should have painted everybody the same colour and then they wouldn't fight.'

DAVID RICARDO (AGED 4)

'Everybody knows that yellow, orange and red induce and represent ideas of joy and of riches.'

EUGÈNE DELACROIX

'Anyone who sees and paints a sky green and pastures blue ought to be sterilized.'

ADOLF HITLER

'Pure draughtsmen are philosophers and dialecticians. Colourists are epic poets.'

CHARLES BAUDELAIRE

'Dear friend, theory is all grey, and the golden tree of life is green.'

WOLFGANG GOETHE

'Colour is nothing but a sensation and has no existence at all.'

OGDEN ROOD

'... there isn't a colour I wouldn't use except Chartreuse.'

SEYMOUR CHWAST

'My mother warned me to avoid things coloured red.'

CLAES OLDENBURG

'Draughtsmen may be made, but colourists are born.'

EUGÈNE DELACROIX

'Colour is a creative element, not a trimming.'

PIET ZWART

'I want to know one thing. What is colour?'

PABLO PICASSO

'Colours are light's suffering and joy.'

WOLFGANG GOETHE

'Grey hairs unlock closed doors.'

JOHN McCONNELL

'Painters use red like spice.'

DEREK JARMAN

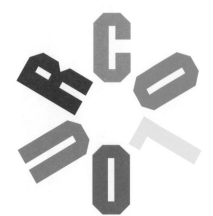

Colour spectrum :

The system of arranging colours in a circular spectrum running from yellow to green to blue to violet to red to orange to yellow again, demonstrates the principle of mixing two different colours to obtain a third.

For the colour letters opposite the orange was made by overprinting the magenta with the yellow, and the green by overprinting the yellow on the blue, and the purple by overprinting the blue on the magenta.

Medieval physicians used colour spectrums to diagnose disease by keying different colours to different afflictions. Comparing the colour of a urine sample to the chart, the physician would identify what the patient was suffering from.

Colour Terminology :

Hue is the attribute which distinguishes one colour from another – it comes from the Old English for 'beauty'. *Tone* is the position a *hue* holds on the scale from light to dark. *Tints* and *shades* are variations of *tones*. *Intensity* refers to the purity of the colour.

Primary colours are those which can be mixed to produce all other colours. *Primaries* are not always the same.

Prismatic primary colours are produced by light and come in four hues : red, blue, green and yellow. Project them so they mix together and you get white.

Pigmented primary colours are used in paints and inks, and have three hues : red, blue and yellow. Mix them together and you get black. Printers generally use magenta, cyan, yellow and black inks to print colour pictures in books and magazines. Psychologists employ specific hues and tones for diagnostic purposes : orange, red, dark blue, blue-green and bright yellow.[1]

The Bezold Effect :

Butt two colours up next to each other and they can create a third optical hue, or at least create a third in our minds as an after-image. Pointillist artists such as Seurat, who painted with dots, put yellow and blue dots next to each other which optically mix into a green when seen at a distance. [2]

The discovery of perceptual colour mixing by Wilhelm von Bezold led to the 4-colour printing process. Colour printing uses tiny dots of primary colours to mix colours, shades and tints. The picture reproduced on a postcard thus looks just like the scene – or, for that matter, the artwork of the pictures in this book.

The McCollough Effect :

Look hard at a pattern of vertical red and black stripes. Then quickly shift to look at a pattern of vertical and horizontal black and white stripes. The horizontal lines still look black and white, but the vertical ones appear green – Irish magic.

1. *Colour*. Mitchell Beazley (London 1980)   2. Josef Albers. *Interaction of Colour*. Yale University Press (New Haven & London 1963)

Weber-Fechner Law :

One might assume that to make an equal scale of *tones* from white to black, one adds an equal amount of black for each step. Wrong. An equal progression requires the amount of black to be doubled at each step. For example, using transparent grey film the first step has one layer, the second needs two, the third needs four, the fourth eight, and so on. It's an interesting concept.

Take a sheet of paper, fold it in half. Fold it again (the double fold has now become four) and continue until it's folded fifty times. You probably don't have enough time so estimate the thickness. Most guess anything from inches to feet, or centimetres to metres; in fact the folded paper would just about fit between the earth and the sun. It would be about 100 million miles thick. You don't believe me? Try it.[1]

Vizier Sissa Ben Dahir claimed a humble reward from King Shirham for inventing chess. All he asked for was a grain of wheat to be placed on the first square of a chess board, two grains of wheat on the second, four on the third, and so on. The King graciously agreed, delighted at such a bargain, until he realized he had unwittingly committed all the wheat in his kingdom. This is one of many similar stories.

The Greek Jinx Wheel :

This disk has a pattern of different coloured stripes and patches on each side. It is made to whizz around by pulling a loop of string passed through two holes near the centre. Legend tells how the Greeks used these devices to enchant their bored lover – quite how, I can't think – anyway by spinning the disk the colours optically fuse into just one.

The Benham Top :

This is a disk with a pattern of black lines on a white background. When spun clockwise (five to ten revolutions per second) the black lines turn blue, green and red, from the centre outwards. Spun anti-clockwise the colour order is reversed. It's not magic. It's flicker. Brain cells can't absorb quickly enough and so give out the wrong reading.

Colour instrumentation :

When colours are butted up they change *hue*. Optically green looks yellower and warmer next to yellow, bluer and colder next to blue.

M.E. Chevreul, in 1839 or thereabouts, received complaints that the colours in his tapestries of classical paintings were inaccurate. He realized that although the colours of the threads were correct, they optically changed viewed from distance. By simplifying the palette of coloured threads from 30,000 to 1,420 – a financial benefit of 95.3 per cent – he converted the discrepancy between physical fact and optical reality to commercial advantage.

The profit and loss diagram for an annual report, opposite, was based on this principle. The two vertical turquoise bars are exactly the same colour, as can be seen by the bottom bar, and only appear different because of the colour of the backgrounds.

1. R.L. Gregory. *The Intelligent Eye.* Weidenfeld & Nicolson (London 1971)

'Can you lend me the Theory of Colours for a few weeks?' requested Beethoven referring to Goethe's opus. 'It is an important work. His last things are so insipid.'

BRILLIANT, GORG
VIVID, FLAUNTING,
GLOWING, GLARING
SCREAMING, SHRIE
MELLOW, MATCHI
PASTEL, SOBER, D
CONSTANT, COLOUR
PARTLY-COLOUR
KALEIDOSCOPIC,
TATTOOED, DYE
DAUB AND SCRU
HIGH-KEYED COLO

OUS, PAINTED, GAY
E AR A WAY,
LURID, LOUD,
ING, MARCHING, PROUD
G, DEEP AND SOMBRE,
AD AND DULL,
UL CHROMATIC,
D AND PRISMATIC,
VARIEGATED,
, ILLUMINATED
BLE, DIP AND DYE,
UR, COLOUR LIE.

It was Pytheas the Greek mariner who first called the ancient blue-woaded Brits *Prettanoi* (*Brittania*) – 'painted ones'. Yves Klein patented a synthetic blue in 1960 as IKB (International Klein Blue), although he mistakenly – or deliberately – incorrectly specified the formula. Tree frogs in the Antipodes are changing colour from green to blue owing to atmospheric pollution. There is a book entitled *The 750 Commonest Colour Metaphors in Daily Life*. Harold Nicolson was telling Proust about the 1919 Peace Conference. 'Yes, Yes,' said Proust impatiently, 'but what was the colour of the blotting paper?' Nicolson couldn't remember. Colette only wrote on blue stationery and was fussy about the exact shade. Alexander Dumas [père] wrote his novels on blue paper, his poetry on yellow, and non-fiction on pink. And Cyril Connolly wrote his notes in green ink. Personally I wouldn't trust anyone who wrote in green ink but I guess that's as much a foible as doing so.

Georgiana Burne-Jones (1904): 'This year began an increase of intimacy with Mr (now Sir Lawrence) Alma-Tadema and his family, and though distance prevented frequent meeting, personal friendship steadily strengthened. At rare intervals they would join us at lunch on Sunday, bringing bright life and warm kindness with them. One of these times was remembered by us all as the day of the funeral of a tube of mummy-paint. We were sitting together after lunch in the orchard part of the Grange garden, the men talking about different colours that they used, when Mr Tadema started us by saying he had lately been invited to go and see a mummy that was in his colourman's workshop before it was ground down into paint. Edward [Burne-Jones] scorned the idea of the pigment having anything to do with a mummy – said the name must be only borrowed to describe a particular shade of brown – but when assured that it was actually compounded of real mummy, he left us at once, hastened to the studio, and returning with the only tube he had, insisted on our giving it a decent burial there and then. So a hole was bored in the green grass at our feet, and we all watched it put safely in, the spot was marked by one of the girls planting a daisy above it.'

Wim Crouwel: 'Leaf green, sandy and earthy colours, ochre – too scorched. I can't stand them. For me, dark colours always have to be cool. Cool grey, for instance. I once did a booklet that the client insisted on having dark brown. It still makes me absolutely miserable to think about it. The typography was perfect but the colour was wrong. A revolting, sultry, earthy colour.'

Bridget Riley: 'Of course, we saw all the great monuments – Sakkara, El Giza, Karnak and Luxor. But I couldn't help noticing how the strips of vegetation on each side of the Nile stood out against the white escarpment of the desert – it was like the settings and bands of their ancient jewellery ... I saw the role those reds, blacks, blues, turquoises and whites played in ancient Egypt's daily equipment, their wall hangings, illuminations, sarcophagi – they were the colours to celebrate life and wellbeing, the gifts of sunshine.'

Will Alsop (3.43 pm 9 November 1997): 'The sky from Albert Bridge – London Paynes Grey, Elephant Grey, Slate, Bright Blue, Magenta & Pink plus a Rainbow.'

Robert Mangold: 'I am attracted to generic or "industrial" colours; paper bag brown, file cabinet gray, industrial green, that kind of thing.'

Rem Koolhaas: 'A Dutch friend asked me if I would like to see the tulip fields. Inwardly I really did not want to see the tulip fields. For some reason I thought that seeing so many tulips – red, yellow, white, purple – would be too much. In any case I did not want to see tulips. My friend persuaded me to go with him. I am glad that he did. He brought me into a deep view. When we rode along the roads which moved through the tulip fields I began to understand Mondrian. I always thought him to be an international painter; I found him to be a Dutch painter. It was not the colour of the tulips but the density of the sand and earth where the bulbs were planted which reminded me of Mondrian. It was the atmosphere of opacity. The place, the land, the earth was dense opacification. The coloured flowers were not the issue, it was the infinite penetration and the compaction of trapped light crystals in the earth which illuminated the air into a grey solidity ... *Dutch grey*.'

Caroline Hightower: 'A military unit marches proudly into battle with its *colours* fluttering in the wind. A storyteller *colours* his narrative with adjectives, verbs, point of view. Certain things *colour* our thoughts and judgements. The tonal qualities of music have *colours*. A unique individual or character is described as *colourful*. Or even *colourless*. And there is no more direct a challenge than to show one's true *colours* ... Colour generates emotional and intellectual responses.'

Alfred Wallis (to Jim Ede, 30 November 1935): "i do not put Collers what do not Belong, i Think it spoils The pictures. There have Been a lot of paintins spoiled By putin Collers where They do not Blong."

Red has always posited problems. These ads appeared in *The Magnet, Billy Bunters Own Paper*. 'The Best School Story Paper.' Price 2d. 1937

For the purist black and white are not colours, but light and dark. 'White', said Renoir, 'does not exist in nature.' On the other hand Van Gogh said he'd noticed 'no less than twenty seven blacks' in a painting by Franz Hals. ✍

John Tyndall, who discovered why the sky is blue, wrote: 'What we see is dust suspended in our shell of air, quadrillions of prisms shattering pure sunlight into spectra. Blue is the colour that scatters. The moon's sky is black and the sky over Mars is red.' ✍

Island of Panarea. The brilliant hues of the June flowers punch holes in the landscape like flecks of scratched emulsion in a colour transparency. ✍

Washington DC. Still remember a downtown corner Singer sewing machine shop. It was painted inside and out in sharp green and pulsating orange. The shopkeeper's exuberant interpretation of corporate colours. ✍

Arrived in Milan one evening. Was whisked off to a party given by a Sr. Bianchi (Mr White), an architect. The huge apartment was totally white: walls and ceilings, carpets, lights, door knobs, chairs, pictures. All the guests were dressed in white, the food was white, the wines were white. The dressing room had clear glass cupboards containing white shirts, knickers, suits, socks and shoes ... and a solitary colour patterned tie, which (together with my blue shirt and jeans) made everything else whiter. ✍

Sometimes I squeeze my eyes tight shut. And see blotches of sulphurous yellow on patches of pale lilac. Wow! ✍

Morocco. 1988. Driving through the Atlas Mountains. Vivid impressions of rusted earth, sulphurous sand, purple rocks, limegreen strata, turquoise bushes, indigo tarmac. It's the minerals — not my lurid imagination. ✍

Bologna. cool pale grey shutters open against deep apricot coloured walls. ✍

Villa Igiea, Palermo, Sicily. Spring 1988. Siesta time: I look down from the balcony over a garden of pineapple palms, hibiscus, oleander and bougainvillea. Flagged paths, lichened statuary, dappled shadows. Register the scene in my head in black and white, squiggles, scribbles, splodges, splatters, smudges and blots. Lie down, doze off, and dream it all in colour. ✍

Skopelos, Greece. Holiday. On the first morning I woke up early and went out to test the temperature. Whammo! It was warm and the field outside a mass of blue flowers. I went to the beach. When I came back the flowers had gone. Their moment was a few minutes early morning. Too short. ✍
PERHAPS THEY WERE THE PALE ALMOND FLOWERS DESCRIBED BY PATIENCE GRAY [1] AS '... LIKE PLUMES OF SMOKE, LIKE SIGHS, LIKE VAPOUR, HAD MADE A SIGN, THEN VANISHED'. ANYWAY I PRESERVED THEM WITH THE EYE OF MEMORY. THEY ARE ON THE NEXT PAGE. EACH A DIFFERENT BLUE, AND MADE BLUER BY THE YELLOW FLOWER. ☞

1. Patience Gray. *Work Adventures Childhood Dreams*. Edizioni Leucasia (Lecce 1999)

BLUE MOVIES IN FULL COLOUR.

A SIGN IN A GERMAN PORN SHOP WINDOW

IN THE RED · RED CARPET · RED CENT · RED RAG · RED HERRING · PAINT THE TOWN RED · RED BRIGADE · RED LETTER DAY · RED LIGHT · REDNECK · RED TAPE · RED CROSS · RED HANDED · RED ALERT · SCARLET WOMAN · SCARLET PIMPERNEL · SCARLET FEVER · ORANGEMAN · ORANGE ORDER · LIVID PINK · SHOCKING PINK · TICKLED PINK · PINK ELEPHANTS · IN THE PINK · PINK POLITICS · JAZZ BLUES · BLUEBLOOD · ONCE IN A BLUE MOON · BLUE STOCKING · BLUE FIT · FEEL BLUE · BLUE MURDER · BLUE PENCIL · BLUE FILM · BLUEBEARD · BLUE MOOD · BLUE FUNK · CORDON BLEU · TRUE BLUE · MOOD INDIGO · GREEN ENVY · GREEN PARTY · GREENBACK · GREENFINGERS · GREENHORN · GREENTHUMBS · GREEN BELT · GREEN ROOM · BLACKBALLED · BLACK MOOD · BLACK MAGIC · BETE NOIRE · BLACKOUT · BLACK LOOK · BLACK SHEEP · BLACK DEATH · BLACK HOLE · BLACKGUARD · BLACK AND TANS · BLACK MARIA · BLACK COMEDY · BLACK WATCH · BLACKJACK · BLACKMAIL · BLACKLEG · BLACK COUNTRY · BLACK BOOK · BLACK AND BLUE · BLACKSHIRTS · BLACK TIE · IN THE BLACK · BLACK MASS · BLACK POWER · BLACKLIST · BLACK SPOT · BLACK MARKET · GREY MATTER · EMINENCE GRISE · PURPLE HEART · PURPLE PROSE · PURPLE PASSION · SHRINKING VIOLET · YELLOW PERIL · YELLOW STREAK · YELLOW-BELLY · YELLOW PRESS · BROWNED OFF · BROWN STUDY · BROWN NOSE · SILVER SCREEN · SILVER WEDDING · SILVER LINING · SILVER TONGUE · GOLDEN RULE · GOOD AS GOLD · GOLDEN EGG · GOLDEN FLEECE · GOLDEN MILE · GOLDEN SECTION · GOLDEN AGE · GOLDEN HANDSHAKE · WHITEWASH · WHITE RAGE · VIRGIN WHITE · ETC ·

'From the pictures sent in for exhibition it is clear that the eye of some men shows them things other than as they are — that there really are men who on principle feel meadows to be blue, the heavens green, the clouds sulphur-yellow … Either these 'artists' do really see things in this way and believe in that which they represent — then one has but to ask how the defect in vision arose, and if it is hereditary the Minister of the Interior will have to see to it that so ghastly a defect shall not be allowed to perpetuate itself — or, if they do not believe in the reality of such impressions but seek on other grounds to impose them upon the nation, then it is a matter for a criminal court.' Extract from a speech delivered by Adolf Hitler at the inauguration of The House of German Art in 1937.

Among mammals only primates see in colour. Birds, fish, reptiles and insects have colour vision, horses, cats and dogs do not. Bees can't see red.

Horses can't see colours but bees and snakes can, and some people can see colours which others can't. I have a friend who can't tell the difference between brown and green. He is a devotee of *Trivial Pursuit*, a general knowledge board game. You throw a die, move a counter, and end up on a colour. Your fellow player then takes a card and asks you the question keyed to that colour. The answer is keyed to the same colour. When we play I'm never sure whether he actually asks me the right question, or even gives me the right answer. Inherited colour blindness affects about one man in 12 and one woman in 200. A wide disparity explained by Horner's law: colour-blind fathers have colour-normal daughters who are the mothers of colour-blind sons. The most common defect is red-green blindness. Actually a misnomer since although most can distinguish between reds – crimson, scarlet, vermilion – their problem lies in colour 'richness'. They identify red with the same enthusiasm most of us greet *khaki*. They also have difficulty with green. Colour defects seem related to habitat or environment. In remote regions, the Arctic and equatorial forests, defective colour vision only affects one in fifty. This disability increases the denser the population and more urban the area. So much for that ikon of colour communication, the London Underground map.

Never mind, we all need something to work against. Paradoxically, colour disability hinders writers more than artists. The painter can use whatever colour he likes. But the author has to be able to describe sunsets, flowers, clothes, or whatever, with a degree of accuracy. Anyway the fact is colours are a product of the mind, not of reality. Who knows whether my red is your red? Even if two colour experts were asked to dress up a Father Christmas, and one asked to pick the coat and the other the trousers you can be sure the top wouldn't exactly match the bottom. Birds and bees can see colours unknown to humans: colours generated by the ultraviolet wavelengths. A raven, seen by another bird, instead of appearing plain and dark, has a dazzling plumage of blue, violet and purple. And swans, which to us appear kind of white, are seen as a shimmering spectrum. Not only will we never see these colours, but we'll never reproduce them because for the human eye they do not exist. This dotted colour circular image is reproduced from a test card used for colour-blind tests. Those with normal colour vision see the number 42. Those with red deficiency only see 2 and those with green deficiency only see 4. At least they do if the colour in this book is accurate. Disadvantage can also be advantage. In World War Two, those with severe red-green colour-blindness were pressed into service as bombadiers, because of their ability to 'see through' camouflage.[1]

PARSING

Illustration. S. Isihara. *Tests for Colour Blindness.* Kanehara Shuppan (Tokyo 1960)   1. Oliver Sachs. *Anthropologist on Mars.* Picador (London 1995)

COLOUR IS A POWER WHICH DIRECTLY INFLUENCES THE SOUL. COLOUR IS THE KEYBOARD, THE EYES THE HAMMER, THE SOUL IS THE PIANO WITH MANY STRINGS. THE ARTIST IS THE HAND WHICH PLACES, TOUCHING ONE KEY OR ANOTHER TO CAUSE VIBRATION IN THE SOUL. IT IS THEREFORE EVIDENT THAT COLOUR HARMONY MUST REST ONLY ON A CORRESPONDING VIBRATION IN THE HUMAN SOUL.

W. Kandinsky. *Concerning the Spiritual in Art*. Wittenborn Schultz (New York 1947)

pink and poets

Colours have always had associations beyond their hues. You can see red, feel blue, or be considered green. After Irish independence in 1925 the new government began to remove all the monuments and insignia left behind by the British. One formidable item was the bright red iron pillar box which bore a royal coat of arms implacably cast in its body. Short of the wherewithal to replace this conspicuous facility, they painted them bright green and thereby effectively made them Irish. In America, holding elections among the illiterate Navajo Indians the government assigned each candidate a colour. What they hadn't realized was that Navajo allocate to colours a hierarchy of importance, so since blue is good and red bad, the results had little to do with the candidates' popularity. Leonardo da Vinci related yellow to earth, green to water, blue to air and red to fire. Monet reckoned that fresh air was violet and Kandinsky that black and white were silent. Charles Dickens, eulogizing Winsor & Newton's paints, wrote of 'Chrome and Carnations, and Crimsons, loud and fierce as a war-cry, and Pinks, tender and loving as a young girl'. A 1960s gay rights placard declared equally enthusiastically that 'black and blue are beautiful'. During the 1930s the painter Amédée Ozenfant, intrigued with colour metaphors, decided to record colour words which expressed an idea or feeling. He randomly selected five pages from the works of fifty French poets commencing with Baudelaire and ending with Cocteau. He then tallied up the number of times they occurred. Pink or Rose (hue not flower) came tops. The primaries of blue, red and yellow came next with a 55 per cent preference for blue but only 18 per cent for yellow. Of the three secondary colours only green was mentioned. Orange and purple didn't turn up at all. I don't quite know what conclusion to draw except that they do say that 'if you're in the pink, everything seems rosy!'

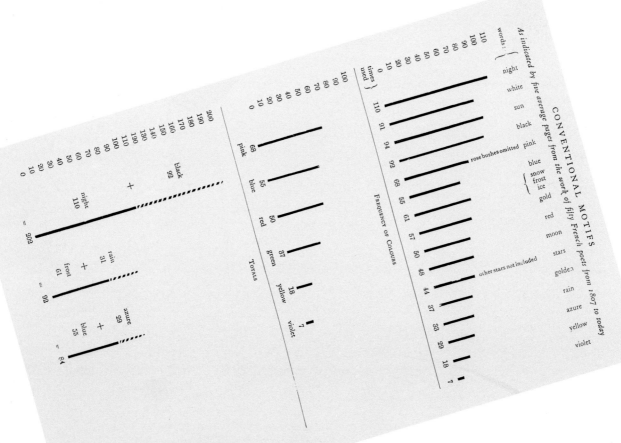

Page from Ozenfant's *Foundations of Modern Art*. Dover Publications (New York 1952)

'I saw

a sunset in Querétaro

that seemed

to reflect

the colour of a rose

in Bengal.'

JORGE LUIS BORGES

Stephen Leacock   'It may be those who do most dream most.'

Dreaming is what happens when the lunatics take over the asylum

One does not dream, one is dreamed

I am sometimes confused as to whether I actually did something, or thought I'd done it, or whether I was dreaming I did it. I guess you know what I mean.

Philosopher René Descartes was bewildered when he realized there were no conclusive indications to distinguish whether he was awake or asleep. He would have been even more confused had it occurred to him he might have been a character in someone else's dream. That happened to Chuang Tzu who dreamt he was a butterfly. And when he woke up he didn't know whether he was a man who dreamt he was a butterfly or a butterfly that dreamt he was a man. Hindus believe they are in Brahma's dream, just as Aborigines believe they are in the dreams of deities. The Aborigines' problem is that if the deities wake up they won't exist.

A contemporary version has it we are a dream in the circuitry of a sleeping computer. And when the computer runs down (after a billion years or so) we will wake up to find we are a different intelligence from that which we had been dreaming we were – when we were a dream in a machine.[1] An alternative thought is that maybe we are only the shadow of somebody else, in someone else's dream.

I find it all too complicated. The trouble with working on your imagination with your imagination is you end up with smoke and mirrors, not sure who, where, or what. After being shot (1968) and almost terminated by Valerie Solanis, Andy Warhol said his life had become a dream as he wasn't sure whether he was really alive or dead. 'It's sad,' he complained, 'I don't know whether to say hello or goodbye.'

Lucid Dreams

Helen Keller, blind and deaf from infancy, dreamt of a pearl. This she described as 'a smooth exquisitely moulded crystal' with the 'velvety green of moss, the soft whiteness of lilies'. She could never have seen or remembered a pearl, a lily, or moss. She was not unique. There are many instances of people dreaming things they have never seen, or of participating in events centuries past or future happenings.[2]

I MUST GET UP!

WHY?

7-7

Calman

1. D.R. Hofstadter and D.C.Dennett. *The Mind's I*. Harvester (Brighton 1981)

'I'll let you be in my dreams if I can be in yours', sang Bob Dylan, unaware that some people can do just that. According to a recent scientific paper [3] three participants who were attending a course on dream research decided to meet up in a dream. Their *rendezvous* was on a specific bench in a particular park at a particular time. That night two of them dreamt they met and had a lengthy conversation while waiting for the third to turn up. He didn't appear.

The next day the two independently wrote down their recollections and found they tallied; they then searched out the third party. Before they were able to say anything he apologized for not turning up, he'd forgotten to fix the appointment in his mind before falling asleep.

Since we spend about twenty-five years sleeping and seven per cent of that dreaming, just imagine all the *rendezvous* one could make.

Nightmares

If you had a dream about green monsters you'd assume you'd overdone it the previous evening. Perhaps you did, but not necessarily so. Ancient peoples terrorized by fearsome prehistoric creatures in the dark of night may have had the same dream. Passed down generations over millennia the stream of consciousness in some deep part of your brain could have received it from them. Jung came to this conclusion [4] after seeing illustrations of dream images reproduced in medieval books which were identical to those recounted by his patients. Most scientists think this is nonsense. As far as they are concerned dreaming is no more than neural house cleaning.

Do Androids dream of electric sheep? ✱

All mammals dream except anteaters and dolphins. Dolphins never completely sleep as the left and right halves of their brain take it in turns. While one side is asleep, the other is wide awake. Giraffes only just qualify as they only sleep for five minutes every twenty-four hours, so their dreams can't amount to much.

An expert reckons that people who use their visual imagination during the day – artists, designers, architects, photographers, film directors and the like – rarely have spectacular mind-blowing technicolour dreams. These,

paradoxically, tend to be bestowed on those whose daily work is more predictably routine.

If the mouse dreams dreams which would terrify the cat, and geese dream about maize, it could be that dreams are an expression of wish fulfilment. Certainly I find going to bed with a problem and pulling my imagination over my head before falling asleep often results in waking with a solution. A blind date in the land of nod can be more productive than working in the light of day. The problem is remembering.

✱ Philip K. Dick, science fiction writer, workaholic and pharmaceutical dropout, wrote *Do Androids Dream of Electric Sheep?* This was adapted by Ridley Scott for sci-fi classic film *Blade Runner*, which in turn took its title from a story by William Burroughs.

A confession

One night I had a strange dream about dwarfs with pointed hats and nubile ladies. I was sharing an apartment with a medical student. In the morning I told him about it. He laughed, took down a book by Freud (*The Interpretation of Dreams*), found the page, and showed me an account of an identical dream. And I mean identical. If the average person has an average of four dreams a night how many repeats of the same dream are going on?

Night shift

Shiro Kuramata designed two chairs in a dream but only remembered one of them. 'Perhaps the other one was better,' he ruefully commented. The one he remembered he called *Apple Honey* after the jazz number. Lewis Carroll had the same problem and made a cardboard alphabetic stencil which he called a *nyctograph*. He kept this under his pillow so he could jot down his dreams in the dark without having to get up and light a candle. Similarly Charlie Chaplin, who composed his film music while asleep, had a recording device so he could wake up, hum a few bars, and go back to sleep.

However, not everybody treats dreams as a source of creative potential: 'I don't get ideas during the night', says Erno Rubik, inventor of the dreaded cube, 'I don't suddenly wake up with new answers to design problems. I sleep well and deeply.'

In *The Act of Creation* Arthur Koestler wrote: 'The most fertile region seems to be the marshy shore, the borderland between sleep and full awakening, where the matrices of disciplined thought are already operating, but have not yet sufficiently hardened to obstruct the dreamlike fluidity of the imagination.'

Those states of limbo between falling asleep and waking up seem the most conducive conditions for ideas to outflank the sentinels of commonsense and float to the surface. I find mine often emerge under the shower or whilst contemplating marmalade and toast at breakfast. The image of a woman standing on a quay, staring out to sea in *The French Lieutenant's Women*, 'rose in my mind one morning when I was still in bed half asleep,' wrote John Fowles. Ray Bradbury said scenes for novels come into focus in the half-awake state before he gets up. Illustrator Seymour Chwast says he often gets ideas 'just after the alarm goes off'. Paul McCartney wrote the song *The Yellow Submarine* '… in that twilight zone just as you're drifting off to sleep'. And the designer Massimo Vignelli told me he gets his while shaving, which, he emphasized, is the reason why he doesn't have a beard.

It could be that we dream all the time without realizing it because consciousness makes such a noise we're not aware of what's going on. After all to daydream one has to tune out the static.

The asylum

Edward O. Wilson '… dreaming is a kind of insanity, a rush of visions, largely unconnected to reality, emotion-charged and symbol-drenched, arbitrary in content, and potentially infinite in variety. Dreaming is very likely a side effect of the reorganization and editing of information in the memory banks of the brain. It is not, as Freud envisioned, the result of savage emotions and hidden memories that slip past the brain's censor.'

Note. One night I woke up laughing. I'd been dreaming about a situation in which one of the characters told a joke. I hadn't heard it before. Recently I had a another dream in which one of the characters related something which had happened in one of their dreams. Dreams within dreams.

2 · J.W. Dunne. *An Experiment with Time.* A.&C. Black (London 1927)   3 · Celia Green. *Lucid Dreams.* Institute of Psychophysical Studies (Oxford 1968)   4 · Carl G. Jung. *Man and his Symbols.* Aldus Books (London 1964)

DAYDR

EAMS

MOONLIGHTING

A dream heralded the birth of Jesus and the philosophies of Muhammad and Buddha. Hannibal dreamt his destiny was to conquer Rome and Bismarck that his was to found the German empire. Here are some others: **Luis Buñuel** told Dali about a dream in which a cloud sliced the moon in half 'like a razor blade slicing through an eye'. **Dali** responded he'd dreamt about a hand crawling with ants. Out of these two dreams the surrealist film *Un Chien Andalou*[1] was born. **Jasper Johns**, helping Robert Rauschenberg decorate windows in the New York store Bonwit Teller, told him he'd dreamt of painting the stars and stripes. Rauschenberg suggested he did. Soon after Robert Blake died he appeared in a dream to his brother – **William Blake** – and gave instructions for a new etching technique. These were so precise that Blake immediately sent his wife out to buy the materials. Most seemingly spontaneous ideas are probably the unanticipated result of previous work or thought. Anyway what is certain is that dreams often release the mind to look at things in new ways. ' I turned my chair to the fire and dozed', related **Friedrich Kekule** [another version has him nodding off on a Clapham omnibus[2]] describing how he envisaged the *Benzine Ring*. '... the atoms were gambolling before my eyes ... twining and twisting in snakelike motion ... One of the snakes had seized hold of its own tail and the form whirled mockingly before my eyes ...' The image of a snake biting its own tail is such an ancient and archetypal symbol it even has a name: the OUROBOROS. Other revelations which arrived in dreams include ... **René Descartes** (philosopher): the principles of analytical geometry. **Richard Wagner** (composer): the prelude to *Das Rheingold*. **Albert Einstein** (physicist): the connection of time with space. **Samuel Taylor Coleridge** (poet): stoned out of his skull on opium, the idea for *Kubla Khan*. **Alfred Russel Wallace** (naturalist): his theory of evolution. **Giuseppe Maria Mitelli** (calligrapher): the *dream alphabet* (1683). **Otto Loewi** (chemist): the chemical mediation of nerve impulses. **Robert Louis Stevenson** (writer): the plot of *Dr Jekyll and Mr Hyde*. **Elias Howe** (inventor): the first sewing machine. **Igor Stravinsky** (composer): the score for *Petruschka*.

1. Luis Buñuel. *My Last Sigh*. Alfred Knopf (New York 1983)   **2.** *The Faber Book of Science*. Ed. John Carey (London 1995)

Haiku of Basho	'You the butterfly – I, Chuang Tzu's dreaming heart.'
Gunter Rambow	'Our thoughts and dreams possess no typographic system. We dream in pictures, feelings and imaginary awareness.'
Friedensreich Hundertwasser	'When one dreams alone, it is only a dream. When many dream together, it is the beginning of a new reality.'
D.H. Lawrence	'Sleep seems to hammer out for me the logical conclusions of my vague days, and offer them to me as dreams.'
Jorge Luis Borges	'Writing is nothing more than a guided dream.'
Tchaikovsky	'The germ of a future composition comes suddenly and unexpectedly ... it takes root with extraordinary force and rapidity ... frequently in a somnambulistic state ...'
Amédée Ozenfant	' ... dreams are not a panacea. Dreams are another reality ... and the proof is that nightmares are intolerable.'
Peter Bogdanovich	'I used to dream in black and white until I made a color movie, and then I dreamt in color.'
George Bernard Shaw	'You see things; and you say, "Why?" But I dream things that never were; and say, "Why not?"'
W.B. Yeats	'The visible world is no longer a reality and the unseen world is no longer a dream.'
André Breton	'If dreams are a translation of waking life, equally waking life is a translation of dream.'
Edgar Allan Poe	'All that we see or seem is but a dream within a dream.'
Jean-Michel Folon	'With most people dreams appear only in one's sleep. But in my case dreams go on and on in endless succession, during both sleeping and waking hours.'
Alexander Herzen	'You can waken men only by dreaming their dreams more clearly than they can dream themselves, not by demonstrating their lives as geometrical theorems.'
Brian Eno	'Dreamed I was a song. Disappointing to wake and find myself a man in a hole.'
Dino de Laurentiis	'Often I dream of work problems and how to solve them.'
Philippe Starck	'... I don't work. I just dream. My best office is my bed.'
Arthur O'Shaughnessy	'We are the music makers, / And we are the dreamers of dreams ... Yet we are the movers and shakers / Of the world forever, it seems.'

A truly
poetic
canvas
is an
awakened
dream

RENĖ MAGRITTE

Photograph. Nick Knight

Plato called pictures: 'Dreams for those who are awake.'

EVAPORATE
THEY
REALITY
INTO
MASSAGED
ARE
IDEAS
UNLESS

Don Marquis

'An idea isn't responsible for the people who believe in it.'

Someone once asked the mathematician Alfred North Whitehead, 'which is more important, ideas or things?' 'Ideas about things,' Whitehead instantly replied.

An attitude which is not always shared. I once worked for a marketing director who treated ideas with vehement suspicion. At best he considered them gimmicks, and generally subversive ones at that. We soon parted company. Without new thoughts you can only progress in diminishing circles and I hear he is now down to selling carpets. However, in one respect he was right. Ideas *are* subversive. And they come in various guises. Here are three:

Lethal ideas can seize control of the mind like the catchy tune in a story by Arthur Clarke. Once lodged they block off potential alternatives and masquerade as the only viable solution. I think of them as lethal because they can be compared to a particularly nasty insect which flies up the nostrils of wildebeest and lays eggs that turn into maggots, which eat the brains, so the animal gallops around in circles until it dies of exhaustion.

Promiscuous ideas are always auditioning, they never give up. I'm often put out when looking through my old scribbles, or articles on other designers' work, to see one of them, when I thought I'd only just thought of it.

Fertile ideas are the kind which take root and spread seeds. Their influence is gradual and imperceptible, much as the flutter of a butterfly's wings in Peking which causes a storm in New York a week later.

Roger Sperry, who is a neurophysiologist, points out that ideas help evolve new ideas. 'They interact with each other and with other mental forces in the same brain, in neighboring brains, and, thanks to global communication, in far distant, foreign brains. And they also interact with the external surroundings to produce *in toto* a burstwise advance in evolution that is far beyond anything to hit the evolutionary scene yet, including the emergence of the living cell.'

Michael Ignatieff writing[1] about philosopher Isaiah Berlin noted that 'there was a strong analogy between what Berlin learned from Toscanini and what he was to learn from Bertrand Russell: that artists and thinkers of greatness have a core idea, which, however complex the adumbration and defences of it may be, is always simple. Once found it unlocked the nature of a work.'

Question
Where do you get your ideas?

Answer
I don't. They get me!

1. Michael Ignatieff. *A life of Isaiah Berlin*. Vintage (London 1998)

Ideas create new ways of thinking. As Mies van der Rohe explained, the Bauhaus, wasn't a school but an idea – 'only an idea', he said, 'could spread so far.' No wonder the Nazis closed it down. 'Resistance to new ideas', cautioned Bertrand Russell, 'increases as to the square of their importance.' Not everyone shares this view. 'Style and structure are the essence of a book;' wrote Vladimir Nabokov, 'great ideas are hogwash.' Then there is the inevitable nerd who, like a character in a Woody Allen movie, says, 'Let's take this concept and turn it into an idea'.

'Why is it', a correspondent complained in a letter to the *New York Times*, 'no one has any idea, concept or thought anymore? Nowadays it's always a "notion", the teeniest of ideas.' A complaint which echoes a malicious comment made by a colleague on a fellow academic who left the University of Chicago to become treasurer of Macy's. A move, he said, which proved he'd abandoned ideas for notions.

The difference is one of weight. A notion is a small idea, a brainwave, a cute whim, a cockamamie thought – something of small consequence and little stamina. It generally conforms to that well-known rule that the length of the description is inversely proportional to the amount of illumination. Real ideas on the other hand are of a different order. They have dimension and are resilient and flexible. Like a genuine panama hat which can be rolled up and passed through a wedding ring.

Ideas with big ideas are concepts. A concept amplifies an idea into a scenario in which all the unrelated bits and pieces dovetail neatly into place. There is an inevitability about whatever a concept embraces, it has a singular solid spherical shape, it is impossible to knock over.

Concepts tie thoughts together, form bridges between one intelligence and another, provide a common point of reference. With a concept, explains the ancient Chinese rule of painting, the brush can spare itself the work.

Note. La Pelosa. Puglia, Italy. Trawling with the hairy crab (La Pelosa) and fishing around for ideas have a lot in common. The hairy crab is small, soft-shelled, and densely covered with tiny bristles. First you have to find one, then tie a piece of string to a leg, toss it over the side of the dinghy, and slowly trawl the shallows. For the octopus, somewhat surprisingly, the crab is a delicacy. The trick is, just as the octopus envelopes it with its tentacles, to jerk it out of the water. Reluctant to let go, the octopus tightens its grip, the bristles act as hooks, and both arrive on board.

Drawing. André François

Sol LeWitt's truffle

Sol LeWitt, American conceptual artist, believes in superiority of idea over object. In 1987, he sold an intangible concept [an idea for an artwork that doesn't actually exist] at auction – for the concrete sum of $26,400. Legal ownership was indicated by a typed certificate, which specified that the artwork ['10,000 lines about 10 inches long, covering the wall evenly'] should be executed in black pencil. The owner has the right to reproduce this piece as many times as he likes. If you reproduce it you'd only have a fake – despite the fact that LeWitt would not have picked up his brush in either case.

brilliant ideas   like truffles

are rare **and only possible** **given special conditions**

IN-SPIRATION originally meant receiving a breath of divinity. In modern parlance psychoanalysts refer to it as 'a moment of insight' and behaviourists 'an act of intuition'; most of us rely on the metaphoric 'bolt from the blue'.

'The idea seems absurd, but I can find no flaw in it.' Johannes Kepler

An experience when an unanticipated and spontaneous idea suddenly pops up into the head from nowhere. An unnerving sensation that, rather than us making something happen, something is happening to us.

'I execute the drawing almost with the irresponsibility of a medium.' Matisse

Ever since Archimedes leapt out of his bath shouting *'Eureka'* – I've found it – recorded instances of creative lightning flashes have become legion. James Watt was struck with the idea of the steam engine while watching his kettle; Leo Szilard the sudden illumination of a neutron chain reaction (or how to make an atomic bomb) while waiting at traffic lights in Southampton Row.

'Develop an infallible technique and then place yourself at the mercy of inspiration.' Zen maxim

How such connections spring to mind are guesswork but they seem to favour those who have a promiscuous curiosity and chronic attraction to problems.

'Personally I always preferred inspiration to information.' Man Ray

The only certainty is that inspiration cannot be summoned up by an act of will. To labour towards it, is, in effect, to move in the opposite direction.

'The fact is that I don't think up most of what I write. It's dictated to me. I wonder who by?' Pirandello

As Nietzsche put it : 'A thought comes when it wills, not when I will it.'

Doppler Effect : the tendency of stupid ideas to seem smarter when they come at you rapidly.

'If I were to give an award for the single best idea anyone has ever had, I'd have to give it to Darwin, ahead of Newton and Einstein and everyone else. It's not just a wonderful scientific idea; it's a dangerous idea. It overthrows, or at least unsettles, some of the deepest beliefs and yearnings in the human psyche.'

Daniel Dennett

'Designers often hear the answers to their questions as shades of variation or confirmation of their predetermined intentions. I know I do myself. I blot out the communication on offer with the deafening sound of my own ideas.'

Michael Wolff

'You hear people all the time saying ridiculous things like, 'I could write a book', or, 'I could compose a piece of music'. Well, of course they couldn't. They might have an idea in their head, but it's realising that idea that counts.'

Vivienne Westwood

'Inspiration, the muse experience, is like telepathy. Nowadays one hardly dares to say that inexplicable phenomena exist for fear of being kicked in the balls by the positivists and the behaviourists and other hyperscientists.'

John Fowles

'Almost all really new ideas have a certain aspect of foolishness when they are first produced.'

Alfred N. Whitehead

'There's an enormous difference between beating a notion to death and beating an idea into shape.'

Rich Saul Wurman

'Yesterday an idea is mine, today it is yours, and tomorrow it belongs to the whole world.'

Konstantin Stanislavsky

Once you've had a baby you can't put it back.

Drawing. Andrea aged 6. Nanette Newman. *Lots of Love.* Collins (London 1975)

BUT THE IDEA
OF THE NEST
IN THE BIRD'S MIND,
WHERE DOES IT
COME FROM?

Quotation. Joseph Joubert

Statistics state that in London you're never more than seventy feet away from a rat. I often feel the same about finding a solution to a problem. You can't come up with the answer but know that it's hanging around somewhere.

Everything is connected to everything else and searching for solutions often requires being alert to spot the unlikely connections …

Billy Wilder once asked Charles Eames to design a *chaise-longue* so he could take forty winks in his office; it was not, he emphasized, to be used as the proverbial casting couch. Shortly afterwards Eames happened to visit a lighthouse where he noticed a narrow bench used by the keeper for taking a nap. This encounter influenced the form of his design.[1] Le Corbusier liked watching Westerns and his famous *chaise-longue* was prompted by a scene where a baddie was lounging in a rocking chair on a saloon porch with his feet propped up on the hitching rail. In hindsight such connections seem obvious but at the time we seldom recognize them.

However, outside of connections, where ideas come from and how they announce themselves is unpredictable. Some arrive with the force of being hit over the head with a thick stick, others emerge slowly like the Chinese courtesan who covered herself with a thin layer of grain and then let a hungry duck eat away until her charms were revealed. They can turn up like a row of lemons on a fruit machine, or just drop into one's mind between random thoughts. The only thing for certain is, like cats, ideas don't come when called.

It's necessary to regularly hoover the mind of detritus to give ideas space to fertilize. The poet Schiller used to keep rotten apples under the lid of his desk so he could take a sniff of their pungent bouquet when he needed to find the right word. 'A few places are specially conducive to inspiration – automobiles, churches – private places,' writes John Updike, 'I plotted *Couples* almost entirely in church.' Frank Lloyd Wright described how he derived the roof for his church at Madison [Wisconsin] from the shape of his hands at prayer. The wife of Eero

Saarinen told a friend, who told me, where the architect got his idea for the design of the Kennedy TWA Air Terminal (1955-62). One morning, she said, she gave him half a grapefruit for breakfast. He looked at it intently – ate it – and then turned it upside down. Using one hand he squeezed it to form indentations, turned it over, smiled, and went off to the office. Le Corbusier used to keep a crab shell by his drawing board. It was, he once casually mentioned, the origin of the roof of his church at Ronchamp.[2] Ivan Chermayeff does much of his thinking in taxis, Lou Dorfsman on planes and Steve Guarnaccia on the subway. Designers also talk of getting ideas when they are in the sleep borderland, in a state of exhaustion or just waking up. Philippe Starck claims he suddenly thought of the design for his *Docteur Globe* plastic café chair just as the 'fasten-seat-belts' sign went out on a flight to Tokyo.

In *Critique* magazine Marty Neumeier writes: 'If idea-making can't be reduced to a system, perhaps it can be expressed in a formula. Like the workings of the internal combustion engine, the conceptual process can be seen as a series of controlled explosions that drive ideas forward. In a car engine, when fuel is mixed with fresh air and ignited by a spark, the wheels turn and the car accelerates. In the human mind, when a problem is mixed with a new perspective and exposed to intuition, the wheels turn and we arrive at a new concept. Problem + fresh perspective x intuition = concept. An example of this formula in practice is the invention of the printing press. Gutenberg could not figure out how to press a large number of letter seals onto a single sheet of paper at the same time. One day at a wine festival (after sampling a glass or two), he began to look carefully at a wine press. Suddenly he realized that the wine press, with minor alterations, might be transformed into a printing press. *Mein Gott!* The simple mixture of two ideas, the letter seal and the wine press, sparked by a little imagination, produced one of the greatest inventions of the Renaissance.'[3]

Here are some other responses:

George Lois: **'It's hard to remember how or when you get an idea.'** *Milton Glaser:* **'I find ideas occur at any time, anywhere, while I am working, while I'm not working. I depend on ideas to generate themselves while I'm not paying attention to the problem, which is the way I've always worked.'** *George Giusti:* **'The idea sprouts in some hidden corner of my subconscious.'** *Federico Fellini:* **'The idea for a film comes first out of the mind like a very fine piece of thread. One thinks, and perhaps it becomes a piece of string!'** *Aaron Copland:* **'The source of an initial musical idea comes as a gift from heaven. A direct link with some unknown source much like manifestations of automatic writings.'** *Philippe Starck:* **'... I am just a copier, an imposter. I wait, I read magazines. After a while my brain sends me a product.'** *William S. Beck:* **'Ideas come by day, by night, by chance, by work and by play. They come in dreams, in hallucinations, in seminars and saloons.'** *Helmut Krone:* **'Good ideas announce themselves. A bell rings.'** *Bob Blechman:* **'I find that ideas crystallize in off hours, off moments, when I am totally relaxed. Usually it is at the very end of the day when I am exhausted. That is when I get my best ideas.'** *Henry Wolf:* **'You can never get the split second when it happened.'**

ideas on ideas

1. Digby Diehl. *Supertalk*. Doubleday (New York 1974)   2. Geoffrey Broadbent, Richard Bunt, Charles Jencks. *Signs, Symbols, and Architecture*. John Wiley & Sons (Chichester 1980)   3. *Critique* magazine, Spring 1997

Since Alex Osborn of the advertising agency Batten, Barton, Durstine & Osborn came up with the idea of 'brainstorming' in the late 1930s, business has been busy trying to wed creativity to commerce. Unfortunately the very nature of business tends to stifle creativity as the very competition it fosters establishes one of the biggest blocks :

the fear of making a mistake.

Brainstorming emerged in the 1950s with a great fanfare as the answer to everybody's creativity problem. In point of fact, it was never the answer to anybody's creativity problem, and at its worst it is actually hostile to the creative process because it leads to the proliferation of ideas exclusive of merit. However, brainstorming has genuine advantages at certain stages of problem solving. For one thing, it's a handy reminder of how rigid we get and how hard it is to free ourselves of rational bindings.

Brainstorming is the technique in which a group tries to make a dent in a problem, by very rapidly throwing up a barrage of ideas. The rules of the game require that it be played in a short period of time, usually signalled by a timer, that all ideas be written immediately on a blackboard or flipchart where everybody can see them; and that – most important of all – there be no censorship, no shooting ideas down at the time they appear. No idea, no matter how preposterous, expensive, irresponsible, or even stupid it may seem, is rejected at the time it's expressed. All ideas are put on the board for later consideration.

'... for any group used to working rationally, it's very difficult to brainstorm without practice. For me, brainstorming is almost always agonizingly difficult, because I have a tendency to want to edit things on the way out. So a lot of ideas never get out.'

Ralph Caplan

The human brain can only generate 30 watts.

The Wassily Chair. 'In one of those Newton-and-the-Apple flashes of the blindingly obvious, Marcel Breuer was smitten, whilst out riding on his brand-new Adler bicycle, with the potential of tubular steel as a material from which to fashion modern furniture.' He reckoned that since he was already sitting down pedalling around Dessau, the same structure would do for sitting down at home. So he designed a tubular steel chair. He named it the Wassily, after his friend at the Bauhaus, the painter Wassily Kandinsky.[1]

The Safety Razor. Cornflakes were invented by Dr Kellogg as nutritional therapy for his mental patients. Watching all those faces happily munching away it suddenly occurred to him that since most people are comatose at the start of day it would be ideal stuff for breakfast. A staggeringly successful diagnosis which, combined with the principle of regular consumption, made him a fortune. King Camp Gillette in pursuit of a similar idea – something one would use once a day and then throw away – methodically worked through the alphabet listing every possibility. This proved a waste of time. The idea of the safety razor didn't arrive through reasoning but through a transcendental moment when Gillette realized that a razor wasn't *an object* but *a sharp edge*. 'In that moment I saw it all,' said Gillette, '… more in pictures than in conscious thought.'[2]

The Bubble Lamp. In the late 1940s a design status symbol was the spherical Swedish hanging lamp. It was extremely difficult to make as it had a silk covering sewn on a wire frame. It was also extremely expensive. George Nelson, hearing there was a sale at Bonniers, rushed off to buy one for his new office. The price was ludicrous. As he was departing (empty handed) a picture suddenly popped into his mind that he'd seen in the *New York Times* some weeks before: Liberty ships (which transported war supplies from the States to Britain) being mothballed. This was done by covering the ships with nets and spraying with plastic. He rushed back to his office and designed the Bubble lamp.

Guarding the Flame. 'The best idea in the world is worth precisely dick if it doesn't make it through the gauntlet of carpers, lawyers, clients, and the dark forces of bean counters …' *Richard Seymour*

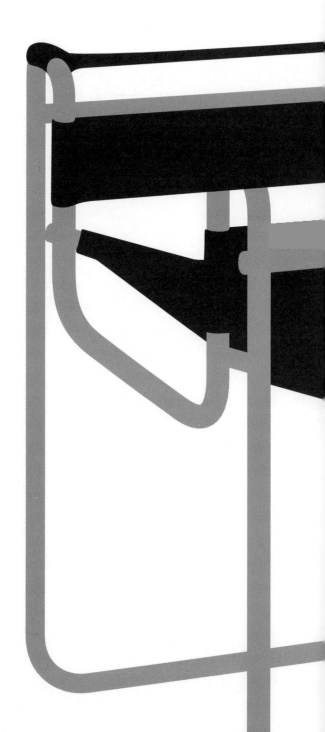

 1. Deyan Sudjic. *Cult Objects*. Paladin Books (London 1985) **2.** Hannah Campbell. *Why did they Name it?* Fleet Press Corp (New York 1964)

'BETWEEN
THE IDEA
AND THE REALITY.
BETWEEN
THE MOTION
AND THE ACT.
FALLS
THE SHADOW.'

T.S. Eliot

THE DISTANCE BETWEEN GETTING AN IDEA AND PUTTING IT DOWN IS LONGER THAN THE LENGTH FROM YOUR HEAD TO YOUR HAND.

No man is an island,
entire of itself;
every man is a piece
of the continent,
a part of the main.
— John Donne

Snap

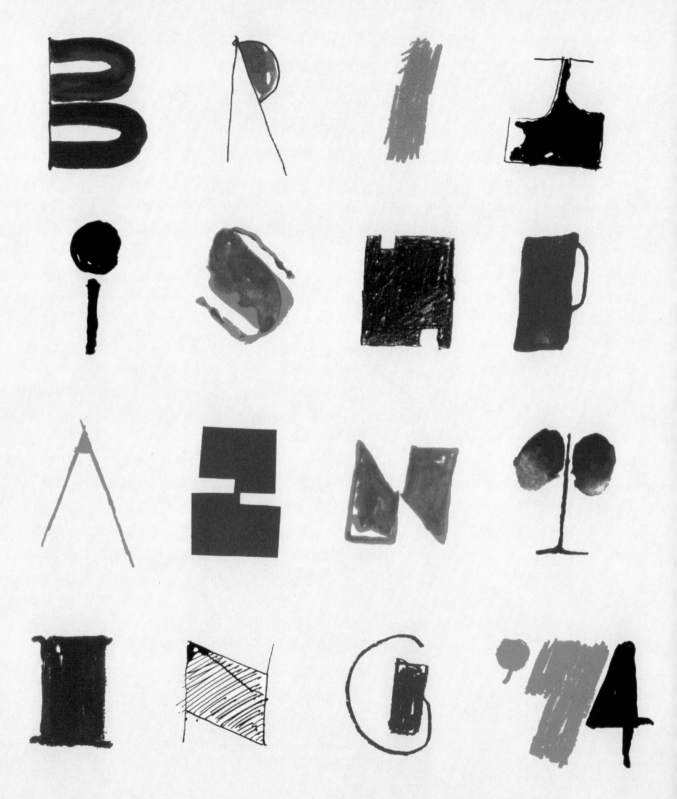

Image. Exhibition poster

Snap. Identical discoveries and inventions made independently but concurrently include the evolutionary theory of species, calculus, the telephone, the telescope, photography, the planet Neptune and the Rubik Cube. The distance between originality and duplication is often minimal, particularly when the different parties are on the same train of thought.

In the 1970s NBC Television commissioned Lippencott and Margulies, an American design office, to design a new corporate symbol.[1] After considerable expenditure and months of work involving behavioural scientists, market researchers, graphic designers, and God knows who else, they produced a solution, a device based on the letter N. At the same time a small radio and TV network in Nebraska came up with the same graphic solution at minimal cost and by one man.

The popular press went to town. David and Goliath, value versus cost, and all the rest of it. Of course they didn't talk about the real issue which was one of confidence, or, more exactly, the lack of it.

The large corporation, which had a lot at stake, had to convince itself that the new design was appropriate and suitable. Or put another way, a lot of suits insecure in their individual aesthetic judgement when it came to assessing the qualities of a letter N, had to ensure that no one was going to laugh them out of office.

They wanted to cover all the options. This required the designers to produce a *myriad* of ideas, each rendered in a vast number of variations and permutations. Up in Nebraska the guy probably fiddled around a bit, thought one solution looked nice, slept on it, and sent it off to be registered next day. Who knows, perhaps someone at Lippencotts had come up with that particular N before the man in Nebraska?

In an out-of-court settlement NBC bought exclusive rights to the symbol. They had to pay 55,000 US dollars in cash and supply the Nebraska network 500,000 US dollars worth of television equipment. As any designer knows, there but for the grace of God ...

1. Wally Olins. *The Corporate Personality.* Design Council (London 1978)

The Hundredth Monkey Syndrome

Wild monkeys on an isolated island off Japan were introduced to the sweet potato. Unfamiliar with this new food they were unable to cope, getting them covered with sand and dirt. Luckily there was a monkey genius in the community who washed the potatoes in a pool, and then ate them. A ritual which was gradually adopted by the others.

At a certain point something quite extraordinary happened. The habit suddenly and spontaneously occurred, without any rational explanation, in several other isolated and unconnected monkey colonies.

Lyall Watson, a scientist intrigued with paranormal affairs, suggested the following explanation: 'Let us say, for argument's sake, that the number was ninety-nine', he was referring to monkeys washing potatoes, 'and that at eleven o'clock on a Tuesday morning one further convert was added to the fold in the usual way. And that this addition, the hundredth monkey, was the impetus which carried the know-how across a threshold into the common pool of monkey instincts.'[1]

Note. Most of the stuff in this book has been acquired. That is to say I've read bits here and there and stuck them together to record a bit of information, voice an opinion, arrive at a conclusion or raise a query. Since noting this monkey story I've come across another account of the monkey genius. This one says he, she, or a colleague in the colony, must have swum to other islands and told them how to wash potatoes. This account doesn't mention how the monkey learned to swim, so my money stays on the previous version.

1. Lyall Watson. *Lifetide.* Hodder & Stoughton (London 1979)

The Blaenau Ffestiniog Syndrome

A similar situation to the monkey colony occurred in Wales where the traditional metal bar cattle grid has confined sheep for decades. Apparently flocks near the small town of Blaenau Ffestiniog have recently learned to cross cattle grids by tucking up their little legs and rolling over the bars. In sheep terms this represents a giant leap in reasoning power.[2]

The authorities, anxious to contain this flamboyant behaviour, have taken steps, a journalist ironically wrote in the local newspaper, 'to isolate them so they don't go to market and boast about their grid-rolling activities to other sheep'.

By the way, the British Standards Institute issued a specification some years ago which required all cattle grids to have a narrow ramp for hedgehogs — so they don't fall between the bars attempting to cross from one side to the other.

The Blue Tit Syndrome

The blue tit was the first bird to peck the metal foil tops off milk bottles to get a drink. This scam was first recorded in Southampton in 1921 and by some twenty years later every blue tit was at it.

This behaviour did not gradually emanate or spread out from Southampton but arose suddenly and independently in random places all over the British Isles. Those who study blue tits can't account for this. It can't be explained by tits passing on the information to other tits – they dislike travelling.

‖**Syndrome** (si·ndrŏ˘m, si·ndrŏmi). 1541. [mod.L. – Gr. συνδρομή, f. σύν SYN- + δρομ-: δραμεῖν run.] 1. *Path.* A concurrence of several symptoms in a disease; a set of such concurrent symptoms. 2. *transf.* or *gen.* A concurrence; a set of concurrent things 1646.

Knowledge can be unconsciously transmitted from one mind to another. If one person discovers something it becomes easier for another person (or many others), faced with the same issues, to arrive at similar solutions. In an effort to understand this phenomenon – known as Morphic Resonance – a complex experiment [1] was set up. In essence it took the following form.

Two figurative (representational) drawings were converted into two abstract (non-representational) images which disguised the original subjects by eliminating all the pictorial details. For example a picture of a zebra is representational, the same picture when radically simplified ends up looking like a bunch of abstract stripes.

One of the figurative drawings and its abstract counterpart were televised, as a pair, to a British audience of eight million viewers. The viewers were shown the abstract image first, then the drawing, and then the abstract once again. Not surprisingly, after they had seen the figurative drawing, they found it easier to recognize the abstract version.

A few days later television audiences in Europe, South Africa, and North America were shown the same two abstract images, but this time without the figurative drawings. They were then asked to identify the subjects that the abstracts brought to mind.

Their answers produced two astonishing results.

Seventy-six per cent guessed the subject of the abstract image which had been televised (with its figurative drawing) to the British audience. But only nine per cent could guess the subject of the second abstract. This suggests that once some people know something, it's easier for other people to know or understand as well.

Another surprise was this. The guesswork response of audiences in Europe and South Africa was more or less equal. However, in America and Canada which lie some hours later to the west, only a few guessed the subjects of the two abstract designs. Perhaps time zones placed them 'out of tune'?

This is one of the abstract images. What is it? [SEE P533].

Note. I was at a public lecture given by Professor John Maynard Smith, an authority on evolutionary biology. At question time a woman stood up and asked; 'Professor, can you comment on Rupert Sheldrake's theories on Morphic Resonance?' Maynard Smith hesitated, and then replied: 'I think it's a load of rubbish.'

   1. Rupert Sheldrake. *A New Science of Life*. Blond & Briggs (London 1985)

Illustration. Morgan Sendall

INDUS VALLEY
EASTER ISLAND
INDUS VALLEY
EASTER ISLAND
INDUS VALLEY
EASTER ISLAND

B R A I N W I R I N G

If widely separated cultures more or less share the same art forms, there are four possibilities: **1** The peoples have gradually spread out across regions. **2** Separated peoples have experienced shared feelings and so responded in the same way. **3** It occurs through a racial memory, or a collective subconsciousness, in which certain ideas and archetypes are innate. **4** It's purely coincidental. All possibilities, in effect, fit the Brainwiring hypothesis. [SEE P467]. Outside of an unlikely amazing coincidence, a connection appears to exist between the Indus Valley script and the Easter Island pictograms. Their close similarity could be the result of archetypal images, something dredged up from a remote ancient racial memory. If not – then there is a mystery. The facts are these: Easter Island is isolated in the middle of the Pacific and located half way around the globe from the Indus Valley which lies in the north of Pakistan. That's a vast distance. And there is a chronological gap of at least 2,500 years between the arrival of the first settlers to Easter Island in the thirteenth century and the last dated inscription of the Indus script. That's a vast period of time. According to Easter Island folklore their ancestors arrived on the island with sixty-seven inscribed wood panels; only fifteen remain today. See below. Known as Kohau-rongo-rongo (talking wood), the panels are inscribed with rows of pictograms incised with a shark's tooth. On each successive row the symbols (men, birds, fish) alternate the direction they face and are sometimes drawn upside down – a kind of Polynesian boustrophedon. [SEE P173]. To date both scripts remain largely undeciphered. The few comparative illustrations shown on the left– there are many many more – are reproduced from a seminal work on the subject.[1] They demonstrate that the characters are uncannily similar and virtually interchangeable. Despite this similarity the experts dismiss any connection between them on the basis that knowledge transfer across thousands of miles and held in suspension for two and a half millennia is beyond credibility. Who could argue with that? On the other hand, I guess that whatever monkeys can do [SEE P81], so can humans. An aside: Over a period of 500 years the Polynesians who settled on Easter Island erected more than 900 gigantic stone heads up to 30 feet tall, some weighing as much as 65 tonnes, carved out of volcanic rock. The original settlers had found a forested paradise, covered in palm trees. Over time the islanders cut down the trees to provide logs to move the statues. Eventually there were so few trees left they could no longer reproduce and the remaining forest died out. As the island lost its vegetation, most of the population died too, possibly in a series of inter-clan wars for the dwindling resources. Now the island is a bare grassy moor, stripped of all trees, a mute witness to the vanity of human endeavour.

1. David Diringer. *The Alphabet*, Vol 2. Hutchinson (London 1968)

THIS IMAGE FOR A MUSIC CATALOGUE ECHOES
A FAMOUS ADVERTISING CAMPAIGN BY SHELL IN
THE 1930S – 'THAT WAS SHELL THAT WAS' – AND
RE-EMPLOYS THE DOG CALLED NIPPER.

Illustration. Jones Thompson

George Santayana   'Those who cannot remember the past are condemned to repeat it.'

... one of his

most treasured possessions

was a miniature sweet pea

with pale green leaves

and tiny sky-blue flowers.

The seed it came from

was the grandchild of a seed

that had been found

in a tomb of

one of the Pharaohs.

[**Extract.** Obituary of Berthold Wolpe, designer and typographer]

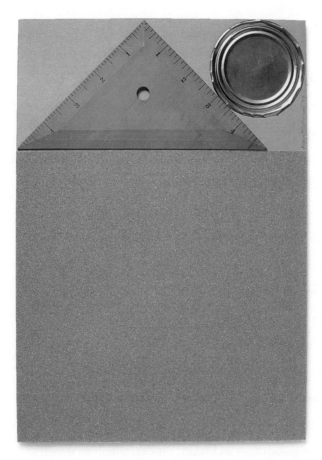

Cheops

design genes

Motifs are seldom irrational. Take the lotus. This has five petals. These have variously symbolized the five senses, the five digits, the four limbs and the head, the zenith and four points of the compass, and a number of other things. A myth is not a fiction but a structure to express elusive experiences or share philosophical ideas.

Adopted by the ancient Egyptians as a symbol of sun worship, the motif of the lotus travelled east to Persia and onwards through India to China. On the way local civilizations percolated the motif through their own cultures to produce a variety of hybrid designs, some of which made a return journey to the west undergoing yet further transmutations.

→ When the lotus infiltrated ancient Greece it conjugated with the palm to make the palmette. Over time palmettes became linked with other palmettes to create a continuous loop device, a useful attribute when painting around a pot as loops could be stretched or squashed so the decorative strip would neatly meet up the other side.[1]

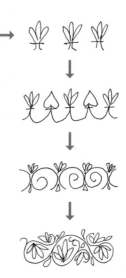

This simple linking design literally branched out into an elaborate decorative scroll of stems and stalks terminated by leaves and blossoms. This scroll motif then emigrated to the east once more where fanciful interpretations converted the foliage into peonies, pomegranates, parrots and other indigenous flora and fauna, thus extending its design frontiers from a scrolled border into a decorative field of undulating free-flowing arabesque patterns. The appropriately named arabesque then travelled back to the west to ornament the Alhambra in Spain, become a Paisley pattern in Scotland, an overture by Bizet and the title of a film featuring Audrey Hepburn and Cary Grant directed by Otto Preminger. Once a motif gets going its genes tend to spread.

   1. E.H. Gombrich. *The Sense of Order*. Phaidon (Oxford 1979)   **Drawing opposite.** Alberto Giacometti

Mondrian based his famous painting Boogie Woogie on the view looking down at the Manhattan streetscape from the 90th floor of a skyscraper. 'The statues by Giacometti outside the Musée Picasso in Antibes', wrote Graham Greene, 'remind me of my only meeting with the artist in his Paris studio where he showed me the origin of many of his works — the Roman statuettes, a few inches high, fished out of the Seine.' Mies van der Rohe originally designed his classic Barcelona chair for the King and Queen of Spain. It was displayed in the German Pavilion of the 1929 International Exposition in Barcelona. The seats in The New Savoy Theatre in London are in five colours selected to match the zinnias in nearby St James's Park. And this typeface is used on German street signs.

Surrealists played a game they called CADAVRE EXQUIS (Exquisite Corpse) which assembled words or pictures into

a composition. A player would write a noun on paper, fold it over, pass it to the next person who would add an

adjective or verb, then fold it over, and so on around the table. The last player unfolded the paper to reveal a bizarre

unpredictable phrase – or image. Sort of a visual CHINESE WHISPERS .

An owl was the start of a similar exercise* involving a group of twelve people. The owl was momentarily shown to

the first person, who then had to draw it from memory. The next person was briefly shown the predecessor's rendering,

and then drew it from recollection. And so it proceeded. Gradually the owl morphed into a sort of polar bear and then

into a kind of blob. The blob was shown to someone who hadn't participated in the game. 'What is this'? I asked, 'A

baby,' she replied.

Mundane contexts can also develop unlikely expressions. Take the buttonhole. In past times the thread which

*

Similar exercises beginning with the same owl can be seen in Edi Lanners's book : *Illusion*. Thames & Hudson (London 1977)

reinforced button holes got ideas above its station. It began to decorate the edges. It then spread out to luxuriantly

decorate tunics and create ceremonial military uniforms with gold braid, silver epaulettes, and elaborate trimmings —

the scrambled egg of officialdom. From buttonhole to Brigadier.

Then there is the intellectual play of PASSING THE BUCK. Architect Rem Koolhaas utilized context in his design to

house the Hague National Dance Theatre. Sited in an ugly urban district the structure was deliberately conceived to

echo the surrounding messiness. It was created piecemeal and at random in a calculated response to the constantly

changing brief and specifications.

Life is lived forwards but only understood backwards. The significance of THE LAST SUPPER was not realized by those

around the table, but only by those who viewed it with the hindsight of what was to come. That is probably why the

CADAVRE EXQUIS is also known as CONSEQUENCES.

'Why should we look to the past to prepare for the future? Because there is nowhere else to look!'
JAMES BURKE

  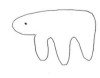 

These were done by students at a design workshop at FABRICA in Treviso, Italy

**A**round about 5000 years ago someone suddenly realized that simply by planting a stick in the ground they could make a shadow and measure the passage of time. The *gnomon* was the name given to the stick which cast the shadows across ancient Sumerian sundials. With a *gnomon* you could tell the time of day, the day of the month, the seasons of the year, the east from the west. You possessed *knowledge* [1] [gnowledge is a tempting thought]. It gave its name to the art of *gnomology*, the *gnomists* who practised it, *gnomic* discourse, and extremely circuitously to *gnomes*. *Gnomes* are a stumpy clever species along with goblins and elfs and sprites and trolls, who live in the interior of the earth. *Gnosis,* in Greek, means knowledge; and the name *gnome* originated with Swiss alchemist Paracelsus, who called *gnomes gnomes,* because *gnomes* know where precious metals like cobalt and gold are found. Despite this attribute *gnomes* are considered naff. They are the sort of garden icon that declares their owner to be lower middle class or even lower. Their usual habitat is the small town garden, with crazy paving painted white at the joins, plastic urns, and ornamental miniature wheelbarrows topped off with a dazzling display of bedding plants in red, white and blue – with some orange and yellow for good measure. Indeed they have such demeaning connotations that The Royal Horticultural Society won't allow them in the Chelsea Flower Show. The list of proscribed articles specifically mentions 'coloured figures of all kinds, *gnomes*, fairies or any similar creatures, actual or mythical'. The *gnome* is on a horticultural blacklist.

apple on a dish

   1. Richard Gregory. *Odd Perceptions*. Routledge (New York 1993) 2. Philip Wilson. *A Surreal Life, Edward James*. Exhibition catalogue, Royal Pavilion, Brighton, 1998

Max Ernst invented **FROTTAGE** by making use of floorboards: 'It all started on August 10, 1925, by my recalling an incident of my childhood when the sight of an imitation mahogany panel opposite my bed had induced one of those dreams between sleeping and waking. And happening to be at a seaside inn in wet weather I was struck by the way the floor, its grain accentuated by many scrubbings, obsessed my nervously excited gaze. So I decided to explore the symbolism of the obsession, and to encourage my power of meditation and hallucination I took a series of drawings from the floorboards by dropping pieces of paper on them at random and then rubbing the paper with blacklead. As I looked carefully at the drawings that I got in this way – some dark, others smudgily dim – I was surprised by the sudden heightening of my visionary powers, and by the dreamlike succession of contradictory images that came one on top of another with the persistence and rapidity peculiar to memories of love.' [SEE P155].

Edward James: 'Salvador Dalí's inventions are curious things, like, for instance, the Pleuvial Taxi. They came out of real occurrences. Dalí and I were waiting one day for a taxi after lunch in Verona. It was pouring, pouring with rain and there weren't any empty taxis. And Gala was somewhere else in the town, getting impatient; she got very cross if she was kept waiting. Dalí got more and more nervous. Finally it stopped raining, and up came an empty taxi, and Dalí said, "It's almost sure to be raining inside the taxi now that it's stopped outside." From that he elaborated the idea of a Pleuvial Taxi. He said, "They'll be very elegant. It will cost more money to be in a raining taxi. Everybody will come to lunch a bit wet, wearing a mackintosh, even on sunny days, because they'll have been in one of my Pleuvial Taxis." He created a Pleuvial Taxi for the first Surrealist show in Paris, with a wax model in it, with snails crawling up her arms. That was the origin of that!' [SEE P447].

The Pleuvial Taxi

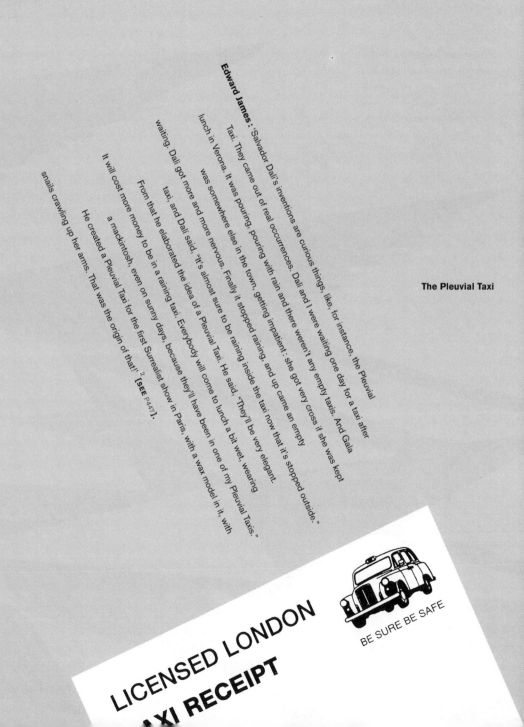

LICENSED LONDON TAXI RECEIPT

BE SURE BE SAFE

This detail is from FLIGHT, a woodcut by McKnight Kauffer, used on a poster to launch a new British newspaper, the *Daily Herald,* in 1916. The caption read 'Soaring to Success – the Early Bird.' Winston Churchill saw it, and commissioned Kauffer to design the flag for the new Royal Air Force. Later, on discovering he was American, he dropped the matter. However, the design led to the bird symbol of Imperial Airways, then that of BOAC, and a variation still persists today as an element in the livery of British Airways Concorde.

This book is
about everything –
well almost everything –
I was never taught.
THE AUTHOR

R.D. Laing

'If I don't know I know, I think I don't know.'

TEACH YOURSELF
IGNORANCE

BY

A. EARNSHAW

ENGLISH UNIVERSITIES PRESS LTD.
LONDON

'Culture is activity of thought, and receptiveness to beauty and human feeling. Scraps of information have nothing to do with it. A merely well-informed man is the most useless bore on God's earth.' *Alfred North Whitehead*

'Where is the wisdom we have lost in knowledge? Where is the knowledge we have lost in information?' *T.S. Eliot*

'We are drowning in information, while starving for wisdom. The world henceforth will be run by synthesizers, people able to put together the right information at the right time, think critically, and make important choices wisely.' *Edward O. Wilson*

'You cannot create a world by hot instinct; only by cold experience.' *John Fowles*

'The Great Green Arkleseizure theory is not widely accepted outside Viltvodle VI and so, the Universe being the puzzling place it is, other explanations are constantly being sought.' *Douglas Adams (The Restaurant at the End of the Universe)*

'The fox knows many things, but the hedgehog knows one big thing.' *Archilochus*

Note. Ring doves instinctively sing the song of their species even if they have never heard another dove. A young cuckoo may never see its parents (who parked the egg in another bird's nest), but a month after they have left the nest, the young ones get together and intuitively take off for the same place. The baby swift never learns to fly, it just instinctively launches itself into the air and then spends the next two years in flight without touching ground.

Illustration. Anthony Earnshaw

the VELCRO factor

At one time the mind was considered a blank page only written on by experience. Today we favour the seed and soil theory. For example distinguishing colour, line, pattern and shape are innate, but doing anything with them can only be learnt.

Knowledge is the only instrument of production not subject to diminishing returns. Furthermore it increases at a spectacular rate. Ninety per cent of all the scientists who ever lived are alive today.[1] 'In the 500 years since Gutenberg invented printing some thirty million books have been printed; and an equal number has been published in the last five years. The quantity of information doubles every eight years. This means by the time a child born today [1970s] graduates from college, the amount of knowledge in the world will be four times as much, and by the time that child is fifty it will be thirty-two times as great. By then ninety seven per cent of everything known will have been learnt since that child was born.'[2]

I'm not quite sure what all this amounts to, but one cynic has suggested that as we find out more and more, about less and less, the point will soon come when we'll know everything about nothing. In any event what is for sure is that the more you know the less you need.

The fact is that the mind thinks with ideas not information, so acquiring knowledge is useless unless one learns how to use it. A dictionary may contain all the words but no one can tell a poet which to choose or what to write.

I love my daddy becorse he give me a good ejukashun

ZOE AGED 6

1. Peter Drucker. *The Age of Discontinuity.* Harper Row (New York 1968)   2. Alvin Toffler. *Future Shock.* Heinemann (London 1970)

'Stare.

It is the way
to educate
your eye,
and more.

Stare, pry,
listen, and
eavesdrop.

Die knowing
something.

You are not
here long.'

Walker Evans

The Banyan Tree (*Ficus virens*) is revered by Buddhists as the *Tree of Knowledge* under which the meditating Buddha gained enlightenment.

We all need a Banyan. Most of us remember someone who opened a door in our minds. 'Why are you drawing the tree like that?' queried the art teacher. I said I didn't know but that was how I felt like doing it. He asked why I felt like doing it like that. I still didn't know. 'You should,' he said, 'otherwise how can you really draw the tree?' I didn't understand. Eventually I did. Of course there are also those who close doors. Making a colour composition an instructor once sharply admonished me, saying '*We* never use orange!' She was a formidable lady and I didn't dare ask why – even now I look over my shoulder if I use orange.

Later I was taught by Josef Albers, painter and colourist, who believed that teaching is a matter of asking the right questions rather than giving the right answers. Not that *he* was exactly open-minded. He used to say Matisse didn't know anything about colour, and regularly picked me out in class to state arbitrarily that the English had no taste. But by then I'd learnt what, and what not, to pay attention to. If your mind is too open people can throw all sorts of rubbish into it.

I also learned something else. When Albers gave a lecture he'd invariably trip over himself as he approached the lectern. He'd also drop his notes. Immediate audience sympathy. I saw him do this at least half a dozen times in nine months. Coincidence?

A few years passed.

'I will introduce you,' said the principal of the design school in Hong Kong, 'then give your lecture but as the audience is Chinese speak slowly. When you've finished I'll ask if there are any questions. There won't be. Then we'll go for lunch.'

I gave my talk. The Principal asked whether there were any questions. There weren't. Over lunch I asked how he knew beforehand. 'Oh,' he said, 'If they'd asked you a question it

'To look
is to
learn,
if you
listen
carefully.'

Per Arnoldi

would have meant you hadn't explained something clearly enough. And that would have meant you would lose face and they are very polite students.'

Did you hear about the rich American explorer who died at the North Pole and whose relatives paid an Eskimo a lot of money to fly back with the body? Once he'd delivered the body, the Eskimo decided to spend the money seeing the States. Speaking no English, he queued up at railway stations and repeated, sound by sound, whatever the traveller queuing in front said when he bought his ticket. The Eskimo saw a lot of places. But eventually, running out of the money, he ended up in a small town in Ohio. And that's where he lived for the rest of his life.

At an international exhibition held in Japan during 1985 one of the main attractions was an incredible tree which bore 12,000 tomatoes. According to the propagator, a Dr Shigeo Nozawa, the tree was capable of growing to a size which could produce up to 100,000 tomatoes. Normally plants carry 20 to 25 tomatoes. He explained that the environment was more significant than genes, or whatever equivalent thing tomatoes have, and on the premise that life began in water, he grew his tomato tree hydroponically. He gave it love, care and attention. He talked to it a lot. Dr Nozawa doesn't believe in cloning.

Education, remarked Oscar Wilde, is an admirable thing, but then went on to say nothing worth knowing can be taught. Certainly, received wisdom isn't beyond questioning – the other day I read that when baiting a mousetrap, gum drops are more effective than cheese.

'… you learn that when an eraser falls off the table, you don't jump after it. You keep cool!' observed Saul Steinberg, 'you follow it with the eye, because it keeps jumping until it rests in the most unlikely place.'

Laboratory Rat: **'I have trained that man so every time I press this lever he gives me food.'**] Paul Rand: **'... experience slows you up. It makes you more aware that what you've just tried is no good.'**] Louis-Fernand Céline: **'Experience is a dim lamp, which only lights the one who bears it.'**] John Constable: **'An artist who is self-taught is taught by a very ignorant person indeed.'**] Vaclav Havel: **'We must try harder to understand than to explain.'**] Friedrich Jacobi: **'It is the instinct of understanding to contradict reason.'**] Stanislaw Lec: **'Even his ignorance is encyclopedic.'**] Milan Kundera: **'A question is like a knife that slices through the stage backdrop and gives us a look at what lies hidden behind it.'**] Francis Picabia: **'The known is an exception, the unknown a deception.'**] Emily Dickinson: **'He has the facts but not the phosphorescence of learning.'**] Henry David Thoreau: **'It is only when we forget all our learning that we begin to know.'**] Rémy de Gourmont: **'To know what everybody knows is to know nothing.'**] Albert Einstein: **'The important thing is to never stop questioning.'**] William Lethaby: **'An art school is generated only by the intensity and heat of a common pressure!'**] Confucius: **'If you learn without thinking, you will gain no understanding; if you think without learning, you will lose yourself.'**] Stephen Jay Gould: **'Science is a procedure for testing and rejecting hypotheses, not a compendium of certain knowledge.'**] Hugo von Hofmannsthal: **'Knowledge is little; to know the right context is much, to know the right spot is everything.'**] Rich Saul Wurman: **'A weekday edition of *The New York Times* contains more information than the average person was likely to come across in a lifetime in seventeenth-century England.'**] Robert Graves: **'... introduce, say, a Hebrew scholar to an ichthyologist or an authority on Danish place names and the pair of them would have no single topic in common but the weather ...'**] Buckminster Fuller: **'Many people have asked if the Bauhaus ideas and techniques have had a formative influence on my work. I must answer vigorously they have not.'**] William Blake: **'There are things known, and things unknown: in between are the doors.'**] Doris Lessing: **'... that is what learning is, you suddenly understand something you've understood all your life, but in a new way.'**] Josef Albers: **'To distribute material possessions is to divide them. To distribute spiritual possessions is to multiply them.'**] Jan Tschichold: **'Anyone who does not want to be an apprentice will never become a master.'**] Sir Thomas Beecham: **'You should try everything once, except incest and folkdancing.'**] Anatole France: **'It is enough to open minds, do not overload them. Put there just a spark. If there is some good inflammable stuff, it will catch fire.'**] April Greiman: **'If you're trained in something that's the death of it.'**] Ernest Hemingway: **'The thing is to become a master and in your old age to acquire the courage to do what children did when they knew nothing.'**] Vincent Van Gogh: **'I am always doing what I cannot do yet, in order to learn how to do it.'**] Steven Pinker: **'The contents of the world are not just there for the knowing but have to be grasped with suitable mental machinery.'**] You only learn balance by losing it.

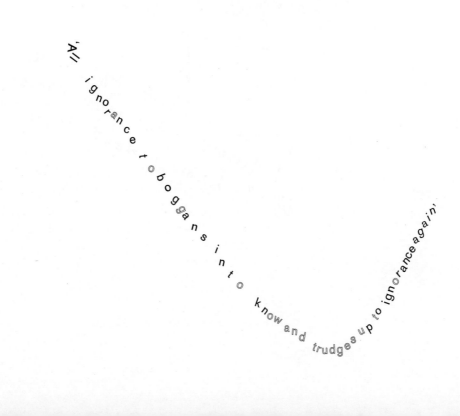

'All ignorance toboggans into know and trudges up to ignorance again'

ee cummings

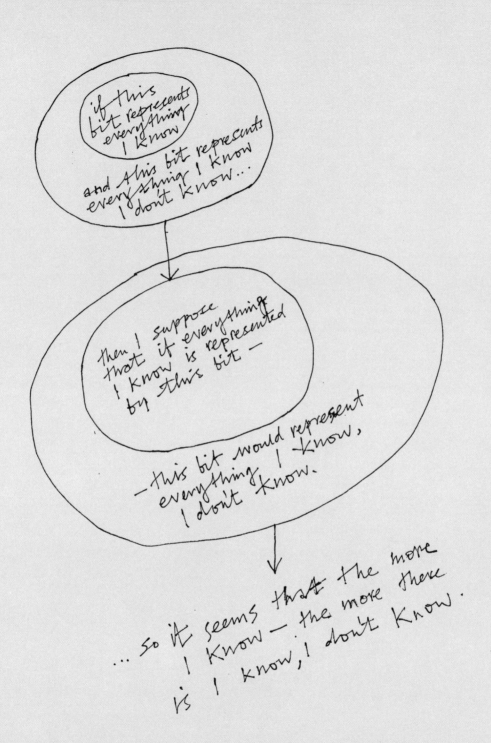

BEWARE OF THE MAN
WHO SAYS HE HAS
TWENTY YEARS' EXPERIENCE
WHEN WHAT HE SHOULD
BE SAYING IS HE HAS
ONE YEAR'S EXPERIENCE
REPEATED TWENTY TIMES.

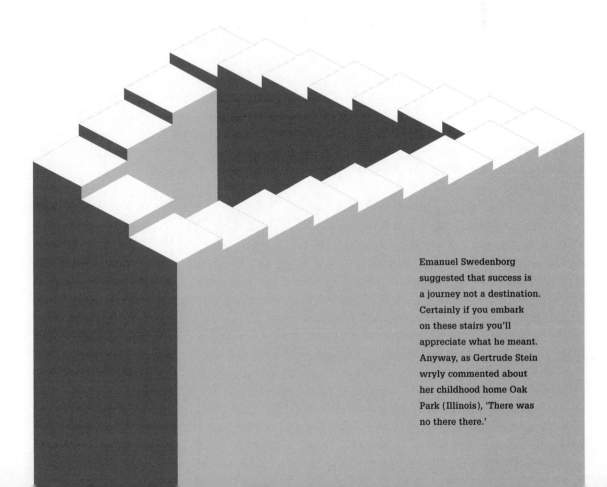

Emanuel Swedenborg
suggested that success is
a journey not a destination.
Certainly if you embark
on these stairs you'll
appreciate what he meant.
Anyway, as Gertrude Stein
wryly commented about
her childhood home Oak
Park (Illinois), 'There was
no there there.'

always
the
beautiful
answer
who
asks
a
more
beautiful
question.

ee cummings

Suddenly I heard a door slam and looked around and there was Mr Wright in his cloak and his pancake hat and his cane coming out of his apartment at the end of this desert camp. He saw me standing there – there was nobody else – and he was obviously in a very good mood, so he came by. He looked out at the desert with me and indulged in a certain amount of chit chat. Suddenly he said, 'George, do you know what architecture is?' I thought, Oh boy, this is why I've been following around this old man for seven or eight years. I said, 'Uh, I think, Mr Wright, that there's not much point in my trying to tell you, but if you'll tell me, I'd be very much obliged.' That was the right answer: he didn't want me to tell him whether I knew what architecture was, he couldn't have cared less. But, like a lot of other people in this neighbourhood, he liked the sound of his own voice, so I said 'What is architecture, Mr Wright?'

He looked around and on the terrace, which was a rough stone terrace, somebody had left a kind of triangular hole which was part of a whole system of little walls, very pretty, in which they had planted a paloverde tree. A paloverde tree is a desert tree with green bark on it, which is why it's called the green stick or pole tree. It doesn't have leaves, it has spines, which is characteristic of desert vegetation. Leaves evaporate too much and they don't make out well in desert climates. So here was this very pretty little tree, and at that season it was covered with kind of butter-coloured little blossoms, prettiest damn thing you ever saw.

He waved his cane at the paloverde tree, and he said, 'Architecture is a little bit like that paloverde tree coming into bloom.' And I said, 'Is that really what architecture is, Mr Wright?' I don't know when I've felt so disappointed. He said, 'Yeah, it's sort of like that, it's like this wonderful new tree coming into bloom.' Then he wandered off, swinging his cane, heading for his next victim, whenever he could pick one up. And then he stopped suddenly, very abruptly, and turned around and he said, 'Well, George, it isn't exactly like a paloverde tree coming into bloom. It's more like a boy falling in love with a girl or a girl falling in love with a boy.'

I said, 'Thank you very much.' And I thought, You old blaggard, I've been coming out here for years trying to get the thing right from the horse's mouth, and you tell me it's like a paloverde tree or a boy and a girl. I could've figured that out staying in Europe. Well, the fact was this marvellous old man had told me all he knew. Took me about ten years to figure that one out. But there wasn't anything else.

Everything else was just technology.

**Keeping
body
and
soul
together
under
water** [1]

Jerzy Kosinski

'Last year, while vacationing in Bangkok, a Venice of the Orient, I became aware of the ease and freedom with which the Thais approach the water. One day, at my hotel, I saw a middle-aged Thai lower himself into the deep end of the pool, but just when I expected him to start swimming, he brought his feet together, placed his hands along his thighs and with his head above the surface, began to float upright as if standing on a transparent shelf.

Approaching the pool, I examined him closely – several feet of water separated him from the bottom – and there was no device to keep him afloat. "Excuse me," I asked, perplexed, "Why don't you sink?" "Why should I?" said the man, "I don't want to." "Then why don't you swim?" "I don't want to swim," said the man. "What do you do to buoy yourself like that?" I asked. "Can't you see?" said the man, "I do nothing." "But what's the trick?" I asked, watching his every move. "Being oneself. That's the trick," he said, shifting in the water. His thighs spread, his feet tucked under him, his hands clasping his shins, he became motionless, gently bobbing with the movement of the water.

"Being oneself – that's all?" "That's all," he agreed. "But when I'm myself and do nothing I drown," I objected. "To drown is to do something," said the man. "Do nothing. Be yourself." "Easily said! Is there a place where I could learn it?" I asked. "There is," he replied, a bit impatient. "Water." "But do you know someone who can teach me how to?" "I do. You can teach yourself," said the man with emphasis, as he turned away.'

1. Jerzy Kosinski. *Observer* colour supplement, June 1984

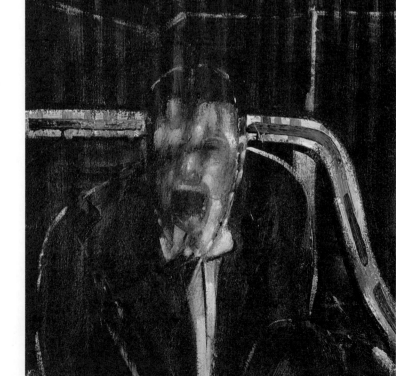

Painting. Francis Bacon, *Man Screaming*, 1952

The bark is the song of the dog

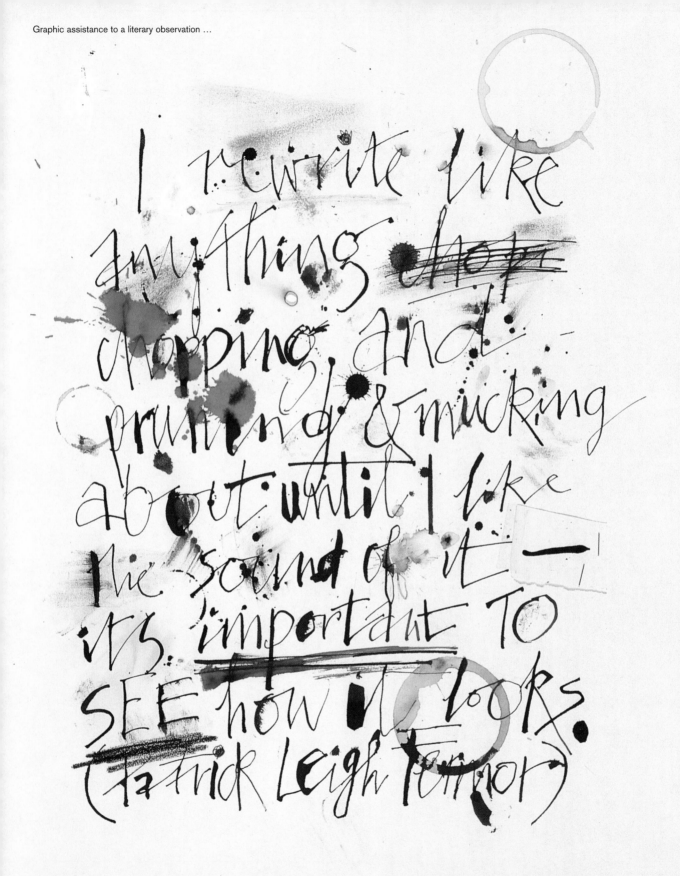

I rewrite like anything ~~Now~~ chopping and pruning & mucking about until I like the sound of it — its important TO SEE how it looks.
(Patrick Leigh Fermor)

PSSTTT

If you ask me what
I came to do in this world,
I, an artist,
I am
'I live
'I live
lou

I will answer you:
here to
but I'd

Emile Zola

Heh-hegggggggggggggggggggggghhhhhhh

It's one of those ungodly contralto cackles somewhere out there in the audience

'Boooo! . . . Yegggghhh! .

BRAAANNNNNGG!

The alarm

Hehheheh . . . unnnnhhhh-hur

They erupt with those belly sounds he hates so much.

Aaaaaah, aaaahhhhh, aaaaahhh

Thumpathumpathur

'N-n-n-n Ohhhhh.

She jerked her shoulder away from him.

Tom Wolfe. *The Bonfire of the Vanities.* Jonathan Cape (London 1988)

hhhhhhh!

'Craaaaasssssssh!'

said Maria, weeping with laughter.

. Yaaaggghhh! . . .

There's a terrific commotion on one side of the stage.

BRAAANNNNNGGGGG!

the noise of the alarm – was overpowering.

hh . . .

h, aaaahhhhh, aaaaaahhhhhhhh.

Sherman realizes it's himself, gulping for air …

athumpathumpathumpathumpathumpa

The noise of the airliners taking off pounded down so hard, he could feel it.

Some exuberant onomatopes by Tom Wolfe

FLAT NOISE. Flicker, blink and cuddle are effective interpretative word echoes of physical movements. Similarly the verbal sounds of sneer and mellifluous call to mind what they mean. [SEE P384]. So do names such as pussy (sound symbolism) and cuckoo (onomatopoeia). Onomatopoeia is the grand evocative term for words which imitate sounds: tick tock, choo choo, bark, miaow, oink, splat, clunk, bang, buzz, cackle, clatter, hiss, murmur, pop, sizzle, whiz, tinkle, whoosh, zoom. A parallel example is the graphic vernacular of speech balloons, think clouds and go faster stripes. Whereas onomatopoeia works through instinctive associations the graphic devices are only understood because everyone knows the visual language of comics and cartoons. The sound of battle was conveyed in the message opposite written by Futurist Filippo Marinetti from the front-line trenches in 1915. The typography echoes the staccato clatter of bullets, explosive thud of bombs, whine of shrapnel and shriek of shells. The composition expresses panic and confusion —— the fractured language of disassembled thoughts. A pictorial metaphor of violence.

24.2.1974 Leeds
A man in a new overcoat and an astrakhan hat, the weekend shopping in his arms, walking along the pavement barking loudly like a dog.

Ian Breakwell's Diary. 1964-1985

In Japan pigs don't 'oink oink' they 'boo boo'. And in Indonesia the dogs don't 'bark' they 'gong-gong'.

Drawing. André François

SCRABrrRrraaNNG

Ho ricevuto
il vostro libro
mentre bombardam
il monte Coro
F.T. ...

Paa piiig
Paaak
Piing
bombardam

futurista

GRAAAAG

tam-tumb
tumb tumb-tumb-tumb-tumb-tumb
-tumb ffffrraaah tatatatata... rrrrrraaah
tatatata PUUM PAMPAM

TRAG

SIMULTANEITA ESPLOSIONE

10000 esplosioni

ISONZO
campestre intre fresco
DOLCE DOLCISSIIIIMO PACIFICO

grazie e ai suoi arder
lasci augun

Guerra ai
tedeschi!!
compagni
verdi   sdraiato

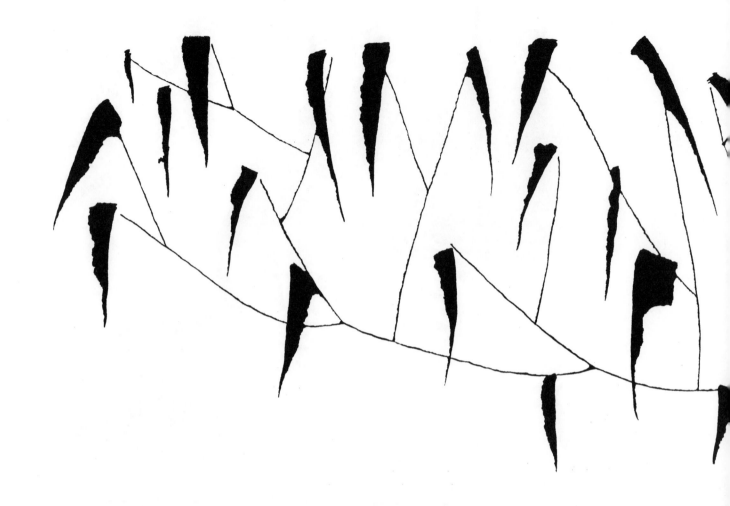

This is the Caribbean **Shak Shak** tree
distinguished by lack of leaves and abundance
of long black beans. It's the rattle and rustle of
the beans in a mild breeze – the **shak, shak,
shak, shak** – which gave the tree its name.
Actually this drawing is not of a specific **Shak
Shak** but more the character of the tree. The
pen tracing the routes of the branches and the
twist and flick of the nib rendering the beans.

DOWN WITH DOGMA

Fish are the last to recognize water.

This drawing illustrates the *Flat Earth* column in *The Independent on Sunday* newspaper. This photograph is the first whole body X-ray of a living person and was taken in 1907. The lady was fully dressed with rings, necklace, bracelet, hatpin, button boots with nailed-on heels, and a whalebone corset. An image of a paradigm which accepted exposing and displaying her most intimate self, at a time when nudity was only publicly accepted in the domain of the demi-monde and artist's model.

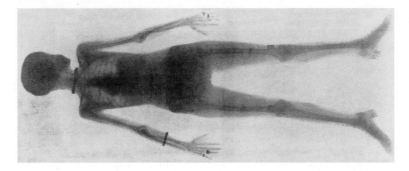

Illustration. David Littleton   **X-ray.** William Morton

'Each man makes his own world.' *Emerson*

The Pangloss Syndrome : For fish the world is water; for one old lady it was a tortoise. At a public lecture a well-known scientist (some say William James, others Bertrand Russell) described how the earth orbits around the sun, which orbits around the stars, so on and so forth. At the end of the lecture, up jumped a little old lady: 'Absolute rubbish', she said, 'the world is a flat plate supported on the back of a giant tortoise.' The lecturer with a superior smile asked, 'and so, what is the tortoise standing on?' 'You're very clever, young man, very clever,' said the old lady, 'but it's tortoises all the way down.'

In the mythology of native Amerindian peoples they live on Turtle Island.

Although paradigms provide a sense of continuity and stability they also breed resistance to new ideas. St Augustine – 'give me chastity and continency, only not yet' – even withdrew to a monastery to avoid the temptation of curiosity.

Theologians unwittingly refer to St Augustine's request as his 'ejaculatory prayer'.

At the reception given for Galileo to demonstrate his new discovery, a guest refused to look through the telescope in case he faced an unwelcome truth. On hearing Darwin's theories on evolution the wife of a bishop remarked that, even if true, she hoped the congregation didn't hear about it.

'Theology is the effort to explain the unknowable in terms of the not worth knowing.' *H.L. Mencken*

In 1925 a Tennessee school teacher was indicted by a court for teaching Darwin's theory of evolution. A Gallup Poll in 1986 reported that 67 per cent of American teenagers believe in angels. About the same time a Mr Wilbur G. Voliva (of the Apostolic Catholics in Zion) flew around the world and remained convinced it was 'as flat as a saucer'. Cosmas, a much travelled merchant [and scholar] who lived in Alexandria during the early part of the fifth century AD, thought the world was a flat parallelogram with a length double its width. All such views neatly encompassed by South Africa's President Botha who, responding to an interviewer with irritation, stated: 'My mind is made up, so don't confuse me with facts.'

'Who is born square will not die round.' *Neapolitan proverb*

When imagination circles around the wheel of faith the mind bends reality to fit the paradigm. As Dr Pangloss concluded, we have spectacles because we have noses. It's not an uncommon condition.

'We are all a product of the choices we make.' *Albert Camus*

the belly button problem

Early painters of religious subjects faced a major issue: should Adam and Eve have navels? If they did, they must have had a mother. If they didn't, they looked silly. A sprig of foliage with the fig leaf usually got around the problem.

In the seventeenth century James Ussher, Archbishop of Armagh and Professor of Theological Controversies, figured out that mankind began (Adam and Eve getting it off together) at noon, Greenwich mean time (I assume), on 23 October 4004 BC. The time and date of 9am on 26 October is also frequently incorrectly quoted. Such mistakes are perpetrated when people blindly copy things out of other people's books! Anyway the Archbishop came to his conclusion by adding up the ages of the couple's descendants from the Old Testament.

I was on a train to Cologne. Checking a map in the corridor to see how much further I had to go, I saw a railway station called Neanderthal. Who'd have thought of naming a station after a species of prehistoric man? I speculated in naming stations for the new London underground line to Docklands: Piltdown, Lucy, Oetzi, Java. The place – of course – was named after the primitive skull discovered there in 1856. A mere three years before the publication of Charles Darwin's *On the Origin of Species*. At the time everyone, well almost everyone, believed Adam and Eve were the very first human beings. The apelike creature, they concluded, must therefore have been a deformed arthritic cripple from medieval times. Or perhaps, someone suggested, the skeleton of a Cossack pursuing Napoleon's retreating army. All of us, as Norman Nicholson irritatingly points out, are inclined to make 'the pretension to be the uncommon exception to the universal bondage'.

Evolution theory was respectable long before Darwin, although always tempered with the implication that a divine hand was at work. Even Darwin demurred when Karl Marx wanted to dedicate *Das Kapital* (Volume One, English translation) to him by feebly responding to his request that his wife would be upset to see such a godless work dedicated to him.

To reconcile the disparity between faith and fact, Philip Henry Gosse wrote *Omphalos* [1857], subtitled *An attempt to Untie the Geological Knot*. The *Omphalos* (Gk navel) was a stone in Delphi which the ancient Greeks believed located the centre of the world. Although science in the nineteenth century had established that the earth had been in existence for billions of years, religious conviction held that Genesis only occurred some six thousand years previously. The answer to this conundrum was provided by Gosse who, being both brilliant naturalist and religious fundamentalist, came up with the notion that the world was a divine illusion created by God.

The birds and the bees, flowers and plants, sunsets and rainbows, he proposed, were invented to enrich and ennoble our lives. The act of creation included accounting for the inexplicable aspects of the past. Adam suddenly appears aged 33 (with navel) born of no mother. The skeletons of Glyptodonts (which I erroneously imagine as hairy hippopotomuses with long legs) exist in a mountain gorge in France – yet there could never have been Glyptodonts, since we know they lived before Adam and Eve. The scenario was neat, irrefutable and ludicrous.

The book was received with derision. One aspect they gleefully wanted him to explain was fossilized excrement. No problem, responded Gosse, God placed petrified turds within his created history to complete the illusion.[1] A point of view as rational as that held by a man in a pub who confidentially leans over to his friendly neighbour and says: 'Excuse me, but I think you've had quite enough to drink – your face has become rather blurred.'

Note. Symi, Greece. I dropped a crumb. An ant interrupted its staccato scurrying to carry it off across the roughly paved courtyard. It dragged a piece of fodder as large and surely as heavy as itself, up and down cement ravines between the edges of high stone slabs, around huge lumps of gravel and deep holes, dodging towering clumps of weed. For an idle moment I imagined being that ant living in that hard grey landscape. Another world within my world.

---

1. Stephen Jay Gould. *The Flamingo's Smile*. Penguin (London 1991)

a paradigm shift

Illustration. Medieval man breaks through into the modern world

LONDON

PARIS

ROMA

AMSTERDAM

During a tedious moment during a television documentary on a schoolroom of chanting children in China, I noticed a strange map on the wall. All the bits and pieces seemed to be in the wrong places until I spotted Peking in the centre. On early maps Jerusalem often occupied pole position, but nowadays, as any commercial airline route map clearly demonstrates, the middle of the world is where *you* live.

Although many early maps of the Mediterranean put Africa at the top and Europe at the bottom, eventually someone must have decided the other way up was better. The world is round, so there is no top or bottom, although we think there is. Being *'on top'*, or *'over and above'*, is preferable to being *'put down'*, or *'beneath notice'*. Thumbs up are better than thumbs down. *Down under,* they even refer to the Northern Territories as *'The Top End'*.

A bias also operates between East and West. I can't understand why we insist on referring to Japan and China as the Far East. From Canada, the orient, so to speak, indisputably lies to the west. It's the Chinese who should consider Europeans and Americans to be orientals. By the way, on the *Mappa Mundi*, the oldest surviving medieval map, the Garden of Eden is positioned in the Far East, hence the term ORIENTATION.

While making a film in China in 1972, Antonioni attempted to send a telegram home, but the clerk in the post office at Nanking had never heard of Italy. When Antonioni wrote the word out for her, she looked at it sceptically, then hurried off to consult her colleagues. On a wall map, they finally managed to pick out the thin peninsula which bore the name. Having located it, they burst into contagious laughter at its dwarfish size.[1]

And then there's the one about an American and a Chinaman who struck up a conversation at a bar. Suddenly the American knocked the Chinaman off his stool and shouted, 'take that for Pearl Harbour.' Somewhat shaken the Chinaman protested he was not Japanese. The American apologized, explained that orientals all looked the same to him, introduced himself as Mr Goldberg, and bought him a drink. A few minutes later the Chinaman threw his drink in the American's face and shouted, 'That's for the Titanic'. The American angrily riposted that the Titanic hit an iceberg. 'So', said the Chinaman, 'Goldberg, Steinberg, Iceberg – they all sound the same to me.' A corny joke but a pertinent reminder of the blinkers imposed by paradigms.

Saul Steinberg's cover for *The New Yorker* magazine mocking the insularity of Manhattanites (shown left), says it all. In fact it was so pertinent that it has been plagiarized all over the world to illustrate local paradigms. Some are shown here. Steinberg was extremely unamused. He even sued Columbia Pictures for using a version in their publicity for a film. And won damages. I have illustrated these blatant copies because their paradigms are more interesting than their plagiarisms.

TOO FAR EAST IS WEST

1. Peter Conrad. *Modern Times, Modern Places.* Thames and Hudson (London 1998)

In India they worship cows ... In Argentina they BBQ 'em ...

Design. Imprint Graphic Design

In  ... **they see things differently.**

Photograph. Hein Gorny, Untitled (c.1930). If it required a title my suggestion would be **CONFORMITY**

From the dedication page of *The Autobiography of a Dog Trainer* by Lt.-Col. G.H. Badcock, foreword by Lady Kitty Ritson. Other books by Lt.-Col. G.H. Badcock: *Disobedient Dogs, The Understanding of a Dog, Man and his Gun Dog, The Training of Retrievers and Spaniels, The Early Life and Training of a Gun Dog, The Care of Domestic Animals.*

A book review in *Field and Stream* (1959), a magazine devoted to outdoor pursuits. Although written many years ago, *Lady Chatterley's Lover* has just been reissued by the Grove Press, and this pictorial account of the day by day life of an English gamekeeper is full of considerable interest to outdoorminded readers as it contains many passages on pheasant-raising, the apprehending of poachers, ways to control vermin and other chores and duties of the professional gamekeeper. Unfortunately one is obliged to wade through many pages of extraneous material in order to discover and savour those sidelights on the management of a Midland shooting estate, and in this reviewer's opinion the book cannot take the place of J.R. Miller's *Practical Gamekeeping.*

'When I was little', says Jean Cocteau, 'I believed that foreigners could not really talk at all, but were only pretending.' And, as a child, Clarence Day remembered being deeply shocked when he found a Bible printed in French. 'Imagine', he said, 'the Lord talking French.'

By the end of the nineteenth century the physical sciences had progressed to such an extent that Lord Kelvin believed that all that remained to be done was to measure physical constants to the next decimal place in accuracy. Even the Prussian Patent Office closed down on the assumption there was nothing left to be invented.

General Gordon of Khartoum (and *Cloud Cuckoo Land*) was convinced that the Seychelles were the Garden of Eden and the native *coco-de-mer*, a nut shaped like female private parts, was the *Forbidden Fruit*, grown of course by the *Tree of Knowledge*. By the way the average weight of temptation is 25 to 30 lbs.

A bishop landing on a remote island found a hermit chanting aloud, 'Cursed be the Lord, cursed be the Lord, cursed …' Reprimanding him he told him to sing 'Praised be the Lord' instead. As the bishop was sailing away he was amazed to see the hermit running across the water towards the boat. Climbing on board the hermit tearfully asked the bishop to repeat the prayer as he'd forgotten the right words.

There is nothing more difficult to take in hand, more perilous to conduct, more uncertain in its success, than to take the lead in introducing a new order of things,' wrote Machiavelli, 'because the innovator will have for enemies all who have done well under the old conditions, and only luke-warm defenders who do well under the new.'

The Western Wall, better known as the Wailing Wall, is in the old city of Jerusalem. Here orthodox Jews gather to pray and stick notes into the cracks between the masonry. Requests, notes of gratitude, that sort of thing. The Israeli telephone company has a special service which enables you to fax in a message which will be stuck in the wall on your behalf.

In ancient Delphi a round stone called the *Omphalos* (navel) was kept in the Temple of Apollo. This, the Greeks believed, lay beneath the North Star and marked the centre of the world. Actually at that time it certainly did. [SEE P106].

Lady Caroline Lamb, in the embraces of her unattractive husband, is reputed to have said, 'Oh, to be in England now that April's there.' I don't know who was eavesdropping – apt choice of word don't you think?

Explorer Sir Richard Burton paid a visit to a sheikh in the desert. As the sheikh rode out to welcome him his wife tumbled off her camel, her clothes slipped up, and she revealed all. Disaster? No. The sheikh was pleased because she kept her face covered while she fell. Actually, having read his biography, Burton probably recognized her anyway.

There's a story that David Hockney's mother, who lives in Leeds, was visiting her son in Los Angeles. Being shown the sights under the blue skies and bright sun she was heard to keep muttering, 'What a shame, what a shame. Such a beautiful day and not a washing line to be seen.'

Newspaper clip: In Afghanistan, the Taliban recently [1998] banned women from wearing white socks as they draw attention to the ankles.

A tribe of Indians in a remote part of the Amazon assumed they were the only people in the world. When they were discovered in 1943 the trauma of learning that they were not unique was so severe, they almost died out.

A few years ago some wood carvers were flown from Indonesia to London to reconstruct a rice barn at the Museum of Mankind. When asked their impression of the city, they said that what really astonished them were the dogs exercising people on leads.

Lady Gough's Etiquette (published 1863) : 'The perfect hostess will see to it that works of male and female authors be properly separated on her bookshelves. Their proximity, unless the authors happen to be married, should not be tolerated.'

Have you heard about the man who complains that his wife overcooks his steak because she thinks he likes it too rare?

How to boil a frog:

The cockroach condition:

The chicken effect:

Note. Sales were falling and the client decided the fault lay in the package design. I had, he said, a completely free hand. However, every proposal I made he thought too radical, too different, regularly referring to the average taste of which he considered himself arbiter and spokesman. In short he was unable to accept change. Eventually in frustration I facetiously reminded him of the proverb which states people can get killed crossing the road — because they don't want to let go of their umbrellas. He didn't get the point.

My mother ses she's cold and then she makes me put on a coat

Colin aged 7

Ladders and walls:

Quotation. Nanette Newman. *Lots of Love.* Collins (London 1974)

Throw a frog into a saucepan of boiling water and not surprisingly it jumps right out. Ease a frog into a saucepan of cold water and it will contentedly slurp about. Turn on the heat, but at first keep it low. Then *slowly* increase the temperature so that *imperceptibly* the water gets *warmer*, and *warmer*, and *warmer*. And the frog *dozier* and *dozier* and *dozier* – until it boils.

Conclusion : When someone raises the temperature watch your back.

A scientist worked for years trying to teach a cockroach to respond to verbal commands. Eventually he succeeded in getting it to leap over his finger whenever he told it to jump. Once it had learned this, he pulled off its front legs. When he then commanded the cockroach to jump again it took a deep breath and just managed to clear the man's finger. He then pulled off the middle legs and on the command to jump it just about managed to stagger over. Finally he pulled off the back legs. But when told to jump, the cockroach just lay there, legless.

Conclusion : When all a cockroach's legs are removed, deafness occurs.

A man visits his doctor as he's worried about his wife who is getting acutely deaf but refuses to acknowledge it. The doctor says he can't help unless he knows how deaf she really is and suggests, when she isn't looking, the husband stands at the opposite end of the room and asks her a question. If she doesn't respond, to take three paces forward and ask again, and so on. When the husband gets home he finds she's cooking. Fortuitously the kitchen is extremely large. Standing as far away as possible he asks what's for supper. She doesn't reply. He advances three paces and asks again. No response. He takes another three paces and leaning forward shouts in her ear. Startled, she shouts back, 'Chicken.' And then adds, 'for christsakes, what's wrong with you? I've already told you three times.'

Conclusion : Don't believe everything you hear.

One often thinks one is climbing towards a solution only to eventually discover that the ladder has been leaning against the wrong wall. Sometimes this happens because one didn't look where one was going, or was receiving the wrong information, or because one addressed the situation with an invalid preconception.

Conclusion : If you don't realize you've picked the wrong wall, then when you've reached the top you're convinced it's the right answer.

'How delightfully
the fishes
are enjoying themselves',
exclaimed Soshi.

'You are not a fish',
commented his friend,
'how do you know
that the fishes
are enjoying themselves?'

'You are not myself',
answered Soshi;
'how do you know,
that I do not know,
that the fishes
are enjoying themselves?'

Taoist dialogue

IFMANDOESNOTKEEPPACEWITHHISCOMPANIONS, PERHAPSITISBECAUSEHEHEARSADIFFERENT

DRUMMER.LETHIMSTEPTOTHEMUSICWHICHHEHEARS

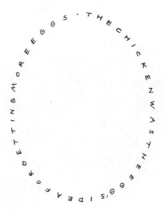

THE CHICKEN WAS THE EGG'S IDEA FOR GETTING MORE EGGS ·

Samuel Butler

Patrick Hughes

'The hen is only the egg's way of making another hen.'

Machina Sapiens. Designing creatures has been going on a long time: God created Adam from dust. Rabbi Loew made the *Golem* out of clay. Pygmalion carved a sculpture of Aphrodite, fell in love with it, and brought her to life as *Galatea*. Daedalus designed sculptures animated by liquid mercury. Hero of Alexandria constructed dancing figures activated by steam and weights. Albertus Magnus had an automaton servant which Thomas Aquinas, convinced it was the work of the devil, attacked and reduced to scrap. Leonardo da Vinci made a lion to greet Louis XII when he arrived in Milan – a triumph of mechanics which walked towards the king and tore open its chest to reveal a fleur-de-lys emblazoned on its heart. In the eighteenth century Jacques de Vaucanson invented a mechanical duck which quacked, paddled, waddled, ate and defecated. And Jacquet-Droz (who inspired Mary Shelley to write *Frankenstein*) created a puppet which could write, 'I do not think, therefore I am not.' Another famous automaton was a turbanned chess-playing robot known as *The Turk*. At least everyone had accepted it as a robot until it was revealed to be operated by a dwarf, some say a legless Pole, who really was a master chess player. *Tik-Tok* was born in 1907 in the book *Ozma of Oz*. A plate bolted on his metal back said, 'Thinks, Speaks, Acts, and Does Everything But Live.'

The word *Robot* (Czech for serf) was appropriated from *Rossums Universal Robot*, a surrealist play by Karel Capek produced in the 1920s, and later popularized by sci-fi writer Isaac Asimov. In the film *Metropolis* (1927), Professor Rotwang designed a robot which worked continuously and never tired or made mistakes; an idea which appealed to big business. In 1939 Westinghouse had produced *Electro* and his dog *Sparko*. *Electro* could walk, talk, and count. *Sparko* wagged his tail and could sit up and beg. Unfortunately one night someone left the door open and *Sparko* ran outside. Attracted by the lights of a car, he homed in and was crushed to death.

Since then we've had *Speedy, Cutie, Daleks, Nomad, R2D2, Blade Runners, Terminator* and less happily *Acoustic Kitty. Acoustic Kitty* was a real cat, a 1960s product of 25 million dollars' research and technology internally wired to eavesdrop. One day the CIA tried to persuade her to cross the road and enter the Soviet embassy, but only succeeded in disorientating her. And so, like *Sparko*, she took off, got run over, and written off.

By 1970 Marvin Minsky, a godfather of Artificial Intelligence, was predicting that within the decade a machine would 'read Shakespeare, grease a car, play office politics, tell a joke, have a fight'. He was an optimist. Machines haven't got much further than putting other machines together, let alone thinking up interesting ideas. However, if and when human engineering develops creatures like the *Replicants* who feature in *Blade Runner,* we might not be able to distinguish 'cyber' people from 'meat' people. At that point, it has been suggested, the ultimate test is to interview them from behind a screen. If you can't tell whether you're talking to a machine or a person, you have to accept it's a person …

Here is an alternative suggestion :

Can you imagine loving one?

Can you imagine wondering if it loves you?

If the second question doesn't occur to you :

One of you isn't human!

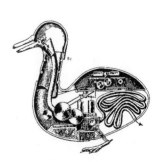

VAUCANSON'S DUCK

Daniel Hillis: 'I have programs that have evolved within the computer from nothing, and they do fairly complicated things. You begin putting in sequences of random instructions, and these programs compete and interact with each other and have sex with each other and produce new generations of programs. If you put them in a world where they survive by solving a problem, then with each successive generation they get better and better at solving the problem, and after a few hundred thousand generations they solve the problem very well. That approach may actually be used to produce the thinking machine.'[1]

1. John Brockman. *The Third Culture*. Touchstone (New York 1996)

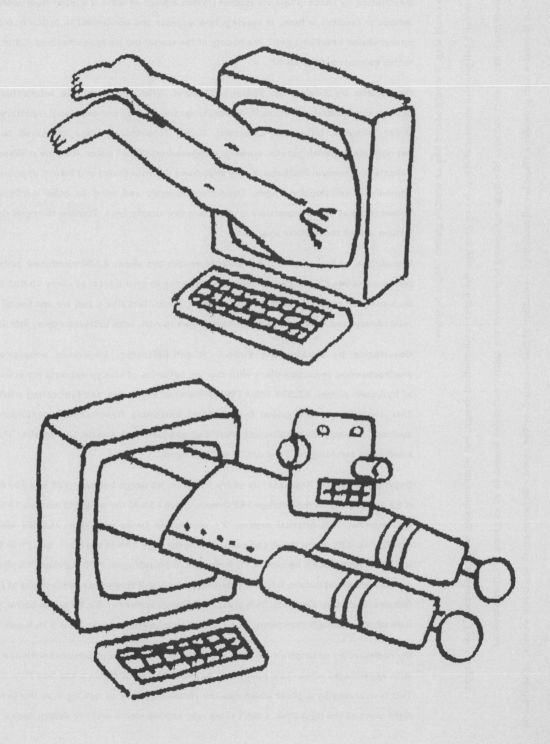

Can robots Kama Sutra ?

Illustration. Seymour Chwast

Description by Karen Blixen: 'What is man, when you come to think upon him, but a minutely set, ingenious machine for turning, with infinite artfulness, the red wine of Shiraz into urine?'

Description by Shakespeare via Hamlet: 'What a piece of work is a man! How noble in reason! how infinite in faculty! in form, in moving, how express and admirable! in action how like an angel! in apprehension how like a god! the beauty of the world! the paragon of animals! And yet, to me, what is this quintessence of dust?'

Description by Edward O. Wilson: 'Cultural. With indeterminate intellectual potential but biologically constrained. Basically a primate species in body and emotional repertory (member of the Order Primates, Infraorder Catarrhini, Family Hominidae). Huge compared to other animals, parvihirsute, bipedal, porous, squishy, composed mostly of water. Runs on millions of coordinated delicate biochemical reactions. Easily shut down by trace toxins and transit of pea-sized projectiles. Short-lived, emotionally fragile. Dependent in body and mind on other earthbound organisms. Colonization of space impossible without massive supply lines. Starting to regret deeply the loss of Nature and all those other species.' [1]

Description by Steve Jones: 'A C-class Mercedes has about 4,500 numbered parts, some of them (screws and the like) repeated several times over to give a total of some 10,000 individual items. Men and women have about 70,000 working genes. Just like a car, we are full of duplication and redundancy; and many components have begun to rust, with battered copies littering the DNA.' [2]

Description by Buckminster Fuller: 'A self-balancing, 88-jointed adapter-base biped: an electrochemical reduction plant with storage batteries of energy extracts for activating thousands of hydraulic pumps, 62,000 miles (100,000km) of capillaries, self-lubricating crushers and cranes. This whole mechanism guided from a turret containing stereoscopic rangefinders, olfactory and auditory sensors, air-conditioning inlet and exhaust, and a main fuel intake. The whole system needing no servicing for 70 years, if well-managed.'

Description by Rem Koolhaas: 'In every 100 men, 95 weigh between 127 and 209 lb. (for women it is 95 and 195 lb). In the average 162 lb man, about 43% of the weight is muscle, 14% is fat, 14% bone and marrow, 12% internal organs, 9% connective tissue and skin, and 8% blood. The weight distributes: 47% in the trunk and neck, 34% in the legs, 12% in the arms, and 7% in the head ... man is 65% oxygen, 18.5% carbon, 9.5% hydrogen, 3.3% nitrogen, 1.5% calcium, 1% phosphorus, 0.35% or less each of potassium, sulphur, chlorine, sodium, and magnesium, with traces of iron, iodine, zinc, fluorine, and other elements. This gives him enough water to fill a 10 gallon barrel, enough fat for 7 bars of soap, enough phosphorus for 2,200 match heads, and iron for a 3 inch nail.' [3]

My rudimentary description: 'A tube with a hole at each end punctuated with apertures and fitted with appendages whose sole purpose is to generate and maintain a one-way flow through the pipe. This is overseen by a ghost which has the elementary task of making sure the two ends are in the right place at the right time. I can't think why anyone would want to design such a silly product.'

'If a machine could sing, it would sound like an electric guitar.' Roger Scruton

'The computer can't tell you the emotional story. It can give you the exact mathematical design, but what's missing is the eyebrows.' Frank Zappa

'We are survival machines – robot vehicles blindly programmed to preserve the selfish molecules known to us as genes.' Richard Dawkins

'... a mysterious theater which provides a stage for all exchange – whether of matter, mind, or the sense – between inner and outer worlds.' Michel Leiris

'Life is any self-perpetuating pattern of chemical reactions.' J.B.S. Haldane

'Eating is a silly thing. In order to get food into your stomach you've got to push it through your face.' Dagwood (Blondie comic strip)

1. Edward O. Wilson. *Consilience*. Little Brown (London 1998) 2. *Daily Telegraph*, Friday 26 March 1999 3. Rem Koolhaas and Bruce Mau. *S,M,L,XL*. 010 Publishers (Rotterdam 1995)

'while you and I

      have lips and voices

which are for kissing

      and to sing with,

who cares if some

      one-eyed son of a bitch

invents an instrument

      to measure spring with?'

ee cummings

Curiosity killed the ...

Curiosity is the mother of intelligence.

Emotional Intelligence

Intelligence makes us self-conscious. We think about thinking, we know about knowing. So far no other animal, vegetable or mineral has this ability.

Emotional intelligence (EQ) is self-awareness, the who and what we are. If you are good at reading your own feelings, then you are likely to be good at reading other people's. If you aren't, success in life is limited. The kind of people who lack EQ are psychopaths, rapists and child molesters.

Emotional intelligence is being able to deal with human relationships without becoming subsumed by them. To be able to control our desires rather than giving in to them.

The Marshmallow Test : Four-year-olds were called individually into a room where a kindly old gentleman (psychologist in disguise) gave each a marshmallow. He then said he had to leave for a few minutes but they could eat the marshmallow. However, if they didn't eat it, they'd get an extra one when he got back. Well, some could and some couldn't. Years later it was discovered that those children who waited were more socially adjusted than those who didn't. The latter still had trouble postponing gratification, were argumentative, had low self-esteem, coped badly with stress.

I saw this in a scientific journal. Sounds like a load of rubbish to me. A really greedy kid would hang on as long as possible to garner an extra treat. And if the children had claimed they were hungry, the kind old man might have sprung a few more up front. Analytic hindsight lacks the acumen of punter's foresight.

Artificial Intelligence

Someone has suggested that intelligence is what you use when you don't know what to do. That's a relief to know because I was brought up to believe that intelligence was the major ingredient in everything I was no good at. Latin, physics, algebra and other schoolboy nosegrinders.

Intelligence has been given a fixed value so it is easier to grasp, in consequence we treat it as something specific rather than as a convenient label. It's a fallacy to think people can be neatly ranked from ape to Einstein. Those who compose intelligence tests can only measure skills similar to their own; as Alfred Binet (father of IQ testing) said : *'intelligence is what my tests measure.'*

Conventional IQ tests would be useless in assessing the spatial intelligence of a Rudolf Nureyev, the musical intelligence of a Philip Glass, or the visual intelligence of an Alexander Calder.

Originally the designing of artificial intelligence (AI) programmes was based on logical deduction and rational response. In consequence it was easier to mimic the thought process of a chess master concerned with determined patterns, than a child which imagines randomly and makes improbable analogies. [SEE P120].

To be comparable to the real thing artificial intelligence has to accommodate subjective as well as objective processes. And that's about the unpredictable and irrational – in other words behaving like humans. We are overly impressed by the ability to calculate and rationalize, and inadequately impressed by the ability to see possibilities and make connections.

And connections, as Adam and Eve discovered, are what life is about.

Question : Do you think computers have made creative people redundant?

Computerspeak

During the 1940s Alan Turing envisaged that by the turn of the century humans would have conversations with computers. He was optimistic. Nevertheless fifty years later five out of ten people were fooled in a contest which pitted their wits against a bank of computers. Two of which responded for themselves; the others were remotely controlled by humans. Each dialogue was restricted to a single topic.

This is one exchange, I don't know whether of machine intelligence or operator's wit, but I can guess.

Person:
'Have you ever had a dry martini?'

Computer:
'I drink one before dinner, sometimes during dinner. I don't like martinis after dinner.'

Person:
'What about wines?'

Computer:
'Mostly I drink relatively young burgundies of modest fame, such as Savigny-les-Beaunes and Pernand-Vergilesses.'

If this really was machine intelligence, then it is a pretentious mechanical snob.

Deep Blue

In 1996 Gary Kasparov – arguably the greatest chess player ever – was beaten by a machine whose capacity for calculation leaves the human brain standing. Whereas Kasparov can evaluate three moves a second, IBM's Deep Blue can evaluate millions. Nevertheless such is the complexity of chess, this still only provides for five moves ahead.

The advantage is reversed when it comes to improvisation, and Kasparov won the second game by this strategy. I think he lost the rest of the matches and apparently at the end of the session, accused the machine of cheating – maybe it has already aquired human characteristics.

Intelligence is a matter of *conceptualizing* rather than *calculating*. In the unlikely position of the game shown here black has the advantage of two rooks and a bishop, and white the wall of impregnable pawns. Impregnable that is, provided they refrain from taking the black rook. All the white king has to do is to move aimlessly from square to square until, in frustration, black concedes a draw.

A computer would find it difficult to understand a strategy based on calculated irritation.

PARALLEL PROCESSORS

Half a million hungry army ants moving through a forest can progress 200 metres a day and cut a swathe 20 metres wide. Taking off on a bearing roughly 123 degrees anti-clockwise from the previous foray, the swarm sticks to one course. If it meets a stream it will move along until it can cross over, then turn back along the opposite side to reach the point where it can continue on the original course.

This uncanny sense of purpose and direction is not apparent in the individual, nor does the group have any discernible hierarchy. Evidently ants have a collective intelligence which acts in much the same way as cells in the human brain. That is to say the whole is greater than its individual parts. Something which biologist Lewis Thomas called a kind of live computer with crawling bits for wits.

Indeed ants are so much like human beings as to be an embarrassment. They farm fungi, raise aphids as livestock, launch armies into war, use chemical sprays to alarm and confuse enemies, capture slaves, engage in child labour, exchange information ceaselessly. They do everything but watch television.

And here is one (circa 2000) with a micro-chip.

Photograph. Andrew Syred

David Ruelle

'What we call intelligence is the activity of the mind and takes place in the brain. Intelligence guides our actions on the basis of what we perceive from the outside universe, and the interpretation of visual messages is therefore part of it.'

A.N. Whitehead

'Insistence on clarity at all costs is based on sheer superstition as to the mode in which human intelligence functions. Our reasonings grasp at straws for premises and float on gossamers for deductions.'

Scott Fitzgerald

'The test of superb intelligence is the ability to hold two separate ideas in mind at the same time and still retain the ability to function.'

Aldous Huxley

'Man is so intelligent that he feels impelled to invent theories to account for what happens in the world. Unfortunately, he is not quite intelligent enough, in most cases, to find correct explanations. So that when he acts on his theories, he behaves very often like a lunatic.'

Douglas Hofstadter

'It is an inherent property of intelligence that it can jump out of the task which it is performing, and survey what it has done ...'

Jean Baudrillard

'The sad thing about Artificial Intelligence, is that it lacks artifice and therefore intelligence.'

R.L. Gregory

'I suspect that thinking about intelligence has been strangled through not disentangling the what-is-given from the what-needs-to-be-discovered senses of intelligence.'

Willard R. Espy

Haikus show I.Q.s.
High I.Q.s like haikus. Low
I.Q.s – no haikus.

The haiku is a Japanese verse-form consisting of seventeen syllables – five each in the first and third lines, seven in the second – to which the reader adds his own associations and imagery.

← 'Sorry, I forgot and cut them off.'

Put yourself to the test

Try this mini I.Q. test to find out if you are eligible for membership to Mensa, the high I.Q. society. Four out of these five questions right and you will probably qualify. Which is the odd one out in each of these five questions? Answers are upside down at the base of this advertisement.

1
17 15 14 13 11
a b c d e

2
Z L T V Y
a b c d e

3
.5 1.5 2 2.5 3.5
a b c d e

4
a b c d e

5
a b c d e

To learn more about Mensa and how to take the Mensa entrance tests, return the coupon to Mensa, Freepost, Wolverhampton WV2 1BR (no stamp required)

The grammar of the advertisement text wouldn't get a member of Mensa past a rudimentary English test, but that's nothing to do with IQ – just common sense.

This is the logotype of a Welsh brewery. [**SEE**P117].

Philippe Starck

'I am my brain's publisher.'

'The workings of the brain more closely resemble the living ecology of a jungle than they do the activities of a computer or any machine we could possibly imagine.'

Gerald Edelman. Neuroscientist

'... brains were designed to understand hunting and gathering, mating and child-rearing: a world of medium-sized objects moving in three dimensions at moderate speeds. We are ill-equipped to comprehend the very small and the very large; things whose duration is measured in picoseconds or gigayears; particles that don't have position; forces and fields that we cannot see or touch ...'

Richard Dawkins. Evolutionary biologist

'... digital technology and networks are part of the evolution not just of the human species, but of the planet itself. The planet is going to be networked, and a billion brains are going to be connected together, and that will have a profound impact on humans, and on the planet – unlike any that we have seen before.'

Louis Rossetto. Publisher. *Wired* magazine

'... here is the relaxing thought: computers will not take over the world, they cannot replace us, because they are not designed, as we are, for ambiguity.'

Lewis Thomas. Pathologist

(late night thoughts on listening to Mahler's *Ninth Symphony*)

'The brain is like a kaleidoscope where, as soon as one changes activity, the whole configuration may alter.'

Susan Greenfield. Neuroscientist

The seat of one's intellect is determined by culture. Ancient Egyptians located thought in the heart, Homeric heroes in their bellies, we think that we think in our heads, and now scientists think thinking can be done in a box – or more specifically in a machine.

Although they more or less know how the brain works, where our thoughts come from, or how we register memories, remains a mystery. One can't look inside a brain and say: *'Aha'*, here we have a Muslim fundamentalist, or a concert violinist, or a dominatrix, or a whatever. And that is a major problem to resolve before one can design a facsimile brain.

Apparently it's not a matter of size, weight or dimension. Neanderthals had larger brains than modern man and look what happened to them. [SEEP7]. The average brain weighs about the same as a kilogram bag of sugar. If squashed flat it would cover four sheets of typing paper, a chimp's would only fit on one, a monkey's on a postcard, and a rat's on a stamp.[1] And we're talking about one and a half litres of protein and fat – the most remarkable structure in the universe.

Actually to talk of a brain as a single entity is a simplification. The organ has three layers: the earliest and ancient part, the intermediary piece, and the modern bit. These have been referred to as the alligator, the horse and the man. The alligator responds to primitive urges such as anger, fear and lust. The horse copes with the commonplace needs. The man is the cortex – the top and most recent layer – which deals with more elevated thoughts like love, greed, ethics and envy.

Plato: *'When the gentler part of the soul slumbers and the control of Reason is withdrawn ... the Wild Beast in us ... becomes rampant.'* Henry David Thoreau: *'We are conscious of an animal in us which awakens in proportion as our higher nature slumbers.'* Freud called the beast within us, the *Id* [Latin for 'it'].

This model gets across the idea but obviously evolutionary development is more fuzzy than divisional, so the Triune Brain is an oversimplification rather than a real description.

1. Chris Stringer & Robert McKie. *African Exodus*. Jonathan Cape (London 1996)

'The brain is silent, the brain is dark, the brain tastes nothing, the brain hears nothing. All it receives are electrical impulses – not the sumptuous chocolate melting sweetly, not the oboe solo like the flight of a bird, not the tingling caress, not the pastels of peach and lavender at sunset over a coral reef – just impulses.' [2]

After Albert Einstein died his brain [2.75 lbs] was carefully removed and examined. No one could find anything exceptional, although one bit seemed bigger than average and a groove shallower. Incidentally his eyeballs are in the possession of a Dr Abrams who keeps them in a safety deposit box, in New Jersey. Anyway a journalist following up the brain examinations interviewed a Dr Harvey in Kansas who had become its custodian. Dr Harvey slices bits off and sends them to interested scientists – one recipient relates how he received his by parcel post in an old mayonnaise bottle. A surgeon in Osaka keeps his in a Twinings tea can on his desk. Neurologists are evidently not a classy crowd.

The journalist said he was flabbergasted when the doctor casually pulled out a cardboard box, took out a jar, and showed him the remainder of Einstein's brain. He probably would have been equally gobsmacked if he'd visited The Institute of the Brain in Moscow. This holds jars containing the pickled brains of Lenin (in Room 19), Stalin, Sergei Eisenstein, Tchaikovsky, Mayakovsky, Gorky, Andrei Sakharov and others. The Institute hasn't made any startling discoveries from their brain tests either.

One lost opportunity perhaps occurred with Walt Whitman who had thoughtfully bequeathed his brain to the American Anthropometric Society. When it was ready for analysis a nervous assistant dropped it and it splattered all over the floor. The brain of America's greatest poet ended up being thrown into the garbage.

What seems to be generally accepted is that the brain functions as the crossroads of mind and body – an instrument which thought finds useful. An apparatus with which we think, we think.

Rather than a neat organized circuitry system waiting to succumb to formal scientific analysis, the brain appears to be made up of Rube Goldberg/Heath Robinson mechanisms. Or as an eminent computer scientist puts it, 'a collection of kludges', which he goes on to describe as 'a hodge-podge of a range of odd ball things that cause us to be intelligent'. [3] Another view is that the brain is a confederacy of dunces, each only bright enough to handle one small part of what's coming from the senses. Not surprisingly, it is exceedingly difficult to grasp and understand.

Best understood is the visual area of the brain, which is at the back of the head and takes up 30 per cent of the cortex, compared with 8 per cent for touch and 3 per cent for hearing. Here features such as colour, edges and angles are handled by different cells. The shape of an apple is recognized by one lot, its colour by another, and whether it's dropping on Newton's head by another.

The opening paragraph of *The Astonishing Hypothesis*, a book [4] on the brain and consciousness: *' "You", your joys and your sorrows, your memories and your ambitions, your sense of personal identity and free will, are in fact no more than the behaviour of a vast assembly of nerve cells and their associated molecules. As Lewis Carroll's Alice might have phrased it, "You're nothing but a pack of neutrons."'*

Since brains, like rocks, are made up of atoms which obey the laws of physics, it follows that those in our head are no exception except that they must be organized in a very particular way. In just what way we do not know, but this does raise the possibility that the brain may not be capable of providing an explanation of itself. In other words …

<u>… if our brains were simple enough to be understood, then we would be too simple to understand them.</u>

'A girl with brains ought to do something else with them besides think.' Anita Loos (Gentlemen Prefer Blondes)

2. Diane Ackerman. *A Natural History of the Senses*. Phoenix (London 1996)   3. John Brockman. *The Third Culture*. Touchstone (New York 1996)   4. Francis Crick. *The Astonishing Hypothesis*. Charles Scribner's Sons (New York 1994)

Each of us is always in two minds about everything.

Our brains are divided into two hemispheres. The left concentrates on analytical, logical and verbal activities, the right on the emotional, musical, spatial and intuitive.

Simplistically the left is a doer and the right a dreamer.

Our actions and responses are handled by a cross-over system. The left hemisphere is linked to the right eye, right ear and right hand. And the right hemisphere *vice versa*.

People who have suffered brain damage on one side or the other end up only being able to draw pictures with their left hand and write words with their right. The right hemisphere knows no words.

In an experiment with patients, who for some ghastly reason had had the two halves separated, the word HEART was flashed on a screen. The HE was positioned to the left of the patient's nose and ART to the right. Normally anyone asked what they saw would respond 'HEART'. However, when asked what *they* saw these patients responded 'ART' – the section of the word seen by the right eye and interpreted as a word by the left and vocal side of the brain.

They were then offered two cards. One carried the HE, the other ART.

Asked to point with the left hand to one of the cards which corresponded to what they had just seen on the screen, they invariably pointed to 'HE' – a response by the right spatial side of the brain.[1]

Paradoxically, if both hemispheres are all right life can be twice as complicated, as we're unaware of which half is upstaging the other.

1. Lyall Watson. *Lifetide.* Hodder & Stoughton (London 1979)

**'You would not want to have a
date with a right hemisphere.'**
Michael Gazzaniga

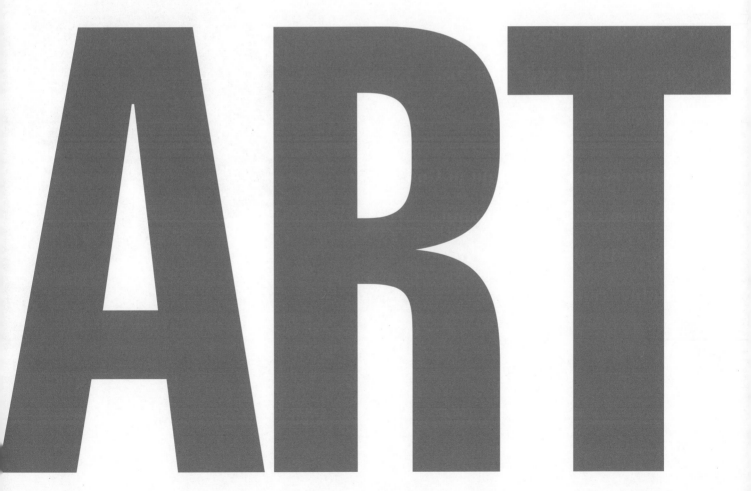

The brain is wider than the sky,

For, put them side by side,

The one the other will include

With ease, and you beside.

The brain is deeper than the sea,

For, hold them, clue to clue,

The one the other will absorb,

As sponges, buckets do.

The brain is just the weight of God,

For lift them, pound for pound,

And they will differ, if they do,

As syllable from sound.

'One's not half two', ee cummings pointed out, 'It's two are halves of one.'

HIABLM

HAL was the computer which took control in Stanley Kubrick's film epic *2001: A Space Odyssey.* It may be coincidental but alphabetically H precedes I, A precedes B and L precedes M.

Designed by Will Burtin for the Upjohn Pharmaceutical Company in the 1950s, this was the first brain you could walk into and have a look around. Will Burtin left Germany in the early 1930s to work in Holland. Albert Speer got in contact and asked him to return and work in his studio in Berlin. Burtin had a better idea – he immediately left for New York.
[SEE P14].

'The central offices of McDonald & Co contain a small room that has the specific function of stimulating creativity. It is a very special sort of space: nothing about it resembles the work environment or the rest of the building – nor any other space on earth. It is an atmosphere that takes one into another dimension: directly inside the human head. People who come in can lose themselves on a big cushion in the form of a brain.'
Piera Scuri[1]

'The interlinking of human beings that began with the emergence of language has now progressed to the point where information can be transmitted to anyone, anywhere, at the speed of light. Billions of messages continually shuttling back and forth in an ever-growing web of communication, link billions of minds together into a single global brain. And although this network may not yet be as complex as the network of cells in our own brain, if our development continues to accelerate, there is every reason to suppose that the global brain's complexity will parallel that of the human brain in the early years of the next millennium.'
Peter Russell[2]

Question:

Why did the chicken cross the road?

Answer:

Because a road-crossing triggered a neuron in the chicken's cerebral cortex which activated a group of walking-pattern units in its brainstem, which in turn sent rhythmic groups of electrical impulses to motor neurons in the spinal cord …

1. Piera Scuri. *Late Twentieth Century Skyscrapers*. Van Nostrand Reinhold (New York 1990)   2. Peter Russell. *The Awakening Earth*. Routledge & Kegan Paul (London 1982)   **Photograph.** Ezra Stoller

'My brain, it's my second favourite organ.' Woody Allen

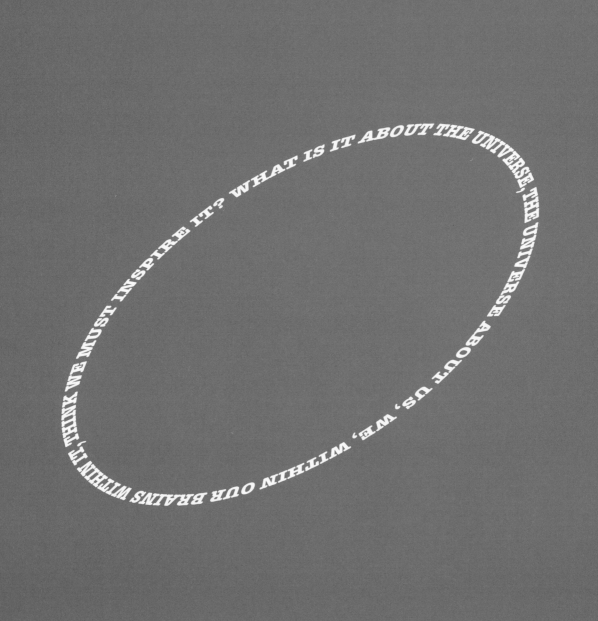

WHAT IS IT ABOUT THE UNIVERSE, THE UNIVERSE ABOUT US, WE, WITHIN OUR BRAINS WITHIN IT, THINK WE MUST INSPIRE IT? WHAT IS IT

1. Bob Brier. *The Murder of Tutankhamen.* Weidenfeld & Nicolson (London 1998)   2 & 3. Bart Kosko. *Fuzzy Thinking.* Flamingo (London 1994)   **Poem:** May Swenson. *The Universe*

Mummification. The objective of mummification, at least that practised by ancient Egyptian embalmers, was to preserve the body in as good a condition as possible for the next life. As the body would be resurrected in the afterworld appearance was as important as having all of one's bits and pieces. To avoid putrefaction, dehydration required removing the internal organs which were kept in separate vessels. The exception to this practice was the brain. A probe was shoved up the nostrils to break into the cranium. The embalmer then inserted a wire up into the brain, twisted and twiddled it around to reduce the brain into a liquid mush which drained out through the nose. This stuff was then thrown away. The Egyptians thought the brain quite useless as thinking and the soul inhabited the heart.[1]

Your brain changes. Three pounds of meat changes. It changes a little bit every time you see an image or hear a sound or feel a surface or taste a flavour or walk a new ground. Everything you sense changes your brain. Your brain measures things and those things change your brain. It learns new changes and forgets or unlearns old changes. A single photon of light changes your brain. TV ads and movies and books and talks and ad jingles and all the stuff that your mind eats change your brain. It changes right now as you read this. Your brain starts out with about 100 billion neurons or brain cells and ends up with several billion fewer. That's about as many stars as are in the Milky Way galaxy or as many galaxies as are in the known universe. The neurons do not act as computer memory sites. No cell holds a picture of your mom or the smell of lime or the idea of God. You can pull out any cell in your brain and your mind will not change. You could pull out a few million cells at random and not miss them. Pull a few wires or circuits out of a computer and it crashes. What counts is the wires between the cells. They count for about 40 per cent of your brain mass. We call these wires synapses or neural connections. Each neuron in your brain can connect up to 10,000 other neurons. That gives us synapses in quadrillions. Learning and memory lie in the great tangled webs of synapses. Not in cells, in webs. Take a drink of scotch and lose a few hundred neurons and a few million synapses. Learning is change. In brains, learning is change in a synapse.[2]

Cryonics. 'The early cryonics movement drew scorn from scientists and the press because it could not explain how future science might revive the unthawed dead. The freezing process damages tissue as the water between cells turns to ice and punctures the cells. In the 1980s the rise of nanotechnology showed how cryonics might work. Thaw a dead brain and then rebuild it a molecule at a time with tiny nano-robots or nanobots. As of 1993 there were over 30 patients in cryonic suspension. Most have suspended only their brains. The idea is that if nanotechnology can repair freezing damage and rejuvenate the dead brain, it can grow a lean young body from the head stump too.'[3]

the creeping crumb

I dislike ginger biscuits. You know that moment when a child bites on something which it doesn't like, and its face suddenly crumples? That's what ginger biscuits did for me. I only mention it because I was attending one of those business meetings where the mind is inclined to slide about and I noticed a ginger crumb on the table. I saw it move – I was not surprised. Reality intruded. Actually it was a tiny orange spider. I think they're called money spiders.

What, I imagined, would it look like seen face to face? A glistening ginger apparatus of flashing eyes, gnashing teeth, menacingly jumping up and down with a diabolical cluster of legs and claws? Or, perhaps, no more than a basic passive assembly of simple features, a fragile arrangement of limbs and joints? I scrawled it down with the intention of portraying it one way or the other but never got round to working it up. I came across my doodle the other day. Here it is on the right.

Weight for weight the silk of the common spider is five times stronger than steel. Its strength derived from a structure of proteins and flexibility from a pattern of molecules.

'The same combination of order and disorder,' physicist Richard Feynman[1] explains, 'as that exploited and achieved by Japanese sword makers through tempering and sintering.' The web, itself, is an engineering miracle. An elegant, concentric, polygonal structure, with a diameter many times greater than its weaver, delicately angled in space, and stabilized by a single sensitive tensile thread.

How do spiders conceive, know how to design, instantly construct and repair such a web? How does she – spiders are always she – know where to construct it? The site can't be pre-programmed although some predisposition to environmental circumstance must be involved. She spins her web, sits at the centre, and waits. 'Does she know what she's waiting for? Does she dream of succulent moths and foolish mayflies? Or does she wait with her mind a blank, idling, thinking of nothing at all. Until, that is, the tell tale tug sends her scurrying down one of the radial struts to sting the struggling insect?'[2] No one knows.

A pinprick is roughly the size of a spider's brain. That's where it all happens. Makes you think. Doesn't it?

The instincts of small creatures go way beyond human capabilities. Take the Tunisian desert ant. This tiny creature can wander across the desert sands for up to 50 metres until it stumbles across the remains of a dead insect, whereupon it bites off a piece and takes it directly back to its nest – a hole no more than one millimetre in diameter. How does it find its way back? By the process the Apollo astronauts used to plot their course to the moon: dead reckoning (strictly 'ded' reckoning from 'deductive' reckoning). The idea of dead reckoning is to calculate your position relative to your starting point from a knowledge of your speed and your direction of travel. Some ants lay down a scent trail to keep track of their path but not the Tunisian desert ant. If it is moved after it finds the food, it will head off in exactly the direction it should have to find its nest if it had not been moved ...[3]

 1. Richard Feynman. *'Surely You're Joking, Mr Feynman.'* Vintage (London 1992) 2. Carl Sagan, Ann Druyan. *Shadows of Forgotten Ancestors.* Arrow Books (New York 1993) 3. *The Guardian*, 24 August 1999

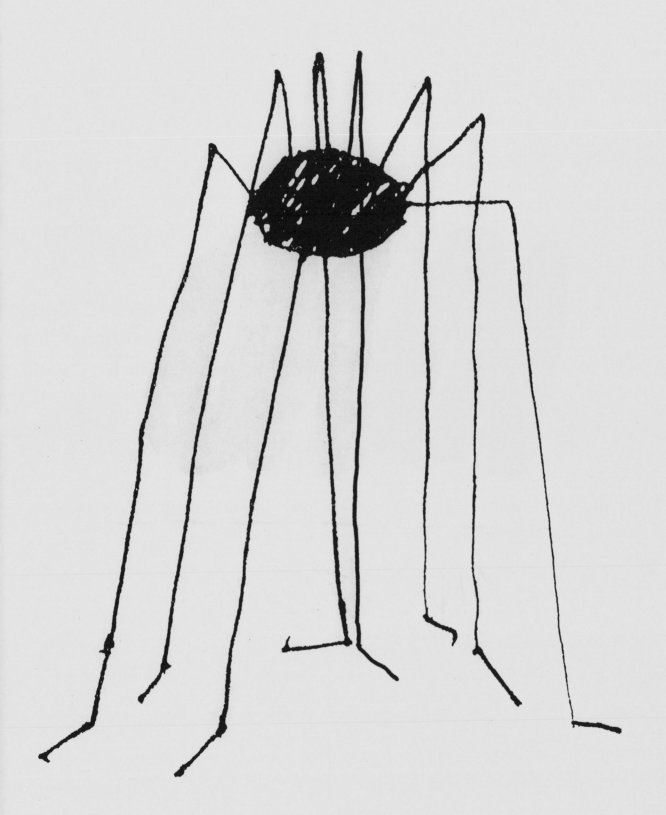

Racquel Welch

'The mind can also be an erogenous zone.'

1. K. Popper and J. Eccles. *The Self and its Brain*, Springer (Berlin 1977)   2. Richard Dawkins. *The Selfish Gene*. Oxford University Press (Oxford 1976)   3. Diane Ackerman. *A Natural History of the Senses*. Phoenix (London 1996)

Philosopher Karl Popper proposed that the mind has three tiers.[1] The first is occupied by things one can see and touch. The second houses the conscious and unconscious states. The third accommodates thoughts and ideas. For example language exists as writing in the first, as electrical impulses in the second and as literature in the third.

Many of the thoughts which occupy this third tier seem innate rather than acquired. Evolutionary biologist Richard Dawkins calls these *memes* (pronounced like cream). Whereas genes carry data in a linear mode through physical reproduction, *memes* spread laterally from one mind to another in a spatial momentum of their own. The difference is that whereas Plato may or may not have one of his genes still circulating, many of his *memes* are still alive in our minds today.[2]

Actually we assume thoughts inhabit the mind although no one knows exactly where, since the mind seems to be everywhere but nowhere in particular – hence all those references to 'the ghost in the machine' and 'the horse in the locomotive'.

We assume the mind is located in the head, but the latest findings in physiology suggest that the mind 'travels the whole body on caravans of hormone and enzyme, busily making sense of the compound wonders we catalogue as touch, taste, smell, hearing, vision.'[3] After reading this explanation I closed my eyes and concentrated on trying to locate just where my mind was … it certainly didn't feel like it was cruising. Predictably enough it seemed to be inside my head. Not hovering up front, nor around the back, but fuzzily floating in the middle towards the top. Hot air rises. I opened my eyes and then tried to concentrate in the same way again. I couldn't, a gear shift had taken place – the world intruded. It's difficult to explain, try it and you'll see what I mean.

Perhaps it all works quite differently. Imagine the brain as a television set, the mind as the picture, and thoughts as programmes transmitted from another source. Perhaps we all unconsciously draw on a collective pool containing our past experiences and those of others. We call it intuition.

By the way, have you noticed that it's the brain which sleeps while it's the mind which dreams?

Two monks
were watching a flag
fluttering in the wind.

One said,
'It's the wind that moves'

The other said,
'I disagree, it's
the flag that moves.'

But a Zen patriarch
standing nearby, said,
'It's not the wind,
nor the flag...

it's the mind,
that moves.

'If you work on your mind with your mind, how can you avoid an immense confusion?' *Seng Ts'an*

'The mind is like an umbrella – it functions best when open.' *Walter Gropius*

'The soul is an abstraction and the brain is an organ. To speak of the mind is to blend the two.' *Anthony Smith*

'An intellectual is someone whose mind watches itself.' *Albert Camus*

'We know more about the interior of stars than the process going on in our heads.' *Richard Gregory*

'The no-mind not-thinks no-thoughts about no-things.' *Buddha*

'The cultivation of the mind is a kind of food supplied for the soul of man.' *Cicero*

'The hand is the cutting edge of the mind.' *Jacob Bronowski*

'Mind is something we experience, rather than something we observe.' *Lyall Watson*

'Our body is a universe teeming with galaxies of its own.' *Jean Cocteau*

'… mind oscillates between sense and nonsense, not between right and wrong.' *Carl Jung*

'Some people think computers can't.' *Marvin Minsky*

'Cogito, ergo sum.' The philosopher Descartes distinguished mind from matter by characterizing the former as that which thinks. Today one scientific endeavour is to invest matter (hardware) with the attributes (software) of mind. It will be a difficult task.

Consciousness is synonymous with awareness and involves the same cerebral gavotte as that played between attention and short-term memory. Mind is consciousness with knobs on. The mind can fit disparate elements together to make cohesive objects. Encompass the notion of size from atoms to milky ways, comprehend time and leap over seconds as nimbly as millennia. Reconstruct what no longer exists and call it the past, guess at what might happen and call it the future. A realm in which we can wonder, reflect, regret or enjoy.

Although living in a computer age most of us back off at the thought that a machine will eventually acquire an analogue of the mind. At best, we maintain, the computer can only be a moron. Well maybe, or maybe not. In the 1930s Alfred North Whitehead said it would take ten thousand years to get to the moon. In 1940 the scientific adviser to the British Government stated man would never fly faster than sound. And until the 1950s the possibility of heart transplants was inconceivable.

Predictions are notoriously unreliable. So consider the potential of a machine which is not only skilful enough to monitor itself but which has begun to simulate. One which builds models of reality and then runs strategies through them, one which can predict outcomes and select the most favourable course to follow. Once it can do this the next logical move is to jump from performing by rote to acting by reasoning. If that happens then a machine could be said to have acquired consciousness.[1]

In which case Descartes's famous dictum, *'I think, therefore I am'*, could be amplified to; *'I think that I think, therefore I think that I am.'* If a machine gets that far it will certainly have a mind of its own. However, this postulation carries its own spanner in the works – as Gödel's theorem states: *'no system can explain itself, and no machine can understand its own workings.'* That is equally applicable to a human system.

There are differences between machine and mind. Computers can blink but they can't wink. They can't convey the wealth of information provided by a look, a nod, a shrug, a smile, or a twinkle in the eye. They can't feel pain, get depressed or have giggles. A computer scans bit by bit while the mind looks at everything at once. The more computers know the slower they get; the more the mind knows the faster it operates. Our brains make extensive use of chemicals which have a dimension of flexibility not yet modelled in silicon.

Anyway I find process of more interest than technology. If one can garner some insight into how the mind works then perhaps one can use it rather better. As actress Judi Dench observed: *'Unless you know your character's mind, it's a hollow sound you make.'*

'Is the mind more

like a fancy system

of domino chains

or

a bathtub full of

spring-loaded mousetraps?

I'm betting on the latter.'

1. Lyall Watson. *Lifetide.* Hodder & Stoughton (London 1979)

Douglas Hofstadter

The mind's eye

Do you mind?

I don't mind

Mind you

Mind out

What is mind? No matter! **What is matter?** Never mind!

Mind how you go

Mindful

Mindless

Singleminded

Simpleminded

Absentminded

Author: Sometimes I have written down a pearl I've noticed somewhere-or-other and shoved it in my pocket – only to realize later that I omitted to register the name of the author or source. That accounts for some of the observations on this and other similar pages which are uncredited.

Mind to brain is as whistle is to steam engine.

There is a view that the universe more closely resembles a great thought than a great machine, and that mind is not a chance intruder into the realm of matter but something else which has a similar shape.

What is really miraculous is that most of the time we can effortlessly distinguish between seeing something, imagining it, dreaming about it and hallucinating it.

Mind could be thought of as a mental bootstrap which summons up all sorts of things from an accumulated wealth of experiences and memories. The echoes and whispers of the past. Something which reassembles and composes fragments into the images and thoughts we have of the present and imagine for the future.

Stephen Hawking can hear but can't talk. He only has movement in two fingers of his left hand and communicates by typing and a computer screen. He suffers from motor neurone disease. Yet despite this appalling disability which physically isolates him from the world he juggles the universe in his mind, conjectures with notions of infinity, curved space-time and black holes in which matter disappears up its own singularity. He explores the universe from a wheelchair.

Douglas Hofstadter suggests that mind is a pattern perceived by a mind which is circular but neither vicious nor paradoxical.

Will the silicone chip ever be capable of understanding the irony in Dali's absurd surrealist image in which a man put a stone on his head, and went for a walk in the park, and while on his walk passed a statue that also had a stone on its head?

Thomas Huxley: 'How it is that anything so remarkable as a state of consciousness comes about as a result of irritating nervous tissue, is just as unaccountable as the appearance of the Djin, when Aladdin rubbed his lamp.'

Steven Pinker: 'Our bafflement at the mysteries of the ages may have been the price we paid for a combinatorial mind that opened up a world of words and sentences, of theories and equations, of poems and melodies, of jokes and stories, the very things that make a mind worth having.'

Colin McGinn: 'Somehow, we feel, the water of the physical brain is turned into wine of consciousness, but we draw a total blank on the nature of this conversion. Neural transmissions just seem like the wrong kind of materials with which to bring consciousness into the world.'

Andrew Marvell: The mind, that ocean where each kind/Does straight its own resemblance find.'

Chief Eagle, Teton Sioux: The mind is like a tepee. Leave the entrance flap open so that the fresh air can enter and clear out the smoke of confusion.'

David Chalmers: The ineffable sound of a distant oboe, the agony of an intense pain, the sparkle of happiness or the meditative quality of a moment lost in thought. All are part of what I am calling consciousness. It is these phenomena that compose the real mystery of the mind.'

Joseph Campbell: The "collective unconscious" doesn't refer to any sort of "group mind" into which we are all piped, but rather to a piece of our psyche that inherits experiences and impressions of our ancestral past in much the same way as we have inherited an appendix. Race memories stretching back to distant ancestors which we experience in the form of archetypes – Earth Mother, the Hero and so forth – which is why they appear in myths all over the world.'

John Horgan: '... what hope is there that computers will ever mimic our more subtle talents, like recognizing a college sweetheart at a cocktail party and instantly thinking of just the right thing to say to make her regret dumping you 15 years ago.'

Ambrose Bierce: 'A mysterious form of matter secreted by the brain. Its chief endeavour being to ascertain its own nature, the futility of the attempt being due to the fact that it has nothing but itself to know itself with.'

Samuel Johnson: 'A system, built on the discoveries of a great many minds, is always of more strength than that which is produced by the mere workings of any one mind ...'

Julian Huxley: 'Like the earth a hundred years ago, our mind still lies in darkest Africa, unmapped Borneos and Amazonian basins. In relation to the fauna of these regions we are not yet zoologists, we are mere naturalists and collectors of specimens.'

James Clerk Maxwell: 'The only laws of matter are those which our minds must fabricate, and the only laws of mind are fabricated for it by matter.'

Diane Ackerman: 'Consciousness, the great poem of matter.'

Acknowledgement to Magritte.

'How do you know
but every bird
That cuts the airy way
Is an immense world of delight,
Closed to your senses five?

William Blake

Chinese proverb

'The soul has no secrets that conduct does not reveal.'

Has anybody said publicly how nice it is to write on rubber with a ball-point pen? The snow, ink-rich it is to write on rubber with a ballpoint pen? The snow, but, ink-rich line, rolled over a surface at once dense and yielding, makes for a multidimensional experience no single sheet of paper can offer.

Extract. Nicholson Baker. *The Mezzanine.* Granta Books (Cambridge 1986)

Extract from a Letter	HELEN KELLER	'Smell is a potent wizard that transports us across thousands of miles and all the years we have lived.'
Modern Painters	JOHN RUSKIN	'… to see clearly is poetry, prophecy, and religion, all in one.'
The Physiology of Taste	ANTHELME BRILLAT-SAVARIN	'Those … from whom nature has withheld the legacy of taste, have long faces, and long eyes and noses, whatever their height there is something elongated in their proportions. Their hair is dark and unglossy, and they are never plump; it was they who invented trousers.'
Enchiridion	EPICTETUS	'God gave man two ears, but only one mouth, that he might hear twice as much as he speaks!'
A Natural History of the Senses	DIANE ACKERMAN	'Our skin is a kind of space suit in which we manoeuver through the atmosphere of harsh gases, cosmic rays, radiation from the sun, and obstacles of all sorts.'

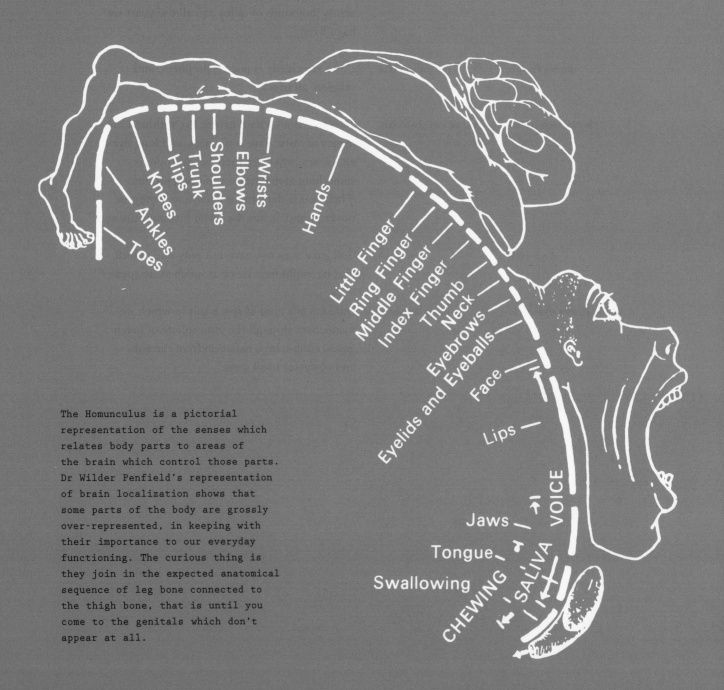

Knees
Hips
Trunk
Shoulders
Elbows
Wrists

Ankles

Toes

Hands

Little Finger
Ring Finger
Middle Finger
Index Finger
Thumb
Neck
Eyebrows
Eyelids and Eyeballs
Face

Lips

Jaws

Tongue

Swallowing

CHEWING

SALIVA

VOICE

The Homunculus is a pictorial
representation of the senses which
relates body parts to areas of
the brain which control those parts.
Dr Wilder Penfield's representation
of brain localization shows that
some parts of the body are grossly
over-represented, in keeping with
their importance to our everyday
functioning. The curious thing is
they join in the expected anatomical
sequence of leg bone connected to
the thigh bone, that is until you
come to the genitals which don't
appear at all.

Are you a sensuist or a sensualist?

25.3.1975 London: Farringdon Road, EC1
A man with one leg considerably shorter than the other,
lurching along whistling 'I Could Have Danced All Night'.
Ian Breakwell's Diary. 1964-1985

'since feeling is first

who pays any attention

to the syntax of things

will never wholly kiss you.'

ee cummings

'Sensations

are rapid

dreams.'

Santayana

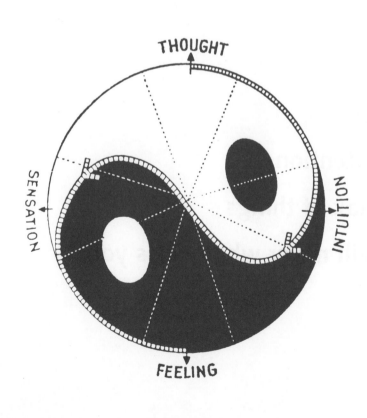

'What does music really express? It's not about the sensations apprehended from the external world but about the intimations, intuitions, dreams, fantasies, emotions, the feelings within ourselves ...'

Michael Tippett

'Music draws upon feeling and thinking, joining the emotional with the rational.'

Yehudi Menuhin

Carl Jung maintained there are only two types of basic personality: those who react to external situations by giving a measured thoughtful response, and those who react to internal stimuli and give a knee-jerk response. Most of us oscillate between the two. The differences in personality are determined by the swings and roundabouts of thinking. Diagramming this with the *Yin Yang* symbol, Jung suggests personalities are shaped by **feelings** and **thoughts**, while **sensations** colour the details and **intuition** interprets the currents. **Feeling:** Looking through a telescope an astronomer grumbled that it was going to rain. His assistant asked how he knew. 'Because', said the astronomer, 'my corns hurt.' **Thought:** 'In thinking', wrote Plato, 'the soul is talking to itself.' **Sensation:** Two people can look and marvel over the same star but nobody ever shared a splitting headache. Sensations can be exclusive. **Intuition:** 'My hand is simply "a tool controlled"', said Paul Klee. 'It's not my head that's functioning, but something else, something higher and more remote, somewhere.' **Conscience:** An inner voice which tells us how we are performing. It also warns us that somebody else may be looking in.

QUALIA

[THE QUALITY OF A THING]

Pathologist Lewis Thomas matched the ancient *Seven Wonders of the World* with a contemporary example.[1]

'My Fifth Wonder is the olfactory receptor cell, located in the epithelial tissue high in the nose, sniffing the air for clues to the environment, the fragrance of friends, the smell of leaf smoke, breakfast, nighttime and bedtime, and a rose, even, it is said, the odour of sanctity. The cell that does all these things, firing off urgent messages into the deepest parts of the brain, switching on one strange unaccountable memory after another, is itself a proper brain cell, a certified neuron belonging to the brain but miles away out in the open air, nosing around the world. How it manages to make sense of what it senses, discriminating between jasmine and anything else non-jasmine with infallibility, is one of the deep secrets of neurobiology.'

A snail slithering across my morning kipper is something I'd find instinctively repulsive, while a blob of vermillion paint on a warm grey background might be deeply satisfying. Even sensations generated by the same object vary. Lukewarm water will feel hot to a cold hand, and cold to a hot hand. Such sensations are called *qualia*. The taste of claret to you that I will never know. The colour of red to you that I can never share. The recall of a fragrance to me that you can't experience.

For a baby the world is a *'hallucinogenic perfumery'*, divines Diane Ackerman.[2] And then goes on to describe *'... a creamy blur of succulent blue sound, smells like week-old strawberries dropped onto a tin sieve as mother approaches in a halo of color, chatter, and a perfume like thick golden butterscotch.'* From what I remember, and as a grandfather observe, she's got it on the nail.

Smell was the first sense. <u>We think, because we smelled</u>. Smell, generated in the primitive brain, is the one sense indelibly printed in the memory. As agent of recall the nose is the one. *'I remember the first time I went to India,'* reminisced painter Bridget Riley. *'I stepped off the aircraft into the warm velvet of the Bombay night and was engulfed by the smell of frangipani, jasmine, petrol, urine – an inextinguishable compound'.* As a child Saul Steinberg recalled he got *'high on elementary*

things, like the luminosity of the day and the smell of everything – mud, earth, humidity, the delicious smells of cellars and mould, grocers' shops.' Neil Armstrong recalls the moment he stepped back into his craft –

'... there was a distinct smell to the lunar material – pungent, like gunpowder or spent cap-pistol caps. We carted a fair amount of lunar dust back inside the vehicle with us, either on our suits and boots or on the conveyor system we used to get boxes and equipment back inside. We did notice the odor right away.'[3] In the book, *The English Patient*, the nurse tells how her father would take his dog's paw in his hand and sniff, as if it was a bouquet. It revealed, he expounded, *'the aromas of a garden, a field of grasses, a walk through cyclamen – a concentration of hints of all the paths the animal had taken during the day'.*

For myself distant memories are less refined. One scene instantly arrives via a whiff of pea soup – wartime school supper. The fragrance of freshly mown grass conjures up the chore of rolling the cricket pitch. The pungent aroma of Gauloises, my first trip to France. The stale stink of boiled cabbage – the proximity of a cheap English boarding house.

Commercial perfumes are concocted from artificial and natural sources. Although Marilyn Monroe only wore perfume when she went to

1. Martin Gardner. *Great Essays in Science*. Oxford University Press (Oxford 1985)   2. Diane Ackerman. *A Natural History of the Senses*. Phoenix (London 1996)

this is a picture of your tongue ...

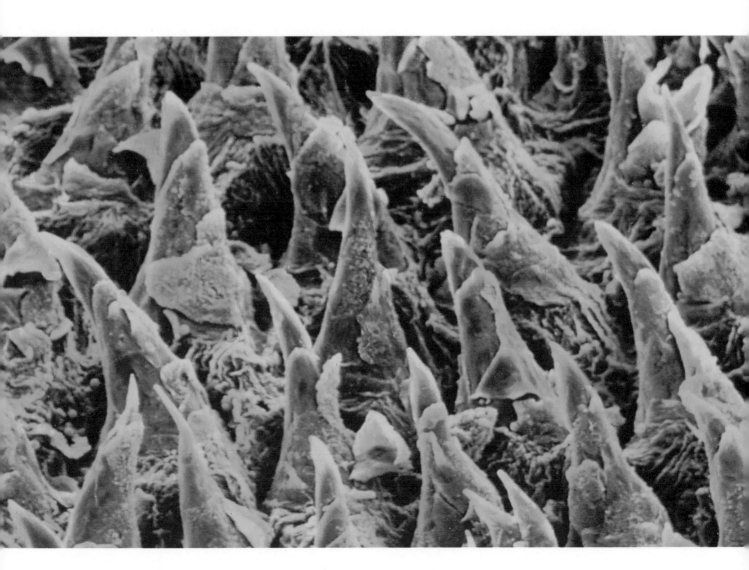

3 . John Carey. *The Faber Book of Science.* Faber & Faber (London 1995)   **Photograph.** Pietro Motta.

'... consciousness or sentience, the raw sensation of toothaches and redness and saltiness and middle C, is still wrapped in a mystery inside an enigma.'   Steven Pinker

and this is a picture of your eyeball.

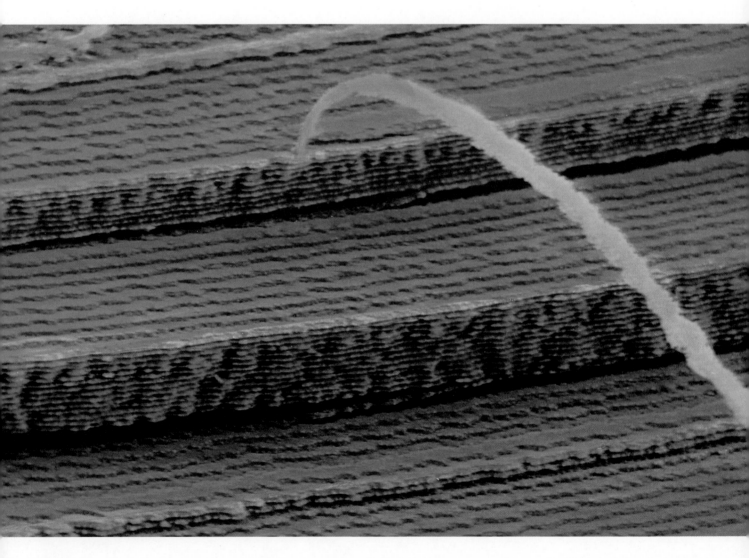

Photograph. Pietro Motta. *Cells of the lens of the eye*

'follow your bliss' suggested Joseph Campbell

bed, she probably didn't know it contained secretions from a civet's anal glands. Except Chanel No. 5, of course, one of the first synthetic fragrances and created way back in 1922.

Actually I have a problem with smell. Mine is blunt rather than acute. All those smoking years probably. Those who are deprived of two senses are called deaf or blind, but what is the word for those who can't smell?

Hearing has become less acute along the long evolutionary road. Nevertheless we still flinch at the scratch of a nail or screech of blackboard chalk – excruciatingly unpleasant sounds, which, it is suggested, trigger an instinctive response to the sound of a predator's claws on a nearby rock.

Readings of individual blood pressures show we are affected by music. Music can arouse energy, eroticism, calm, pensiveness, sorrow, dance, pride, laughter, irritation, a feeling of belonging. It can also arouse mental states of which we may prefer not to be reminded.

We live inside a two-metre-square envelope of skin. Our largest organ. We call emotions *feelings*. We like to keep *in touch*, can be *profoundly touched*. Problems can be *thorny, ticklish* or *sticky* and often need to be *handled* with kid gloves. Touch is the first sense to ignite and the last to burn out: indeed we even talk of *losing touch*.

Our tongue is only sensitive to sweet, or sour, or salty, or bitter flavours. Paradoxically sensations

of taste are created through smell. As restaurant critic A.A. Gill commented : *'Nothing is as redolent of time and place and the passing seasons as eating the food of your childhood miles from home.'* Extending this thought, perhaps deeper ancestral memories dictate why we prefer steaks served at the body heat of a freshly killed animal.

The majority of our sense receptors are in the eyes. Sight so dominates our intellectual practices that we construct diagrams so we can *see* what is happening, *see* if something is possible, and try to imagine situations in the mind's *eye*. Maybe the struggle to make sense of what we *saw* gave us the ability to think abstractly.

One factor which distinguishes us from other creatures is awareness of *self*. A *feeling* of being individual and behaving beyond instinct. This will o' the wisp fleeting *feeling*. When we say we *feel* numb – we *feel* nothing. *Feeling* takes place in our bodies which have internal landscapes, within external landscapes. One populated with other creatures and objects which in turn have their interior landscapes …

… so who are *we* who inhabit these fragile bodies around whom the world is displayed?

Note. I'm on vacation by the shore. I have time on my hands. I close my eyes. I block out distractions, thoughts, sensations. I concentrate on the sounds I hear. It's difficult to hear with focus. Gradually I become aware of layers upon layers of overlapping noises. The muffled rumble, sharp slap and sibilant hiss of breaking waves. The bustle and rustle of leaves. The coo, hoot, twitter and chirp of birds. The distant grind and groan of a car. Strident shouts, the cries and chatter of children on the beach. A steady hum from the hotel – an air conditioner perhaps. The jangle in the undergrowth – drones, clicks, whirs, creaks, squeaks and other insectoid scratchy noises. Unidentified squeals, snorts, bangs, honks and whistles. More practice, and bigger ears, I could get to hear grass grow.

SUCK IT AND SEE

Synaesthetes* are crosswired. They feel shapes, smell noises, see flavours, hear colours. Coloured hearing seems to be the commonest of the mix-ups. Liszt, Wagner, Scriabin ('D Major was yellow') and Goethe all saw musical notes in colours. For Anthony Burgess an oboe was 'silver-green lemon juice' and a flute 'light brown and cold veal gravy'. Wassily Kandinsky heard sunsets and saw music. 'Absolute green', he was sure, is the same as 'the placid middle notes of a violin'. As a writer Rimbaud had typographic leanings and felt that the letter *A* was a 'black hairy corset of loud flies'.

Here are some other examples of synaesthasia culled from a newspaper article: Rosie Young: 'Numbers are especially vivid to me,' she confides, 'my parents ran a small hotel and I felt each room had a colour because of its number. Room 12 was bright blue, Room 11 black, and Room 13 green.' Gillian Murphy: 'All words have colours for me. Sing is yellow; jump is black; walk is blue with white around the a …' Ms Young: 'Tuesday, Wednesday and Thursday are crimson, scarlet and burgundy. June and July are dark blue, and January is a dark green. 1 to 10 have different colours, 1 is black and so 11 is black. 788 is brown and pink and pink; 701 is brown and white and black. Letters also have colours, and sometimes the first letter of a word gives the word a colour. Waterloo is deep red and London is Yellow.' Most synaesthetes see, or allocate, the same colours for vowels: I is white to pale grey, U is yellow to light brown and O is white.[1]

Alexander Theroux listed things that he felt 'seemed' yellow: 'maiden aunts, gumdrops, diffidence, the letter H, all women's poems (except Emily Dickinson's, which of course, are red), lewd suggestions, debt, the seventies, Nat "King" Cole's song *China Gate*, sadness, the Yale English department faculty, the name as well as the country of Brazil, August, the House of Congress, the word "hills", lampshades, physicians, insurance agents, the thin, squealing noises of children in playgrounds ("… making fun of life", according to folklorist Iona Opie), political compromise, the state of Nebraska, illness in general, old wagon wheels, whispering, and the vapid name Catherine.'[2]

I see what he means. And empathize with a lady who feels a kiss evokes thoughts of orange sherbet. And Clive James who maintains that papaya tastes yellow. However, although one might think that for synaesthetes reality must be recurringly unfamiliar, a world without certainties and governed by sensual responses that are unpredictable and random, perhaps the rest of us are in that condition.

* One in 25,000, it is said 1. *The Independent*, 30 June 1992 2. Alexander Theroux. *The Primary Colours*. Picador (London 1995)

'I invented the colour of vowels', wrote Arthur Rimbaud. 'A is black, E, white, I, red, O, blue, U, green.' And Rabelais said, '... We saw red words, green and azure words, black and gold words ...'

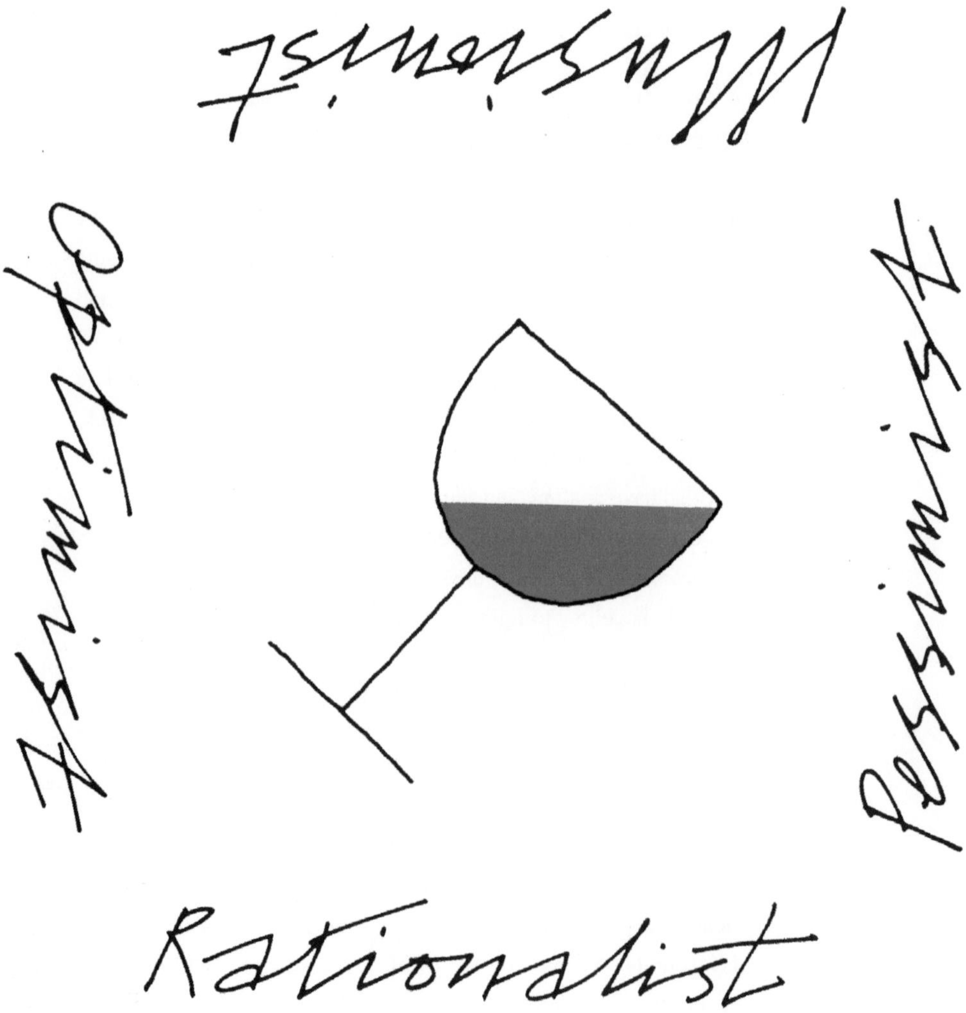

Illusionist

Optimist

Pessimist

Rationalist

The Fletcher *Personality Diagnosis* diagram

'Among the many characteristics which have been identified as peculiar to the human species – language, laughter, politics, love and cruelty – the one which is often overlooked is the capacity to be delighted and diverted by the exercise of the senses. Although these systems were evolved to furnish reliable knowledge of the external world, man is unique in exploiting them for sheer enjoyment. In fact a large proportion of his energy and ingenuity is spent on re-arranging the external world for the express purpose of providing more delightful perceptions. Even in communities which live on the margins of subsistence, scarce resources of time and energy are dedicated to the pleasures derived from decoration and ornament, and in more developed societies the amount of labour devoted to such provisions is taken to be one of the most significant measures of its civilization.'

Jonathan Miller

Extract from Foreword to *The Paradox Box*. Redstone Press (London 1999)

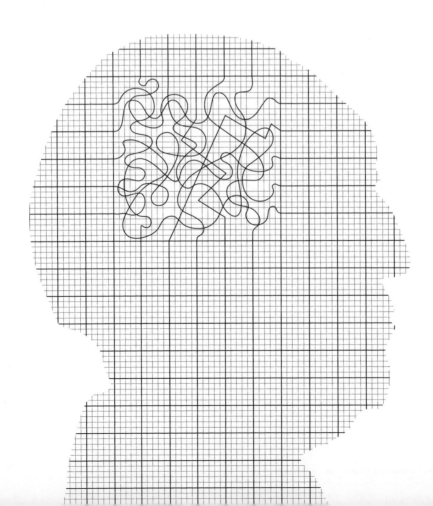

Thinking is drawing in your head.

We don't think in words. The temptation to equate thinking with language is because words are more palpable than thoughts. After all — I'm thinking — if I couldn't talk to myself how would I know what I was thinking?

Thinking is hard work; few engage in it.

For those who do there are a number of ways of sorting, each with advantages and disadvantages.[1] They can be broadly categorized:

Natural thinking. This is fluid and undirected, it wanders and meanders, is subject to repetition and generalizations. The sort of thinking that goes on when we don't think we're thinking.

Logical thinking. This selects a route and follows it to its conclusion. With this approach the solution is largely predetermined, so if you head off in the wrong direction you can end up painting yourself into a corner.

Pattern thinking. This confines thoughts to operate within given rules. Therefore solutions are limited by the possibilities available within the pattern.

Lateral thinking. This is purposeful in intent without specific aim. Freewheeling so it can reveal solutions which might have been overlooked in other approaches.

Grasshopper thinking. Most of the time our thinking jumps around alternating and mixing between reasoning which adheres to measurable responses, and imagining which allows unpredictable currents to play around with data. Producing an electrico/chemical sludge.

In *Ulysses* James Joyce exploited the fact that we don't think in words, and even if *Ulysses* is so complex as to be inaccessible (at least to me), it must still be a gross simplification of the mush of muddled thought constantly churning, tumbling and swirling around in our heads.

Edward de Bono: 'For hundreds of years we have believed that if something is logical in hindsight, then logic should have been enough to get the idea in the first place. This is complete and total rubbish.'

1. Edward de Bono. *The Use of Lateral Thinking.* Jonathan Cape (London 1967) & Edward de Bono. *I am Right You are Wrong.* Penguin (London 1991)

Paradoxically education allocates more value to logic and analytical skills than to imaginative conjectures. Thus law is held in esteem whereas art, or design, is considered a fiddly, fussy, arty-crafty activity of minor intellectual endeavour. An attitude with an attitude — particularly perverse since analysis looks backwards while design looks forwards.

Language also plays its part. Have you noticed that when we don't agree with someone we say: 'I don't think so'. The '... think so', literally indicating a proscribed route.

The conventional thinking we are taught (and conditioned to think) employs what Edward de Bono calls 'rock logic'. Rocks being solid, hard, permanent, inert and unchanging.* Like bricks, rocks can be added on top of one another to build structures. However there is also 'water logic'. This is fluid and flows according to gradient (context), and assumes form according to space (circumstance). If you add one rock to another, you get two; if you add water to water, it changes shape. Rocks analogous to a page of accounts and water to a piece of poetry.

The former has units which add up to a conclusion, the latter has images which conjure up a perception. One isn't better than the other; it's courses for horses.

To move from hod to pail Edward de Bono suggests inserting an equivalent of the mathematical zero into our thinking. [SEE P ░░░]. He suggests 'po', a neologism derived from hy'po'thesis, sup'po'se, 'po'ssible, 'po'sition and 'po'etry. Confronted with a sticky situation one inserts 'po' into the equation, instead of giving a knee-jerk res'po'nse. This allows for time to generate new thoughts and ex'po'se fresh perceptions. 'Po' can open the mind to reveal 'po'tentials outside of conventional thinking and analytic evaluation.

The world we have made around us is a result of the level of thinking we have done thus far, unfortunately it has also produced problems we cannot solve on the same level of thinking at which we created them.

*Actually rocks have their place. One day, a Tibetan Lama was speaking to a group of monks and, to make a point, pulled out a large jar, set it on the table in front of him, produced a few fist-sized rocks, and placed them, one by one, into the jar. When no more rocks would fit inside, he asked, 'Is this jar full?'. Everyone said, 'Yes'. He reached under the table and pulled out a bucket of gravel, dumped some in and shook the jar, the gravel worked between the rocks. Again he asked: 'Is this jar full?' The monks were catching on. 'Probably not,' one answered. 'Good!' he replied and reached under the tabel and brought out a bucket of sand. He dumped the sand into the jar until it filled all the crevices. Once more he asked: 'Is this jar full?' 'No!' the monks shouted. 'Good!' He said and grabbed a pitcher of water and poured until the jar was filled to the brim. Then asked, 'What is the point of this illustration?' One young monk responded, 'The point is, no matter how full your day you can always fit some more things in.' 'No,' the speaker replied, 'the point is that if you don't put the big rocks in first, you'll never get them in at all. What are the priorities in your life?'

'MAN'S A KIND
OF MISSING LINK,
 FONDLY THINKING
HE CAN THINK.'
PIET HEIN

Drawing. André François

The best thoughts are the most delicate,
fastest, trickiest to capture.
Lepidoptera so different on the wing,
than when caught, killed,
and proudly displayed.

Randy Read

LATERAL THOUGHTS

Since Aristotle, logical thinking has been exalted as the most effective way to use the mind, but it's not much help in generating new ideas. You have a chance to look at things from different angles if you manoeuvre the mind like that Australian bird which – according to Ripley – can fly upside-down and backwards.* Turning problems on their head can frequently convert them into solutions.

Here are a few :

Eighteenth-century tariffs imposed by France against imported pottery were based on weight and expanse of painted decoration. The British potters countered by punching out patterns, and Leedsware came to look like lace, and although full of holes cornered even more markets. At the height of disillusion over Vietnam, one bright senator suggested the best way to get out of the mess was to declare victory and withdraw immediately. A husband on learning his wife had lost her credit card didn't trouble to report the loss because the thief didn't spend as much as she did. Then there is the Irish Duelling Pistol in the Tower of London. This has a single barrel with stocks and firing mechanisms at each end – a ploy to reduce duty on the import of firearms. The importer, on receipt, cut it in half and ended up with a pair of pistols. The Nijo Castle in Japan is celebrated for its Nightingale Floor. This is cunningly constructed so that even with the lightest step the boards emit a squeak – to warn of the approach of assassins. The Shilla kings of the ancient Korean empire were buried in tombs covered with loose rocks and stones which created huge mounds. When robbers tried to dig a hole the space immediately filled with rubble.

THOUGHTS

Thoughts are the least
Silent things I know.
They jostle and nudge
And vie for position,
Single spies, battalions.
Exploding bladderwrack,
Long linked lines of
Genetic information
Multi-tracked
As a cream slice.

Sarah Lidell

According to Tass news agency (1996) when Muscovites park their cars they remove wipers and mirrors, otherwise they're stolen. Left with little else to purloin, thieves now extract windscreens. To counter this, an entrepreneur offers a service which neatly cracks the screen in two – on the passenger's side – so as not to impair the driver's visibility. As Dadaist Francis Picabia observed, our heads are round to allow thoughts to change direction.

A draw in a World Cup football match is resolved with a penalty shoot-out to decide the winner. To the unacquainted the shoot-out is when a member of one team elected to be goalkicker confronts the goalkeeper of the other. Each team [alternately] takes five kicks at goal, and the team which scores most goals wins. Anyway, after the 1998 World Cup which had several shoot-out results, the clamour of protest was considerable. This letter, in the *Daily Telegraph's* correspondence pages, expressed, I thought, a creative and new perception of manipulating an established pattern.

SIR — Perhaps the penalty shoot-out before the match. This might help eliminate some of the teams, should be taken by goes adopted match would be on negative tactics when the onus won't to be particularly. The longer the shoot-out the into extra time. The more leading the team that lost. The more attack-minded. The more would become. NEIL HOAD match went on without Brighton the more open it would.

* Or like the Wryneck. A woodpecker which can turn its head full circle to pick up scurrying ants. By the way Ripley was of *Believe it or Not* fame, a syndicated cartoon strip.

Oblique Strategies is the name of a pack of cards designed by Brian Eno and Peter Schmidt to resolve creative blockages and other dilemmas. For instance one card reads 'Honour thy error as a hidden intention.' The cards have their own website with a button to click that produces a card at random.

Not all roads lead to Rome.

A foreigner driving through Ireland stopped in a small village and asked a local the way to Dublin. After considerable thought the Irishman replied he couldn't say since he wouldn't have started out from there in the first place.

When a Persian poet was asked a similar question, he replied : 'I fear you will not reach Mecca, O Nomad, for the road which you are following leads to Turkestan.' Obviously not a nice place to go.

The pointy bits

In addition to women and trifle, King Farouk of Egypt liked gambling. He often made up for bad luck with bluff and bluster. Once he bet £10,000 on a hand of three kings. The stakes escalated and, when his opponent was called, Farouk faced a full house. He laid down his three kings and began to gather in the chips. 'But, Your Majesty,' his opponent protested, you only have three kings.' 'No,' replied Farouk, 'I am the fourth.' And that settled that.

 While staying in the country with friends one wet weekend the husband proposed we pass the time playing cards. A graduate of Harvard Business School, he suggested a game called Eleusis which he remembered being used to test the problem-solving ability of students. The game followed the same pattern as whist but as each player's turn came round to deal, he or she invented a set of simple rules without telling the others. For example, six of clubs were trumps, or whatever. Naturally to have a chance of winning you had to quickly spot the rules.

When it was my turn I decided the winning hand would be whichever had the most graphic pointy ends on the cards facing each player. Thus a five of diamonds would yield a score of seven. A nice touch, I thought, to include the little ones under the figures. I won several games because no one could guess the rules. For some reason when I explained my system everyone was furious!

Zugzwanged

Zugzwanged is a chess term which describes how black, owing to white's extra move in starting the game, is forced into playing a losing move. This match follows a similar ploy.

A stranger challenges two Grand Chess Masters to a tournament. He proposes playing both at the same time and bets he will either beat one of them or at least force a draw. He offers a large sum of money to tempt them and they agree. Each champion is then seated at opposite sides of a room behind a screen so neither can see the other's board.

The first Grand Master opens the game by moving white Queen's pawn forward two squares. The challenger studies this for a moment and then crosses the room to the second Grand Master and opens against him with the same move. The second Master responds by shifting his black Queen's pawn forward two squares. The challenger returns to the first Master and repeats the very same move. The first Master responds by sliding another pawn forward and the challenger returning to the second Master repeats the same move. So it continues.

The two Masters, each increasingly baffled by the expertise of the challenger, reach an impasse and are forced to concede a draw. The challenger collects the cash. Not bad for someone who didn't know how to play chess.

A potzer, according to Stanley Kubrick who was a chess hustler in Washington Square during his youth, is a chess term for a weak player with an inflated ego.

Black is white [1]

Once upon a time an impoverished merchant fell into debt. The ugly old money-lender fancied the merchant's beautiful daughter and offered to cancel the debt if he could have her instead. That proposal didn't go down too well so he cunningly suggested they let providence decide.

It so happened they were all standing on a path strewn with black and white pebbles. The moneylender suggested they put a black and a white pebble in a bag, and that the daughter then took one out without looking. If it was black she would become his, if white she could stay with her father. In either case the debts would be cancelled but if they didn't play along with the idea then he'd throw dad into prison. Reluctantly they agreed.

The money-lender bent down, selected two pebbles, and popped them in the bag. However, the girl noticed he cheated by picking up two blacks. He told her to close her eyes, put her hand in the bag, and pick one out. She did, but pretending to fumble dropped it on the path. 'Oops', she exclaimed, 'never mind, if you look in the bag you can tell which one I took by the colour of the one that's left.'

Russian Joke

Mikhail Gorbachev was having lunch at Windsor Castle during his visit to Britain. As the guests were working their way through the hors-d'oeuvres he was horrified to spot one of his *apparatchiks* sliding one of HM's gold spoons into his sleeve.

At first, Gorby was outraged. But then, struck with a bright idea, started to work his own spoon towards his pocket. Unfortunately it struck his glass and as the tinkle resounded everyone around the table assumed he was about to make a speech.

Scrambling to his feet, clutching his spoon, and thinking quickly, he announced: 'I will now perform a magic trick.' Holding up the spoon, he said, 'see this gold spoon? I will put it in my breast pocket, like this, and Vladimir Ilianovich down there, will produce it from his sleeve!'

1. Adapted from Edward de Bono. *The Use of Lateral Thinking*. Jonathan Cape (London 1967)

'... A DOOR' Ralph Waldo Emerson

'The thought and the thing
thought about are one
and the same.'
Parmenides

'Sometimes I am,
sometimes I think.'
Paul Valéry

'To think is not enough; you must
think of something.'
Jules Renard

'Discovery consists of seeing what
everybody has seen and thinking
what nobody has thought.'
Albert Szent-Györgyi

'The irrational is not
necessarily unreasonable.'
Sir Lewis Namier

'Think like a man of action,
act like a man of thought.'
Henri Bergson

'A great many people think they
are thinking when they are merely
re-arranging their prejudices.'
William James

'Life consists in what a man is
thinking all day.'
Ralph Waldo Emerson

'All modern thought is permeated
by the idea of thinking the
unthinkable.'
Michel Foucault

'He who seeds a thought, harvests
a destiny.'
Zen saying

'What we cannot think,
we cannot think;
we cannot therefore say
what we cannot think.'
Ludwig Wittgenstein

'Thinking is a skill, not
intelligence in action.'
Edward de Bono

'To think that I am not going to
think of you any more is still
thinking of you. Let me then try
not to think that I am not going to
think of you.'
R.D. Laing

'There is no expedient to which a
man will not resort to avoid the
real labour of thinking.'
Sir Joshua Reynolds

'Thinking and spoken discourse
are the same thing, except that
what we call thinking is, precisely,
the inward dialogue carried on by
the mind with itself without
spoken sound.'
Plato

'... what turns the cranks in my
head is not information, but ideas,
hypotheses, creative solutions that I
might not have come across before.
I can't get those from a computer.
I can get those only by thinking.'
Clifford Stoll

I sat down in a tropical sunny clime with an orange juice. Instantly this banana bird alighted on my glass. When a bird fixes you with that hostile beady eye what's he/she thinking? Nothing, a birdologist would say – he/she is merely registering whether you're predator or prey. Rubbish. This little bastard was clearly assessing whether it could snatch another drink before it got a backhand.

Birdbrain or not, there is a lot going on in birds' heads. For instance, in the Arizona desert, eagles hunt in pairs, one flushes out the cottontails while the other swoops in to take them out. Greek eagles are so smart that they sweep out of the sky, snatch up tortoises, take them way up high and then drop them on rocks so they crack open. A return dive collects the snack. All requiring considerable skills including evaluation, identification, co-ordination, calculation and planning. I know a lot of people who can't do that.

Actually maybe the banana bird was only making sure I drew his/her best profile.

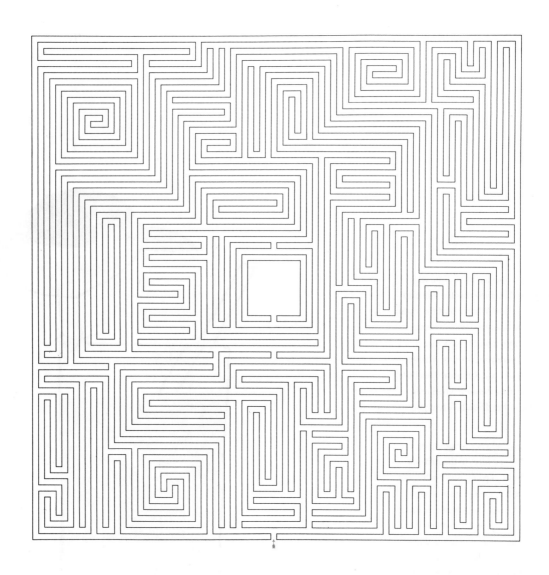

Roman Proverb   'If you don't know where you are going all roads lead there.'

Trying to solve most problems is like trying to assemble a jigsaw without first seeing the picture on the box. One knows a solution exists providing all the bits and pieces are put together in the right way.

Goethe said that everything has been thought of before and the real problem was to think of it again. Here are a couple of examples.

The architect of the *Duomo* in Florence died without leaving plans for constructing the enormous dome. That left a quandary as no one could figure out how to do it, so the *Duomo* was built without a dome. A hundred years later someone came across an early document which described how they built the dome of the *Pantheon* in ancient Rome by filling the space between the walls with earth. A neat piece of lateral thinking [SEE P143] finessed by scattering coins in the earth so once the building was finished the enthusiastic populace was invited to carry away the earth and rubble. For some reason the authorities didn't adopt this scheme and held a competition instead. Brunelleschi came up with the answer by tapping an egg on a table so it dented, and then stood it up on end. He got the job.

The *Santa Trinita* bridge in Florence, dynamited during the last war, was reconstructed from photographs and Ammannati's original drawings. One difficulty was that the curves of the arches didn't conform to standard geometry. Some speculated that they were catenary curves, the shapes produced by the loop of a chain, others that they derived from the shape of a violin. Finally someone suggested they were drawn freehand by someone brighter than Ammannati.* They were right. When Cosimo I commissioned the bridge he was also talking with Michelangelo on other matters. The original design of the triple curves can be found carved in the Medici tombs on Michelangelo's sarcophagi of *Night and Day, Twilight and Dawn.*[1]

'Reverse engineering' is a technique for the unravelling of a problem; the reasoning works like this. You are confronted with an object which you don't understand, yet was obviously designed for some specific purpose. You then attempt to analyse the object in terms of what problem it would be good at solving. 'Reverse thinking' works on the same principle.●

Diderot: 'Michelangelo gave to the dome of St Peter's at Rome the most beautiful shape possible. The geometer De la Hire, struck by this shape, drew it to scale, and found the outline to be the curve of the greatest resistance. What was it inspired that particular curve in Michelangelo, among the infinity of others he might have chosen?'

The art in solving problems is to identify the rhinoceros, and then adopt the right method of approaching it. Easier said than done. I often take a problem to bed, set it up centre stage in the mind, and focus on it as I'm falling asleep. Sometimes a solution reveals itself, sometimes it doesn't, but it's more fun than counting sheep.

Problems can be of our own making and trading on experience to resolve them can be a mistake. That's what happened to the scientist, engineer and designer who were arguing about the height of a church tower when a man passed by holding a barometer under his arm – one of life's small coincidences – and joined in the debate. To resolve matters he challenged them to find the answer by using his barometer. The scientist took a long time carefully measuring the barometric pressure at the bottom and top of the tower, and then calculating the height by the difference. The engineer, scorning this lengthy procedure, climbed up the tower, judged how much the barometer weighed, dropped it over the edge and worked out the height by timing how long it took to hit the ground. The designer popped into the church and offered the barometer to the verger in exchange for a look at the building plans.

*Michelangelo commenting on the sculpture of *Neptune* in the Piazza della Signoria: '*Ammannato, Ammannato, che bel marmo hai rovinato.*' ('What a beautiful piece of marble you've ruined.')

The *grook*, above left, is a kind of humanist *haiku* invented by Piet Hein.

1. Mary McCarthy. *The Stones of Florence*. Penguin (Harmondsworth 1972)

Problems
worthy
of attack
prove
their worth
by hitting
back

The simplest route to a solution is usually the best. How the Chinese artefact of delicately carved ivory balls within ivory balls is made appears to defy explanation. Designer Henry Steiner, who lives in Hong Kong, decided to find out. A Chinese working in his studio had a friend, who had a friend, who knew someone in a souvenir factory. Money changed hands, and Henry met a ballmaker willing to part with his trade secret. Here it is : A solid sphere of ivory is clamped in a lathe. A drill routs out conical holes pointing to the centre at fixed points around the sphere. Then, another drill, with a right-angled blade, is inserted into the holes. With a circular motion it cuts sideways at different depths. A tidying up and the resulting balls within balls are free to revolve around within each other.

Cosmetic solutions are those which are expedient rather than effective. This old joke makes the point. A man being fitted for a suit complained that one of the shoulders wasn't cut properly. The tailor suggested he slightly turn his body. That improved it, but the back developed a bulge. Never mind said the tailor, just lean forward a bit. This solved that, but the left trouser leg tended to rise. Keep your knee bent and it will look all right, said the tailor. The suit now fitted provided the man stood askew instead of upright, lent forward, and hobbled when he walked. Passing him in the street a lady remarked to her companion how lucky the poor cripple had found such a good tailor.

Of course if the only tool is a key then every problem is a lock. James Riley (1849-1916), responsible for the expression 'a life of Riley', was a dedicated alcoholic. In an effort to keep him sober friends once locked him in a hotel room for a couple of hours before he was due to give a lecture. He responded by calling room service for a double scotch and a straw. When it arrived he asked the waiter to bend the straw, poke one end through the keyhole, and stick the other end in the glass.

Assumptions inhibit shaking out answers. This riddle is only a riddle because of an assumption. A man lives in an apartment on the twentieth floor. Every morning he gets in the elevator and pushes the ground floor button, is taken down, gets out, and goes to work. In the evening he returns, enters the elevator and pushes the button for the tenth floor. He gets out and walks up the stairs to the twentieth. Why on returning home doesn't he ride straight up to his apartment? Maybe he's a half-hearted fitness freak? Actually he isn't. ·ʇǝƃpıɯ ɐ s,ǝH

Then there was the American woman who got into the textbooks for having made 548 visits to 226 physicians and receiving 164 different diagnoses. Her problem was she didn't understand her problem. And why do opera singers have a lot of trouble with their knees?

Then there is the **BIG PROBLEM** – who are you? There is an endemic human tendency for self-deception. We all think we're one kind of person when we're somewhat different (especially viewed by others) than we imagine we are. You – the reader – no doubt feel you're an exception.

● An alternative definition holds that 'Reverse engineering' is the dodgy science of copying a technical function without copying the legally protected manner in which that function is accomplished in a competitors product. Phew !

'Invent a better mousetrap, and you create the problem of mouse disposal. Incite the world to beat a path to your door, and you create the problems of traffic control, of quality control, of distribution control, of inventory control, of self control.'

Ralph Caplan

'A problem left to itself dries up or goes rotten. But fertilize a problem with a solution – you'll hatch out dozens.'

N.F. Simpson

'The sharks I dodged, the tigers I slew, what ate me up was the bedbugs.'

Bertolt Brecht

'It has long been an axiom of mine that the Little Things are infinitely the most important.'

Sherlock Holmes

'You've got to take the bull by the teeth.'

Samuel Goldwyn

'It isn't that they can't see the solution, it is that they can't see the problem.'

G.K. Chesterton

'A problem well stated is a problem half solved.'

Charles Kettering

Lenny Bruce said you can't get snot off a suede jacket. Of course you can – if you use the right solution.

'When you're up to your ass in alligators it's hard to remember you're there to drain the swamp.'

American cop

'If one finds the quintessence of a problem, one will have better access to an irreducible solution.'

Emilio Ambasz

'As I begin to dissect a problem, the solution always seems to emerge – sometimes as though it were staring me in the face.'

Woody Pirtle

'There are children playing in the street who could solve some of my top problems in physics, because they have modes of sensory perception that I lost long ago.'

J. Robert Oppenheimer

'We all agree that your theory is mad. The problem that divides us is this: is it sufficiently crazy to be right?'

Niels Bohr

'The problem, not a theory nor a style, determines the solution!'

Karl Gerstner

'Our cause is a secret within a secret, a secret that only another secret can explain; it is a secret about a secret that is veiled by a secret.'

Jafar al-Sadiq

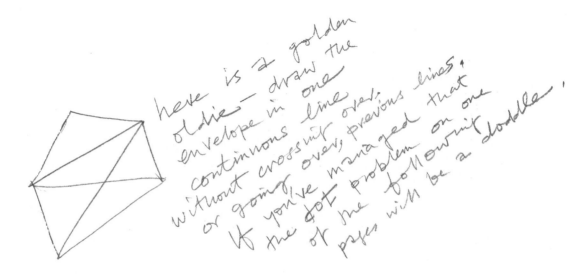

here is a golden oldie – draw the envelope in one continuous line without crossing over, or going over previous lines. If you've managed that the dot problem on one of the following pages will be a doddle.'

So how do they get Teflon to stick to the pan?

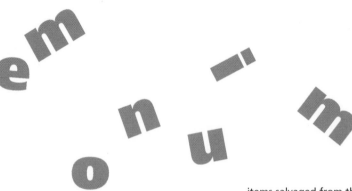

Once upon a time there was a computer programme called Pandemonium – a word invented by John Milton to name the capital of Hell in *Paradise Lost*. Anyway the programme featured a bunch of demons (*Pan demonium*) who, when faced with a problem would excitedly jump up and down saying, 'Me! me! me!', 'Let me do it!', 'I can do it!' After a brief struggle one would win and try to fix it. If that didn't work another would take over, the premise being that the mind throws everything at a problem to see what works rather than sorting it out methodically. An endorsement of the proposition that several heads are better than one.[1]

I once took part in an exercise done by corporations to demonstrate the benefits of teamwork. The group were the partners of Pentagram, an international design practice of intelligent, bolshie, innovative, assertive, creative, competitive, bloody-minded but entertaining individuals.The exercise was based on how well we would deal with a life-threatening disaster. The following account is much simplified.

The situation is this. A small group of people have survived a plane crash in a remote region of Canada. Everyone is badly shaken but uninjured and fortuitously dressed in insulated clothing and heavy boots. Collectively their personal possessions include: $153 in bills, 2 half dollars, 4 quarters, 2 dimes, 1 nickel and 3 new pennies; 1 pocket knife (2 blades and an awl which resembles an ice pick); one stub lead pencil; and a map.

In addition to this stuff a search of the wreckage yields: magnetic compass, gallon can of maple syrup, 1 sleeping bag (arctic type) per person, bottle of water purification tablets, 20 x 20 foot sheet of heavy-duty canvas, 13 wood matches in a metal screwtop waterproof container, 250 feet of quarter-inch braided nylon rope (50lb test); 1 operating 4-battery flashlight, 3 pairs of snowshoes, fifth of rum (151° proof), safety razor shaving kit with mirror, wind-up alarm clock, hand axe, 1 aircraft inner tube (punctured) for a 14-inch tire, book entitled *Northern Star Navigator*.

The assumption is that the number of people doing the exercise is the same as the number of survivors. Also that everyone has decided to stick together and the items listed above are in good order. The scene, so to speak, is set.

We were divided into three groups and the challenge was for each individual to rank the items salvaged from the plane in importance of use. Consideration of items from the list of the personal possessions may have relevance to the ranking.

I can't remember my reasoning but I put the matches top, then the canvas and sleeping bag. The alarm clock came bottom. Obviously I mistook the survival strategy for a camping holiday. Anyway once everyone had individually completed their rankings the next requirement was for each of the three groups to discuss and evaluate the results between themselves. This is where the significance of more than one head came into play.

For instance some viewed the canvas sheet as a protection against the weather, others as a device to catch dew and rainwater. Some chose the maple syrup for its metal can, and the clock for its spring – a fish hook perhaps? A group ranking was then listed by mutual consensus. Not surprisingly this was a different order to that of the individuals.

There was also, it was finally revealed by the convenor, a ranking composed by a survival expert. Each of the groups was nearer to the expert's ranking order than any of those produced by an individual.

1. John Brockman. *The Third Culture*. Touchstone (New York 1996)

This task was a typical challenge which confronted
applicants seeking to pass the tests posed by the
British Army Officer Selection Board. It appeared
in a recruitment advertisement in 1975.

A TYPICAL COMMAND TASK.

One member of an 8-man group of applicants has the
problem explained to him by the Officer. (Each member
of the group has a turn at leading the group through a
different problem.)

He then has a few minutes to figure out a solution
before explaining it to his group and getting them to
implement it. The problem is to switch the cans (17″ high
and filled with sand) which are at **A** and **B**.

The group must be split into two teams of 4 each.
Each team is then assigned to a can and mustn't touch the
other team's can. Neither can they use the other team's

platform **C** or **D**. They must each use their own route.
Nobody and nothing may touch the ground on the left of
the start line **E**. Behind which both teams must start.
Jumping from one platform to the other isn't allowed.

There is a rope lashing **F** on the platform **J** and two
planks **G** each one long enough to bridge the gaps **C-H**,
H-J and **J-D**. And between the start line and the two
nearest platforms.

Time allowed to interchange the drums is 10 minutes. It
doesn't matter where the men, the planks or the rope end up.
Go to it.

Your blind spot …

Viewing a situation in conventional terms can sometimes create problems which don't actually exist.

This is neither trick nor test, but a demonstration of the human tendency to make assumptions.

The requirement is to link all the dots in four straight lines without lifting pen from paper. Angles are permitted but not wobbles or bends. [SEE P533].

[SEE P147]

Photograph. Henri Cartier-Bresson (Athens 1953)

Michael Bierut

'If you want to get lucky … it pays to be ready.'

BRIC●LAGE

I'm told that the Tully River Aborigines have never made the connection between coition and pregnancy. For them the ultimate act of creation – childbirth – is one of divine chance.

Perhaps chance, reflected Joseph Joubert in his notebooks,[1] *'is a role that providence has reserved for itself in the affairs of the world, a role through which it could make certain that men would feel they have no influence.'* Well maybe, but now with Chaos Theory even chance itself might be less unpredictable, as mathematician Ian Stewart implies when he says, *'Chaos is when any determinist system ... has a solution that is so complex and so irregular that it appears to be random unless you know a lot of hidden information about what it is doing.'*[2]

Chaos Theory proposes that <u>the end result always depends on an initial condition</u>. A popular analogy is billiards or pool. If you hit a ball in a specific spot at a specific velocity it follows a specific track, ricochets around and ends up in a specific place. However if you started again, with everything precisely where it was the first time, but hit the ball minutely differently, the resulting pattern of play and end result would not be the same. The ball will end up somewhere else. Factors such as dust on the ball, the humidity in the air, the player's frame of mind, whether he's wearing new shoes, all play a part in effecting the result.

For myself I bank on *bricolage*. The *bricole* was a medieval military machine for throwing stones. Nowadays the term refers to a shot in billiards which doesn't turn out as intended but is nevertheless successful. Luck, say those who know, is a talent.

The picture opposite is of Aries the Ram, a character from the Zodiac. In drawing it I had difficulty with the configuration of the horns and eventually had to resort to photographic reference. Revelation. Rams have horns which grow in such variety of frenzied angles and crooked curves they defy imagination – and my skill. I settled for *bricolage*. Tightly gripping a dip pen, I closed my eyes, gritted my teeth, and did a couple of awkward scrawls. I hope they look convincing.

1. *The Notebooks of Joseph Joubert.* North Point Press (San Francisco 1983)   2. Melvyn Bragg. *On Giants' Shoulders.* Hodder & Stoughton (London 1998)

Strap

a piece of toast

— buttered side up —

to the back of a cat.

Throw the cat

out of the window.

Will the cat land

on its feet

or will

Murphy's Law

apply ?

Finger of God. The superstitious or primitive mind does not acknowledge chance, or accident or caprice. A change of wind, expiring flame, or breaking bow, are all occurrences fraught with meaning.

Paradoxically the sophisticated mind does believe in chance. John Cage composed music by consulting the *I Ching*, or showing the orchestra drawings and asking them to play whatever came into their heads. Jean Arp made unpredictable compositions by tossing pieces of paper onto a board (*Squares Arranged According to the Laws of Chance*). Jackson Pollock swung cans of paint to make artworks out of unforeseen dribbles. Damien Hirst throws gunge into his vitrines so it can predictably rot into unpredictable scenarios. More inventively a friend once sealed a pizza in a plastic bag and hung it up in the Italian sun all one summer, with spectacular results. David Bowie – following Tristan Tzara's instructions opposite – slices up texts which he reassembles to create lyrics.

More adventurously, the Boyle Family create 'paintings' by reproducing small patches of the world in dense meticulous detail. They select their sites at random. A blindfolded person throws a dart into a large map of the world. Then the Boyles call someone who lives near to wherever the dart pinpointed – perhaps the curator of a nearby gallery – and asks them to throw a dart at the local map, again blindfolded. The Boyles pack their bags and travel by air, sea and land until they're standing on the spot. Then one of them takes a right-angle and hurls it into the air. The place it lands becomes the first corner of the new work.

Writer Raymond Queneau was not an advocate of chance. 'Another very wrong idea that is also going the rounds at the moment,' he complained in the 1930s, 'is the equivalence that has been established between inspiration, exploration of the subconscious, and liberation, between chance, automatism, and freedom. Now this sort of inspiration, which consists in blindly obeying every impulse, is in fact slavery.' [SEEP275].

For sure luck is not going to resolve problems whose solutions lie within fixed patterns. These are as immune to chance as the possibility of a whirlwind reassembling the scattered debris of a crashed plane, or making a watch by putting all the parts in a box and shaking it. Even if someone could, there's zero chance of it also ending up with the right time. A blindfolded person given a Rubik Cube and asked to make a move each second could take forever as it can be twisted into 40,000,000,000,000,000,000 different states. I copied all these noughts very carefully so you can take my word for it. However, for those in the 'know' the moves can be done within fifty turns and, by the extremely deft, in thirty seconds. The benefit of knowledge over the potential of chance.

Of course it all depends on how one defines chance. I'm informed that if you thoroughly shuffled a deck of cards and in dealing they came up in four suits each sequentially running from ace to king, this arrangement would be just as likely as any other. Well maybe, but I'd be gobsmacked.

Anyway, as a designer, I deal with both random and fixed patterns. Experience painfully informs me that my instinctive inclination to rely on impulse rarely pays dividends. Nevertheless, with the optimism of a chancer, I usually have a go.

To make a Dadaist poem

"Take a newspaper.

Take a pair of scissors.

Choose an article as long as you are planning
to make your poem.

Cut out the article.

Then cut out each of the words that make up

this article and put them in a bag.

Shake it gently.

Then take out the scraps one after the other in
the order in which they left the bag.

Copy conscientiously.

The poem will be like you.

And here you are a writer, infinitely original
and endowed with a sensibility that is charming
though beyond the understanding of the vulgar."

Tristan Tzara

I make sunrises. An attempt to capture that moment

when the sun suddenly arrives with a

ssssssssGLOOP and BOING

like a cork popping out of a bottle.

The method is to brush in a stroke of colour, then

to rapidly daub a spot just above – touching the edge of the sea.

Whoomf. It's sudden death, it works or it doesn't, it's a chancy business.

Flip Wilson Theory. During the 1970s a group of enthusiastic physicists and computer whizz-kids got together to outwit the roulette wheels of Las Vegas. The wheel operates with a 44 per cent advantage to the Casino which is a significantly larger ratio to beat than in any other extant gambling system. The challenges they faced included the invention of computers small enough to fit into shoes, elaborate clandestine communication devices, and mind-boggling equations and crunching calculations:

'Finely machined and oiled, the disk of a roulette wheel suffers little decay in its velocity. A roulette ball, on the other hand, confronts numerous opportunities for entropic degradation. As it drops from orbit and arcs toward a rendezvous with the spinning rotor, it passes through a veritable minefield of galactic booby traps. It encounters friction from the track on which it turns. It faces wind resistance drag, and the ineluctable pull of gravity. Analysing the ball's trajectory would still be relatively straightforward were it not for further complications. Several metallic diamonds, pitched either horizontally or vertically, decorate the surface of a roulette wheel. On hitting a diamond ... a roulette ball will be knocked off course. It may be lofted higher in its trajectory, or dropped straight toward the wheel, where it faces even more interference from the metal frets that separate the cups.' [1]

The enthusiasts were moderately successful but eventually gave up. Having got wind that advantageous gambling odds might be breached by computer technology the State of Nevada made it illegal (1985) to carry any device into a casino capable of predicting the outcome of gambling games. Anyway, the roulette busters went on to bigger things by helping define the complex principles of Chaos Theory.

The forefather of the computer, Charles Babbage, had had a similar notion some 140 years earlier. Although his analytical machine was a crude behemoth operating with holes punched out of card, gears and cranks, it embodied most of the basic elements of the modern computer. Almost all we know about his machine comes from the writings of Lord Byron's daughter, Ada Augusta, the Countess of Lovelace. She combined good looks with a head for mathematics and, with Babbage, tried to work out a scheme for beating the odds at the races.

The Quail Game. In ancient Greece a game of chance centred on a quail. It worked like this. You drew a chalk circle about the size of a large plate on the table. You then found a quail with clipped wings, and put it in the centre of the circle. The next thing needed was a spoon. Everyone put money on the table and the first punter sharply rapped the quail on the head with the spoon. If the quail didn't back off and stayed in the circle, the punter collected the money. If the quail did, he passed the spoon on to his neighbour.

'You can't expect to hit the jackpot if you don't put a few nickels in the machine'

Flip Wilson

1. Thomas A Bass. *The Newtonian Casino.* Penguin (London 1991)

This jolly verse by Arthur Stanley Eddington is composed of 118 letters and 29 words. By tossing the letters on the page they ended up like this. However often I try, in no way are the letters likely to end up in the same pattern as on the opposite page. Mind you any one composition is as likely as any other. [SEE P152]. The letters were made out of bone by Napoleonic French prisoners of war incarcerated in Dartmoor prison. I bought them in Portobello Market during the early 1960s thinking I'd find a use for them one day.

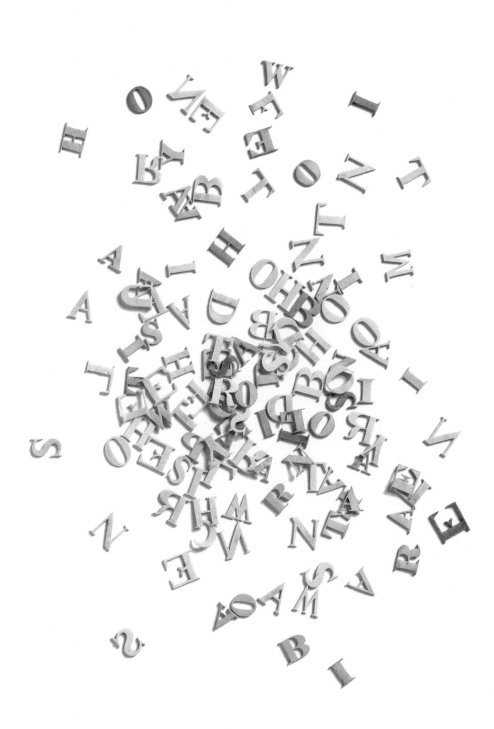

THERE ONCE WAS
A BRAINY BABOON
WHO ALWAYS BREATHED
DOWN A BASSOON
FOR ‒ HE SAID ‒
IT APPEARS THAT IN
MILLIONS OF YEARS
I SHALL CERTAINLY
HIT ON A TUNE

Ecremage. Float pigment over an oily liquid and draw a shape on the surface with a stick, or whatever. Drop a sheet of paper on top, and lift off to expose the image it has picked up. A technique which exploits chance to create unpredictable effects and was used to achieve the marbled paper shown opposite.

Decalcomania. Spread ink or paint over a non-absorbent material, such as acetate, porcelain or glass. Cover with paper, massage or rub or draw on the back of the paper, lift to reveal an unpredictable transfer as with ecremage.

Fumage. Create residual and unimaginable effects by passing paper or canvas or a plate over a smoking candle. You could also try a firework!

Froissage. Screw up paper, smooth it out and immerse in colour inks. The creases absorb the ink and generate haphazard wrinkles, tracks, threads, webs and gossamer.

Coulage. Pour molten metal or hot wax or chocolate into cold water. Watch it solidify into fantastic shapes. Hold your own sculpture exhibition.

Collage. Assemble and stick down miscellaneous bits and pieces of printed ephemera like tickets or labels, or excerpts cut out of newspapers, magazines and books. The chance factor lies in what you can make out of what is to hand.

Montage. Compose scenarios using photographs, or elements thereof, to create new and unforeseen situations. Not that chance comes into play when an unscrupulous photomontage can be deliberately produced to deceive the viewer into believing that the scene portrayed is real.

Decoupage. Decorate a wall or screen by papering with printed pages. As the patterns created by the juxtaposed subjects are largely random, there is a vague degree of chance involved in the outcome of the overall appearance.

Grattage. Scrape or scratch wet or dry paint to conjure up a magical image.

Frottage. Place a sheet of paper on a textured surface, say a plank of wood. Rub over the surface with crayon, pencil or charcoal to achieve bizarre effects.

Collins English Dictionary: **FROTTAGE.** 1. The act or process of taking a rubbing from a rough surface, such as wood, for a work of art. 2. Sexual excitement obtained by rubbing against another person's clothed body.

A grapefruit
is a lemon
that had
a chance
and took
advantage
of it.

Oscar Wilde

John Milton

chance governs all

It may be that the whims of chance are really the importunities of design

Mary McCarthy

Louis Pasteur

chance favours the prepared mind

The things we bring off by chance – what power they have

Robert Bresson

Paul Klee

Make chance essential

You never get a second chance to make a first impression

Will Rogers

Stéphane Mallarmé

chance will never be abolished by the throw of a dice

We can't leave the haphazard to chance

N.F. Simpson

André Breton

chance ... baffles its way through man's unconscious

Design. James Cross. Symbol for IDEAS, student congress in Australia

A person without imagination is like a teabag without hot water.

Self-awareness and the creative urge distinguish us from other creatures. To create requires that something can be envisioned before it can be caused. This is called *Hellenic Imagination* after Prometheus, the Greek god, credited

Edward O. Wilson dubbed imagination the Promethean gene

with the discovery of the magical power of being able to imagine the future by projecting a horizon of possibilities.

Like the white Queen in *Through the Looking Glass*, it is helpful to believe six impossible things before breakfast.

Imagination is the active ingredient of thinking

'What

Imagination jumps from present facts to future possibilities

is now proved

Imagination forms mental pictures of things not present

was once

Imagination conceives of situations not yet in existence

only imagined.'

Imagination conjures up correspondences and analogies

William Blake

'Imagination is intelligence with an erection.' *Victor Hugo*

Note. A friend of mine was reading the draft copy of this book. 'Can people really see purple cows?' she mischievously asked me. I'd just been on holiday and in reflective moments had watched a tree outside the place I was staying. In the early morning its trunk was pale grey, the leaves silhouetted dark indigo against the bright pale sky. Late afternoon, in catching the edge of the sun the trunk turned vermilion, the leaves a dark Winsor green. At sunset the trunk was sepia while the upper branches became pink and the leaves become a tinge of deep brown. In winter the leaves will have gone – but the trunk will probably be dark greeny grey flecked with silver bark. My answer was 'yes'.

'Ah, yes!
I wrote the Purple Cow
     I'm sorry, now, I wrote it!
But I can tell you anyhow,
     I'll kill you if you quote it!'

To imagine is like flying a kite. The mind, loosely tethered, is free to be blown about. Usually the direction it takes just happens but sometimes by tweaking the string it can arrive at an unlikely destination. Take Einstein who, struck with the thought of riding on a shaft of light in outer space while looking at himself in the mirror, interpreted the imagery to come up with the principles of his *Theory of Relativity*.

Imagination, an unimaginative person once wrote, is what happens when a drunk loses his watch and has to get drunk again to find it. Although fantasy and make-believe flourish in childhood they rapidly atrophy as one is moulded to fit the adult's grey consensus of reality. A child, out on a walk with its mother, suddenly points and cries out, 'Look, a purple cow.' The mother, perhaps rather tired and domestically harassed, snaps, 'Don't be silly.' And then delivers the crunch line: 'There's no such thing as purple cows.'

So the child, a vagabond in the backwoods of rationality, is brought up to see the world in the prosaic terms of grown-ups and eventually forgets it ever saw a purple cow. Now purple cows walk around unseen by anyone.

'I never saw a purple cow,
     I never hope to see one;
But I can tell you, anyhow,
     I'd rather see than be one!'

Quotations. Frank Gelett Burgess. *The Burgess Nonsense Book*. Frederick A. Stokes Company (New York 1901)

'Consolation from imaginary things is not an imaginary consolation.'
Roger Scruton

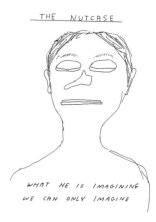

THE NUTCASE

WHAT HE IS IMAGINING
WE CAN ONLY IMAGINE

Photographer Brassaï [who claimed he invented nothing but imagined everything] recorded a conversation[1] with Picasso in 1943 in which he said: 'If it occurred to man to create his own images, it's because he discovered them all around him, almost formed, already within his grasp. He saw them in a bone, in the irregular surfaces of cavern walls, in a piece of wood. One form might suggest a woman, another a bison, and still another the head of a demon.' *Conversations with Picasso*

'If you look at certain walls covered with stains and built of mingled stones … you will … discern provinces with their mountains, their rivers, rocks, trees, plains, great valleys, hills in many aspects … battles and the swift movement of faces and singular expressions, clothes and innumerable other things.' Leonardo da Vinci

'Both fantasy and imagination concern unrealities; but while the unrealities of fantasy penetrate and pollute the world, those of the imagination exist in a world of their own, in which we wander freely and in full knowledge of the really real.' Roger Scruton

'Sometimes
we see a cloud
that's dragonish;
A vapour sometime
like a bear or lion,
A tower'd citadel,
a pendent rock,
A forked mountain,
or blue promontory
With trees upon't,
that nod unto
the world,
And mock our eyes
with air …'

William Shakespeare
(Anthony and Cleopatra)

'To see a World
in a Grain of Sand
And a Heaven
in a Wild Flower
Hold Infinity
in the palm
of your hand
And Eternity
in an hour.'

William Blake

Illustration. David Shrigley   1. Edward O. Wilson. *Consilience*. Little, Brown (London 1998)

'How nice it would be to have enough imagination to live in a dream world.'

Ken Pyne

half a word is enough for a *quick* ear

Even a few lines can trigger
our imagination. It really is
quite astonishing that our
perceptual apparatus can
bridge the distance between
a scribble and a three
dimensional object. In this
sketch a living, breathing,
middle aged couple doing
the samba.

the view from my room

This scene is a souvenir of a place where I once stayed. By looking at it I can remember the smell of bougainvillea on hot afternoons and the sound of the surf sliding up and down the beach. It's a kind of scratch'n'sniff card for my imagination.

Philip Roth delivered these remarks at The National Book Critics Circle in

1988: 'The imagination has a conscience all of its own; you wouldn't want it

as a friend. This butcher, imagination, wastes no time with niceties: it clubs

the fact over the head, quickly it slits its throat, and then with its bare hands

it pulls forth the guts ... By the time the imagination is finished with fact,

believe me, it bears no resemblance to a fact.' Comments well substantiated

by the Fortean Times, a periodical which reports on weird things such as

woman gives birth to fish, lawnmower shoots man, a house that bleeds,

tomatoes which use the telephone, man clubbed to death by a cucumber. Not

figments of the imagination, the editor claims, since all articles are endorsed

with place, date and time of the happening. In an age where science is seen

to explain everything, he says, awareness of the inexplicable is important.

No wonder imagination has been described as a warehouse of facts managed

by a poet and liar. However, sometimes there could be an explanation for

such phenomena. The examples quoted in the book The Nature of Things[1]

(subtitled The Secret Life of Inanimate Objects) may make you think twice.

As G.K. Chesterton explained, the function of the imagination is 'not to make

strange things settled, so much as to make settled things strange'.

1. Lyall Watson. *The Nature of Things.* Hodder & Stoughton (London 1990)

While Tibetan monks pray for two weeks before their

mandalas to transform them into three-dimensional floating palaces of light, with *Virtual Reality* one only needs to push a button. *Virtual Reality* is a technology which electronically converts physical and mental impulses into a computerized facsimile; a digitalized *doppelgänger.* By putting on some electronic gear you automatically get plugged into cyberspace, a world of controllable illusion. The brain, anxious to optimize the illusory sensations, grants them the credibility normally reserved for real experience. At the moment the tools are rather crude, but it works like this: The *Datasuit* projects an image of the body out into space, the *Eyephone* conjures up the vistas, the *Dataglove* interprets your gestures. Tilt your hand to the left, you look to the left; point your finger, and you move forward. You are in effect free to go where you like and do what you will. Using the software of world knowledge one could conduct a symphony orchestra or do a bit of brain surgery. The more imaginative participants might mix imagery and sensations, play with time and space, or engage in auto-eroticism – a field of fantasy referred to as *Tellydildonics*. The options are seemingly limitless: jog around the moon, swim through banknotes, sit on the rings of Saturn, be a piano and play yourself. Technology, said Max Frisch, was the knack of so arranging the world that we don't have to experience it. In much the same way, Virtual Reality bestows a sensation of achievement without the real experience. I guess that presented with the option of walking around a *Virtual Florence* rather than the real Florence, many people would choose the former. They'd prefer the homogeneous version rather than being in an old smelly city with traffic congestion and pigeon shit all over the place. There's an anecdote about Kierkegaard standing rapt in thought in a municipal flower bed. An irascible park keeper arrived and demanded to know what he was doing there. 'What are any of us doing here?' replied the sage. His imagination didn't need an electronic substitute.

'What I love about virtual reality is the notion that computers could provide a way for people to share their imagination with each other in new ways. I am not interested in replacing the physical world or creating a substitute for it. I am excited about the notion that you could get beyond this dilemma that we all live with; namely, that we have infinite imagination and are completely free so long as we retreat into our heads, into our dreams, into our daydreams, and make everyone else disappear, but as soon as we want to share this with other people, we become very much not free. I would like virtual reality to provide a way out of that dilemma, where you have a world that's fully objective like the physical world, but also completely fluid like the imagination.' Jaron Lanier (*computer scientist*)

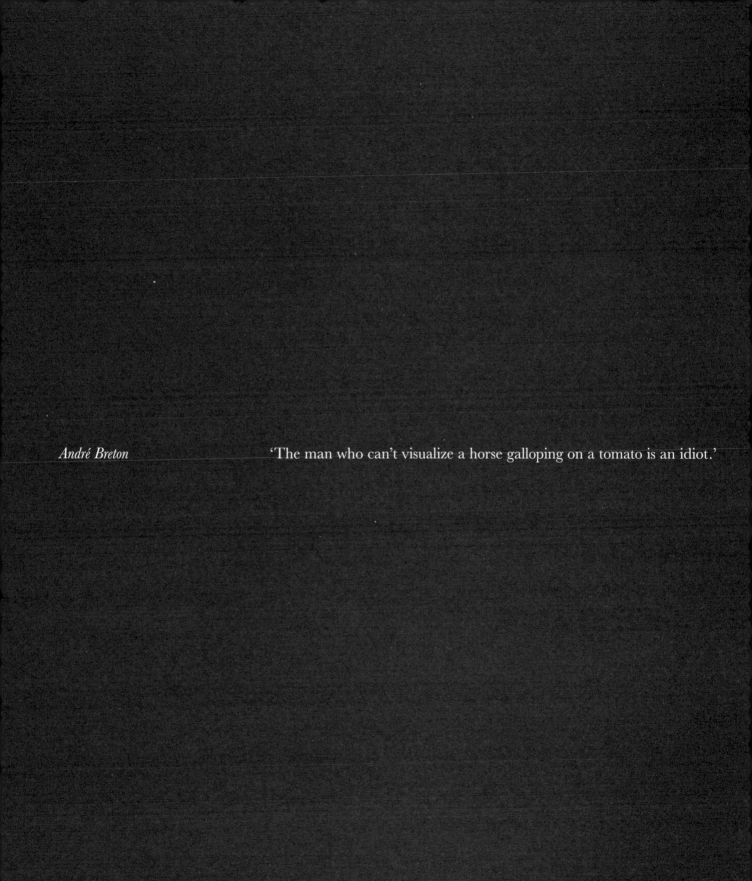

André Breton   'The man who can't visualize a horse galloping on a tomato is an idiot.'

A poem
is like a face
which one seems
to be able
to visualize clearly
in the eye
of memory…

Stephen Spender

I see what you mean

In William Golding's novel *The Inheritors*, the Neanderthals always say 'I had a picture' instead of 'I've just thought of something.'

Anthropologists agree that for once a novelist got it right. The terms *'Show me'*, or *'I see what you mean'* indicate a connection between sight and subject which is very real. After all, the highest compliment we pay to people of foresight is to call them visionaries or seers.

Unless we can visualize something we are unable to think about it. E.M. Forster (or his aunt) once remarked, *'How can I tell what I think until I see what I say?'* And Thoreau, *'You can't say more than you see!'* One cannot separate one from the other, any more than the child who, describing his drawing, said he just thought a thought and drew a line around the think. Children's drawings are invariably interesting because of this innocence and because they do not attempt to impress. Being untutored they are unadulterated, and therefore are a direct and unfiltered transmission of a thought.

Visual thinking is a 'mental graphic system' which Steven Pinker describes as 'operating by rotating, scanning, zooming, panning, displacing and filling in patterns and contours'.

An extension of visualizing is pictorial thinking – or imaging – which is the ability to conjure up something in the mind's eye, move it around, change it, and make judgements. A capacity which can be externalized by models, drawings, diagrams, or whatever.

Henry Moore visualized solid shapes and then mentally looked around them to assess weight and volume. Beethoven composed in his imagination, listening to the strings and then feeding in the brass. Hans von Bülow, travelling by train from Hamburg to Berlin, read Stanford's *Irish Symphony*, previously unknown to him, and then conducted it that evening without a score.[1] Nikola Tesla, inventor of the electric motor, designed in his head and was able to instruct his machinists with such accuracy that when all the components were assembled they fitted perfectly. To test the machine he put it together in his mind, let it run, and hours later mentally dismantled it to visualize the wear and tear.[2]

Unless the whatever-it-is can be clearly visualized, fiddling around on a bit of paper isn't much help. Designer Vico Magistretti first runs up a chair or lamp in his imagination and only uses a pencil *'after I have created what I have in mind'*. He never does a technical drawing and has one assistant who, so he told me, only has one arm.

However, when it comes to externalizing a mental mirage by putting it down on paper or screen other factors come into play. One thickness of line as opposed to another may enhance or degrade the translation. A slip of the pen or accidental smudge may adulterate or add frisson. The intervention of the hand in the translation from image in the mind to realization on a surface is an engagement requiring skill.

Whenever Hollywood makes films of well-loved books the producers are often criticized for altering the storyline and picking the wrong actors. The image doesn't match the imago – the idealistic picture in the mind. As John Fowles sees it, 'the cinematic visual image is virtually the same for all who see it; it stamps out personal imagination.' In *Anna Karenina* Tolstoy never actually described what Anna looked like. This could hardly have been an oversight. After establishing that she was beautiful Tolstoy left the reader to create their own notion of what that was.

1. John Carey. *The Faber Book of Science*. Faber & Faber (London 1995) 2. Lyall Watson. *Lifetide*. Hodder & Stoughton (London 1979)

'Only rarely will I sketch a number of studies; those I do in my mind. I never see a product or a house as drawings, but rather as a three-dimensional entity I can hold before my mind's eye and turn around or move into. Once the mental image is formed, then, and only then, do I draw it up in one of the notebooks that I carry with me constantly.'

EMILIO AMBASZ

'... one should not put pencil to paper before having visualized what one wants from all angles ... I have come to work by a series of mental images ... the drawing board enables me to give effect to those images.'

ETTORE BUGATTI

'My subject enlarges itself ... and the whole, though it be long, stands almost complete and finished in my mind, so that I can survey it, like a fine picture or a beautiful statue, at a glance.'

WOLFGANG AMADEUS MOZART

'From the distant days when I wanted to be a graphic artist, I have an odd habit of tracing what I see with a mental finger or pen – outlining a shoe or foot, drawing diagonals across window panes, tracing a certain pattern while my real finger slightly twitches. This too, this idiotic tic, is my self.'

JOHN UPDIKE

'A bee puts to shame many an architect in the construction of her cells, but what distinguishes the worst of the architects from the best of the bees is this, that the architect raises his structure in imagination before he erects it in reality.'

KARL MARX

'When I play, I turn the pages in my mind; I even see the coffee stains.'

ARTUR RUBINSTEIN

'Disney has now made its contribution to the history of architecture', proclaimed the **New York Times** referring to Isozaki's Team Disney Building at Epcot in Florida. 'An extraordinary composition of geometric forms: intensely colored, fragmented boxes set at clashing angles.' Arata Isozaki has never seen the finished building ... Disney officials had implored him to come and see it, but Isozaki demurred. 'But you haven't seen it finished,' they said. 'Yes I have,' replied Isozaki. 'I saw it when I designed it. I saw it in my mind.'

Ceci n'est pas une pipe.

imaging

Visualization of ideas is experienced, not deduced. Milton Glaser recounts a telephone conversation when he was asked to design a poster for the Sony corporation. The only stipulation, his caller stated, was to include their current slogan: 'Sony Tape. Full Color Sound.' At that very moment, Glaser recalls, 'the mental picture arrived fully formed, not by a sequence of thoughts, or analysis and conclusion, but instantly.' Magritte captioned one of his works depicting a pipe: 'This is not a pipe.' Indeed it isn't – it's a painting of a pipe or to be more accurate the picture shown here is a photograph of a painting, or even more precisely the reproduction of a photograph transferred off a printing plate by small inked dots. Now I'm into this analysis I might as well keep going because what you really see is an upside down image flipped left to right on the back of your retina, an electrochemical hallucination in the head. A contrived visual echo of the visualization in Magritte's mind when he painted the picture back in 1928! And the cigar on a poster by Woody Pirtle which says it isn't, is an ironic image prompted by Magritte's pipe.

'When you telephone your mother in another city, the message stays the same as it goes from your lips to her ears even as it physically changes its form, from vibrating air, to electricity in a wire, to charges in silicon, to flickering light in a fiber optic cable, to electromagnetic waves, and then back again in reverse order. In a similar sense, the message stays the same when she repeats it to your father at the other end of the couch after it has changed its form inside her head into a cascade of neurons firing and chemicals diffusing across synapses.' STEVEN PINKER [1]

Esto no es un cigarro.

1. Steven Pinker. *How the Mind Works.* Penguin (London 1998)

Sony Tape. Full Color Sound.

Two Creative Blocks

Creative block occurs when the mind is locked into overdrive and no amount of manoeuvring to change direction makes any difference. No innovative thoughts, no mental jumps, no creative impulses. That's the extreme condition, but even in normal circumstances we think along tramlines.

Two figures diagram two aspects of a free-standing three-dimensional object.[1]

Front elevation

Side elevation

Can you draw it in three dimensions?

If you can't here are some clues. The front elevation indicates that the small rectangle inside the large one is either a projection or a hole. The side elevation tells us that it is a hole, and that the hole is a slot. So how come that in the front elevation the small rectangle doesn't extend all the way from left to right?

Having got this far most people give up, but a few will 'figure it out' and end up with a three-dimensional object which looks like this ...

That's one answer – but there's a more elegant interpretation:

This second solution can only be achieved by visualizing the object holistically, as a thing in itself, rather than as a sum of bits and pieces. One has to be able to imagine a feature which is not even indicated. In turn that means opening up the mind to provide an arena in which the imagination can play.

Now you know how to go about it, can you visualize what kind of single form could completely fit, and pass right through, each of the holes represented by the three white shapes on the page opposite?

Here is a clue. The piece would have to be square, triangular and round – all at once. If you can't visualize what <u>that</u> looks like you're in trouble. [SEE P533].

 1. Victor Papanek. *Design for the Real World*. Thames & Hudson (London 1972)

Note. If somebody is deliberately unpleasant to me, I employ the ultimate private put down. I visualize them as they probably looked a million years ago. A scenario where it's difficult to distinguish whether they're chimp or human, where they tend to shamble on two legs or amble on all fours, when their anus is as prominently exposed as their nose. They look faintly familiar and smell rather strong. I have a private smile and exit as soon as possible.

● The Washburn Equation was originally devised to describe the extent to which various blotting papers soak up ink. A similar equation $L = \gamma \times Dxt \over 4x\eta$ calculates the assimilation of coffee or tea when dunking various kinds of biscuits. Apparently assimilation enhances the flavour of gingernuts, digestives, and other biscuit varieties. The t in the equation indicates how long coffee takes to be absorbed. D is the diameter of the holes the coffee passes through. The γ is the surface tension, and one of the other figures the liquid viscosity. ● I wanted to illustrate this page with Il Gabinetto del proprio niente, a marvellous drawing by Saul Steinberg demonstrating the art of memory. It is in a catalogue published by the Whitney Museum in New York in 1978. However, much of it is out of focus and illegible. The original is in a private collection. So private I can't find out who they are to ask for a decent print. The world is full of anal retentives. ● 'I have a memory like an elephant,' confided Noël Coward; 'in fact, elephants often consult me.' [SEE P28].

MEMORY

One afternoon in 1909 Marcel Proust dipped a biscuit into his tea ●. A small gesture which triggered off a detailed recollection of past events and childhood memories. He put it all down in *A La Recherche du Temps Perdu*. Sometimes making a sudden connection between the similar or disparate illuminates the memory. ■ I can still distinctly remember, when I was ten, my teacher (Mr Willink) telling the class how to remember the conjugation of Latin verbs. He said you had to visualize a tree, then the branches, the twigs, leaves, fruits and flowers. You stuck a word on each and then fixed the picture in your mind. Fifty years later I can't recall the verbs but I remember the tree. ■ There are of course many instances of prodigious memory such as Cyrus, King of the Persians, who could call every soldier in his armies by name. Legend attributes the art of memory to the Greek poet Simonides who, so the story goes, was chanting a panegyric at a banquet in honour of his host Scopas. Unwisely he also praised Castor and Pollux. Scopas took umbrage and said he'd only pay half the fee and the rest was up to the twin gods. They must have heard him. Shortly afterwards a messenger entered the hall and told Simonides there were two visitors waiting to see him outside. Just as Simonides left, the roof collapsed and crushed everyone to death. The relatives were unable to recognize the bodies but Simonides, recalling where everyone sat, was able to indicate who was who. Have you noticed that when trying to explain how we go about doing something, we often start by saying '*in the first place I would ...*' ■ The secret of lengthy oration lay in the visual *aides-mémoires*. Orators would invent imaginary palaces to hold in their mind, structures of rooms, courtyards, alcoves, arcades, fountains, statuary, pediments, architraves, columns, all enriched with ornament and decoration. Elements would be sited in light or shadow, be high or low, positioned near or far. By fastening each part of the discourse to these features in order and sequence, orators were able to memorize speeches of immense detail and of amazing length[1] ●. I can't even remember which sock I put on first when I get up in the morning – the left or right. ■ Giulio Camillo took the idea further and built a tiny wooden theatre. A physical example of a memory palace. The theatre could just about accommodate two people, contained an auditorium divided by seven gangways which rose in seven steps, and was dense with ornamentation, decorations, small sculptures and carvings, little drawers filled with notes. Everything, from structure to content, held specific meanings, associations and references. It was a *Theatre of Knowledge*, an encyclopedia of everything known at the time. It was also a dangerous occupation during the sixteenth century – Camillo was burned at the stake. ■ Nowadays it's hardly necessary to commit anything to memory. But those who are interested in furthering their mental powers, or in continuing the tradition, join societies such as *The Brain Club*, which treat memory as mental callisthenics ●. One member, a Mr Carvello, memorizes telephone books. People give him their name and address, he closes his eyes, calls up the pages in his head, and then he gives them their telephone number. Another member can memorize – on single sighting – the sequence of numbers and suites after thirty packs of cards have been randomly shuffled together and then spread out. ■ Both are spectacular feats but unless you have something to say you're only talking to yourself. ■ I have a terrible memory but gain dubious satisfaction from a comment I read that 'a retentive memory may be a good thing, but the ability to forget is the true token of greatness.' No doubt said by somebody else with poor memory.

PALACES

1. Frances Yates. *The Art of Memory*. Routledge & Kegan Paul (London 1984)

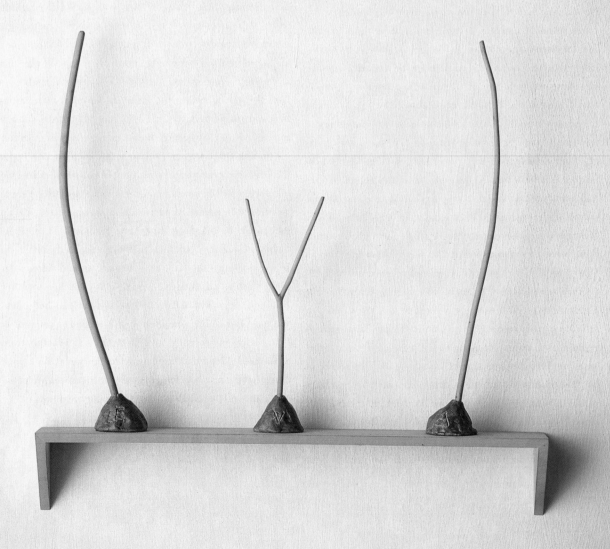

POLTERGEIST TAKES A SHOWER
AFTER DIP IN OUTDOOR POOL

Observation. David Shrigley

Joseph Joubert   'Music has seven letters, writing has twenty-six notes.'

'Until writing was invented, man lived in acoustic space: boundless, directionless, horizonless, in the dark of the mind, in the world of emotion, by primordial intuition, by terror. Speech is a social chart of this bog. The goose quill put an end to talk. It abolished mystery; it gave architecture and towns; it brought roads and armies, bureaucracy. It was the basic metaphor with which the cycle of civilization began, the step from the dark into the light of the mind. The hand that filled the parchment page built a city.'

Marshall McLuhan

'... writing put commandments, laws, agreements on record. It made the growth of states possible. It made a continuous historical consciousness possible. The command of the priest or the king and his seal could go far beyond his sight and voice and could survive his death.'

H.G. Wells

'What man, indeed, can compose a fitting hymn of praise for the learning of letters? It is by such knowledge alone that the dead are carried in the memory of the living.'

Diodoros of Sicily

'The discovery of the alphabet will create forgetfulness in the learners' souls, because they will not use their memories; they will trust to the external written characters and not remember of themselves ... You give your disciples not truth but only the semblance of truth; they will be heroes of many things, and will have learned nothing; they will appear to be omniscient and will generally know nothing.'

Plato

'... from the invention of letters all polite intercourse and music proceeded and reason and justice were made manifest; the relations of life were defined, and laws were fixed; governors had a lasting rule to refer to; scholars had authorities to venerate; the historian, the mathematician, the astronomer, can do nothing without letters.'

Henry Noel Humphreys

'We know not when, and we cannot guess where, there dawned upon some mind the fact that all the words which people uttered are expressed by a few sounds. Hence, what better plan than to select from the big and confused mass of ideograms, and all their kin, a certain number of signs to denote, unvaryingly, certain sounds? That was the birth of the alphabet, one of the greatest and most momentous triumphs of the human mind.'

Edward Clodd

'Alphabets, like musical scales, or fingers and toes, or stars and constellations, or stone circles, or abacuses, or sea waves, or comets and eclipses, or genealogies, or bird and fish migrations, owe their interest and appeal to a combination of regularity and chance.'

Edwin Morgan

'... the idea of representing each single sound by a single unvarying symbol ... is the kind of sudden intuitive perception which single men like **Newton** have more than once accomplished, even when others did the elaborating and the perfecting.'

David Diringer

'The civilization of the image is drawing to an end: the victory of the computer will actually establish an alphabetical civilization; the computer is gradually transforming the picture screen into a letter screen.'

Umberto Eco

'I would rather write 10,000 notes than one letter of the alphabet.'

Ludwig van Beethoven

'IN THE BEGINNING WAS THE WORD.' MYTHOLOGIES INVARIABLY ATTRIBUTE THE INVENTION OF WRITING TO DEITIES. THE CRETANS TO ZEUS, THE JEWS TO YAHWEH, THE SUMERIANS TO NABÛ, THE ARABS TO ALLAH, THE MAYANS TO ITZAMNA. THE EGYPTIANS TO THOTH, WHO, AS AN IBIS, SCRATCHED MARKS IN THE SAND WITH HIS BEAK. THE GREEKS TO HERMES, WHO GOT THE IDEA SEEING CRANES FLYING ACROSS THE SKY. THE CHINESE TO EMPEROR HUANG TI, WHO THOUGHT IT UP SEEING TRACKS MADE BY BIRDS IN THE SNOW. THE INDIANS TO GANES, THE ELEPHANT GOD WHO BROKE OFF A TUSK AND USED IT AS A PEN. SANSKRIT, THE MOST ANCIENT OF SCRIPTS, WAS SAID TO DERIVE FROM THE SKULLS WHICH BEADED KALI'S NECKLACE. THE CHRISTIANS CREDITED GOD AS DESCRIBED BY DANIEL DEFOE IN HIS ESSAY: 'AN INQUIRY INTO THE ANTIQUITY AND ORIGIN OF LETTERS PROVING THAT THE TWO TABLES WRITTEN BY THE FINGER OF GOD ON MOUNT SINAE WAS THE FIRST WRITING IN THE WORLD AND THAT ALL OTHER ALPHABETS DERIVE FROM HEBREW.' AND ALL THIS HAPPENED, HE WROTE, 2515 YEARS BEFORE THE BIRTH OF CHRIST.[1] [SEE P106] THE TRUTH IS MORE PROSAIC. WRITING WAS INVENTED BY ACCOUNTANTS, A SYSTEM OF MARKS TO REGISTER TRIBUTES, TAXES, DEBTS AND TITHES. ONLY EVENTUALLY DID IT COME TO RECORD IDEAS. BY TRANSCENDING THE LIMITATIONS IMPOSED BY TIME AND SPACE, WRITING BECAME THE FOUNDATION OF CIVILIZATION. WITHOUT IT THERE WOULD BE NO BIBLE, NO MAGNA CARTA, NO BILL OF RIGHTS, NO BOOKS. **HISTORY BEGAN WITH WRITING.** BEFORE THAT EVERYTHING WAS '**HEARSAY**'.

1. Johanna Drucker. *Alphabetic Labyrinth.* Thames & Hudson (London 1995).

The letters of our alphabet are derived from a script invented, or at least developed, by the Phoenicians. Their neighbours, the ancient Greeks, adopted this for their own use and by translating Phoenician letters into Greek, *aleph* (A) and *beth* (B) becoming *alpha* and *beta*, gave the world the *alphabet*.

'All characters were originally signs and all signs were once images. Human society, the world, man in his entirety is in the alphabet. Masonry, astronomy, philosophy, all the sciences start here ... **A** is the roof with its rafters and traverse-beam, the arch, or it is like two friends who embrace and shake hands. **D** is the back, and **B** is a **D** on a second **D**, that is a 'double-back' - the hump; **C** is the crescent, is the moon, **E** is the foundation, the pillar and the roof - all architecture contained in a single letter. **F** is the gallows, the fork, **G** is the horn, **H** is the facade of a building with its two towers, **I** is the war-machine that throws projectiles, **J** is the plough, the horn of plenty, **K** signifies one of the basic laws of geometry (the angle of reflection is equal to the angle of incidence), **L** is the leg and the foot, **M** is the mountain, or the camp with its tents, **N** is the door, closed with a cross-bar, **O** is the sun, **P** is the porter carrying a burden, **Q** is the croup and the tail, **R** signifies rest, the porter leaning on his stick, **S** is the snake, **T** is the hammer, **U** is the urn, **V** is the vase (that is why **U** and **V** are often confused). I have already said what **Y** signifies. **X** signifies crossed swords, combat – who will be victor? Nobody knows - that is why philosophers used '**X**' to signify fate, and the mathematicians took it for the unknown. **Z** is the lightning – is God ...' Victor Hugo

A schematic of the Phoenician letters. The seminal version is the inscription on the sarcophagus of King Ahiram of Byblos (1000 BC). Incidentally, the town which gave its name to the Bible.

'Among the great calligraphers may be found signs straight as hanging needles and marks round as dewdrops. One also finds signs jagged as lightning flashes or like falling rocks. There are signs inclined like flying birds or galloping beasts. Characters look like dancing phoenixes, like crawling serpents, like precipitous crags, like abrupt peaks. Some of them are as heavy as thick clouds.' Sun Kuo-t'ing

'I find many mysterious relationships among the twenty-six characters of our alphabet ... W like a bird in flight, Z like a bolt of lightning.' *Wolfgang Weingart*

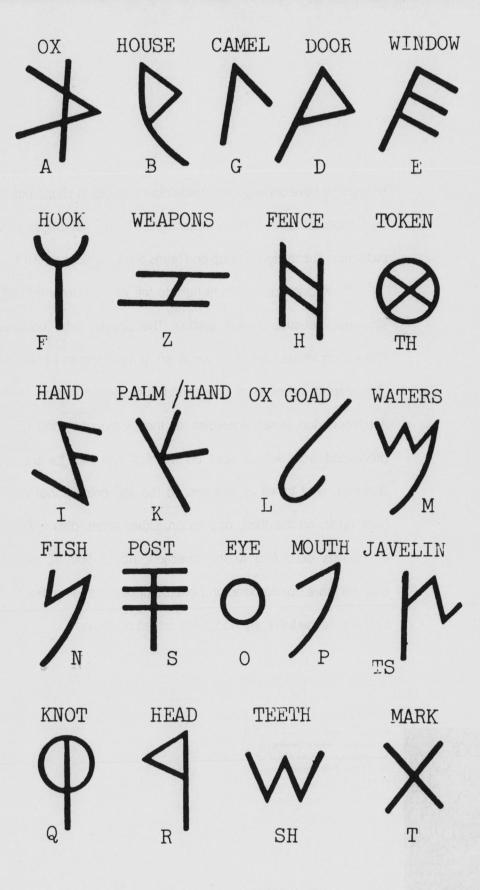

OX HOUSE CAMEL DOOR WINDOW

A B G D E

HOOK WEAPONS FENCE TOKEN

F Z H TH

HAND PALM/HAND OX GOAD WATERS

I K L M

FISH POST EYE MOUTH JAVELIN

N S O P TS

KNOT HEAD TEETH MARK

Q R SH T

'Pictures and letters are really blood relations.' E.H. Gombrich

Pictograms have undergone considerable changes in shape before they ended up as the letters we recognize today. **A** began as a pictogram illustrating the head and horns of an ox. It looked like this : ∀ . Phoenician scribes wrote right to left and so drew the ◁ sideways because it was quicker. The Greeks, who adopted Phoenician letters, generally wrote left to right and so turned the ▷ around, although at one period they used a system called Boustrophedon, which translates 'as the ox ploughs', and which proceeded from left to right on the first line [so ▷ pointed likewise], right to left on the second [so ◁ pointed that way], back again on the third, and so on. Other letters also reversed themselves according to the direction. About 500 BC writing became more standardized and letters stopped changing direction. By that time the letter **A** had finally settled on its horns.

Actually Boustrophedon can follow three methods. The lines reverse but the words don't. The words reverse as well as the lines. The letters reverse as well as words and lines.

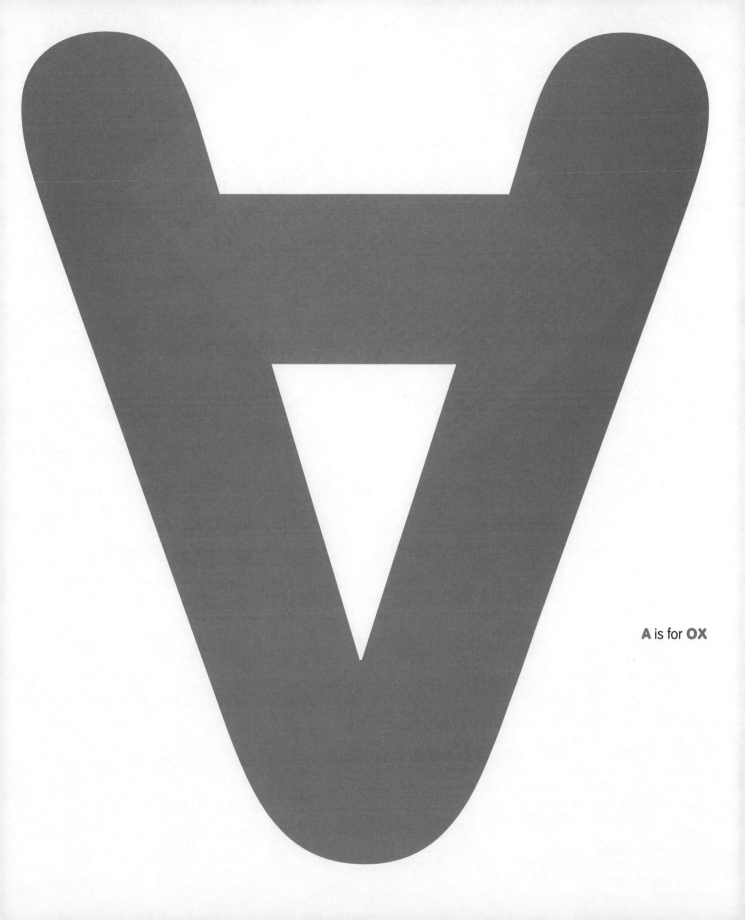

A is for **OX**

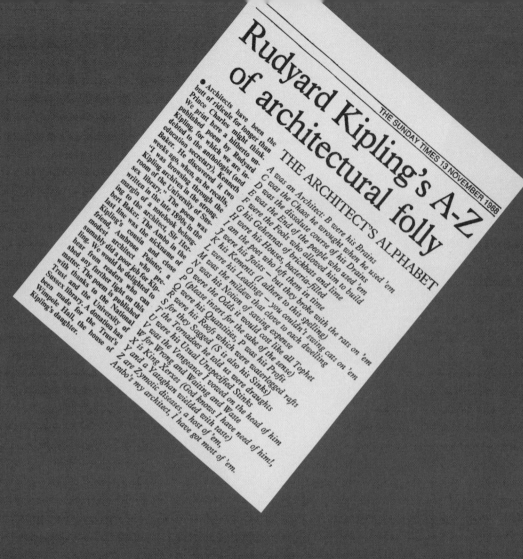

ANACHRONISM, bacchanal, carpet-monger,
dilettante, eccentric, flibbertigibbet,
galumpher, heterosexual, inaniloquist,
jaywalker, knucklehead, Londoner,
marionette, nyctaphile, optimist, punster,
quidnunc, romantic, stargazer, Taurean,
unicyclist, voyeur, weirdo, xenophone,
yodeller, zetetic, late Thirties, seeks
female companionship.

ZINGARO, yodeller, xenophobe, wisecracker,
voyager, utopianist, trentagenarian,
soliloquist, romantic, quidnunc,
pyrrhonist, oddball, nucivore, marionette,
Londoner, kafkaphile, jaywalker,
individualist, heterosexual, guruphobe,
fatalist, eclectic, dreamer, caucasian,
bacchanal, atheist, seeks female
companionship.

Two classified ads from the Lonely Hearts column. *Time Out* Magazine.

The Greeks were probably the first to marry writing with speech. Originally they **NLYWRTWTHCNSNNTS** and didn't

separate words. Over time, to help pronunciation, they invented the vowels **AEIOU** and used spaces to separate words. Thus

the previous gobbledygook would be written **ONLY WROTE WITH CONSONANTS**. Successive cultures chopped and

changed the alphabet by amending, adding and dropping letters to accommodate differing glitches and sounds.

Spurius Carvilius Ruga (about 230 BC) invented **G** by adding a stroke to **C**. The **W** was created in eleventh-century scriptoria

by combining **U** and **U** – to make **double U** [**W** – got it?]. By the way James Thurber once asked a friend if she could think of

a word in which **u** appeared three times. She couldn't, but thought it must be **unusual**. It was and it wasn't. In the Middle

Ages the **j** was made by extending the **i**. Letters invented much later like the **X**, **Y** and **Z**, just got tacked on the end of the

alphabet. Italian still retains the 21 letter Latin alphabet but polygot English has acquired 26. With these 26 characters

403,000,000,000,000,000,000,000,000 [1] pronounceable words are possible. Another source computes the

number as **620,448,401,733,239,439,360,000,000**. Take your pick. The letters most frequently employed are :

e , **t** , **a** , **i** , **s** , **o** , **n** , **h** , **r** , **d** , **u**. Other permutations can be found in Firmage's **ABECEDARIUM** [2] and Jean Cocteau

mischievously suggested that even the greatest literary masterpiece was really no more than an alphabet in disorder.

Names for letters derived from the original sound of the name of the object portrayed by that letter. For example **A** is called **'A'**

because that's how Phoenicians pronounced **'ALEPH'** – their name for ox. [SEE P173] But why do we say **'Bee'**, **'See'**, **'Dee'**, **'Eee'**,

then **'Ef'**, and then **'Gee'**, and then **'Aitch'**? The sequence of **A** to **Z** was established when letters were used to count. **A** stood

for one, **B** for two, **C** for three, and so on. When you got to **Z** you started again doubling up, **AA** etc. [SEE P ꝑ] The earliest record

of alphabetic order is Psalm thirty-seven where verses follow the Hebraic sequence. When travelling, a tenth-century Grand

Vizier of Persia had his library of 117,000 books carried by 400 camels walking one behind the other in alphabetical order. [3] I

don't know whether by author or subject. And have you noticed that famous people die in alphabetical order? At least

according to the obituary columns. 'I am the **ALPHA** and the **OMEGA**, the first and the last, the beginning and the end.'

[Apocalypse of St John]

1. Richard Gregory. *Odd Perceptions*. Routledge (London 1988)   **2**. Richard A. Firmage. *The Alphabet ABECEDARIUM*. Bloomsbury (London 2000)   **3**. Alberto Manguel. *A History of Reading*. HarperCollins (London 1996)

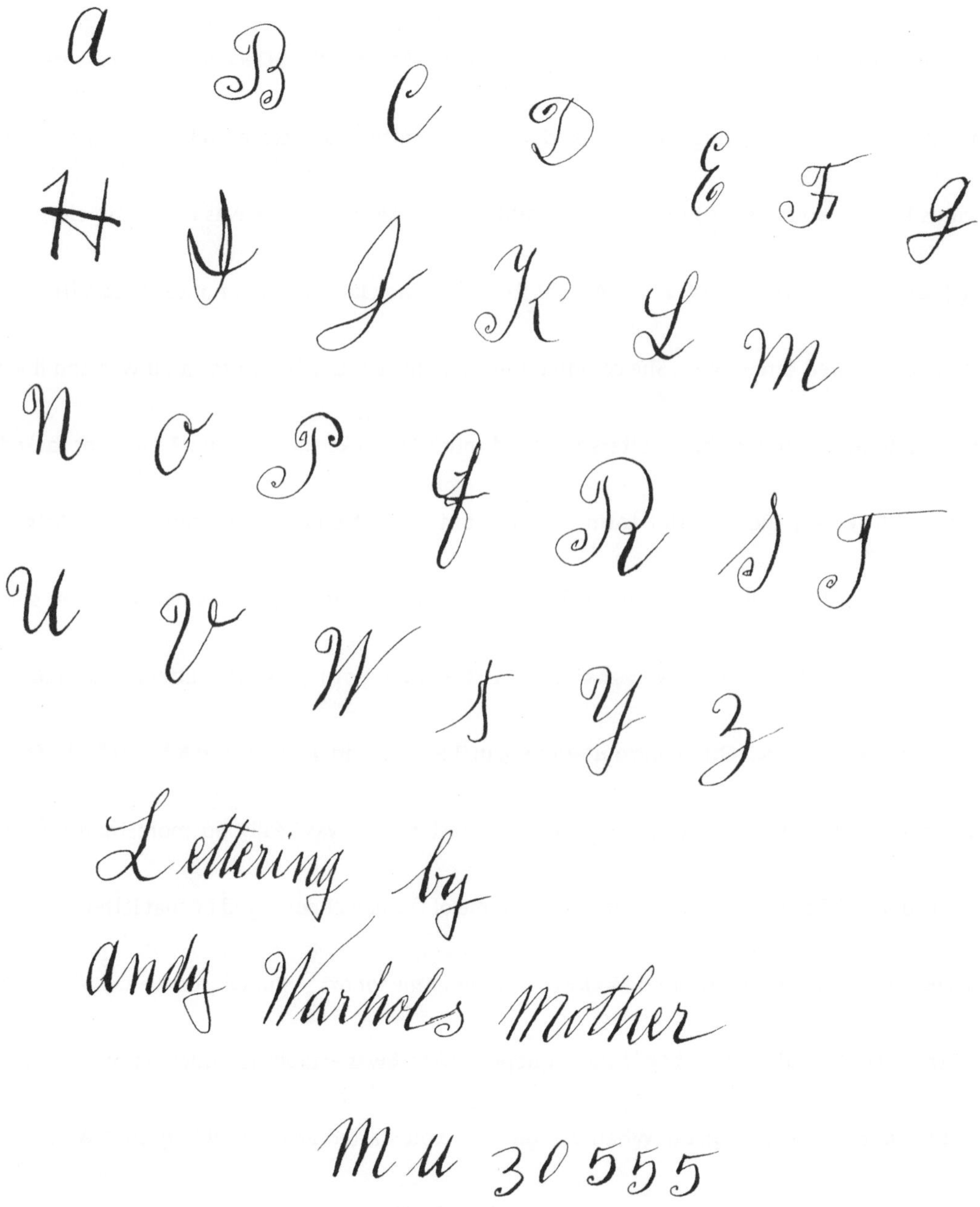

A B C D E F G
H I J K L M N
N O P Q R S T
U V W X Y Z

Lettering by
Andy Warhols Mother

MU 30555

ABCDE
FGHIJK
LMNOP
QRSTU
VWXYZ

Pretzels nibbled by Lou Klein and family

In 1678 Athanasius Kircher, Renaissance polymath, claimed to have seen the alphabet (including the ligature Æ) in the veins of a rock. Perhaps he did. Italian designer Italo Lupi found his alphabet on a beach.

Sight so dominates
our intellectual practices
that we construct
diagrams and charts
so we can 'see
what is happening',
'see if something
is possible',
try to imagine it
'in our mind's eye'.

Illustration. Henryk Tomaszewski

Goethe   'The hardest thing to see is what is in front of your eyes.'

**'To translate the invisible wind by
the water it sculpts in passing.'**

Robert Bresson

'The Eye That Never Sleeps' the slogan of Pinkerton's (private detective agency) gave birth to the term 'Private Eye'.

Taking notice

Theoretically[*] everybody is capable of
remembering everything that ever happened
to them and perceiving everything that's
happening around them. Luckily this never
occurs. Exposure to information of such
overwhelming magnitude would mean closing
down our mind entirely or taking leave of
reality altogether. A situation which strongly
encourages us to only absorb what we want
or need and block out the rest.

A scientific paper entitled *What the Frog's eye
tells the Frog's brain* details how frogs were
wired up to see what they see. Not much
actually. Mainly a matter of light interference,
the looming shadow of a predator or something
edible flying by. The frog's universe is screened
down to the minimum needed for survival. For
them there are no glorious sunsets, no leaves
in the wind.

We also only notice things which are directly
relevant to our daily business. In consequence,
we tend to reduce our environment to visual
muzak – a perpetual symphony of colours,
shapes and patterns.

Blinkered by habit we glance around rather
than look with acuity. In effect the eye sleeps
until the mind wakes it with a question.

[*] The word THEORY derives from the Greek word 'TO BEHOLD'.

Mirage in the mind

The information gathered by a blind man
through his other senses is severely limited
compared to what he might have gained
through sight. With sight he could see the stars.
Or more precisely see a presumed reality by
way of a fabricated picture.

The Greeks assumed that light entered the eye
bringing with it what we see and the beauty
of nature. They were wrong.[1] Nature is a dull
affair, *'soundless, scentless, colourless;
merely the scurrying of material, endlessly,
meaninglessly'.* Even light comes as invisible
wavelengths. It's the brain which does all the
work, parses the spectrum, sorts out the shapes
and lines, puts everything together to form a
mental picture.

What happens is this. Light waves arrive on
the retina, this translates them into tiny upside-
down images. Millions of receptors carve these
up into messages which race off to several
billion cells. These interpret the data and send
back messages to project the images the right
way up. That's what you see in the mind's eye.

Actually that's not quite true. The picture
translated by the retina and the image
projected in the mind's eye are not necessarily
the same. During the process language and
culture act as prisms to bend and shape our
view, so although we all start out seeing the
same things each individual unconsciously
creates their own interpretation. Therefore
although we think of the world as an entity
existing outside our head it's only a mirage in
the mind. *'If I look at the external world',* said
Dylan Thomas, *'I see nothing or me.'*

There are even doubts about that. A current
scientific controversy, also an ancient
philosophical one, still queries whether mental
images are a depiction of reality, a hypothesis,
or whether they even exist.

On the prow of every *luzzo* – Maltese fishing
boat – you will see the painted eye of Osiris
who wards off evil spirits. Osiris was god of
fertility and the dead.

1. Stephen Jay Gould. *The Urchin in the Storm*. Collins Harvill (London 1988)

See-saws 👁 to **see** one's way through 👁 to **see** a way out of a situation 👁 to **see** the point of something 👁 to **see** what I mean 👁 to **see** reason 👁 to **see** someone off 👁 to **see** hope 👁 to **see** a point of view 👁 to **see** what one can do 👁 to **see** things my way 👁 to **see** it's put right 👁 can't **see** the wood for the trees 👁 wait and **see** 👁 over**see** 👁 to **look** down on someone 👁 to **look** up to someone 👁 to **look** someone up 👁 to **look** sharp 👁 to **look** someone over 👁 to **look** something up 👁 to take a **look** 👁 to take a **look** see 👁 to get a **look**-in 👁 to keep a **look**-out 👁 it **looks** like 👁 a **look**-alike 👁 if **looks** could kill 👁 she's a good **looker** 👁 out**look** 👁 over**look** 👁 **look** in 👁 things are **looking** up 👁 **eye**witness 👁 **eye**-opener 👁 **eye** contact 👁 the mind's **eye** 👁 the third **eye** 👁 a sharp **eye** 👁 a good **eye** 👁 private **eye** 👁 keep an **eye** on things 👁 easy on the **eye** 👁 more than meets the **eye** 👁 my **eye**! 👁 an **eye** to the main chance 👁 keep a weather **eye** open 👁 cock-**eyed** 👁 buck-**eyed** 👁 pie-**eyed** 👁 **eye**ful 👁 **eye**wash 👁 **eye**sore 👁 **eye** catching 👁 **eye**sight 👁 fore**sight** 👁 hind**sight** 👁 in**sight** 👁 out of **sight** 👁 second **sight** 👁 over**sight** 👁 un**sightly** 👁 **sightseeing** 👁 unfore**seen** 👁 unfore**see**able 👁 over**view** 👁 **view**points 👁 super**vision** 👁 **seers** and **vision**aries 👁 ETC

Sit with your back to the engine

Most people live with a bag over their head. They treat sight as a convenient method of avoiding bumping into things or watching television. Even the venturesome tend to see things in terms of something else. An acquaintance visited an architectural pleasure, subtly lit, exquisitely furnished, the walls hung with sparkling artworks. Breezing in he glanced around and asked, 'How much did *this* cost?' It's not that he's a nerd, show him a kumquat and he salivates. Play a Puccini aria and he radiates. But he's got tin eyes.

Another symptom of bagged head is fixed view. Art critic Brian Sewell is of the *'I know what I like'* school. He spends a lot of time in warfare with his colleagues – critics criticizing critics – I like it. Anyway he isn't totally ungenerous and apparently changed his will to bequeath his eyes to a rival art critic.

Most people's lives are like sitting facing forwards on a train where everything rushes past in a blur, instead of sitting with their back to the engine in visual comfort to let the landscape scroll by. Of course one can be less passive – driving on a motorway, claimed Reyner Banham, was like *'cresting through parallax like a surfer'*.

'Looking is giving a direction to one's sight,' observed Leonardo da Vinci. *'A bird is an an instrument ... it opens its wings quickly and sharply, bending in such a way that the wind... raises it. And this I have observed in the flight of a young falcon above the monastery at Vaprio, to the left of the Bergamo road, on the morning of 14 April 1500.'*

In contrast, most of us faced with a scene look at it rather than look into it. What you see and what you notice aren't the same thing. You will, of course, have noticed the deliberate mistake in the preceding paragraph – and it's not a spelling mistake.

Picture blind

There is a tribe in the Cameroon who have no pictorial art at all, and only make bands of geometric designs. When shown a photograph of a snake or an elephant it doesn't mean anything to them, the images could equally well be of cooking pots or missionaries. They are picture blind.[1]

In comprehending pictorial representation much is acquired through familiarity with paintings, drawings and photographs, rather than being a trait which is inherited. Mind you, my two-year-old grandson instantly recognized himself in a photo, and his mother too. And he hasn't been to art school or taken a course in visual communications.

Have you noticed that although plenty of people confess they have *'no ear'* for music you don't come across many who admit they have *'no eye'* for painting? Something to remember when looking at a picture we don't understand – and react angrily, feeling that we are being fooled. Perhaps rubbishing something because one doesn't understand it is a remnant of a survival instinct which threatens the unknown before it threatens you. As that famous Irish rugby player Willy McBride maintained, *'It always pays to get your retaliation in first.'*

Of course, it could just be, to quote a character in an Agatha Christie novel: *'if you don't see what a thing means, you must be looking at it the wrong way round.'*

'Strolling is the gastronomy of the eye. To walk is to vegetate, to stroll is to live.'

Honoré de Balzac

1. Nigel Barley. *The Innocent Anthropologist.* Penguin (Harmondsworth 1986)

Mindscaping

I have a penchant for scenarios which juggle with the natural order of things. Sometimes one discerns an incongruous situation; at other times it is camouflaged by commonsense. If I spot one, my first move is to put it down on paper before it gets forgotten.

One such sketch shows how, by looking at a scene in a certain way, a palm tree in the foreground aligns with one in the background and that by mentally squashing space the smaller seems to be propping up the larger. Another shows a palm balanced on the horizon, or maybe the horizon supporting the palm. The cluster of palms (right) ravels leaves with overlaps and transparencies to create several possible realities.

Closing each eye in turn gives such obviously different views that I find it surprising that stereoscopic vision was unknown to the ancient Greeks. They never realized that the two views combine into a single perception.[1] Anyway, in addition to the pair of eyes, there is the third eye located in the forehead (the pineal gland), the mind's eye which inhabits the brain, and what I like to think of as the nomad eye.

Assume you're lying on a beach. You're bored and to entertain yourself you play a mental game of sightseeing. You float your nomad eye high above the ground, move it around, look down, look behind things, and look back at yourself. The two eyes perceive, the third eye divines, the mind's eye composes, the nomad eye explores. Not many people know they have one.

1. R.L. Gregory. *Odd Perceptions*. Methuen (London 1986)

Jack can see he sees
    what he can see Jill can't see
and he can see
    that Jill can't see that she can't see
but he can't see WHY
    Jill can't see that Jill can't see.

R.D. LAING *(Knots)*

ACUITY IS SEEING THINGS OTHERS MAY OVERLOOK – IF YOU SEE WHAT I MEAN.

A MONK
ASKED HIS TEACHER
'WHAT IS MY SELF?'

HE ANSWERED
'SOMETHING HIDDEN
WITHIN YOUR SELF'.

THE MONK
ASKED
WHAT THIS WAS.

THE TEACHER
OPENED AND CLOSED
HIS EYES.

ZEN SAYING

'Do not assume – look!'   General Joe Stilwell

'If you do not raise your eyes you will think you are at the highest point.'   Antonio Porchia

'… the most important instrument of thought is the eye.'   Benoit Mandelbrot

'Every period has its own optical focus.'   László Moholy-Nagy

'Images have had a great influence on realities.'   Joseph Joubert

'Love comes in at the eye.'   W.B. Yeats

'Every man mistakes the limits of his vision for the limits of the world.'   Arthur Schopenhauer

'To gaze is to think.'   Salvador Dalí

'There are so many ear people and not many eye people …'   Damien Hirst

'One hundred tellings are not as good as one seeing.'   Chinese proverb

'Originality is simply a fresh pair of eyes.'   Woodrow Wilson

'The eye is not satisfied with seeing, nor the ear filled with hearing.'   Ecclesiasticus 1:8

'What is a man's eye, but a machine for the little creature that sits behind in his brain to look through.'   Samuel Butler

'… to unveil is to enchant.'   Shigeo Fukuda

'It is only with the heart that one can see rightly. What is essential is invisible to the eye.'   Antoine de Saint-Exupéry

'What you see is what you see.'   Frank Stella

29.1.1976. London: Moorfields Eye Hospital
The line of women in dressing gowns and black glasses hiding
bandaged eyes sit in their armchairs staring at the colour
television. On screen two American cops in black glasses stare
back at them.
Ian Breakwell's Diary 1964-1985

'What is originality? To see something that has no name … hence cannot be mentioned although it stares us in the face.' Friedrich Nietzsche

'I shut my eyes in order to see.' Paul Gauguin

'There is a difference if we see something with a pencil in our hand or without one.' Paul Valéry

'I paint what I know, not what I see.' Pablo Picasso

'Among a hundred men there is one who can think, but only one among a thousand can see.' John Ruskin

'Vision is the art of seeing things invisible.' Jonathan Swift

'The aspects of things that are most important for us are hidden because of their simplicity and familiarity.' Ludwig Wittgenstein

'I only have eyes for you.' Al Dubin

'Seeing is equivalent to knowing, thinking and also understanding. It is with this intuitive insight that I create.' Tak Igarashi

'Never look at the Brass, it only encourages them.' Conductor's axiom

'Seeing is not believing. Believing is seeing.' Robert Pirsig

'Isn't life a series of images that change as they repeat themselves?' Andy Warhol

'Men as a whole judge more with their eyes than with their hands.' Niccolò Machiavelli

'Man is a seeing creature who sees with his thoughts and thinks while seeing. ' Otl Aicher

'The entire course of our life depends on our senses, of which sight is the most universal and most noble. ' René Descartes

Alain de Botton[1]: 'Though constantly looking at people, one rarely forms new impressions of them, impressions implying the registration of novelty rather than the confirmation of prejudice. At only a few stages do we actively sketch a picture of someone – on first meeting, after a long absence, in the course of a furious row, after an illness, something to break the laziness of photographic habit.' **Italo Calvino**: 'We live in an unending rainfall of images. The most powerful media transform the world into images and multiply it by means of the phantasmagoric play of mirrors. These are images stripped of the inner inevitability that ought to mark every image as form and as meaning, as a claim on the attention and as a source of possible meanings. Much of this cloud of visual images fades at once, like the dreams that leave no trace in the memory, but what does not fade is a feeling of alienation and discomfort.' **Sean Cubitt**: 'It is a fallacy that seeing comes naturally. Even (and perhaps especially) in a culture so deeply visual as ours, we have to learn to see … Yet we spend no time at all teaching our children how to look at the visual culture in which they live … You can't always believe what you hear, but you'd better believe your eyes. Hearsay is well and good, but we'd sooner talk to an eyewitness.' **Charles Darwin** (impressions of the Brazilian rainforest): 'If the eye attempts to follow the flight of a gaudy butterfly, it is arrested by some strange tree or fruit; if watching an insect, one forgets it in the strange flower it is crawling over; if turning to admire the splendour of the scenery, the individual character of the foreground fixes the attention. The mind is a chaos of delight …' **Georges Braque**: 'No object can be tied down to any one sort of reality; a stone may be part of a wall, a piece of sculpture, a lethal weapon, a pebble on a beach, or anything else you like, just as this file in my hand can be metamorphosed into a shoehorn or a spoon, according to the way in which I use it. The first time this phenomenon struck me was in the trenches during the First World War when my batman turned a bucket into a brazier by poking a few holes in it with his bayonet and filling it with coke. For me this commonplace incident had a poetic significance: I began to see things in a new way.' **Galileo Galilei**: 'As I stinted neither pains nor pence, I was so successful that I obtained an excellent instrument which enabled me to see objects a thousand times as large and only one thirtieth of the distance in comparison to the naked eye.' **Stephen Jay Gould**: 'Primates are visual animals. No other group of mammals relies so strongly on sight. Our attraction to images as a source of understanding is both primal and pervasive.' **Edward Hopper**: The number of automobile registrations in the USA tripled during the 1920s. American painter Edward Hopper, one of the new drivers, chronicled a new landscape as seen from being seated in a car. A limited and restrictive vision but nevertheless a different one. Views of roads diminishing into the distance, scenes framed by the rear window, rows of houses paralleled by curbs. **Claude Monet**: 'Whenever you go out to paint try to forget what objects you have in front of you – a tree, a house, a field, or whatever … Merely think, here is a little squeeze of blue, here an oblong of pink, here a streak of yellow, and paint it just as it looks to you, the exact colour and shape, until it gives your own naïve impression of the scene before you.' **Paul Cézanne**: 'The same subject seen from a different angle gives a subject for study of the highest interest and so varied that I think I could be occupied for months without changing my place, simply bending more to the right or left.' **John Steinbeck**[2]: 'The Morgan Library has a very fine eleventh-century *Lancelot* in perfect condition. I was going over it one day and turned to the rubric of the first known owner dated 1221, the rubric a squiggle of very thick ink. I put a glass on it and there imbedded deep in the ink was the finest crab louse, *pfithira pulus*, I ever saw. He was perfectly preserved even to his little claws. I knew I would find him sooner or later because people of that period were deeply troubled with lice and other little beasties – hence the plagues. I called the curator over and showed him my find and he let out a cry of sorrow. *"I've looked at that rubric a thousand times,"* he said. *"Why couldn't I have found him?"'*
My mother: I made my weekly telephone call to my mother. 'What have you been up to this week', she asked – as usual. 'Nothing much,' I responded – as usual. Then adventurously said, 'I've been putting a book together.' 'Oh, what's it about?', she queried – with vague interest. My mother wasn't into reading, she equated it with working. 'Well', I improvised, 'it's about *seeing*.' 'Oh, I *see*' – she said. Then changed the subject. 'Are you *looking forward* to going on holiday next week?' 👁👁 The eye is constantly probing space. Take a scene, say a restaurant. Within a fraction of a moment the eye may focus on the silhouette of a waiter across the room, catch a reflection in a glass, note a crumb on the table, the glint of your companion's hair, a glimpse of a gesture. An assembly of impressions we register but rarely record. As the saying goes, in one eye and out the other. Here is one I did record. *'At this moment,'* I scribbled on the back of the hotel menu, *'I'm in a restaurant waiting between courses, scrutinizing a basket of fruit on a small round table. The green-grey of a pear against a beige wall, the sharp green of an apple overlapping the yellow-green of a lemon, a purple-black fig juxtaposed with a damasked plum,'* – I'd had a couple of stiff drinks – *'The sharp edge of a chair cutting the soft curve in the hang of a white tablecloth, the shadow thrown by a table leg darkly tinting a floral patterned carpet.'* A sensation Wordsworth described as eye music. I put the menu in my pocket.

1. Alain de Botton. *The Romantic Movement*. Picador (London 1995)   2. *Steinbeck. A Life in Letters*, ed. Elaine Steinbeck and Robert Wallsten. Heinemann (London 1975)   **Illustration**. CBS symbol. Design. William Golden (1951)

Illustration. Bob Gill

Note. Goethe thought thinking more interesting than knowing, but not so interesting as looking. Certainly when confronted by a boring conversation my concentration is inclined to fold its arms and divert itself by observing the visual dialogues of my surroundings: the chit-chat between dappled sunlight and a chintz fabric, the point of contact between the edge of a near chair and the silhouette of a far lampshade, the dissolving outline of a face as it passes in front of a bright light. As Georgia O'Keeffe pointed out, "nobody sees a flower — really — it is so small — we haven't time — and to see takes time, like to have a friend takes time."

Out of sight

'I see nobody
on the road,'
said Alice.

'I only wish
I had such eyes,'
the king remarked
in a fretful tone.

'To be able
to see Nobody!
And at that
distance too!

Why, it's as much
as I can do
to see real people,
by this light.'

Stereo vision was discovered by physicist Charles Wheatstone in 1838. Until then everyone assumed that we have two eyes for the same reason we have two kidneys: as a spare if the other gets damaged.

Each human eye has more than a million connections to the brain, which has more than ten thousand million cells, each of which has ten thousand further connections. The mechanism is in a constant state of change, losing millions of linkages every twenty-four hours. Luckily everything is renewed at least ten thousand times but not surprisingly, things can go radically wrong …[1]

We forget that we *learn* to see. We are not given the world but make it through experience, categorization and memory. Sometimes it all goes doolally. A man, born blind, had a successful operation which gave him sight. But sight for him meant a bewildering chaos of light and colour. He could only distinguish things through touch. Another patient could only see shapes and details but not both at the same time, so couldn't tell the difference between a ball of string or a salad bowl. Neurologist Oliver Sachs writes of a patient who was so confused that he looked at him with his ears rather than his eyes and took hold of his wife's head because he thought it was his hat. In another extreme case someone was struck blind and lost the very concept of seeing … they had absolutely no notion of colour, light or dark, no visual memories.

Then there was the maniac who stalked a famous singer thinking her responsible for the dead bodies which floated up through the floor at his home and communicated by changing the colour of their eyes. He killed his mother and father by shooting them in the eyes and was eventually captured in a room with seven television sets – tuned into static with eyes drawn on the screens with a black felt pen.

Different creatures see differently. The female praying mantis attacks anything smaller which moves. Males are smaller, thus a target. Since mating requires both proximity and movement – in this case a lethal combination – he is obliged to slowly creep closer, and closer, out of sight. If she turns in his direction he freezes. She doesn't perceive things if they don't move so if a male is raising a leg when she sees him, he keeps it like that until she looks away. If he makes it with a jump he's OK. If he misses, he's a snack!

The eye has arisen *de novo* some forty separate times in the history of its evolution which began well before 540 million years ago. Experiments reveal that beginning with a piece of 'virtual' skin, a computer can replicate the entire sequence from skin to eye in 400,000 generations.[2]

And then there is the extinct marine reptile, a species of ichthyosaurus, which had eyeballs one foot wide – bigger than the eye of the giant squid. Trilobites [SEE P329], crustacean-like creatures that inhabited the oceans for three hundred million years, had eyes made of crystal – or to be more precise calcite.[3] The same stuff as the white cliffs of Dover.

Of course what an eye sees depends on the creature looking through it. Beware of the catoblepas that can kill with a glare and the basilisk that kills with a look.

28.6.1985. London: St John Street, EC1
'A man is staring at a puddle. He inspects it from three different positions. Then he walks away, sighs, shrugs his shoulders and says: "With puddles like that there's no hope for us."'
Ian Breakwell's Diary 1964-1985

 1. R.L. Gregory and E.H. Gombrich. *Illusion in Nature and Art.* Duckworth (London 1973) 2. Steven Pinker. *How The Mind Works.* Penguin (London 1998) 3. Richard Fortey. *Trilobite!* HarperCollins (London 2000)

The photographer Robert Frank spent 1955 criss-crossing the United States, photographing cafeterias, flophouses, shoe-shiners, public lavatories, the abraded faces of retirees, assembly lines in Detroit. In the South a sheriff asked him what his business was. 'I'm looking,' he replied. He was given an hour to get out of town and in Arkansas spent three days in gaol for the same offence – observation. 'To look' was un-American.

Alfred Stieglitz. 'Photography is a fad well nigh on its last legs, thanks largely to the bicycle craze.'

Susan Sontag. 'Photographs may be more memorable than moving images, because they are a neat slice of time, not a flow … Each still photograph is a privileged moment turned into a slim object that one can keep and look at again.'

Flâneurs. Charles Baudelaire described walking down city streets in the 1850s as an adventure, more dramatic than any play, richer in ideas than any book. One should become, he suggested, a *flâneur* (a stroller or saunterer). *Flâneurs* don't have any practical goals in mind, aren't walking to get something, or to go somewhere. What *flâneurs* are doing is looking. Opening their eyes and ears to the scene around them, wondering about the lives of those they pass, constructing narratives about the houses, eavesdropping on conversations, studying how people dress and street life in general. *Flâneurs* relish what they discern and discover.

The Decisive Moment. 'To me, photography is the simultaneous recognition, in a fraction of a second, of the significance of an event as well as of a precise organization of forms which give that event its proper expression.' *Henri Cartier-Bresson*

Photograph. Henri Cartier-Bresson. *Place de L'Europe* (1932)

'Poets will know what I mean by slantwise: it is a way of looking through a difficult word or phrase to discover the meaning lurking behind the others.'

Robert Graves

ONE CAN LOOK AT SEEING $\begin{bmatrix}\text{SEE}\end{bmatrix}$ ONE CAN'T HEAR HEARING

Note from Marcel Duchamp's *The Green Box*

Sketch of street markings

Mae West

'It's always better to be looked over than overlooked.'

Memory of Sandy Lane Beach
in Barbados - late March 1991.

Illustration. Dr Martin's watercolour and sandpaper

Impressions, fragments, memories of places. How often has one seen a gem, an oddity, a surprise, a piece of information, an idea, only for it to dissolve in the memory and be forgotten. A visual encounter lost forever. Here are just a few of those I've kept and noted down.

Buenos Aires (1988). Reminiscent of Barcelona in the early 1950s. The single-decker *colectivos*, Mercedes buses, are still made in the style of the late 1940s. Flash Gordon grilles, moulded fenders, chromium trims, streamlined mascots, enamelled insignia, Mickey Mouse lettering and go faster stripes. The contemporary graffiti (political) are carefully painted. In lines, outlines, block-lettered, imitation stencil. No sloppy aerosol around here. Victorian cast-iron poster frames (imported from Birmingham) mounted on pedestals edged with thick-roped borders painted dark green, topped off with a cartouche displaying the city coat of arms in heraldic colours. One poster threatened the opening of a Wimpy. Yellow plastic paraboloid phone booths reminiscent of the 1960s – a bureaucrat's notion of modernity. A city of styles.

Stockholm. Black domes and cupolas, steep zinc roofs, battened, cleated and braced against snow and ice. Façades coloured in discreet greys, washed salmon pinks, faded lime greens, pale ochres, tints of terracotta. The quays packed with steamers, ferries, boats. Subway stations, excavated out of rock, masquerading as sets for *Lohengrin*. Convex traffic signs – you have a clue of what's coming up left and right. Land and sea, sentiment and severity.

Sydney. Cantilevered shop canopies; red-roofed suburbs; corrugated iron; wrought-iron balconies; shovel-shaped pavement corners; 'walking trouser' pedestrian crossing signs; half- and full-flush loos; bottle shops; overhead trains; Strine; the pale cream and barley sugar Opera House variously referred to as 'an old Olivetti Lettera 44 after an office party' or 'a broken Pyrex casserole dish in a brown cardboard box'.

Barcelona. Vast banks of birds wheeling over the port. The feel of the textured pavement under your shoes along the Paseo de Gracia. Truncated corners of buildings at cross-roads. Art Nouveau shop façades. The smashed crockery embedded in the walls of Gaudí's Parc Güell. The ridiculous Sagrada Familia.

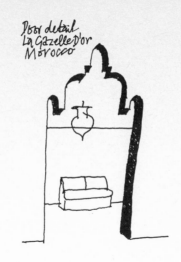

Door detail La Gazelle D'or Morocco

SEQUOIA ARIZONA

Blackened Snapper [Bajan delicacy]

ROMA

Fire Island Pines. A modish summer community (gay ghetto) on a long narrow strip of sand some fifty miles from New York. No roads, no cars, not many ladies either. Narrow undulating board walks thread through pines, poison ivy, and a thriving deer population. The planks are edged in white so you don't fall off the edge at night. Houses the haute couture of the 1950s, very classy domestic architecture. Sharp-edged, juxtaposed volumes, silver-bleached wood cladding. Large plate-glass windows, spacious interiors, glimpses of Knoll, Laverne and Miller furniture, Noguchi lamps, Ellsworth Kellys, Calder mobiles. Solari chimes, sundecks, swimming pools, Italian market umbrellas, barbecues. Fluttering flags, Japanese fish, colonial weather vanes, funky house names.

New York. Custard yellow cabs, scarlet fire hydrants, a cacophony of street signs clustered on intersection poles. The city authorities are against feet : NO STANDING, NO STANDING ANYTIME, and incongruously for Manhattan, NO STANDING EXCEPT WHEN HORSEDRAWN. NO PARKING signs come with qualifications : 8AM-11AM TUES-FRI, 7AM-4PM SCHOOL DAYS. DON'T EVEN THINK OF PARKING needs no qualification. Here are some others : TOW AWAY ZONE, RED ZONE FINE $185. SNOW ROUTE (looks odd in July), TRUCK ROUTE, CLEAR FIRE LANE, BUS LANE - BUSES ONLY. All with arrows up, down, left or right, or both ways.

Tokyo. Right-angled and diagonal corner to corner street crossings (zebra striped) yield six pedestrian routes. Extremely narrow tall buildings layered with shops, minuscule bars, offices, apartments, enormous glittering signs. Cabs : each signifying its company identity by the design, shape and colour of the illuminated plastic bobble on the roof. The doors open by remote control; the interiors furnished with antimacassars, translucent plastic covered seats, tiny television sets and drivers with white gloves.

Bangkok. Enormous hoardings of posters painted *in situ*. Lurid colours captioned with luxuriant curvaceous scripts. The hubbub, neon and nubility of Patpong. The temples which predated Disneyland by hundreds of years. Sadly becoming the armpit of the Orient.

Fort Worth (Texas). Signs around town : Chicken Fried Chicken, Fudge Love, Pain Management, Fried pies and Art Gallery, Environmental Contractor.

Airship at St Barts.

Looking towards
Santa Monica beach
from Room 832 Loews
Hotel 10.XI.89

Sydney Bridge built in 1931

A walk (London). Walking to work over the last few years (it's just round the corner) I've become pavement aware. They used to be paved with large irregular York stone slabs which looked great – especially when wet in the rain. Gradually they have been replaced (repairs to underground pipes) with rectangular cement paviors or even in dismal asphalt. Further repairs are introducing even smaller paviors. Easier to lift and replace, but dreary in the rain and dispiriting to the eye.

Berlin. Stayed at the Hotel Alexander [c.1990], just off Ku'damm, an Art Deco wet dream. I cut myself shaving laughing, thinking how to describe it – I can't. Went to a major Picasso exhibition in the Mies National Gallery. Some of it crude, much of it careless, most of it brash. Then every so often – whammo – an immaculate drawing, painting or sculpture. Concluded his genius was lack of inhibition. A drive around East Berlin. A cityscape designed by dogmatic bureaucrats: mean, cheap, nasty, degrading, depressing and dull. Judging by the faces of the citizens, who can doubt that urban environments affect the human spirit?

Delphi. I haven't been to ancient Delphi in Greece but this comment by journalist Geoffrey Smith touched a chord. 'It is,' he said, 'the raw material of unalloyed magic for those with eyes prepared to see and minds ready to imagine.'

Orange (Provence). Taken on a balmy summer evening to a concert in the Roman theatre. A shock on entering to be confronted by a vertical wall of faces. A totally different sensation to seeing the theatre empty with the spaciousness of rising tiers and the odd seated tourist putting everything into scale. And from where, in those times, could so many have come to fill the tiers? Yesterday I was looking at a treatise by Geofroy Tory (1480-1533), designer of Champ Fleury alphabets. Describing the proportions and pictorial associations of letters, the D, he said, is in the image of 'a theatre stage, like the one I saw in a city near Avignon … This stage, which is straight at the front and circular at the back, can well be taken as the letter D.' Was he referring, I wondered, to the Théâtre Antique just north of Avignon, in Orange?

Turkey. Rousseau-like growling lions and tigers painted on the front grills of the trucks. And the ubiquitous split arrow. Why, I wonder, the bottom half? [SEE P201].

Sicily-Concordia

metaphor of a fig tree

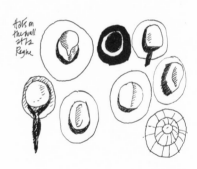

Hats on
the wall
at the
Reyne

tables at REMETZO/Spetses

Zihuatanejo (Mexico). Architect Ricardo Legoretta's Hotel Camino Real (now Westin Ixtapa). A painted raw concrete structure. Dominantly coloured with a ginger diarrhoea brown juxtaposed with glowing mauve and hysterical pink walls, niches of French ultramarine, nuclear yellow window apertures. The restaurant enveloped in a luminous vermillion and oyster white - a cooler shade of condensed milk. Altogether a colour triumph.

Door hinge. Sometimes I feel like a hinge. I'm always going somewhere or coming back, entering a situation or leaving it. Living in the cracks of the door jamb, in between one space and another.

Jerusalem. Being shown around the new Supreme Court, a building of pale honey-coloured stone, by a friend – Yarom Vardimon. He stopped; 'look at the pavings,' he said. I looked. 'What do you see?' he asked. 'Well, uhm, ah, not much, apart from the nicely hammered texture.' 'Of course,' he replied testily, 'but look at their handwriting.' Sure enough, the stipple of each pavior was slightly different from the next – the effect of how each mason held his chisel and wielded his mallet. With time and patience, by reading the stones, one could have calculated the number of masons who'd worked on the site. On Saturday the hotel hung a sign on an elevator which stated The Shabbatt Elevator. During Shabbatt (Sabbath) the orthodox Jew doesn't do anything – not drive a car, not cook a meal, nor push a button. This particular elevator moved up and down all day, automatically stopping at each floor. I'm undecided whether that's lateral thinking or cheating.

Brazil. I haven't been there probably because I've read that it's home to the bloodsucking fishlet known as *candiru*. This swims up a man's urine stream and lodges itself in the urethra with a ring of retrorse spines preventing its removal. One of the very rare circumstances in which doctors perform a peotomy. You've guessed right.

Udaipur (Rajastan). The hotel on an artificial lake, confronted by a half-submerged statue. The palace with elephant parking bays, corrugated snake-like channels in the pavings so the rain ripples off the terraces, intricately carved window screens so the women could observe without being observed, the small room with tiny bits of glass embedded in the dome to magically create stars when you light a candle in the evening.

PALM TREES ON VENICE BEACH LA.

BAR TABAC DES ALPILLES

View from Katia restaurant

Bruno Munari having ice cream at Salgeri in Verona

24·4·72

Los Angeles. Dilapidated trees on Venice beach. The view from the Getty Museum reveals a permanent sulphurous yellow smudge over downtown. The Getty Museum a stage-set masquerading as a solid structure. One day, in the near future, when they have concreted over the world, everywhere will look like Los Angeles but not necessarily with the sun. As Noël Coward (and Fred Allen) commented, California was a nice place – if you were an orange.

Otranto. A small sleepy port on the eastern heel of Italy. The cathedral encapsulates the human polarities of construction and destruction. In 1165 Panaleone designed and laid out a huge mosaic – the Tree of Life – on the floor of the the nave. It illustrates the history of the world from Adam and Eve to his own time. In 1480 the Turks besieged Otranto. Eventually it capitulated and the Vizier, enraged by their resistance, had the Archbishop sawn in half and decapitated all 800 inhabitants. Their skulls and bones are jammed together in glass-fronted cupboards behind the altar.

Klondikes. There have always been cities which attracted entrepreneurs in search of wealth and fame, bread and butter. When I'm in Manhattan I can imagine I'm in ancient Alexandria, Tyre, or Constantinople. Walk down Fifth Avenue and you'll see why. The fat, skinny, swarthy, blonde, black, smart, decrepit, sharp-eyed. Hopeful, desperate, complacent, resigned. You hear English, Spanish, Ethopian, Hindi, Yiddish, Cantonese, Korean, Swahili. [SEE P392].

A Restaurant. One evening I dined in a new local Chinese restaurant of ineffable sadness. An open rectangular space. The top half capped with off-white speckled acoustic ceiling tiles punctured by recessed lights spreading an even and unrelenting bluish glow. Pale peach walls unrelieved by kitschscapes or knick-knacks. The bottom half of the room layered with salmon sheened tablecloths dotted with clusters of condiments, plastic ashtrays, and pinched tin vases holding a lonely scrawny flower. A visit to the toilet revealed diluted toffee-tinted marshmallow tiles, pink-tinged fluorescent strip lights, a blush mirror, yellow toilet rolls, and an insubstantial silver-tinselled decorative door handle. Service came with a well-meant smile, dark blue polyester suit, white nylon shirt, awkward collar, tasteless tie. The meal was indescribable.

Impressions noted by others. Miami is a shopping centre with live-in customers. Tokyo is the world's biggest video installation. London Docklands isn't a real place – it's a building developers' theme park. Mark Twain on Bermuda: it has many sights but they are easily avoided. And painter Francis Bacon, receiving an invitation to visit Switzerland: 'What for,' he ungraciously responded, 'to see all those effing views?', and declined. And El Dorado in Venezuela, I've read, is a dump.

Out of season. Strange sojourn in an expensive hotel by a beach, in the semi-tropics. In the cavernous empty marble reception a white grand piano cabled to a black box plugged into a socket playing anodyne melodies at happy hour. The ivories and black keys eerily play by themselves. In the dark pink bathroom mirror, one appears as tanned as a local – the truth is otherwise – every silver lining has a cloud. In the evening, outside the window, the garish neon electrochemical colours along the deserted promenade clash and meld with the liquorice and melba sunset. Corpulent pelicans crashland on the sea and deftly swivel on impact to brake with their bums.

Moscow. Pitched green roofs. Basins: hot tap always on the right … almost always. Doilies, & doilies, & doilies. Condiments: one hole for pepper, several for salt … well usually. Shape of military caps. Stalls selling prescription spectacles. Matryoshka dolls. Dismal gravy-brown interiors. Cyrillic. Men have gallant manners (my wife tells me). Striking-looking young ladies. Myriads of officious old ladies sitting around fulfilling some function or other. Formula One speed subway escalators. 'Health thro' strength' statuary. Kitsch ornaments. Holding up hand in street to signal cruising drivers for a negotiably priced taxi ride. More magnificent nineteenth-century buildings than I thought. Plus brain-dead politbureau architecture. Restoration time for churches. Rare: drinking water, decent postcards, cafés. Surprising number speak good English. Restaurants: you are fed rather than served. Bolshoi Theatre: seating is on upright chairs fixed with a lateral wood joist to establish rows. The curtain densely embroidered with stars, hammers and sickles and CCCPs.

Burt Lancaster checking the menu at da Franz: Venice Biennale

Terraced hills northern cyprus

Golden Bee Supper 8·10·96 Souvenir for Serge Serov

Hotel Restaurant. I was in the darkly lit opulent Hotel Ritz restaurant in Barcelona late one evening. The service was extremely slow. To pass the time I mentally drew the place: Hard edges cutting into soft shapes, shadows fuzzing and fading. Lights blurring and twinkling, folds creased, billowed or crumpled. Sharp corners and wobbly curves. Colours accentuating, blending and jumping. When we try to explain visual matters through words our ears come so far forward they blinker our eyes. I sympathize with the man who said that he couldn't actually describe a hippopotamus but he'd sure recognize one if he saw one.

Toronto. Black squirrels.

Scottish Highlands. Gorse (Yellow). Heather. Bracken. Bagpipes. B&B. Sheep. Pebbledash. Bagpipes. 1950s. Red-grey granite. Tartan. Pebbledash. Knobby people. Shortbread. Theme Park. A damp rockery. Bagpipes. Rain & wet. Mist & damp. Cold & chill. Pebbledash. Tacky souvenirs. Bagpipes. Arran sweater patterns. A damp rockery.

Bequia. Grenadines. Guernsey cows grazing among the palm trees. [SEE P491].

Venice. Peggy Guggenheim's Alexander Calder's silver bedhead. S. Maria de Miracole. Bilaterally asymmetric gondolas. Gondola rowlocks. Terraced roof decks. Secret gardens. Gently stencilled Bodoni street names. Vaporetti station for Ghetto signalled in Hebrew. Carnival mask shops. Foot bridges. Façades. Pink, ochre, deep terracotta, deep green shutters.

'How these curiosities
would be quite forgott,
did not such idle fellowes
as I am putt them downe.'
John Aubrey

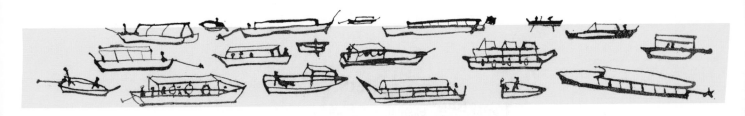

River of Kings - Bangkok - as
seen from room 1512 at the
Oriental Hotel.

Illustration. Indian ink and industrial tape

Language of flowers

From Alice M. Fennell

Sir, While stopping at Harrow-on-the-Hill tube station, I noticed that when the Daffodils are closed up they shake their heads. And that when they are opened out they nod there heads! I dont think that any body has noticed this, so that I think I'm the only one who has noticed it.

Yours sincerly,
ALICE M. FENNELL (aged 8),
Rickmansworth, Hertfordshire.
March 28.

The Times, 1 April 1988

Wallace Stevens

'Realism is a corruption of reality.'

Illustration. French agricultural magazine

'... art changes our understanding of the conventions by altering our perceptions.' *Sol LeWitt*

Maurice Saatchi: 'In his film *Rashomon*, Kurosawa showed us four very different versions of "reality". In twelfth-century Kyoto, a couple are ambushed: the wife is raped, the husband killed. After the event four people recall the attack. By altering the perspective and order of events for each character, we perceive the unreality of their contrasting perceptions. This is perhaps why English law would not rely on any of the versions provided by Kurosawa's witnesses. Our legal system prefers the principle of *mens rea*, the guilty mind. What matters is not what was perceived in the eyes of observers, but what was perceived in the mind of the accused.'

'Reality is a creation of the nervous system.' *Harry Jerison*

Robert Pirsig: 'We build up whole cultural patterns based on past "facts" which are extremely selective. When a new fact comes in that does not fit the pattern we don't throw out the pattern. We throw out the fact.'

'Perception of the strange is hindered by strangeness; recognition of the familiar is prevented by familiarity.' *Hugo von Hofmannsthal*

Virginia Woolf: 'We are floating in a medium of vast extent, always drifting uncertainly, blown to and fro; whenever we think we have a fixed point to which we can cling and make fast, it shifts and leaves us behind; if we follow it, it eludes our grasp, slips away, and flees eternally before us. This is our natural state and yet the state most contrary to our inclinations. We burn with desire to find a firm footing, an ultimate, lasting base on which to build a tower rising up to infinity, but our whole foundation cracks and the earth opens.'

'... the worth of sights is dependent more on the quality of one's vision than on the objects viewed.' *Alain de Botton*

Ian Stewart: 'Reality is only one possible state of the universe from an infinite range of potential states, a slender thread of the actual winding through the space of the potential.'

'Love is a delightful interval between meeting a girl and discovering that she looks like a haddock.' *John Barrymore*

David Ruelle: 'When we open our eyes we receive an enormous amount of information from the outside world. But because this outside world has a lot of structure, the messages received by the eyes are highly redundant. The visual system … performs data compression. This data compression begins at the level of the retina, and even before reaching the visual cortex the visual messages are already highly processed and compressed. What we see are interpreted images, interpreted by a visual system that has been shaped by natural evolution to cope with a certain type of outside physical reality.'

'Reality. The dream of a mad philosopher. That which would remain in the cupel if one should assay a phantom. The nucleus of a vacuum.' *Ambrose Bierce*

Quercy: 'One can affirm the presence or perception of an object when it is present and perceived, when it is absent and perceived, when it is neither present nor perceived.'

'The spectacle has changed, but our eyes are the same.' *Joseph Joubert*

Aldous Huxley: 'To be shaken out of the ruts of ordinary perception, to be shown for a few timeless hours the outer and the inner world, not as they appear to an animal obsessed with words and notions, but as they are apprehended, directly and unconditionally, by Mind at Large – this is an experience of inestimable value to everyone.'

'To have *discernment* (precision in perception).' *Robert Bresson*

'This world is only in my imagination; the only reality is the imagining.' *Gyorgy Kepes*

Cesare Pavese : 'A true revelation, it seems to me, will only emerge from stubborn concentration on a solitary problem. I am not in league with inventors or adventurers, nor with travellers to exotic destinations. The surest – also the quickest – way to awake the sense of wonder in ourselves is to look intently, undeterred, at a single object. Suddenly, miraculously, it will reveal itself as something we have never seen before.'

'Perceptions ... are according to the measure of the individual and not according to the measure of the universe.' *Francis Bacon*

Daniel Boorstin : 'We have used our wealth, our literacy, our technology, and our progress to create the thicket of unreality which stands between us and the facts of life ... experiences of our own contriving begin to hide reality from us ... transforming us from travellers into tourists.'

'Truth is like a diamond cut with many facets, each of which can be cut, polished and set to advantage.' *George Santayana*

Josef Perner : 'There is a difference between knowing that something has happened, remembering that it happened, and thinking that it happened. The representations are linked with the human ability to understand how others view the world, and through this to an understanding of how an individual views his or her world.'

'... We are surrounded by screens ... the artist is the one who pulls them down.' *Jean Renoir*

Robert Pirsig : 'The culture in which we live hands us a set of intellectual glasses to interpret experience with, and the concept of the primacy of subjects and objects is built right into these glasses. If someone sees things through a somewhat different set of glasses or, God help him, takes his glasses off, the natural tendency of those who still have their glasses on is to regard his statements as somewhat weird, if not actually crazy.'

'Our habits of inspection and our view of the world are reconfirmed each time we concentrate our vision or avert our eye.' *Julian Barnes*

Emilio Ambasz : 'I am interested in daily rituals: the ritual of sitting in a courtyard, slightly protected from your neighbour's view and the strong wind, gazing up at the stars; the ritual of the father sitting on his bed and seeing his children playing in another room ... an acknowledgement that there exists a certain distance between generations ... made up of people of different ages, with different modes of perception and ways of seeing reality.'

'Art must take reality by surprise.' *Françoise Sagan*

Vaclav Havel : 'We have to abandon the arrogant belief that the world is merely a puzzle to be solved, a machine with instructions for use waiting to be discovered, a body of information to be fed into a computer in the hope that, sooner or later, it will spit out a universal solution.'

'In this universe of mirrors and metaphors, man reflects and parallels all the realities ...' *John Fowles*

Julian Schnabel : 'A painter's job is to invent new ways that form can be looked at, to organize things in a way so that people notice things they didn't before. It's about letting your mind go somewhere new. Hopefully, what paintings do is give you an opportunity to inhabit another part of yourself and to see the world in a new light.'

'Fiction reveals truths that reality obscures.' *Jessamyn West*

The proposition that
half a glass of wine
could be perceived as
being half full or half
empty, depending whether
one was an optimist or
pessimist, could — by an
iconoclast — be rendered
thus...

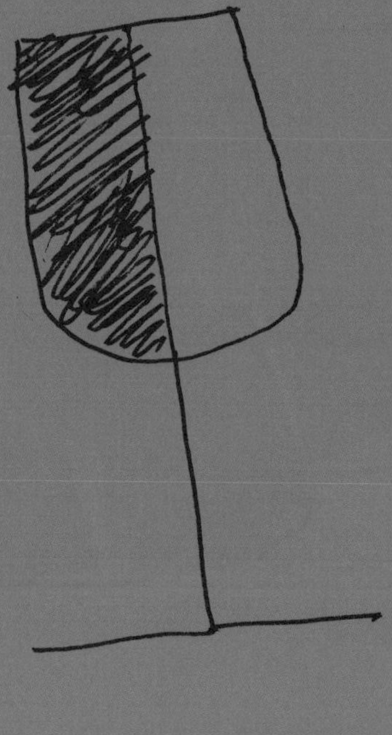

The NECKER Cube

Nummulites are fossilized shells. Lots of them are littered around the Pyramids and the ancient Greek geographer Strabo thought they were remains of rations dished out to slaves who were building them. After all why else would there be seashells in the desert? In 1838 the first dinosaur bone was discovered, or more accurately phrased, identified as such. Suddenly they were turning up all over the place and museums soon became stuffed with dinosaur bones. The point is that they didn't just suddenly appear, the fossils had been there all the time, they just hadn't been recognized for what they were.

We don't see what we see. We see what we want to see.

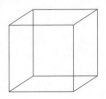

This Necker Cube, as it is called in scientific circles, demonstrates that we can see something in two different ways although what we're looking at remains unchanged.

Imagine that the cube is made of translucent glass so that in looking you can't tell the front surface from the back surface. In other words back or front is dependent on what you think it is ...

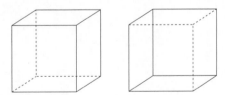

Same picture, different perception!

The image opposite is a favourite illustration from the 'now you see it, now you don't' school of perceptual psychology. Look at it in one way and it's a profile of an unattractive lady with a hooked nose. Look at it in another way and it's a side view portraying a young girl with her face turned away. When the mind has seized on one view, it's amazingly difficult to get it to switch one's perception to see it from another point of view.

Reality is perception – not a reflection of truth.

Drunken man reels
into a pub carrying
a goose under his arm.

'Who's that pig?'
asks the publican
with distaste.

The drunk slurs in reply,
'this is not a pig,
it's a goose.'

'I know that,'
says the publican,
'I was asking the goose.'

ɷ

An old man dies
and wakes up in a
strange ethereal world.

The first thing he sees
is another old man with
a curvaceous young lady
sitting on his lap.

'This must be Heaven!'
he exclaims,
'Is she your reward?'

'No,' replies the
other old man,
'We're in hell and
I'm her punishment!'

A parallelepipedom is a regular solid bounded by six plane surfaces – a cube for example.

Looking out of the window of a train as I was passing through the Devonshire countryside, I was struck by the thought that maybe all those sheep grazing in the fields really were only half an inch high (12.5 mm). When I arrived at my destination I checked the height of a man on the station concourse. Discreetly (and quickly) holding out my thumb, at about one hundred paces away, I took his measure. He was one inch tall (25 mm). Whatever height you think you are is evidently an illusion. Some years later on one balmy evening under the stars in Turkey I was having a drink and gazing at the crescent moon. I noticed that it mirrored the crescent made by its reflection on the surface of my wine, as seen from an angle over the rim of the glass. Recalling the Devonshire sheep got me wondering how big the moon was. Holding out my arm (discreetly once again) I measured it between thumb and forefinger. A doubletake. It was barely an eighth of an inch (4 mm). And to think that this tiny thing was not only the subject of innumerable songs but also the symbol of the Islamic world.

Mind sets

In Plato's allegory of the human condition, we are tied to chains in a dark cave, able to see a passing parade of objects we think real but which are only the shadows cast by the objects. Since the Renaissance it has been held that the world is a tangible phenomenon slowly being unravelled by science. An alternative view is that it's a mirage, a construct of the imagination. A web of ideas, a fabric of our own making.[1]

Stephen Hawking: 'We see the universe the way it is because if it were different, we would not be here to observe it.' And, on a less metaphysical plane, Werner Heisenberg: 'What we observe is not nature itself, but nature exposed to our method of questioning.' Or plainly put, what a piece of bread looks like depends on whether you're hungry or not. Our notion of reality is moulded by our parents, schooling and culture. Since we all come from differing backgrounds so do our perceptions of things. That is not to say we experience totally different things but different aspects of those things. The Hindu's view of a cow in no way corresponds to that of a canning factory meatpacker, and in Istanbul they keep their pigs in the zoo instead of making them into sausages. We build our own models[2] of reality. Even those created by Newton or Einstein or fashioned by Picasso or James Joyce, are merely alternative versions of the same hologram. To alter our particular personal construct requires a substantial leap of imagination as we need to see things from a new angle. And only when this is expressed through a creative action, can it be experienced by others. At which point their perceptions can also change.

Tolstoy described it this way: first one had to evoke a feeling in oneself; and having evoked it in oneself by means of movements, lines, colours, or words, then one had to transmit that feeling so others could share the same feeling. When Picasso showed his portrait of Gertrude Stein to someone (probably Alice) they remarked it didn't look much like her. It will, prophesied Picasso. Of course now it does. Another oft-quoted story makes the point. Seeing *Les Demoiselles d'Avignon* at an exhibition opening a man approached Picasso (who was hanging around) and asked why he didn't paint people the way they looked. 'Well, how do they look?' asked Picasso. The man took a photograph of his wife from his wallet and handed it over. Picasso looked at the picture; then handing it back, said, 'She is small, isn't she. And flat too.' What things look like is a convention not a truth, as how we see things is a weird amalgam of observer and observed. We have to accept the uncomfortable fact that much of what seems real to us is governed by our own perceptions. During his lifetime Van Gogh couldn't give his paintings away yet eighty years after his death *Sunflowers*, all fourteen of them, was sold for £24.75 million. The painting hadn't changed but aesthetic and visual attitudes had. Now the artworld considers there is a strong possiblity that it is a fake. Naturally the owners, a Japanese Corporation, won't even countenance such allegations. Of course you may find all this sort of thing a bit tedious and prefer to be a goldfish. The awareness of a goldfish is about four seconds, so it never gets bored as each trip around the bowl is a new journey. It has advantages.

★
Bishop Berkeley was the very same Bishop after whom Berkeley in California was named. And Zenon Pylyshyn – he's a cognitive scientist not a character out of a sci-fi novelette – reckons that rocks are smarter than cats because rocks have the sense to go away when you kick them.

1 · Joseph Chilton Pearce. *The Crack in the Cosmic Egg.* Lyrebird Press (London 1973)   2 · Howard Gardner. *Art, Mind and Brain.* Basic Books (New York 1982)

There is a theory that when you aren't looking at

something it doesn't exist. A situation obliquely analagous

to a blind man in a dark room looking for a black cat

which isn't there. Certainly when I look at something, then

shut my eyes, I can't see whatever it is — so can't be sure that

it's still there. I could give it a kick to reassure myself like

Samuel Johnson who, on hearing Bishop Berkeley* declare

that reality was only a state of mind, kicked a rock to

disprove him. But what I kick might be something else, so

all I know is that when I open my eyes — it's come back

again. I'm reminded of the Lennon-McCartney lyric which

asks : 'What do you see when you turn out the light ? —

I can't tell you, but I know it's mine.'

Salvador Dali invented the term
The Paranoiac-Critical Method
to describe transformations of
one image to another.

' ... I was looking for an address
in a pile of papers when suddenly
I was struck by a reproduction
of a face I thought was by
Picasso ...' said Dali referring
to the postcard shown here.

If you look at the postcard this
way round – through half closed
eyes – exert some imagination,
and you'll see what Dali meant.

Dali reproduced the illusion in an
oil painting he called *Paranoid
Face* which is shown on the page
opposite.

Paranoid Face (1934/5)

Perception is how we see the outside from the inside.

This is undertaken by networks of brain cells which each deal with shapes, colours, forms and so forth. One particular set of cells responds to horizontal lines, another to vertical and diagonal lines, and another to angles and corners. Some cultures have a bias for one or the other.

In industrial urban societies the environment basically consists of lines and angles. Rectangular buildings and boxy rooms, elevated power cables, straight or curved roads, and parallel tracks of railways. We live in a geometry of linear perspective. Zulus, on the other hand, have a circular culture. They live in round huts with round doors, they even plough in curves. Cree Indians don't like right-angles or curves. They prefer diagonals and live in lodges built like wigwams, complicated structures of poles built every which way at every conceivable angle.

Why such preferences exist, or persist, hasn't been adequately explained but it could be a matter of what you get used to. Stanford psychologists raised two batches of kittens. Some were brought up seeing only vertical stripes and others seeing only horizontal stripes. When they grew up they were released and spent the rest of their lives seeing the world either in vertical or lateral terms. [SEE P105]. This implies that environments also shape our preferences, but doesn't explain why some cultures prefer to be rectangular or curvaceous or angular to begin with.

I'd like to be a Gecko, not permanently, but for ten minutes or so. Geckos are charming small lizardy creatures with suction pads for feet. They live vertically. Walls are their *terra firma*. For them trees grow sideways, hills are sky, pavements are walls. Our heads may be in the clouds but our feet are always on the ground and even if you wear spectacles which make you see the world upside down, you adjust in a day or so, and see everything the right way up. Take the glasses off and you'll have another few upside-down days until everything reverts back to normal.

'Things,' said film director Robert Bresson, 'are made more visible not by more light, but by the fresh angle at which I regard them.'

Physicists are notorious for their lack of scientific rigour in comparison to mathematicians. A meticulous mathematician, a sloppy physicist, and an even sloppier astronomer are walking in Scotland. They see a black sheep in the middle of a field. 'Look,' exclaims the astronomer, 'all Scottish sheep are black!' 'No, no!' the physicist responds, 'Some Scottish sheep are black!' The mathematician shakes his head, 'Gentlemen, all we can truly say is that in Scotland there exists at least one field, containing at least one sheep, at least one side of which is black.'

Silhouette of Nevsky Prospect in St Petersburg

Street markings, Pembridge Road, Notting Hill, London

Images can often be ambiguous. This jotting records a scene I saw of holidaymakers frolicking in the ocean. It only occurred to me afterwards that someone might interpret it as the gruesome aftermath of a chainsaw massacre.

The split arrow. I've noticed that just using the bottom half is the norm throughout the Arabic-speaking world.   I don't know why.

Fletcher (flecher, flechier) is the trade name for an arrow-maker.

Philip Guedalla   'I had always assumed that cliché was a suburb in Paris, until …

… I discovered it was a street in Oxford.'

|| **Cliché** (kliʃe).
pple. of clicher s
the sound prod
on the molten
perh. the i
block ; a ca
type of a v
b. fig. A
place pl

832. [Fr., subst. use of pa.
ereotype, said to be imit. of
ced by dropping the matrix
netal (cf. G. *klitsch* slap, clash,
med. source).] A stereotype
t or 'dab'; *esp.* a metal stereo-
ood-engraving used to print from
ereotyped expression, a commo
rase 1892.

Cliché, French for printing block, is a graphic means of repetition *ad infinitum* or, as Marshall McLuhan put it, a ditto device. 'I want to be a machine,' declared Andy Warhol, called his studio 'The Factory', and turned out up to eighty canvases a day, each of which looked much like the next. An art form which ironically echoed the repetitious commercial messages which assail us every day. And Max Ernst used the cliché as a creative instrument by assembling montages from old steel engravings.

Clichés survive long after the conditions that produced them are dead. We go on about pigs in pokes and dogs in mangers, whatever they are, but nevertheless we still know what the cliché signifies. Clichés are not to be sneezed at, as Sam Goldwyn appreciated when, on hearing a complaint that a script was full of them, promptly told his director to introduce some more.

Clichés are the fastest way to express something. I know, because I've been faced with a situation when 'my blood ran cold'; have been 'rooted to the spot with fear', have 'stood at the edge of an abyss', and a few other dodgy situations I'm too embarrassed to mention. Although I detest obviousities it's difficult to think of less hackneyed phrases which carry the same emotional charge. Although irritating, the cliché is probably better than anything else you can think of to replace it.

This letter, written to a newspaper in a debate over the use of clichés by a certain Mr Graham Hopkins, says it all: 'It's the same old story isn't it? In a nutshell, we've had all and sundry who, by and large, and with all due respect, can't see beyond the end of their noses. They're in their ivory towers telling us that clichés are nothing to write home about (Call me old fashioned, but ... G2, January 2). I say hold your horses. I might rock the boat and ruffle some feathers, but in this day and age, the conventional wisdom smells fishy to me. Indeed, you might think I've got bigger fish to fry or that I've got a chip on my shoulder, but clichés are meat and drink to me. Sure, they can stick out like a sore thumb, but mark my words (and let me say this loud and clear) a good, bad or indifferent cliché, time and time again, can warm the cockles of your heart. I could bang on about this until the cows come home, but at the end of the day, when the chips are down, a cliché is par for the course. I realise that I've got my work cut out but there's no two ways about it: to some, clichés might stink to high heaven, but I'll use them until hell freezes over.'[1]

Writer Alain de Botton holds another view suggesting that clichés are inadequate since they do no more than 'inspire us to believe that they adequately describe a situation while they're merely grazing its surface'.[2]

The oldest (and commonest) visual cliché is the pointing finger. To point is vulgar, at least that's what my mother taught me. A social attitude she shared with film director John Ford who said it was only socially permissible to point at pimps, pastries and producers. He was, of course, referring to Hollywood producers. Those obese, cigar-chomping philistines, bent on sacrificing art in catering to the lowest common denominator.

The second oldest visual cliché has to be the pictorial arrow. Driving from Rome to Brescia artist Jean-Michel Folon, reckoned he counted over a thousand different versions.[3] A clear indication that to provoke an immediate response to an authorative instruction – the cliché is essential. However, remember this, in creative endeavour one benchmark which separates sheep from goats is the ability to stroke a cliché until it purrs like a metaphor.

Photograph. Herbert Spencer. 1. *The Guardian*, 3 January 2001 2. Alain de Botton. *How Proust can Change Your Life.* Picador (London 1997) 3. George Nelson. *How to See.* Little, Brown (Boston 1977)

The enormous sculpture of the hand of the emperor Constantine (c. 4th century), Piazza del Campidoglio, Rome

Photograph. Arnold Schwartzman

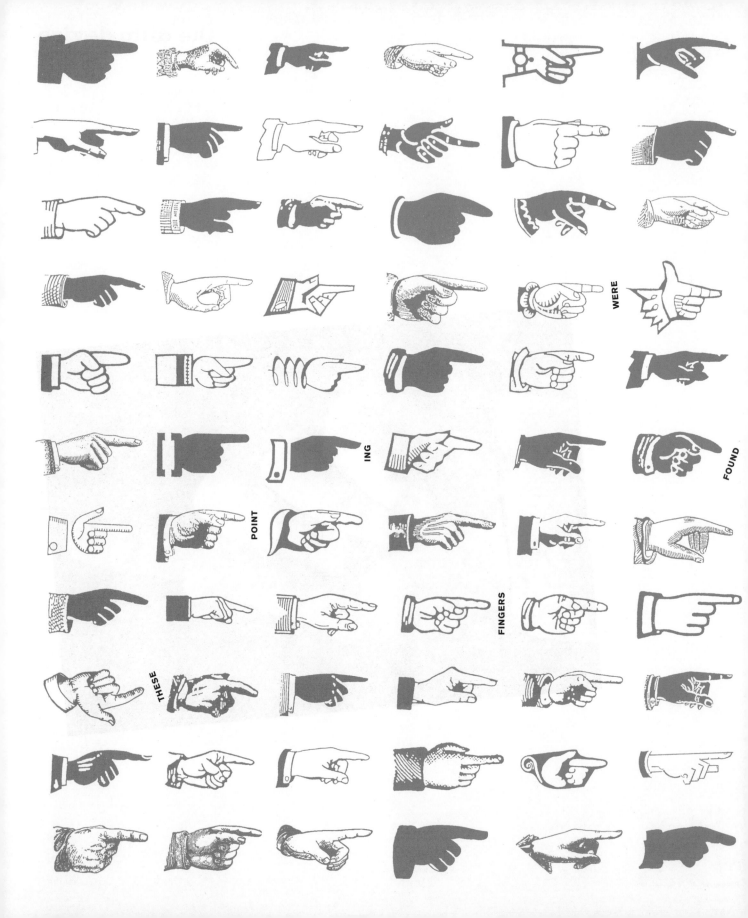

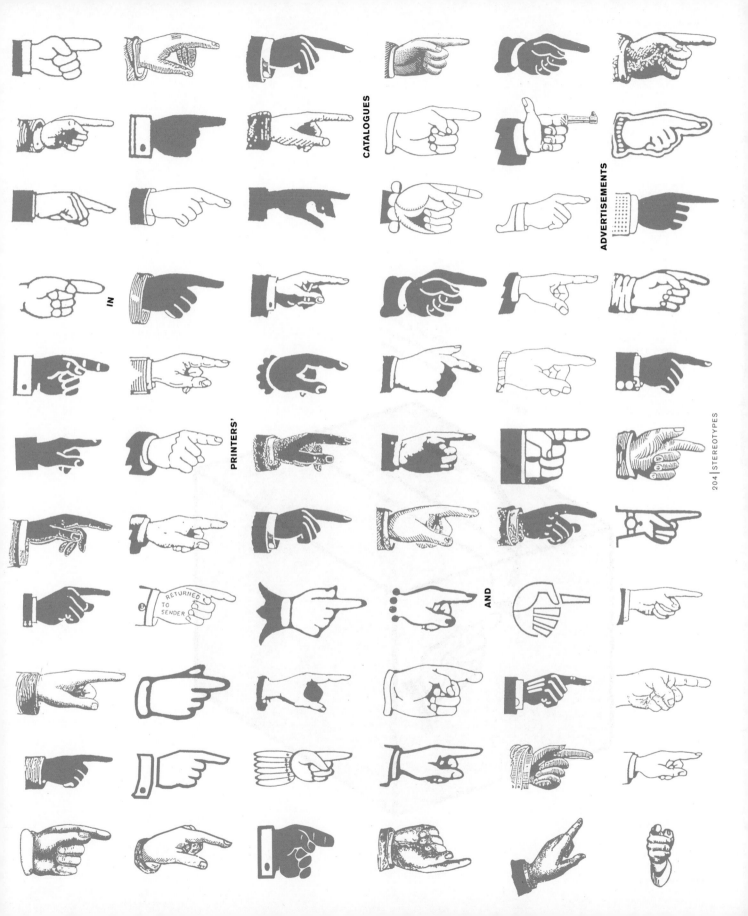

CATALOGUES

ADVERTISEMENTS

IN

PRINTERS'

AND

RETURNED
TO
SENDER

These visual clichés printed on a transit carton were intended to convey information to the illiterate, or to bypass language barriers.

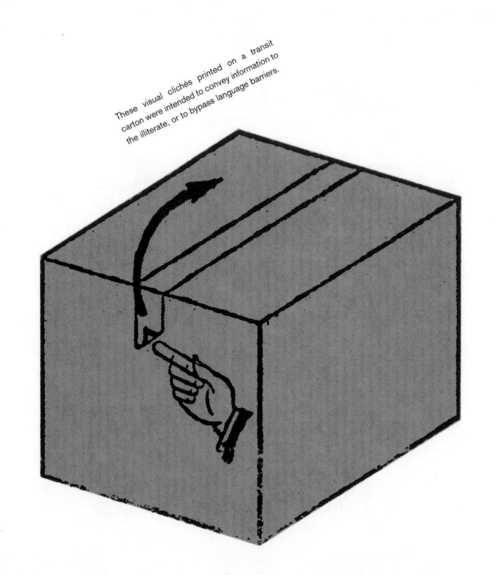

'A CLICHÉ IS A BANKRUPT IDEA.'
John McConnell

'I TAKE A CLICHÉ AND TRY TO ORGANIZE ITS FORMS
TO MAKE IT MONUMENTAL. THE DIFFERENCE IS OFTEN
NOT GREAT, BUT IT IS CRUCIAL.'
Roy Lichtenstein

'EVERYTHING HAS BEEN SAID BEFORE BUT BECAUSE NO ONE
LISTENS YOU ALWAYS HAVE TO SAY IT AGAIN.'
André Gide

'THE CLICHÉ IS DEAD POETRY.'
Gerald Brenan

over the top

Brasilia.

Exciting!
From Tropitone

Here is contemporary
Bauhaus design to enhance
your lifestyle. A dramatic
statement inspired by that
most beautiful South
American capital. And it's only
one of seven complete
groups of casual furniture in
an almost infinite number of
colors. Send $3 for our
48-page full color catalog
and the name of your
nearest dealer. See why
people say, "Tropitone.
Probably the finest."

Tropitone **East**: P.O. Box 3197,
Sarasota, FL 33578
West: 17101
Armstrong, Irvine,
CA 92714

tropitone

I recently came across this advertisement in
a magazine. It leaves no stone unturned. It's
way over the top, or, as they say in Berlin,
there's more than one way to bake a parrot.

The poster shown opposite was designed by
Jan Tschichold in 1938. At the time it was an
innovative orchestration of graphic invention:
the photographic negative, spectrum of colour,
typographic juxtapositions and the asymmetric
composition. Today's inventions usually end up
as tomorrow's clichés.

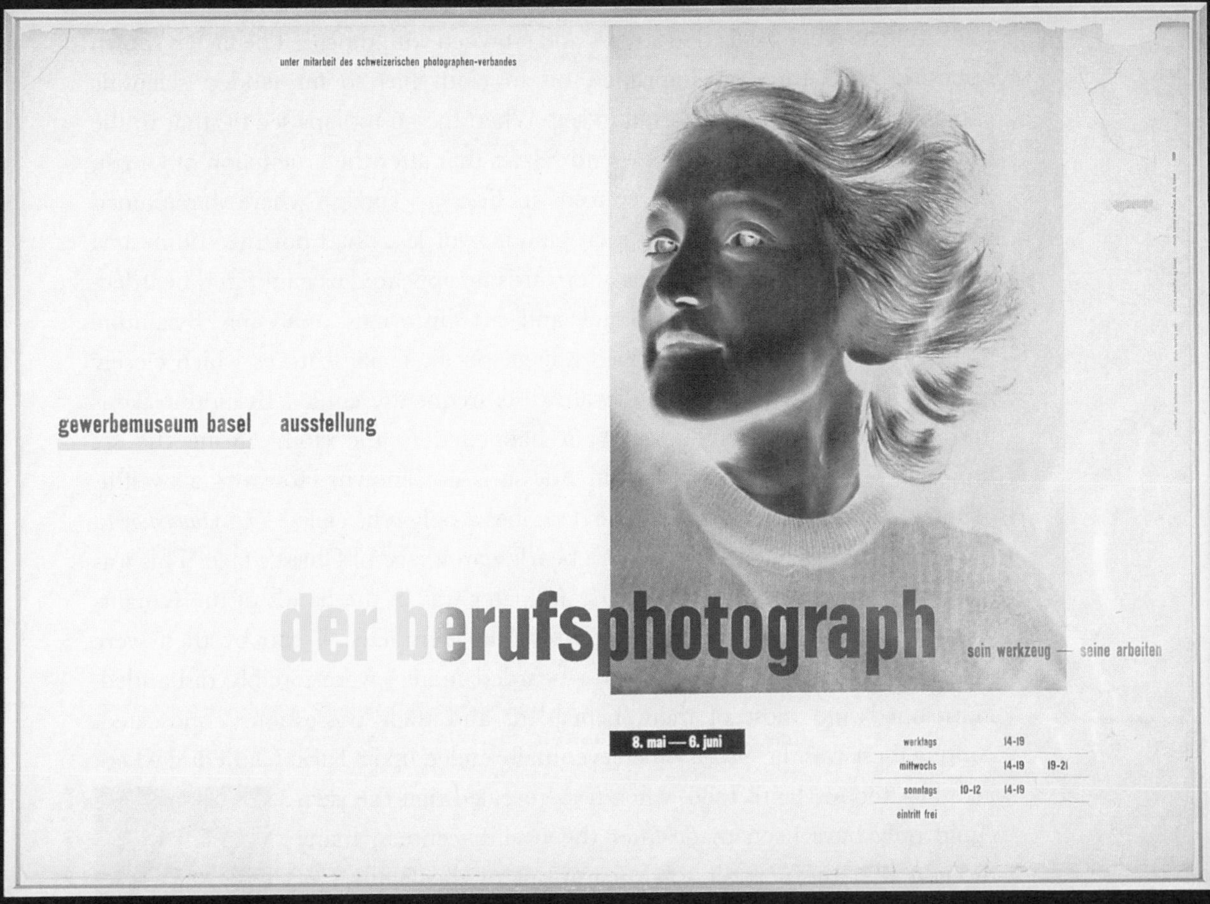
unter mitarbeit des schweizerischen photographen-verbandes
gewerbemuseum basel
ausstellung
der berufsphotograph
sein werkzeug — seine arbeiten
8. mai — 6. juni
werktags 14-19
mittwochs 14-19 19-21
sonntags 10-12 14-19
eintritt frei

Byzantine mosaic of Christ before 600 AD

'His eyes were yellow if you believe Piero della Francesca and blue if you trust Cima da Conegliano. Giovanni Bellini painted them brown. Caravaggio avoided the issue entirely by showing them closed. The fact is that there is no description of Christ in the Bible: not a word. Indeed, there is no description of Christ anywhere in any contemporary or near-contemporary document relating to or describing His life. Nothing. We do not know if He was fat or thin, bearded or bald, handsome or ugly. No one who knew Him, or even who knew someone who knew Him, no apostle or evangelist or Jewish historian, has left us an inkling. And yet, even in these notably godless and devilish days, nine out of ten of us would recognize Him immediately if we saw Him in the street. We think we know exactly what Jesus the Nazarene looked like. Art has given Him a face.'[1] Man's ideas of his gods have always been relative. Xenophanes noted that the Ethiopians envisaged their gods as black and snub-nosed while the people of Thrace as blue-eyed and red-haired. Nowadays everybody pictures Jesus as gaunt with long mousy brown hair and a beard. The *Turin Shroud* is a yellowish piece of cloth just over 14 feet long and some $3^1/_2$ feet wide, which bears a faint negative image of a man's body which had been whipped and speared, with stains indicating he'd been nailed to a cross and crowned with thorns. The face is shown opposite. How this was imprinted on to cloth has so far eluded scientific explanation, but there it is for all to see. When the custodians see fit, that is; the last time was a few years ago. Legend relates that after the crucifixion of Christ, his burial cloth was sent to a convent in Edessa (Turkey) where it remained hidden for six centuries. Before then paintings of Jesus had portrayed him as a clean-shaven Greek god, whereas afterwards he appeared as gaunt and bearded. This switch is hardly coincidental and art historians analysing Byzantine paintings of that era have identified fifteen specific facial features which closely match those on the *Shroud*. Medieval artists frequently copied Byzantine ikons and so created the stereotype. What happened to the cloth during the six hundred years after its discovery in Edessa is not known. However, a twelfth-century chronicle in Constantinople describes a holy relic called *The Mandylion* (a portrait not done by hand) as a cloth bearing an image of Christ's face. This was acquired by the rapacious crusaders, and later was in the hands of the Knights Templar. In the early fourteenth century the Templars – who by then were reputed to worship the portrait of a bearded man – were forcibly disbanded, imprisoned and most of them beheaded, and their possessions confiscated. Among these was the *Shroud* which eventually ended up in Turin Cathedral where it resides today.[2] Until 1988, when tests revealed that the yarn could only have been made after the twelfth century, many thought that the portrait was an imprint of the features of Christ himself. Some disagree and Shroudologists, a whacky cult, are convinced that the image is of Leonardo da Vinci.

Byzantine ikon of Christ. c. 700 AD

1. Waldemar Januszczak in *The Sunday Times*, 3 April 1994   2. Liam Butler. *The Shroud of Turin*. Butler & Thompson (London 1979)

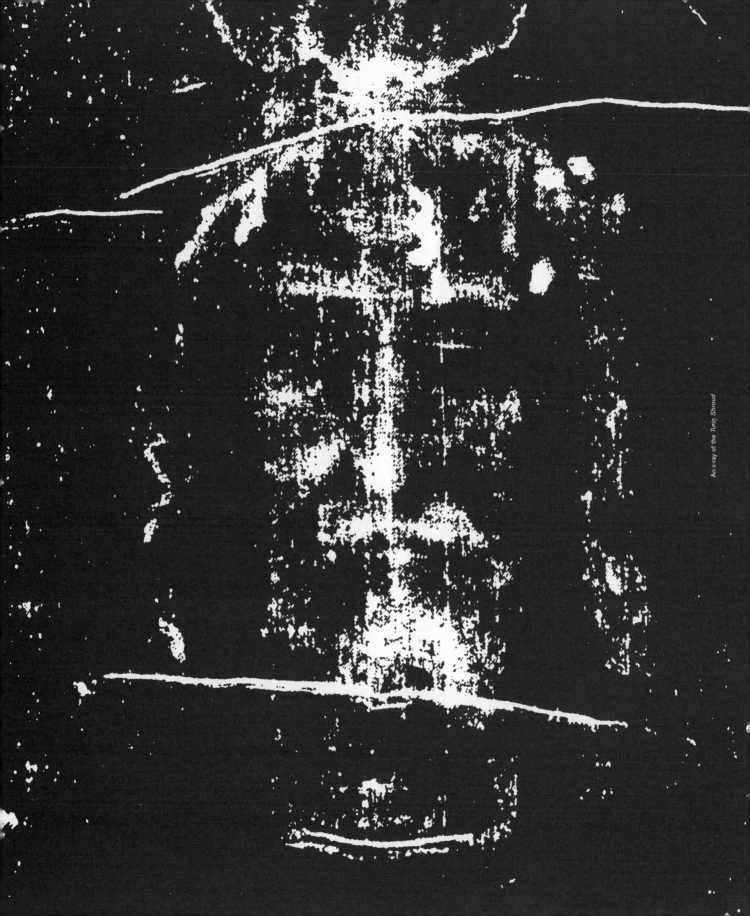

An x-ray of the *Turin Shroud*

When office cleaner Patricia Cole looked at the other side of the dirty rag used to polish a brass rail in the planning office of Leeds City Council, the image of Jesus looked back. The *Rag of Leeds* might seem feeble compared to the *Shroud of Turin* but perhaps this is only due to age and provenance. The Catholic Church also possesses two large cloths known as *Veronica's Veil* or *Handkerchief*, and the *Vernicle*, said to be relics which bear an image of Christ's face. Originally there were three but I'll come to that in a moment. The legend of *Veronica's Veil* is similar to that of the *Shroud*, but with a twist. After the original cloth disappeared from a monastery in Turkey it turned up years later in three different places. One was kept in Sainte Chapelle, Paris, until it vanished during the French Revolution. Another was kept in the Vatican until it also disappeared in mysterious circumstances, and the third still resides in a convent at Genoa. This one is publicly shown on Ascension Day and kept the rest of the time in a shrine which can only be opened with eight keys in the possession of eight local notables. Perhaps the elaborate security is an anxiety that it might go missing again – only to reappear in several other places. Recently someone mischievously pointed out that *Vera* [true] and *Icon* [image] combine to sort of spell *Veronica*. Then there is the *Vernicle*. Actually there are also several *Vernicles*, the most venerable of which has been hidden for 300 years in one of the piers supporting the dome of St Peter's in Rome. I don't know which one. Something tells me I might have got all this muddled up, but then I wouldn't be the first. Anyway, the one which had been in the Vatican has just turned up [1999] in the tiny village of Manoppello in the Apennines. The professor of Christian art history at the Vatican's Gregorian University thinks the relic is genuine. Enlarged digital photographs have been used to compare the veil with the face on the Shroud; the faces are the same shape, both have long hair, a tuft on the forehead, and the beards match. The Regius Professor of Divinity at Oxford University said: 'The Gregorian University is quite respectable, but I think the claim about the veil is totally absurd … I'd put it on the same level as seeing the face of Muhammad in a potato.'

THE RAG OF LEEDS

You too have shared Diego's vision. The picture you see is a tacky souvenir. A cheap lithographic colour reproduction on paper glued onto plastic imitation wood, the cracks carefully rendered and the surface an even glossy finish. The printing plate was created from a negative film, which had been taken of a colour photographic print, which had in turn been produced from a negative film, probably duplicated from another negative film, which perhaps had been taken of the original painting. The faithful believe the painting itself was created by divine transference directly onto Diego's cape. An image of the vision he'd seen with his own eyes on a mountain nearly 500 years ago. Sort of the same one you see before you now.

Our Lady of Guadalupe hangs in the Basilica of Guadalupe in Mexico City. The life-size painting of the Virgin is the most popular, or at least most visited, Catholic shrine after the Vatican. The story goes that the Virgin appeared in a vision to an Indian peasant called Juan Diego in December 1531 and imprinted an image of herself on his cape. The canvas of the picture is the cloth of his cape. † Painted without evidence of brushstroke, the woven cactus cloth shows no deterioration even after four and a half centuries. It's easy to believe, believers say, that the picture was not painted by human hand. I've never seen the picture and these descriptions are garnered from second-hand sources. † The artwork is said to have even yet more curious features. † If you look closely into a human eye you can see three tiny reflections of yourself, two appear the right way up and are reflected from the front and back of the lens, and the third upside down reflected from the cornea. In 1979 (and in 1981) the painting was carefully examined by experts who confirmed various beliefs about the materials, dates and so forth. They also made computer-enhanced photographic prints of the eyes. These magically revealed three images of a tiny human figure as described above. And, furthermore, I quote, the tiny mirrored figure 'is that of a man dressed as an Aztec peasant might have been in the early sixteenth century'. † According to the book[1] from which I gleaned this revelation, the analysis was serious, authentic, and documented. I haven't checked to verify myself but there's nothing to stop a sceptic doing so.

Rory Carroll in Rome

The Vatican was thrown on to the defensive yesterday after the Virgin of Guadalupe, one of the Roman Catholic church's most powerful icons, was accused of being a con.

The attack came not from secular scholars, but the very clerics who for decades watched over the Guadalupe shrine, which draws millions of pilgrims each year.

In a letter leaked to the press, the former abbot of the basilica in Mexico City, Guillermo Schulenburg, warned Pope John Paul II not to canonise Juan Diego, a native American whose vision of the Virgin 500 years ago was decisive in converting Latin America to Christianity.

In the face of centuries of devotion, ecclesiastical research and plans to make him a saint next year, Mr Schulenburg said that Diego had never existed except as a tool to convert native Americans.

He warned that there was insufficient evidence that the vision of a dark Madonna — adopted as Mexico's patron saint — appeared on Diego's cloak in Mexico City in 1531.

OUR LADY OF GUADALUPE

1. Lyall Watson. *The Nature of Things*. Hodder & Stoughton (London 1990)

The Guardian, 19 December 1999

On his way home from China Marco Polo saw a rhinoceros in Java. He assumed it was a unicorn although he recorded his surprise at its appearance which was less elegant than he thought and its disposition less gentle. Albrecht Dürer's woodcut of a rhinoceros which he did in 1515 (shown below), was of an animal he'd never actually seen. He copied it from a sketch done by someone else. Relying on this second-hand evidence he endowed the beast with a spike on its neck, armoured plates and scaly legs. This imaginative picture so took hold in the public mind that 300 years later when James Bruce published his so-called first drawing of a real rhinoceros, it still looked more like Dürer's than the real thing.[1]

When we create a stereotype it can become a truth.

Take the Panda. We think of it as an attractive playful creature. Soft, furry, cuddly, cute black and white patches, large eyes with an engaging look. In fact the myth doesn't match the reality. The Panda is a smelly dedicated eating machine. It spends 60 per cent of its time devouring bamboo, 40 per cent resting, and defecates continuously. Indeed it does so on such a prodigious scale that it is said to confound the mathematical ratio between input and output.[2]

Rhino: *symbol for the Suzuki four-wheel drive vehicle,* **Panda:** *symbol for the* World Wide Fund For Nature *(Design by Sir Peter Scott and Landor Associates)*

 1. E.H. Gombrich. *Art and Illusion.* Phaidon (London 1960) 2. Stephen Jay Gould. *An Urchin in the Storm.* Collins Harvill (London 1988)

Ikons

Appearance is an essential component of corporate culture. One major American corporation even instructs its recruitment officers to ensure that prospective employees 'look like us' ... whatever that means. Probably grey.

Erich Fromm proposed that social ikons are really projected self-images, and then wickedly suggested that *Mickey Mouse* is an unconscious psychological portrait of the average American. Well, maybe he's right, but it doesn't explain why Americans chose a baldheaded eagle* for their national emblem, the British a squashed dog and the French a chicken?

Perhaps to compensate for the chicken the French also have the *Marianne*, a statuette which represents the Republic and which with an eye on progress – or at least fashion – is fashionably updated: Bridget Bardot was replaced by Catherine Deneuve, who was replaced by Ines de la Fressange, who was replaced by ... I've lost track. Anyway I find that is an altogether more attractive concept than

that dreamt up by the Poles who, in 1939, elected the Virgin Mary to be Queen of Poland – mind you, the German tanks had just begun to roll across the frontier.

When the figure representing Britannia was introduced on the coinage Charles II had the Duchess of Richmond and Lennox act as the model for the portrait. She was his mistress. The latest Britannia which appears on a new issue of postage stamps (1995) is the wife of Barry Craddock. He's the illustrator.[1]

Religious icons are particularly bizarre as they are metaphors which became clichés which ended up as convictions. How else can one account for the popular biblical texts which illustrate Jesus with delicate raised hands, gentian blue eyes, bobbed blonde curls and cherubic lips. Not exactly a good-looking Jewish boy, more of an image which prompted Woody Allen to call him the *Pansy from Palestine*.

* American comedienne Joan Rivers claimed that the spread-eagle which also represents California was modelled on a well-known tinseltown actress.

1. Julian Barnes. *Letters from London*. Picador (London 1995)

An *imago* is
an image of
the parent
buried deep in
the subconscious
from infancy.
The word comes
from the wax
busts of parents
which the Romans
carried in funeral
processions.

Two grandmothers meet in a park.

One is pushing a pram.

'What a beautiful grandchild,' says one.

'That's nothing,' says the other,

reaching for her purse.

'I'll show you her picture!'

THIS

COMMERCIAL

FABERGÉ

EGG

IS

MADE

OUT

OF

GOLD

FOIL

SAVED

FROM

INNUMERABLE

CIGARETTE

PACKS.

Thomas Watson Jr (Chairman IBM, 1961-1971)   'Good design is good business.'

SHOP SIGN IN SANTA MONICA: 'QUALITY DOESN'T COST MORE, IT PAYS MORE.'
ROBERT PIRSIG: 'QUALITY IS A DIRECT EXPERIENCE INDEPENDENT OF AND PRIOR
TO INTELLECTUAL ABSTRACTIONS.' PAUL RAND: 'QUALITY DEALS WITH THE
JUDICIOUS WEIGHING OF RELATIONSHIPS, WITH BALANCE, CONTRAST, HARMONY,
JUXTAPOSITION, BETWEEN FORMAL AND FUNCTIONAL ELEMENTS – THEIR
TRANSFORMATION AND ENRICHMENT. FURTHER, IT IS CONCERNED WITH IDEAS
NOT TECHNIQUES, WITH THE ENDURING NOT THE EPHEMERAL, WITH PRECISION
NOT FUSSINESS, WITH SIMPLICITY NOT VACUITY, WITH SUBTLETY NOT BLATANCY,
WITH SENSITIVITY NOT SENTIMENTALITY.' HENRY ROYCE: 'THE QUALITY REMAINS
LONG AFTER THE PRICE IS FORGOTTEN.' LÁSZLÓ MOHOLY-NAGY: 'WITH THE
MASTERY OF MATERIALS, THE MOVE TOWARDS OBJECTIVE QUALITY BEGINS.' JOHN
RUSKIN: 'QUALITY IS NEVER AN ACCIDENT: IT IS ALWAYS THE RESULT OF
INTELLIGENT EFFORT.' DUC DE LA ROCHEFOUCAULD: 'IT IS NOT ENOUGH TO HAVE
GREAT QUALITIES; ONE MUST MAKE GOOD USE OF THEM.' EDWARD DE BONO:
'THE QUALITY OF LIFE IS FUELLED BY OUR PRODUCTIVE WEALTH.' JEWISH
PROVERB: 'NEVER MIND THE QUALITY FEEL THE WIDTH.' [OR: 'NEVER MIND THE
CONTENT FEEL THE CONTROVERSY.']

Triage (trɑi·ėdʒ). 1727. [– (O)Fr. *triage*, f. *trier*; see TRY *v*. -AGE.] The action of assorting according to quality.

Warhol's shoes. Barry Trengove went from London to New York to be art director of I. Miller, the classy American shoe company in the 1960s. He arrived on a Friday and went to the office. The company was moving over the weekend and he wanted to check on where to report on Monday. Passing down a corridor, he noticed that the walls were hung with the original shoe illustrations done by Andy Warhol for advertising campaigns in the 1950s. The movers were shifting out furniture and had begun to stack the pictures in a corner. Finding the foreman, Barry enquired what was happening to them. 'They'll be thrown away tomorrow,' he said. 'Um,' said Barry, 'I'd quite like them.' 'Well,' said the foreman, 'come in the morning at nine, five bucks and they're all yours.' Barry didn't sleep all night. He was back there bang on nine. 'Sorry,' said the foreman, 'the rubbish was collected earlier than expected!' *He probably regretted losing five bucks.*

Adding value. Business is motivated by profit. However, when asked how to improve the profit margin executives respond differently. The accountant will recommend reduction of costs, the engineer the purchase of better equipment, the marketing director an increase in advertising, the salesman more consumer choice. Rarely does anyone suggest that one way to increase the ratio between cost and sales is by making the product more desirable. *Well, how do you do that?* Assuming all other factors are reasonable you have to add a value and project an image which reflects that attribute. 'The consumer is not a moron,' said David Ogilvy, 'she's your wife.' And added, 'You can't bore people into buying your product, you can only interest them in buying it.' In my experience cost myopia is an almost ubiquitous corporate disease, a symptom of which is to cut costs. As anyone in the world's oldest profession knows, that situation can become terminal. *If all other things are equal, only one product in the market can be the cheapest.*

The crab. Chuang-tzu was an expert draughtsman and when the Emperor asked him to draw a crab he replied saying that he needed five years, a country house and twelve servants. The Emperor agreed. Five years later he pleaded for yet more time. The Emperor agreed again and gave him a further five years. At the end of the ten years Chuang-tzu took up his brush and in a single stroke drew a crab. The most perfect crab ever seen. The Emperor was delighted. *I've never met a client like that. Mind you, I'm no good at drawing crabs either.*

Assessing value. When Whistler was in litigation with Ruskin, who'd accused him of throwing a pot of paint in the public's face, he was asked how he could possibly justify charging two hundred guineas for two days' work. His reply was that the sum was not for two days' work but for a lifetime's knowledge. He won the case but was only awarded costs of a farthing. Equating creativity with money has always been a dodgy business. I like the way Saul Steinberg finessed the conundrum. The story goes that an enthusiastic young lady editor at a book publisher wanted him to illustrate a book-jacket. After a great deal of persuasion she got her boss to agree, although he insisted the fee would be beyond the budget. She telephoned Steinberg, described the job, explained there was a low budget, and appealed to him to accept. Not wishing to disappoint her, but having experienced tight-fisted publishers, he proposed that if his illustration was accepted he wouldn't charge. But if it wasn't, he'd charge a fee guaranteed to make the publisher's eyes water. *Predictably, the offer was declined.*

Theory of ruin value. There's a folk story about three stonecutters who were asked what they were doing. The first replied he was working to make a living. The second said he was the best stonecutter in the country. The third, with a visionary gleam in his eye, said he was building a cathedral. Albert Speer shared the same vision but went one step further by paradoxically propagating the *Theory of Ruin Value*. This meant build solid – lots of stone, lots of marble. He disdained steel and reinforced concrete because they didn't weather well. The principle being, since nothing lasts for ever, in thousands of years' time the ruins of Berlin would look so impressive that they would automatically transmit a sense of past Nazi grandeur. The eventual ruins were not what he had in mind. *As Joseph Brodsky commented (some forty years later) 'Ruins are the most persistent form of architecture.'*

Bernie Cornfield's calling card. In the 1960s a design group were asked to design a business card for an international (and infamous) financial entrepreneur. He wanted something simple, nothing fancy nor expensive. We agreed on a £25 fee (it was a long, long, long time ago) plus travel expenses. A few days later the proof was ready. Bernie called from Zurich and asked to see it over breakfast at the Dorchester in London. He didn't turn up. We ate his breakfast. A note followed asking us to be in Geneva the following week. We arrived in Geneva to learn he was on his way to Singapore. More days passed. A telex arrived. This fixed a time between flights in Frankfurt air terminal one winter Sunday at the crack of dawn. When we arrived – you guessed it – the bugger was in Johannesburg. Eventually, after further broken appointments, we presented his card. He was pleased but indignant about the price – the travel expenses were in the region of £1000. A lot of bread at the time. *Some only count the cost, and don't see the value.*

La Contessa. La Contessa is rich, and has homes in Gstaad, Barbados, New York, and no doubt other places as well. Actually she doesn't have a house in New York; she has two apartments. She lives in one and holds cocktail parties in the other which is at the top of the Trump Tower. She says the view is so spectacular. *Some see the value and don't give a toss about the cost.*

Commercial art. After the war Cassandre and Leupin met in the street. Both were on hard times. 'How much do you charge for a poster?' asked Leupin. 'Oh,' Cassandre replied, '5000 francs,' or whatever it was. 'That's strange,' Leupin said, 'so do I.' And then asked, 'And how many have you sold recently?' 'None,' Cassandre replied. 'That's strange,' said Leupin, 'neither have I.' In the late 1980s I was at a design conference in Aspen (Colorado) and saw an original print of a poster (*Normandie*) by Cassandre for sale in a smart gallery. It was, I thought, as amazing as the price. I thought about it all night and concluded that I had to have it. Next day I called a taxi. It arrived, and as I had one foot in the door I was accosted by David Hillman. 'Where are you going?' 'To the art gallery,' I innocently replied. 'Ah,' he said, 'You like the poster?' 'Uhm, well, yes.' 'How much is it?' he asked knowingly. I told him it was $1,500. He fell about laughing and said I'd dropped a nought off the end. I got out of the taxi. *With hindsight, as with other opportunities, I should have gone for it.*

The Brief.[1] The creative designer interprets briefs as starting points rather than finishing lines. He feels his way by challenging assumptions, finding chinks in the specifications and reaching through to discover the plums. It's an unknown journey. Trying to guess how long it will take and what it might cost is a toss-up between experience and faith. Not a good basis for negotiating a business transaction. A designer commissioned to design a product to a rigid brief and fixed fee meticulously went to work. Eventually he presented his solution. The clients were delighted. They took him to lunch. Over coffee the designer casually mentioned he'd produced another idea outside the brief, but if they wished to know what it was he'd expect an additional fee. Consternation and curiosity mingling with the euphoria of lunch, they agreed. When they saw the alternative they were even more delighted. *The aim is not to give the client what he thinks he wants, but what he never even dreamt he wanted.*

Officialdom. During the 1920s, the American Customs brought a suit against the sculptor Brancusi. They claimed he'd tried to avoid duty on raw materials by calling his bronze *Bird in Space* a work of art. A reasonable action as regulations specified that works of art are 'imitations of natural objects … in their true proportions'. As the prosecutor pointed out: 'M. Brancusi claims that this object represents a bird. If you met such a bird while out shooting, would you fire?' *The lesson is never argue with customs officials.*

The Kiss. Rodin's famous marble clinch *The Kiss* was originally presented to the town of Lewes in Sussex by an art dealer. The nude couple was displayed in the town hall but after complaints that it was having 'a prurient effect' on soldiers stationed nearby (I'm not sure what that meant but it was obviously dangerous) the local dignitaries leapt at the excuse to return it to the donor. It was stored in stables until the Tate Gallery in London bought it in 1953 for £5,500. *In 1999, 85 years later, Rodin's most celebrated sculpture returned to Lewes. The Council redecorated the town hall and strengthened the floor. Dozens of local businesses and individuals contributed to the cost of bringing it home.*

Lucky Strike. 'In March 1940, George Washington Hill walked into my office unannounced and said, "You Raymond Loewy?" I said, "Yes, I'm Raymond Loewy." He then took off his jacket, kept his fishing hat on, sat down and threw a packet of *Lucky Strikes* on my desk. "I'm from *American Tobacco*." (He was the president.) "Someone told me that you could design a better pack, and I don't believe it." "Then why are you here?" I asked. He looked at me for a moment, grinned, and we were friends. Without further ceremony, he pulled an attractive cigarette case out of his pocket. "*Cartier*," he said. "Only the French can make this. And look at these suspenders! *Cartier*, too." "So are these," I said, showing my own, which *Cartier* had made for me. "Well," he said, "what about that package? Do you really believe you can improve it?" "I bet I could," I answered. We bet fifty thousand dollars. He left, and in April the new *Luckies* pack was adopted, with resulting sustained large sales increases, creating at the same time a new look for cigarette packaging. On the old green pack, the *Lucky Strike* red circle (the target) appeared on only one side. Knowing they sold in the millions, I decided to display the target both sides so that the name *Lucky Strike* would be seen twice as often. I replaced the green with a shiny white and the pack looked more luminous; it was also cheaper to print and the smell which the green ink had given off was gone.' As *Time* magazine declared: '*Loewy streamlines the sales curve.*'

Tulipmania. Four hundred years ago the tulip was introduced into Holland from Turkey. It quickly caught the fancy of Dutch society, becoming the fashionable garden plant highly prized for exotic beauty. Mounting demand led to fierce competition, prices rocketed. Old masters were ten a penny but the *Black Tulip* was to die for. Frenzied trading became known as *Tulipmania* – collective madness which saw people offer anything to acquire the rights to tulips not yet grown, the first futures market. A single 'Semper Augustus' tulip bulb fetched 4,500 guilders plus a horse and carriage. Another exchanged for two loads of wheat; four loads of rye; four fat oxen; eight fat swine; 12 fat sheep; two hogsheads of wine; four barrels of beer; two barrels of butter; 1,000 pounds of cheese; a marriage bed with linens, and a wagon to haul it all. Today's flower people will be delighted to hear that the rare buttercup *Ranunculus ophioglossifolius*, which only grows on a tiny nature reserve at Badgeworth in Gloucestershire, was saved from extinction (1992) when permission to build a vehicle-washing plant on the site was refused. '*Once man believed he could make his own pleasures; now he believes he must pay for them.*' wrote John Fowles. '*As if flowers no longer grew in fields and gardens; but only in florists' shops!*'

A kangaroo walks into a bar and orders a whisky. 'That will be £3,' says the bemused barman, muttering, 'We don't get many kangaroos in here.' 'At £3 a drink – it's no wonder,' replies the kangaroo.

1. Kenneth Grange. *Boilerhouse* Catalogue

BUY 2 GET 1 FREE

Value paradox. It bothered Adam Smith, father of economics and author of *The Wealth of Nations* (1776), that diamonds were expensive while water was cheap, the former being useless and the latter essential. Rarity accounted for price but not value. Diamonds have to be dug up, meticulously cut, carefully polished, skilfully mounted. All you need for water is a pail. It's really a question of currency and at the height of the transatlantic slave trade the cost of two slaves in Lagos was one cowrie shell. I'm told that a bar in Colombia had a menu which read: *Bread with butter: 100 pesos. Bread with margarine: 80 pesos. Bread without butter: 60 pesos. Bread without margarine: 40 pesos.*

Junk design. I worked in Barcelona for a year in the 1950s. At lunch I used to have a *bocadillo* at a bar on the corner of Ramblas and Plaza Catalunya. The interior was panelled in mahogany, the circular bar had a good thick brass rail. The brasserie was furnished with bentwoods and small round marble-topped tables. The *tapas* were memorable. I was there a short while ago and went for a nostalgic drink. It now belongs to a fast food chain. The bar had gone, the interior was tricked out in formica, polystyrene cups, junk food. *Why does throughput have to be at the expense of what one is put through?*

Kudos factor. A designer produced a calendar for an African bank. He illustrated it with pictures of buffalo, gnu, kudus, antelope etc lifted from currency notes issued by various African states. He was surprised that so many of the different banks favoured animals to embellish the currency until it occured to him ... *in Africa, status equals wealth equals cattle.*

Wombats. A WOMBAT is not only a Australian marsupial but also an acronym for Waste Of Money, Brains And Time. 'Every day I face an onslaught of tawdry products, mindless logos, gratuitous graphics, witless signs, institutional notices, illiterate brochures, impenetrable forms, portentous job titles, dehumanizing rituals, and impersonal letters that have no expression, or life, or even competence. What is it that generates this cornucopia of life-threatening debris? What suppresses the inclusion of delight, sensuality and even common-sense?' *'Why is environmental responsibility seen as cost, and short-term expediency considered more practical than boldness and imagination?' asked design consultant Michael Wolff. And then, 'Why is cool and reason more acceptable than passion?'*

Anecdote. There is a story about a window cleaner who was doing the offices at one of Britain's largest design studios. After spending an inordinate amount of time polishing one of the windows he leant into the studio and, with a conspiratorial wink at a designer fiddling around with his pencil and pad, asked if his boss knew that that was all he ever did all day?

'All works of taste must bear a price in proportion to the skill, taste, time, expense and risk attending their invention or manufacture. Those things called dear are, when justly estimated, the cheapest.'
JOHN RUSKIN

'All day long I add up columns of figures and make everything balance. I come home. I sit down. I look at a Kandinsky and it's wonderful! It doesn't mean a damn thing!'
SOLOMON GUGGENHEIM

'There is no wealth but life.'
JOHN RUSKIN

'Customers may be tough but consumers are pushovers.'
RALPH CAPLAN

'We work not only to produce but to give value to time.'
EUGÈNE DELACROIX

'There is hardly anything in the world that some man cannot make a little worse and sell a little more cheaply ...'
JOHN RUSKIN

'... good design is good business, but good business may not always be good design.'
MICHAEL BIERUT

'Free advice isn't worth paying for.'
MY ACCOUNTANT

'My capital is time, not money.'
MARCEL DUCHAMP

'Hollywood is a place where they'll pay you a thousand dollars for a kiss, and fifty cents for your soul'.
MARILYN MONROE [attributed]

'No good deed remains unpunished!'
PROVERB

INDUSTRIALISTS,

WHO TURN THE AMAZONIAN JUNGLE INTO USELESS TUNDRA

OR CEMENT OVER HALF THE PLANET,

ARE NOT, FOR SOME REASON,

MACHINE-GUNNED *EN MASSE*,

NOR CAPTURED AND EXHIBITED,

NOR DO THEY HAVE THEIR TEETH EXTRACTED

AND CARVED INTO LITTLE MEN.

HEATHCOTE WILLIAMS

What we see is often more of a visual assumption than a visual truth. If you casually look at these two faces there is little to note except that each appears to be looking in a different direction. However, if you cover their faces up – except the eyes – both pairs are revealed to be identical and looking in the same direction.

Groucho Marx

'Who are you going to believe, me or your eyes?'

A

'Do not adjust your mind, there is a fault in reality.'   *Graffiti*

Baron von Münchausen lived so completely in his fantasy world that he confused fact with fiction, reality with illusion. We also live out our lives in the shadows between fantasy and reality, swayed by preconceptions, prone to assumptions, oscillating between paranoia and pollyanna.

The things people believe can be quite extraordinary. A few years ago someone suggested that the more intelligent a bird or animal the better it tasted when cooked. That's about as sensible as thinking that because a rose smells better than a cabbage it makes better soup. Even that expert of deduction Arthur Conan Doyle believed in fairies, despite the fact that the photographs taken by two little girls at the bottom of their garden in 1917, which had convinced him, were revealed to be fake. In some quarters it is still held that Walter Sickert was Jack the Ripper. Perhaps he was.

Although such fanciful opinions could be considered eccentricities, there is a very real condition called Capgras's syndrome in which sufferers believe that someone they know has been replaced by an identical impostor. [SEE P431]. The same credibility gap is created by the optical illusion.

Here the difference between what we see and yet know can't possibly be, leads us to think we are 'seeing things' or that we 'must be dreaming'.

The power of illusion lies in its untranslated immediacy through a suspension of disbelief. This can be artificially contrived, like *Pepper's Ghost*, a Victorian stage effect conjured up with mirrors and projections to create an appearance of reality that completely fooled audiences. Or it can be like a trick performed by Houdini : Four men wheel a large cabinet on stage followed by Houdini leading an elephant. Houdini ushers the elephant into the cabinet, and closes the door. He waits a moment, then opens the door again – the cabinet is empty. Twenty men wheel the cabinet off stage. So, where is the elephant ? Or it can be a natural phenomenon like the *Fata Morgana*,[*] a mirage occasionally seen in the Straits of Messina off Sicily, when ships and cities are seen suspended up-side-down in the sky.[1] Or it can be similar to something experienced by a Tom Stoppard stage character. He said that although to anyone standing on the platform at Paddington station it seemed that the train had left Paddington – for the seated passengers the observable phenomena indicated that Paddington had left the train.

[*] The crusaders on the their way to the Holy Land imagined the illusory scene to be the legendary citadel of *Morgan Le Fay*, King Arthur's evil sister, who lured sailors to their doom. However, there are no illusions which fool all of us all of the time or even most of it, because if there were – they would be a reality. Maybe some are.

1. Edi Lanners. *Illusions*. Thames and Hudson (London 1977)

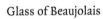

Glass of Beaujolais

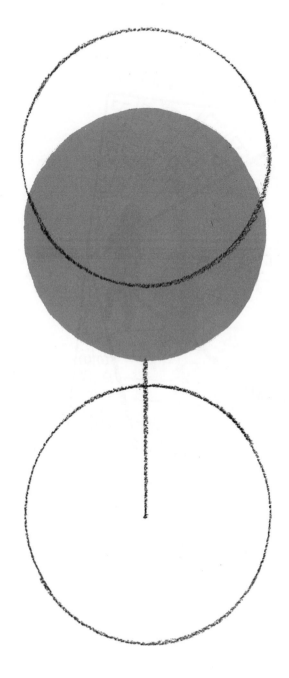

Illustration. Victorian advertisement

'It is the theory which decides what we can observe.' Einstein

A perceptual paradox

The disappointment of holiday snapshots is that they appear undramatic in contrast to our vivid memory of the glorious panorama. The reason is that a camera only records the scene presented. It doesn't have the human capability which amplifies reality to make things larger than life. What makes the difference is our perceptual apparatus which automatically increases the scale of whatever we're looking at according to its distance from our eyes.[1] It works like this:

In physical terms an image **halves in size** each time its distance from the eye is doubled.

In perceptual terms an image **increases in size** the further away it is from the eye.

The difference between what we see, and what we think we see, is clearly demonstrated in a mirror. We have the impression that the reflection of our face is the size it really is. Actually it's half. Put your forefinger and thumb to your chin and the top of your head in the mirror, and then bring your hand back and compare this measure to your actual face. For the more technically minded, use a ruler.

Pairs of things look much the same size whatever their distance. An outstretched hand will look almost exactly the same size as the other hand which is held out at half the distance, unless you overlap them.

In the illustration below depth is conveyed by the perspective created by the tiles, and so one automatically assumes the figures diminish in size the further away they are. In fact the reverse happens – the furthest figure appears to get larger. Our perceptual apparatus is unable to reconcile the conflicting information presented by the illusion of three dimensions, rendered in two dimensions on a flat surface. It therefore settles for what it thinks it should see. Actually the three figures are the same size.

Remember the Russian saying : He lies like an eyewitness.

'Seeing is deceiving. It's eating that's believing.' James Thurber

1. R.L. Gregory & E.H. Gombrich (eds.). *Illusion in Nature and Art.* Duckworth (London 1973)

Snapshot of the Five Fingered Mountain in Cyprus.
The photograph diminishes the contours just as
the drawing – with considerable artistic licence –
exaggerates them. (see previous page).

Illusion. 'God created it and placed it between the seeds, the fruits, flesh, and the palace of the mouth, and from this tastes were born; between the flowers and their smells, and from this perfumes were born; between hearing and sounds, and from this was born harmony, melody, etc.; between the eyes and objects, and from this were born colours, perspective, beauty. It is a small bit of nature that amuses itself by giving us pleasure through evaporation. It is different from error. If I see colours without seeing any object, as in the air for example, I am in error. In the opposite case, I am under an illusion and still within the truth. All illusion is produced by some emanation and is the effect of a cloud, a vapour, the intervention of a fluid. If the organ is tainted, if the object is improperly disposed or altered in its constituent parts, there is no illusion. One of the two parts is then lacking to set the process in motion, and the play of illusion can no longer work.'

Illusions. 'They can thus be produced only by these effluvia, these invisible outflows, these subtle emanations that maintain the perpetual currents between these different beings. They cannot therefore give and receive agreeable sensations if they do not somewhere produce some loss of substance. Thus, to the condition of change and decline is attached the good of inspiring and feeling pleasure.'

Joseph Joubert [1798]

'Delusion is the abandonment of outer reality in favour of inner wish.' Alain de Botton

Broomstick technology. Although we see the sun rise up in the east and set in the west we now know that actually it's angels that are busy rotating the earth around the sun. It wasn't always like that. Once upon a time everyone thought that the sun revolved around the earth. I find this a reasonable assumption since you're woken up by the sun in the east and whilst you're minding your own business during the day, it passes over your head and drops out of sight in the west. While some illusions <u>look</u> more real, others <u>feel</u> more real. The earth spins around its axis every 24 hrs at 1,000 mph and orbits the sun once a year at 66,000 mph. Adding up the spinning and orbiting means you've travelled about 550 miles since you started reading this paragraph. Or, put another way, you're travelling through space at 18.5 miles a second – faster than a bullet. Have a nice day. **'I am a passenger on the spaceship Earth.'** Buckminster Fuller

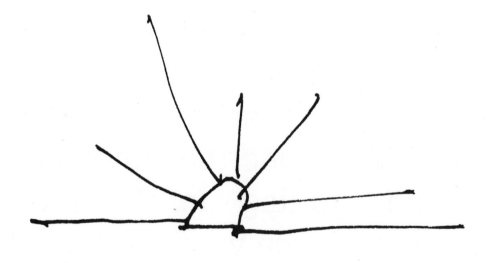

sunset

ready to go. I showed them to someone and explained how I saw the scenario. He looked at me with that 'who *is* this twit?' expression. Maybe he was right; our capacity for self-deception is endemic.

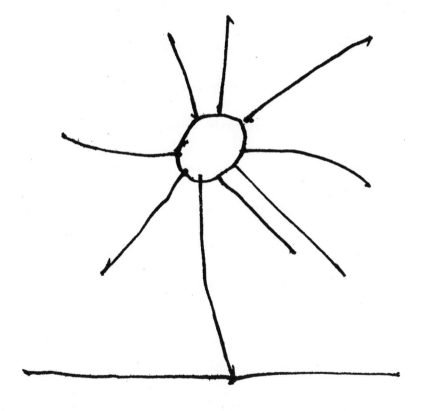

sunrise

[confabulations]

'Confabulation', **said Anthony Burgess**, 'means the replacement of
the gaps left by a disordered memory with imaginary happenings.'

'Nature [confabulation], my dear Sir,' Raoul Dufy once told a critic who was complaining about his liberal use of artistic licence [confabulation], 'is only a hypothesis' [confabulation]. When it comes to challenging visual truths [confabulations] Magritte has no equal. In describing his painting THE HUMAN CONDITION [confabulation] – shown opposite – he said: 'I placed in front of a window, seen from a room, a painting representing exactly that part of the seascape which was hidden from view by the painting. Therefore, the sea represented in the painting hid from view the sea situated behind it, outside the room. It existed for both the spectator, as it were, simultaneously in his mind, as both inside the room in the painting, and outside in the real seascape [confabulations].' Robert Pirsig: 'Laws of nature are human inventions, like ghosts [confabulations]. Laws of logic [confabulations], of mathematics are also human inventions, like ghosts. The whole blessed thing is a human invention [confabulation], including the idea that it isn't a human invention. It's all a ghost, and in antiquity was so recognized as a ghost, the whole blessed world we live in. It's run by ghosts [confabulations].' Two friends left Sheridan, the English wit, rather the worse for drink [confabulated] in front of his house in Berkeley Square. Looking back they saw he hadn't gone in and shouted asking if he was all right. He shouted back he was only waiting until his door went by again [confabulation] and then he'd jump through it. My guess is he missed [confabulation]. Georges Braque explained in his notebooks (1917-47): that 'Writing is not describing, painting is not depicting. Verisimilitude is merely an illusion.'

Painting. René Magritte. *The Human Condition*

Sleight of eye

We are inclined to ignore the commonplace but are alert to the unexpected. Conspicuous change from the norm will catch attention while minor inconsistencies, being of small consequence, are adjusted by imagination to meet our expectations.

'Illusion is in sensations. Error is in judgements.' *Joseph Joubert*

Although frequently reproduced, this image, called the Kanizsa Triangle, always manages to confound me. The image comprises six marks: three linear angles and three incomplete black discs. The white triangle is a phantom only existing in our minds. As the saying goes: absence of evidence is not evidence of absence.

'An actor draws from him what is not really there – illusionist.' *Robert Bresson*

Although we say, 'I wouldn't have believed it if I hadn't seen it,' it would be more accurate to say, 'I wouldn't have seen it if I hadn't believed it.'

Six up, nine down

Jim Coles, he's a carpenter, told me that one of the first
rules taught to an apprentice was six up, nine down. That
is to say, door hinges should be fixed six inches down from
the top and nine up from the bottom. Look at a door which
follows this rule and you'll see the hinges appear to be
equally positioned.

'Optical illusion is visual truth.' *Goethe*

Hollywood – in itself more of a state of mind than a real
place – trades in such illusions. Sets for Westerns were
built in seven-eighths scale so the heroes appeared larger
than life. And the aerodrome scene in *Casablanca,* shot in
a studio, created an impression of distance by cardboard
aeroplanes built on a scale commensurate with the dwarfs
hired to scurry around as mechanics.

'We are the most illusioned people on earth.' *Daniel Boorstin*

On this page are two pencils. Which do you think is the
smaller ? Beware of what you see and what you think
you see.

Potemkin Villages

Lenin to Trotsky:

Now this is the truth, and I can refer you to many authorities. When Catherine II and her royal entourage sailed down the Dnieper River in 1787 to view the New Territories, the Field Marshal Potemkin created sham villages of painted canvas along the river bank to give the distinguished visitors a false impression of reality. We want no more Potemkin villages.

Trotsky to Lenin:

On the matter of the Potemkin villages I must disagree. They were real, and this is the truth, for which I can cite many authorities. The illusion that they did not exist was created by historians, the source of most of our illusions about the past.

Lenin to Trotsky:

Dear Comrade, what does it matter who was responsible, my Field Marshal or your historians? In either event, somebody was rudely deceived.

Lenin-Trotsky. *Pre-revolutionary Correspondence.*

Note, Toyama, Japan. The bar at the top of the hotel was done out in dark colours and dimly lit, with spots softly illuminating tables in separate booths. The floor to ceiling glass window framed the city by night: splats of bright lights; winking neon under a quink sky. I was having a drink with Waldek Swierzy, a Polish designer renowned for his graphic portraits. Gazing over the booths I saw a very small head in a booth across the room. It was in profile, bearded, and immobile. My eye kept wandering back to it; there was something odd which I couldn't quite figure out. I asked Waldek to change places, so I could get a better look … it was three flowers in a vase! When we'd sat down I indicated the head to Waldek, and asked him which nationality he thought the man was. Not a Japanese, he said, perhaps an Indian. Why was I interested? I ordered him another scotch.

Legerdemain

The Gee, the Rick and the Three Card trick.* The confidence trickster, dextrously switching Queen and two Jokers in the three card scam, relies on our expectations to mislead us into assumptions. We are shown the faces of the three cards, we carefully watch as they are turned over, we follow the rapid shuffling, we know where the Queen has ended up, we swear blind we are right and part with money. We are invariably wrong. We think we've been tricked. Actually we have only deceived ourselves. We can't believe we didn't see what we thought we saw.

Illusion is not necessarily deception. The principle of creativity is to show us the world in a new way. 'Art disturbs,' said Georges Braque, whereas 'science reassures.' So whereas the role of the scientist is to correct error, that of the artist is to court illusion. Actors, designers, architects and artists, writers and musicians – all manipulate our perceptions.

The Magus, a novel by John Fowles, was set on an island of manufactured illusions. Through mime, Marcel Marceau created creatures like butterflies, actions like climbing, abstract concepts like bondage. However, to participate illusions have to be translatable. As George Balanchine confessed, in no way could he depict his mother-in-law through dance.

If you think these shapes spell something you've been deluded. They are illusory shadows of invisible forms.

This picture shows a cluster of convex and concave spheres. Turn the image upside-down and all the convexes become concaves and vice versa. The brain assumes there is a single light source from above and responds to the volumes accordingly. Perhaps we instinctively respond to natural light beamed down from the sun and the moon.

R

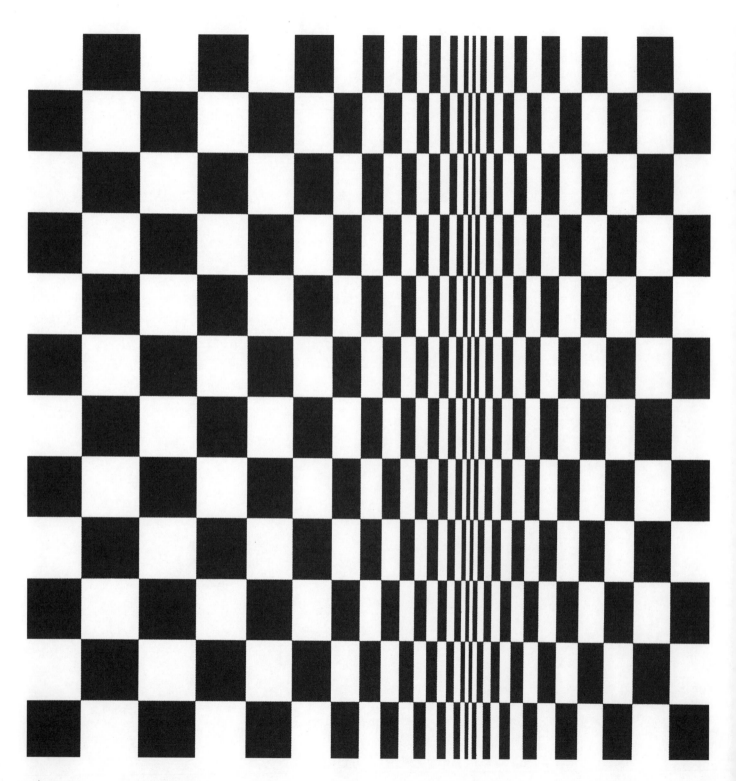

Painting. Bridget Riley

How to geld eyeballs

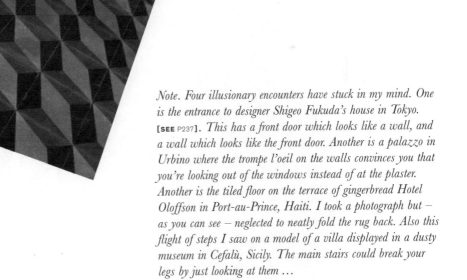

Note. Four illusionary encounters have stuck in my mind. One is the entrance to designer Shigeo Fukuda's house in Tokyo. [SEE P237]. This has a front door which looks like a wall, and a wall which looks like the front door. Another is a palazzo in Urbino where the trompe l'oeil on the walls convinces you that you're looking out of the windows instead of at the plaster. Another is the tiled floor on the terrace of gingerbread Hotel Oloffson in Port-au-Prince, Haiti. I took a photograph but – as you can see – neglected to neatly fold the rug back. Also this flight of steps I saw on a model of a villa displayed in a dusty museum in Cefalù, Sicily. The main stairs could break your legs by just looking at them …

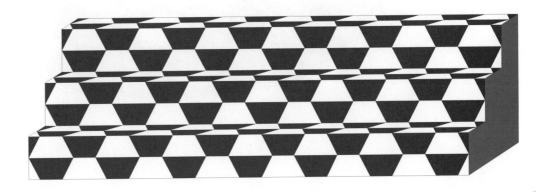

A

Illustration. Peter Brookes. *To Play Cat and Mouse*

Graffiti   'I'd give my right arm to be ambidextrous.'

... reality turns into illusion

semblance changes into presentation

[are you drawn in ...]

[are you thrown out ...]

... traced in magic mirrors

pseudo-spaces are spellbound ...

MAX BILL

Illustration. Josef Albers, Impossible Figure

There are usually two ways of looking at something.

The dilemma here is whether it's passing over one's head, or whether it's going to land on top of it.

'The opposite of a true statement

EMPTY AND BE FULL

is a false statement,

BEND AND BE STRAIGHT

but the opposite of a profound truth

HAVE MUCH AND BE CONFUSED

may be another profound truth.'

HAVE LITTLE AND GAIN EVERYTHING.

Niels Bohr

CHINESE PROVERB

The sentence on the other side of this page is true—

The sentence on the other side of this page is false-

Three kinds of
visual paradox:

**The image which
contradicts itself.**

*A mischievous
painting based on
a cloakroom ticket
by Patrick Hughes.*

**A design which
creates an optical
conundrum.**

*This trademark for
Renault, designed
by Victor Vasarely,
was derived from
a diamond-shaped
hole which was cut
into the bonnet to
cool the engine.*

**The vicious circle
which starts out
and ends up at the
same time.**

*As drawn by
Saul Steinberg
and described by
Nathaniel West:
'It is as if I were
attempting to trace
with the point of a
pencil the shadow
of the tracing pencil.'*

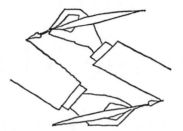

Extremes meet ... since the Creta[n] are liars,' philosophers have built a[...] trying to resolve this particular one [...] to 'wandering the common at night[...]

by day'. I don't know what he concl[...] one thing was certain, which was t[...]

it is not certain, that nothing is cer[...] the visual paradox. Now you see it, [...]

to be impossible, and impossibil[...] conundrums exceedingly irritating [...]

unwelcome challenge to their pe[...] irrelevant. They forcibly remind us [...] seem. 'Art is a lie,' Picasso slyly expla[...]

Epimenides declared: 'All Cretans
discipline out of such paradoxes. In
ertrand Russell said he was reduced
nd staring at a blank sheet of paper
ded but Samuel Butler decided only
at nothing is certain. Including that
ain. The same ambiguities apply to
ow you don't. Possibilities are shown
es probable. Although some find
this could be because they pose an
eptual apparatus – they are not
hings are not necessarily what they
ed, 'that makes us realize the truth.'

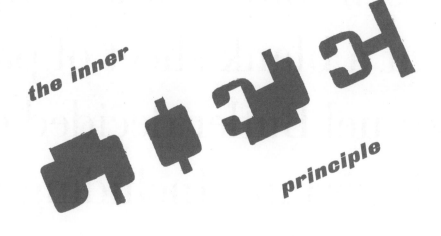

the inner *principle*

Design. Willem Sandberg

Albert Einstein   'The answer is "yes" or "no", depending on the interpretation.'

the **ZEBRA** issue

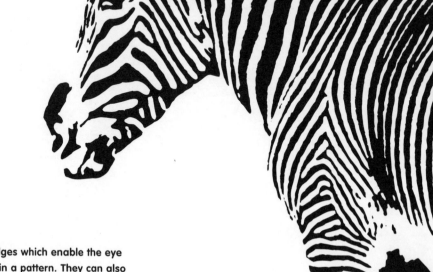

Shapes shape other shapes. Shapes have edges which enable the eye to distinguish objects within space, or areas in a pattern. They can also exist independently in a visual vacuum, like the letters on this page. Although we have the option to see the doughnut or the hole we usually settle for the doughnut. However, the bit we don't usually look at is just as relevant as the bit we do. One cannot exist without the other.

There is no such thing as a zebra or, put another way, there are three kinds of animal which we call zebra although they are not related. There used to be four but the quagga* is now extinct. What they have in common are stripes. The question, you may have guessed, is: is it a white animal with black stripes, or black animal with white stripes? Evolutionist Stephen Jay Gould has written a ten-page essay[1] on the issue. His conclusion is a black animal with white stripes.

For the zebra, unlike the tiger, stripes don't serve to disguise their presence. So why does the zebra have stripes? One persuasive theory is that the stripes control temperature, the black absorbing more heat than the white. The stripes may also help confuse tsetse flies and lions so they do their biting elsewhere. A clutch of zebras in the heat can dissolve their profiles to the extent that one can't tell where one zebra begins or another ends. [SEE P267]. Another benefit is that the foal quickly recognizes its mother's pattern, something David Attenborough calls 'a portable permanent signature'. A barcode of identity.

  1. Stephen Jay Gould. *Hen's Teeth and Horses' Toes.* Norton (New York 1983)

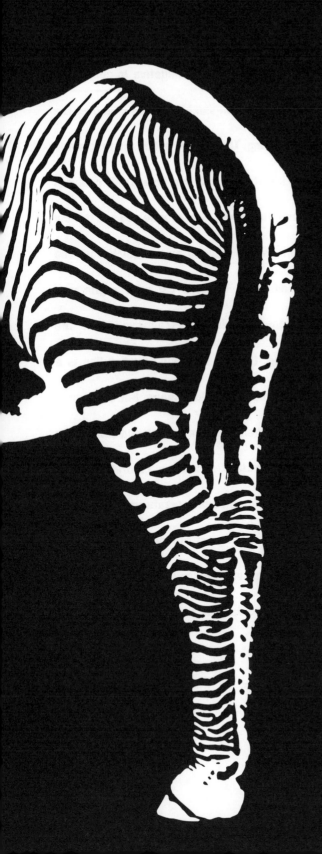

* The last surviving quagga died on 12 August 1883 in Amsterdam Zoo. There is a Quagga Project in South Africa which, by interbreeding related zebra, hopes to re-create the extinct species.

Dutch artist M.C. Escher, maestro of optical double-take, juxtaposes positive with negative to conjure up scenarios which are all object and no space. He is a very popular artist. You see his artworks all over the place. The scientific fraternity find his perceptual conundrums intriguing. The general public are fascinated by the magic rabbits he pulls out of the metaphorical hats. I think his attraction is that he not only conjures up an illusion but also shows how it's done. All without diminishing the magic. Sort of now you see it, now you don't, all at once. Trying to unravel the globby fuzzy morphs is like walking across quicksand. The travelling eye converts birds into fish and vice versa, much as Lewis Carroll's cat with a grin was superseded by the grin without a cat. **NON PLUS SED** comes to mind. As Escher explained: 'The borderline between two adjacent shapes having a double function, the act of tracing such a line is a complicated business. On either side of it, simultaneously, a recognizability takes shape. But the human eye and mind cannot be busy with two things at the same moment … there must be a quick and continuous jumping from one side to the other … I sometimes feel as if I were a spiritualist medium, controlled by the creatures which I am conjuring up … they usually are very difficult and obstinate creatures.' He wasn't an easy man himself and even selected his wife on the theorem that 'the age of the ideal spouse should be half that of the man plus 10'. He is also said to have experienced an epiphany in the Alhambra, in Granada, in 1922. Here the awesome intricacy of the thirteenth-century Islamic tiling set him off compressing figures into increasingly complex tessellations [SEE P261] and forever seeking new ways of making images perpetuate themselves. As they say —— it takes one to make one.

Illustration. M.C. Escher. *Sky and Water 1*

Illustration. William Burges (c.1879)

This is a detail of a tiled wall in the nursery of Cardiff Castle in Wales. The Invisible Prince is portrayed in the foliage. The illustration has a sort of damp charm.

The clipping, one of a puzzle series advertising the beverage Ovaltine, appeared in *Comic Cuts* on 24 March 1945. I found the spade but I'm still looking for all the rest.

There was a fence with spaces you
could look through if you wanted to.

An architect who saw this thing
stood there one summer evening.

Took out the spaces with great care.
And built a castle in the air.

The fence was utterly dumbfounded -
Each post stood there with nothing round it.

Christian Morgenstern

'... in New York you don't get to see them' – art director Tony Palladino is talking about skies – 'because you look up and the buildings are doing this on either side of your face. But I was looking up once, and I said, I'm going to show the world that there are really wonderful skies in New York city. So I had my friend Kathy Phelon take pictures of the skies around 7.30 at night. And just turned them upside down and created castles in the sky. Beautiful'.

In the image on the right by the Japanese designer Shigeo Fukuda, the woman's leg becomes a man's, and vice versa. Fukuda also does personalized drawings for his friends – he did this one for me.

Sketch and poster. Shigeo Fukuda

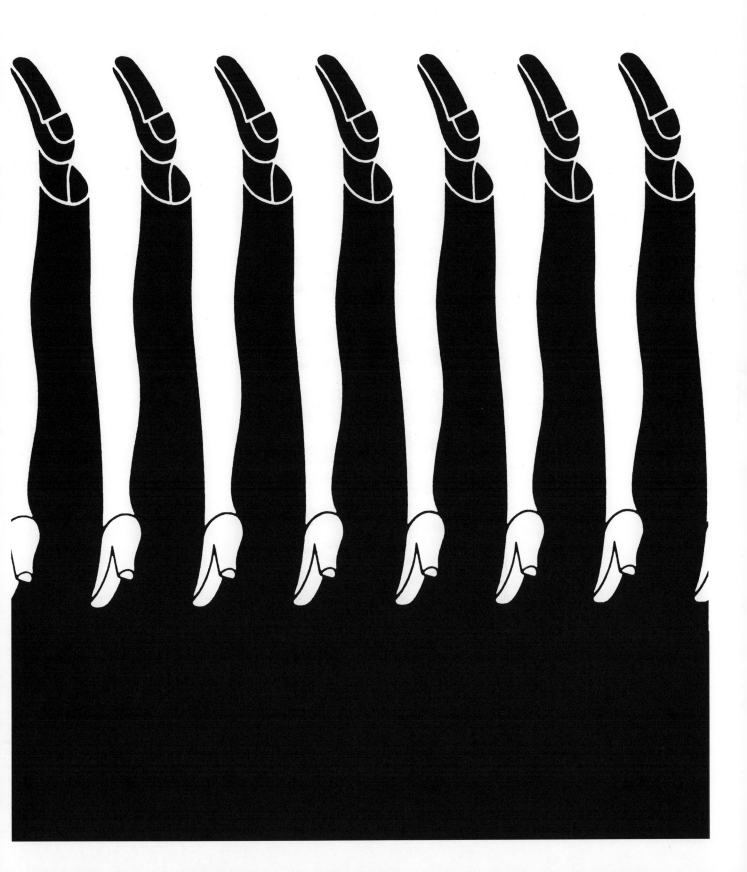

Red on Blue Chair

William Addison Dwiggens   'Symmetry is static – that is to say, inconspicuous.'

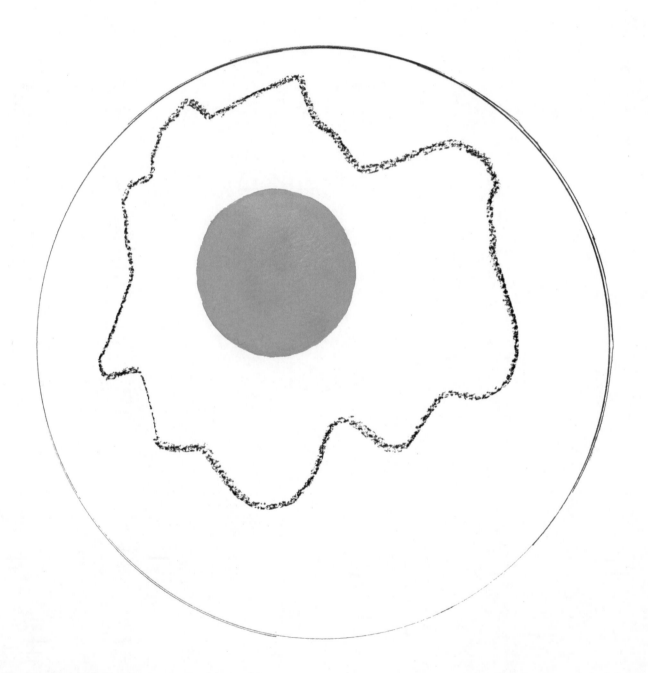

S Y M M E T R I E S.

Letters observe **reflective** and **rotational** symmetries. **Reflective** symmetry occurs when a shape is cut in half, so each half is a mirror image of the other – cut a circle in half and you get two identical semicircles. **Rotational** symmetry is a characteristic of shapes which look the same in different positions – a square turned to sit on its side, or flipped over, or reversed back-to-front, or turned up-side-down. A look at the alphabet reveals that **A H I M O T U V W X Y** have **reflective** symmetry as they more or less look the same although switched left to right. **H I N O S X Z** have **rotational** symmetry as they look the same turned up-side-down. And as you can see **B C D E H I K O X** read just as well when they are flipped over forwards to stand on their heads. **O** and **X** have both **reflective** and **rotational** symmetry. Thus the **O X O** logotype can be turned around any which way. The photograph below is of their erstwhile headquarters in London. The **reflective** symmetry of a chicken's egg [in one plane] can be transformed into the **bilateral** chicken or the **broken** symmetry of an omelette. Other **broken** symmetries are expressed in dappled shadows of foliage, the juxtapositions of a leopard's spots, the speckled pattern on a bird's egg. Symmetries can also be altered by human intervention – pricking a bubble comes to mind. Although the scrambled egg is the ultimate example of **broken** symmetry the fried egg has more to offer. It is **reflective** and **rotational** yokewise, and **brokenly** unsymmetrical eggwhitewise.

Photograph. David Sillitoe. The OXO Tower. London

TIMOTHY

TIMOTHY

CHOICE

CHOICE

THE MOONSHINE CONJECTURE.[1] One problem that attracted mathematician Richard Borcherd was so obtuse that his explanation is usually referred to as the 'moonshine conjecture', scientificspeak for 'a wild guess', or a theorem which seems right but can't be proved, or a concept so complex that only Borcherd could prove it. In this realm of thinking a cube can be rotated to demonstrate 24 distinct symmetries. I've probably got that completely wrong, but whatever it is, it is nothing compared to Borcherd's 'MONSTER'. A frighteningly unimaginable mathematical object which is said to live in 196,883 dimensions and to have 808,017,424,794,512,875,886,459,904,961,710,757,005,754,368,000,000,000 symmetries.

1. John Horgan. *The End of Science*. Abacus (London 1998)   2. Ian Stewart and Martin Golubitsky. *Fearful Symmetry*. Penguin Books (London 1992)

THE THEORY OF EVERYTHING. In the physicists' quest for 'what it's all about', they use the mathematical properties of symmetry as their guide. As science writer John Horgan explains: 'Symmetry became the *sine qua non* of particle physics. In search of theories with deeper symmetries, theorists began to jump to higher dimensions. Just as an astronaut rising above the two-dimensional plane of the earth can more directly apprehend its global symmetry, so can theorists discern the more subtle symmetries underlying particle interactions by viewing them from a higher-dimensional standpoint.'[1] *FEARFUL SYMMETRY*[2] is a readable book compiled by mathematicians Ian Stewart and Martin Golubitsky. The contents pages reveal the breadth of the discipline. Here are some of the subjects listed: The symmetry of a splash. A screw symmetry. Cell divisions in nematode worms. Gastrulation in the frog. The transverse gallop of a cheetah. A feline pronk. Travelling wave in a moving butterfish. Zeeman's catastrophe machine. Symmetries of a cylinder. The in-phase bound of Kangaroo. Apparently there's more to symmetry than meets the eye.

ART LUSTS ULTRA: James Thurber invented a backward tribe called the SESUMARONGI, which

ART LUSTS ULTRA: James Thurber invented a backward tribe called the SESUMARONGI, which

he said exists even though we aren't aware of it. He was referring to our incapacity to read words

he said exists even though we aren't aware of it. He was referring to our incapacity to read words

other than in the accepted direction. An inability which probably prompted Leonardo da Vinci to

other than in the accepted direction. An inability which probably prompted Leonardo da Vinci to

use mirror writing in his notebooks, which possibly explains why Matisse signed his name backwards on

use mirror writing in his notebooks, which possibly explains why Matisse signed his name backwards on

his first painting, and which Dylan Thomas exploited to invent names for characters. As a child

his first painting, and which Dylan Thomas exploited to invent names for characters. As a child

Alastair Reid drove his father mad by calling him REHTAF and the family dog GOD. A poet with a

Alastair Reid drove his father mad by calling him REHTAF and the family dog GOD. A poet with a

penchant for gnomic riddles, he amuses himself by revealing the private language of sauce labels

penchant for gnomic riddles, he amuses himself by revealing the private language of sauce labels

called OTAMOT PUHCTEK and advertisements for MUELONIL.[1] **Looking at the label on a bottle of**

called OTAMOT PUHCTEK and advertisements for MUELONIL.[1] Looking at the label on a bottle of

EVIAN, a mineral water from a town of the same name, I could see his fascination with the game.

EVIAN, a mineral water from a town of the same name, I could see his fascination with the game.

Not many people keep palindromes in their bathroom but I have an American friend who does. I must

Not many people keep palindromes in their bathroom but I have an American friend who does. I must

remember to tell him! In front of the toilet is a mirror, and mounted on the wall opposite (or

remember to tell him! In front of the toilet is a mirror, and mounted on the wall opposite (or

behind one might say) is a travel poster boldly entitled ROMA. Most of us only appreciate fifty

behind one might say) is a travel poster boldly entitled ROMA. Most of us only appreciate fifty

A typographic palindrome I made for my friend ANNA by printing the first two letters and then folding the paper over in half, and rubbing down while the ink was still wet to get a transferred impression (1960).

ANNA

1. Alastair Reid. *Passwords*. Little Brown (Boston 1959)   2. Karl Gerstner. *Compendium for Literates*. Arthur Niggli/MIT Press (Teufen 1974)

per cent of what we read. True palindromes are a particular species which yield the same meaning

backwards or forwards. Some are merely repetitive such as NEVER ODD OR EVEN, or SEX AT

NOON TAXES, or LEPERS REPEL, or the name of a language: MALAYALAM. Others

generate further meanings such as Thurber's PEEL'S LAGER ON RED RUM DID MURDER ON

REGAL SLEEP, which could even be 'an advertising slogan disguised as a line from Macbeth'.

Karl Gerstner, designer and painter, has his own constructed in Latin by poet Andre Thomkins.

ART, SI GERSTNER APPARENTS REGISTRA, which translates (unpalindromically) into ART, IF

GERSTNER WILL REGISTER WHAT APPEARS.[2] The longest single-word palindrome in any

language is in Finnish: SOLUTOMAATTIMITTAAMOTULOS which means 'the result from a

measurement laboratory for tomatoes'. One palindrome I particularly like is A TOYOTA. It also

works in reverse in a mirror – that's ultra smart.

HCTUD - ELBUOD

The Nootka Indians* who lived on the west coast of Vancouver Island used to fish as far away as China and Japan. To get there they navigated by singing.[1] The melody and words keyed to the sun, stars, winds and currents. Not, perhaps, an uncommon practice among early sailing peoples, but here we have a difference. To make the return journey the Nootka sang the songs backwards.

I've never met anyone who could read backwards, let alone sing in reverse. However, I understand that the *Cantabile*, a group of singers who relish challenging conventions, provide a convincing rendition of a scratched 78 record played with a jumping needle, a bizarre version of *Yankee Doodle Dandy* sung in Swahili, and a weird performance of *The Lambeth Walk*. This they sing in reverse order playing the music backwards and the lapel-holding stepping-out routine back to front.

Trying to comprehend in reverse is difficult. Throughout the early 1980s the Russians jammed propaganda radio broadcasts from China. Peking changed tactics and transmitted backwards. The Kremlin stopped jamming. Either they didn't realize what was going on, or — more probably — they assumed it was severe static. Can you possibly imagine what Chinese sounds like backwards? Anyway those in the know recorded and played the tape in reverse.[2]

There used to be an undergraduate society at Oxford called the *Hysteron Proteron Club*. The members, Evelyn Waugh recalled, 'put themselves to great discomfort by living a day in reverse, getting up in evening dress, drinking whisky, smoking cigars and playing cards, then at ten o'clock [in the morning] dining backwards starting with savouries and ending with soup.' In *Time's Arrow*, Martin Amis adopts the same principle to construct a novel. When the narrative begins an old man is expiring in hospital, when it ends he's a new-born vanishing into his mother's body. At meal-times characters regurgitate edibles and spout beverages. Bodily functions are formidable feats of ingestion. Knives heal cuts, pens erase, fists cure black eyes, municipal workers distribute garbage around the streets. Another book, *Counter-Clock World*, employs the same tomb-to-womb device.

* On arriving in the vicinity of Vancouver, Captain Cook asked the local chief the name of the place. The chief, not understanding, replied 'Nu•tka•!' — an expression suggesting Cook go back where he came from. Actually, if you can believe what you read, the entire continent seems to have acquired names in this fashion.

1. Anne Cameron. *Daughters of Copper Woman*. Women's Press (London 1984) 2. *Economist*, 15 November 1986

Buckminster Fuller: 'You've all seen motion pictures run backwards where people undive out the swimming pool back on to the board. I'm going to run a motion picture of you backwards. You've just had breakfast: now, I'm going to run the picture backwards, and all the food comes out of your mouth on to the plate and the plates go back up on to the serving tray and things go back on to the stove, back into the icebox; they come out of the icebox and back into the cans and they go back to the store and then, from the store, they go back to the wholesaler. Then they go back to the factories where they've been put together. Then they go back to trucks and ships, and they finally get back to pineapples in Hawaii. Then the pineapples separate out, go back into the air; the raindrops go back into the sky, and so forth. But in a very fast accelerated reversal of a month, practically everything has come together that you now have on board you, gradually becoming your skin and hair and so forth whereas a month ago it was some air coming over the mountains. In other words, you get completely deployed.' [SEE P115].

These letters were cut out of a carton containing evian, a mineral water produced and bottled in a town of the same name in France. Rearranged and stuck down in reverse order they say something else.

The symbols shown above are encountered every single day of our lives but combining them with their reflected shapes to make symmetrical figures drastically impairs our recognition of them, familiar as they are. ● In contrast the idealized head of Mussolini, sculpted by the Futurist Bertelli, ensures Il Duce is always recognized from whichever side he is seen. It is a three-dimensional palindrome. ● For the Taoists symmetry and repetition were considered fatal, as a treatise on the design of a teahouse firmly indicates. `The various objects for the decoration should be so selected that no colour or design is repeated. If you have a living flower, a painting of flowers is not allowable. If you are using a round kettle, the water pitcher should be angular. A cup with a black glaze should not be associated with a tea caddy of black lacquer. In placing a vase or an incense burner on the tokonoma, care should be taken not to put it in the exact centre, lest it divide the space into equal halves. To break any suggestion of monotony in the room the pillar of the tokonoma should be of a different kind of wood from the other pillars.'[1] ● On the other hand, so to speak, I have a neighbour who is convinced that symmetry (the reflective kind) is synonymous with good taste. He arranges his furniture and plants his terrace accordingly. I'm waiting – we're not on good terms – for an opportunity to inform him that according to the Taoists his aesthetics are stuck between his cranial hemispheres. ● Rich art collector and artist groupy, Peggy Guggenheim, was also asymmetrically inclined as she demonstrated with her mismatched earrings, one by Yves Tanguy and the other by Alexander Calder. [SEE P191]. ● A journalist was having a chat with Giorgio Giugiaro, maestro automobile designer, at a Geneva Motor show in the 1970s when Triumph was launching its TR7 model. According to the journalist, Giugiaro stared for some time at the profile, walked round the car, and then said: 'Oh no. They've done the same thing on this side as well.' [SEE P424]

   1. Okakura Kakuzo. *The Book of Tea*. Charles Tuttle (Tokyo 1956)

beginning up start happy nice eat
196
death war end down finish

Like hiccups, some reversals repeat themselves – the New Year
greeting card for 1961 (opposite) and the French door plate (above).

Others reveal different aspects of the same subject along the
lines of this satirical nineteenth-century caricature. Or create
different scenes with different images like this illustration from
a Victorian children's book.

A popular make of jeans employs the first method to portray the
brand name, albeit a typographically contrived solution.

The second method was employed by a dodgy character in a novel[1]
who tattooed his girlfriend's name on his chest. An unwise move —
she left him soon thereafter — so he was constantly reminded of her
every time he looked down at his navel :

317537

Take note that a truly extraordinary occurrence will happen on the
51st day of the year 2002. On this day the date will be an eight-digit
palindrome: 20. 02. 2002. What is more, at two minutes past eight
on that auspicious evening, the time and date combined will read
20. 02, 20. 02. 2002.

Malcolm de Chazal

'A mirror has no heart but plenty of ideas.'

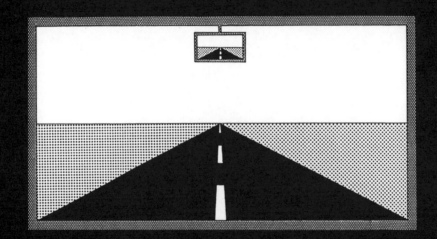

Painting. Patrick Hughes. *Déjà Vu*

Déjà Vu. 'We look at the present through a rear-view mirror,' commented Marshall McLuhan, 'we march backwards into the future.' This painting by Patrick Hughes captures a similar thought and encapsulates it in a timeless moment. The view through a windscreen reveals what lies ahead, the rear-view mirror reflecting what is left behind. A mirror image of the future seen in reverse and the past reflecting what lies ahead.

instrument of illusion

The oldest known mirror is a lump of polished obsidian found in the debris of one of the earliest human settlements dating from 9000 years ago in Turkey. Self-reflection has been with us since the dawn of consciousness. Indeed superstition holds that you can't be sure you're dead until you realize you have no reflection. If you see what I mean.

The mirror made of glass, at the time a miraculous invention, was monopolized by the Venetians who forbade their export on penalty of death.[1] The French King Louis XIV, who owned one valued at three times the price of a Raphael, offered gold and women to tempt Venetian mirror makers across the Alps to live and work in France.

The mirror was also considered to be extremely precious (seven years' bad luck if you broke one) as it had magical properties. For instance, when you look into a mirror which faces another mirror, you are reflected back and forth until you disappear into infinity. It reverses images left to right, but not upside down. When a right-handed person looks in the mirror while shaving, he becomes left-handed. Your reflected image is only half the size it really is, so you never see yourself as you are seen by others. [SEE P489]. And even more disturbing is that the reflection of the person you think you are, isn't you – it's your other you.

One of Saul Steinberg's first drawings was of a man looking in a mirror saying 'Dammit! This isn't me. I got lost in the crowd.' Like Magritte reflecting on the nature of mirrors and how we find and lose our identities. Agnes, a character in a novel by Milan Kundera, looked at it in another way: 'Just imagine living in a world without mirrors. You'd dream about your face and imagine it as an outer reflection of what is inside you. And then, when you reached forty, someone would put a mirror before you for the first time in your life. Imagine your fright! You'd see the face of a stranger. And you'd know quite clearly what you are unable to grasp: your face is not you.'[2]

Anaïs Nin would spend hours writing her diary at her dressing table which had a set of mirrors so she could see herself in triplicate whenever she glanced up. 'I needed to reassure myself that I existed', she explained. She wasn't alone. 'I look in the mirror', says Judy Collins, 'through the eyes of the child that was me.' And Alice B. Toklas wrote that all her life she had

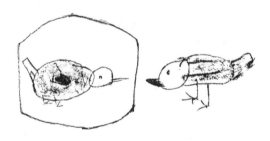

My budgie broke is neck.
It served him rite because
he was always kissing himself
in the mirrer.

Tim aged 6

Illustration. Nanette Newman. *Lots of Love.* Collins (London 1974)   1. Mary McCarthy. *Venice Observed.* Heinemann (London 1961)

looked in the mirror and seen someone else. I know the feeling. While I'm shaving I address this old guy in the mirror and I'm always amazed that, whatever I say, he repeats it exactly.

Mirrors should think before they reflect.

Then there are *metamirs*, metaphysical mirrors which don't obey the law of optics but reproduce your image as seen by the person who stands before you. A generally less favourable image than the one normally reflected or the one you would like to project.

Mirrors also have technical attributes. Painters use them to check their compositions as the reflection provides an alternative view. And in the Renaissance they used convex mirrors to enlarge their angle of vision. In the late seventeenth century amateur landscape painters used the Claude glass to capture the artistic qualities associated with the picturesque. This instrument was a small, portable, slightly convex glass mirror backed with dark foil. When held up to reflect the landscape it was considered to provide optimum framing and a harmonious (albeit tinted) colour scheme.

Black mirrors served a different purpose. '… the object in Madame's drawing room is a black mirror,' wrote Truman Capote[3] after visiting a lady in Martinique. 'It is seven inches tall and six inches wide. It is framed within a worn black leather case that is shaped like a book.' 'It belonged to Gauguin,' she explained, 'they were quite a common artefact among artists of the last century. Van Gogh used one. As did Renoir.' 'What did they use them for?' he asked. 'To refresh their vision. Renew their reaction to colour, the tonal variations. After a spell of work, their eyes fatigued, they rested themselves by gazing at these dark mirrors.' It was a traditional practice of medieval scribes and illuminators to keep polished marbelized stones next to their work, to look at for a while and rest their eyes.

A mirror doesn't reflect things the wrong way round, it reflects what is immediately in front of it. Or rather, as Jonathan Miller explains: 'If I imagine myself facing in the same direction as my reflection seems to be facing, I have to rotate my imagined self through 180 degrees, and when I do so, my right hand is now on the same side as my reflection's left. Hey presto – reversal!'[4]

A pause for reflection.

LOOKING-GLASS, *n*. A vitreous plane upon which to display a fleeting show for man's disillusion given. *The Devil's Dictionary.*

A monkey can't recognize itself in a mirror, but a chimpanzee can. [SEE P9].

'Every mirror is false,' Malcolm de Chazal reminds us, 'because it repeats something it has not witnessed.' Not that that bothered the Nazi propagandists who published this cartoon in the 1930s. The intention was to imply that *The Times* was controlled by Jews. The reflection is as typographically inaccurate (the S and E), as the punning is clumsy … and ballerinas wore tin helmets?

War -„Times"

2. Milan Kundera. *Immortality*. Faber & Faber (London 1991) 3. Truman Capote. *Music for Chameleons*. Signet (New York 1975) 4. Jonathan Miller. *On Reflection*. National Gallery Publications (London 1998) **Cartoon**. Anon

'My deuce,
my double,
my dear image
… what flavour has
that liquor
you lift with
your left hand …?'

*W.H. Auden
on observing himself
in a bar mirror*

'… what I'm trying to do, is Stendhal's definition of a novel, when he says that it's just like walking alongside a road with a mirror. Well for me, the mirror is the camera.'

Louis Malle

A SQUARE PUDDLE

'Philip Quarles, a character in Aldous Huxley's *Point Counter Point*, is a novelist who is planning a musicalized novel of contrapuntal themes. "Put a novelist into the novel," reads one of Quarles's notes. "But why draw the line at one novelist inside your novel? Why not a second inside his? And a third inside the novel of the second? And so on to infinity, like those advertisements of Quaker Oats where there's a quaker holding a box of oats, on which is a picture of another quaker holding another box of oats, on which etc., etc. At about the tenth remove you might have a novelist telling your story in algebraic symbols or in terms of variations in blood pressure, pulse, secretion of ductless glands, and reaction times."'[1] The quaker was not the only one. There was also a nun, at least she looks like a nun, doing the same thing for a brand of cocoa. This classic design illustrating itself on the can repeats itself *ad infinitum*. Actually the curious figure is a cross between a nun and a nurse – no doubt to emphasize that cocoa is good for you. The illustration below is a double double-take, of a double-take, of Bob Gill drawing Bob Gill drawing Bob Gill drawing Bob Gill …

Note. I was having supper in a restaurant, and noticed a couple reflected in a mirror on the other side of the room. They were in deep conversation and – for a moment – I was tempted to wonder whether their conversation was also back to front.

1. Howard Gardner. *Order and Surprise.* Oxford University Press (Oxford 1984)

A better analogy for portfolio insurance might be a medicine that made the situation worse but which automatically gave the patient larger doses as his condition deteriorated .

We live in a world in which the wider uses of markets is stridently advocated for more and more problems. Examples might be tradeable pollution permits or individual personal pensions. Yet such products are based upon the financial assessment of risk. Portfolio insurance shows that, in the well-known City term, 'there's no such thing as a free lunch.'

RUSSELL SPARKES
Fund manager for the Central Finance Board of the Methodist Church and author of The Ethical Investor.

Reflective thought

MIRRORS IN MIND
by Richard Gregory
W.H. Freeman/Spektrum, £25, 302pp. ISBN 0716745119

Mirrors have long been associated with vanity, truth and self-knowledge; with the virtue of prudence and the shades of superstition. We use phrases like 'on reflection' all too readily. The word 'speculation' derives from speculum, Latin for a mirror. We 'inspect' ourselves in a mirror to know how others see us, if back-to-front, remedied if we want nowadays by the camera and screen. Reflection was the cause of Narcissus' watery self-love and early orators like Demosthenes are said to have perfected their skills before, probably, sheets of polished bronze. The mirror in one form or another has always been with us: an alter ego; a spy on our actions; a revealer of hidden thoughts; and, even, the soul. As furniture, it has been an aid to reflecting not only images but light and, with 'walls' of mirrors, falsely extending space. The witch ball, a suspended mirrored globe, was intended to absorb evil spirits. Mirrors were covered on a death in the house to stop the soul's escape to oblivion. The mirror has always been an object of mystery. Richard Gregory, Professor of Neuropsychology and Director of the Brain and Perception Laboratory at Bristol University from 1970 to 1988, successfully and entertainingly unravels many of its properties and spells.

From the reviewer's standpoint as an art historian, the mirror has long been a fascination. It is also more common in painting than the author leads us to believe. His chapter 'Mirrors in Art' dutifully refers to the National Gallery's van Eyck, *The Marriage of Arnolfini*, and Velasquez' *Rokeby Venus*, with its out-of-focus mirrored image of Venus' face which relates, perhaps, to other focal depth tricks of the Caravaggio school. His *Las Meninas* in the Prado is mistakenly reversed but is this sent to try us? Whether by accident or design, slides get projected back to front without an average audience noticing. Painters often use a mirror placed against a work in progress to judge its probity. Mention is made of

famous left-handed painters: Holbein, Picasso, Klee and Leonardo – who penned his notebooks in 'mirror-writing' but not, as claimed, Raphael. Self-portraits by right-handed artists, being mirror images, often fudge the hand doing the painting, when shown. Rembrandt changed his hands over in the Kenwood self-portrait, the unintentioned left-handed posture being visible only in x-ray. Degas and Dali are mentioned but more could have been devoted to Magritte's most intriguing 'mirrambiguity', *La Réproduction Interdite*, and other works.

Much of the rest of this book consists of substantial studies of visual and mental perception which comprise an admirable if highly technical foil to the writings of Sir Ernst Gombrich, a friend of the author, from *Art and illusion* onwards. There is a useful chapter on techniques of mirror manufacture, 'Making and using mirrors' and (more challenging) on 'Handedness', with wider implications. Alice's relief on emerging from the looking glass can be shared with some exultation on reaching the final page of this fascinating study – so many doors of perception are opened and we are conducted through them with great erudition and not without some of Magritte's humour and wit.

JOHN COOPER
Art historian and lecturer

René Magritte, La réproduction interdite
(Not to be reproduced), 1937.

79

 [SEE P259].

Painting. Anna Pugh

THERE WAS A MAN

WHO BECAME

SO INTRIGUED WITH

WATCHING SALAMANDERS,

THAT HE ENDED UP

AS A SALAMANDER

WATCHING THE MAN

HE WAS.

JULIO CORTÁZAR

17.3.1974   7.25 p.m. Leeds-London train

The woman in the corner seat wears a green velvet coat trimmed with imitation fur, and knee-length maroon suede boots. She falls asleep, sinking into the corner of the seat. Her red velvet skirt slides up around her thighs; her mouth falls open and is reflected in the window, superimposed on the night landscape outside. The train runs parallel with a motorway: cars and lorries rush into her mouth, their headlights on full. She wakes up coughing.

Ian Breakwell's Diary. 1964-1985

Wann, an Anglo-Saxon word which has no modern equivalent, re

Fealo referred to the glint of a shield or the sparkle of the sea. In

source), lumen (a beam or ray), colour which was the effect on

effect until the discovery of transparent glazes enabled painters

of metal, the shimmer of silks, the glow of burnished silver and th

quality – the fascination of mirrors and beads for the natives is e

an Irish scribe: 'Pleasant to me is the glittering of the sun upor

writes,[1] 'I love the constancy of shine on the edges of moving obj

in the grayness of their rotation …' Light (Gk phos, photos) has

'I've seen the light,' or 'it dawned on me.' We recognize a saint

bulb over his head. And brilliant people are bright – not dim.

  1. Nicholson Baker. *The Mezzanine.* Granta Books (Cambridge 1990)

ed to the gloss on a raven's wing or the sheen off a coat of mail.

dieval times the properties of light were categorized into lux (the

rface, and splendour – the reflected lustrous quality. An elusive

epresent the glitter of diamonds, the lustre of pearls, the sheen

parkle of crystal. Shining, particularly if iridescent, has a magical

ed by a note jotted in an illuminated ninth-century manuscript by

ese margins, because it flickers so.' Similarly, Nicholson Baker

. Even propellers or desk fans will glint steadily in certain places

r properties. When we suddenly understand something, we say

is halo, an individual who has a flash of inspiration by the light

Photograph. Martin Parr

William Feaver   'Pattern, the fruit of design, can be seen as the measure of culture.'

An ancient Egyptian craftsman manipulated nature by tracing the spots off a leopard's skin, and then reversing them to make a pattern of pale ivory patches set into black ebony. The design forms the seat of King Tut's stool. Actually what you see on this page are shapes I traced off the ancient design, which had been traced off that leopard skin 3300 years ago. In some way the process of re-enactment gave me the feeling of sharing something with the past — creating an echo. This wall is in Ayia Triádha, a monastery in Crete. A recent renovation of cement and pink paint decorating a plain surface with stunning simplicity; an impromptu texture which man has been doing for thousands of years. No equipment, no tools, just gouging and flicking damp mud walls with the thumb. An economic gesture which captures sunlight to create a texture of ever shifting random highlights and shallow dark patches.[SEE P270]. Addendum. Visiting the monastery a year later I checked up on the wall. Silly me. It had been smoothly plastered and painted a pale ochre. The pattern had, it seems, been no more than a rough rendering to key the plaster.

Different
patterns can
be made by
manipulating
a single
shape.

This odd
looking
floor tile
demonstrates
the premise
on the
following
pages.

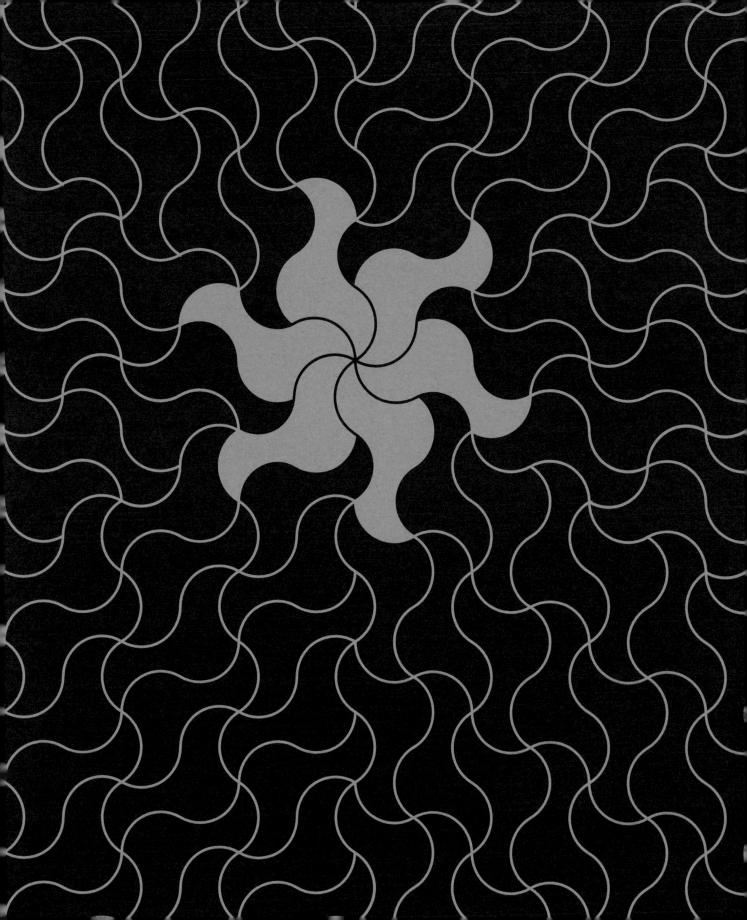

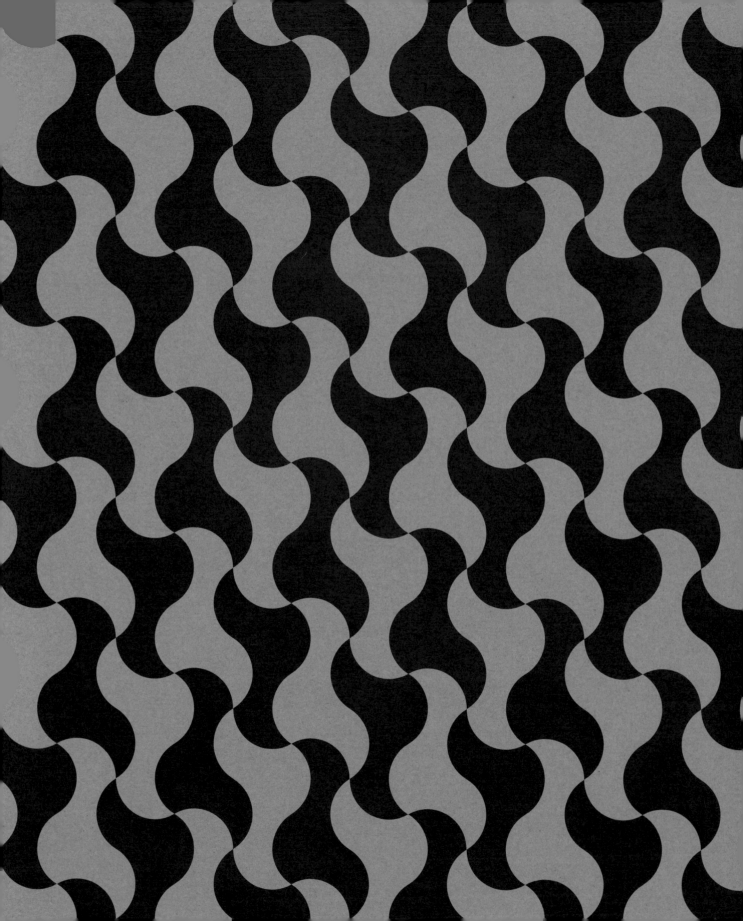

This framed Victorian case of samples – nuts and bolts, nails and screws, cleats and clamps – was mass-produced for stock display in ironmongers and hardware stores. The customer could identify and point out which items he required. Not so long ago one such shop was undergoing refurbishment and modernization. This item was put out with the other rubbish. A friend of mine did them a favour and carried it away. It was so heavy he had to park it with me. I did him a favour and hung it on my living-room wall. It's a notable example of pattern as advertising, and advertising as art. The reverse side is equally spectacular. All the screws and nails are held in place by thin wires threaded through the backboard and fixed in place with blobs of silver solder.

bowerbirds & bacteria

In nature decoration always has a practical purpose. In Australia male bowerbirds build stick structures up to three metres high which they decorate with orchids, shells, butterfly wings, bird feathers, bottle tops, toothbrushes, whatever they can find. They also colour them with fruit juices by using fibres held in their beaks. To build a seductive bower, Jared Diamond explains, the bowerbird must be endowed 'with physical strength, dexterity and endurance, plus searching skills and memory – as if women were to choose husbands on the basis of a triathlon contest extended to include a chess game and sewing exercise.'[1] Made to attract females, they obviously work in that respect as the promiscuous bowerbird has an astonishingly high score. There's a clue somewhere in there.

Alberti described ornament as an additional brightness and someone else, who exactly I don't recall, reckoned that ornament is lumpy and pattern smooth. Convention insists on a clear separation between applied and fine art. Ruskin described architecture as decoration of structure and Pugin said that one should never construct decoration. The decorator should stylize, the painter should not. A flower on a wallpaper should be flat, a flower in a picture three-dimensional.

Antoni Gaudí had no such hang-ups. The undulating façade of his Casa Batlló in Barcelona (43 Paseo de Gracia, corner of Arago) is speckled with coloured fragments of ceramic and glass, punctuated by fluid balconies, and culminating in a reptilian tower capped by a cross. The façade is supported on giant columns resembling elephants' feet and the chimneys have tiny mirrors that sparkle in the sun. Anthony Burgess described it in similar terms: '... balconies like carnival masks, lizardy roof-tiles, roughcast walls stuck all over with fairy money, pillars like limbs, stone dripping like stalactites ...'

The interior is a grotto of polished sea shell in *café au lait* and turquoise, penetrated by a light shaft of pale blue tiles shading into darker hues to reduce glare. Apart from the floors, no surface is flat, and no line is straight. 'The corners will vanish, and the material will reveal itself in the wealth of its astral curves,' Gaudí noted in his diary. 'The sun will shine through all four sides and it will be like a vision of paradise.'

In the 1920s architect Adolf Loos dogmatically stated 'culture is synonymous with the removal of ornament from utilitarian objects'. And went on to say that 'lack of ornament is a sign of intellectual power.' However, advocacy of glass and concrete boxes was not his only eccentricity – he always pressed his trousers sideways and asked to be buried in a cube mounted on a plinth when he died. He was.

The making of patterns introduces a degree of control into the chaotic world. Akin to tidying up and putting things in order, it is probably a by-product of plaiting and weaving. Perhaps it began by someone noticing the imprint left by a basket in the earth, the foliage of a tree against the sky, the tracks of a bird in the snow, the speckle of a pebbled beach.

The squiggly pattern shown right was contrived by Ettore Sottsass who was prompted by pictures of swarming bacteria. *Bacterio* is a product of the 1970s Memphis movement in Milan, a style which reinvented the conventions of pattern and form by utilizing and glamorizing the tacky and tawdry. [SEE P319].

1. Jared Diamond. *Guns, Germs and Steel.* Jonathan Cape (London 1997)

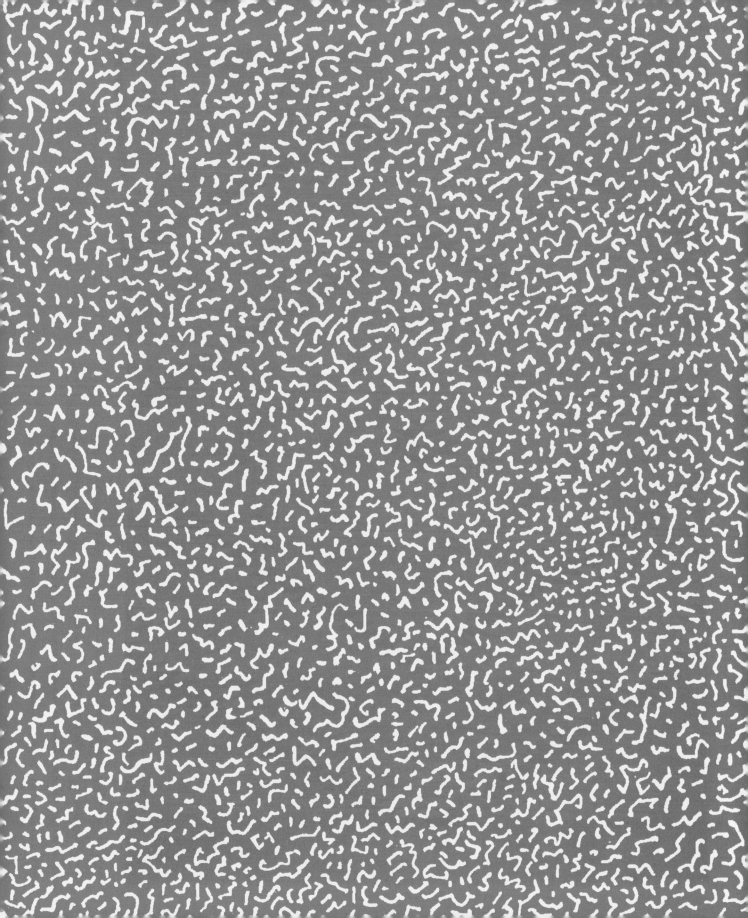

Serape. Courtesy of Joshua Baer & Company, Santa Fe

In the 1880s the railroad arrived in the American Southwest along with barbed wire [SEE P307], blue jeans [SEE P56] and canned food. The railroad also brought machine-spun synthetic-dyed knitting yarns produced in Germantown, Pennsylvania. The Navajo liked the uniform quality and bright colours. In this eyedazzler serape (circa 1885, and measuring 74 by 54 inches), two trains run in opposite directions along the top and bottom.

MAGIC CARPETS. Edward James was the mega-rich patron of René Magritte, Pavel Tchelitchew, Leonora Carrington, Salvador Dalí and Balanchine. He was also a poet, art collector, bizzare interior designer as his house in Sussex testifies, founder of a craft school in Sussex and builder of a surrealist palace in the Mexican jungle. James was that rare personality – an enthusiast. One of his artefacts that comes to mind is a carpet woven with a pattern of his wife's wet footprints. Whether as an act of expediency, or homage, or novelty, I have no idea. Anyway, after a fracas with his wife Tilly Losch, a tempestuous Austrian ballet dancer, he divorced and had the design replaced with the paw prints of his dog.[1] [He cited Prince Serge Obolensky, who played rugby for England 1936, came up with the idea of adding Tabasco sauce to the Bloody Mary in New York, and died at the controls of a Hawker Hurricane in 1940.] The footprints appeared decades later as cement stepping stones in the grounds of Xilitla, his concrete El Dorado in Mexico. The designs of traditional carpets are less fickle but equally whimsical. The ethnic carpet is an ecology of fanciful creatures, exotic birds, stylized flowers, arabesques and sacred signs: the flame of Zoroaster, the loop of the river Jumna, the elephant's footprint, the imprint of a fist on wet plaster – pictorial echoes of the cultures which made them. During the occupation of Afghanistan by the Russians, flora and fauna were replaced by helicopters, Kalashnikovs, tanks and grenades. And for good reason. The carpet can be a child's primer: don't hurt that, pointing at a flower; don't touch that, pointing at a scorpion – or a grenade. 'Paradise' is derived from the Persian word for garden, and the Sassanid kings created a perpetual paradise in their huge carpets, lined with canals and populated with birds, trees and flowers. All picked out in gold and silver thread and studded with jewels. Even the poor nomad wandering a barren and hostile desert could carry his imaginary paradise in a two-dimensional Eden. By pitching his tent and unfolding his woven garden he could create an instant oasis. When it was time to move on he rolled it up, put it under his arm, and rode off into the sunset.

Note. You know if you are in an English hotel of indifferent category because of the vomit carpets with tortured florals, bilious colours and patterns of mind-numbing insensitivity. Clumpy, crude, crass interpretations of delicate, elegant, fragile flowers. Favoured colours are distressed maroons, and violated violets nestling in custard and mustard yellow foliage. A generalization I admit, but you'll know what I mean when you see it.

1. Nicola Coleby (ed.). *A Surreal Life: Edward James.* Exhibition Catalogue, Royal Pavilion (Brighton 1998)

'It is a constant idea of mine, that behind the cotton wool (of daily reality) is hidden a pattern; that we — I mean all human beings — are connected with this; that the whole world is a work of art; that we are parts of the work of art.' Virginia Woolf *(A Sketch of the Past)*

The Euclidian world is neat and orderly. A geometric structure of lines, circles, triangles and squares; spheres, pyramids and cubes. The sort of neat man-made place we have when an architect has got his hands on a shopping mall.

In the fractal world everything is tangled and mangled. Fractals are fuzzier than a line, never quite fill a plane, inhabit geometry which mixes dimensions, and create an environment which is grainy, wiggly, wrinkled and uneven. A chaotic landscape of marks and tracks inflicted by the passage of time. Something more like a hallucinatory experience than a real place.

The Mandelbrot Set is an aspect of fractal geometry. This is when a tiny detail (a fractal) within a pattern is magnified and displays another pattern which is a replica of the first. And when a tiny detail of this is magnified it yields yet another identical pattern, and so on — ad infinitum. Many phenomena from cloud formations to stock-market fluctuations have this property.

patterns of chaos

The conundrum explored in a scientific paper called 'How Long is the Coast of Britain?' explains how selecting a piece of the coastline on the page of a map, one imagines how it might look viewed through a telescope from outer space, or even through a microscope. You would find the contours more or less look the same. Counterfeiters take note — I am informed paper money is being designed using fractal patterns which blur when copied. [SEE PP432&511].

It transpires that patterns in nature are made up of layer upon layer upon layer, like the exquisite dessert *mille foglie*, and no matter how much you enlarge or reduce them they never change. For a more accurate instance — cauliflowers, where each floret of the edible bit resembles the whole.

Fractal observations have been around for quite a while. Fourteenth-century Italian painter and scribe Cennino Cennini : 'If you wish to acquire a good style for mountains, and to have them look natural, take some large stones, sharp-edged and not smooth, and copy them from nature, applying the lights and darks as the rule prescribes.'

As one enthusiast says, 'if you like fractals it is because you are made of them. But if you can't stand fractals, it's probably because you can't stand yourself.' It happens.

Fractal. Professor Mario Markus at the Max-Planck-Institut

Pattern: Roger Penrose   1.   Douglas Hofstadter, *Metamagical Themas*, Penguin Books (London 1986)   2.   John Brockman & Katinka Matson, *How Things Are*, Phoenix (London 1996)

PARQUETS

Over the years William Huff, an American professor of architecture, has orchestrated the creation of linear patterns with his students.[1] He calls them PARQUETS, after the style of wood flooring. His PARQUETS also tessellate – smart word for tiles which pattern an infinite plane – but his can be exceedingly disconcerting as their irregular groupings change and fluctuate as the eye travels around zooming in and out, trying to get a lock on what it's looking at. Such patterns create a visual pseudo-chaos in which shapes cluster, configurations dissolve, the eye flickers, the mind gets dizzy. They have been neatly described by Louis Kahn, another architect, as 'the religion of the ordered path'. [SEE P382] The PARQUET principle is illustrated above, although this is a pattern with a difference – I'll come to that in a moment. Mathematician Ian Stewart claims there are ' ... precisely seventeen different types of repeating pattern that can fill a plane and two hundred and thirty different types of pattern that can fill three-dimensional space.'[2] I believe him. Supposedly they can all be found among the Islamic patterns which richly decorate the Alhambra in Grenada. [SEE P234] If the simplest pattern is the chequerboard and its three-dimensional expression of interlocking cubes, then the most complex pattern must be one invented [and patented] by Sir Roger Penrose. This is the one illustrated here and, as you can see, generates mind-boggling variations. A-crazy-quilted-kaleidoscope-of-facets. Even a computer trying to calculate all the combinations would develop a serious headache. You can discern truncated cubes, wonky polygons, skewed parallelograms, weird trapezoids and other geometric astonishments. [SEE P241] A pattern on Prozac. Speaking of which a well-known commercial corporation which manufactures toilet rolls must have seen the pattern somewhere [where?] and thought it rather attractive. It also thought the design would enhance the appearance, texture, appeal, and sales of their product. Sir Roger came across one of these enhanced toilet rolls. He was not amused. He started legal proceedings. A pattern with a patent.

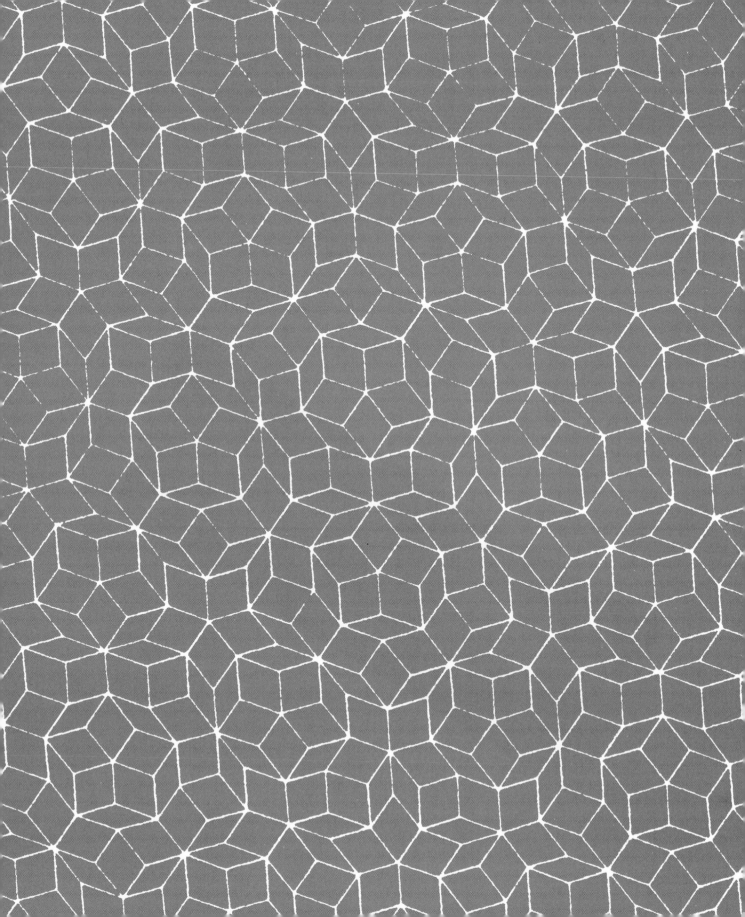

I cut this off a roll of sticky industrial tape. The camouflage pattern — I guess — is intended to disguise the fact it is a piece of sticky industrial tape.

James Joyce

'Interpretations of interpretations interpreted.'

Born to live in open savannah, among tall wavering grasses and under the hot sun, the tiger is encaged in a utilitarian zoo. Industrial ceramic washable tiles and a barren polished cement floor. Can you comprehend the crushing insensitivity of the grey bureaucrats which condemns a wild animal to live in this monstrous environment?

Photograph. Britta Jaschinski

Photograph. Ronald C. James (1966)

'I spilt spot remover
on my dog
and he disappeared.'

JACK BENNY

Camouflage, Parisian *argot* for a puff of smoke in the face so the thief could quickly nick your wallet, operates by either making the conspicuous inconspicuous or the inconspicuous conspicuous. A chameleon-like ability to merge into the background like the fluffy white-feathered Ptarmigan in arctic and alpine snow or the Praying Mantis (Devil's Blossom) masquerading as a flower or leafy twig to attract and gobble up insects.

The objective of camouflage is to mislead rather than conceal. To disguise rather than to hide. Take the butterfly. The edible Viceroy has adopted a guise to imitate the inedible Monarch. As a caterpillar the Monarch consumed enough noxious poisons to sicken any untutored predatory bird. Another species of butterfly illustrates flowers on its wings so it merges into the flora and foliage. Then there is the smart moth – *Stenoma algidella* – which masquerades as a bird dropping.[1]

Countershading is another subterfuge. A gazelle is darkest on the back which is always in sunlight and lightest underneath the belly which is in shade. In favourable lighting the three-dimensional form can appear flat, of uniform shade, and entirely disappear. The penguin is also dressed in tuxedo for good reason. It may look comical standing up but when swimming the white front blends with the pale sky when viewed from beneath and the black back merges with the dark depths when seen from above.

Disruptive patterns use bars, stripes, spots, blotches, splotches, dapples and patches, to fragment silhouettes. The striped tiger merges imperceptibly into long grass to await an unwary passer-by.

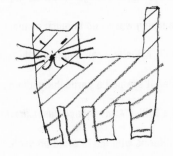

Confrontational marking works on the contrary principle. This is typified by a particularly large (and nasty) spider in Australia which only fancies small insects, and so spins a large white cross on its web to warn off larger flying items. The little ones can't see it. A more sympathetic species spins white zigzags as a signal to butterflies to avoid entanglement.

In *The Cruise of the Snark* Jack London describes skimming 'in a chromatic ecstasy' over a Pacific reef; however, the conspicuously iridescent coloured vibrant fish of the Great Barrier Reef aren't intended to delight the eye. They are extremely poisonous. By flaunting their presence, they warn predators to avoid making a fatal culinary mistake.

1. Stephen Jay Gould. *Bully for Brontosaurus*. Penguin (London 1996)

A slash of angular blacks
Like a fractured edifice
That was buttressed by blue slants
In a coma of the moon.

Wallace Stevens

At the Royal College of Art, during the early 1950s, the student joke was that the teaching wasn't up to much as most of the staff had been in the army camouflage unit. Actually, I can remember thinking that if camouflage was the art of deception, then it seemed a particularly appropriate qualification. 🐌 In the days of the Raj the British Army rubbed dust (*khaki*) on their scarlet jackets and dyed their white uniforms with tea to avoid presenting targets. Just as the Scots ghillie and stalker wore tweeds which have colours echoing mist, heather, gorse and bracken. During the First World War the protagonists employed artists to design camouflage to disguise installations but the first official military camouflage unit was French. Fashionable Parisian portraitist Guirand de Sceuola was appointed to supervise the artists, among whom were André Dunoyer de Segonzac and Jacques Villon. The German Expressionist Franz Marc, best remembered for his blue horses, decorated nine tarpaulins to hide artillery from spotter planes and ecstatically wrote to his wife that he painted each of them in differing styles from Manet to Kandinsky! Neither Marc nor his artworks survived. 🐌 In the Second World War designer and painter Willi Baumeister was forbidden to paint abstracts by the Nazi authorities. Caught at work one day by an official, he adroitly explained that the pictures were experiments in camouflage. The inspector was so impressed he recommended him to the military – a response obliquely analogous to the dubious story about the

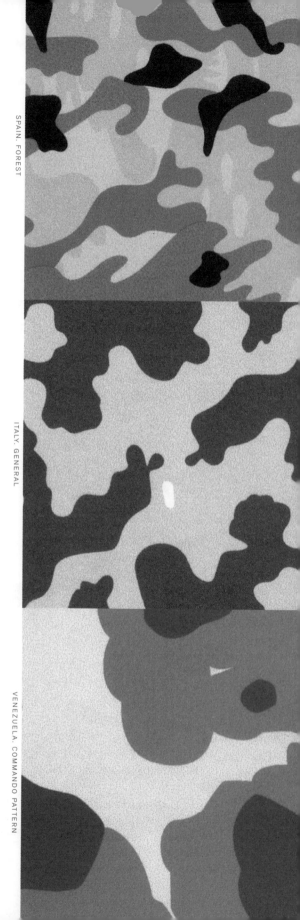

SPAIN. FOREST

ITALY. GENERAL

VENEZUELA. COMMANDO PATTERN

GABON. GENDARMERIE

USA. CHOCOLATE CHIP 1970s

ZAIRE. 1970s

Highlander confusing a sheep with a Wren in a duffle coat. ᔥ US army doctrine had long held that camouflage was a passive response to warfare, and only introduced it during the 1940s with their classic 'frog' pattern. This was created by one Norvell Gillespie, a gardening editor for *Better Homes and Gardens* magazine. However, the use of camouflaged uniforms only became the norm during the Vietnam War. ᔥ The largest collection of camouflaged uniforms was made by Dr Jean Borsarello but eventually he sold them. *'C'est trop,'* he said, 'There used to be just one army camouflage per country. Now there are five or six – Russia has 25!' Perhaps another reason was that ownership of Nazi memorabilia is illegal in France. ᔥ Since the objective of camouflage is deception, this creates a paradox because at the same time one has to distinguish friend from foe. Patterns and colours need to be distinguished. Thus, ironically, camouflage has become distinctive, each country favouring its own design. ᔥ Another characteristic of the genre is matching names with designs : Jigsaw, Splinter, Ragged Leaf, Pine Needles, Falling Rain, Brushstroke, Duck Hunter, Plane Tree, Tigerstripe, Woodland, Clouds, Night Desert, Chocolate Chip, Oak Leaf.[1] ᔥ Anyway, conventional camouflage is on its way out. In the future disguise will be acheived by a myriad of micro-dot light-sensitive chemical sensors impregnated in material to respond to all kinds of environment. Man will, in effect, become chameleon. ᔥ

THE HUNTER

The hunter crouches in his blind
'neath camouflage of every kind,
And conjures up a quacking noise
To lend allure to his decoys.
This grown-up man, with pluck and luck
Is hoping to outwit a duck.

Ogden Nash

1. Tim Newark, Quentin Newark, Dr J F Borsarello. *Brassey's Book of Camouflage*. Brassey's (London 1996)

breeze. But there was no breeze: the trees and bushes were not moving.

Or were they?

Thorne had the sense that something was wrong. Something right before his eyes, something that he could see but couldn't see. With the effort of staring, he began to think his eyes were playing tricks on him. He thought he detected a slight movement in the bushes to the right. The pattern of the leaves seemed to shift in the moonlight. Shift, and stabilize again.

But he wasn't sure.

Thorne stared forward, straining. And as he looked he began to think that it wasn't the bushes that had caught his eye, but rather the chain-link fence. For most of its length, the fence was overgrown with an irregular tangle of vines, but in a few places the regular diamond pattern of links was visible. And there was something strange about that pattern. The fence seemed to be moving, rippling.

Thorne watched the fence, pushing against it.

Maybe there's an animal inside the fence, he thought. Maybe it is moving, he thought. But that didn't seem quite right.

It was something else. . . .

Suddenly, lights came on inside the store. They shone through the barred windows, casting a geometric pattern of dark shadows across the open clearing, and onto the bushes by the tennis court. And for a moment—just a moment—Thorne saw that the bushes beside the tennis court were oddly shaped, and that they were actually two dinosaurs, seven feet tall, standing side by side, staring right at him.

Their bodies seemed to be covered in a patchwork pattern of light and dark that made them blend in perfectly with the leaves behind them, and even with the fence of the tennis court. Thorne was confused. Their concealment had been perfect—too perfect—until the lights from the store windows had shone out and caught them in the sudden bright glare.

Thorne watched, holding his breath. And then he realized

that the leafy light-and-dark pattern went only partway up their bodies, to mid-thorax. Above that, the animals had a kind of diamond-shaped crisscross pattern that matched the fence.

And as Thorne stared, the complex patterns on their bodies faded, the animals turned a chalky white, and then a series of vertical striped shadows began to appear, which exactly matched the shadows cast by the two windows.

And before his eyes, the two dinosaurs disappeared from view again. Squinting, with concentrated effort, he could just barely distinguish the outlines of their bodies. He would never have been able to see them at all, had he not already known they were there.

They were chameleons. But with a power of mimicry unlike any chameleon Thorne had ever seen.

Slowly, he backed away into the shed, moving deeper into darkness.

"My God!" Levine exclaimed, staring out the window.

"Sorry," Harding said. "But I had to turn on the lights. That boy needs help. I can't do it in the dark."

Levine did not answer her. He was staring out the window, trying to comprehend what he had just seen. He now realized what he had glimpsed the day Diego was killed. That brief momentary sense that something was wrong. Levine now knew what it was. But it was quite beyond anything that was known among terrestrial animals and—

"What is it?" she said, standing alongside him at the window. "Is it Thorne?"

"Look," Levine said.

She stared out through the bars. "At the bushes? What? What am I supposed to—"

"Look," he said.

She watched for a moment longer, then shook her head. "I'm sorry."

"Start at the bottom of the bushes," Levine told her. "Then

Experimental camouflage patterns being tested in the Nevada desert in 1944

'WHEN YOU'VE BEEN SOMEWHERE
FOR A WHILE, YOU ACQUIRE THE ABILITY
TO BE PRACTICALLY INVISIBLE.
THIS LETS YOU OPERATE
WITH A MINIMUM OF INTERFERENCE.'
JENNY HOLZER

DAZZLE

The text on this page is set in *Kabel* typeface, designed in 1920 by Rudolph Koch and so named to commemorate the laying of the first cable from Europe to America.

'On a cold morning early in 1917, Lieutenant Norman Wilkinson was in a railway carriage travelling to Devonport to rejoin his unit, a Royal Naval Volunteer Reserve motor launch section. Through the window he watched the way the progress of the train across the landscape caused the colours and shapes of the fields and trees to vary continuously; it suddenly occurred to him that ships could be painted overall in abstract patterns of colour in a way that would confuse the eye and the judgement of anyone seeing them against the sky through a submarine periscope.'[1] Wilkinson came to the conclusion that although it was impossible to camouflage a ship at sea, it was possible to cause confusion. To judge where and when to fire torpedoes the predatory submarine had to assess the distance, direction and speed of the target. DAZZLE PAINTING was intended to confound this judgement. Designs were painted on models and tested against backdrops in the basement of the Royal Academy in Piccadilly. The principle was to optically alter physical features. Ships were painted with different patterns and designs which folded around construction points, formed illusionary shapes to imply non-existent structures, created misleading angles and split flat areas into bands and slices. These shapes were then painted in pale colours, juxtaposed with black and greys, to blend ship with sky and water. Tricked out in a medley of aggressive arcs, stripes and lozenges in various tones, the vessels presented a bewildering target. Peering through a periscope at a convoy it was difficult to see which piece belonged to which section and which section to which ship. It must have been an amazing sight. Ships appeared to bend and plunge, be both coming and going and zig-zagging in all directions at once. By the way, HMS BROKE, the first British ship to be camouflaged in this way, was accidentally rammed on her first excursion. I guess that means the design was particularly effective, although with a name like that what did the captain expect? In peacetime Norman Wilkinson was your conventional artist of grey naval patrols on sparkling seas, although one of considerable reputation, and one of his seascapes hung in the smoking room of the TITANIC. Edward Wadsworth, who in one year supervised the patterning of 2000 ships, although never actually creating one of the designs, later came to fame as a Vorticist painter.

Extracts from Marinetti's Notebook. 28, 29, 30 June 1918. Genoa: The ships are camouflaged with dynamic lines and acute angles very similar to the dynamic lines of Boccioni and Balla. They have been done in this fashion to defend themselves from the German submarines ... The port of Genoa is like an exhibition of futuristic paintings.[2]

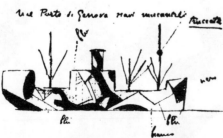

1. Paul Atterbury. *Antique Collector*, vol. 46. April 1975   2. F.T. Marinetti. *Taccuini*. Il Molino (Bologna 1987)   **Illustration.** Sketch by Marinetti, Linocut by Edward Wadsworth

Greek coffee

Gertrude Stein

'I like a view but I like to sit with my back turned to it.'

The quality of a design depends on the economy of means used to achieve it. The bending of a piece of wire to create a paper clip gets high marks, the clearing of fifty-five square feet of Brazilian rainforest to graze enough beef to make a hamburger doesn't. Perhaps the optimum principle of *'less is more'* is the FULL MOON THEATRE near Montpellier in France. This is a natural amphitheatre lit entirely by directed and reflected moonlight, a dramatic arena of minimum human intervention.

The first move in any creative process is to introduce constraints. This brings potentials into focus which may be overlooked in more generous conditions. *'All I need to make a comedy,'* said Charlie Chaplin, *'is a park, a policeman and a pretty girl.'* He didn't mention an agile mind but that was implicit. In 1923 Moholy-Nagy composed three abstract paintings with industrial colours on graph paper by calling a sign factory and dictating the specifications over the phone. At the time that was a radical idea. An art critic (with less restraint) reviewed the results in a newspaper: *'don't talk about coldness, mechanization; this is sensuality refined to its most sublimated expression ...'* Critics are not noted for constraint.

Another scenario is related by the writer Ralph Caplan[1] who was attending a seminar on creativity some forty years later. *'One part of the project involved architects who were asked to perform an exercise which consisted of designing a building, based on a set of modular plastic cubes, which came in a rich variety of colours. They all went to the storehouse so they could pick out their cubes and they went back to studios and designed something.'* Caplan records that afterwards he heard Eero Saarinen ask Philip Johnson which colours he had picked. *'Black and white'*, Johnson said. *'What about you?'* *'White,'* replied Saarinen. Less can be more than enough. *'Affluence offers the kind of freedom I am deeply suspicious of,'* wrote Charles Eames, *'It offers freedom from restraint, and it is virtually impossible to do something without restraints.'* For a while photographer Martin Parr [SEE P253] even restricted himself to only take photographs on grey days when it was raining or bad weather. G.K. Chesterton was even more reductionist: *'Art is limitation; the essence of every picture is the frame.'* For Georges Braque art was not extending limits but knowing them better, an axiom exemplified by Hokusai with his thirty-six views of MOUNT FUJI, and by Monet with his thirty variations on the façade of ROUEN CATHEDRAL. By the way, when in London Monet did about a hundred sketches and paintings of CHARING CROSS and WATERLOO bridges. He stayed in rooms 508 and 509 at the SAVOY HOTEL. Both have views of the Thames. Incidentally, before 1900 in Britain, there were only 23 different building materials in common use and now there are well over 2,000 – is the architecture any better?

An aside: Wassily Kandinsky, artist, teacher and believer in theosophy, spent much of his life exploring line, form and colour. While at the BAUHAUS he sent a questionnaire (right) to all the members of the school to gauge their views on the synesthetic relations between shape and colour. [SEE P137]. The majority chose yellow for the triangle, red for the square, and blue for the circle. ▲ ■ ● This confirmed Kandinsky's thesis. In the year 2000 I copied his questionnaire and gave it to 18 students at FABRICA, a school of design, photography and music housed in a building by Tadao Ando just outside Venice. They were from a variety of backgrounds and countries. 7 students responded ▲ ■ ● , 4 ▲ ■ ● , 4 ▲ ■ ● , 2 ▲ ■ ● and 1 ▲ ■ ● . I don't think Kandinsky would have been too happy.

The brief was to produce a colourful, happy poster to commemorate an annual event when classy furniture manufacturers invited classy architects and designers to visit their showrooms. The intention, while plying them with food and drink, was to show off the latest products.

I could, the client said, do whatever I liked. Bad news. Open-ended problems need boundaries to avoid any unnecessary excursions and limit the area of creative play. So the first move was to set these up. Where one draws the boundaries affects the rules, the type of game and the nature of its outcome.

I settled for the three basic shapes of circle, triangle and square. And the three primary colours of red, blue and yellow. I also threw in grey to create a handicap.

These elements constituted the players, the rules were budgets and deadlines. The game was to add pencilled lines to convey a lighthearted day. The score was the degree to which prosaic ingredients were successfully converted into party pieces.

By the way a game, according to the celebrated formulation by Wittgenstein, consists of the rules by which it is played. So if you want to win — make up the rules. [SEE P143].

Fachgebiet (Beruf): ....   Zu Untersuchungszwecken
Geschlecht: ....   bittet die Werkstatt für
Staatsangehörigkeit: ....   Wandmalerei des Bau-
                                           hauses Weimar, folgende
                                           Aufgaben zu lösen:
                                           1. Füllen Sie diese drei
                                              Formen mit den drei
                                              Farben Gelb, Rot und
                                              Blau aus. Die Farbe soll-
                                              te die jeweilige Form
                                              ganz ausfüllen.
                                           2. Geben Sie, wenn mög-
                                              lich, eine Erklärung für
                                              Ihre Farbverteilung.
                                           Erklärung:

    1. Ralph Caplan. 'Notes on Creativity'. *STA Journal* (winter 1980)

gravestones
St. Thomas
Winchelsea

'Nature uses as little as possible of anything.' *Johannes Kepler*

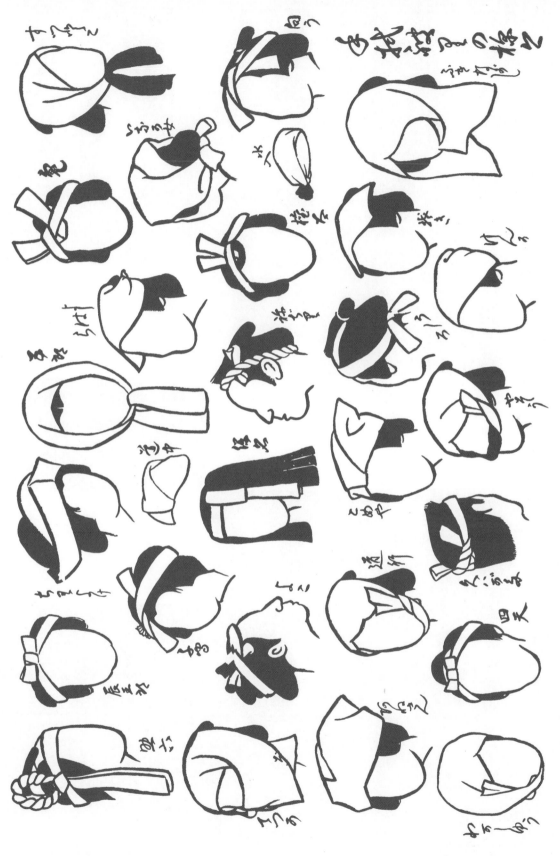

Making do. The Japanese *tenugui* is a length of cotton, in the proportion of one to two. With imagination and dexterity it can be whichever style of headgear you fancy – here are a few. These crude illustrations are from a cheap broadsheet I found on a stall selling *tenugui* in a Tokyo street market.

Mies van der Rohe
Less is more*

Frank Lloyd Wright
**Less is only more
when more is no good**

Norman Foster
Achieve more with less

Robert Venturi
Less is a bore

Gianni Versace
Less is a snore

Gianfranco Ferré
For me more is more

Theo Crosby
Less is less

Newspaper headline on
a political appointment –
More of less

Rodney Kinsman
**Less is more – providing you
had more to begin with**

Ivana Trump
**As you get older
less is always more**

Kingsley Amis
More means worse

Ettore Sottsass
**I'm for maximalism,
minimalism is very protestant**

William Shakespeare
More matter with less art

✳ Actually from *Andrea del Sarto* by Browning

'Brevity is the soul of lingerie.'
Dorothy Parker

'You can't create unless you're willing to subordinate the creative impulse to the constriction of a form.'
Anthony Burgess

'The more constraints one imposes, the more one frees oneself of the chains that shackle the spirit.'
Igor Stravinsky

'Much more would be done if people believed less was impossible.'
Malesherbes

'The economy of means is founded on the richness of thought.'
Henryk Tomaszewski

'Great effects with little means.'
Beethoven

'Simple is better than complicated. Quiet is better than noisy. What is close at hand is better than what has to be sought.'
Dieter Rams

'Infinite use of finite means.'
Humboldt

'The fewer limitations the artist imposes on his work, the less chance he has for artistic success.'
Alexander Solzhenitsyn

'Expression through compression.'
Robert Bresson

'The art of art, the glory of expression and the sunshine of the light of letters, is simplicity.'
Walt Whitman

'Everything that is exact is short.'
Joseph Joubert

'Imagine a piano having seventy-five different sounds. This is the situation of painters.'
Salvador Dalí

'"More of a good thing" isn't necessarily better.'
Michael Macrone

'Maximum meaning = minimum means.'
Abram Games

'I want … to write for large bunches of people about how much pleasure there is in things no bigger than a fly's eye.'
Clifford Odets

'Parsimony is a criterion of good theory.'
Edward O. Wilson

'The problem about art is not finding more freedom, it's about finding obstacles.'
Richard Rogers

'Liberating power of constraint.'
P.D. James

'Give me a laundry list and I will set it to music.'
Gioacchino Rossini

'How can you govern a country which has 264 different kinds of cheese?'
General de Gaulle

'Elimination is the point of departure.'
A.G. Fronzoni

'Entities ought not to be multiplied except from necessity.'
William of Occam

'Without firm limits there is no play.'
Rem Koolhaas

'Conciseness in art is a necessity and a grace.'
Edouard Manet

'Limit gives form to the limitless.'
Pythagoras

'Romance is still necessary, ornament is necessary and simplification is not better than complexity.' Milton Glaser

'There is less in this than meets the eye.'
Tallulah Bankhead

Note. Three of nature's little economies: The Darkling Beetle conjures up moisture where there appears to be none. Even in Africa's harsh Namib Desert, there is a tiny amount of dew that appears at daybreak. As condensation forms on its shiny exoskeleton, the beetle tilts forward, sending the moisture down its body and into its mouth. The Amazon Moonflower, I've read, grows on the bank of the upper Rio Negro in Brazil and only blossoms once a year — during the night. I came across the Milk Weed in the Australian rainforest while staying at an excruciatingly expensive hideaway hotel. The gardener tidying up the place called it a weed. Anyway, it has ten irregular dark green leaves which surround a tight cluster of stamens. Each leaf is 'printed' with a hot pink petal creating an illusionary flower.

This brush is from the Caribbean island of Grenada. The end of a stick of bamboo is shredded into fibres and bound to create a fan of bristles.

Illustrations made from the classical Chinese tangram puzzle involving arrangements of the same seven pieces.

These pages are from *What a Life!*, a satirical autobiography of an Edwardian gentleman based on illustrations taken from the catalogue (1911) of a London department store.[1]

This entertaining figure, representing the cut-and-paste technique used in producing the publication, appears on the title-page. In a deadpan preface the authors comment: 'One man searching the pages of *Whiteley's General Catalogue* will find only facts and prices; another will find what we think we have found – a deeply moving human drama.' The chronology of this human drama extends from childhood to marriage, with chapters on London, a diamond burglary, romance, travel and wedded bliss.

64   WHAT A LIFE !

Ponto, the watch dog, seemed dazed. He had been drugged, the detective said.

He also pointed out that the horse's neck was strangely swollen.

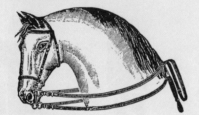

THE STOLEN DIAMONDS   65

The detective next interrogated the whole house party, although some were in *déshabille*.

70   WHAT A LIFE !

But at this moment the detective returned; in a disguise calculated to baffle the keenest observer.

The contents of the mysterious bag having been analysed,

THE STOLEN DIAMONDS   71

he showed us that the ring was movable,

and drew our attention to the fact that there were signs of a struggle.

He then showed us the print of a blood-stained hand on the wall,

ELISION. The *Oulipo*,[2] founded in 1960, is an exclusive French literary club whose membership is by invitation only. It was founded by Raymond Queneau, who also wrote popular lyrics for Juliette Greco. Members have included Georges Perec, Marcel Duchamp and Italo Calvino. Literature is limited by the structure of language and the conventions of writing. The *Oulipo* are committed to imposing yet further restrictions as they hold that constraints increase creative potential. Hence their choice of *Oulipo*, an acronym of *Ouvrier de Littérature Potentielle* – Workshop for Potential Literature.

One favoured device is the lipogram. This is a composition which omits certain words or letters. The early Greek poet Tryphiodorus wrote an epic of 24 books (the Greek alphabet has 24 letters), each of which left out one of the letters. Similarly Lope de Vega wrote five novels, each of which dropped one of the five vowels. Ernest Vincent Wright wrote *Gadsby* without using the letter e. Similarly Georges Perec wrote the 300-page *La Disparition* (translated as *A Void*) without an e, and *Les Revenentes* in which e was the only vowel used. Perec also composed a palindrome of 500 words and wrote poems composed with the principles of Schoenbergian serialism. I don't know what that means but I'm sure it's not as entertaining as *The Great-Ape-Love-Song* – another *Oulipo* work – which only uses words from the *Tarzan Dictionary* of ape-speak by Edgar Rice Burroughs.

In *One Hundred Thousand Billion Poems* Raymond Queneau introduced ten sonnets, each with fourteen lines, written in such a way that the reader could choose to replace each line from one of the nine other poems. The reader could thus compose some 100,000,000,000,000 different poems, all adhering to the immutable rules of the sonnet.

'I dream,' wrote Italo Calvino, 'of immense cosmologies, sagas and epics all reduced to the dimensions of an epigram.' And went on to write, in *Six Memos for the Next Millennium*, of his ambition to edit a collection of tales consisting of one sentence only. Unfortunately he never came across any which matched his favourite by Augusto Monterroso: *'Cuando despertó, el dinosauro todavía estaba allí'* ('When he woke up, the dinosaur was still there'). I don't know if his collection also included Arthur C. Clarke's favourite book title: *Shut up, he explained*.

Mind you, the distance between constraint and masochism is paradoxically narrow. For example, Nicholson Baker's notion of writing an essay solely on the books visible in the background of a photograph in a mail-order catalogue. Or designer Edward Fella composing a typographic poster using only typefaces whose names rhyme. Let alone the thought of that eccentric British General, Orde Wingate, who, as a form of self-imposed discipline, used to read *Pride and Prejudice* in a cold bath. And of course I would have made this book shorter if I'd had more time.

1. E.V. Lucas and George Morrow. *What a Life!* Methuen (London 1911)   2. *Oulipo Laboratory*. Atlas Anti-Classics (London 1995)

Illustration. University of Waseda Library, Tokyo

Agnes, a character in a novel[1] by Milan Kundera: *'If you put the pictures of two different faces side by side, your eye is struck by everything that makes one different from the other. But if you have two hundred and twenty-three faces side by side, you suddenly realize that it's all just one face in many variations and that no such thing as an individual ever existed.'* She then goes on to analyse the faces which appear in a popular magazine.

Copying Agnes, or rather Kundera, I decided to make a similar review looking through the pages of *Hello* magazine (4 April 1998). Admittedly a periodical totally devoted to society celebrities, but nevertheless an indication of the relationship between how you look and who you are. From cover to cover I counted no fewer than 569 faces. This sum includes three crowd scenes, six dogs, one horse, and a couple of cartoon characters. Not a bad score for one issue.

Inventories of human emotion can be arranged under eight main headings: happiness, sadness, fear, anger, surprise, disgust, interest and shame. All unconsciously conveyed by instinctive arrangements of facial features. The words for happy, sad and angry vary throughout the world but the facial expressions which accompany these emotions are the same. A New Guinea tribesman will interpret a smile, a frown or a snarl of the average upwardly mobile traveller on the New York Subway with as much accuracy as a fellow passenger.

James Shreeve: *'Faces are exquisitely expressive instruments. Behind our facial skin lies an intricate web of musculature, concentrated especially around the eyes and mouth, evolved purely for social communication – expressing interest, fear, suspicion, joy, contentment, doubt, surprise, and countless other emotions. Each emotion can be further modified by the raise of an eyebrow or the slight flick of a cheek muscle to express, say, measured surprise, wild surprise, disappointed surprise, feigned surprise, and so on. By one estimate, the 22 expressive muscles on each side of the face can be called on to produce 10,000 different facial actions or expressions.'*[2]

These seventeenth-century Japanese illustrations catalogue a few of the many make-up designs used by actors in *Kabuki* theatre to portray characters. They create an identity and graphically express the role. Within the topographic constraints of a face the graphic permutations are virtually unlimited.

Do you ever play that game of surreptitiously looking at total strangers in some crowded place and wondering what they're thinking? Even this crude, furtively jotted sketch of a man I saw in a restaurant captures a moment of his thoughts. To tell the truth I don't think it looks much like him – but it registers his hubristic expression.

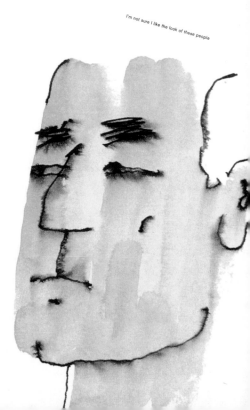

I'm not sure I like the look of these people

1. Milan Kundera. *Immortality*. Faber & Faber (London 1991)   2. James Shreeve. *Neanderthal Enigma*. Viking (London 1996)

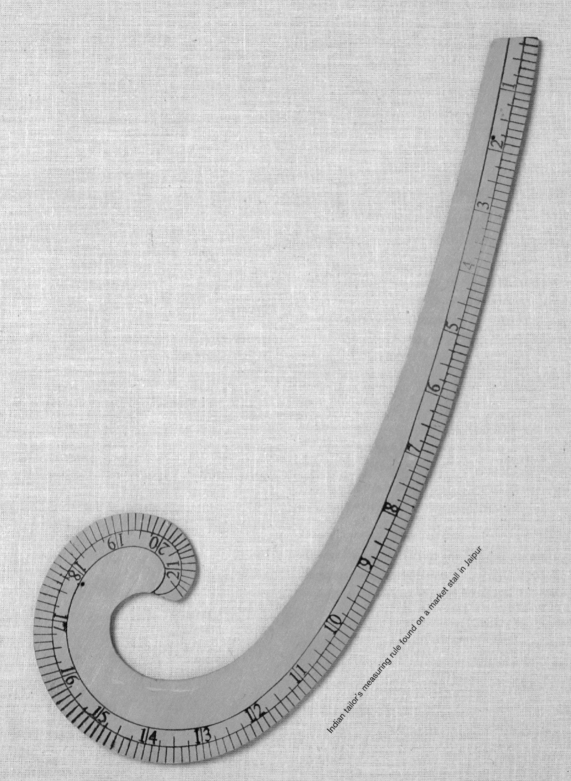

Indian tailor's measuring rule found on a market stall in Jaipur

Protagoras   'Man is the measure of all things.'

Plato proposed that the world is composed of : tetrahedra, cubes, octahedra, dodecahedra, icosahedra. Today we speak of atoms and molecules. Beliefs in a hidden architecture.

The Philosopher in *Sophie's World*: 'This was the period when Socrates walked through the streets and squares talking with the Athenians. He could thus have witnessed the rebirth of the Acropolis and watched the construction of all the proud buildings we see around us. And what a building site it was! Behind me you can see the biggest temple, the Parthenon, which means *The Virgin's Place*. It was built in honour of Athene, the patron goddess of Athens. The huge marble structure does not have a single straight line; all four sides are slightly curved to make the building appear less heavy. In spite of its colossal dimensions, it gives the impression of lightness. In other words, it presents an optical illusion. The columns lean slightly inwards, and would form a pyramid 1,500 metres high if they were continued to a point above the temple. The temple contained nothing but a twelve-metre-high statue of Athene.'[1]

Are there any criteria for the number of segments in a citrus fruit?
● Leonardo of Pisa, otherwise known as Fibonacci, investigated the population growth of rabbits around 1220 AD and deduced the series 1 . . 2 . . 3 . . 5 . . 8 . . . (1+2=3, 2+3=5, 3+5=8, etc) to model it. Later investigators have found that the series is very common in the plant world. For example, the number of petals per ring in a daisy flower follows this model, in which the ratio of the last number in the series to the penultimate approaches 1:1.618, the golden section of the visual arts. It would be surprising if such a fascinating rule does not apply in some way to citrus fruit. *Ted Webber, Trinity Beach, Australia.*

Notes & Queries. *The Guardian,* 1 July 1998

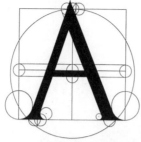

loganberry, the Parthenon, a Chinese Ming vase, a fugue or the human body seem to have little in common but are all part of the grand scheme of things. Not surprisingly, since we are a component, there is a conviction that certain proportions are more pleasing than others. We like things in proportion and when something seems exaggerated we think of it as out of proportion. There is a canon of proportions which Euclid defined as follows : 'Cut a finite line so that the shorter part is to the longer part, as the longer part is to the whole.' This is the Golden Section.

It seems that this is how the whole world is put together. Transcribing the Golden Section into a rectangle can generate a logarithmic curve found in shells and flowers, in the rates of organic growth and other harmonious compositions. Plato concluded that all creative endeavour was an unconscious desire to create these proportions. Pythagoras discovered that dividing a vibrating string into halves, thirds, quarters and fifths produces a sequence of harmonious notes, and Polykleitos was the first sculptor to use this canon to create a figure of harmonious proportions. The original, called *Doryphoros,* no longer exists but a Roman copy in Naples's National Archaeological Museum is an accurate facsimile. Harmonious proportions between man and architecture were later refined by Vitruvius.

However, knowing your proportions is a matter of grammar not language. When Iktinos and Callicrates designed the Parthenon they first got the canonical proportions right, but then fiddled them so the building looked right. Their methods included *entasis* [Greek for stretching], the imperceptible swelling of the columns so they appear parallel, the adjustment of the intervals between columns so they appear equal, the platform made higher in the centre so it seems level. A *ménage à trois* of theory, practice and perception.

Leonardo da Vinci, it is said, invented proportionally sized spoons so he could mix colours to achieve exact shades. An apprentice couldn't quite get the hang of it and asked one of the others how the master used them. He was told he didn't.

1. Jostein Gaarder. *Sophie's World.* Phoenix (London 1995) **Capital letter.** David Lance Goines

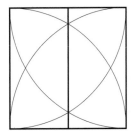

The Golden Mean

Start with a square
and draw an arc
from each of the
four corners.

Where the arcs cross
draw a vertical line
cutting the square
in half.

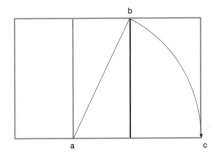

The Golden Section

Place the compass at
the point (a) where the
vertical line meets the
base and draw an arc
(b-c). Join up the
points to construct the
Golden Rectangle.

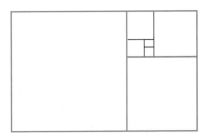

The Golden Rectangle

The rectangle can be
further divided to repeat
the same configuration
ad infinitum.

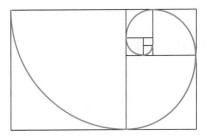

The Golden Spiral

Draw arcs from the
corners of the squares
to create an ever-
growing spiral.

One accessible book about the *Golden Mean*: György Doczi. *The Power of Limits*. Shambhala Publications (Boulder, Colorado, 1981)

A lady

visited Matisse

in his studio.

Inspecting

one of his

latest works

she unwisely said:

'But, surely

the arm

of this woman

is much too long.'

'Madame,' The artist

politely replied,

'you are mistaken.

This is not a woman,

this is a picture.'

Leonardo da Vinci's copious notes [1] on the proportions of the human figure cover every conceivable combination. Here are a few: The span of a man's outstretched arms is equal to his height. The ear is precisely as long as the nose. The big toe is the sixth part of the foot. From the chin to the starting of the hair is a tenth of the figure. From the junction of the palm of the hand as far as the tip of the middle finger a tenth part. From the chin to the top of the head an eighth part. And from the pit of the stomach to the top of the chest is a sixth part. And from the fork of the ribs as far as the top of the head a fourth part. And from the chin to the nostrils is a third part of the face. And the same from the nostrils to the eyebrows, and from the eyebrows to the starting of the hair. And the foot is a sixth part, and the forearm to the elbow a fourth part. Etc, etc, etc, etc, etc, etc, etc, etc, etc

1. *The Notebooks of Leonardo da Vinci.* The Reprint Society (London 1954)

THE PARETO PRINCIPLE: THIS MAINTAINS THAT 80 PER CENT OF RESULTS FLOW FROM 20 PER CENT OF THEIR CAUSES. THE PRINCIPLE HAS UNIVERSAL APPLICATION. FOR INSTANCE 20 PER CENT OF PRODUCTS ACCOUNT FOR 80 PER CENT OF PROFITS; 20 PER CENT OF MOTORISTS CAUSE 80 PER CENT OF ACCIDENTS, AND 80 PER CENT OF THE HUMAN BRAIN IS DEVOTED TO PROCESSING VISUAL DATA.[1]

Big Nudes

Visual Arts Gallery
209 East 23rd Street
New York City

1. Rupert Cringely. *Accidental Empires.* Penguin (London 1996)

Poster. Milton Glaser

Note. Some years ago I had quarry tiles laid on my kitchen floor. A few years later I extended the size of the room and laid more quarry tiles. The first lot came in inches, the second lot were metric. The difference where they meet is quite discernible. At first I went ape, but now I'm reconciled to treating the mismatch as a cultural landmark.

I came across this illustration in a nineteenth-century French book on medicine.

It is the kind of picture that can make one feel extremely uneasy and very uncomfortable.

The source of our discomfort is the unnatural disfiguration or – put another way – the aberration from what we think of as a natural proportion.

Perhaps a reaction deeply rooted in the human psyche generated by nature's blueprint principles regarding the survival of the fittest.

'... a building', explained Le Corbusier, 'is many men thick.'

The oldest human footprints were left about 3.6 million years ago by a man, woman and child in Tanzania. The length of a foot is about 15 per cent of a person's height, thus we know these creatures were a metre to a metre and a half tall.

Once upon a time man measured by his own scale, so whether for a tall Viking or diminutive Pygmy, things were made to suit human proportion. Henry I decreed [1101] that the Saxon gryd or girth, the circumference of the body, was the exact length of his arm. The distance from the tip of his nose to the end of his outstretched middle finger he called a yard. The inch was fixed by the length from knuckle to the end of his thumb. The foot was contributed by King John, who, stamping his foot, said: *'Let this be the measure from this day forward.'* And so it was.

The French Revolution did away with that and invented a bureaucratic system devoid of individuality or personality. A pace was standardized into a metre, which was calculated as one ten-millionth the distance from the equator to the Poles.

This measure was fixed by the length of a metal bar kept in a vault. That seemed neat and tidy but science soon proved as inconsistent as human nature. In the pursuit of accuracy the metre was later amended to 1,650,763,830 times the wavelength of orange light, then expressed in terms of the speed of light travelling in a vacuum, which you'll be fascinated to learn is 1/299,792,458 of a second.[1] Today it's probably something else as they've found out the speed of light was less between 1928 and 1945 than it is today. You have to be a cybernoid to relate to any of that. Anyway all of this was of limited interest to the housewife wanting to buy a length of cloth or elastic.

Come to think of it, to be metrically consistent they should have inflicted a ten-hour clock as happened in Fritz Lang's film *Metropolis*.

Roman architect Vitruvius believed that buildings should conform to the measures of man, an idea revived with enthusiasm during the Renaissance ...

'Four fingers make one palm, and four palms make one foot, six palms make one cubit, four cubits make once a man's height, and four cubits make a pace, and twenty-four palms make a man's height, and these measures are in his building.'

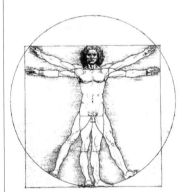

By relating body to geometry, Vitruvian Man was born. However, the idealistic proportions portrayed by Leonardo's *Homo Vitruvius* were both vertically and horizontally challenged as no one is that perfect. Art historian Kenneth Clark even observed that from the point of view of strict geometry, *'a gorilla might prove to be more satisfactory than a man'*.

The Japanese *tatami* is a mat of woven dried grass roughly measuring six feet by three. A size naturally related to the body as it was used as a mattress. The size of a room would be determined by the number of *tatami* mats it was to contain. The *tatami* became the basis for building proportions. Although the proportion remains consistent (one ken long and half a ken wide) the *tatami* varies in size. The Kyoto ken (1.97m) is the peasant measure while the Tokyo ken (1.82m) was the imperial size. In Japan aesthetic standards are often flexible within a common theme.[2]

In 1945, Tokyo, then a city of wood houses, was burnt to the ground. If you walk around nowadays you may notice that the space between some new buildings is just about wide enough to stick your fist in. A relic of times when a minimum distance between town houses was established for fire protection, which in turn fixed boundaries. So although the dimensions of the skyscrapers are metric, their boundaries are determined – at least in my mind – by *tatami* mats.

Paradoxically, it's now illegal to import inches and feet (human scale) measuring instruments into metricized modern Japan.

For centuries Buddhist priests have eaten from a set of small bowls which, when stored, nestle inside each other. They are of a size and shape which can easily be held in the hand. They have a double skin of thin red lacquered wood, which conserves heat and yet is cool to handle. Bowl size is related to the calories and proteins required to preserve a balanced diet. For example, the largest bowl is for rice, the next for fish, the next for vegetables, the smallest for sauce. A Japanese friend tells me this is nonsense. The bowls were used to beg for alms. He should know – he's a successful businessman.

Travelling to New York from Le Havre on a cargo boat in 1945, Le Corbusier utilized his time to refine a system of harmonious proportions based on the human figure. He called it *The Modulor*. Personally I find his writings impenetrable and calculations incomprehensible, but deduce that the principle is an amalgam of imperial measures and metrics, all related to the Golden Mean.

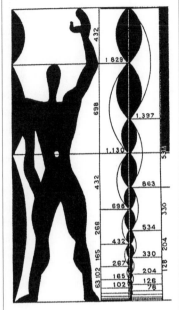

'Take a man-with-arm-upraised,' he writes,[3] *'2.20 metres in height, put him inside two squares, 1.10 by 1.10 metres each, superimposed on each other; put a third square astride these first two squares ... With this grid for use on the building site, designed to fit the man placed within it ... you will obtain a series of measures reconciling human stature and mathematics ...'*

Anyway a whole generation of architects grew up drawing his blobby people in their architectural perspectives.

And did you know that the average flea can jump one hundred and fifty times its own height?

'Smell of autumn ... heart longs for the four-mat room.'

Haiku of Basho

1. Stephen Jay Gould. *The Flamingo's Smile.* Penguin (Harmondsworth 1985) 2. Kiyosi Seike. *The Art of Japanese Joinery.* Weatherhill (New York 1977) 3. Le Corbusier. *The Modulor.* Faber & Faber (London 1954)

Idly contemplating the back label of a 250 gm jar of MARMITE I was amazed to learn that 'THIS JAR CONTAINS APPROX 62 SERVINGS'. Amazed because I had difficulty in imagining someone precisely knifing out the right amount of the stuff to evenly cover 62 standard slices of bread.

The I-don't-care scale

2 jots	=	1 tittle
3 tittles	=	1 continental
2 continentals	=	1 tinker's dam
4 tinker's dams	=	1 damn

Linear measure

2 hops	=	1 skip
2 skips	=	1 jump
24 jumps	=	1 stone's throw
3 stone's throws	=	1 piece
12 pieces	=	1 way-the-hell-and-gone

Applause scale

2 salvos	=	1 accolade
2 accolades	=	1 triumph
3 triumphs	=	1 ovation (sitting)
4 ovations	=	1 lionization
2 lionizations	=	1 outtasight

Paprika measure

2 dashes	=	1 smidgen
2 smidgens	=	1 pinch
3 pinches	=	1 soupçon
2 soupçons	=	too much paprika

Political opponent's measure

2 nincompoops	=	1 fathead
2 fatheads	=	1 incompetent
3 incompetents	=	1 opportunist
2 opportunists	=	1 machiavelli

Alcohol beverage measure

2 fingers	=	1 tot
2 tots	=	1 shot
2 shots	=	1 slug
4 slugs	=	1 snootful
2 snootfuls	=	1 night in jail

Altercation scale

2 tussles	=	1 fray
3 frays	=	1 fracas
2 fracases	=	1 skirmish
2 skirmishes	=	1 fight

Historical invective scale

2 scamps	=	1 rascal
3 rascals	=	1 knave
2 knaves	=	1 varlet
4 varlets	=	1 scoundrel
2 scoundrels	=	1 charlatan

Measure for Measure *Joe Ecclesine*

When a friend drew the sizes of all Vincent Van Gogh's paintings he found that the size of the canvas fluctuated in proportion to Van Gogh's finances. And that for landscapes Van Gogh always chose a size he could carry under his arm.

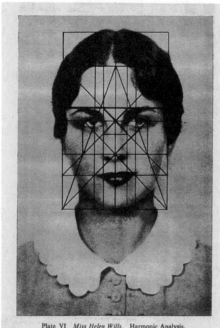

Plate VI *Miss Helen Wills*. Harmonic Analysis.

experting...

'Vitality, ideal proportion

and classical beauty

be damned!'

Francisco de Goya

A friend in Hong Kong is convinced that the Chinese view all animals in terms of food. After all the Chinese don't greet you by saying 'good afternoon' but ask 'have you eaten?' He once took his small American nephew and a Chinese girl to the zoo. On seeing a gorilla the small boy was transfixed with fright – the girl merely enquired what it tasted like.

There's a Chinese axiom that you can eat anything if you cut it up into small enough pieces. This not only applies to dogs and snakes but metaphorically can be applied to any issue. Then there is Interdeterminism Theory which holds that measuring alters our concept of whatever is being measured. For instance in particle physics, just looking at a minute substance can change the way it behaves. This elliptically brings me to the art historian's obsession with analysis.

At art school I acquired a small thin scholarly treatise on the *Golden Mean*. It was an exceedingly dry publication[1] which diagrammed ancient Greek vases, dissected Assyrian ziggurats and covered Renaissance paintings with grids. The text was composed of square roots, complex equations, Fibonacci scales and mathematical formulae. One painting was illustrated with a manic network of lines which related everything to anything thus demonstrating the harmony of the composition. It almost terminated my interest in art.

The analysts are still at it. A doctor, according to a recent newspaper report, maintains that Degas had myopia, astigmatism, a blind spot and a divergent squint. This, he concluded, accounted for his inclination to crop figures awkwardly, portray people from unusual views and distort conventional perspective. The doctor doesn't mention that Degas was a perceptive fellow or the influence of the newly discovered camera.

It would be difficult to think of a painting so universally revered as Leonardo's *Mona Lisa*. When first exhibited in New York during 1962 she

1. Matila Ghyka. *Geometric Composition and Design*. Tiranti (London 1952)

to death

L.H·O·O·Q

was seen by more than one million visitors, each spending an average of 0.79 seconds before the enigmatic smile. They were probably unaware, according to Giorgio Vasari (1568), that while painting the *Mona Lisa* Leonardo 'employed singers and musicians and jesters to chase away the melancholy that painters usually give to portraits. As a result … there was a smile so pleasing that it seemed divine … those who saw it were amazed to find that it was as alive as the original.'

The painting was stolen by an employee at the Louvre in 1911, but for a variety of reasons suspicion fell on Apollinaire, who spent a few days in prison as a suspect. Marcel Duchamp preferred arm's length vandalism, and bought a tacky postcard reproduction to which he added a moustache and beard and a caption LHOOQ. Pronounced in French this is a crude comment. The picture above is my version of his version.

A medical consultant, obviously unaware of, or disregarding, Vasari's comments, has diagnosed the enigmatic smile as a distortion caused by a 'classic complication of Bell's palsy occasionally incurred by pregnant women'. And during the 1980s a psychiatrist came up with the notion that the *Mona Lisa* is a self-portrait of Leonardo da Vinci himself – without beard. Working with overlays to form a composite face and then reversing and superimposing the transparent image over a reproduction of the *Mona Lisa*, revealed, he said, 'a self-portrait in inversion, both with regard to laterality and gender'. Just imagine that! Thank God they can't all be right.

When Keats [who was 5 feet 3 ¼ inches short] complained that Newton tried to unweave the rainbow, implying no mystery no magic, he had a point. Analysis is commencement of conformity and creative paralysis. Analysis also looks backwards while design looks forward. As with life, it's important to realize the direction one is facing.

'There was an awful rainbow once in heaven:
We know her woof, her texture; she is given
In the dull catalogue of common things.
Philosophy will clip an Angel's wings,
Conquer all mysteries by rule and line …'
John Keats

Triple composition:

The Mona Lisa

International flags

A jigsaw

To bring the features into focus hold at arm's length.

[**SEE** P283].

Jigsaw design. Shigeo Fukuda

Puccini

'Music is noise submitted to order by wisdom.'

I have an affliction. The symptoms become apparent at
the dinner table. It starts with a compulsion to reorganize
the view of the scene in front of me. To fractionally shift
a wine glass so it overlaps another to make a more
satisfying juxtaposition. Once that has been enjoyed, one
might move a stray toothpick to neatly bisect the shadow
thrown by the wine bottle. Sliding a knife up under the
toothpick will establish a balance, and the odd pea – or
small piece of bread – can adjust the equilibrium. Now
comes the tricky bit. To realign the increasingly delicate
arrangement one may have to bring bulkier objects into
play. A salt cellar perhaps. At this moment I'm usually
sussed by my dining companion. They tend to favour
what they think of as table manners over what I think
of as niceties of composition.

The composition opposite is an invented scenario. The
situation occurred to me when I noticed a lemon lying
on a table next to a banana. The shadow of the lemon
prompted the notion that it was balancing on the end of
the banana. Mentally moving more fruit (and shadows)
into the scene made the composition more interesting
and as soon as it felt right I transferred it from mind
to paper. Now my quandary is this: if the quick and
crude colour rendering gets across the thought, is that
sufficient? Or do I spend hours trying to improve the
presentation? I suspect not.

*Note. Lunch with Massimo Vignelli in Tokyo. The
main course arrived on a plate which appeared to have
been broken in half. Actually each half belonged to a
different design and style of plate. Laid across this
broken dish was a fish, or at least two halves of a
fish. Actually it was the front half of one fish and the
back half of another fish. It was delicious; it was also
exceptionally expensive. When we finished Massimo
casually inspected the bottom of each broken plate –
they were Rosenthal!*

PICTURE - SCAPING

American perceptual psychologist J. J. Gibson has written that a picture **'is a surface so treated that a delimited optic array to a point of observation is made available that contains the same kind of information that is found in the ambient optic arrays of an ordinary environment.'** Well that sounds a lot of fun. Personally I prefer the description by Maurice Denis who remarked that a picture, **'before being a battlehorse, a nude woman, or some anecdote, is essentially a plain surface covered with paint in a certain arrangement'**. Or Henri Matisse's comment that, **'Composition is the art of arranging in a decorative manner the various elements at a painter's disposal for the expression of his feelings.'** José Ortega y Gasset simply suggested it was like looking at a window and then gradually becoming aware of the garden beyond – the window being the form and the garden the content. At the turn of the century Monet created a garden at his house in Giverny. He planted trees, shrubs and flowers, and by diverting a stream made a large pond. Slowly it all took shape: water-lilies, clumps of iris, weeping willows and a replica of a Japanese bridge entwined with green wisteria. It required six full-time gardeners and gossip claimed that Monet read more horticultural catalogues than reviews by art critics. When completed it became the subject of more than 200 paintings. Over the years Monet received many visitors including some Japanese aesthetes who were reassured by a Japanese inscription painted in blue, on a flowerpot, congratulating Monet on behalf of all Japan for having been one of the first painters in the West to abandon perspective. Ian Hamilton Finlay composed his garden the other way around. He took landscapes off the canvas and put them back into nature. His garden in Scotland is created from a painting by Claude Lorrain. It also has a footbridge inscribed with a huge facsimile of Lorrain's signature which I construe as a dubious confirmation that nature imitates art. In 1938 Sergei Prokofiev wrote the music for the film score of Sergei Eisenstein's film *Alexander Nevsky*. Eisenstein provided Prokofiev with stills as it was being filmed. Prokofiev used the silhouette of the landscape and the shapes of the human figures in these scenes as a pattern for positioning the notes on the stave. He then orchestrated around these notes. I also like the thought of Brazilian composer Heitor Villa-Lobos looking at the mountains outside his window, choosing a vista, sketching the outline on music paper, and using it as the basis for a melodic line. The portrait opposite is of President Woodrow Wilson constructed by Brigadier General Mathew C. Smith and 21,000 officers and men at Camp Sherman in Ohio.

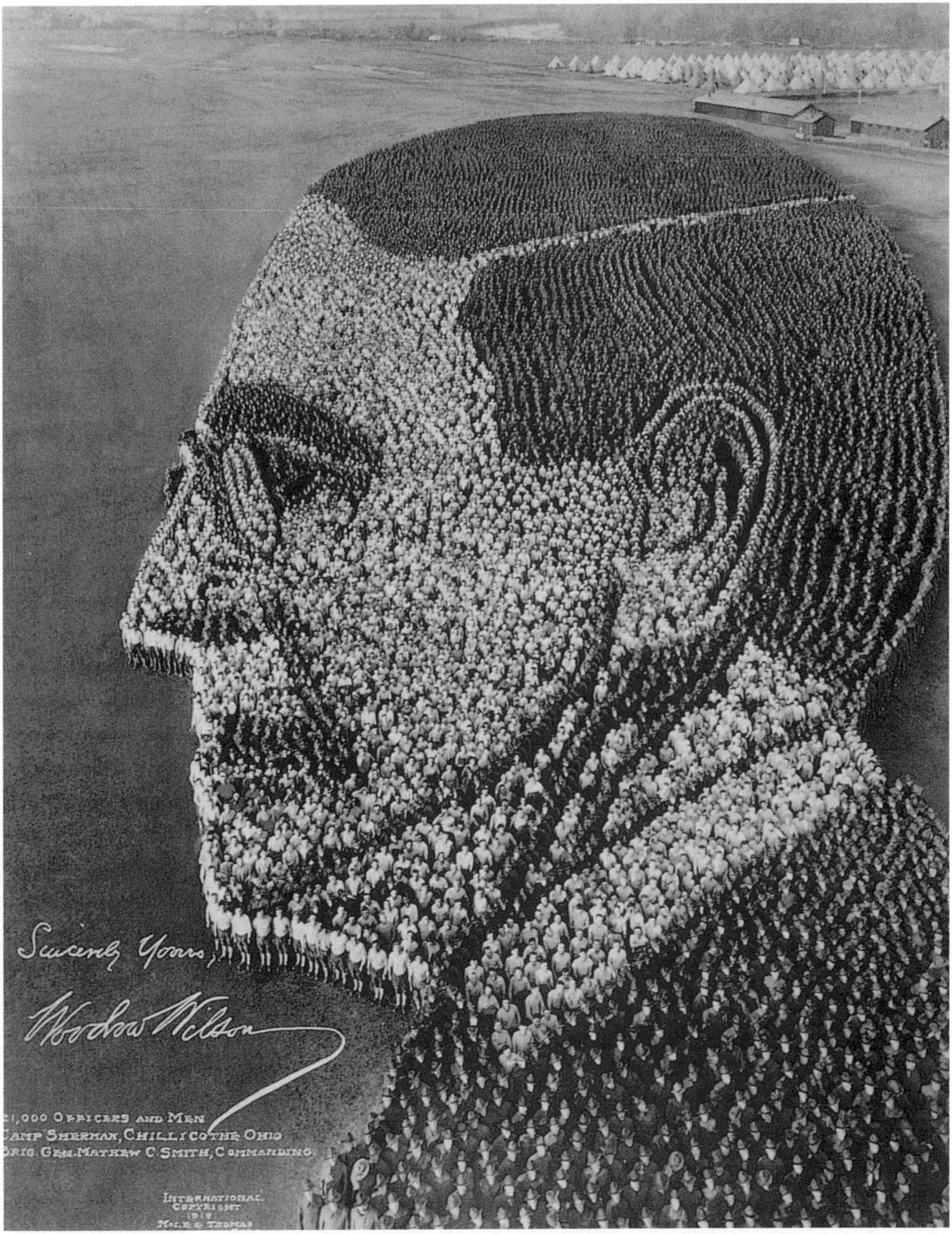

Sincerely Yours,

Woodrow Wilson

21,000 OFFICERS AND MEN
CAMP SHERMAN, CHILLICOTHE OHIO
BRIG. GEN. MATHEW C SMITH, COMMANDING.

INTERNATIONAL
COPYRIGHT
1918
MOLE & THOMAS

Excerpt from a review of a book by novelist Nadine Gordimer: '... note the way the author opens the plot, arranges the magical correspondences, finds the fixed points, and sets them in a broad open space where many drifting, always to the point, things can wander.' Contrived compositions can introduce dimensions unobtainable in less constructed contexts. Here are some more literary examples: Italo Calvino's The Castle of Crossed Destinies is composed as a Tarot game, and his If on a Winter's Night a Traveller as a novel about reading a novel. Miorad Pavic's The Dictionary of the Khazars and Landscape Painted with Tea are constructed as dictionary and crossword puzzle respectively. John Fowles's The French Lieutenant's Woman has its own critical apparatus, Walter Abish's Alphabetical Africa is in alphabetical order, and Martin Amis's Time's Arrow [SEE P243] employs reverse chronology. In André Gide's The Counterfeiters, the novelist is writing a novel into which he plans to put himself as a character. In him, ee cummings wrote a play about a playwright writing a play about a playwright. Alfred Jarry wrote L'Amour absolu to be read as three different stories: the vigil of a condemned man the night before his execution, the monologue of a man who imagines he's condemned to death, and the story of Christ. While in The Garden of Forking Paths, Jorge Luis Borges presents a metaphysical spy story as an endless Chinese novel within a dozen pages. A critic describes Nicholson Baker's writing as 'undertaking a long journey conducted with your face six inches from the ground'. As a genealogy of thoughts one of his books, Vox, solely narrates a four-hour dialogue on a telephone sex line, while in another, The Mezzanine, a whole life could be constructed by interrogating the intimacies of industrial design during a lunch hour – the smooth ascending of an escalator, the perforations of a paper towel. James Joyce claimed Ulysses was so topographically accurate that Dublin could be rebuilt – pubs and all – should it ever be burnt to the ground. A systematic work, it is also an encyclopedia of styles, references and interpretations such as medieval exegetics – the correspondences of chapters with parts of the body, the arts, colours, and symbols. Georges Perec in Life. A User's Manual takes a cross-section of a typical Parisian apartment building and allocates a chapter per room. We are told about each apartment and its inhabitants, in intricate detail. The building is like a chessboard on which Perec passes from one square to another in knight moves to land on each square in turn. There are 99 chapters – an intentional incompleteness.

Aboriginal artwork consists of lines and dots and circles composed with textures, areas and shapes. Whatever the subject the design is as schematized as a circuit diagram. One modern version (they're also into acrylics) painted by Joshua is titled Qantas Dreaming. Joshua had once been flown from Australia to Amsterdam, via London, to take part in a scientific congress on ethnic cultures.[1] The painting begins with straight lines which turn into a rectangular maze and terminate in wiggles. He explained that the maze was Heathrow and the wiggles his ride by subway and taxi to the hotel. Amsterdam was indicated by a large circle bounded by four small circles linked by squiggles to a box. Not exactly a sacred site but, in Joshua's mind at least, a place of mysterious activities. The experiment consisted of Joshua singing his Dreaming, a Catholic monk performing a Gregorian chant, a Tibetan lama reciting Mantras and an African who sang a tribal story. Apparently the recording apparatus registered the effect of different melodies on the rhythmic structure of the brain, something aborigines have been doing on bark for 30,000 years. This artwork shows a Space Tracking Station [1967], and as it was composed on the ground could, appropriately enough, be viewed from any angle.

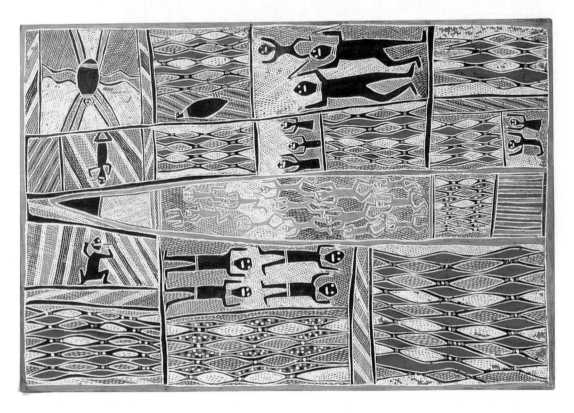

1. Bruce Chatwin. *The Songlines.* Jonathan Cape (London 1987) **Illustration.** Mungurrawuy Yunupingu. *Space Tracking Station*

Design. Benoit Jacques

OCR-A, one of the first optical character recognition typefaces, was designed to meet the criteria set by the U.S. Bureau of Standards. It was introduced in 1968. The font was developed to facilitate the automatic processing of large quantities of numbered forms by machines rather than by people – cheques and accounts in banking for example. OCR-B, the European version, designed by Adrian Frutiger, is slightly easier to read. This text is in OCR-A. The adjacent text is in OCR-B.

GENERATIVE MUSIC: The computer has progressed from a step by step contraption to one in which everything is connected to everything. A complex of parallel architectures. Furthermore, like brain cells, the bits and pieces can organize themselves to behave on a higher level than the individual parts. Daniel Hillis, computer scientist, has designed programmes which are so fast they re-enact the span of human evolution in minutes. His models emulate evolutionary patterns in anticipation that they will generate intellectual abilities similar to our own. One such ability is creating music. Composer Brian Eno[1] feeds his synthesizer musical seeds.'First I choose a note, then I can change the attack, the decay, the timbre. I choose notes from a scale, and assign probabilities. For example, I might tell it not to choose the flattened fifth a lot, but to use a lot of the major third. I might tell it to leave a lot of gaps in the music, or to use a lot of dotted notes ...' He calls it generative music because it's independent of human jurisdiction. The idea came from 'screensavers' which invade monitor screens while the computer is at rest. These produce their own ever-changing patterns where motifs interact without predictable outcomes or time frames. 'These blooms are not meant to be cut, arranged and displayed,' the composer says. The musical result has been described as '... drifting lines of consonant electronic melody, a soft clanging like church bells under water, gentle patterns shifting and recombining with a moire* effect.' It's possible, Brian Eno suggests, that 'our grandchildren will look at us in wonder and say: "You mean you used to listen to exactly the same thing over and over again?"'

1. Brian Eno. *A Year With Swollen Appendices*. Faber & Faber (London 1996)   *This Anglo-Saxon font doesn't have accents.

Joe Colombo's spoon

Most of us hoard bits and pieces. Those things which we think will be of use one day, things of sentimental value, things which belong to other things – a nut without its bolt.

During the 1960s Joe Colombo, one of the first of many famous Milan designers, designed the plastic cutlery for Alitalia. The design was in use until the late 1990s. Until recently I kept the knife, fork and spoon in a drawer along with a single brass door hinge – after all I might come across its companion – a decorative swizzle stick from a forgotten celebration, a washbasin plug which doesn't fit anything, and all the other paraphernalia you can see here.

In one of my periodic clearouts I braced myself to lift the lid off the garbage bin and dispense of these artefacts forever. At that very moment, like St Paul, I saw the light – superglue.

Of course anybody could assemble a composition out of accumulated rubbish. But what counts is knowing where and how to stick what, and which to stick next to which.

Joe Colombo's spoon is securely bonded in the bottom right-hand corner.

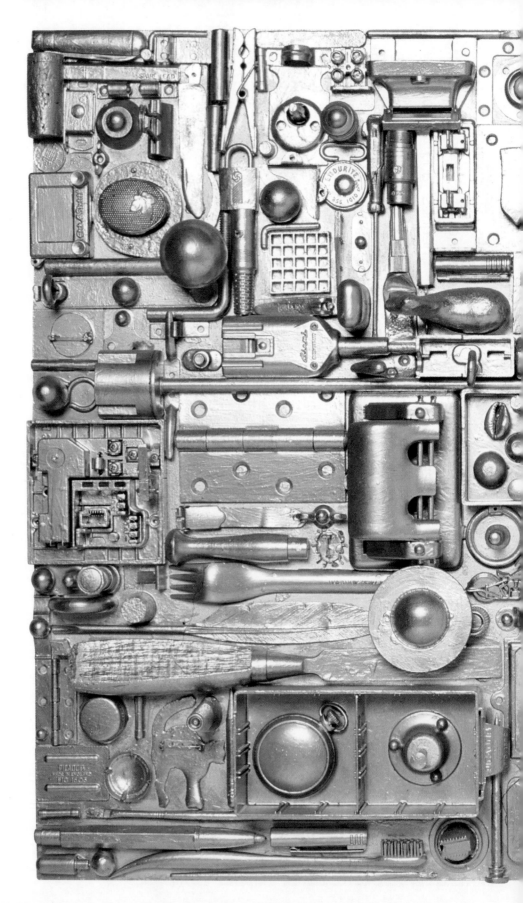

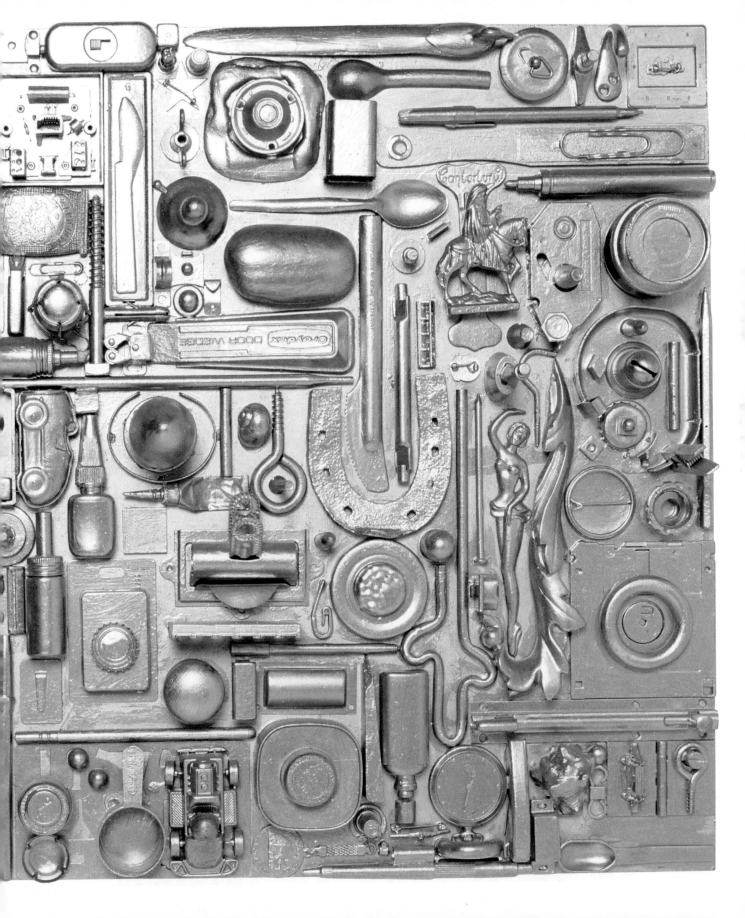

Saul Steinberg improvising at the Long Man of Wilmington in a photograph by Lee Miller (c.1954). Cut into Windover Hill on the chalk Downs in Sussex, is a giant figure, 70m (230ft) tall carrying a staff in each hand. The Long Man of Wilmington has been identified variously as a local giant, a Roman soldier, a Saxon haymaker. Whoever he was, he most likely dates back 2,000 to 2,500 years.

W.H. Auden

'To you, to me, Stonehenge and Chartres Cathedral …

… are works by the same Old Man under different names: we know what He did, what, even, He thought He thought,

A ziggurat is a stepped pyramid.

At Chichén Itzá in Yucatan, Mexico, the Temple of Kukulkan (also known as Quetzalcoatl) is a 100-foot-high ziggurat with four flights of stairs, each with 91 steps. Counting the top platform as one step, the total number comes to a significant 365.

The design and solar orientation of the structure had been calibrated with a degree of precision calculated to achieve an objective as dramatic as it was esoteric:

'On the spring and autumn equinoxes, regular as clockwork, triangular patterns of light and shadow combined to create the illusion of a giant serpent undulating on the northern staircase. On each occasion the illusion lasted for 3 hours and 22 minutes exactly.'[1]

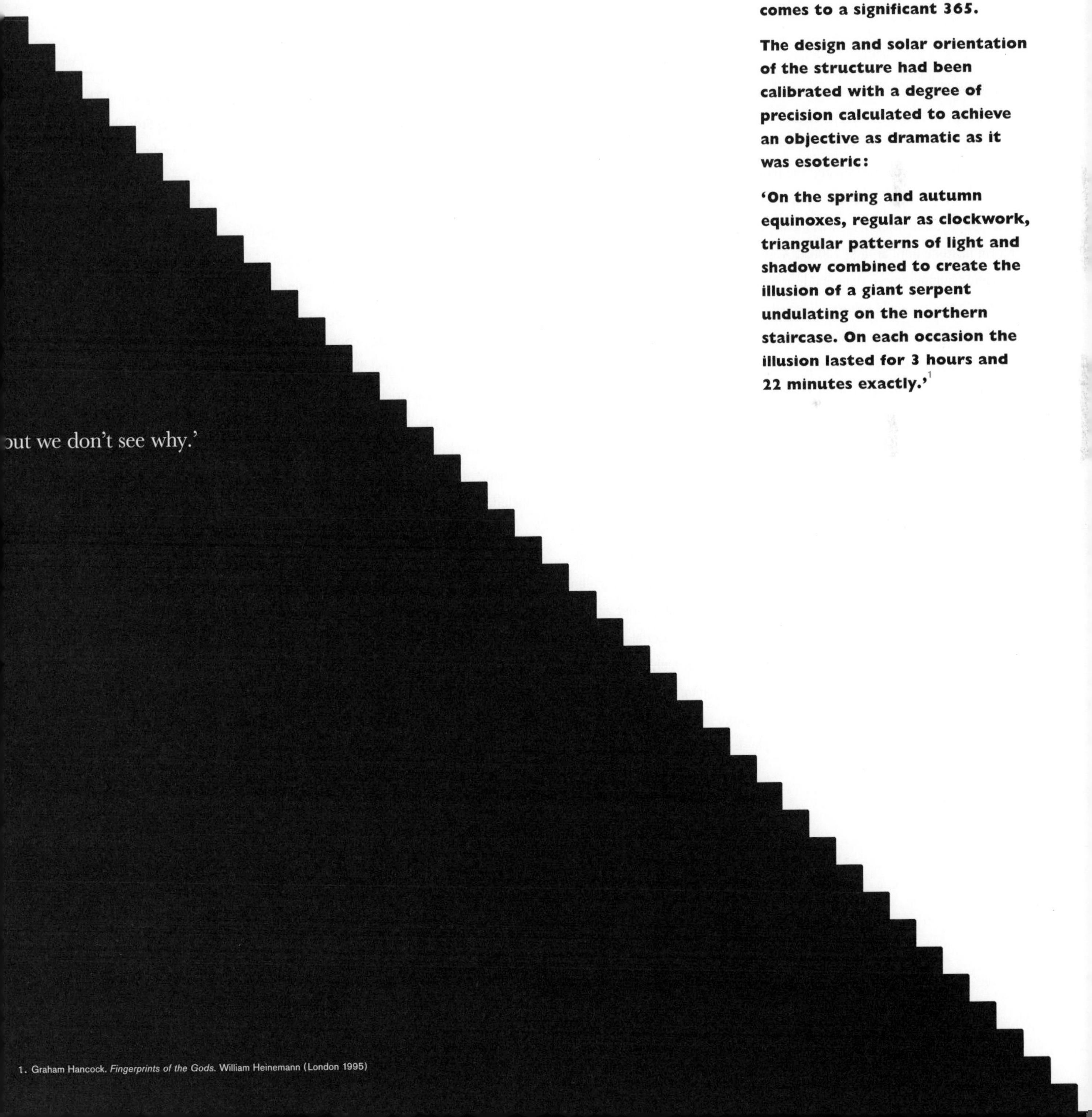

but we don't see why.'

1. Graham Hancock. *Fingerprints of the Gods*. William Heinemann (London 1995)

The Great Pyramid at Giza was not even on the drawing board when the wooden henge at Stanton Drew in Wessex was built about five thousand years ago. The builders were near-contemporaries of those who invented the sail in Egypt, the wheel, bronze casting and the plough in Mesopotamia, and writing in Sumer. None of which were known in Britain. Stonehenge itself existed but like the temple at Stanton Drew was made of wood and did not assume its final form in stone until around 2000BC. Avebury in Wiltshire was built earlier. The ancients humped more than 600 four-metre high, 35-ton stones from the Marlborough Downs while others, chopped out of the Welsh hills, were dragged to the river Avon and floated upstream. Quite why they took the trouble is a mystery as such an enterprise wasn't lightly undertaken.

The very thought that ancient man had the knowledge and technology was inconceivable to subsequent societies. 'It is remarkable', wrote Horace Walpole, 'that whoever has treated of this monument has bestowed on it whatever class of antiquity he was particularly fond of.' The superstitious believed they were conjured up by Merlin through 'skill in Magick', Sir Christopher Wren thought they'd been 'spewed forth by a volcano' and Samuel Pepys asserted they 'grew out of the ground'. The clergy considered the stones works of the Devil and toppled a lot over. When re-erected in 1938 one revealed a medieval accident, the crushed corpse of a barber with his scissors still in working order and coins dated 1307. Others saw the stones as a source of building material and you can still see bits and pieces in the walls of Avebury village. Certainly Avebury was a very special place. On the site of a small circle nearby, long since destroyed, nineteenth-century field workers came across a large ancient burial ground. The bones have now also vanished – a local physician ground them up to use as a medicinal potion for the locals.

Inigo Jones thought Stonehenge the ruin of a Roman temple and Thomas Hardy romanticized it as the 'Temple of the Winds'. Anyway Stonehenge has its own mystery. Excavations have unearthed amber from Scandinavia and blue beads from Egypt. Even more surprising are the discoveries in 1953 of an eroded outline of a dagger on one of the sarsens and barely discernible shapes of double-headed axes cut on others. Some maintain that these are too similar to those found in Mycenae in the Aegean to be coincidental. A clue, perhaps, as to where the building expertise came from. Others dismiss any link although there are certainly similar designs on stone sites in the north of France.

The stones weren't just cobbled up and the structure clearly indicates a sophisticated mind and skill at work far beyond the ordinary: the intricate plan, the east-west orientation, the accuracy in the placement of the 81 45-ton sarsen stones, the juxtaposition of blue and grey granite stones, their shaping, the mortice holes, and grooving to hold the lintels in place, the tooling and dressing on the inner side of the stones, the employment of measures which included the inch, foot, cubit and megalithic yard. [SEE P281].

Stonehenge is unique – it is the only large stone structure in Europe of its period – yet its intricacy suggests already existing skills. Perhaps these were brought by a colleague of Daedalus visiting ancient Britain or a local who had been to Greece. Or achieved in isolation? Whatever the case writer John Fowles[1] came to this conclusion: 'For what an artist's intuition is worth, it feels to me like the creation of one man's mind, a stroke, or a series of strokes, of single genius. What he did was not to change the function of Stonehenge, but its symbolic expression. Only very great artists perform that kind of magic.'

Why spend so much energy and to what purpose? Perhaps it stands for that eternal physical expression – something of me shall survive.

1. John Fowles. *The Enigma of Stonehenge*. Summit Books (New York 1980)   A message found behind a wall during building refurbishment at Tate Gallery, London in 1985. Redstone Press Diary 1999

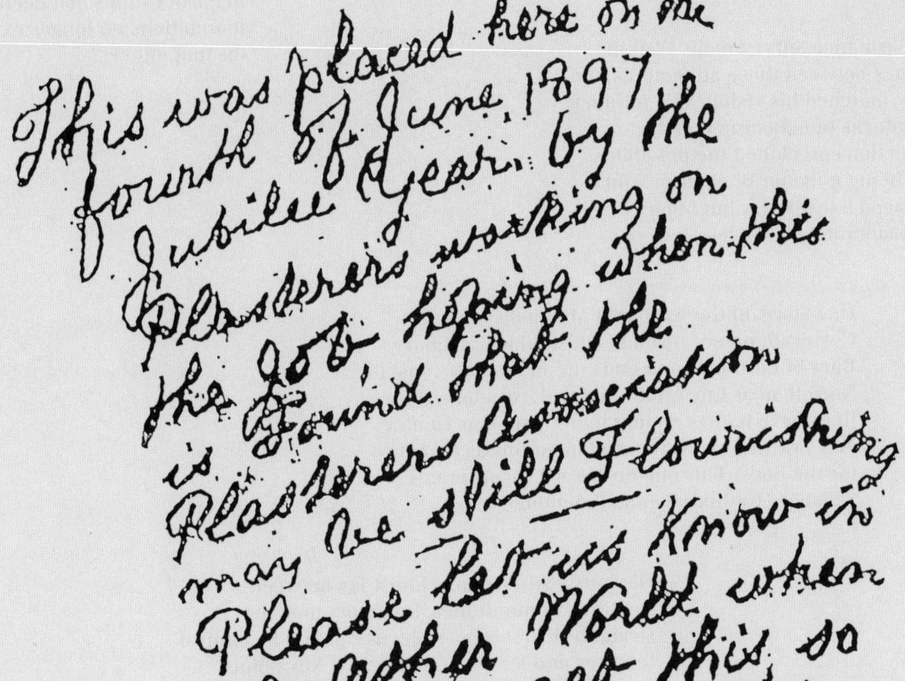

This was placed here on the fourth of June, 1897 Jubilee Year, by the Plasterers working on the Job, hoping when this is found that the Plasterers Association may be still Flourishing Please let us Know in the Other World when you get this, so as we can drink your Health.

Signed W Gallop
F Wilkins
H. G. Chester
A. Pickernell
Secretary

Leylines. In the early 1920s Alfred Watkins was riding across the hills west of Hereford when suddenly, in a moment of transcendent perception, he saw something no one had seen for thousands of years. A network of straight lines superimposed on the landscape. Ancient tracks, alignments of cairns, stone circles, medieval crosses and churches. Traces of an ancient Britain whose very existence has been forgotten.[1]

Checking with Ordnance Survey maps Watkins drew straight lines between these alignments and found the reality matched his vision. The number of man-made features punctuating these lines and their intersections precluded the possibility of the locations being a matter of chance. Some could only be traced a few miles but others extended for considerable distances.

One starts in the west at St Michael's Mount in Cornwall, passes through Glastonbury, Avebury, Bury St Edmunds and ends up on the east coast in Norfolk near Lowestoft. Many places along these lines have names ending in 'ley', such as Henley and Crawley, so Watkins adopted this as a name for the lines. This one on the left incorporates Salisbury Cathedral and Stonehenge.

Mr Briggs is a dowser. With his wire coat-hanger he traced the foundations of a thirteenth-century church in Northumberland which had been demolished 600 years ago. Archaeologists know because they dug down and had a look. They can't make out how he does it, and Mr Briggs doesn't know either. He thinks it's an instinct, a sixth sense. Furthermore, he found he could pick up the outlines of ancient structures which in earlier times had been destroyed and whose foundations no longer existed. He can't account for that either.

Obviously when dense forest lay between scattered communities, travellers took the straightest routes possible, navigating by natural features and landmarks placed at key points.

Less easy to explain is why sites which lie on these lines frequently have exceptional concentrations of natural energies. Water diviners have located underground springs and psychics experienced mysterious sensory currents. More pragmatically the magnetic activity is unusually high. Indeed a prehistoric site was recently discovered through a wobble on a magnetic survey. It has been named the Conebury Anomaly.

The implications are that early man not only knew much more than we think but had an intensely close relationship with nature which we have lost. Well most of us.

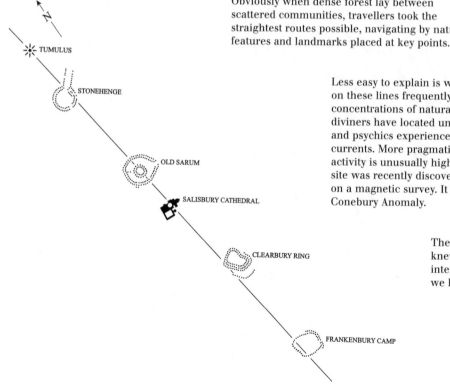

N

TUMULUS

STONEHENGE

OLD SARUM

SALISBURY CATHEDRAL

CLEARBURY RING

FRANKENBURY CAMP

1. John Michell. *The View over Atlantis.* Sago Press (London 1969)

The Saintbury Ley. On the edge of a hill in the Cotswolds, a short ley runs 5.5km (3.5 miles) through the village of Saintbury. Beginning at a cross beside a road junction, it follows a road (or vice versa) to Saintbury Church, and a Bronze Age round barrow, and beyond this the ley passes through a Neolithic long barrow and a pagan cemetry, before ending at the ancient farmstead of Seven Wells.

'We all live within the ruins of an ancient structure, whose vast size has hitherto rendered it invisible. The entire surface of the earth is marked with the traces of a gigantic work of prehistoric engineering, the remains of a once universal system of natural magic, involving the use of polar magnetism together with another positive force related to solar energy.' *John Michell* the **FENG-SHUI** tendency

In 1955 Adrian Boshier, a sixteen-year-old boy, walked into the African bush only equipped with a pocket knife and a bag of salt. He lived alone in the wilderness for the next twenty years. He learned to camp with considerable care after unpleasant experiences with snakes and floods. He also found that some places exerted appeal while others did not. They **felt right** or they didn't. He eventually concluded that **what mattered was not what you like, but what likes you.** I've got a problem with this because I'm never sure whether **when things look right they feel right**, or whether **when they feel right they look right**. In either case it's really all been sorted by the Chinese **art of placement**. This art divines and interprets the forces of nature and cosmic powers to enhance our bodies and minds through design. Born out of the 3,000-year-old **I-CHING**, the art of **FENG-SHUI** is based on **geomancy** – a mix of geometry, geography and psychology. Practitioners use an octagonal template called the **BA-GUA** to assess an area as large as the floor of a building or as small as a desk-top. Used as a compass the template divides space into key areas each of which have a bearing on career, family, wealth, and so forth. To use the **BA-GUA** as a compass, point it towards the front of the house, room or desk. The area concerned with wealth is in the far left corner. The direction, layout and placement of objects within these areas are important. Flowers are good, curves are good, crystal and glass are good. Spikes are bad, angles are bad, sharp is bad – and **at all costs avoid crazy paving**. Clutter and darkness are also likely to cause problems: you need to tidy up, add light, and introduce positive items like plants and wind-chimes and mirrors.

Blank areas can be enriched by hanging mirrors. If they are placed on opposite walls you double up the options. Don't let energy flow straight through the house so it disappears out the other end – but deflect it with mirrors. Mirrors are important. [SEE P248]. When building the Hong Kong Bank the directors showed the plans to a **FENG-SHUI** expert who subsequently asked the architect to realign various features. 'We all worked together very happily', said the expert, a Mr Lung. The Bank of China tower in Bejing (Peking) doesn't meet **FENG-SHUI** approval. 'Too many triangles', says expert Sung Siu-Kwong. 'Triangles mean danger, not many people like them, except for the Egyptians.' Trade at the Sheraton Hotel in Singapore failed expectations and a **FENG-SHUI** consultant advised replacing the boring entrance with an articulated façade of doors. The casements were ripped out and replaced. From then on, business took an upward turn. The last time I was there I paid the new entrance a visit. The design looked all right but the finish wasn't very good.

Geomancy also works in Manhattan. A New York designer was robbed six times, sent a plan of his office to an expert in Hong Kong. The resulting instructions were to install a tank with six black fish and hang up a red clock. He did what he was told. No more break-ins. In the 1990s **FENG-SHUI** became fashionable and there is even a popular magazine of the same title. I predict it will go the same way as **MAH-JONG**. Anyway, '**maximize the benefits of your environment**' and '**be regular and orderly in your life**', Gustave Flaubert advised, then you can '**be violent, and original in your work**.'

1. Lyall Watson. *The Lightning Bird*. Simon & Schuster (New York 1982)

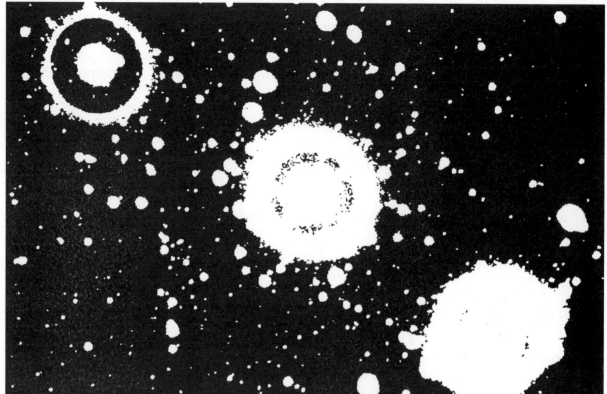

The stars of Orion's Belt. Note that the small star is not in line with the other two.

Bird's-eye view of the pyramids at Giza. Note that the small pyramid is not in line with the other two.

1. Robert Bauval & Adrian Gilbert. *The Orion Mystery*. Mandarin (London 1995)

✳ It must have been a source of wonderment to the ancients for the stars to disappear during the day, only to reappear in the same place the next night. Fu Hse, legendary founder of geomancy, was one of the first to record correspondences between stars and landscape: 'Looking up he contemplated the images in the heavens; looking down he discerned the patterns on the earth.'

✳ The last survivors of the Seven Wonders of the World are the pyramids outside Cairo at Giza. *The Orion Mystery*[1] is a best-seller about these pyramids, replete with speculations on their purpose, structures, meaning and significance. Seemingly written on the gallop, the book is dense with reference and littered with repetition. No easy read. Nevertheless it proposes an intriguing conjecture.

✳ The premise is that the pyramids are a map on earth of Orion's constellation of stars in the sky. The spin of the earth has a slight wobble so the night sky of ancient Egypt is different to tonight's but calculations imply the image postulated was correct for the time.

✳ Personally I find constellations don't even vaguely shape up to their names, and that includes Orion The Hunter. In Orion's case they say two stars mark the shoulders, three mark the belt, and a couple sort of mark the knees. Linking these together diagrams the figure of Orion. Actually Orion is a product of light, time and imagination. The individual stars are separated by inconceivable distances and time frames. One which marks the shoulder is 350 light years away, the other 420 light years. Those making the belt are 1,500 light years away. And the light emitted by a star marking the leg started out over a millennium ago. The speed of light is 186,282 miles a second[2] — a light year is longer than you need to know.

✳ The heaven on earth phenomenon has also fitted the Cambodian temples of Angkor Wat to the constellation of Draco. And the celestial plans of the Mayan cities of central America. Even the profile of the Sphinx is said to mirror the constellation of Leo, and we even have our own site in Glastonbury.* Who knows whether these are genuine discoveries or fanciful speculations?

✳ In an observation concerning *Treasure Island,* Robert Louis Stevenson wrote: '... here is an inexhaustible fund of interest for any man with eyes to see, or tuppence worth of imagination.' He was anticipated by Dr Dee, Elizabethan scholar, astrologer, magician and alchemist, who was convinced that Glastonbury in Somerset reflected the twelve figures of the heavenly Zodiac. These were discernible by joining up certain stars, and by seeing them echoed in ancient tracks, earth mounds, hills, valleys, marshes and the river. Aerial photographs reveal the outlines alluded to, but whether they are a reality or merely mirror romantic expectations, depends on your frame of mind.

✳ Glastonbury was a sacred place important in antiquity. Folklore has King Arthur buried on the Isle of Avalon (Glastonbury is on reclaimed marshes), along with St David of Wales and St Patrick of Ireland. During the 1920s local sculptor Katherine Maltwood read even further meanings in the outlines. 'They marked', she wrote, 'the travels (or travails) of King Arthur and the Knights of The Round Table in their quest for the Holy Grail.' More recently John Michell has written a meticulously detailed book[3] which connects the Glastonbury Zodiac to ley lines and Chinese dragon lines. I remember driving to Glastonbury for the first time, through the valleys and hills just outside the town, and sensing an undercurrent about the place. A figment of my imagination? An echo from the ancient past? Romantic expectation? Whatever it was I reflected that we can still be starstruck, be starry-eyed, have movie stars, or star in something or other.

✳ Perhaps there is no answer because there is no problem. [SEE P302]. The scientific establishment dismiss such conjectures. The two photographs shown left are as they appear in *The Orion Mystery.* However, the stars photograph points north, while the top of the pyramid photograph points south. Another academic wit created the Leo Masterplan. This neatly diagrammed the constellation of Leo with New York by the lines joining up the Statue of Liberty, Grand Central Station, The Public Library and other city landmarks.

2. George Johnson. *Fire In the Mind.* Viking (London 1996)   3. John Michell. *New Light on the Ancient Mystery of Glastonbury.* Gothic Image (Glastonbury 1990)   * **Glastonbury: Celtic** for *Glaston* [woad] and *bury* [earthworks]

THE NAZCA LINES. The Pampa de Ingenio, a plain of sand and stones, lies in the Peruvian desert south of Lima. The surface is scored with mysterious tracks, some as narrow as a footpath, others as wide as an airport runway. The designs were made during a 1000-year period between 500 BC and 500 AD. They consist of hundreds of straight lines extending up to five miles, vast triangles, trapezoids, spirals, zigzags and labyrinths. Criss-crossing these are giant contours of birds, fish, animals and insects. One of these is an identifiable species of spider which copulates with its hind leg, and since the anatomical details of this particular spider *(Criptocellus simonis)* are only visible under a microscope, that introduces yet a further mystery. Why and how they were made is still speculative. The Nazca Indians who made them had immense skill since they could only visualize the pictorial result in their minds. The drawings make little sense viewed from the ground and were only discovered by accident during an aerial survey in the 1930s. Seen from a light aircraft 'you can only gasp with amazement at their scale and the imagination of their makers,' wrote Bruce Chatwin.[1] Fantasist Erich von Daniken reckons they are a relic from a time way beyond antiquity, when extraterrestrial intelligence established a space terminal in Peru. However, anthropologist Maria Reiche, who lives in Peru and has devoted her life to unravelling Nazca culture and surveying the lines, contemptuously dismisses this notion.[2] In her opinion they were an astronomical calendar. Many of the lines closely relate to movements of the sun, moon and stars, and the spider's configuration is an earthly diagram of the Orion constellation. [SEE P295]. Another view holds that they were a graphic attempt by early man to signal to the divinities in the skies. Recent research favours the drought theory. This holds that the desert alignments are related to sources of water in the Atlas mountains, and that the tracks and totemic animals were processional routes to ritualistically summon up rain in a devastatingly long period of acute drought. Whatever their purpose it is doubtful they were conceived as art since no one could have seen them. Not that it's a prerequisite of art to be seen. Medieval churches have frescoes and carvings placed so high up that they're almost out of sight and only dimly lit by stained glass – artworks conceived not for man but for the glory of God. Bach used numerical references to biblical texts which can be deduced from the score but are inaudible during performance. The desert lines are only one expression of this ancient culture. They made gruesome sacrifices, had elaborate rituals, and sported pointy heads. We are the same people as they were, our bodies are not that different, our brains are the same size, but in our different ways of expressing thoughts and anxieties and fears and skills we are worlds apart. Or are we? How come our national newspapers all carry articles on astrology?

 1. Bruce Chatwin. *What am I Doing Here?* Jonathan Cape (London 1988)   2. *Peruvian Ground Drawings.* Exhibition catalogue, Kunstraum (Munich 1974)

A geoglyph

Photograph. Cornell Capa

AUSTRALIAN ABORIGINES BELIEVE EVERYTHING EXISTS FOR A REASON. EVERYTHING HAS A PURP

ALSO BELIEVES HE IS LIVING IN A DREAM OF HIS FOREBEARS - TOTEMIC FIGURES WHOSE SPIRITS

BEINGS COME IN MANY GUISES: MYTHOLOGICAL HEROES, CURIOUS CREATURES (WITCHETTY

DESERT ORANGE DREAMING), AND EVEN DISTURBING PHYSICAL MANIFESTATIONS (COUGH DREAMIN

CUSTOMS, RITUALS, SONGS AND TERRITORIES. THEN THERE IS THE MYSTERIOUS LABYRINTH OF

KNOWN AS DREAMING-TRACKS OR SONGLINES. THE ABORIGINES BELIEVE THEIR ANCESTORS

FLEXED THEIR LIMBS, TOOK A STEP FORWARD, SANG THEIR NAME, AND THEN WALKED OFF SINGIN

CREATURES, AND EVERYTHING ELSE. EACH CLAN CONSIDERS THE LAND THROUGH WHICH THEIR

TRAVERSE HUNDREDS OF MILES, CROSS OTHER SONGLINES, PASS THROUGH REGIONS WHER

BUT ONCE THE SONG IS COMPLETED, THAT IS THE BOUNDARY. A FACTOR ABORIGINES FIND IM

IF AN ABORIGINE SEES ANOTHER'S FOOTPRINT, THEY CAN IDENTIFY TO WHOM IT BELONGS. INDE

VEHICLE, DATE AND TIME, AND EVEN THE NUMBER OF PASSENGERS.[2] NOW HERE IS A REALLY C

WHICH THE SINGER IS ON 'WALKABOUT', AND THE SACRED SITES ON THE ROUTE ARE IDENTIFIED

LANDSCAPE MEANS ONCE A SONG IS COMPLETED THAT MARKS THE END OF CLAN TERRITORY - BU

DIFFERENT LANGUAGE. SINGING THE WORLD INTO BEING GIVES A REAL MEANING TO THE PLA

MYTHOLOGIES, FOR EXAMPLE THE NAVAJO INDIANS WHO BELIEVE EVERYTHING WAS HO

 1. Bruce Chatwin. *The Songlines.* Jonathan Cape (London 1987) **2.** Marlo Morgan. *Mutant Message Down Under.* Thorson (London 1995)

HERE ARE NO FREAKS OR ACCIDENTS, ONLY MISUNDERSTANDINGS AND MYSTERIES. THE ABORIGINE

SSED ON THROUGH EACH GENERATION OF EACH PARTICULAR DREAMING CLAN. THESE ANCESTRAL

DREAMING, POSSUM DREAMING), FRUITS AND PLANTS (CHEEKY YAM DREAMING,

CHINESS DREAMING, EVEN DIARRHOEA DREAMING). EACH CLAN ALSO HAS ITS OWN MYTHS,

IBLE TRACKS WHICH CRISSCROSS AUSTRALIA.' THESE ARE FOOTPRINTS OF THE ANCESTORS,

ED THEMSELVES OUT OF MUD FROM A PRIMORDIAL WATERHOLE, FORMED THEIR BODIES,

WORLD INTO EXISTENCE. THE SKY, SEA AND LAND, THE ROCKS, WATERHOLES, GUM TREES,

LINE PASSES AS THEIR TERRITORIAL BIRTHRIGHT. THIS ANCIENT TOPOLOGY MIGHT

SPEAK OTHER LANGUAGES. IN THE CONVENTIONAL SENSE THERE ARE NO FRONTIERS

LY CONFUSING IF TRAVELLING ACROSS COUNTRY BY TRUCK. WITHIN A SMALL GROUP,

EY HAVE BEEN KNOWN TO TELL FROM THE TRACKS MADE BY TYRE MARKS, THE SPEED, TYPE OF

US THING: THE MELODY OF THE SONG REFLECTS THE NATURE AND CONTOURS OF THE LAND OVER

PUNCTUATION OR PORTION OF THE SONG. THE INDIVISIBLE RELATIONSHIP BETWEEN SONG AND

MELODY CAN BE CARRIED ONWARDS BY THE NEXT CLAN IN THEIR SONG, EVEN IF SUNG IN A

INOUS AXIOM THAT 'EACH DAY IS THE FIRST DAY OF YOUR LIFE'. MANY CULTURES HAVE SIMILAR

INTO EXISTENCE BY COYOTES – THEY EVEN CALLED THEM SONGDOGS.

Photograph. © 1991 George Wingfield. Crop circle at East Kennet, Wiltshire, 27 July 1991

Crop Circles. Usually occur in windless conditions, mainly at night in low undulating landscapes when the air, disrupted by cold, triggers off a small whirlwind which flattens crops into circles.

That's one explanation, there are others.

'... of the myriad theories, which themselves would make an astonishing sociological study, the most vehement are those which hope to explain the circles within the context of current orthodoxy,' writes Michael Glickman. *'The whirlwind, the hoax, animal behaviour, agricultural chemicals, secret military radiations have all been enlisted to give us comfort. None of them work! This phenomenon vehemently resists analysis ... something here appears to be tugging, gently but firmly, at the foundations of our carefully constructed mechanistic paradigm.'* [1]

Crop circles, agriglyphs to the cognoscenti, have probably always existed. Perhaps it was their mysterious arrival which endowed certain sites with sacred significances. Possibly they were templates for wood henges and stone circles? Perhaps they are the origin of that folksy souvenir the corn dolly, an ancient fertility symbol made from twisted corn.

The popular press rubbish the whole thing as a hoax. Anyway in the summer of 1992, to corroborate or disprove this scepticism, twelve teams attempted to produce crop circles in a field of wheat, within five hours, and at night. The designs had to imitate fifteen typical crop circle features – here are some of them:

The Grapeshot Circle: the crop must spread radially from centre to perimeter. **The Circle:** must show no evidence of having been entered. **The Triple Lay:** at the junction of the shaft with the inner ring the stems should weave at right-angles. **The Gap:** at least seven feet must be left between the central shaft and the two parallel strips. **The Swirl:** the swirl in the main circle should be at least eighteen inches off the geometric centre. **The Mini Ring:** no more than 12 inches thick with the lay of the corn half clockwise and half anti-clockwise. **The Downward Bend:** there should be an area of at least two square yards where the crop is bent downwards. **Bent at the Nodes:** there should be a sheaf or a single stem near the centre of the circle bent half way up the stem.

The results were convincing but inconclusive. After all, proving you can fake a £5 note doesn't prove that all £5 notes are fake. [**SEE** P432].

'The more thoroughly you describe, the more you will confuse. It is necessary to draw as well as describe.' Leonardo da Vinci

1. Michael Glickman. *Pentagram Papers 21* (London 1993)

Avebury Truslœ 9 June 1991

Hazeley Farm Fields 3 August 1990

Ogbourne Maisey 11 July 1991

Westbury July 1990

Etchilhampton Hill 29 July 1990

Silbury Hill 27 July 1991

Diagrams of crop circles in various locations recorded by Michael Glickman and Wolfgang Schindler. Other configurations can be found in his book: *Crop Circles.* Wooden Books (Powys 2000)

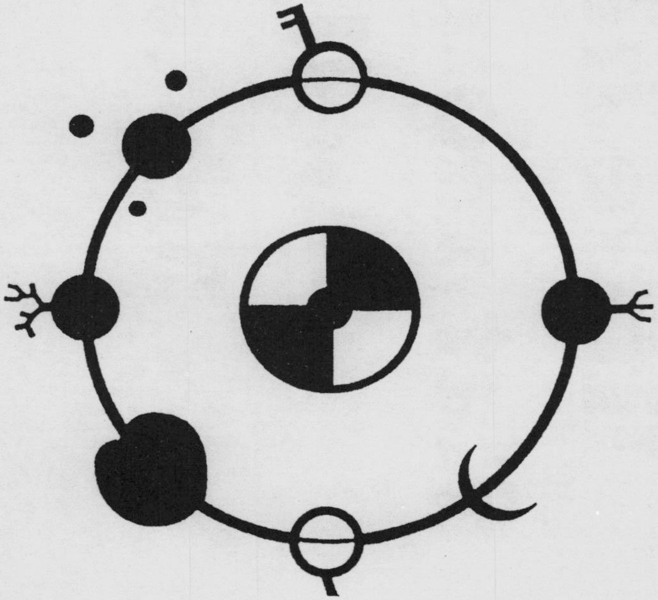

Alton Barnes 9 July 1992

Alton Barnes 12 July 1990

Exton 4 August 1992

Telegraph Hill 16 June 1990

Silbury 17 August 1992

'Ask a toad what is beauty ... he will answer that it is a female with two great round eyes coming out of her little head, a large flat mouth, a yellow belly and a brown back.'

Voltaire. *Philosophical Dictionary*, (Paris 1794)

Stendhal   'I do not feel I have wisdom enough yet to love what is ugly.'

beauty is a flavour of quark

For the sub-atomic physicist – says *Brewer's Dictionary of Twentieth Century Phrase and Fable* – beauty is a flavour of *quark*. Quark (rhymes with pork) is a nonsense name coined by physicist Murray Gell-Mann from the line 'three quarks for Muster Mark' in *Finnegans Wake* by James Joyce.

Photograph. David Doubilet

This fish isn't the sort of creature you feel you want to stroke and take home for a pet.

To be candid it looks horrible.

Yet it looks like this for a very good reason.

If it looked any different it probably wouldn't still be around.

The nightingale doesn't sing for our delectation but is merely announcing her availability to fellow nightingales. Ironically, our appreciation of aesthetics is rooted in Wordsworth's 'red in tooth and claw', and appears to be a by-product of survival attributes and sexual attraction.[1] The aerodynamic bird, the streamlined cheetah, the armoured stag, the flamboyant peacock.

Somewhere along the ancestral line a sensibility crept into the human psyche. Monkeys, for instance, don't give a banana about aesthetics. They don't respond to visual harmony or even like one kind of music more than another – actually they prefer silence. However, they *are* aroused by colour. They like blues and greens (sky and trees?), dislike yellows (lions?), and red (blood?) really upsets them.[2]

Sexual attraction is linked to favoured features. These are genetically accumulated since they are more desirable. The female bird of paradise fancies the males with the longest tails. Nobody knows how they came to be equipped with such a colourful presentation but, as Richard Dawkins surmised, 'For me the peacock's fan … is clearly the product of some kind of uncontrolled, unstable explosion that took place in evolutionary time.' I'm not quite sure what that means but female peacocks seem to inherit the attraction for long tails and pyrotechnics, which is why her sons are show-offs and have long tails. And so it goes.

The reasons for other physical features are less easy to categorize. Why are gentlemen said to prefer blondes? CLAIROL advertising slogan: 'If I only have one life let me live it as a blonde.' Did giraffes grow long necks so they could eat the leaves at the top of acacia trees? Or to get a better view and thereby acquire a taste for acacia leaves? Either way, when it comes to choosing mates the giraffe's preference is for long necks. Acacia trees also have survival strategies. To avoid being munched to death they evolved long, sharp thorns. Giraffes then developed longer tongues. Acacias then evolved toxins in the leaves to create an arboreal alarm system. When a giraffe begins munching, the tree releases a chemical into the air which causes other acacias to increase toxin production. The smart giraffe avoids trees downwind.[3]

In contrast, have you heard about the Japanese bricklayer who always placed a rose next to him when he worked, so he could look at it from time to time, and savour the aroma?

1. Stephen Jay Gould. *The Flamingo's Smile.* Penguin (London 1991)   2. John Brockman. *The Third Culture.* Touchstone (New York 1996)   3. Michael Crichton. *The Lost World.* Arrow Books (London 1997)

In 1882 Oscar Wilde was met by reporters when his ship arrived in New York harbour, and delivered a perfectly cadenced lecture. 'I am here to diffuse beauty,' he said (condescendingly). 'Beauty is nearer than most of us are aware. It's a wide field which has no limit, and all definitions are unsatisfactory. Some people might search and not find anything. But the search, if carried on according to right laws, would constitute aestheticism.' Most people's criterion of beauty lies somewhere between Cleopatra's nose and the ugly baby – a baby so ugly that the mother hung a pork chop around its neck so the dog would play with it. Philip Sassoon used to haul down the Union Jack over his house late in the afternoon because he thought the colours clashed with the sunset. Some find a chair beautiful to look at because it's comfortable to sit in, others find it comfortable because it's beautiful to look at. William Morris told someone who complained about one of his chair designs that if he wanted comfort he could go to bed, and when in Paris did his writing (some say Maupassant) in the restaurant of the Eiffel Tower so he could avoid looking at it. Actually it is neither ugly nor beautiful. Its function was to symbolize a world fair by being the highest man-made structure in the world (at the time), and to serve as a monument of technical abstraction by the exercise of joining base to pinnacle. Anyway Morris was no less eccentric than a character in John Le Carré's novella, The Tailor of Panama, who found the bougainvillea in his neighbour's garden so lovely he wanted to bite it. Sir Francis Galton [Victorian and founder of Eugenics] tried to quantify the geographic distribution of female beauty: 'I prick holes, unseen, in a piece of paper, torn rudely into a cross with a long leg. I use its upper end for good, the cross arm for medium, the lower end for bad.' – apparently he secretly did this under his overcoat – '… place, and date … classifying the girls I passed in streets or elsewhere as attractive, indifferent, or repellent … I found London to rank highest … Aberdeen lowest.' Chaucer was more direct: 'With buttokes brode and brestës rounde and hye.' Nowadays scientists quantify beauty into units called helens. A millihelen is just about enough beauty to launch one ship. Some consider beauty a manufactured value rather than an intrinsic quality. Andy Warhol thought 'all is pretty' and Picasso (and Constable) claimed he never saw an ugly thing in his life. Heinrich Heine ironically remarked that he once knew a woman who resembled the Venus de Milo, the figure displayed in the Louvre. 'Like her,' he said, 'she is extremely old, has no teeth, and has white spots on the yellow surface of her body.' For myself I think it comes down to that indefinable feeling which the ancients must have thought of as 'the sympathy of things'.

ATTEMPT TO RENDER MIDWAY POINT BETWEEN
BEAUTY AND UGLINESS

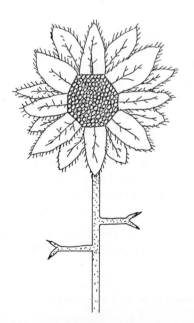

Illustration. David Shrigley. Photograph. Richard Billingham.

AN ART CRITIC REVIEWING RICHARD BILLINGHAM'S PHOTOGRAPHS OF HIS PARENTS [THIS ONE IS OF HIS MOTHER] IN THEIR TINY TACKY APARTMENT CONCLUDED THAT: 'EVERY WRONG WITH THE PICTURES IS RIGHT WITH THE WORK, EVERY FAILURE OF THE IMAGE A SUCCESS FOR THE ART. SUCH IS THE AESTHETIC OF OUR TIMES: A DESIRE IN EFFECT OF FUCKING UP SO COMPLETELY, AND YET WITH SUCH CONFIDENCE AND CONTROL, THAT ONE'S MEDIUM EXPANDS.'

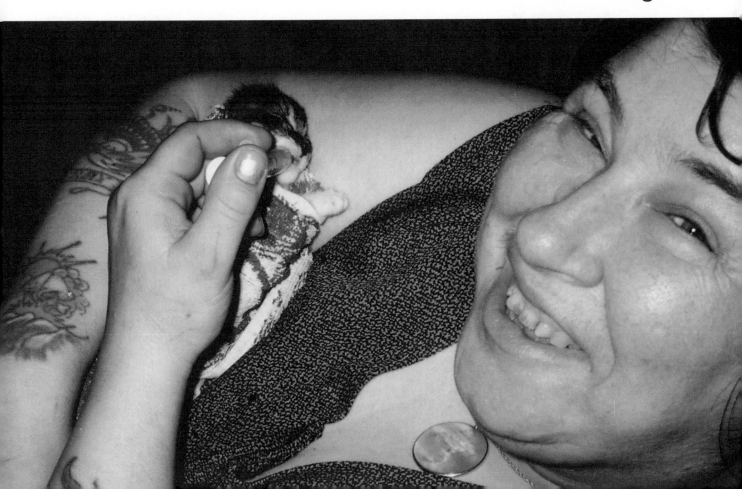

George Nelson : 'We have brainwashed ourselves into equating the new with the good, and the newest with the best, and the only remaining holes in the synthetic padding wrapped around our uneasy convictions are those intermittent fits of modernistic anxiety, so often expressed in nostalgic fads which fill the stores with "provincial" furniture, "early Aztec" TV sets, "Art Nouveau" lampshades (made of paper and imported from Hong Kong), distempered dishwashers and refrigerators.'

Illustration. Barbara Jakobson's Airstream

'Aesthetics is for the artist, like ornithology is for the birds.' In Greek *techne* meant 'skill'. The

BEN SHAHN (SOME SAY BARNETT NEWMAN)

ancient Greeks didn't separate art from *techne*, but called all artists and craftsmen *technitai* (makers). Today we don't have it quite so together. The engineer generally works from inside out, concerned how the whatever-it-is will perform, while the designer usually works from outside in, concerned how people will use and feel about it. They rarely meet up. That leaves a fuzzy bit in the middle. Massimo Vignelli, a New York designer, had a Rolls Royce. He liked the idea that the loudest noise was made by the clock but he didn't appreciate having to spend a fortune on having to have the car disassembled to change a sparking plug. He sold it. Details aren't details, they're the product. In *Zen and the Art of Motorcycle Maintenance*, Robert Pirsig writes : 'Technology is simply the making of things and the making of things can't by its own nature be ugly or there would be no possibility for beauty in the arts, which include the making of things. If you have to choose among an infinite number of ways to put it [motorcycle] together then the relation of the machine to you, and the relation of the machine and you to the rest of the world, has to be considered. "Sounds like art," the instructor says. "Well, it is art," I say. This divorce of art from technology is completely unnatural. It's just that it's gone on so long you have to be an archaeologist to find out where the two separated.' David Hockney said that 'art moves you and design doesn't – unless it's a well-designed bus.' Well actually he's wrong and anyway designers have admired a bus since the early 1930s. The *Airstream*, dreamed up by Wally Byam, was a streamlined polished metal projectile which became such an icon that Marcel Breuer even built one into his house. Neither simply a vehicle, nor simply an aesthetic experience, the *Airstream* satisfied on both counts simultaneously. The Japanese don't have a word for art, they use a word synonymous with function, purpose and aesthetics – *geijutsu*. In the West we mistakenly perpetuate the idea that there is a clear-cut distinction when it's more a matter of shading than dividing. The diagram[1] concocted by Arthur Koestler could be redrawn from automation to craft, art to engineering, or from any other two points you care to think of.

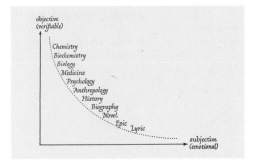

1. Arthur Koestler. *The Act of Creation*. Hutchinson (London 1964)

'Following a chimpanzee through a forest in Tanzania a monkey watcher saw it stop beside a waterfall. Whether it was going there or incidentally passing by is not clear but it was a stunning sight. At first the chimpanzee seemed lost in contemplation. Then it began jumping up and down, running around, calling out, and generally expressing enough excitement to merit an explanation. Although the chimpanzee could have had no practical interest in the waterfall it obviously held an interest, a curiosity, some kind of communication. Perhaps millions of years ago, in the infancy of the human spirit, something evoked a similar response from a very similar animal. Something that made it stop in its tracks overcome by a sense of wonder.'

Melvin Konner. *The Tangled Wing*. Penguin (Harmondsworth 1984)

Soviet Generalissimo Toukatchewski (1920s) on Versailles: 'The foundations you live on are rotten. As for Latin and Greek civilizations, what filth! … These things, harmony and measure, are what must first of all be destroyed. I only know your Versailles from pictures. But that too elaborately designed park, that finicking architecture resulting from too much geometry, is hideous. Has it never occurred to anyone in your country, to build a factory between that Palace and the ornamental water? … You lack taste or else you have too much of it, which comes to the same thing.'

Edward Fella: 'I don't like to use terms like "good", "bad", "beautiful", "ugly", because they continually take on different meanings. The eighteenth century thought that beauty was in the eye of the beholder, but it's in the culture of the beholder. Every culture has its own standards of beauty.'

Bernard Berenson: For years I had been inquiring, excavating, dredging my inner self, and searching in my conscious experience for a satisfying test. I needed a test to apply to artifacts that I thought I admired but could not hypnotize or habituate myself to enjoy with complete abandon, while the worm of doubt kept gnawing at the felicity of the ideal paradise. Then one morning as I was gazing at the leafy scrolls carved on the door jambs of S. Pietro outside Spoleto, suddenly stem, tendril and foliage became alive and, in becoming alive, made me feel as if I had emerged into the light after long groping in the darkness of an initiation. I felt as one illumined, and beheld a world where every outline, every edge, and every surface was in a living relation to me and not, as hitherto, in a merely cognitive one. Since that morning, nothing visible has been indifferent or even dull. Everywhere I feel the ideated pulsation of vitality, I mean energy and radiance, as if it all served to enhance my own functioning.'

Confucius: 'A common man marvels at uncommon things; a wise man marvels at the commonplace.'

Jules Henri Poincaré: 'The scientist does not study nature because it is useful to do so. He studies it because he takes pleasure in it, and he takes pleasure in it because it is beautiful. If nature were not beautiful it would not be worth knowing, and life would not be worth living. I am not speaking of course of that beauty which strikes the senses, of the beauty of qualities and appearances. I am far from despising this, but it has nothing to do with science. What I mean is that more intimate beauty which comes from the harmonious order of its parts, and which a pure intelligence can grasp … Intellectual beauty, on the contrary, is self-sufficing and it is for it, more perhaps than the future good of humanity, that the scientist condemns himself to long and painful labours.'

Antonio Salieri (on hearing Mozart's Serenade for Thirteen Wind Instruments): 'It started simply enough: just a pulse in the lowest registers – bassoons and bassett horns – like a rusty squeezebox. It would have been comic except for the slowness, which gave it instead a sort of serenity. And then suddenly, high above it, sounded a single note on the oboe. It hung there unwavering – piercing me through – till breath could hold it no longer; and a clarinet withdrew it out of me, and sweetened it into a phrase of such delight, it had me trembling.'

Ian Stewart: '… there is a kind of deep beauty, and some of the really best mathematics in the world, when you understand it, gives you this wonderful feeling that it is elegant, that it draws upon all sorts of wonderful areas that you had not realized were connected. It is like a musical composition where, somehow, everything comes together and you get this feeling of complete inevitability.'

Ralph Waldo Emerson: 'Beauty must come back to the useful arts … It will come, as always, unannounced, and spring up between the feet of brave and earnest men … [It is the instinct of genius] to find beauty and holiness in new and necessary facts, in the field and roadside, in the shop and the mill.'

Amédée Ozenfant: 'We must be grateful to the dictionary "Larousse", for so exactly revealing the common error. Beauty: "What is pleasing to the eye or spirit." Masterpieces are practically never pleasing. Their effect upon us is too striking for the definition of "pleasing" to have any true application. If M. Larousse had looked at the Sistine Chapel, Notre Dame, the Parthenon; if he had heard the "Pastoral Symphony", Bach, or read Shakespeare or Sophocles, all beautiful things, would he have called them pleasing? The editor of the Dictionary must have been thinking of comic opera. No doubt his favourite writers and painters are the free and easy collaborators to *La Vie Parisienne*. All we can say is that the feeling of elevation gratifies us. To say it pleases us is, as an explanation, inadequate. The truth is that a masterpiece inevitably calls forth strong emotion: some feel pleasure because of this emotion, but others feel pain: we must have nobility ourselves to be able to support grandeur.'

Seventeenth-century writer: '… a skilful and expert limner [illuminator, painter] will observe many elegancies and curiosities of art, and be highly pleased with several strokes and shadows in a picture, where a common eye can discern nothing at all; and a musical artist hearing a consort of exact musicians playing some excellent composure of many parts, will be exceedingly ravished with many harmonical airs and touches, that a vulgar ear will be utterly insensitive of.'

American tourist (on being shown around Windsor Castle): 'What a lovely castle', she enthused, 'such a pity they built it so near that nasty Heathrow airport.' The same tourist who thought the Tate Modern had the 'earmarks of an eyesore'.

Note. Walking through Kensington Gardens, I passed an acutely unattractive couple. He looked like a stuffed sock. Short, pallid and hairless, he wore gold wire glasses on a button mushroom nose and had the mouth of a goldfish. She was equally unfortunate. They were holding hands. There's no doubt about it, aesthetic values are subjective. After all she must think he's a rather sexy fellow.

Returning from an
errand one drizzling
autumn Sunday
morning I saw a
damp dirty white
carton dumped on
the wet pavement.
A plaintive message
printed on its side
caught my eye,
I tore it out and
took it home.
Here it is.

Three Japanese Tenets

Suki: *Subtle Elegance.* The attraction of the unusual or idiosyncratic. A primitive mask, an obscure agricultural tool. *Suki* is the attraction and fascination exerted by the unfamiliar.

Wabi: *Tranquil Simplicity.* The quality of natural colours, materials, forms and textures. Plain clay pots, woven baskets. *Wabi* is the voluntary spirit of poverty, appreciation of the commonplace and the unselfconscious, the fine line which precariously separates beauty from shabbiness.

Sabi: *Patina of Age.* The enhancement of the ravages of time. The castle ruin, the armless statue. *Sabi* achieves its ultimate when age, wear and tear bring something to the very threshold of demise.

SHABBY CHIC

Material poverty but spiritual richness. Odd, misshapen, awkward. Quiet, tranquil and calming. Unstudied but inevitable looking. Understated and unassuming. Rich in raw texture. Rough tactile sensations. Simplicity but not simple. Sober, modest, unencumbered. Discoloration and attrition. Rust, tarnish, stain, warping, shrinking, shrivelling, cracking, nicks, chips, bruises, scars, dents, peeling.

'We affirm that the world's beauty is enriched by a new beauty: the beauty of speed,' declared the **Futurists**. Not a view shared by **Baroness Blixen** alias **Isak Dinesen** alias **Pierre Andrezel**, who always travelled by rail or ship – 'One does not travel in a plane,' she declared, 'one is merely sent, like a parcel.' **Le Corbusier's** dictum that 'The house is a machine for living in' prompted **Frank Lloyd Wright** to mutter, 'Yes, but only in so far as the human heart is a suction pump.' **Cyril Connolly:** 'Speed is the only new sensation since the Palaeolithic.' **Roland Barthes:** '… cars today are almost the exact equivalent of the great Gothic cathedrals: I mean the supreme creation of an era, conceived with passion by unknown artists …' **J.K. Huysmans:** 'Look at the machine, the play of pistons in the cylinders: they are steel Romeos inside cast-iron Juliets.' **Marinetti:** 'a roaring motorcar that seems to run on shrapnel is more beautiful than the Victory of Samothrace.' **Benito Mussolini:** 'It is Marinetti who instilled in me the feeling of the ocean and the power of the machine.' **Alfred Barr:** 'Machines are, visually speaking, practical applications of geometry.' **Fritz Schumacher** [of *Small is Beautiful*] **:** 'A crank is a piece of simple technology that creates revolutions.' **Norman Bel Geddes:** 'Keats wrote a few immortal lines about a Grecian urn. Had he known about it he could as well have written them about an aeroplane.' **Marshall McLuhan:** 'One generation's technology is the next generation's artform.' The first public sculpture of a car still stands in a park by the Port Maillot in Paris.

When taken for a drive in the country Matisse always insisted on travelling at five kilometres an hour – walking pace – so that he could get a sense of the trees.

'When I was a child, I
Loved a pumping engine.
Thought it every bit as
Beautiful as you.'

W.H. Auden

'Ettore Bugatti gave up painting in 1899 to concentrate on the design and manufacture of cars, whose streamlined bodies sculpted the whirlwind. The painter Francis Picabia hurtled around Paris in a succession of luxurious cars, to which he had racing carburettors fitted. He began, docilely enough, with a Ford, advancing to a Citroën, a Rolls-Royce and a Hispano-Suiza. During the First World War, he managed to turn this automotive obsession to good account, and got himself reprieved from the trenches by obtaining a post as the general's chauffeur. The next war was less propitious for him. The rationing of fuel in 1940 obliged him to downgrade from a sleek Nash car to a less greedy Opel. Then, back-pedalling even further, he had to settle for a bicycle. Rather than humanizing machines, Picabia mechanized human beings. His nude portrait of an American girl, made in 1915, was a diagram of a spark plug : a device for generating a brisk and instant erotic fire.'

Peter Conrad. *Modern Times, Modern Places.* Thames & Hudson (London 1999)

CURATORS' EGGS

> 'Mr Henry Tate has withdrawn his generous offer to give his collection of pictures to the public, in consequence of the failure of the Treasury to fulfil his conditions as to the building in which it should be lodged. We are inclined to think that his conditions were too severe and too peremptory. The State cannot properly make such sacrifices as he demanded for any collection of pictures which a generous donor expects to be appreciated at his own high and perhaps extravagant estimate.'
> *The Spectator* (12 March 1892)

On the first Sunday that the British Museum opened its doors to the public (a term invented by the gentry), a portly greengrocer backed into a Greek amphora – the one which inspired the ode by Keats – knocked it off its pedestal and smashed it to bits. An unfortunate move confirming Baudelaire's opinion that 'sculpture is the stuff you bump into when you step backwards to admire a painting.' Anyway, the accident confirmed that the idea of popularizing art had been a dreadful mistake. Luckily the amphora was eventually stuck together again.

Even by the turn of the nineteenth century such matters were an exclusive indulgence for an élite minority and confined to specific areas of creative activity. Stonehenge was still considered of such marginal interest that it was auctioned (1915) for £6,600 to a Mr Chubb (three years later he gave it to the nation), and a rare rock collection was used as building hardcore for a public urinal in Bewdley, Worcestershire. Today buildings of architectural merit are protected and restored, and artefacts entombed in museums. But paradoxically they show a way of life that we have made almost impossible. The situation is worsened by the beautyspot syndrome described by art critic Robert Hughes as 'the insoluble paradox of museum going, which is that famous art gets blotted out by the size of its public ...'

On the dubious principle that consumption is a measure of culture Coca Cola has a $15 million corporate museum in Atlanta. This houses and displays old bottles, signs, advertisements declaring 'The Ideal Brain Tonic' and 'Coke is it', and stuff like that. Other corporate shrines include such places as Frederick's of Hollywood Lingerie Museum, The Tupperware Visitors' Centre and Museum in Orlando, Colonel Harland Sanders's Kentucky Fried Chicken Museum in Louisville and a McDonalds Museum with fake food and plastic mannequins which is located somewhere or other. Ironically, whoever said civilizations are remembered by artefacts, not by bank balances, was quite right.

Curios are often allocated artistic merit and I'm told that Ripley's 'Believe It Or Not!' Museum in Los Angeles has shrunken heads from New Guinea, costumed fleas, petrified mermaids, miniature paintings on olive seeds, artwork on lint, the world's smallest violin, potato chip drawings, an eight-legged pig, a picture of the Last Supper in toast.

The line between what has aesthetic value and what hasn't, and what's worth keeping and what isn't, is subjective and relative. An Aboriginal bushman might be mystified as to why his codpiece is on display in the Pitt Rivers Museum in Oxford, just as the journalist who found the collection of barbed wire in the Museum of Miscellanea in Alabama risibly banal. However, in *The Americans*, Daniel Boorstin rated barbed wire as indispensable for the rapid development of the Wild West and one of the most effective and widespread low-technology materials of all time. The 1874 patent stated that the invention was designed to look like a thorn hedge. Like thorns themselves, the new product diversified into (among many others) Griswold's Savage, Blake's Body Grip and Brink's Stinger. The patentee almost lost his millions because rivals claimed that he had merely copied the living world. [SEE P518].

Of course there is a more focused attitude. 'This book presents a theory of modern culture', begins philosopher Roger Scruton's introduction to *An Intelligent Person's Guide to Modern Culture* – go for it Roger – and then goes on to define a cultivated person. 'You don't have to be familiar with the entire canon of Western literature, the full range of musical and artistic masterpieces or the critical reflections which all these things have prompted. But it would be useful to have read *Les Fleurs du mal* by Baudelaire [in the original I assume] and T.S. Eliot's *Waste Land*. I shall also assume some familiarity with Mozart, Wagner, Manet, Poussin, Tennyson, Schoenberg, George Herbert, Goethe, Marx and Nietzsche.' On those criteria I score an embarrassingly low figure but, of course, I haven't had time to get round to them.

'In Europe, museums smell of town halls,' said Saul Steinberg, 'and in America they smell like banks.'

Henry Tate was
immortalized by
introducing a
commodity of
brutal capitalism.
Cane to crystal,
crystal to granular
solid, and this to
a white cube.
A product produced
in astronomical
quantities, but
which quickly
disappears when
placed in hot water.

I saw this small figure
at the back of an
antique shop in
Bologna in 1959.

The label, tied on the
wrist, carried an
exorbitant price
equivalent to five
pounds sterling
– I balked.

The following year
I returned to the same
shop. The figure
was still in the same
corner. The price
was the same. He
now hangs over my
television set.

E.H. Gombrich 'Consider the symbols e = mc². This simple equation is the product of a theory as beautiful as a Mozart concerto.'

Robert Grudin ' ... like gravity, beauty is a force whose existence is inferred from its apparent effects ...'

William Hogarth ' ... variety without confusion, simplicity without nakedness, richness without tawdriness, distinctness without hardness and quantity without excess.'

Marcel Janco 'The coarse is nearer the truth than the delicate; an insult more effective than a compliment; a smell acts more surely than a perfume; the art of the uncivilized cave dweller is grander than today's; ugliness is more beautiful than beauty.'

John Keats 'Beauty is truth, truth beauty.'

Javier Mariscal 'I have felt the same vibrations before a painting by Tàpies, a Dick Tracy comic, a package of Camels or a traffic sign ...'

Jeff Koons 'My work has no aesthetic values, other than the aesthetics of communication.'

Michelangelo 'Beauty is the purgation of superfluities.'

Hippolyte Taine 'Ugliness can be beautiful, but beauty is still more beautiful.'

Helena Rubinstein 'There are no ugly women, only lazy ones.'

C.F.A. Voysey 'Never look at an ugly thing twice. It is fatally easy to get accustomed to corrupting influences.'

Alfred Tennyson 'Science grows and Beauty dwindles.'

Larousse defines beauty as 'that which is pleasing to the eye or spirit'. However, beauty isn't necessarily in the eye of the beholder ...

Leon Battista Alberti '... the harmony and concord of all the parts achieved in such a manner that nothing could be added or taken away or altered except for the worse.'

Francis Bacon 'There is no excellent beauty that hath not some strangeness in the proportion.'

William Blake 'Exuberance is beauty.'

André Breton 'Beauty will be erotic veiled, explosive fixed, magic circumstantial, or will not be.'

Edmund Burke 'Sublime is great and beauty is small and smooth.'

Tibor Kalman 'I'm not against beauty, it just sounds boring to me.'

Will Burtin 'Beauty is not necessarily a matter of form or style, but a result of order achieved.'

Italo Calvino Crystal and flame: 'Two forms of perfect beauty that we cannot tear our eyes away from, two modes of growth in time, of expenditure of the matter surrounding them, two moral symbols, two absolutes, two categories for classifying facts and ideas, styles and feelings.'

Coco Chanel 'Art is ugly things that become beautiful and fashion is beautiful things that become ugly.'

Salvador Dalí 'Beauty is simply the total consciousness of our perversions.'

Serge Gainsbourg 'Ugliness is superior to beauty, it lasts longer.'

SHOP SIGN SEEN IN CONNECTICUT

Aussie observation

'As flash as a rat with a gold tooth.'

A piece of architecture

'Antonio Gaudí's last work, the unfinished *Sagrada Familia*, soaring over Barcelona like a congealed eruption of pink and gold-flecked porridge, is one of those highly questionable architectural "masterpieces" that the world could well have done without. It is, so we are invited to believe by the more lachrymose of its partisans – and there are many – the embodiment of a passionate, highly personal view of architecture. Meat and drink to the architecture-is-frozen-music school. They love its "art", its symbolic content and its hyperactive inventiveness. To me, however, its looming presence is oppressive, not to say toe-curlingly embarrassing, ever more so as Gaudí's self-appointed heirs labour to finish the unfinishable in ever more kitsch style. It has become a testimony, not to Gaudí's undoubted genius, but to the grotesque metamorphosis that overtook him as the *Sagrada Familia* crowded everything else out of his mind in the closing years of his life when he turned into a nail-sprouting Howard Hughes recluse, living in its unfinished crypt. *La Sagrada Familia* is no work of genius, more a brilliant idea converted into banality.'

extract from an article by Deyan Sudjic [1]

6.2.1975 Bristol–London train, near Bath, Somerset
By the side of the railway track is a white house which has a new antique door with an inset leaded window and polished coach lamps on either side. The husband is cleaning the car on the gravel drive leading from the five-barred gate. The wife is polishing the handle of the wishing well. A bull is looking at them over the garden wall and sticking out its big red tongue.
Ian Breakwell's Diary 1964-1985

Superficial but omnipotent

'"Good Taste is better than bad taste," remarked Arnold Bennett, "but bad taste is better than no taste." It has never been discovered whether Bennett himself had any taste, although his most tangible legacy, the *Omelette Arnold Bennett* – made with smoked haddock, cream and Parmesan cheese – tastes pretty good to me. You, however, may read the list of ingredients and grimace. The difference between my pleasure and your revulsion is "taste". Superficial but omnipotent, the most mysterious of human phenomena, taste can be seen to explain everything. Indeed, taste is so firmly woven into every aspect of our lives that all the common sayings about taste from antiquity onwards (to each his own) indicate that any discussion about taste is taboo: it is supposedly a purely subjective phenomenon and all tastes are equally valid. There are honest, brave and truthful men, God-fearing and good fathers, who choose to wear grey patent-leather slip-ons and tight pale-yellow polyester shirts and brown Terylene ties. Their wives may bake like angels and be exemplary mothers, even if they choose to decorate their sitting-rooms with paintings on black velvet and little gilt wall sconces with red velveteen shades. Such admirable folk are happy, well-adjusted and secure in the knowledge that they have good taste, and act accordingly. We, who scorn what they like, can take comfort from the fact that by identifying their taste as bad we immediately confirm our own taste as good. And that's the trouble with taste. All the discussions quickly reduce to the entertaining, though uninstructive, scrap between good taste and bad taste. Good taste/bad taste is a game that diverts us from questions of: what is taste? where does it come from? how does it operate?'

extract from an article by Loyd Grossman [2]

1. *The Sunday Times*, 15 December 1991   2. *The Guardian*, 24 December 1991

The most famous item designed by Charles
Eames is an easy chair in moulded plywood
with leather upholstery. It is elegant and
comfortable and right, and whenever there is
a new book or exhibit about design, this chair,
Chair 670, usually has a place, summing up
all that is good about design in the twentieth
century as precisely as Hepplewhite spoke for
the eighteenth. Although it first went on sale
in the 1950s, it has that curiously dateless look
characteristic of a classic. As an article in *Time*
magazine said about him, 'Wherever in the
world Eames goes, for whatever enterprise he
and Ray are engaged on, people mention the
chair. A slightly weary look comes into his eyes
as this celebrated ghost of the past intrudes
into his current enthusiasm.' It isn't the chair
he liked best: he mentions another chair, on
slender steel legs designed in 1945. He didn't
originally intend the easy chair to go into
production. 'I made it as a present for Billy
Wilder. Billy had made a picture in East
Germany and found a Marcel Breuer chair and
brought it back to me, and this was a return
present.' Quid pro quo.

The untouchable icon of modernism, collaged
with floral patterns to ironically reflect the
axiom: *De gustibus non est disputandum.**

* There is no arguing about taste

Question: *'What do you think of Eames?'* Response: *'What are they?'*

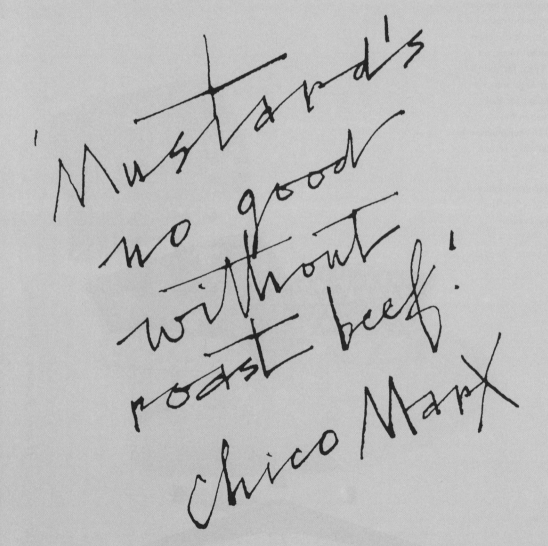

'Mustard's no good without roast beef.'

Chico Marx

Mammoths. Russian scientists have dined off mammoth steaks cut from carcasses preserved under Siberian ice for 50,000 years. I don't know if they enjoyed them but at various times I've balked at marinated crocodile, rocky mountain oysters, stir-fried puppy, smoked emu and reindeer sausage, so have sympathy for a Japanese tourist confronted with Irish stew and a greasy spoon. A reaction, I guess, much the same as sharing a meal with an Eskimo who scrapes gunk from between his toes to garnish your blubber, or being welcomed by tribesmen in Sarawak who (so I've read[1]) expect to savour your snot as a sign of esteem.

Oysters. In the film *Spartacus*, it is 76 BC, Laurence Olivier is chatting with his servant Tony Curtis. *'Do you eat oysters?'* asks Olivier. Curtis replies that he does. *'Do you eat snails?'* he asks next. Curtis replies that he doesn't. Then Olivier tosses in a real poser. *'Do you consider the eating of oysters to be moral and the eating of snails to be immoral?'* *'I don't think so,'* says Curtis. *'Of course not,'* snaps Olivier. *'It's a matter of appetite, isn't it?'*

Gastronomes. Even cannibals, gastronomes of the old school who prefer the simple natural diet of the pre-pork period, have their preferences. Certainly the bloodthirsty Caribs, who gave their name to the Caribbean, and through a variant of their name – *Canib* – gave us the word 'cannibal', had discriminating taste. They considered the French delicious, the English reasonable, the Dutch tasteless and the Spanish inedible – too stringy and gristly. Nowadays there aren't many cannibals around although Anthony Burgess wrote about once enjoying *'a crisp piece of roasted meat'* while visiting a tribe in New Guinea and being proudly informed they fed unwanted children to the pigs. He was immediately *'as sick as a dog'* but later explained it wasn't that his stomach had objected – but that his culture had intervened. An acquaintance told me humans taste like chicken. How did *she* know? Her great-great-uncle worked as a missionary among cannibals, and had asked them. Throughout most of human history we have been cannibals. The evidence of this is what archaeologists call 'pot polish'. This is the effect on human bones caused by being stirred in a cooking pot. *'It was a theory of mine'*, wrote Paul Theroux,[2] *'that former cannibals of Oceania now feasted on Spam because Spam came the nearest to approximating the porky taste of human flesh … "Long pig" as they called a cooked human being in much of Melanesia. It was a fact that the people-eaters of the Pacific had all evolved, or perhaps degenerated, into Spam-eaters. And in the absence of Spam they settled for corned beef, which also had a corpsy flavour.'*

Zoo food. In 1870 when Paris was under seige from the Prussians, the citizens, tired of rat and cat *fricassés,* turned to the zoo for sustenance. Victor Hugo was sent joints of bear, deer and antelope by the *Jardin des Plantes*. Kangaroo was consumed at the fashionable *Chez Brébant* restaurant, and wolf steaks served by the best butcher in *Faubourg St Honoré*. The hippo survived because it failed to meet the reserve price of 80,000 francs, but Castor and Pollux, two young elephants, went straight in the pot. One resident Englishman noted: *'I have now dined off camel, antelope, dog, donkey, mule and elephant, which I approve of in the order in which I have written.'*

Pastied cornish. *'The most proactively constructive word I can think of for Cornish catering'*, food critic A.A. Gill exclaims, *'is … Yeeeuuuuurrrrchhh.* [**SEE** P101]. *And any restaurant that wants to quote me on the menu can. Almost without exception, it's vile.'*[3]

Two oddities. Ludwig Wittgenstein always ate an identical meal for breakfast, lunch and dinner. Maybe he was indifferent or it was a matter of taste. I have no idea. In any case, whether of the palate or aesthetic preference, taste is more a matter of what you think than what you fancy. Take a Brahmin: if the shadow of an Untouchable falls across his dinner plate he has to throw it away.

Note. My mate Brian, who likes his food and drink, had to lay off alcohol for a few months. 'Have you any idea', he regretfully asked me, 'what it's like to have oysters with a glass of water?' I didn't. Didi, an Italian friend, lived close to Kensington Gardens and ran his kitchen off the sage, thyme and rosemary growing amongst the manicured shrubs around the Albert Memorial. And he expertly barbecued steak on a purloined London roof slate.

1. Guy Davenport. *Geography of the Imagination*. Pan Books (London 1984) 2. Paul Theroux. *The Happy Isles of Oceania*. Hamish Hamilton (London 1992) 3. *The Sunday Times* Style Magazine, 5 September 1999

Personal values. Taste is not a universal truth. It is only a reflection of what Immanuel Kant called *'a personal value for the agreeable'*. Nevertheless all values observe some kind of criteria and taste is no exception. The visitors' book for an exhibition on *Taste* held at the Victoria & Albert Museum was predictably inscribed with witticisms. One smart entry recorded *'Good taste is not having the audacity to inflict your opinion on other people.'* An unkind cut, since the curator wrote in the catalogue, *'Taste is the same as manners.'* Perhaps he was right – after all, Baudelaire confessed what he found seductive about bad taste was *'the high-born pleasure of giving offence'*.

Anecdote. Renoir asked Cézanne why he wore such an awful cravat. Cézanne replied that if it was in bad taste he wouldn't be wearing it. Disraeli was equally positive and suggested that Sir Charles Barry should have been hanged for his design of the Houses of Parliament, but at the same time disagreed with whoever it was who described the Nash terraces in Regent's Park as *'a violent digression from true taste'*. Today both properties are protected by legislation.

A preference. In 1840 Edgar Allan Poe wrote *The Philosophy of Furniture,* an essay on good taste. His preference was for the English style of the period: *'a glory of wallpaper, figured rugs, marble-top tables, tall narrow windows with dark red curtains, sofas, antimacassars, vases, unfading wax flowers under bell jars, a rosewood piano, and a cozy fireplace.'*

The bag lady. One wouldn't consider the clothing worn by a bag lady as being in good or bad taste, however, one might take another view of a hysterical outfit sported by a well-off matron. Taste comes into play when the degree of investment exceeds a reasonable return. Aristotle Onassis could be said to be suffering a shortfall when he had the bar stools on his yacht upholstered in whales' foreskins. When the intention is to create one effect, but it only succeeds in projecting another, then aesthetic sensibilities could be judged to be out of alignment. Actually most people can't tell the difference between what looks right and what doesn't. But because taste is considered a desirable value nobody admits to not having any – taste that is. As has been variously claimed, good taste depends on how close it is to what one personally likes, or doesn't like.

A letter. Poet Osip Mandelstam wrote from Switzerland in 1906: *'I have strange taste: I love the patches of reflected light on Lake Leman, respectful lackeys, the silent flight of the elevator, the marble vestibule of the hotel and the Englishwomen who play Mozart with two or three official listeners in the half-darkened salon. I love bourgeois, European comfort and am devoted to it not only physically but emotionally.'* He eventually died in a Siberian prison camp after years of hardship. A tragic ambivalence with contradictory allegiances to physical and spiritual well-being which exists in all of us.

A feeling. *'Taste gives a sensuous feeling, not an aesthetic emotion,'* Marcel Duchamp decided, and *'Taste presupposes a domineering onlooker who dictates what he likes and dislikes, and translates it into beautiful and ugly.'*

Zurich. Forty years ago it was virtually impossible to find a decent watch – a plain white face printed with twelve respectable typographic figures. At the time I was passing through Zurich and seeing a likely watch in a shop window, I went in and enquired the price. It was astounding. The shop assistant said they had a similar but cheaper version. It was indeed similar. But the face instead of being plain had a sheen as it was rendered like a white silk quilt. Disappointed I turned to leave. *'You English,'* she said, addressing my departing back, *'have no taste!'* A barb which suddenly, and agreeably, made me realize I didn't actually need a watch. Indeed I didn't wear one for twenty years.

'The enemy of art is good taste.' *Marcel Duchamp*

'Taste is institutionalized to guarantee its goodness.' *Ralph Caplan*

'A good apple is better than an insipid peach.' *Leigh Hunt*

'I have the simplest of tastes … I am always satisfied with the best.' *Oscar Wilde*

'Taste is the feminine of genius.' *Edward Fitzgerald*

'Good taste is as boring as good company.' *Francis Picabia*

'Standardization means industrialized violence to individual taste.' *Alvar Aalto*

'Good painting is like good cooking; it can be tasted, but not explained.' *Maurice de Vlaminck*

'We all need a splash of bad taste.' *Diana Vreeland*

'Taste, like style, is the man himself.' *Roger Scruton*

'If I had my life to live over again I'd live in a delicatessen.' *Woody Allen*

Trauma in Toyama. At a formal gathering of notables and designers in Japan, I was informed that the delicacy in a small bowl placed before me was extremely rare. No doubt it was also diabolically pricey. You were meant to swallow it. An appreciative inspection disclosed a glutinous mobile mustard colour substance embracing a pulsating malevolent purple blob. Expectantly watched by my hosts I conjured up an enthusiastic smile, and quickly knocked it back. A year later I attended the same dinner, but this time with Massimo Vignelli, a fellow designer from New York. The identical dish arrived. Massimo politely smiled, nodded and bowed, but omitted to take a close look. As he was raising the bowl I whispered the bad news in his ear. As previously the hosts were attentively watching, he blanched, but kept going. He's still not forgiven me. After I'd been in Japan for a week – *sashimi, sushi, shabu, tempura* – I felt an unreasonable yearning for fish and chips! I scanned the international menu in the hotel coffee shop. Obviously it catered for those in similar circumstances and listed: *sauerkraut, paella, spaghetti ... fish and chips*. I looked around guiltily, didn't see an acquaintance, and quickly ordered. Eventually the waitress arrived with a vast white plate elegantly setting off three miniscule fish, traversed with three extremely thin chips. In London, a month or so later, a Japanese designer came to stay with me. He brought his own breakfast, shyly explaining he'd called the Japanese embassy beforehand to ask where he could buy a particular noodle. I felt less silly about fish and chips.

The picture rail. I have a childhood memory of a family conference held in front of a hissing gas fire to pick a wallpaper to redecorate the front room. For the working class the front room was usually only used Sunday evenings or to receive visitors. Anyway, several evenings were spent poring through a thick, heavy sample book held together by nuts and bolts. The final choice, I vaguely recall, was the colour of pale porridge embossed with a bubble texture speckled with flecks of orange. The frieze prompted further discussion. The frieze, I should explain, was a two-inch-wide strip of decorated *anaglypta* which topped off the wallpaper. The space between frieze and ceiling was roughly twelve inches and painted the same colour as the ceiling – usually cream. Actually a frieze is a poor man's picture rail. The frieze was an update on the Victorian wooden rail. The picture rail was profiled to accept large brass hooks which held the cord of picture frames to display chromoliths of stags at bay and other highland scenes.

Giftware. During the 1960s I regularly drove to a publisher's offices in Mayfair and often had to stop at the traffic signs on an intersection with Oxford Street. On the corner was a large chinaware gift shop. I developed such an obsessional hatred for all those ginger cats and coy figurines that I promised myself I would throw a brick through the shop window. I found a brick and kept it under the seat. The shop has long gone. I never threw the brick. I am ashamed. I had the courage but was too mean to pay the inevitable fine.

Heals Department Store. I was in the furnishing department. In walked a newly married young couple. You can always tell. They inspected the sofas and were tentatively trying out one or two when the salesman arrived. He exuded confidence, was solicitous, brisk and efficient. They had a chat. He bounced around on a few items, stepped back to admire them, ran his hand over the contours. The couple were bemused. I was riveted. The husband nodded his head, she pursed her lips. Eventually the salesman alighted on a particularly repellent piece. She wasn't sure, the husband was unnerved, the salesman was convinced. As I left, I saw them signing a cheque.

QUESTION : 'What is bad taste?'   ANSWER : 'A distressed flavour.'

Illustration. Karl Arnold

The Kumquat Factor. Kumquats are tiny chinese oranges. They are delicious, succulent, a touch bitter. You like them or you don't. Deeply nailed into the you or YOU is the *like/don't like* feeling. It is not rational or even shared, as a lot of people like Kumquats. Just as they *like/don't like* the colour puce, or bugs, or the sound of wind in the willows. If someone doesn't like spinach you will never ever persuade them that they do ... as Clarence Darrow expostulated : '*I don't like spinach, and I'm glad I don't, because if I liked it – I'd eat it, and I just hate it.*' Now here's a thought. Like Darrow I hated spinach – but now I sort of like it. Maybe it's because I'm not who I was. [SEE P486].

'Excellence and the avant-garde are designed for the sophisticated palate.' Steven Pinker

'I do not think I shall ever forget the sight of Etna at sunset; the mountain almost invisible in a blur of pastel grey, glowing on the top and then repeating its shape, as though reflected, in a wisp of grey smoke, with the whole horizon behind radiant with pink light, fading gently into a grey pastel sky. Nothing I have ever seen in Art or Nature was quite so revolting.'

Evelyn Waugh

'There's only one thing worse than bad taste, and that's good taste!' *Raymond Savignac*

This image, which I think of as a hysterical sunset, was prompted by two contrasting memories.

The spectacular technicolour sunsets in Santa Barbara which are akin to slashing your wrists in a bowl of milk, and a pyrotechnic sunset over the Great Barrier Reef conducted in a tropical storm and orchestrated in a monochrome of blacks, greys and whites.

'It's better to make a creative mistake than a stagnant work in good taste.' *Philippe Starck*

Susan Sontag. *Writer*
'Camp is bad to the point of being laughable but not to the point of being enjoyable.'

Léon Krier. *Architect*
'The *kitsch* object is not beautiful, it merely stands for beauty and value. It is the *ersatz* for all those values which are said to be unaffordable to the masses: Art, Taste, Authenticity, Luxury, Craftsmanship, etc. However, with the exception of some confused intellectuals, few people are deceived by the true nature of the *kitsch* object. To glorify *kitsch* as being better than the real thing underestimates, to say the least, the level of man's intelligence and sense of dignity.'

Veronica Lee. *Journalist*
'Appreciating crap is a fine art.'

A.A. Gill. *Journalist*
'Garnish is horrible. The artfully arranged sprig of green or the deep-fried basil leaf says more than you ever want to know about the kitchen and the chef's raised pinky. It's the visual equivalent of the aspirant H set upon the vowel, the corner of the pursed lip dabbed with the serviette. Garnish is edible doily.'

Peter Fuller. *Art Critic*
'... if a man said that a mass-produced, cold white, Woolworth's bowl was as 'good' as a great Bernard Leach pot, I could not simply assent that he was entitled to his taste: rather I would assume that some sad occlusion of his aesthetic faculties had taken place.'

Fran Lebowitz. *Journalist*
'Your right to wear a mint-green polyester leisure suit ends where it meets my eye.'

Roger Scruton. *Philosopher*
'Kitsch delights in the tacky, the ready-made, and the cut-out, using forms, colours and images which both legitimize ignorance and also laugh at it, effectively silencing the adult voice. Such art eschews subtlety, allusion and implication, and in place of imagined ideals in gilded frames it offers real junk in inverted commas. It is indistinguishable in the end from advertising – with the sole qualification that it has no product to sell except itself.'

Anton Beeke. *Designer*
'Art breaks your heart,
Only kitsch makes you rich.'

kissin' cousin to camp.

One difference between erotic and kinky is this. A feather used with delicate and tantalizing effect is erotic whereas using the whole chicken is kinky. When the capital of invention runs out, creative inflation sets in – and you get kitsch. Liberace was kitsch. Described by a journalist as a 'winking, sniggering, snuggling, chromium-plated, scent-impregnated, luminous, quivering, giggling, fruit-flavoured, mincing, ice-covered heap of mother love', Liberace showed he also had teeth, sued the newspaper, and won. His lifestyle included glass grand pianos, electric candlesticks, and a ring comprising a miniature gold record player with a moving turntable. At an affair celebrating the American centennial he arrived in a Rolls Royce painted with stars-and-stripes, wearing an ermine robe with red, white and blue hot-pants, to conduct the orchestra holding a candelabra. On another occasion (at the age of 62) he made an entrance by soaring above the stage at Radio City trailing a cape of silvery scales. And for an Easter performance he emerged from a giant Fabergé egg in a cape of pink turkey feathers. His genuine popularity undeniably reflects most people's preference for the ersatz over the real thing, for candy rather than pickle. On the other hand, as The Encyclopedia of Bad Taste puts it: 'At its most delicious, bad taste is impudent ... it provokes anxiety because it breaks taboos ... it's a walk on the wild side of popular culture.' Something along the lines of Elizabeth David's comment on encountering a dish of sardines stuffed with sultanas – discordant but stimulating. This clock (a Christmas present from my friend Nancy) hangs in the bathroom. Although I gaze at it once a day while shaving I haven't yet hit on any way of improving it; by improving I mean making it better within the context in which it was conceived —— enhancing, as Baudelaire put it, 'a phosphorescence of putrescence'.

Tony Willet, publisher of *World of Interiors*, at home.

'We have become a nation of dreamers when it comes to our homes. Our appetite', writes a journalist in *The Times*, 'for pictures of other people's homes, with suitably revealing text, seems insatiable. Few of these magazines are entirely unpalatable. Nevertheless, some taste better than others, and *World of Interiors* is a truffle among the mushrooms.'

We're talking about a very classy magazine. The publisher, seen at home in this photograph, has his own theory for the huge success of the magazine. 'There's a time when you grow out of experimentation, minimalism, having nothing to sit on, sleeping standing up. By middle age you should have decided what you want to do. And the older one gets, the more traditional one becomes.' In the pages of *World of Interiors*, fading grandeur rather than contemporary design is the style. 'We come across so many houses that are ghastly,' confides Tony Willet, 'they have had millions of pounds spent on them and they look dreadful,'[1]

twinset and pearls provincial

1. *The Times*, 19 February 1999

Italian tenor Andrea Bocelli has sold more records than Pavarotti.

Illustration. Conceived by Tak Igarashi and drawn by Mick Haggerty

Pablo Picasso

'God ... invented the giraffe, the elephant, the cat ...

… He has no real style. He just goes on trying things.'

this-is-how-it-should-be-ness

Style is the particular in spite of the general – the difference between Howard Keel and Ray Charles singing *Some Enchanted Evening*. Style amplifies content with personality and at its best has *panache* and a confidence in expression: Greta Garbo or the Bugatti Roadster. At its worst it is merely mannerism, a confection, a snail in puff pastry:

> Advertisement: 'Pierre Cardin, that name synonymous with style, is the individualist's choice. His fragrances are crisp and spicy, with a touch of the erotic and exotic. They are sophisticated and refined, with a hint of classicism.' Whew!

I had an acquaintance who held me personally responsible (as a designer) for the inadequacies of his smart Italian lamp. His frustration centred on changing the light bulb, which required several screwdrivers, electrical pliers, an extra pair of hands and probably several hours' work. By focusing his irritation in my direction he was expressing the deeply rooted belief that design is synonymous with style. Actually the reverse is true. Creating cosmetic appearance masquerading as functional performance is mannerism. Mannerism only disguises the degree to which a problem was not solved rather than the degree to which it was.

The original mind aims for the centre but the stylist can only rework the circumference. Locked into a repetitive mode they are condemned to end up victims of their own trademark. They are recognized by their mannerism, not by their achievements. Without their corset they lose shape. Do you know about the sea squirt? This roams the sea seeking a rock to cling to for the rest of its life; when it finds one, it grabs hold. Since it no longer needs its brain, it eats it.

This-is-how-it-should-be-ness was coined by Charles Eames to refer to things which stand outside style. An antique three-legged stool was made that way so it could stand on crooked floors. Similarly, an axe handle has no style – because it has no mistakes.

'I loathe mannerism.'   *Henri Cartier-Bresson*

*Note. Suppers at Vieste, Italy. Ulla and designer
Willy Fleckhaus spent the summers at their spectacular
medieval tower by the sea in Puglia, Southern Italy. As
holiday neighbours we frequently came to supper. Balmy
evenings, flickering candles, Vivaldi recordings, local
wine, the lapping of the sea and a vertical supper. Half
a dozen large white shallow dishes with chunky stems
standing on top of each other created a tower. One began
with the top dish, olives (to accompany the aperitif),
moved down to the second – antipasto – to the third
with proscuitto, and so on, and so on, slowly all the
way down to the fruit.*

'In a Greenwich Village night club, Fats Waller had just

finished playing and singing his way through a stunning

twenty-minute set which included Honeysuckle Rose,

Sweet Georgia Brown, I'm just Wild about Harry, Basin

Street Blues, Body and Soul, Somebody Love Me,

and Blue Turning Grey over You. Perspiring, laughing,

loving the applause, Fats left his piano and walked over

to the bar where he encountered a fashionably dressed

woman. "Oh", she said, "Just the man I want to see.

I'm sure you can answer my question. Tell me Mr

Waller, what is swing?" Fats reached for his drink with

one hand, mopped his face with the other, looked the

woman squarely and replied. "Lady, if you gotta ask,

you ain't got it!"'   Art Tatum

AVANT-GARDE USUALLY ENDS UP AS OLD HAT

There are no functional reasons why a car should regularly change shape. Following the tenet that form follows function, every Chrysler used to be built with a high roof so that a man wearing a hat could sit upright. In those days proper people wore hats. Resisting the trend to lower and more streamlined automobiles, the chief executive declared that Chrysler 'built cars to sit in, not piss over.'[1] The company almost went to the wall because hats went out of fashion. Fashion is something which can become unfashionable. An ephemeral attraction for a particular style at a specific time for a number of people. An attraction deliberately created by commercial enterprise or mysteriously generated by intangible whim – like the millionth Chinese who decided to wear his Mao jacket back to front. Either way fashion is meant to be fun. Well, usually. In *Recueil de décorations intérieures*, written during the Industrial Revolution, the authors complained that fashion was dictated by mass production combined with compulsory change through obsolescence – the commercial enterprise effect. Advocating a return to functionalist principles they wrote that a chair should be dictated by the human shape, and illustrated the one shown below to make their point.[2] Much, much more recently, at a Milan Furniture Fair, one exhibitor made the startling announcement that his new chair was 'an object to sit in'. And then went on to elaborate: ' ... elusive of all traditional typological forms it is an hermetic and pregnant object, like a symbol deeply embedded in the past.' Gosh. The Carlton sideboard, illustrated right, is a product of the Memphis movement which flowered in Milan during the 1970s. For many it was a miasma, for others a whiff of fresh air. Either way it challenged preconceptions, and was a deliberate exercise in creating a style. The intention was to elevate popular taste (synonym for bad), and endow tacky materials (synonym for cheap), with cult status (synonym for I know and you don't). It was all the vogue for about five years. Now pieces turn up in antique shops. Clearly we are all prisoners of style and period.

Illustration. Percier and Fontaine chair. 1812   1. David Abodaher. *Iacocca*. Macmillan (New York 1982)   2. E.H. Gombrich. *The Sense of Order*. Phaidon (Oxford 1979)   This text is typeset in Avant Garde.

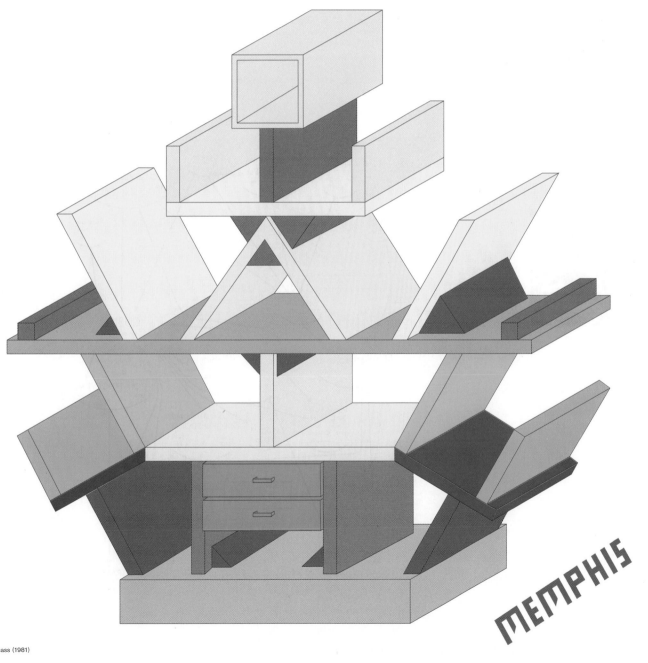

Sideboard. Ettore Sottsass (1981)

1898

1905

1906

1950

1962

1969

1973

David O. Selznick :

'There are only
two classes –
first class
and no class.'

Arthur Miller :

'An era can be said
to end when its
basic illusions
are exhausted.'

Amédée Ozenfant :

'When a particular
kind of feeling is
dominant in
certain epochs,
the distribution
of certain "modes"
creates what is
known later as
its style.'

Misha Black :

'Style is the signal
of a civilization.
It is impossible for
man to produce
objects without
reflecting the
society of which
he is a part.'

Catalogue cover. MOMA, New York

László Moholy-Nagy :

'Every period has its
own optical focus.'

QUESTION: Can anyone explain in a single short sentence what postmodernism is — without resorting to rudeness or cynicism?

□ TODAY'S interpretation of yesterday's vision of tomorrow. — M Stilton, London E5.

□ PESSIMISTIC wishful thinking. — John Gardner, Brasenose College, Oxford.

□ REVOLT against such seminal modernist figures as Joyce and Eliot, Stravinsky, Le Corbusier, Picasso and their descendants; a declaration of independence that seeks to blur traditional distinctions between high and popular culture. — Andrew Hoellering, Thorverton, Exeter.

□ RECOGNITION that our understanding of the world around us is shaped by a wide variety of influences as diverse, yet having a fundamentally similar effect upon our consciousness, as ancient Greek tragedy and Bugs Bunny cartoons. — Kenneth Corn, United World College of the Atlantic, South Glamorgan.

□ HOW ABOUT a three-word, a two-word and then a one-word definition? The three-word version is Jean-Francois Lyotard's: "Incredulity towards metanarratives." By this Lyotard means that the postmodern condition has rejected the certainties of large schematic perspectives (eg of Marx, Freud), replacing them with discontinuity, fragmentation ephemerality. . .

The two-word definition is by Linda Hutcheon, who identifies postmodern fiction as "historiographic metafiction". By this she means fiction that talks about itself, the writing process (metafiction), and explores the relationship between history and narrative (historiography). Examples include John Fowles's The French Lieutenant's Woman and Graham Swift's Waterland.

The single-word definition (which may, unfortunately, be both rude and cynical) is by a recent undergraduate of mine, and requires no gloss: "crap." — (Dr) George McKay, Department of Cultural Studies, University of Central Lancashire.

i s m s

Style is the physiognomy of an era. 'We are the two greatest painters of our time,' the elderly Douanier Rousseau is said to have addressed youthful Pablo Picasso, 'you in the Egyptian style, I in the modern style.' In the seventeenth-century cultural virtuoso John Evelyn described Gothic as 'sharp Angles, Jetties, narrow Lights, lame Statues and other Cutwork and Crinkle Crankle.' Somewhat later art critic Robert Hughes called David Hockney the Cole Porter of figurative painting. There are visual ingredients which indelibly mark epochs. Those shapes, colours and devices which appeal to one generation and which are usually spurned by the next. 'Nature's aim is man, man's aim is style,' pompously but accurately enunciated Theo Van Doesburg. And predictably christened his new art movement De Stijl. The Impressionists inherited their tag (1874) from the title of a painting by Claude Monet – IMPRESSION, SUNRISE. A critic seeing an Italianate bust surrounded with paintings by Matisse commented : 'Donatello chez les fauves' [Donatello among the wild beasts]. Apollinaire described the ballet PARADE (1917), a collaborative effort by Picasso, Cocteau, Satie, Massine and others as 'une espèce de sur-realisme'. The ponderous nineteenth-century Austro-German style took its name from Papa Biedermeier, a cartoon figure which satirized the middle class. In 1908 Henri Matisse disparagingly called Georges Braque's paintings 'petits cubes', hence Cubism. Art Deco was derived from the Exposition Internationale des Arts Décoratifs held in Paris in 1925. Bauhaus was coined from the German for building and house, and Dada the French for hobby horse. Charles Jencks pinpointed the post-modernist movement as starting in 1972 when the Pruitt-Igoe apartments in St Louis were dynamited because no one would live in them. Zeitgeist is academic jargon for the cultural characteristics of an era. The immediacy and ephemeral nature of graphics unconsciously typify the times in which they were born as you can see from the Pepsi logos. Commercial signatures need to keep pace with the times. Pepsi started life with elaborate penmanship redolent of leisured days and today has ended up on the bottle cap to reinforce branding. The stuff inside has remained more or less the same even though surface graphics reflect seventy-five years of changing tastes. 'Being modern', a flapper exclaims in a Noël Coward play, 'only means twisting things into different shapes.'

Jean Muir 'I prefer to think of fashion as a verb.'

Newspaper review: '"Josephine's is Sheffield's intimate nitespot" – it says on the complimentary ticket. The ticket offers 'Nite life London style' – whatever that is, hopefully not mugging, rioting or arson, but music, bubbly, a good time. The doors open at 9pm – by 11 o'clock it's bursting. Bouncers guard the doorway. Big blokes, big as buses. They scrutinize you from head to toe. The management guarantee a "select clientele". "Dress with style", it warns on the door. The bouncers enforce the rules vigorously. Everyone is inspected. If they don't like the look of you, they turn you away. No longhairs, no jeans, no casual jackets, shirts with buttons all the way down the front.'

Coco Chanel 'Fashion is architecture: it is a matter of proportions.'

Darwin Rig: Darwin Region Tourism Association, 1992: 'Life in the Top End [Northern Australia] calls for tropical ease in clothing styles. Most establishments welcome casual clothing, but often specify no T-shirts and no thongs. More strict regulations apply for the evenings, when *Darwin Rig* is the recommendation. For women this means either day or "after five" dress, casual but elegant. For men, long trousers and a collared shirt.'

Jean Cocteau 'Fashion is what goes out of fashion.'

De Nîme: Levi Strauss made durable trousers of denim (*de Nîme* from Nimes) for prospectors in the 1850s California gold rush, while bib overalls can be traced back to philosopher Herbert Spencer who invented them in the 1870s. He wanted to create a utilitarian one-piece suit. His own was tweed with buttons from crotch to neck.

E.H.Gombrich 'A fad is less than a fashion. If it were a fashion people would copy it.'

Two memories: In Mexico, in the late 1950s, the fashion cognoscenti wore mobile jewellery. This involved welding a precious stone onto a beetle's back, fixing a short slender gold chain to a leg and fastening the other end to a lapel. The tethered beetles crawled around and occasionally were rewarded with a crumb. At least that's what I saw the lady do at the next table. Ten years later – sitting in a restaurant in Paris – I noticed half of the women had a thin mascara line drawn down the centre of their nose.

Yves Saint Laurent 'Fashion is a kind of vitamin for style.'

By the way, did you hear the comment of the fashion designer who, driving through the countryside and glimpsing a herd of Friesan cows through the window, sneered: 'Yuk! Black and white, last year's colours.'

Cecil Beaton 'Fashions are ephemeral, but fashion is enduring.'

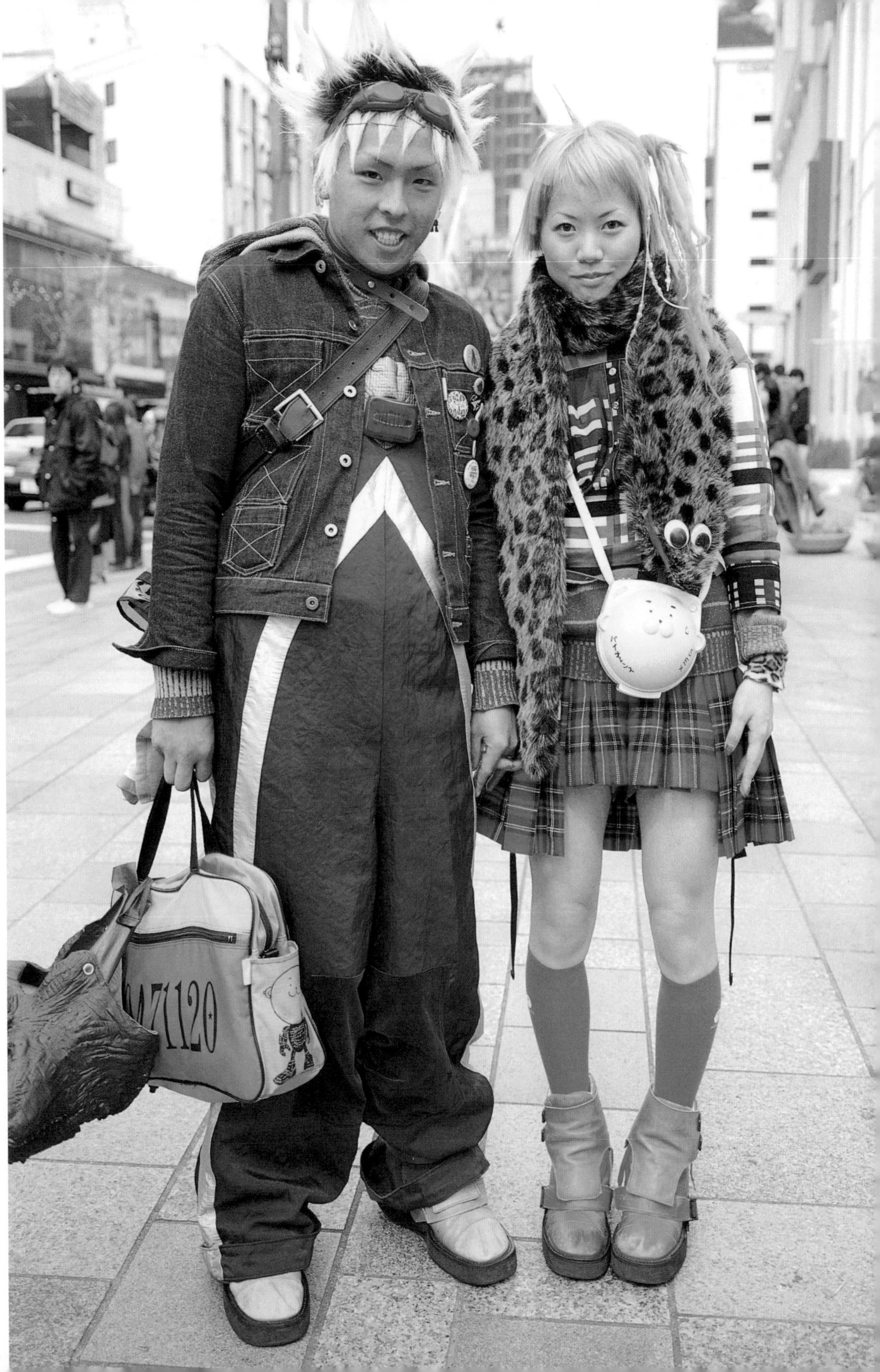

Photograph. Shoichi Aoki. Japanese street fashion

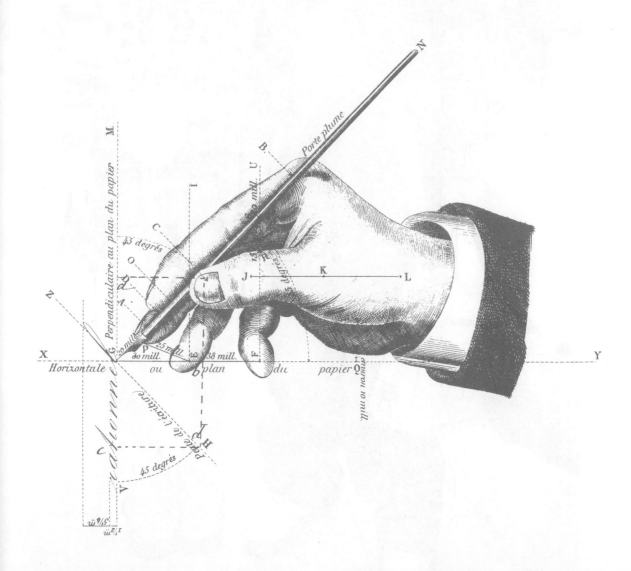

French proverb

'There is no such thing as a pretty good omelette.'

'Whatever we do, whatever we work at, our only rescue is to concentrate completely on it and to try and achieve perfection. The Greeks called it virtue. That's all we want. That's all we are capable of.' *A.G. Fronzoni*

Perfection is an imaginary state distinguished by its improbability. A much-quoted chauvinistic example is living in an English cottage with American central heating, a Japanese wife, a Chinese cook, and a French mistress. A notion of imperfection is a country where the Germans are the police, Finns the comedians, Italians the army, Belgians the pop singers, Spanish run the railways, English are the cooks, Irish the waiters and the language is Dutch. Like most generalizations, both examples contain a germ of truth.

Georg Staehelin is in Zurich gazing out of the window. He sees two workmen in the street manoeuvring an extremely large and unwieldy wooden triangle. He picks up the phone and dials my number in London. Being a Swiss designer he sussed out what was up and to entertain me describes the scenario. Laying down the triangle, the workmen carefully line it up with the kerb and draw chalk lines across the road. Then they paint in the pedestrian crossing.

I live in London at the end of a mews which is also a cul-de-sac. Some of my neighbours keep their dustbins outside their garages but to hide the clutter they usually front them with a row of potted plants. One day looking out of an upstairs window, I see a man appear at the top of the mews with a makeshift contraption – a bucket of yellow paint mounted on a wheel. He has come to paint the yellow 'no parking' line which borders the houses along each side of the mews. Lining up the wheel, which transfers paint to cobbles, he proceeds in a reasonably straight line until he encounters the potted plants. At this point he awkwardly manipulates his machine so that the yellow line erratically curves and wobbles around the contours of the

pots. Once clear of these impediments he proceeds in a straight line back up the mews.

The Duchess of Windsor used to get four servants to hold the corners of a bed sheet to take it upstairs after it had been ironed. She couldn't bear the thought of fold marks. And Anouska Hempel, who personally oversees her eponymous London hotel, insists that the orchids all have to face in the same direction. If you feel these two examples somewhat picky, how about Max Ernst's father? He painted a picture of his garden and omitted a tree as it spoiled the composition, but then was so overcome with remorse at this offence against realism that he cut the tree down. Michael Cimino was similarly obsessive, and after making *Heaven's Gate* and driving United Artists bankrupt by spectacularly exceeding the budget he commented : 'If you don't get it right, what's the point?' I agree, but there again tunnel vision is also a symptom of acute myopia.

'Thomas Eakins, American realist painter ... was so in love with the specific,' writes art critic Robert Hughes,[1] 'that one scholar managed to compute, from the sun's angle, the time and date of the scene depicted in one of his paintings of rowers training on the Schuylkill, *The Pair – Oared Shell*; they went under the bridge, give or take a few seconds, at 7.20pm on either May 28 or July 27, 1872.' An attitude somewhat different to that of film-maker, poet, writer, painter Derek Jarman, who when asked how he managed to do so many things, replied, 'I was lucky, I wasn't born a perfectionist.'

Of course too scrupulous an accuracy can impede the imagination, and although commonsense admires precision, the intelligence of exactitude does not exclude the pleasure of inexactitude. The subtle imperfection that testifies to the presence of the shaping hand. A point Ruskin made remarking that Turner spoilt his early paintings by filling in all the canvas to finish them. Certainly Michelangelo used to leave some roughness on

a finished sculpture just to show the marks of his tools, and the authentic Persian rug usually contains a deliberate fault on the principle that only Allah is perfect. A friend tells me that in South Africa, or more specifically in Kimberley, they inspect diamonds under skylights angled and tinted precisely to match those in the diamond cutters' workshops in London. Well that's what he told me.

Swiss designer Bruno Monguzzi relates being buttonholed by Antonio Boggeri who ran a famous influential design studio in Milan during the 1950s. Summarizing his story : 'Boggeri, thin hands raised in the air, one day confided in me,' recalls Bruno, 'about his Cobweb Theory. Like a cobweb, Swiss graphics were perfect, but often perfectly useless. A cobweb only becomes useful when a fly has infringed its meticulous structure.' An echo of the observation by the philosopher in the *Crock of Gold*, who declared 'Nothing is perfect. There are lumps in it.'

When perfection is the aim there is no end in sight, and so the trick is knowing when to finish and how to stop. A Japanese folktale tells of a father watching his son tend the garden. After pruning the plants and removing weeds, he swept the steps, washed the lanterns, sprinkled water on the mosses, and combed the gravel. After a while the son declared he had finished, and that it was perfect. The father smiled, stepped into the garden, and shaking a tree scattered gold and crimson leaves all over the ground 'to add a brocade of autumn'.[2] And to throw in another oriental pearl of wisdom – what the caterpillar calls 'the end', the rest of the world calls 'a butterfly'.

The Interference Fit. The skilled cabinet maker, having made mortice and tenon, will drill a hole through them to insert a peg. The hole made in the mortice is slightly off centre so that when the peg is driven home the misalignment creates extra torsion. This examples the art of the deliberate mistake.

zebra crossings and a brocade of autumn

The PERFECT NIPPY

Cap correctly worn,
monogram in centre.

Ribbon clean and pressed.

No conspicuous use of make-up.

Teeth well cared for.

Hair neat and tidy.

Clean and well laundered collar
correctly sewn in.

Dress clean and tidy.

Badge clean and securely sewn.

All buttons sewn on with
red cotton.

Fastening to have Hooks,
Eyes and Press Studs,
which should be securely
sewn on and fastened.

Clean and well laundered cuffs,
correctly sewn in.

Point well pressed.

Clean hands.
Nails well manicured.

Clean, well laundered apron,
correctly worn.

Dress correct length.

Plain Black Stockings.

Well polished plain shoes.
Medium heels for comfort.

J. Lyons & Co. Ltd.

Lyons Cornerhouses were an extensive chain of teashops and restaurants in London and other major cities. Founded at the turn of the century, they formed part of city life until their demise in the late 1960s. The Lyons waitress, or 'Nippy' as she was known, was formally dressed in a specific style. Lyons worked extremely hard to maintain this dress code as expressed through this instruction issued to its staff in 1937.

1. Robert Hughes. *Nothing if Not Critical.* Penguin (London 1992)   2 . Okakura Kakuzo. *The Book of Tea.* Charles Tuttle (Tokyo 1956)

THE WEIGHT OF EXACTITUDE

'For the ancient Egyptians, exactitude was symbolized by a feather used as the weight on the scales used for the weighing of souls. This light feather was called Maat (goddess of the scales) and its hieroglyph also stood for a unit of length – the 33 centimetres of the standard brick – and for the fundamental note of a flute.' *Italo Calvino* [1]

THE LOST VARNISH OF CREMONA

The Stradivarius is the epitome of perfection. Antonio Stradivari made at least 550 violins and 'every single one has a transcendent quality, that something which influences the way people play.' One contemporary violin-maker believes the secret is in the varnish. The recipe is now lost as it was written inside the Stradivari family Bible, long since destroyed. Subsequent attempts to analyse it chemically have proved fruitless. It may be something to do with the thin layer of volcanic ash which was brushed into the wood as a smoothing agent. Or perhaps an ingredient in the varnish of mica and what appears to be finely-ground particles of chitin, prepared maybe from insect wings. There are also 'tantalizing traces of organic compounds that could be bedroom residues, sweat, or pheromones of the master's own breath'.[2] Violinist Nigel Kennedy reinforces the legend that these amazing instruments have a life of their own. 'They are emotional things,' he enthuses, 'each with its own personality. And I'll tell you another interesting thing … they all play their very best in the hills near Cremona.'

Feather. Thomas Bewick   1. Italo Calvino. *Six Memos for the Next Millennium.* Jonathan Cape (London 1992)   2. Lyall Watson. *The Nature of Things.* Hodder & Stoughton (London 1990)

'It's astonishing that cats always have two holes cut in their coats in exactly the same place as their eyes.'

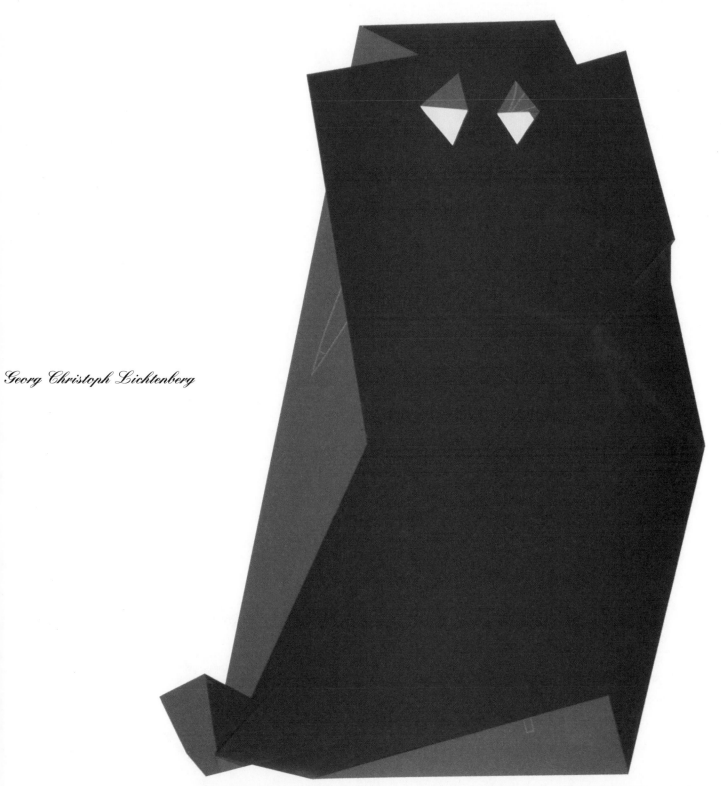

Georg Christoph Lichtenberg

The cat was conjured up by folding a sheet of old typewriter carbon paper — an exceedingly difficult task as the carbon comes off and the thin paper has a wilful static.

The reverse side of the sheet happened to be printed in a linear pattern. By carefully manoeuvring the folds, the two slots fold back to provide the eyes with lashes.

'Trifles make perfection, but perfection itself is no trifle.' *Shaker proverb*

'Perfection does not exist – only the evolution towards it.' *Motto, Ferrari Formula One (1975–6)*

'A work is perfectly finished only when nothing can be added to it and nothing taken away.' *Joseph Joubert*

'Everything is vague to a degree you do not realize till you have tried to make it precise.' *Bertrand Russell*

'A little inaccuracy sometimes saves tons of explanation' *Saki*

'...doing a large number of totally insignificant things that nobody else sees, every time without compromise.' *Herb Elliot*

'...to be animated with an angelic spirit: for such perfection could not be without a soul.' *Giulio Camillo*

'The thing about discipline, is not doing a small number of significantly large things well, it is doing a large number of totally insignificant things that nobody else sees, every time without compromise.' *Herb Elliot*

'... in Egypt there were such excellent makers of statues that when they had brought some statue to the perfect proportions it was found to be animated with an angelic spirit: for such perfection could not be without a soul.' *Giulio Camillo*

'A careless shoe-string, in whose tie/I see a wild civility/Do more bewitch me than when art/Is too precise in every part.' *Robert Herrick*

'What is perfection? It is when in a certain construction it cannot be done better, when form and content meet.' *Marcel Marceau*

'Perfect has always been a word of both intimidation and fragility. An egg, perfect yet fragile.' *Rich Saul Wurman*

'The grace of imperfection is worth more than graceless perfection.' *Alex von Wuthenau*

'Even imperfection itself may have its ideal or perfect state.' *Thomas de Quincey*

'Perfection has one grave defect, it is apt to be dull.' *Somerset Maugham*

Perfect, *in its most familiar sense, means* **flawless**; *in an earlier sense, it meant* **complete**.

UNFINISHED DRAWING OF CAMPSITE

FRANCE-TIR - 60, rue René Boulanger, PARIS

Photograph. Bob Maude

The person you love is 72.8% water.

At 4.29 pm on 9 February 1927, Eduard-Wilfrid Buquet filed his patent for the Flexible-arm Office Lamp at the Ministry of Commerce and Industry in Paris. They are now reproduced in a numbered limited edition. Mine is no. 170. It cost an arm and a leg, needs polishing daily, the joints tightening once a week and bulbs are exceedingly difficult to find. Why did I acquire it? Because I like it.

I have no idea why St Catherine of Siena wore her particular relic, a leather ring made from Christ's foreskin. Nor why villagers in western India pray to fossilized dinosaur eggs, believing them to be Shiva's testicles. Or on what basis young brides in Cairo are convinced that the butcher's calves' knees are an aphrodisiac. What I do know is that we like things for what they represent, not for what they are. A distinction confirmed by the statistic that the person you love is 72.8% water. [*]

When Alberto Santos-Dumont, the Brazilian aviator, was idly chatting to Louis Cartier over a glass of wine at Maxim's in Paris, he languidly complained about the difficulty of consulting a pocket-watch while using both hands to keep a dirigible under control. Cartier came up with a slim rectangular watch held on to the wrist with a leather strap. An innovation which converted watch from instrument to accessory. Today you can buy wrist-watches with multi-dials, a calendar, stop-watch, body temperature gauge and other conveniences. An excess capacity solely introduced to massage the ego of the owner.

When people leaf through advertisements showing cars standing on scrunchy gravel in front of stately homes, or nonchalantly parked in stable courtyards, they don't see pictures of new cars but images of old money. Form invariably exceeds function. Products always have residues of subjective decisions by designer or maker. To make it cheaper, or attractive, feel good, give pleasure. In turn the consumer also invests a product with unpredictable values.

Status usually takes precedence over function and appearance over performance. Why else would Mrs West of San Antonio, Texas, have requested in her will to be buried in her mink behind the wheel of her red Ferrari? Eventually she was. And Jack Kerouac, beat poet, buried as he'd asked, in his red plaid jacket and red bow tie. And why do the burial lots with a view over the ocean in a cemetery at Santa Barbara cost more than those which don't?

There are also products which attract a cult following like Mont Blanc pens and Ray Ban sunglasses. However, products promoted as cult objects such as Rolex watches or Burberry raincoats never make it. If the *cognoscenti* are conscious of being manipulated the magic evaporates. Of course it's not only what people read into things, it's also how things are conceived to be read. Ettore Sottsass said he designed the Olivetti Valentine typewriter not as a mere machine but 'to keep poets company on Sunday afternoons in the country.'

Just about everything we acquire is endowed with a significance, and our whole outlook can be deduced from the values we attach to the objects we treasure – often for reasons we don't know.

The Independent on Sunday, 9 May 1999

'The game hunter spent three hours to track and kill a fully grown giraffe. "It was", he explained, "a skinny 20-year-old sterile bull who had been disowned by the herd ... It takes six men eight hours to skin, dismember and joint a fully grown African male giraffe (1.5 tonne, 5.2m tall) ... one moment the giraffe's head is sticking out of the undergrowth in the veld; a few months later it is sticking out of a living-room wall in Louisiana." The hunter's trophy yielded: a stuffed giraffe head and neck, a giraffe-skin rug, four giraffe-skin standing lamps four novelty giraffe napkin holders. [SEE P314]. "I could have had me some nice authentic giraffe-skin ashtrays as well," the hunter later commented, "but I'm anti-smoking."'

* Another source says 65% water, 25% oxygen, 10% nitrogen   **Illustration.** *The Little Book of Calm*, Paul Wilson. Penguin Books Australia Ltd

Collecting was Rembrandt's passion. He spent huge sums on his collection, even when he could ill afford it. Besides the 65 albums of prints and drawings by eminent European artists, he had Japanese lacquer work, Chinese porcelain, exotic baskets, shells, minerals, stuffed animals, busts of the twelve Roman emperors, Venetian glass and Oriental weapons.

The Surrealists were fond of ambivalent things like the ambiguous *Coco de Mer* and classified them accordingly. One so-called **Perturbed object** was a deformed wine glass contorted by heat. An **Interpreted object** was an oval wheel made by an apprentice to demonstrate his skill. André Breton had one in his collection of oddities. **[SEE** P365**]**. Other categories included **Phantom objects**, **Involuntary objects**, **Dreamed objects**, **Fetish objects** etc. In the contemporary antiques business fetish objects are known by the less lurid title of 'association items'.

I'm attracted to **Visually tactile** objects: The Luxo lamp, Braun shaver, the Wassily chair. **[SEE** P77**]**. '**This-is-how-it-should-be-ness**' objects: the clothes peg, paper clip, ball of string. **Untutored taste** objects: uninhibited folk art, the fairground horse, the cigar label, the bus ticket. **Objects which carry the visual insult of vulgarity**: the kitsch souvenir, mantelpiece art, the McGill seaside postcard.

I've kept a shopping list from the last time I was in Singapore [21 March 1986]: Bought some presents for friends but as I can only buy what I like, I always need two. One for myself. Here it is: three clusters of strong dried tea packaged in bamboo leaves. A dozen packs of Darkie Toothpaste. A rubber man, (twelve inches high) marked out with acupuncture points. Cheap plastic mantelpiece icons of *Ganesha* (the elephant god) coloured in livid pinks, pulverizing mauves, intense oranges and vibrating blues. **[SEE** P56**]**.

Design critic Karrie Jacobs has a clearer evaluation. 'I have prejudices,' she states, 'my Olivetti manual typewriter, the descendant of one designed by the sculptor Nizzoli in 1950, though its practical value has diminished, is still a favourite possession. On the other hand, I left my still-functional Philips coffee maker behind the last time I moved. I think that's an accurate characterization of the products of the two companies. Olivetti makes products that are imbued with value that goes beyond their function. Philips products have very little value aside from their function. If they possessed some sort of cultural identity, if they were, say, Dutch rather than global, it would be different.'

Then there are those who collect for simpler reasons. For instance the rule for collectors of Mickey Mouse memorabilia is simple: the longer the snout, the better – the more rat-like, the more it is worth. **[SEE** P335**]**. Similarly, the 1930s version of Donald Duck, which boasts an extra-long bill, is regarded as more valuable than the short-billed character of the post-war years.

'There is no stone in the street and no brick in the wall that is not actually a deliberate symbol,' observed G.K. Chesterton long before the academic enthusiasm for semiotics took hold, 'a message from some man, as much as if it were a telegram or a postcard.'

Note. Stavros Beach, Akrotiri, Crete. Lying in a stupor on a beach one very hot afternoon, eavesdropping on the conversation of a couple of couples lying 45 degrees off my elbow towards the edge of the sea – a few feet away. They were Americans having an afternoon off work from the NATO airbase nearby. One of the girls, from someplace in the Midwest I gathered, said she collected Monopoly games. She had, she claimed, sets from Vienna, Paris, Taiwan and lots and lots of other places she couldn't remember. Did she have the one of London, one of the male couplets asked? She didn't. In fact she wasn't sure there was one. Did she have the New York board? She wasn't sure about that either. **[SEE** P519**]***. I fell asleep. When I woke up they'd left.*

bric-a-brac

In the Grotte du Trilobite, near Les Eyzies in France, is a cave in which one of the earliest Europeans secreted a trilobite as a revered relic. Trilobites were extremely ancient wood-louse looking creatures. I bought my fossil off a vagrant in the Atlas mountains. The things people collect are rarely dull because they were acquired with the heart. They say something about you. Many of my friends have a penchant for visual bric-a-brac. In Hong Kong Henry Steiner has a comprehensive collection of airline sick bags. In Buenos Aires Ronald Shakespear hoards tins of a particular brand of baking powder. In Los Angeles Arnold Schwartzman has drawers full of steel record needle boxes. In Tokyo Shigeo Fukuda has a cabinet packed with Western plastic food. In Holland Pieter Brattinga stacks shelves with *kokeshi* dolls. In Paris Olivier Mourgue used to have a wall packed with industrial gloves. In New York Rich Saul Wurman [or his wife] had a collection of erotic Mexican folk art. Tom Geismar goes for robot toys. In London Theo Crosby had a multitude of tribal masks. And I recently read that pop star Michael Jackson's public relations agent denies his client tried to buy the bones of the Elephant Man. The whole thing can obviously get seriously out of hand. I don't see myself as a collector, at least not in Delft china or chinoiserie mode, but am irresistibly drawn to humble objects which fulfil some odd, obscure or even forgotten purpose. Here are a few of such artefacts that I can't bear to bin.

Fossil of a trilobite which is about 540 million years old. Trilobites existed for a span of three hundred million years. Man so far has only survived half a percent as long.

A Japanese wood vice (5 inches longest side) for gripping a jade chop while the carver produces an ideogram. The wedges around the central square hole can be rearranged to accommodate a variety of chop sizes.

This wooden contraption comes from Mexico. Some of the rings revolve. It is used, in some mysterious fashion, to make chocolate. Actually I think it's a tourist souvenir – tacky imitation of an honest utilitarian tool. I still like it.

A perforated tin box from Karachi. Parsees fill the box with chalk and bang it down on the doorstep to deposit an image – in this case a fish. An ancient Zoroastrian religious custom – they told me.

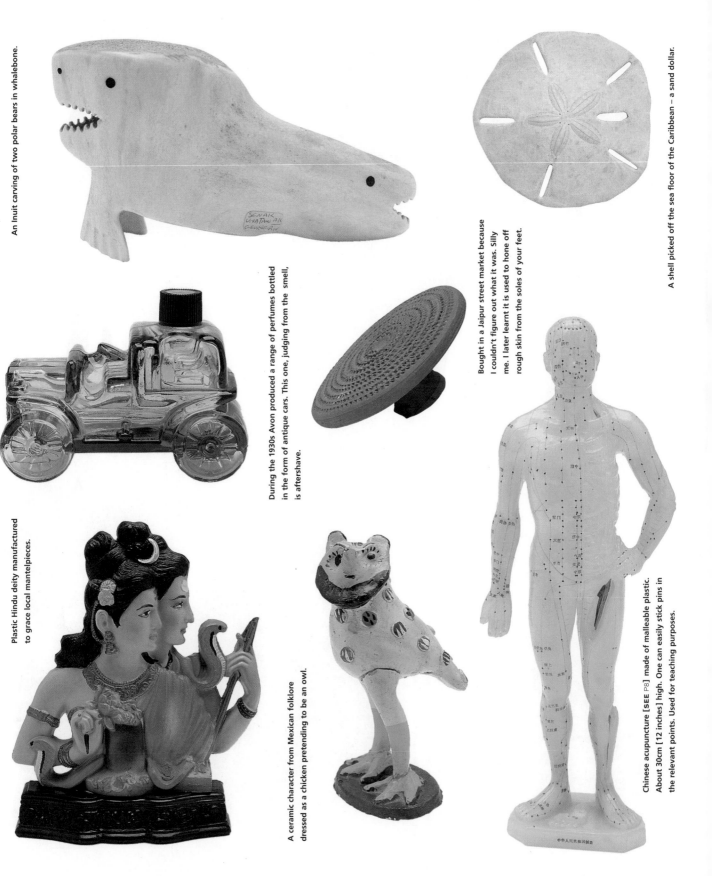

An Inuit carving of two polar bears in whalebone.

A shell picked off the sea floor of the Caribbean – a sand dollar.

During the 1930s Avon produced a range of perfumes bottled in the form of antique cars. This one, judging from the smell, is aftershave.

Bought in a Jaipur street market because I couldn't figure out what it was. Silly me. I later learnt it is used to hone off rough skin from the soles of your feet.

Plastic Hindu deity manufactured to grace local mantelpieces.

A ceramic character from Mexican folklore dressed as a chicken pretending to be an owl.

Chinese acupuncture [SEE P8] made of malleable plastic. About 30cm [12 inches] high. One can easily stick pins in the relevant points. Used for teaching purposes.

Italian liqueur bottles. I had two bottles of the fish. I gave one to designer Saul Bass. The gentleman with the spout on his head is King Umberto.

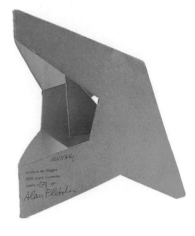

A travelling sculpture made of card and produced in a limited edition of 300 by Bruno Munari. He gave me this one – it is signed and numbered 59.

A contemporary *Kachina* doll made by the Hopi peoples of Arizona.

Sicilian clay whistle masquerading as a cyclist.

This wood block was used to form something. A busby? A muff? I've no idea. It comprises separate numbered pieces which slot together. It has a stamp with the name of a manufacturer in Birmingham – long disappeared. It is 30 cm [12"] high. A tool to resolve some mysterious need.

I was asked to write an article of *'no more than ten pages'* on the Swiss designer Jean Robert. He had won a prize and the piece was for the catalogue. My God – I couldn't write ten pages on myself! I decided that the solution was to get Jean to do the work instead. So, in answer to my question: *'What do you like?'*, he sent me this inventory. This was a long long long time ago. But I hope he hasn't changed his mind. [SEE P40]

'To watch first printed proofs. Pencils and paper. Piet Zwart's work. Colour swatch books. Reciprocal esteem with a client. 1917–1930 Russian posters. A friend who asks me for a copy of a job I have done. Games and puzzles. Guy Bourdin, French fashion photographer. Starting a new job. Swiss posters 1940–1958. Solving a design problem. Jim Nutt, American artist. Wall graffiti. Finishing a job in time. Steinberg drawings. Crazy ideas. Markus Raetz, Swiss artist. Duane Michals, American photographer. Enthusiasm. Simon Rodia, Italian emigrant artist, who built the 'Watts Tower' in Los Angeles. Man Ray's work. The Olivetti corporate image. Finding good ideas. Johannes Gutenberg. The French cartoonists, Bosc and Sempé. Talking about new projects. Colour pencils. Karl Gerstner's work. All typefaces if they are well used. 'Metropolis' by Fritz Lang. To be asked if I want a coffee during a meeting. Herbert List, German photographer. Neon signs. Film of Sergeij Eisenstein 'Que viva Mexico'. Kurt Schwitters's work. Getting paid quickly. Claes Oldenburg, American artist. To look through design magazines. Seymour Chwast's work. Good printers. Lucian Bernhard, German poster designer. The packaging design of the French cigarettes 'Boyards'. Herbert Matter, Swiss designer. Ladislav Sutnar, Czech designer. The advertising campaign for 'St Raphael' by Charles Loupot, France. Architectural and engineering drawings. Kazumasa Nagai, Japanese designer. Franciszek Sarowieyski, Polish designer. Sears Tower in Chicago. Black and white photos. Kati Durrer, my girl friend. Comic strips and cartoons. Typographic books. Eadweard Muybridge's work. <u>And here are some things I don't like very much</u>: Dry felt pens. Unpaid bills. Arriving late at meetings. Too much theory about design. A bad printer. Actual Swiss and Russian posters. Tight schedules for a job. Untidy tables. Bad taste. Giving a presentation. Microgramma typeface. Losing a good client. Undertaking a corporate identity programme for a company which is too big. Typing letters. Swiss television advertising. Making my own artwork. Purple and yellow together. A cup of coffee which drops on my artwork. Marketing people with no feelings. Mistakes. When I urgently need art material and it's out of stock. Swiss designers who still think Swiss design is the best in the world. Clients who try to reduce my invoices. Friends who don't give me back the graphic books I loaned them.' JR

A FETISH IS A STORY MASQUERADING AS AN OBJECT

The shape [object] was made by superimposing the letters **SEMIOTICS**. [**SEE** P440].

Extract from a review of *Wonders and the Order of Nature* by Lorraine Daston and Katherine Park (*London Review of Books*, 7 January 1999)

Stephen Greenblatt: 'The contents of the Wunderkammern ...

coconutshell goblets, elaborately carved ivory knick-knacks,

seashells, bits of coral, antique coins and cameos, stuffed

armadillos, geodes and fossils, polished rocks that looked like

landscape paintings, unicorn horns, birds of paradise,

aberrant fruits and monstrous animals, anamorphic pictures,

mechanical ducks that quacked and flapped their wings, Indian

featherwork capes, Turkish shoes, barnacle geese that grew on

trees in Scotland, mummified hands, dragons' teeth, ostrich

eggs and so on and so forth. They are likely to evoke in us

something like the laughter that the passage in Borges aroused

in Foucault: a shattering, liberating laughter, "breaking up

all the ordered surfaces and all the planes with which we are

accustomed to tame the wild profusion of existing things".' [SEE P2].

This sign

fell off a telegraph pole

in Sicily

– just as I was passing by.

Advertising Slogan

'Every status has its symbol.'

> A picture is a representation
> or an interpretation.
> A symbol is the fruit of marriage
> between the two.

One of the most ancient symbols[1] is the spiral. It comes clockwise, counterclockwise, singly, in pairs, in clusters. No one knows exactly what it represents, perhaps those inexplicable natural forces: the swirl of smoke, the vortex of water, a mysterious pull of energy. It can hardly be coincidental that such vast quantities of spiralled snail shells are found buried at ancient sacred sites all over Europe. More enigmatic still are the almost equally common 'cup and ring' marks. These are circles, or hollow depressions, often penetrated by a line. They appear scratched on stone megaliths from Malta to Scotland. Their ubiquitous presence suggests that they also had a common significance among ancient peoples. Fertility seems a bit obvious; maybe they were diagrams of prehistoric stone circles? Anyway, whatever these marks represented was more than a sign – they are :

> The visible appearance
> of an invisible meaning.

Perhaps a clue lies in Australia. Aborigines paint *tjuringas,* interlinked dots and circles which represent sacred paths and spots in the landscape. Those on a 'walkabout' find their way by consulting such patterns. Colin McCarthy, Australian scientist, explains that his aboriginal friends say magicians use the *tjuringas* to divine messages from afar, to foretell the arrival of strangers, the approach of violent storms, and other drastic changes of weather. It would seem reasonable to assume that what the aborigine can do today, ancient man did yesterday.

> A sign is less than
> the concept it represents,
> whereas a symbol
> stands for something more.

'An idea, in the highest sense of the word, cannot be conveyed but by a symbol.'
Samuel Coleridge

Opposite:
These spirals are from the megalithic site at New Grange in Ireland, and are about 5000 years old. An experienced dowser says such sites are usually located on blind springs. And such springs usually occur over geological faults which often have magnetic emanations. [SEE P293].

Overleaf :
Robert Smithson's Spiral Jetty is constructed on the Great Salt Lake in Utah. Completed in 1970 the design took 6,000 tonnes of granite delivered in 300 truckloads. The piece is submerged during winter and exposed during the summer when the water evaporates and leaves salt on the black rock. It is like a huge archaic landscape symbol. I suppose the point was the pointlessness of it all. In 1973 Smithson was killed when the helicopter inspecting one of his works crashed.

1. Janet and Colin Bord. *Mysterious Britain.* Paladin Books (London 1978)

anything has the potential to be a symbol

In 1953 Julius and Ethel Rosenberg were executed in America as Russian spies. To keep their contacts clandestine they used a cardboard Jell-O box torn in two halves. Both pieces were given to two individuals so they could identify each other when they met. If the halves matched all was well. It was the unpredictable results and the degree of informational complexity of tearing which made it foolproof.

When two people in ancient Greece made a contract they broke something in half so each party could be identified by fitting their half to the other. A broken plate or whatever. The two pieces were called *symbola* (from *symballein*, to join together), a word which eventually came to mean something which represented something else. By way of example: take a small plain disc of cheap metal, stamp a head on one side and a number on the back, and you have a coin. Give it a name, say a dollar, and it immediately acquires a value far in excess of what it cost or was worth. Furthermore, with a name it can be talked about in its absence and everyone knows what it is. It has become a symbol.

Symbolism is the currency of cultural chit-chat. We think and speak in symbols, and the ability to conceive and respond to them creates that *milieu* of ideas, myths and values which we call culture. Some symbols are universally understood such as numerals – 1, 2 and 3 – while others are only understood within certain groups or societies: chemical or alchemical symbols, freemasons' insignia and paraphernalia.

An elderly gentleman once told me that before the Second World War in Budapest, then an elegant, sophisticated city, if you wanted female companionship for the night you left your umbrella on the hotel bed before leaving for dinner. If you did that in London the most you'd probably get is wet. In England and America salt shakers have one hole and pepper shakers lots of holes.* Watch out in Italy, it's the other way round. In America you flick the switch up to put on the light, in Europe you push it down. At a hotel in Tokyo I asked the reception for a map of the city. It was covered with little swastikas. I asked the lady behind the desk what they meant – *Shinto* shrines she said!

Anyway, once established, symbols assume a power of their own. In the Cultural Revolution the Red Guards tried to change the traffic lights so that red signified go and green stop. They were unsuccessful. The same happened when the Chinese army abolished insignia on uniforms. What took their place was a hierarchy of pens prominently displayed in the breast pocket – the number, colour and size indicating rank.

Anything has the potential to be a symbol. Even a rodent. A caricature produced Mickey Mouse, popular affection elevated him into a movie star. In Walt Disney's *Fantasia* (1940) he even mounted the podium in a concert hall to shake hands with Leopold Stokowski. From Hollywood he graduated into a national symbol. Symbols can be considered dangerous. In 1933 he was banned in Nazi Germany, in 1937 in the Soviet Union, in 1954 in East Germany. All to no avail as the little bugger is now everywhere. More than a symbol, he's a mega-billion dollar industry.

* According to etiquette pepper is to be used directly sprinkled over food whereas salt should be heaped on the side of the plate. Hence the salt cellar. Only recently has salt acquired additives to make it sprinklable.

avec :

Gérard Philipe	**P**	le poète
Roger Blin	**M**	Monsieur Diable
Maria Casarès	**a**	l'amoureuse
Michel Michalon	**A**	l'ami
rôle réparti	**H**	l'antidote
Marie Leduc		la bandeuse
Noëlle Chavrence	☽	la communiante
Maurice Petitpas	👁	le fébrile
Malcome	**∞**	l'illuminé
Claude Buré	⇆	l'impératif
Alain Rigaud	☞	l'index
rôle non tenu	☇	le mino
Jean Œttly	**O**	l'ome
André Coffrant	ß	le potache
Michel Retaux		le tapageur
René Alone	**m**	l'intérim
		(ventriloquie de Monsieur Diable).
	W	des voix

WHAT'S THIS ?
- IT'S A SYMBOL

WHAT DO IT MEAN?

- IT MEAN 'DARREN IS A FUCKING
                        MORON'

(LONG SILENCE, DARREN THINKS)

NO IT DOESN'T ?

- YES IT DOES

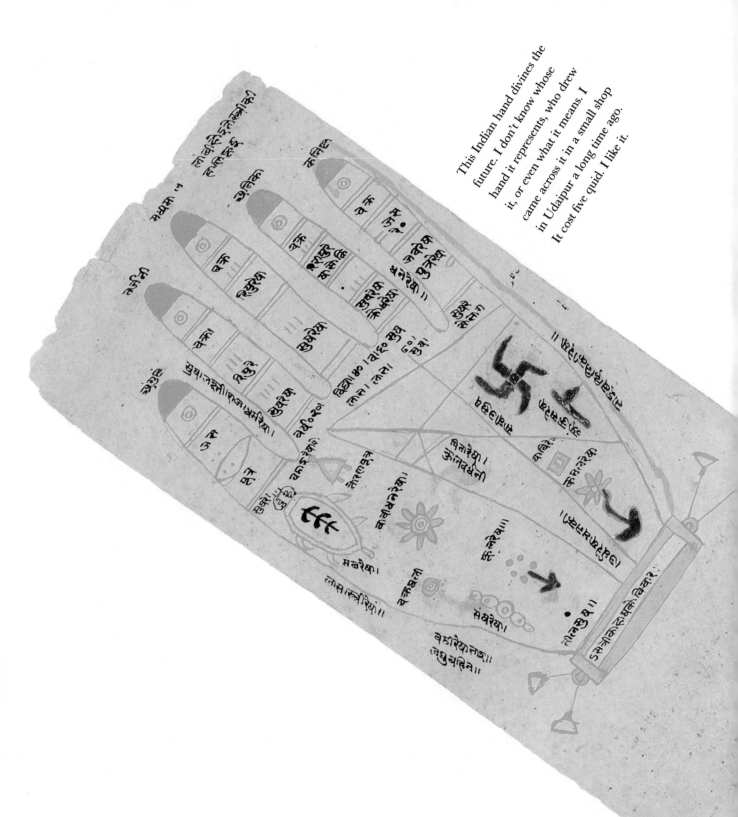

This Indian hand divines the future. I don't know whose future, who drew it, or even what it means. I came across it in a small shop in Udaipur a long time ago. It cost five quid. I like it.

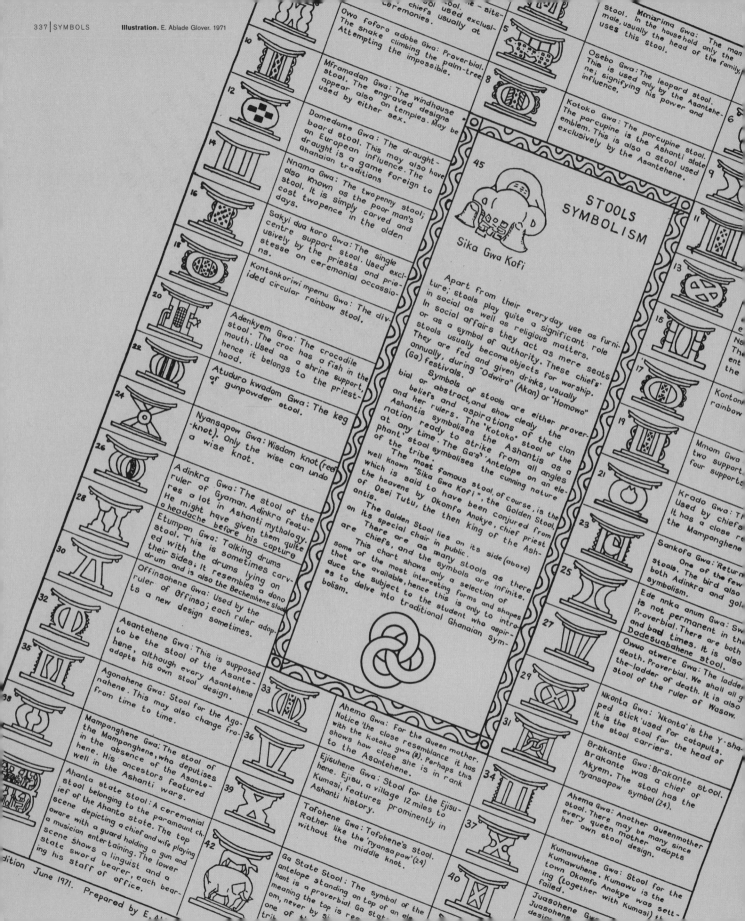

STOOLS SYMBOLISM

Sika Gwa Kofi

Apart from their everyday use as furniture, stools play quite a significant role in social as well as religious matters. In social affairs they act as mere seats or as a symbol of authority. These chiefs' stools usually become objects for worship. They are fed and given drinks, usually annually, during "Odwira" (Akan) or "Homowo" (Ga) festivals.

Symbols of stools are either proverbial or abstract, and show clearly the beliefs and aspirations of the clan and her rulers. The "kotoko" stool of the Ashantis symbolises the Ashantis as a nation ready to strike from all angles at any time. The Ga's "Antelope on an elephant" stool symbolises the cunning nature of the tribe.

The most famous stool, of course, is the well known "Sika Gwa Kofi", the Golden Stool, which is said to have been conjured from the heavens by Okomfo Anokye, chief priest of Osei Tutu, the then king of the Ashantis.

The Golden Stool lies on its side (above) on its special chair in public.

There are as many stools as there are chiefs, and the symbols are infinite. This chart shows only a selection of some of the most interesting forms and shapes that are available, hence this is only to introduce the student who aspires to delve into traditional Ghanaian Symbolism.

Mmarima Gwa: The man stool. In the household only the male, usually the head of the family, uses this stool.

Osebo Gwa: The leopard stool. This is used only by the Asantehene; signifying his power and influence.

Kotoko Gwa: The porcupine stool. The porcupine is the Ashanti state emblem. This is also a stool used exclusively by the Asantehene.

Owo foforo adobe Gwa: Proverbial. The snake climbing the palm-tree. Attempting the impossible.

Mframadan Gwa: The windhouse stool. The engraved designs appear also on temples. May be used by either sex.

Damedame Gwa: The draught-board stool. This may also have an European influence. The draught is a game foreign to Ghanaian traditions.

Nnama Gwa: The twopenny stool; also known as the poor man's stool. It is simply carved and cost twopence in the olden days.

Sakyi dua koro Gwa: The single centre support stool. Used exclusively by the priests and priestesses on ceremonial occasions.

Kontonkoriwi mpemu Gwa: The divided circular rainbow stool.

Adenkyem Gwa: The crocodile stool. The croc has a fish in the mouth. Used as a shrine support, hence it belongs to the priesthood.

Atuduro kwadom Gwa: The keg of gunpowder stool.

Nyansapow Gwa: Wisdom knot (reef-knot). Only the wise can undo a wise knot.

Adinkra Gwa: The stool of the ruler of Gyaman. Adinkra features a lot in Ashanti mythology. He might have given them quite a headache before his capture.

Etumpan Gwa: Talking drums stool. This is sometimes carved with the drums lying on their sides. It resembles a dono drum and is also the Bechemhene stool.

Offinsohene Gwa: Used by the ruler of Offinso; each ruler adopts a new design sometimes.

Asantehene Gwa: This is supposed to be the stool of the Asantehene, although every Asantehene adapts his own stool design.

Agonahene Gwa: Stool for the Agonahene. This may also change from time to time.

Mamponghene Gwa: The stool of the Mamponghene, who deputises in the absence of the Asantehene. His ancestors featured well in the Ashanti wars.

Ahanta state stool: A ceremonial stool belonging to the paramount chief of the Ahanta state. The top scene depicting a chief and wife playing oware with a guard holding a gun and a musician entertaining. The lower scene shows a linguist and a state sword bearer, each bearing his staff of office.

Ahema Gwa: For the Queen mother. Notice the close resemblance it has with the Kotoko gwa (9). Perhaps this shows how close she is in rank to the Asantehene.

Ejisuhene Gwa: Stool for the Ejisuhene. Ejisu, a village 12 miles to Kumasi, features prominently in Ashanti history.

Tafohene Gwa: Tafohene's stool. Rather like the 'nyansapow' (24) without the middle knot.

Ga State Stool: The symbol of the antelope standing on top of an elephant is a proverbial Ga stool, meaning the top is ... om, never by s... one of the ... trib...

Nkonta Gwa: 'Nkonta' is the Y-shaped stick used for catapults. It is the stool for the head of the stool carriers.

Brakante Gwa: Brakante stool. Brakante was a chief of Akyem. The stool has the nyansapow symbol (24).

Ahema Gwa: Another Queenmother stool. There may be many since every queen mother adopts her own stool design.

Kumawuhene Gwa: Stool for the Kumawuhene. Kumawu is the town Okomfo Anokye was settling (together with Kumasi) ing failed.

Jusohene Gwa: Jusohene ... design ...

Sankofa Gwa: 'Return'. One of the few stools. The bird also is both Adinkra and gold symbolism.

Ede nnka anum Gwa: Sw... is not permanent in the ... Proverbial. There are ... and bad times. It is also ... Dadesuabahene stool.

Owuo atwere Gwa: The ladder of death. Proverbial. We shall all ... death. It is also the-ladder of death. It is ... stool of the ruler of Wasaw.

Krado Gwa: Th... Used by chiefs ... It has a close re... the Mamponghene.

Mmom Gwa: ... two support... four supports...

**Konton... rainbow...

**Nsa... The ... ent ... the ...

On 31 August 1935 Aleksey Stakhanov drilled a phenomenal 102 tons of coal in six hours – fourteen times the normal output. Promoted as an industrial hero, he was used to launch the *Stakhanovite* movement. He even had a town named after him. Now we are told that while his propaganda value was exploited, the person behind the image was rapidly discarded. The Stalinist system needed a symbol ... not a real person.

☆ ☆ ☆

Eva Perón was held in saintlike regard by much of Argentina. She died when only thirty-three (1952) and was embalmed for posterity. When President Perón was overthrown the new government, in an effort to distance themselves from the previous regime, hid the body for fifteen years. A testament to her symbolic significance. She was kept in a packing case (marked *Radio Sets*) somewhere in Buenos Aires. There are rumours that the official appointed to look after her engaged in unspeakable necrophiliac activities but that could have been propaganda. Anyway, at one point her body was kidnapped and held to ransom, and when it was retrieved the authorities shipped it off to the embassy in Bonn. Finally, with the help of the Vatican, she was placed in a grave (marked *Maggi*) in Milan. In 1971 the body was returned to Juan Perón, who at the time was exiled in Madrid. Perón returned to power and when he died she was shipped back to Buenos Aires to lie by his side. She is now eight metres below ground in a marble tomb. In contrast Sir Walter Raleigh travelled to enough places when he was alive, but on his death his widow retrieved his head from the public executioner, and kept it in a red leather bag under her bed until she died.

☆ ☆ ☆

Swastika is an Indian word.[1] Cleansed of historical meaning by the Nazis, the swastika was introduced into modern consciousness as an ancestral sign of the Aryan race. It was not the first time it had been appropriated. Madame Blavatsky and the Theosophists embraced it as an esoteric emblem of wisdom from the East. In 1916 it was used by a girls' ice-hockey team in Alberta, and Wilhelm Reich, the psychoanalyst, fancied that it was a stylized image of two people copulating. Finally, since I think it will take generations to shake off its present connotations, it was adopted (1919) by Hitler to represent the National Socialist German Workers' Party. Some say a Nazi in Wilhelm Deffke's studio (known for his Pelikan ink designs) noticed him drawing the ancient eastern device for something or other, stole it, turned it back to front, and used it for the Party. Whatever the case, like a corporate logotype it deals in frozen time and works by direct address.

☆ ☆ ☆

This photograph is replete with messages. The grill of conservatism, the monogram of quality, the Spirit of Ecstasy (mounting the bonnet), the red flag of revolution, the hammer and sickle of labour, the star of destiny.

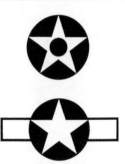

The US Army Aviation mark on combat planes was changed from the first to the second version during the war with Japan, because of confusion with the sign of the rising sun.

This is a stamp used to brand bolts of cotton from the city of Calico in India in the 1800s.

Fylfot (fĭ·lfŏt). 1500. [perh. simply *fill-foot*, a pattern for filling the foot of a painted window.] A name for the figure called also a cross cramponnee (see CRAMPONNEE), and identified with the SWASTIKA of India, the *gammadion* of Byzantine ornament. Also *f. cross.*

1. Malcolm Quinn. *The Swastika: Constructing the Symbol.* Routledge (London 1994)

The photograph opposite was taken by Enzo Ragazzini in a Sicilian church. Votive offerings are small silver or tin replicas given to the church in gratitude for, or hope of, successful cures or avoided disasters. Hands, heads, arms and legs, hearts, lungs, eyes, feet, and other accoutrements.

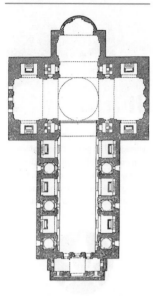

Most churches are a hidden synthesis of symbolism and structure built on the crucifix plan laid out on an axis of west to east.

'Two dark marks on the shoulders of the haddock are, by the legends of many lands, attributed to the Evil One; though by another legend the fish is said to have been the one caught by St Peter, at his Divine Master's command, in the Sea of Galilee, and the marks to have been those of the apostle's finger and thumb, made in holding the fish while he extracted the piece of money for the tribute from its mouth.'
Thomas Parkinson, 1888[1]

CUTUD, Philippines (Reuters, April 1996): 'Eleven people were crucified yesterday in the Philippines while dozens of others flagellated themselves as the country celebrated Good Friday with traditional exuberance. Under a broiling noon sun in Asia's only Roman Catholic nation, the 11 were impaled on wooden crosses as hundreds of people and tourists watched the spectacle in a rice field outside San Fernando. Scores of tourists from the United States, Europe and Japan witnessed the gory annual re-enactment of Jesus Christ's crucifixion 2,000 years ago. Booths selling soft drinks, grilled potatoes, and hard-boiled eggs littered the two-lane road leading to the crucifixion site. Small boys hawked straw hats and giant fans.'

☆ ☆ ☆

The Victory Arch[2] is a monument in Baghdad conceived by Saddam Hussein. This (actually there are two) is constructed with two huge forearms each holding a curved sword. Nets around the base hold 5,000 Iranian steel helmets taken from the battlefield. The swords were forged from captured or abandoned weapons and the arms worked up from plaster casts of Saddam Hussein's very own – they faithfully record every bump and follicle. The monument rises forty metres, the arms are the height of the Arc de Triomphe in Paris. The Iraqis describe it as 'one of the largest works of art in the world' – not bad for something made in Basingstoke.

☆ ☆ ☆

When writer Gerald Brenan stayed in a remote Spanish village during the 1920s, he noticed an unfamiliar coin in his loose change. It was Phoenician and must have been circulating in this isolated community for about 2,000 years. Some symbols keep their original significance through time, while others lose their meaning altogether such as the fringes on Native American Indian shirts, which once represented rain.

☆ ☆ ☆

Sometimes reading meanings into things can get out of hand. [SEE P516]. In *The Complete Works of Marcel Duchamp*, a catalogue raisonné, fifteen pages are devoted to the symbolic content of *Young Man and Girl in Spring* (1911), a vaguely romantic painting. The author manages to find references to Egyptian hieroglyphics, Gnostic texts, the Hebrew Cabbala, Tantric yoga, Greek mythology, Plato, the Upanishads, Buddhism, medieval alchemical texts, Freud and Jung. To the author, this indicated that Duchamp had an incestuous passion for his sister. Actually the analysis tells us more about the author than the artist. [SEE P499].

   1. Robert Osborne. *The Floating Egg.* Jonathan Cape (London 1998)   2. Samir al-Khalil. *The Monument: Art, Vulgarity and Responsibility in Iraq.* André Deutsch (London 1991)

International road signs date from the **1949 PROTOCOL**, the result of a convention held in Geneva in that year. One would assume the mandate directed the officials to arrive at solutions which could be comprehended by the majority of those with average intelligence [SEE P.119]. After all this was the introduction of a new graphic system around the world to help people avoid killing each other on the road. But Murphy's Law prevailed. No one remembers who designed them, but judging from most of the results it must have been a committee. Nevertheless, despite their naïve crudity the pictorial versions register reasonably well. I once attended a lecture by someone who showed slides of hundreds of photographs he had taken around the world of the 'children crossing' sign. The one with two little people holding hands inside a red triangle. None of the details or colours were the same yet each sign was instantly recognizable. I am unfamiliar with the road sign on the right, which appeared in the environs of Beirut during the civil war, but I know what it means. Those which carry ambiguous pictograms are more tricky. Although by now most people understand the significance of the man putting up a large umbrella, the sign that implies low-flying motorcycles actually means something else. Then there are the abstracts which have absolutely no link between form and meaning. In this territory you either know the language or you don't. Apparently many don't. A recent survey unnervingly revealed that only seven per cent of drivers realize a white disk with a red rim means **NO VEHICLES**.

In *The Hitch Hiker's Guide to the Galaxy* the BABEL FISH is something you stick in your ear so you instantly understand any language. Everyone should have one.

In Tokyo the hotel clerk gave me meticulous instructions and drew ideograms on a scrap of paper before I set off to visit Shigeo Fukuda, a designer, who lives on the outskirts of the city. [SEE P237]. Shinjuko station has a throughput of nine million commuters every day, it is very large, very crowded, and has lots of signs and pictograms to help passengers find their way. Failing to relate the marks on my paper to any of the graphics in the station, I cautiously approached a sympathetic looking couple. After a lot of bowing and nodding, I discovered I'd badly miscalculated — they were deaf and dumb. Recognizing the problem, a passerby joined in, he said he spoke English. Maybe he did, but he also had an amazing stutter. Somehow I found my way.

Three hundred years ago Leibnitz recognized the same problem and attempted to encapsulate all human knowledge into symbols so that anyone, anywhere, could understand everything, and everybody understand anybody. He called his system CHARACTERISTICA. His symbols were also to be used like numerals in that they could calculate solutions for every conceivable problem. It proved to be rather more complex than he thought so it never got sorted out. Other moves towards this *lingua franca* include a suggestion by the American Tourist Association to introduce Red Indian HANDAGE, invented languages like ESPERANTO, systems of symbols and pictograms like SEMANTOGRAPHY, invented by Charles Bliss, which comprises a hundred signs, and ISOTYPE (International System of Typographic Picture Education), invented by Otto Neurath. There are countless other systems, and as they prolificated Henry Dreyfuss (visual lexicographer) compiled a data bank. This he published as *Symbol Sourcebook*.[1]

The foreword by Buckminster Fuller gloriously demonstrates the problem: 'Henry Dreyfuss's contribution to a new world technique of communication will catalyse a world preoccupation with its progressive evolution into a worldian language so powerfully generalized as to swiftly throw into obsolescence the almost fatally lethal trends of humanity's age-long entrapment in specializations and the limitations that specialization imposes upon human thinking ...'

Paradoxically the acceleration towards mass communication has revived the need for pictograms and in the small change of international discourse the printed word has been forced to retreat. Stick figures on public lavatories, icons on computers, and traffic signs. Life would seize up without them. Most are crude in conception, ambiguous in signal, parochial in meaning and variable in dialect. One exception was the graphic language for the Munich Olympic Games designed in 1972 and shown opposite. A matrix of shapes, an alphabet of components, a pictorial vocabulary. TRULY A VISUAL ESPERANTO

   1. Henry Dreyfuss. *Symbol Sourcebook*. McGraw-Hill (New York 1972)

Components   Grid   Symbol

Design. Otl Aicher

Scher, Paula Joan
/ b. **2:50**pm **10-6-48** / District of
Columbia / Certificate **#3749586** / Social
Security **#215-53-5794** / Passport U.S.A. **G2357021F**
/ Issue Date **4-24-88** Expires **4-25-98** / Issued N.Y.C. / **125**
East **15** Street, New York, NY **10002-2464** / **212 672-3572** / **59**
Dueling Hills Road, Salisbury, CT **06705-3747** / **203-853-2498** /
Pentagram Design **212** Fifth Avenue, **17**th Floor, New York, NY **10010-**
2739 / **212-683-7000** / Fax **212-532-0181** / New York State / Driver's
License **503721 81534 986438** / **47 W 212713** / August **8, 1998** / **971**
/ Eyes BL / Sex F / **5'3"** / New York City Registration **017897653274690** /
Audi Plate **#6XE8521** / Automobile Club of America **097 W41 127 961** / Polar
Insurance Policy **8965930 B 174** / Amex Corporate **3782-67826969-03123** / Thru
04/98 / Chemical Bank **571160002423-16721** / Privileged Checking **007-398746** /
Super Savings   **059-732654** / National Westminister Bank **028307325:567622198** /
5909:70101   / Blue Cross Blue Shield **215535794** / Bank Americard Visa **4027-**
0248-9774-   **1802** / Thru **09/98** / National Westminister Bank Mastercard **5313-**
7364019-2563   / Thru **08/98** / Diners Club **3875-64540089-3891** / Thru **09/99** /
Discover Card **25**   **51-42355591-0921** / Thru **04/99** / American Express Card **3333-**
434302020-1352 /   Thru **02/99** / American Gold **9261-67139162-5274** / Thru **10/98** /
American Express Platinum **3812-09247362-1835** / Thru **12/98** / Bergdorf Goodman **617-069-**
592 / Bloomingdales **971-2379-453** / Avis **61274-33-05054** / Pan Am World Pass **83257218** /
Cell Phone **917-293-2478** / TWA Frequent Flyer **8623-173-2** / Thru **03/98** / AT&T **874-062-5454-2513**
/ International Number **896352-864-062-5223-7-89** / MCI **C1-124-6351** / AIGA Pat **001792** / Salisbury
Bank and Trust Mortgage **01-93-2010047176** / Marriage License N.Y.C. October **14, 1973 #37295**
4461 / Divorce **9-14-79** Index no **3480679** / Marriage License N.Y.C. June **16, 1989 #47682457** / Con
Ed **54782: 765-0793** / Suburban Propane **047576-3** / Lindell Hardware **4937931** / Decker & Beebe
3759452 / Sony Trinitron **531057** / Craig **UL-4102** / Proton **930-P3007354** / Panasonic **501394795**
/ Magnavox VCR **379670452** / Sony VCR **S1279635** / **RX78566** / **04/30/98** / Tablet
Daily Mfg **50M REM100** / Dr Berczeller AB **1854439** 20mg **RX 3299232** / New York Life
Insurance 47-03956-742 / Chubb 879647594 / Last Will and Testament 874367 / CBS Credit
Union **749653-2G** / Security Alarm System **849375214** Code **1991** / Cartier Warranty
797273 / Olympus **UF1-0746531** / The Haupt Tree Company **0004232** / Smith &
Hawken **#022-01-952** / Key: **H2843J** / White Flower Farm **AC 13972-451** / The
Nation **NAN 000275657054** / Newsweek **00759437921** / Graphis **09473976**
/ Print **15415497361** / HQ **45713654-7** / Federal Express **087145692** /
Bell Atlantic Leasing Corp. **0917-476-9276748** / Grammercy Park Dry
Cleaners **0874** / Palazzetti / 318 Madison Ave, New York, NY 10004 /
Sales Tax **3847857 000** / Order Number **21052** /   Customer
Code **ORIGINALNAME** / Positano Rstr & Cafe **6311**
3285 6000000 / May **11, 1998** / Approval Code **26** /
04/98 / Transaction Type: Sale/ Record of Charge
505155 / Terminal **30030076748** / Food and
Beverage / Base Amount **$49.53** / Tip Amount
$7.50 / Total **$57.03** / Customer
Sign Here

Isidore of Seville (*c*.600 AD)   'Take from all things their number, and all shall perish.'

PAIR =

'Two's a crowd and three's company.' ANDY WARHOL

TWO=2

'2 and 2 equals 22, not 4.' MAN RAY

a baker's dozen

A pencil of lines

An erudition of editors

A rumpus of shapes

A madder of painters

A plagiary of writers

A tantrum of decorators

A click of photographers

A slant of journalists

A gild of directors

An obsolescence of appliances

A brood of researchers

A drift of lecturers

A breakdown of plans

A glut of commercials

A pitfall of fine print

A clutch of second thoughts

An impatience of wives

A squat of daubers

A slouch of models

A blur of impressionists

A pinch of producers

A set of designers

A squad of grids

A blessing of unicorns

A drag of queens[1]

'It must have required **many** ages,' suggested Bertrand Russell, 'to discover that a **brace**∗ of pheasants and a **couple** of days are **both** instances of the **number 2**.'

The most primitive societies only have three **number** words: **one**, **two**, and **many**. For assessing **quantities** of things they have special expressions. Australian Aborigines have a few more and calculate how cold it is by the **number** of dogs they need to snuggle up with to keep warm. A **'five-dog night'** is the coldest you can be. The Chinese often repeat symbols to suggest a **multitude** of things. A forest is a **triplet** of trees, fur a **triplet** of hairs, gossip a **triplet** of women. The Persian general Xerxes calculated the strength of his army by building a low wall around his men and counting them off in **myriads** [ten thousand] at a time.

In the Middle Ages **nouns of multitude** were a prevalent method of labelling **lots** of things. **One** of the **first** printed books, *The Hors, Shepe and the Ghoos*, was shortly followed by *The Boke of St Albans*, a thesaurus of hunting terms, which enabled 'gentylmen' to educate themselves. Both printed by Wynkyn de Worde (apprentice to William Caxton), they were no more than listings containing expressions such as a **covey** of quails, and a **plague** of rats. A best-seller, The *Boke of St Albans* was copied and amplified at least a **dozen** times. We still refer to **pairs**, **couples**, **duets** and **twins**.

Four Oxford dons were flapping along the High Street when they passed a **group** of prostitutes. The quickest [of the dons] muttered **'a jam of tarts'**. The **second** responded with **'A flourish of strumpets'**. The **third** countered with **'an essay of Trollope's'**. Not to be outdone the **fourth** suggested **'an anthology of pros'**, **'a peal of Jezebels'**, **'a smelting of ores'**, and [less happily] **'a troop of horse'**.

It's a game anyone can play: Italians make an explosion, the French an *ennui*, the Irish a point, the Scots a **fifth**, and the English – fish and chips. [**SEE** P282].

∗ **Brace,** in Old French, meant the width of a pair of outstretched arms. This gave rise to the {brackets} used in printing, braces for trousers, and the term for a couple of pheasants.

 NUMBERS

1. James Lipton. *An Exaltation of Larks*. Penguin (Harmondsworth 1977)

By tearing a simple portrait in **half** you get **two** profiles –
an image for Gemini [the **twins**]. Geminis are reputed to
be unable to keep a secret – unlike Scorpios. By the way,
more Geminis are in jail than prisoners of other signs. More
Cancers are alcoholics than other signs, and more Taureans
are accused of murder than other signs. I'm a Libra.

OUNCE

DICE

TRICE

QUARTZ

QUINCE

SAGO

SERPENT

OXYGEN

NITROGEN

DENIM

2
3
4

NUMBERS

Alastair Reid. *How to count from one to ten for children*

UO
RIO
TET

Note. I've not come across the medical term but I reckon that I suffer from numerical dyslexia. If I have to convert yen to dollars or divide a three-figure number, my mind closes up. There are a lot of us around. Mind you, I did invent a number game. You look around a crowded place, say the Tate Gallery on a Sunday afternoon, or over supper in a smart restaurant, and imagine that everyone younger than you – vanishes. I don't play it any more. Who was the idiot who said age doesn't mean anything, except for wine?

Acknowledgements ♥ to Chermayeff, Brownjohn, Geismar

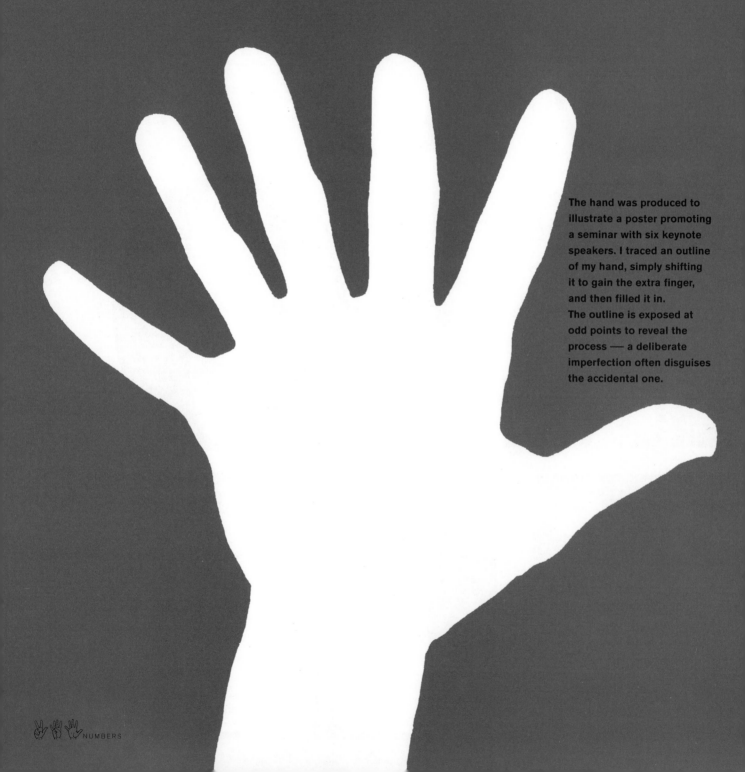

The hand was produced to illustrate a poster promoting a seminar with six keynote speakers. I traced an outline of my hand, simply shifting it to gain the extra finger, and then filled it in.
The outline is exposed at odd points to reveal the process — a deliberate imperfection often disguises the accidental one.

NUMBERS

I	1	LXX	70
II	2	LXXX	80
III	3	LXXXVIII	88
IV	4	XC	90
V	5	XCIX	99
VI	6	C	100
VII	7	CX	110
VIII	8	CXI	111
IX	9	CXC	190
X	10	CC	200
XI	11	CCXX	220
XII	12	CCC	300
XIII	13	CCCXX	320
XIV	14	CD	400
XV	15	D	500
XVI	16	DC	600
XVII	17	DCC	700
XVIII	18	DCCC	800
XIX	19	CM	900
XX	20	XM	990
XXX	30	M	1000
XL	40	MD	1500
L	50	MDCCC	1800
LV	55	MCMLXX	1970
LX	60	MM	2000

NUMBER LETTERS

The ancient Greeks used letters to count. **A** represented **1**, **B** was **2**, and so on. When they got to the end of their **twenty-four**-letter alphabet they began again, so **AA** stood for **25**, **AB** for **26**.

The Romans inherited the method of using letters but to simplify matters introduced particular letters for specific quantities. **V** for **5**, **L** for **50**, and so on. Mind you as a system it was rather unwieldy. For instance if you multiply **LVII** by **XXXVIII** you get **MMCLXVI**. This archaic method still persists in displaying dates such as **MCMXCV** and the hours on clocks. Have you noticed that sundials and clocks usually show **IV** as **IIII**? One suggestion is that **IV** stood for Jupiter – **IVPITER** as it used to be spelt – and that the **IIII** was substituted for **IV** to avoid offending the deity. That sounds too boring to be true. Another suggestion is that **IIII** visually balances **VIII** rather more agreeably than **IV**. I'm not convinced by that either.

A chronogram is a phrase in which letters are used to form a date or numerical reference. During the **Second** World War British intelligence set up the **Twenty** Committee to co-ordinate secret **double** agents. A bureaucratic joke as in Roman numerals **twenty** is **xx** – a **double-cross**.

Nowadays it's much simpler as we can coherently count in **millions, billions, milliards, trillions, quadrillions, quintillions, sextillions, septillions, octillions, nonillions, decillions** and **gigabytes**.

@ 6s & 7s

Here are a number of things. Ionesco said that if one strokes the back of a circle it can turn vicious. Certainly if you put a zero in the wrong place it causes trouble. In Indian antiquity using a dot to indicate 'nothing' and a circle to represent 'something' eventually gave rise to the invention of 'zero'.

The value of nothing ranks among man's greatest intellectual discoveries. The Arab mathematician Abu Abdullah ibn Musa al-Khwarizmi al-Magusi, more economically known as al-Khwarizmi, was born around AD 680 when the golden age of Muslim science coincided with Western Europe's darkest hour. Al-Khwarizmi's treatise on arithmetic was the first book to explain the operations of decimal numerals.

The word zero comes from the Arabic *sifr* [empty] and algebra from al-jabr, which loosely translates as 'bringing together broken parts'. The Arabs introduced numerals into Europe in the twelfth century, and the Italian mathematician Fibonacci wrote about a new sign called *zephirum* which signified absence by presence. The O is nought and naught, nothing, nil, and in tennis – love. Perhaps this comes from playing to win or playing for love [nothing], or maybe because the game was imported from France and the French used the expression *l'oeuf* for 'no score', because a zero resembles an egg. Mispronouncing *l'oeuf* may have changed it to *love*.[1]

The nought enables us to distinguish between **12**, **102** and **120** and thus led to the invention of modern mathematics. The concept of zero was independently discovered by the Mayans in Mexico centuries earlier than it appeared in Europe.

Numbers also have associations outside mathematics. Delacroix, they say, numbered his mufflers, waistcoats and hats to correspond with variations in the weather. Eccentric but understandable. But why **3** cheers, **3** little pigs, **3** wishes, **3** wise men, the Holy Trinity? **4** has variously been said to represent the ancient sigil of Hermes and a visual representation of physically making the sign of the cross. Apart from fingers and toes, **5** stones slew Goliath, **5** loaves fed the multitude, the owl and pussycat went to sea with their worldly goods wrapped in a fiver. The world was made in **7** days, there are **7** deadly sins, **7** wonders of the world, **7** years' bad luck and 7th heaven. Take **9**. This is a very odd number as it's an even number (**6**), on its head. Multiply any number by **9**, add up the figures in the total (**7** x **9** = **63**; **6** + **3** = **9**) and you end up with a **9** or (in large numbers) a multiple of **9**. Reverse the digits (**36**) and you always get a multiple of **9**. Take any number – say **4,321** – and divide it by **9**. The remainder (**1**) will be the same as you are left with when added together (**4** + **3** + **2** + **1** = **10**) and divided by **9**. Creative accountancy no less. Then there's cloud **9**, and a current edition of a slim volume titled *Number Nine*. People nervous of **13** even have a term for their anxiety: *triskaidekaphobia*.

Numbers massaged with statistics become facts, while numbers without statistics become anecdotes. I read that in Russia the average car kills an average **1.5** million insects each average summer. I was stunned. And that one teaspoon of water holds as many molecules as the Atlantic contains teaspoonsful of water. A neat claim but hardly sustainable. And that the average American uses **1/2** inch of toothpaste twice a day. That means **240** million Americans use **1.1** million miles of toothpaste every year – over two round trips to the moon.[2] If stretched out the DNA molecule from a cell would be two metres long. How can something so minuscule that you can't even see it, unravel itself so that you can? Brevity was not characteristic of Marcel Proust and one of his longest sentences in *In Search of Lost Time* would, 'if arranged along a single line in standard-sized text, run on for a little short of four metres and stretch around the base of a bottle of wine seventeen times'.[3]

I doubt you find any of these comparisons helpful. Numbers must be relative to what one can comprehend. Buckminster Fuller's question to a housewife comes to mind. '*Madam*,' he asked, '*do you know how much your house weighs?*' **Aaargh!**

1. Robert Hendrickson, *Encyclopedia of Word and Phrase Origins*, Facts on File (New York 1987)   2. Rich Saul Wurman, *Information Anxiety*, Doubleday (New York 1989)   3. Alain de Botton, *How Proust Can Change your Life*, Picador (London 1997)

SEVEN

The Magical Number Seven, plus or Minus Two A few people are able to remember eight or nine numbers and an equal number five or six numbers. So seven – plus or minus two – represents the ability of almost everyone else. The magical seven also applies to telephone numbers such as names, procedures, shopping items and so forth. Local chunks are the key. One can remember few standardized on seven digits as although longer sequences would have dispensed with area codes [or were] on seven digits as although longer sequences would Simony, one of the world's truly great [computer] programmers, once lamented them. Crumps, clusters and chunks are the ability to remember more things if they are in chunks. For instance 'Charles have been able to remember more things if they are in chunks. For instance 'Charles minus two [computer] I have to really concentrate ... when I was young] I could easily having on his ability to remember ... when I was young] I could easily remember ten different objects in it. I can't do that Simony, could remember 200.[4]

telephone numbers with twenty rooms with each room having ten different objects in it. I can't do that imagine a castle Prpp. Thus whereas only 3 in 2,000 people could easily remember more than nine pieces any more.'... [see Prpp. Thus whereas only 3 in 2,000 people could easily remember more than nine pieces of unrelated data – Simony, could remember 200.[4]

4. Robert X. Cringely, *Accidental Empires*. Penguin (London 1996)

1494

1495

1496

**Numbers
are
the
only
symbols
understood
everywhere
by
everybody**

The idea of using signs to represent different quantities arose in ancient India. The figures naturally grew out of drawing them by finger on boards covered with a thin layer of sand. This enabled markings to be quickly made, changed or wiped out.

The Arabs, who had adopted and refined the Hindu system, moved into Spain during the 8th century and brought their numbers with them. Nevertheless it still took a few hundred more years before medieval Europe used them in preference to letters.

The consequence of this late cultural arrival means we have inherited **3** different ways of counting:

by words (**five**)
by letters (**v**)
by figures (**5**)

China and Japan never had this diversity. Figure and word are represented with the same ideogram.

Unlike letters which have changed shape over their history, figures have kept shape for **100**s of years.

4 is an exception.

Albrecht Dürer unwittingly illustrated this development on **3** of his drawings which are respectively dated **1494, 1495, 1496**. See above

 NUMBERS

1 2 3 4

These numbers were drawn by Giambattista Bodoni in the 1790s

5 6 7 8

9 0

'Four is an interesting number because it is a shape that would arouse the curiosity of a cat,' wrote Saul Steinberg. 'Most numbers are either open or closed. Number **8**, for instance, is closed; a cat has no business to look inside. A cat likes to peer into something that is half open – a little bit open – a mystery. Number **3** is obvious; number **1** is nothing; **5** perhaps is more intriguing, but **4** certainly is perfectly designed and engineered for a cat to look inside and find out what is going on.' Not for nothing are letters and numbers called characters, as Steinberg appreciated when he drew them as personalities. '**5** and **2** might happily get into bed together,' but '**1**, **4** and **7** have no sex appeal.'

Numerosity

As can be seen on the front and back of this envelope the Russian Post Office employs a simple modular grid constructed without curves, to render the numbers for their postal codes.

This diagram appeared in a Russian book[1] published in the nineteenth century. It supported the theory that Arabic and Roman numbers had their origin in the triangle and square within a circle. A notion elegantly interpreted by French calligrapher Jean Larcher 125 years later. His version shown opposite renders the numerals 1 to 0 within this format.

[SEE P480]

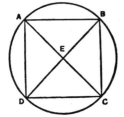

AD = 1
ABDC = 2
ABECD = 3
ABD + AE = 4

 NUMBERS

1. A.S. Pushkin. *Works*, Annenkov (St. Petersburg 1855)

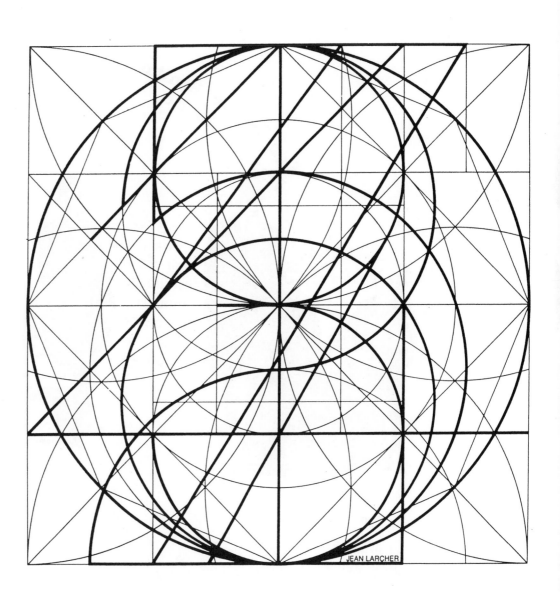

Bonjour **Madame Smith**
Vous avez l'air fâché

Oh!

*C'est que
voyez-vous
ma femme
est un peu
humiliée
de ne pas
avoir eu
raison*

Il y a eu
Monsieur
le Capitaine
des Pompiers
une controverse
entre Mme
et M. Smith

à M. Martin :
*Ça ne vous
regarde pas !*

(A. M. Smith)
*Je te prie de ne pas mêler
les étrangers à nos querelles
familiales*

Oh chérie
ce n'est pas bien grave
Le Capitaine est
un vieil ami de la maison
Sa mère me faisait la cour
son père je le connaissais
Il m'avait demandé de
lui donner ma fille en mariage
quand j'en aurais une
Il est mort en attendant

Design. Massin. This page from Ionesco's *La Cantatrice chauve* typographically echoes a conversation piece.

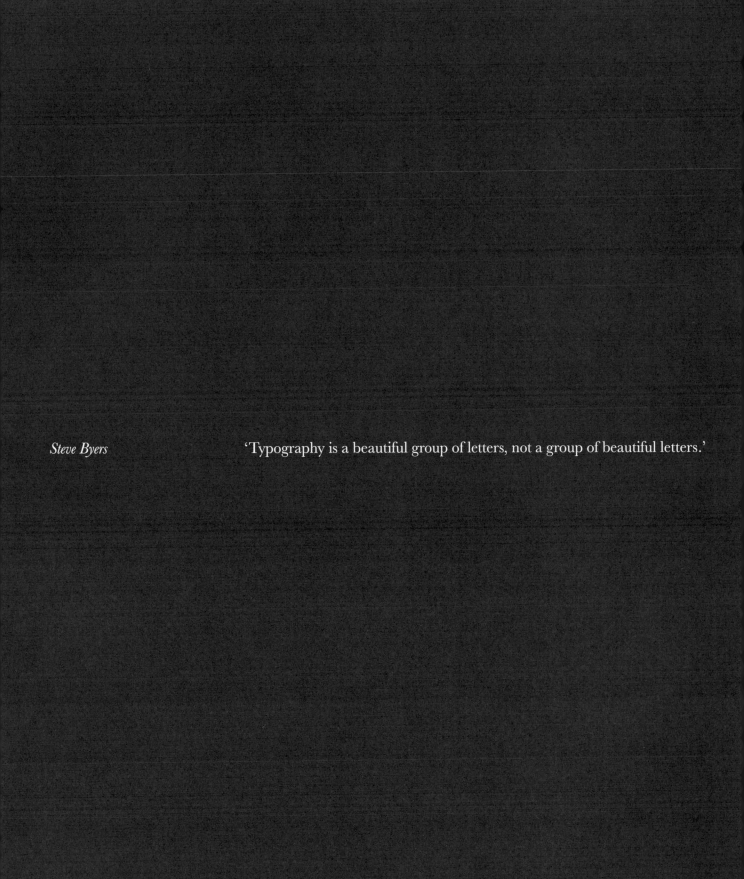

Steve Byers   'Typography is a beautiful group of letters, not a group of beautiful letters.'

Robert Hughes: 'In general, self-consciously *avant-garde* type, like self-consciously *avant-garde* food, is detestable. And we all know that the recent history of type design is littered with the equivalents of those beastly little green discs of kiwi-fruit bearing one quail's liver in a *déglacement* of blueberry vinegar that used to infest New York restaurants a few years ago. Postmodern guck. I am not against experiment but I loathe mannerism …'

Aaron Burns: 'Perfect communication is person-to-person. You see me, hear me, smell me, touch me. Television's the second form of communication; you can see me and hear me. Radio is the next; you hear me, but you don't see me. And then comes print. You can't see or hear me, so you must be able to interpret the kind of person I am from what is on the printed page. That's where typographic design comes in.'

Edward Gottschall: 'Whereas painting, poetry and architecture greatly influenced typeface and typographic design in the early 1900s, the primary influences since the mid-1960s have come from bits and bytes, lasers and fibre optics, electronics, and even photonics.'

Douglas Hofstadter: 'Stylistic moods permeate whole periods and cultures, and they indirectly determine the kinds of creations – artistic, scientific, technological – that people in them come up with … not only are alphabets of a given period or area distinctive, but one can even recognize "the same spirit" in such things as teapots, coffee cups, furniture, automobiles, architecture and so on.'

Beatrice Warde: 'It is sheer magic that I should be able to hold a one-sided conversation by means of black marks on paper with an unknown person half-way across the world. Talking, broadcasting, writing and printing are all quite literally forms of thought transference, and it is this ability and eagerness to transfer and receive the contents of the mind that is almost alone responsible for human civilization.'

Kit Hinrichs: 'I think in terms of three categories of typography: Classics, which transcend all periods of design; Period, which represent former and future eras; and Vogue, which exhibit the most extreme (the best and often the worst) in current typography.'

Jan Tschichold: '… to my astonishment I detected the most shocking parallels between the teaching of *Die Neue Typographie* and National Socialism and Fascism.'

Giambattista Bodoni: 'No other art is more justified than typography in looking ahead to future centuries; for the creations of typography benefit coming generations as much as present ones.'

Matthew Carter: 'It is no more or less difficult to define a letter form on a computer screen than on paper. What PCs have brought is access not to designing type but to making fonts. A font made on a Mac by a graphic designer or a non-professional will work just as well, in the technical sense, as a font manufactured professionally – and that is revolutionary.'

David Ogilvy: 'Do you think an advertisement can sell if nobody can read it? You cannot save souls in an empty church.'

1. Richard Firmage. *The Alphabet ABECEDARIUM*. Bloomsbury (London 2000)   **Comment.** M. Skjei

Most read without *seeing* what they read. In all probability you – the reader – have no idea of the name of this typeface. Not that it's of overwhelming importance. As advertising doyen David Ogilvy once commented, no housewife ever bought a new detergent because the advertisement was set in Caslon. Nevertheless, if a piece of text looks unattractive or difficult to scan, one isn't likely to read it. **[SEE** P400**]**.

Typographers live in a world inhabited by serifs, counters, kerns, ligatures and linefeeds, populated with Egyptian Expandeds, Latin Extendeds and Modern Romans. Wordage is viewed in terms of colour and weight, points, picas and leading. The aesthetics involve space, proportion, scale, balance, harmony and order. **[SEE** P105**]**. As you can *see*, there is more to it than you thought. Furthermore, the opinions held by this fraternity can excite an intensity of passion only equalled by medieval ecclesiastics arguing about how many angels can dance on the head of a pin. Typographers have ideological commitments to symmetrical or asymmetrical arrangements, fervent allegiances to particular typefaces, unremitting hatred of others, and what could be construed as moral attitudes **[SEE** P370**]**; '*Using bold caps*', declared Paul Rand, '*is like wearing belt and suspenders.*' (Hmmm!)

Despite contrary evidence typography is not an esoteric skill practised by a lunatic fringe of the design community; it actually represents, to quote Peter Behrens – who among other things **[SEE** P488**]** was a typographer – '*the most characteristic portrait of a period*'. 𝔒𝔫𝔢 𝔰𝔞𝔩𝔦𝔢𝔫𝔱 𝔢𝔵𝔞𝔪𝔭𝔩𝔢 𝔟𝔢𝔦𝔫𝔤 𝔟𝔩𝔞𝔠𝔨 𝔩𝔢𝔱𝔱𝔢𝔯 𝔱𝔶𝔭𝔢, 𝔞𝔱 𝔣𝔦𝔯𝔰𝔱 𝔠𝔬𝔫𝔰𝔦𝔡𝔢𝔯𝔢𝔡 𝔟𝔶 𝔱𝔥𝔢 𝔑𝔞𝔷𝔦𝔰 𝔞𝔰 𝔱𝔥𝔢 𝔫𝔞𝔱𝔲𝔯𝔞𝔩 𝔢𝔵𝔭𝔯𝔢𝔰𝔰𝔦𝔬𝔫 𝔬𝔣 𝔱𝔥𝔢 𝔄𝔯𝔶𝔞𝔫 𝔰𝔬𝔲𝔩. **[SEE** P63**]**. 𝔥𝔬𝔴𝔢𝔳𝔢𝔯, 𝔢𝔦𝔱𝔥𝔢𝔯 𝔟𝔢𝔠𝔞𝔲𝔰𝔢 𝔱𝔥𝔢𝔶 𝔴𝔞𝔫𝔱𝔢𝔡 𝔞 𝔪𝔬𝔯𝔢 𝔭𝔯𝔞𝔠𝔱𝔦𝔠𝔞𝔩 𝔱𝔶𝔭𝔢𝔣𝔞𝔠𝔢 𝔣𝔬𝔯 𝔭𝔯𝔬𝔭𝔞𝔤𝔞𝔫𝔡𝔞 𝔬𝔯 𝔞𝔠𝔱𝔲𝔞𝔩𝔩𝔶 𝔟𝔢𝔩𝔦𝔢𝔳𝔢𝔡 𝔱𝔥𝔢 𝔫𝔬𝔱𝔦𝔬𝔫, 𝔦𝔱 𝔴𝔞𝔰 𝔡𝔢𝔠𝔯𝔢𝔢𝔡 𝔬𝔫 3 𝔍𝔞𝔫𝔲𝔞𝔯𝔶 1941 𝔱𝔥𝔞𝔱 𝔤𝔬𝔱𝔥𝔦𝔠 𝔱𝔶𝔭𝔢 𝔥𝔞𝔡 𝔟𝔢𝔢𝔫 𝔦𝔫𝔳𝔢𝔫𝔱𝔢𝔡 𝔟𝔶 𝔍𝔢𝔴𝔰 𝔞𝔫𝔡 𝔱𝔥𝔢𝔯𝔢𝔞𝔣𝔱𝔢𝔯 𝔬𝔫𝔩𝔶 𝔯𝔬𝔪𝔞𝔫 𝔣𝔬𝔫𝔱𝔰 𝔴𝔬𝔲𝔩𝔡 𝔟𝔢 𝔲𝔰𝔢𝔡.[1]

Typographers are masons of the printed word. Of fierce independence, many are eccentric, and a few certifiable. John Baskerville refused to countenance the thought of a Christian burial and built a mausoleum in his backyard so he could be buried upright facing east. After he died (1775) his type and punches ended up in Paris and his body in a warehouse. **[SEE** P337**]**. And Eric Gill, devout Catholic, artist, sculptor, typographer and writer, engaged in improbable priapic activities. Not surprisingly with their often odd inclinations and obsessive secretive natures, typographers are perceived by authority as subversive.

Extract of a letter to Berthold Wolpe from the Reichskammer der Bildenden Kunst in Berlin [February 1935]: *'As you are a Non-Aryan and as such do not possess the necessary reliability to create and spread German cultural values, I forbid you to further practice your profession as a graphic designer.'* Berthold quickly left for London. **[SEE** P85**]**. Jan Tschichold was arrested (temporarily) by the Nazis for propagating 'un-German' typography. On release he left for Switzerland. In a letter to Tschichold's publisher the Gestapo wrote that 'for the protection of the German people' all copies of one of his books were to be confiscated. Ten years later he was in charge of design at Penguin Books in London. **[SEE** P206**]**. Paul Renner, who designed the typeface called Futura, was hauled in as a *'cultural Bolshevik'* but managed to get released and smartly transferred to Switzerland. Will Burtin **[SEE** P124**]** turned down an offer from Albert Speer to work for the party and moved to Holland and later the United States. **[SEE** P124**]**. In addition to his collages and performances Kurt Schwitters **[SEE** P432**]** was typographic designer to the city of Hanover, producing stationery and official forms for every kind of municipal activity, from letterheads for the zoo to school timetables, all austerely modern. Seeing how things were going he took off for Norway and later to Britain. Herbert Bayer (and Mies van der Rohe) departed for the US in 1938. In occupied Holland Willem Sandberg used his skills to forge identity cards and survived to become curator of the Stedelijk Museum in Amsterdam. **[SEE** P232**]**. Hendrik Werkman, accused of printing propaganda, was executed by firing squad.

typematters

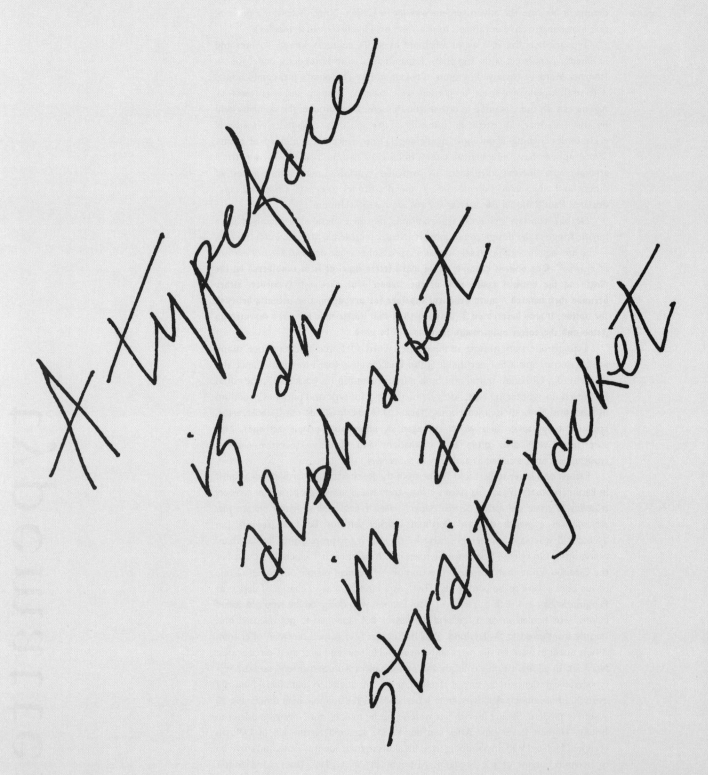

A typeface is an alphabet in a straitjacket

Answer: A terminal condition suffered by letters

The Rule of Swiss typography: When something is not forbidden it is compulsory. **Hermann Zapf:** 'Type is the ligature between author and reader.' **Bruno Monguzzi:** 'Typography is the matrix of graphic design.' **Max Bill:** 'It is the aim of every typographer to endeavour to lessen the incompatibility between the mathematically exact medium on the one hand and the haphazard shape of the text on the other.' **Edward Johnston:** '... to win access for that communication by the clearness and beauty of the vehicle ...' **Robert Massin** [Describing a page by Dadaist Tristan Tzara]: 'This disorganized muddle of words, a deliberate jumble, a real old rag-bag of typefaces which must have made the typographers of the period sit down and weep, is not without beauty and attracts the eye while discouraging us from actually reading it.' **Jan Tschichold:** 'The aim of typography must not be expression, least of all self-expression, but perfect communication achieved by skill.' **Francis Meynell:** 'Printing is the vehicle: legibility is the well greased bearing that allows the wheels of sense to revolve without squealing.' **Zuzana Licko:** '... you read best what you read most.' **Paul Renner** [On his *Futura*]: 'At last, a typeface that captures the spirit of the times.' **Piet Zwart:** '... those faces with a high-handed, personal, idiosyncratic seal should be avoided - their pretentious character opposes the utilitarian task of typography.' **Véronique Vienne:** 'Illegible typefaces are the graffiti of cyberspace.' **Stanley Morison:** 'Typography is the efficient means to an essentially utilitarian and only accidentally aesthetic end.' **El Lissitzky:** 'Typographical design should perform optically what the speaker creates through voice and gesture for his thoughts.' **Paul Rand:** 'Typography is an art. Good typography is Art.' **Steven Heller:** 'Type has become an artistic medium in its own right'. **Eric Gill:** 'There are now about as many different varieties of letters as there are different kinds of fools.' **Friedrich Schiller:** 'Type gives body and voice to silent thought.' **Neville Brody:** 'The traditions of typography are not fun; communication should be entertaining.' **László Moholy-Nagy:** 'Typography must be clear communication in its most vivid form.' **Walter Tracy:** '... legibility and readability are separate, though connected, aspects of type.' **Helmut Schmidt:** 'Typography needs to be audible. Typography needs to be felt. Typography needs to be experienced.' **Ellen Lupton:** 'Typography is the basic grammar of graphic design, its common currency.' **Charles Peignot:** 'In lettering, fantasy is of the essence; in type design, discipline is the first requisite.' **Emil Ruder:** 'A printed work which cannot be read becomes a product without a purpose.'

Josef Müller-Brockman: 'Never combine different type families.' **Jonathan Barnbrook:** 'I try never to use lower-case as I find the shapes boring on the page.' **Ralph Schraivogel:** '… I see type above all as an element of imagery and colour …' **Karl Gerstner:** 'Today everything is stylistically allowable.' **Henry Wolf:** 'I think of type as the bridge between word and picture.' **Frederic Goudy:** 'Type, after all, is merely handwriting divested of the exigences and accidents of the scribes.' **Erik Spiekermann:** '… a text can sound different each time it is dressed in a different typeface.' **Morton Goldsholl:** '… a form that expresses something other than itself.' **Tak Igarashi:** 'To me letters and characters are communication symbols on one hand, and attractive objects that stimulate my sensitivity, on the other.' **Jeffery Keedy:** 'There is no such thing as a bad typeface … just bad typography.' **George Tscherny:** 'Type is for reading – except when it's not.' **Allen Hurlburt:** 'This twisted path to conformity is strewn with the tortured reminders of the vagaries of our typographic taste: Broadway, Agency Gothic, Cartoon, Corvinus, Neuland, Signal and Slim Black, to name but a few.' **Franco Grignani:** 'Typography, like music, must read the senses of listener and viewer.' **Markus Kutter:** '… the typographic image optically orchestrates the content.' **Wim Crouwel:** '… one of the most important and most functional vehicles for ideas.' **Ralph Steadman:** 'As far as I'm concerned all grids belong in the gutter.' **Rick Poynor:** 'Typographic design has always been a broad church: refined on one side of the aisle, much rougher and readier on the other.' **Oswald Cooper:** 'Types too dextrous, like tunes too luscious.' **Marinetti:** 'The typographic revolution was initiated by me.' **Phil Baines:** 'The Bauhaus mistook legibility for communication.' **El Lissitzky:** 'Printed words are seen and not heard.' **Adrian Frutiger:** '… a written thought with an aesthetic form.' **Kiyoshi Awazu:** 'Typography is the root of design.' **Herb Lubalin:** '… type should be read the same way we talk – in a rhythmic, consistent flow.' **Niklaus Troxler:** 'In typography we can observe the passage of time'. **Kurt Weidemann:** '… there has hardly been anything completely new in typography, any more than there has been in cooking or in bed.' **T.M. Cleland:** '… the servant of thought and language to which it gives visible existence.' **Gerard Unger:** 'The essence of reading: not just to know more, but to experience more.' **Kurt Schwitters:** 'There are numerous typographic rules. The most important is: do not ever do it the way someone else does.' **Printers'** axiom: 'When in doubt, set it in Caslon.'

Carlyle wrote that the three great elements of modern civilization were: gunpowder, printing and the Protestant religion.

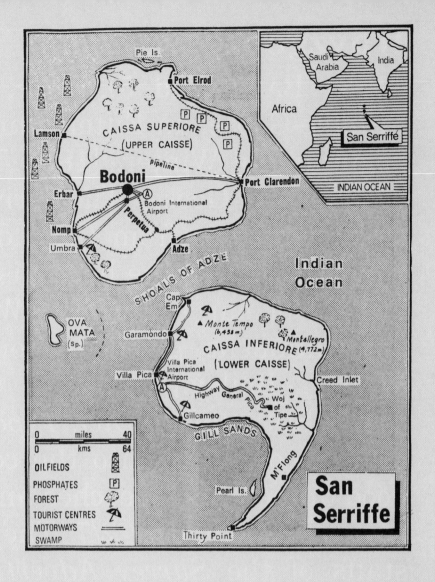

april fool

The Guardian, 1 April 1978

Wayzgoose (ˈweɪz·ɡuːs).

1731 BAILEY (ed. 5), *Wayz*, a Bundle of Straw. W
Stubble-Goose, an Entertainment given to Journey
beginning of Winter. [**1833** TEMPERLEY *Songs*
23 *note* Way Goose.--The derivation of this term is
ly known. It is from the old English word *wayz*,
wayz Goose was the head dish at the annual feast
fathers of our fraternity. 'Wayz Goose, a stubble
entertainment given to journeymen at the be
Winter.'--Bailey.]

1875 SOUTHWARD *Dict. Typogr.* 137 The wayzgoo
consists of a trip into the country, open air amu
good dinner, and speeches and toasts afterwards.
Mirror 23 August. 2/7 The members of the ty
staffs of the *Surrey Advertiser* (Guildford) and
Mirror (Redhill) had their wayzgoose on Saturday
they journeyed to Brighton.

b. *attrib. a* **1880** F. T. BUCKLAND *Notes and Jot*
39 London printers generally have a 'wayzgoose' d
autumn. **1897** F T BULLEN *Cruise of*
372 Carriages were chartered, an enormous
eatables and drinkables provided, and away we w
lar wayzgoose or beanfeast party.

zgoose, a

en at the

he Press

general-

ubble. A

the fore-

oose, an

ning of

generally

ments, a

5 Surrey

graphical

e Surrey

st, when

gs (1882)

er in the

Cachalot'

antity of

t, a regu-

addding
subtrcting
multimultiplying
div id ing

A word can not only represent a meaning – but also reinforce a meaning.

Logotype. Best stores in the United States. Design. Chermayeff and Geismar

Photograph. Paul Nougé. *A New Way of Juggling* (1929)

Lu Ch'Ai   'The end of all method is to seem to have no method.'

He found a formula

for drawing

comic rabbits;

This formula for

drawing comic

rabbits paid.

So in the end he

could not

change the

tragic habits

This formula for

drawing comic

rabbits made.

ROBERT GRAVES

Epitaph on an unfortunate artist

Drawing is looking. Keyboarding is calculating.

The *Australian National Dictionary* defines an artist as a person practised or habitually engaged in an activity which requires little skill, or is reprehensible. The example offered is booze artist. At the beginning of his career Michael Caine was given a small part playing a drunk. He was rather convincing, he thought, staggering about and slurring his speech. The director thought otherwise. A drunk tries to walk straight and speak clearly, he explained, underlining the point that execution without content is merely veneer. Skill is being at one with the purpose in hand. When asked by the Pope for a sample of work, Giotto took a chalk and drew a perfect circle. The Pope got the message and Giotto got the job. Skill appears magical to the uninitiated or incompetent. I still remember being flabbergasted by the seemingly unattainable skills exhibited by the older and experienced fellow students in my first life class. They produced amazing renderings by smudging instant shadows, erasing to make dramatic highlights and conjuring up striking resemblances. A talent, I realized later, much later,

which was really no more than something Anthony Burgess aptly described as 'a small fiddling capacity for producing the conventional and the well shaped'. A Chinese carving of a grasshopper perched on the edge of a cabbage leaf made out of one piece of ivory may seem seductive, but treating skill as product – instead of process – is only pushing pencil. Ever since the ancient Greek painter Zeuxis astonished his audience by painting a bunch of grapes so 'real' that birds tried to eat them, some skills have seemed to be magic. Many people find it exceedingly difficult to draw what they can clearly see. Their usual response is that they can't co-ordinate hand with eye; on the other hand, the very same person may be an excellent knitter or model-maker. The more accurate answer is that they find it difficult to co-ordinate eye with brain. The difficulty arises because our brain is directed towards investing the image, which appears flat on the retina, with the properties of space which is how we see the image in our mind's eye. So by trying to draw a three-dimensional flower on a flat sheet of paper we are reversing the way we naturally see.[1] No wonder drawing doesn't come easily.

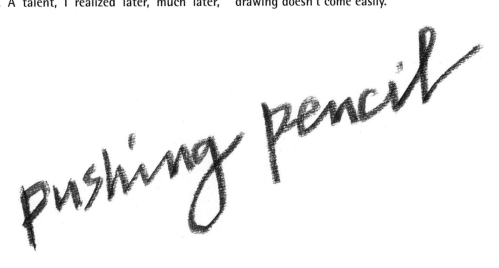

1. Daniel Dennett. *Consciousness Explained*. Penguin (London 1993)

'… measure twice, cut once.' CARPENTERS' MAXIM

'… the learning of a craft takes time, and we all think we're entitled to short cuts.' ANTHONY BURGESS

'… the danger is ever present of mistaking for creative talent what is only a gift for adroit imitation or a highly developed skill in compilation.' REM KOOLHAAS

'One paints with one's head, not one's hands.' MICHELANGELO

'I don't paint with my hands, but my tail.' AUGUSTE RENOIR

'Talent without genius isn't much, but genius without talent is nothing whatever.' PAUL VALÉRY

'There is an art to seeming artless.' CICERO

'Rules are made for baseball players, not baseball players for rules.' ROBERT BIERSTEDT

'It's all one to me: opera, painting, drawing, faxes.' DAVID HOCKNEY

the objective **of skill**

CHINESE PROVERB 'To hear is to forget, to see is to remember, to do is to understand.'

JACOB BRONOWSKI 'The most powerful drive in the ascent of man is his pleasure in his own skill.'

SHUNRYU SUSUKI 'In the beginner's mind there are many possibilites. In the expert's mind there are few!'

BISHOP MAGEE 'The man who makes no mistakes does not usually make anything.'

EDWARD GIBBON 'The winds and the waves are always on the side of the ablest navigator.'

MISHA BLACK 'Design without technique is dilettantism.'

HENRY LONGFELLOW 'If you would hit the mark, you must aim a little above it; every arrow that flies feels the attraction of the earth.'

ANSEL ADAMS 'Photography is a way of telling what you feel about what you see.'

JOAN MIRÓ 'The works must be conceived with fire in the soul but executed with clinical coolness.'

is to make *a dream* **a fact**

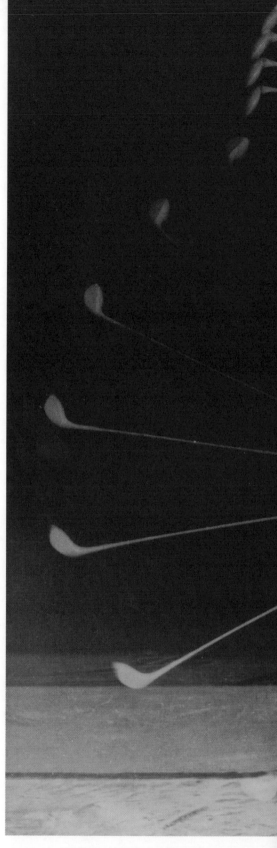

'Flex the knees slightly and, while your upper body inclines towards the ball, keep from bending over too much at the waist. The arms are extended fully but naturally towards the ball without any great feeling of reaching out for the ball … start the club back with that left arm straight, letting the right elbow fold itself against the body … the head should be held over the ball … the head is the fixed pivot about which the body and swing must function.' *Lee Trevino*

'Mister – you'd better find another line of work – this one sure doesn't fit your pistol.' *John Wayne*

'I really believe that everything resides in technique. You can't teach creativity, you can teach technique, and it's from technique that one is able to be creative. This is the terrible mistake of this century, to put creativity first.' *Vivienne Westwood*

'Too bad that all the people who know how to run the country are busy driving taxis or cutting hair.' *George Burns*

Physicist Niels Bohr was an Olympic athlete. Astrophysicist Edwin Hubble was an amateur boxing champion. And in their early days so were Georges Braque, architect Tadao Ando, and movie *auteur* Luis Buñuel, who also married a gymnast who won a bronze medal for France in the 1924 Olympic Games. Writer Albert Camus played in goal for Algeria and singer Julio Iglesias was goalkeeper for Real Madrid's junior team. Ottavio Missoni [of knitwear fame] hurdled for Italy in the 1948 Olympic Games, and designer Marcello Minale won a silver medal for rowing in the 1960 Olympics held in Rome.

Note. I am intrigued to know how, wherever I go in the world, mosquitos always know where to bite me in exactly, and I mean exactly, the same two places.

Multiple-flash photo of golfer Bobby Jones taken by Harold Edgerton (c.1935)

How to do a cave painting :

In a cave at *Pech-Merle* in France there is a prehistoric painting of a pair of spotted horses. It was made like this: The artists pounded charcoal into small pieces, shoved them into their mouths and chewed the bits up with animal fat and lizard oil, diluting the sludge with saliva and water. Working within a scratched outline they spat out gobs which they smudged to form the manes. The lines representing hair were smeared with blackened fingers and twigs. The tails and legs were rendered by spitting the charcoal mixture through a gap formed by two parallel hands, and screening with a hand gave the backs a sharp edge. Body markings and spots were shaped by pursing the mouth to squirt through a hole in an animal skin held at varying distances from the wall. It was arduous work and the entire painting would have taken three to four days with the help of an assistant to hold a lamp. How do I know? Because that's how Australian Aborigines still make rock paintings.[1]

   1. Marlo Morgan. *Mutant Message Down Under*. Thorson (London 1995)

the negative is the score — *but the print is the* [handwritten signature]

ANSEL ADAMS

Before   After 1 hour

The drawings above are by a 64 year old grandmother after just one hour of tuition. *"Yes, You Can Draw!"*

Classified advertisement for an academy which purports to teach people how to draw. And by post too. Personally I think someone made an error as the faces should be swapped around.
The Guardian Education, 21 February 1995

A fourth-century Chinese classic (*Rituals of Chou*) described design as 'a knowledge of auspicious times in the movement of the heavens' – I take this as meaning the right frame of mind. It then got down to the importance of working environment, materials, skill, and the right tool for the right job. According to this treatise it all comes together in *ukiyo*, the engraving of wood printing blocks. The various bits are done by apprentices but the faces are undertaken by the masters, the tricky part being the hairline. But only the most skilled of those can undertake the ultimate – the rendering of a geisha's features as seen through a mosquito net.

The poet Robert Graves, speaking at Oxford in 1962, said: 'Technique ignores the factor of magic; craftsmanship presupposes it. A journeyman, after seven years as apprentice, will get the feel of his materials and learn what quiet miracles can be done with them. A small part of this knowledge is verbally communicable; the rest is incommunicable, except to fellow craftsmen who already possess it. The technician's disregard of this inexplicable element, magic, in painting, sculpture, medicine, music, and poetry – on the ground that it cannot be demonstrated under laboratory conditions – accounts for the present dismal decline in all arts.'

A newspaper article about artists' colourists Winsor & Newton describes how two women spend all day covering sheets of high-grade paper with consistent watercolour washes. These are then cut into tiny sections and stuck on the colour reference charts which you find in the better class of artists' supply shops.

Diodorus Siculus records that 'two sculptors working in different places were each producing one half of a colossal figure; using the "Egyptian system of proportion" they achieved such accuracy that the halves were found to fit without the slightest flaw.'

Drawing is a skill more akin to playing the piano than riding a bicycle. It requires constant practice, whereas if you haven't ridden a bike for years – apart from a wobbly start – it's smooth all the way. Perhaps you've heard about the young man in New York who stops a passer-by and asks the way to Carnegie Hall. The passer-by thinks, shrugs, then replies, 'Practice, passer-by, practice, practice.' Like Debussy, who practised with the piano lid down.

'So with a great musician ... one is no longer aware that the performer is a pianist at all ... his playing has become so transparent ... that one no longer sees the performer himself – he is simply a window opening upon a great work of art.' Marcel Proust

Luis Buñuel's recipe for 'the perfect dry martini' for which he preferred Noilly Prat vermouth and an unspecified English gin: 'The day before your guests arrive, put all the ingredients – glasses, gin, and shaker – in the refrigerator. Use a thermometer to make sure the ice is about twenty degrees below zero (centigrade). Don't take anything out until your friends arrive; then pour a few drops of Noilly Prat and a demitasse spoonful of Angostura bitters over the ice. Shake it, then pour it out, keeping only the ice, which retains a faint taste of both. Then pour straight gin over the ice, shake it again, and serve'.

Medieval German stonemasons believed in three disciplines: First was mastery of technique, secondly the mastery of construction, and finally the mastery of style. The *Geselle* had skills, the *Parlier* had skills and knowledge, the *Meister* had skills and knowledge and creativity.

In Japan many of those who were privileged to wear the work of a grand tattoo master donated their skin to a museum. Tokyo University, I'm told, has three hundred such masterpieces framed and displayed.

A Roman banquet was a stylish affair with guests reclining on couches, slaves serving wine, garlands of flowers to ward off drunkenness, female dancers and roast birds and joints of meat carved in time to music. Young cooks were trained in the skill of musical carving with wooden models of birds and meat, which had slits for the knives.

In *Meetings with Remarkable Men* the mystic Gurdjieff wrote that priestesses in Kurdestan were taught to dance with an elaborate ancient mechanism. His description was extremely detailed but the following gives the gist: the apparatus was a human-sized wooden column mounted on a tripod, with seven branches. Each branch was divided into segments which decreased in length and width according to their distance from the column. Each segment was connected by ivory balls and sockets. These were inscribed with signs which, when matched to other signs on the segments, fixed the positions of various postures. The ritualistic dances were supposedly a choreographic language of ancient teachings. Bruce Lee had a similar apparatus for rehearsing Chinese foot kicks for Kung Fu movies.

With ink and brush the Korean master Yi Su-mun could, in a few strokes, create an impression of wind and rain beating against the branches of a bamboo silhouetted against the full moon. Expertise, or knowing how something is done...can be acquired in a moment but the skill to do it takes time and experience. Despite the instant expertise offered by the camera, most people can't even take a decent snap of their cat.

"mirand R.d.
13th sept 1994
by Gavina
Johnson

Georges Braque   'Perspective is a ghastly mistake which it has taken four centuries to redress.'

Rendered in household paint,
this charming scene was
created by Fred Charles who
lives in Haiti. I like the
colours and enjoy his sense of
abandoned perspective as
the eye leaves the schoolroom.

'I feel an irresistible desire to wander, and go to
Japan, where I will pass my youth, sitting under an
almond tree, drinking amber tea out of a blue cup,
and looking at a landscape without perspective.'

OSCAR WILDE (1882)

Symbol. Design Norman Ives. This symbol for a hotel is both two- and three-dimensional

p e r s p e c t i o n

Predators have eyes in front of their heads, so they can focus on their meal. Prey have eyes each side of their heads to see who's sneaking up. The turbot, being a flatfish, has both eyes on the same side of the head, so the other side can hide in the sand. Human eyes are in front and spaced apart, so we see things from two angles and as three-dimensional objects, not just as flat shapes.

Manipulating the eye to create an illusion of depth has been going on for a long time. Prehistoric artists overlapped bison to indicate that one was nearer than the other. In antiquity sculptors adjusted the angle of carvings placed up high on buildings to look more effective viewed from below. Michelangelo gave David a squint so he looked at his best viewed in either profile. Renaissance painters used linear perspective to create an ordered recession in space.

In 1698 Wang Hui painted a 72-foot silk scroll which recorded scenes the Emperor had observed when he took a trip up the *Grand Canal.* As the scroll is unrolled the panorama appears continuous but is actually an assembly of different perspectives, separated and yet joined, by mists and clouds.

Cubism condensed space and time even further by combining glances taken from different angles at different moments into a single composition. An arrangement without foreground, background, or single light source, packed edge to edge with interlocking forms and overlapped shapes. Some painted, others stuck on. A picture which wasn't meant to look like anything except itself.

De Chirico used perspective to disquiet the eye. In *The Melancholy of Departure* (1914) instead of one vanishing point he used six to clone the various viewpoints.[1] In one series of paintings David Hockney imagined himself standing inside a scene, looking around, and rendering different views. A composition, as if seen from within, but painted on canvas, from without. He also produced *Grand Canyon* (1990s) which comprised sixty abutted canvases, which, he points out, had sixty different viewpoints.

Cultures see things differently. Medieval artists weren't too dim to invent perspective, their perceptions were different.

Patience Gray writes of being aboard an Italian country bus, and experiencing views from such a crazy angle that it verified the pre-perspective conventions of Gothic art : 'what is important zooms up big and close, the rest falls away, small.'[2] An Inuk will depict what he knows rather than what he sees, and show what is underneath the ice as well as what's on top. The Aborigine will indicate what's inside the body, as well as the outside. The Egyptians drew the head in profile but rendered the eye as if seen face on – the body is more recognizable from front than side. However, arms and legs are more clearly described from the side, so that's the way they showed them. The big toe clearly identifies a foot, so they drew all feet as if viewed from the big toe side. Pictorial convention rather than realistic presentation.[3]

In the past the pictorial ambition was to make a three-dimensional world out of a flat medium, whereas today the aim seems to be to make a flat picture out of a three-dimensional reality.

Different times – different points of view.

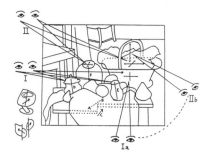

This diagram by E. Loran shows several perspectives in Cézanne's painting *The Kitchen Table.*

1. Robert Hughes. *Nothing if not Critical.* Alfred A. Knopf (London 1990)   2. Patience Gray. *Work Adventures Childhood Dreams.* Edizioni Leucasia (Lecce 1999)   3. E.H. Gombrich. *The Story of Art.* Phaidon (16th edn., London 1995)

Harold Ross, legendary editor of *The New Yorker*, sifting through cartoons submitted to the magazine would sometimes scribble on the artwork, 'Where am I ?' Perspective scratches at the mind like a cat at the door and we 'feel uncomfortable' if things don't 'look right'.

However, when we need to 'put things in perspective' what we really mean is that we prefer situations which conform to 'our point of view'. An unfortunate analogy since a single fixed-point perspective is best contrived by a rigid, upright, one-eyed, motionless person. What we normally see is not like that at all, but a medley of glimpses as we blink, nod, turn our head and move around.

The discovery, or at least the explanation, of linear perspective is attributed to Brunelleschi. In the fifteenth century he demonstrated this illusionary ordered recession of space through painting the *Battistero* in Florence (as seen from the door of the *Duomo*), by cutting a hole in the centre of the painting, and asking a spectator to look through the hole into a mirror held up opposite the picture. By positioning himself the spectator could see in the reflection, that the receding lines on the canvas lined up with those in the view seen through the hole, and that they all converged into a single point. Confirmation of Alberti's definition that a picture was 'a cross-section of the visual rays projecting from the thing observed – if seen from a single vantage point'.

The new discovery appeared to be magical. The vanishing point, fixed where the picture ought to disappear, paradoxically was the organizing principle of what was shown. A two-dimensional surface could be made to appear three-dimensional; large things could be made to look small and small things large; a painting could look like the real thing. Meanwhile the earth which seemed flat was, by a contemporary scientific argument, shown to be round. Illusion and reality have been confused ever since.[1]

' *h! Paolo,* '
Donatello remonstrated with Uccello, *'this perspective of yours is making you abandon the certain for the uncertain.'* Although that seems a contradiction, consider Marcel Duchamp's comment that as two-dimensional shadows are projections from three-dimensional objects, these might in turn be projections from a fourth dimension. Or Ozenfant's observation that *'forms are the consequence of a sort of call from space in which matter infiltrates itself into such space as offers least resistance, and then becomes perceptible.'* Or Apollinaire's conclusion : '... *the wretched trick of perspective, this fourth dimension in reverse ...'*

1. Mary McCarthy. *Stones of Florence*. Penguin (Harmondsworth 1972)

Painting. Alexey Sunduv. *Staying on a Line.* 1986

Photograph. Otto Steinert. *Pedestrian's Foot*

Zeno of Elea   'Whatever exists is in a place – Therefore place exists –

Therefore place is in a place – and so on – ad infinitum.'

LIMBO

'In the collection of the Vatican Museum is a mosaic signed by one Heraclitus. Across a white background is an even scattering of debris: a wish-bone, a claw, some fruit, various discarded limbs of sea-creatures, the remains of fish. It is a copy of a famous mosaic by the artist Sosos of Pergamum, called the UNSWEPT HALL. Sosos, whom the Roman antiquarian Pliny called "the most renowned" of all mosaicists, worked in the first half of the second century BC. He specialized in illusionistic works, trying to turn the unpromising medium of coloured tiles into something lifelike and real. His most famous and remarkable work depicted doves drinking from a birdbath. You could even see their reflections on the surface of the water, says Pliny. A copy was discovered at Hadrian's Villa at Tivoli. It is indeed a fine example of what ancient artists were capable of, achieving a very real sense of the basin's three-dimensional form and burnished metallic sheen. What is so remarkable, however, about the UNSWEPT HALL, is not its illusionistic ambition, but its objective humility. It is a floor that depicts a floor, closing the gap between art and life. This is most obvious, perhaps, with the white tiles, which have a perfect identity with the white tiles of an unswept floor. More honest than the sipping doves, on one level it really is what it claims to be; it is a trick-floor, impossible to clean. But the floor is not really the subject at all. The true theme is an unseen banquet, as we can tell from the strewn litter. And this feast still seems to be going on. There was a pause in Greek banquets between the eating part and the drinking part of the meal, when tables were cleared, floors swept, hands washed and perfumes splashed. Sosos's banquet has not quite reached that stage. Moreover, some of the debris casts rather strange shadows, for it is hovering half a millimetre above the ground, as if it has a little way still to fall.'[1]

1. James Davidson. *Courtesans and Fishcakes.* HarperCollins (London 1997) **Mosaic.** Museo Gregoriano Profano. Vatican

THIRTY SPOKES MEET IN THE HUB,

BUT THE EMPTY SPACE BETWEEN THEM

IS THE ESSENCE OF THE WHEEL.

POTS ARE FORMED FROM CLAY,

BUT THE EMPTY SPACE WITHIN IT

IS THE ESSENCE OF THE POT.

WALLS WITH WINDOWS AND DOORS

FORM THE HOUSE,

BUT THE EMPTY SPACE WITHIN IT

IS THE ESSENCE OF THE HOME.

LAO TSE

no   **thing**   is   *not*   **nothing**

Most people claim they can't draw because their intention gets lost between the head and the hand. Well certainly a skill is involved but more significantly they can't see straight. They look in *ad hoc* fashion, seeing the scene in front of them as a jumble of stuff in a space rather than as a pattern of shapes. One first step in learning to draw is to think of a scene as a flat pattern. Imagine that what you see through a window is imprinted on the sheet of glass. This flattening makes it easier to distinguish the space between things as a **some**thing rather than as a **no**thing. Space is substance. Cézanne painted and modelled space. Giacometti sculpted by *'taking the fat off space'*. Mallarmé conceived poems with absences as well as words. Ralph Richardson asserted that acting lay in pauses. *'I collect silences,'* said Heinrich Boll. *'When I have to cut tapes, in the places where the speakers sometimes pause for a moment – or sigh, or take a breath, or there is absolute silence – I don't throw that away, I collect it!'* Isaac Stern described music as *'that little bit between each note – silences which give the form'*. Franz Kafka warned that '*... the Sirens have a still more fatal weapon than their song, namely their silence ... someone might possibly have escaped from their singing; but from their silence, certainly never.'* And David Hockney on painting his parents: *'They would sit in silence for hours, but then I realized there was some communication ... There are links in silence.'* In contrast art criticism likes to be heard and delights in pretentious prose of the sort parodied by Woody Allen's *'negative space in an airless, godless universe'*. The Japanese have a word (*ma*) for this interval which gives shape to the whole. In the West we have neither word nor term. A serious omission. If the spaces between the stepping stones of images, words or sounds are too narrow, or too wide, even the simplest message can get scrambled in trying to get across. Just like a dish I remember listed on a Greek menu ...

CHICK ENCOOKED IN GREASE PROOFPAPER

Emil Ruder: '… typographers have long recognized the empty spaces of the unprinted surface to be an element of design.'

Jan Tschichold: '… typography is an arrangement of elements … intervals between the groups are as important as the groups themselves.'

Hassan Massoudy: 'In a calligraphic composition there is no such thing as a blank space, there is only black and white, and each space has its own value.'

Pauline Oliveros: 'Any space is as much a part of the instrument as the instrument itself.'

Whospaces

seletters

ealsheep.

icgOudy

How to twist space

Take a strip of paper, give it a twist and stick the two ends together. You now have a *Moebius Strip*. See opposite. The twist converts a two-dimensional flat strip of paper into a three-dimensional model with a curious property. You can pick it up and turn it around so obviously it occupies space, but if you run a finger around the surface (or edge) you end up where you started out. In effect it has neither back nor front, so doesn't occupy space. In which case, how can it be three-dimensional?

'The infinite is a square without corners.' Chinese proverb

One can complicate the notion further. Make a *Moebius* model out of two strips of transparent material, say clear film, then fix them together. Imagine the space between the two as zero thickness. Cut a *swastika* out of black paper, insert it between the strips; slide it around and you'll discover it arrives back where it started except that the prongs have reversed. Slide it around once more and it arrives back in its original form.[1] This implies that if an astronaut made a similar round trip through a slice of space the same situation would occur. Unless he completed a couple of laps his body would be permanently switched left to right. And if the strip was made out of mild steel and magnetized where would the north and south poles be?

'There are two infinities: God and stupidity.' Edgar Varèse

The Rev. Edwin Abbott invented *Flatland* in 1884. This region is a two-dimensional plane populated by squares, circles and straight lines. Social status is determined by the number of sides one has, and moral character by acuteness of one's angle (the more acute, the more degenerate). One day the hero, Square, is startled by the apparition of a point expanding to a circle; in fact circle is Sphere, who enlightens him by taking his brain to other dimensions. To learn what happened next you'll have to buy the book.[2]

'What is it that haunts space where matter is found?' Arthur Eddington

Humans could not exist in *Flatland*. To illustrate this (by analogy) Stephen Hawking produced a diagrammatic cross-section of a dog sliced through the digestive tract from mouth to anus. This demonstrated that a flat dog would fall apart. I was going to show the diagram but figured you could run it up in the mind. [**SEE** P113].

St Augustine pointed out, the world is made **of time** – not **in time**.

ANOTHER THOUGHT : Space is elastic. You are conceived in a point which expands as you grow. Eventually, when your time is up, you collapse and shrink back into a no point situation. Now this is going on all the time all over the world, so if space was a fixed quantity there would need to be a consistent ratio between life and death. Obviously there isn't. I'm lost. Anyway to take possession of a piece of space is our first gesture in life, and we occupy our portion until we depart. But what I want to know is this – who gets mine when I leave?

JORGE LUIS BORGES : 'The steps a man takes from the day of his birth until that of his death trace in time an inconceivable figure.'

LEO LIONNI : 'I am not afraid of death. I just think it's a terrible waste of time.'

BLAISE PASCAL : 'When I consider the short duration of my life, swallowed up in the eternity before and after, the little space which I fill, and even can see, engulfed in the infinite immensity of spaces of which I am ignorant, and which know me not, I am frightened, and am astonished at being here rather than there, for there is no reason why here rather than there, why now rather than then ...'

DIANE ACKERMAN : 'An event is such a little piece of time-and-space you can mail it through the slotted eye of a cat.'

ALFRED NORTH WHITEHEAD : 'It is impossible to meditate on time and the mystery of the creative passage of nature without an overwhelming emotion at the limitations of human intelligence.'

RICHARD FEYNMAN : 'If you think you understand Quantum Theory, you don't understand Quantum Theory.'

INFRA-THIN: Marcel Duchamp was intrigued with the notion of infra-thin. The space between the front and the back of a sheet of paper, the sound made by his corduroy trousers rubbing together when he took a walk.

GROUNDHOG DAY : In the eponymous movie every day begins and ends on the 2nd of February.

'A Moebius strip
Is one-sided,
And you'll get quite a laugh
If you cut one in half,
For it stays in one piece
When divided.'

ANON

1. Martin Gardner. *The Ambidextrous Universe*. Penguin (Harmondsworth 1967)   2. Edwin A. Abbott. *Flatland*. Oneworld (Oxford 1994)

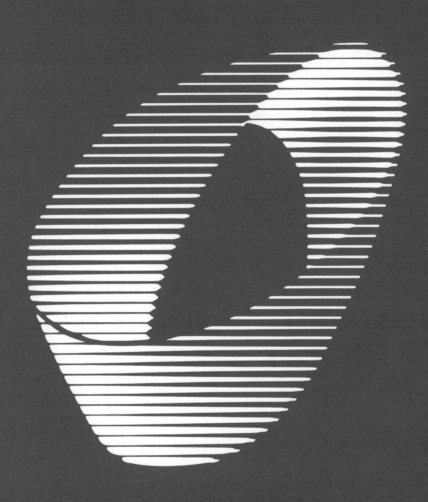

Note. I was having a coffee sitting outside a cafe in a street opposite the British Museum one sunny May morning. A man passed by followed by his shadow. The odd thing is that the next person who passed by was following their shadow. I paid up and left.

There was a young lady named Bright,
Who travelled much faster than light.
She started one day
In a relative way
And returned on the previous night.
Arthur Buller

Never wait for yourself

'There is no difference between Time and any of the three dimensions of Space except that our consciousness moves along it.' H.G. Wells. *The Time Machine.*

The world is not only stranger than we imagine – it is stranger than we *can* imagine. Take the weird branch of scientific inquiry called quantum physics where electrons, protons, tachyons, neutrons, and other kinds of particle exist in unpredictable anarchy. A particle can be in two places at once, travel forwards and backwards at the same time, disappear and reappear in the same instant, have mass but no volume. Then there is all that strange stuff like superstring theory with ten-dimensional loops of energy which occupy a space as small to the atom, as the atom is to the solar system.[1] Indeed there is a proposal that it's only looking at things that gives them an existence and that the universe is no more than a figment of imagination. That is to say if no one looked at the moon it would gradually disappear. I'm mystified how people can work with things they can't see – with microbes, molecules, knots in time, black holes, wormholes and curved space. I have

immense difficulties working with things I can see, which are tangible, flat and immobile. But how is it, I ask myself with dubious self-satisfaction, that I can probably draw a better cat than your leading-edge mathematician? Many scientists predict the universe will end as it began by collapsing back into a single point. If so, at a specific moment, time could reverse and run backwards. Unless we are in a non-linear situation and merely flip back and forth like a coin tumbling through eternity. Time was absolute and unchanging until Einstein equated it with motion, space, length, breadth and height – all at once and in one dimension. A discovery made, the story goes, when he imagined himself sitting on a beam of light holding a mirror in front of his face. Since he and the mirror were travelling at the same speed and direction as light, light could never catch up to reflect his face into the mirror. On the other hand perhaps time is no more than a convenience which stops everything from happening all at once. A category of abstract thought by which the world is practically organized and supposedly understood. For instance they say an

observer with a powerful telescope situated 185 light years away from the earth could be witnessing both the biggest volcanic eruption in history and the Battle of Waterloo at the same time. Mount Tambora in Indonesia erupted with such force that it sent storms around the world and left Napoleon's artillery stuck in a quagmire. The Duke of Wellington, positioned on high ground, was able to mop up the battle. As they say, the essence of action is timing. Time doesn't move or stop any more than length extends or contracts. Time is relative. Not that I find that a comforting thought as when I was a child a year was an eternity whereas nowadays I seem to be having breakfast every fifteen minutes. Perhaps the best way of thinking of it is like philosopher-idler Henry David Thoreau who remarked that 'Time is but the stream I go fishing in.'

'We are bound to perceive objects in the external world as existing in time and space and as being governed by causal relations, and we cannot transcend the limitations which our concepts of space, time, and causality impose upon us.' Anthony Storr

1. Martin Gardner. *The Night is Large.* Penguin (London 1997)

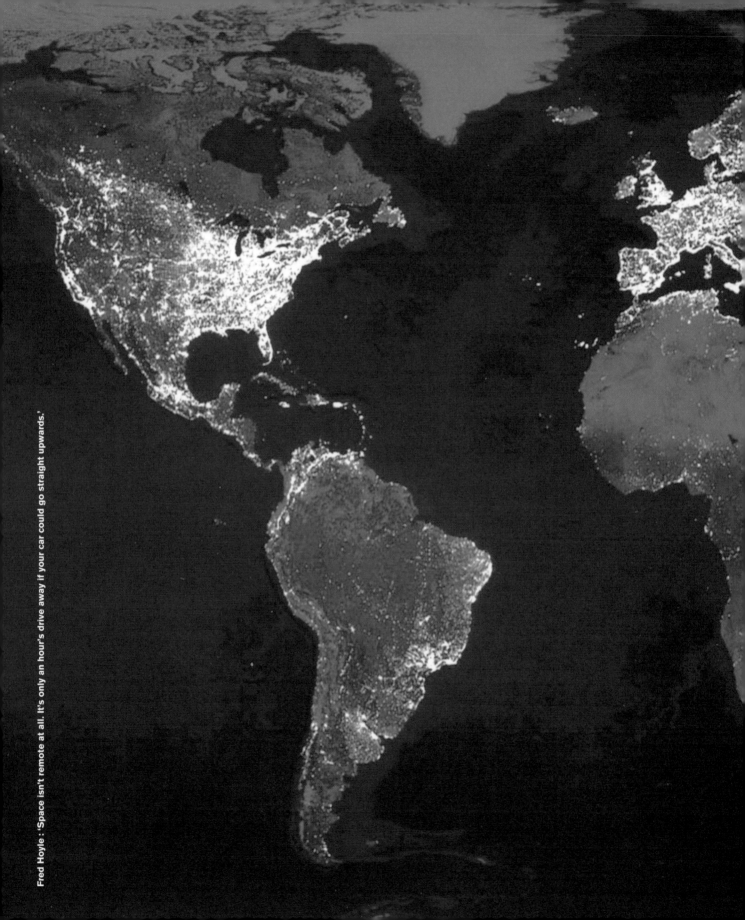

Fred Hoyle : 'Space isn't remote at all. It's only an hour's drive away if your car could go straight upwards.'

Multiple exposure of the world's population centres at night, photographed by America's Defense Meteorological Satellite and released on November 9, 2000

'If light has no age, perhaps time has no shadow.'

ANON

'Echo replies to echo, everything reverberates.'

GEORGES BRAQUE

'Time is to clock as mind is to brain.'

DAVA SOBEL

'Space is in time, silence is in space.'

JOSEPH JOUBERT

'Three o'clock is always too late or too early for anything you want to do.'

JEAN-PAUL SARTRE

'Time is the movement of eternity.'

PLATO

'The future approaches us at 60 minutes an hour.'

RICHARD SEYMOUR

'Time will tell.'

… as my granny used to mutter ominously

'What is past is prologue.'

INSCRIPTION IN THE WASHINGTON MUSEUM

'Danny Hillis and I are putting together the Clock Library, to relengthen civilization's attention span. It will be a physical facility that is both a big slow charismatic clock and something we're calling "a library," which may or may not be recognized as a working library by the time it's actually been built. The Clock Library's function is to help people think about the depth of time both backwards and forwards, and take responsible relationship personally to that. The project is the exact analog of the photograph of the Earth from space from the Apollo spacecraft in the late 1960s, which almost instantly engendered the ecology movement. The trick is to find something that works for understanding time the way that photograph worked for understanding the Earth as a beautiful and fragile planet.'
Stewart Brand[1]

'... staying on the tip of the Cap d'Antibes, in 1948, and walking along the road on the eastern side of the Cap, I had suddenly seen that we had arrived at the subject of the Matisse painting, *Route sur le Cap d'Antibes*, complete with every angle of the road and, again, the pine branches. Edging into a corner of the wall on the landward side of the road, until I felt I could photograph Matisse's subject exactly as he'd seen and composed it, my elbow was pressed hard into the mossy stones of the wall. It occurred to me to peel the moss away from those stones. And sure enough, there I found old palette scrapings of scarlet, ultramarine, violet, lemon and emerald, all oxidizing deep in a small crevice. Thrilled, but not surprised, it was a discovery I still recall with intense emotion. To have the experience of standing precisely where the great painter once saw what he saw – and to know that what he saw was what I now also saw, but saw through his paint, through his brushstrokes, through his selected distortions of the visual data yielded at that exact point in the landscape ... to share an exact experience with a great painter.'
Patrick Heron[2]

1. John Brockman. *Digerati*. Orion (London 1996)   2. Patrick Heron: Selected Writings. *Painter as Critic*. Tate Gallery Publishing (London 1998)

Capsule of a Spent Day

Kingsize duvet cover 'Jane Austen' white appliqué, matching pillow case Two paracetamol 7 Scotties paper hankies peach bloom extra soft Portable Snooze radio Schumann songs with Elizabeth Schwartzkopf Packet azure and silver decaffeinated Lavazza Coffee Bowl Kellogg's Just Right Cereal Semi-skimmed Vital milk Pink grapefruit Independent newspaper Seed catalogue, Chiltern's, from Abelia ('from China . . . rather rare') to Zizyphus ('Buffalo Thorn . . . a S. African greenhouse shrub') Postcard of geisha smoking from David in Japan telling me to stop London Review of Books: Iain Sinclair walking the site of Millennium Dome New book about Dolly the sheep from publishers' publicist London Catalogue of drawings by Karen Killimnick from Louise in Zürich Call for papers for conference in Warwick about Masculinities – 'any fairy tale angle'? Notice of Round Reading Room closure Article about expression 'having a bee in one's bonnet' from Malcolm Jones, folklore scholar, Sheffield, with 17th century pics Notes on appearances of bananas in Restoration letters and verse from Nick Groom, Exeter, with three kisses crossed on top Bill from Toshiba about broken screen of laptop £1300 estimate Roll recycled toilet tissue, lavender blue Sample London bathwater Imperial Leather shower gel Almay Hypo-Allergenic Special Treatments Anti-Perspirant deodorant 'Non-Sting' Body Shop Cocoa Butter Hand & Body Lotion "Melt away dryness with rich moisturization" 2 inches New Icemint Pearl Drops tooth polish Flash universal Cleanser and J-cloth Tweezers Red or Dead platforms, black suede Knickerbox bra and knickers, The Gap red wool jacket Dab Clarins Beauty Flash Balm "youthful radiance" Millen long black skirt, blue-and-white striped Sock Shop tights, black lurex 50 denier, Karen Lancôme Definicils high definition mascara, black Clinique Double Face Powder Matte Neutral Lancôme lipstick, blue violet Bourjois blusher Rosette brune Clinique "quick eyes" pencil, Rouge baroque The Great Frog silver earrings with pink and black feathers Lenscloth and trifocals Toshiba 3400 laptop and clamp from Conrad with pieces of cardboard to make screen work Modem & cable & jack E-mails – more Lady Di and Queen Mum sick jokes Daemon-Typhoon reports failure to deliver message attachment of proofs of short story 'The Belled Girl', from editor Cristina in Hawaii Mug with red rose, 'Labour' Stroopwaffel biscuit BT cordless telephone 188½ miles cable Ream A4 copy paper Uniball micro deluxe pen Black Pizza Hut flyer – new flavour "Spice Girls Special" – Cajun blackened chicken chunks "15% off" Forthcoming gigs at Forum, Highgate West Hill, flyer: Eddie Izzard, Shane MacGowan Chicken and Apricot Pie Cottage Delight "Tangy Pickle with Real Ale" No artificial additives Tomato oregano Virgin olive oil first pressing Aqua Libra "Original" Squeeze Fairy Liquid 3 postcards: standing stones on Dartmoor, Tony Blair and Mother Teresa from Madam Tussaud's, Round Reading Room 3 first class stamps – Enid Blyton's Famous Five 5 second class stamps – "Anniversary of Horror" – Frankenstein, Dracula, Dr Jekyll and Mr Hyde Tampax regular 2 pads with wings Joseph suede and Mongolian lamb trim overcoat, gift of Irène last year Black velvet hat 2 x £1.50 underground from Kentish Town Warburg Institute Reader's Pass Ovid, Fasti Folders images of "Saturn Devouring His Children", Scylla the sea-monster 6 5 x 8 index cards with notes Photocopying swipe card value £5 Bunch 6 lisianthus purple and white Pack 20 Cartier light Squirt Zippo lighter fuel Bottle Jacana 1996 Chardonnay Stellenbosch South Africa Pan-fried Kettle Chips New York Cheddar Pottery bowl by Ann Stokes 15 Sainsbury's Agnolotti with porcini mushrooms Green beans from Mehmet's on the corner Knife and fork and plate from Skyros with mermaid displaying double tail Blueberry Yoghurt – "Virtually Fat Free" 1 William Pear, 1 passion fruit Teaspoon Fortean Times "This summer's crop of crop circles" Lorrie Moore, Self-Help Dr Stuart's Botanical Teas "Vespers" – with Valerian root and hops Quickie Eye Make-Up Remover Pad Clarins Gentle Foaming Cleanser Phial kisses & breath of beloved

Marina Warner (writer)

Humpty Dumpty

'... *my* name means the shape I am –

and a good handsome shape it is, too. With a name like yours, you might be any shape, almost.' In conversation with Alice.

Illustration. Jérome Peignot. *A Flight of Parentheses*

Invisible fields: The Tantra metaphor for the remotest creative sound is the tinkling anklet of a dancer whose movements weave the invisible pattern of the world. There seem to be, although it's no news to ecclesiastics, invisible fields which organize and shape things. A mysterious phenomenon which accounts for the sudden simultaneous banking of a flock of birds, the zig-zag path taken by shoals of fish, the alignment of termite mounds along a north-south axis, the crabwise flight of aeroplanes, mass suicide by lemmings, the mathematical patterns made by elephants when they amble along, the chorus-line legs which react twice as fast as those of individual dancers, identical human cells which can turn into an arm or a leg or a nose. And have you noticed how we *square* our shoulders, *round off* a conversation, think *elliptically*, make a *pointed* argument, receive a *crooked* look, *bend* our mind, *circle* around an issue, *straighten* someone out?

'9 was returning, immersed in thought, from my sketching, when on opening the studio door, 9 was suddenly confronted by a picture of indescribable and incandescent loveliness. Bewildered, 9 stopped, staring at it. The painting lacked all subject, depicted no identifiable object and was entirely composed of bright colour-patches. Finally 9 approached closer and only then recognized it for what it really was — my own painting, standing on its side on the easel ...' WASSILY KANDINSKY (Reminiscences, 1913)

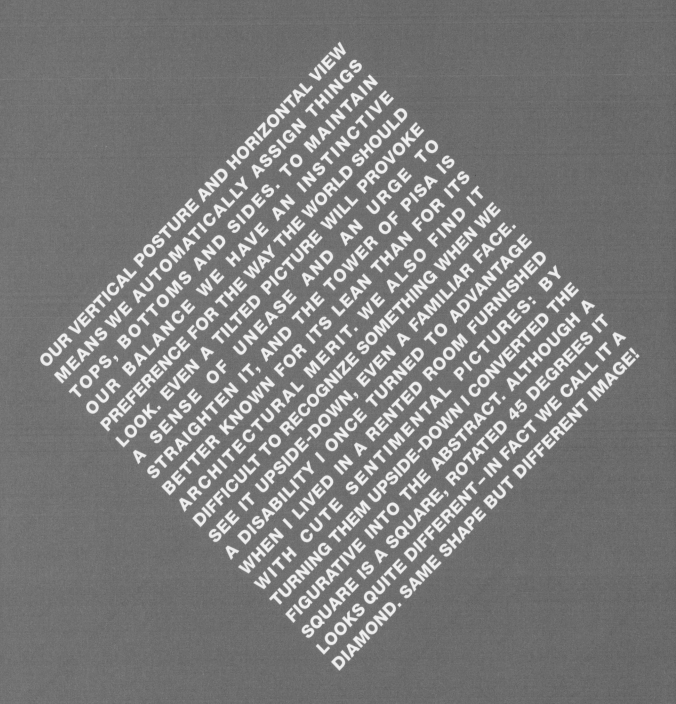

OUR VERTICAL POSTURE AND HORIZONTAL VIEW MEANS WE AUTOMATICALLY ASSIGN THINGS TOPS, BOTTOMS AND SIDES. TO MAINTAIN OUR BALANCE WE HAVE AN INSTINCTIVE PREFERENCE FOR THE WAY THE WORLD SHOULD LOOK. EVEN A TILTED PICTURE WILL PROVOKE A SENSE OF UNEASE AND AN URGE TO STRAIGHTEN IT, AND THE TOWER OF PISA IS BETTER KNOWN FOR ITS LEAN THAN FOR ITS ARCHITECTURAL MERIT. WE ALSO FIND IT DIFFICULT TO RECOGNIZE SOMETHING WHEN WE SEE IT UPSIDE-DOWN, EVEN A FAMILIAR FACE. A DISABILITY I ONCE TURNED TO ADVANTAGE WHEN I LIVED IN A RENTED ROOM FURNISHED WITH CUTE SENTIMENTAL PICTURES: BY TURNING THEM UPSIDE-DOWN I CONVERTED THE FIGURATIVE INTO THE ABSTRACT. ALTHOUGH A SQUARE IS A SQUARE, ROTATED 45 DEGREES IT LOOKS QUITE DIFFERENT – IN FACT WE CALL IT A DIAMOND. SAME SHAPE BUT DIFFERENT IMAGE!

'GOD EVER GEOMETRIZES.' PLATO

'SIMPLICITY OF FORM IS NEVER A POVERTY, IT IS A GREAT VIRTUE.' JAN TSCHICHOLD

'I AM ALWAYS PURSUING THE IDEAL SHAPE ... A RELATIONSHIP BORN FROM THE TENSION BETWEEN THE RAW MATERIALS AND THE SHAPE.' TAK IGARASHI

'GOD ... A GASEOUS VERTEBRATE.' ERNST HAECKEL

'EVERY FORM IS THE PETRIFIED SNAPSHOT OF A PROCESS. THEREFORE, WORK IS A STATION IN EVOLUTION AND NOT ITS PETRIFIED AIM.' EL LISSITZKY

'POETRY IS A SOUL INAUGURATING A FORM.' PIERRE-JEAN JOUVE

'DESIGN IS FORM MADE BY MATERIALS WHEREAS ENGINEERING IS FORM DICTATED BY MATERIALS.' KENNETH GRANGE

'IN THE CIRCLE THE BEGINNING AND THE END ARE COMMON.' HERACLITUS

'... THE B2 BOMBER, DESPITE THE ESSENTIAL UGLINESS OF A MACHINE DEDICATED TO MASS-DESTRUCTION AT ENORMOUS COST, ADDRESSES THE CONSTRAINTS OF ITS TASK (OF COMBINING EXTREME SPEED WITH INVISIBILITY TO ENEMY RADAR) WITH SUCH RUTHLESSNESS THAT, LIKE A VIKING LONG SHIP OR A RENAISSANCE SUIT OF ARMOUR, IT HAS A PURITY OF FORM THAT CANNOT BUT BE INTERPRETED AS BEAUTIFUL.' JOHN PAWSON

'... THE FORM OF AN OBJECT IS A DIAGRAM OF FORCES.' SIR D'ARCY WENTWORTH THOMPSON

Photograph. Quadrant. The B2 bomber

The Turkish puzzle ring

Among my *bêtes noires* are obtuse assembly instructions. Not complex affairs on how to build a stereo, but the small leaflets you receive with Italian light fittings or Japanese toasters.

This brings me to the Turkish puzzle ring. I've never understood how anyone could have visualized the intricate knobby design in the first place. It is impossible to picture in the mind.

Perhaps the three rings, (sometimes there are more), were forcibly overlapped and vigorously hammered together. Alternatively a solid ring could have been partially cut into bands and the remaining portion elaborately carved into interlocking knuckled shapes.

Legend relates that the ring signified betrothal and if it was taken off – for obvious reasons – would fall apart and be impossible to fit together again. Anyway I passed an hour at the bazaar in Istanbul where a helpful, eager shopkeeper showed me how to take one apart and put it together. I had no ulterior motive, merely a curiosity.

PUZZLE RING
Instruction Booklet

Prepared by
EDWARD BASOĞLU

I also bought an instruction booklet as I knew I'd forget the sequence of moves. These, I later discovered, were written and illustrated with a Byzantine sense of humour. That is to say they were incomprehensible — which of course served to reinforce the moral of the legend.

INTRODUCTION

The Puzzle ring consists of four loops which look quite different from each other. Let us get acquainted with them and give each loop a name before we proceed any further :

SINGLE - NOTCH

It has only one notch on either side of the vertex.

DOUBLE - NOTCH

It looks very similar to the single - notch, but has two notches on either side of the vertex.

SMOOTH - CURVE

The main curvature on this loop looks almost like a straight line.

CURLY - CURVE

It is very curly, as the name implies.

Please memorize the names of the loops before reading the instructions.

1 - Shake the four loops until they are clearly separated from each other. Hold either the «single - notch» or the «double - notch» between your fingers. When either one of these two loops is held between the fingers, the other one will form the very bottom loop.

2 - Now use your left hand. Hold the «single - notch» and the «double - notch» between your thumb and the forefinger of your left hand as shown in the sketch.

CAUTION : In the sketch the «double notch» points toward the left plan. If you can not put the ring together this way, try it again by holding he «single - notch» toward the left palm. This is because the four loops in some rings might be positioned differently by the manufacturer.

3 - Pass the «smoothcurve» over the thumb. If the smooth curve is on the opposite side of your thumb pass it over notched loops by lifting first the forefinger and then the thumb.

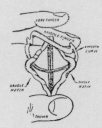

CAUTION

Always keep the curved portions of the loops on the topside; because you will try to fit these curved portions into each other.

4 - Hold the «curly - curve» loop by the bottom. The curved portion should rest on the bottom of notched loops Turn the «curly - curve» toward your body

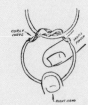

and hold it in position by the aid of your middle finger.

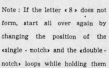

5 — Now bring the smooth - curve toward the curly - curve by turning it away from your body.

When the curvatures of the two loops fit into each other a figure similar to letter « 8 » will form.

Note : If the letter « 8 » does not form, start all over again by changing the position of the «single - notch» and the «double - notch» loops while holding them between the thumb and the forefinger of the left hand.

6 - When the « 8 » is formed hold it at the bottom of the loops by your right hand and leave the other two loops loose.

7 - Transfer the loops making the letter « 8 » to your left hand, in order to have the right hand free for the rest of the work.

Now hold the «single - notch» by the right hand and turn it around until the curved portion is within letter « 8 » Caution : Before you flapp the «single - notch» to the side you must be sure

that its vertex is within the loop of the «double - notch». If necessary, push the double - notch slightly downward.

8 - Flapp the single - notch to the side. This way you obtain a ring made of three loops.

9 - Turn the «double - notch» until you get the curved portion in the letter « 8 »

If necessary ease up the other loops without loosing control over them. Then flapp the double - notch to the side.

Click ; Here is your ring again.

Note. In the eyes of a topologist, a doughnut and a coffee cup are equivalent, because each has only one hole. Either object can be transformed into the other by moulding and without any tearing. A doughnut and a banana don't share this characteristic because one would have to tear the doughnut to mould it into a banana.

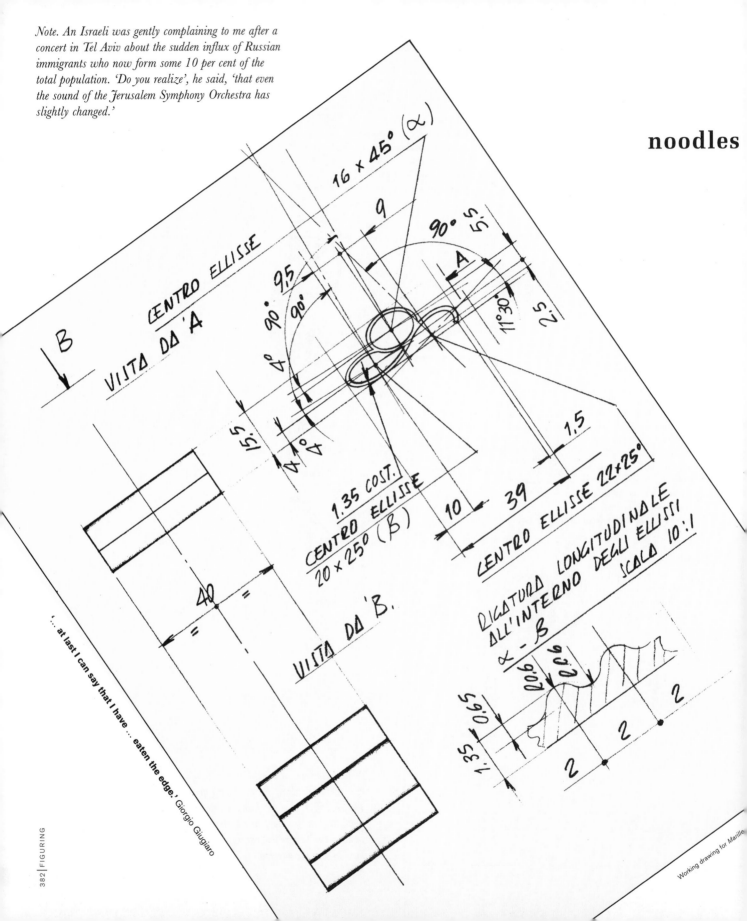

Note. An Israeli was gently complaining to me after a concert in Tel Aviv about the sudden influx of Russian immigrants who now form some 10 per cent of the total population. 'Do you realize', he said, 'that even the sound of the Jerusalem Symphony Orchestra has slightly changed.'

'... at last I can say that I have ... eaten the edge.' Giorgio Giugiaro

Working drawing for Marille

cycloids and squircles

The noodle. *Voiello*, a manufacturer of *pasta*, commissioned designer Giugiaro, who sculpted the *Maserati* and the *Ferrari*, to invent a 'gastronomically relevant' *pasta* for weight watchers. The brief stipulated that 50 grams of the *pasta* should simulate the bulk of 100 grams of *macaroni* – on the plate. Every problem contains unique wrinkles and creating the first new pasta in fifty years was no exception. This required studying the disciplines of drainage, elasticity, swelling and rupture resistance, constant checks with culinary experts, and the production of 35 detailed working drawings. If form is the balance between tension and relaxation then Giugiaro got it right. At a gathering to launch *Marille, Time* magazine reported that a lady journalist exclaimed: 'It is so amusing in the mouth – all movement.' She was sure this was a good thing. The director of *Voiello* simply cried, '*Perfetto!*' [SEE P424].

The cycloid. The curve of The Kimbell Museum vaults, designed by Louis Kahn, in Fort Worth (Texas), is based on the cycloid arc – an elegant curve known as the 'Helen of geometry'. What is that you may ask? Well, Blaise Pascal described it as the line marked by a nail on the rim of a moving rolling pin as it rises from the ground and falls again to meet it. Or, put another way, a curve traced in the air by a point on a rolling disk. If that isn't clear, visit the Museum and inspect the model.

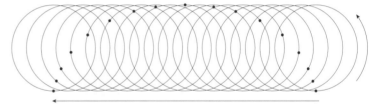

The squircle. The super ellipsoid, I call it a squircle, is an elegant shape which sits somewhere between a circle and a square, or a sphere and a cube. It is a rectangle within an oval without straight sides or corners. Piet Hein, Danish mathematician and poet, defined the precise shape in the 1950s and marketed it as an executive gift called super-egg. Here it is shown actual size. You roll the egg and when it comes to a halt it magically stands up on end. At least that's what it's meant to do. Mine just wobbles over. Most erudite designers possess one. I bought mine in Copenhagen airport. The ellipsoid was first applied by Scandinavian town planners to resolve traffic flows at motorway intersections. The shape also harbours a democratic attribute expressed through the ellipse table, a table where nobody can sit at the head. The squircle was designer Milner Gray's favourite shape in his packaging designs of the early 1950s. Type designer Hermann Zapf also used it as the basis for his typeface called *Melior*.

This page is typeset in the *Melior* font.

Form ever follows function • The **form** follows the

Louis Sullivan

function • **Form** and function are one • **Form** is the

Jean-Baptiste Lamarck　　　　　　　　　　*Frank Lloyd Wright*

external expression of inner content • We do not want

Wassily Kandinsky

form but function • **Form** comes from wonder • **Form**

Paul Klee　　　　　　　　　　*Louis Kahn*

follows emotion • **Form** is not formula • **Form** is not

Hartmut Esslinger　　　　　　　　*Robert McKee*

the goal but the result • **Form** is an extension of

Ludwig Mies van der Rohe

content • **Form** follows function is a statement of

Robert Creeley

'Whether it be the sweeping eagle in his flight or the open apple-blossom, the toiling work-horse, the blithe swan, the branching oak, the winding stream at its base, the drifting clouds, over all the coursing sun, form ever follows function, and this is the law.' *Louis Sullivan. The Tall Office Building Artistically Considered*

sequence, not a path to Enlightenment

Ralph Caplan

'Organizations inescapably have **form**. We cannot actually experience organizations, or convey our experiences of them, without **form** intervening. We cannot even conceive of organizations without evoking (thinking of or perceiving) **form**. The very language we use to depict organizational phenomena is full of references to **form**. thus we re**form** institutions, trans**form** work practices, enhance or measure per**formance**, **formalise** procedures, analyse in**formal** behaviour, **form**ulate strategies, request personnel to wear uni**forms**, fill out **forms** (or **formulaires** in French), and we in**form** and **form** people.'

Rafael Ramírez

Painted wood figure of a Thai dancer

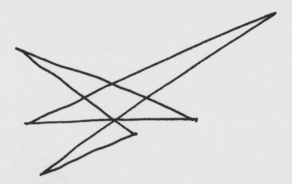

Adam is said to have named the tiger a tiger because it looked like a tiger. On the same principle Christian Morgenstern, poet and mystic, was convinced that all seagulls looked as if their name was Emma. If you think that's a load of rubbish how come, when asked to allocate the names of either **Takete** or **Maluma** to each of these two shapes, everyone invariably gives the same answer?

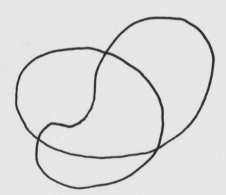

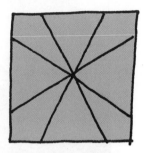

Give someone the above figure and ask them
to pick out a form. If they pick out either of the
two crosses accept them as a friend,

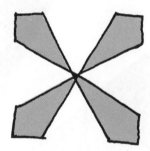
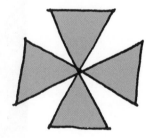

but if they select a form like the one below,
run for the hills.

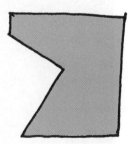

Pessimism Optimism. Futurist painting. *Giacomo Balla*

'urine trail of the bull'

'knees of the tortoise'

'ribs of the giraffe'

'forehead of the zebra'

Whether complex or simple, patterns usually owe their form to an observation or experience or association. The tribal basket makers in northern Botswana give evocative names to the seemingly abstract designs of their patterns : 'flight of the swallow', 'running ostrich', 'urine trail of the bull', 'ribs of the giraffe'. In the pattern they call 'flight of the swallow' one can still discern birdness, but whether the 'knees of the tortoise' was originally based on reptilian wrinkles or the result of a vague association in the mind of the maker, is anybody's guess. The fact is we humans need to allocate names to things so we can get a mental fix. Presented with an unrecognizable shape such as an ambiguous inkblot, or abstract painting, we seek for verbal associations. [SEE P123]. When unable to think of one we confess we can't make 'head or tail' of it. I don't know what the pattern of the basket shown opposite may symbolize or is called, but I know it represents a recent innovation in the ancient art of basket making: it is woven using the multicoloured wires found in telephone cables. [SEE P47]. If you encounter telephonic problems when you're in South Africa you now know why.

In my absence a designer borrowed a large pair of scissors
lying on my drawing table. Before taking them she
conscientiously pencilled a line around the contour and
wrote her name underneath. A graphic way of saying I've
borrowed your scissors! When she brought them back I
indicated towards her outline suggesting that she put
them back on the drawing. She blushed bright scarlet.
Shapes can send messages and create meanings even
on a mundane level. When asked which shape
envelope he preferred Benedetto Croce said he'd
need to know whether it was for a lover's letter or
business correspondence. Fiddling around for a
graphic image to illustrate the cover of a book
on psychology I lit on the idea of a *Rorschach*
ink blot. I wasn't convinced it looked quite
right and asked a friend for his opinion.
'What's it meant to be?' he asked, and then
commented snidely, 'is it a scrotum?' At
that point I knew I'd got it right! Many
years later I used a colourful folded
inkblot on a poster to promote a
photographic colour film. When
people ask me what it means, I just
shrug my shoulders, and ask them
what *they* think.

COLIN FORBES

This is a drawing of a wild / flower, *Lapsana communis*, colloquially known as 'Nipplewort'.

For flat thinkers
the shape of something
is the plane of its form.
Thus a triangle is the
silhouette of a pyramid.

If you think thick,
then shape could be
considered surface volume.
Thus the shape is a pyramid
and the form is the content.

Of course shape and form
can also be a bit (so to
speak) more complicated.

If you can figure this
conundrum out,
you get full marks.

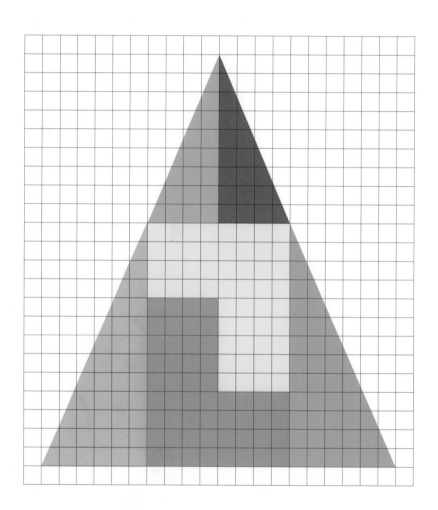

These six pieces make a complete triangle.

content is form

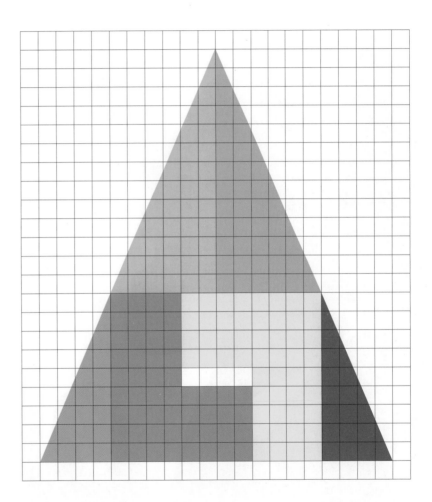

Rearranged the same six pieces make the same triangle — except a bit is missing.

'Language was invented so people could conceal their thoughts from each other.'
Charles-Maurice de Talleyrand

'Language is a mirror of the mind.'
Noam Chomsky

'Language is the dress of thought.'
Dr Johnson

'Language was not made by man, but rather the other way around.'
Francisco Varela

'An artist cannot speak about his art anymore than a plant can discuss horticulture.'
Jean Cocteau

'Ours is a world of words. Our thoughts, our world of imagination, our communication, our richly fashioned culture - all are woven on the loom of language.'
Richard Leakey

'Leafing through my old notebooks, it can happen that I don't understand what I wanted to tell myself, because the notes are more like messages sent by him who I was at a precise moment, to him who he would later be.'
Roland Topor

'A change in language can transform our appreciation of the Cosmos.'
Benjamin Lee Whorf

'Language is the ability to dispatch an infinite number of precisely structured thoughts from head to head by modulating exhaled breath.'
Steven Pinker

'... the harmony between thought and reality is to be found in the grammar of the language.'
Ludwig Wittgenstein

'Language is a dialect with an army and a navy.'
Max Weinreich

'A language makes infinite use of finite means.'
Baron von Humboldt

The photograph is a self-portrait of Dadaist John Heartfield shouting provocative slogans. He had changed his name from Helmuth Herzfelde to spite the Nazi party who were giving him a hard time. Anyway I've borrowed his picture to voice less radical pronouncements.

Ludwig Wittgenstein   'If a lion could speak, we would not understand him.'

LINGO

Isadora Duncan said that if she could have said what she felt, she wouldn't have become a dancer. And Edward Hopper said that if he could have expressed himself in words there would be no reason for him to have been a painter. Then there is the busy Italian waiter who, when asked the way to the toilet, apologized saying he couldn't explain because his hands were full.

Spoken language has its own characteristics. Language, as described by Steven Pinker, is *'the ability to dispatch an infinite number of precisely structured thoughts from head to head by modulating exhaled breath'*. And this happens through what the Patron Saint of the digital revolution, Marshall McLuhan, called an acquired organized stutter. A system of stringing marks together to make words.

A process which he described as …

C,O,N,T,I,N,U,O,U,S and C–O–N–N–E–C–T–E–D

… which has straightened out our minds so they think in linear mode by sequential bits and pieces in a step-by-step process. It's not insignificant that when we don't understand something, we say …

'I DON'T FOLLOW YOU'

We are blueprinted for speech and wired into a sort of universal mental software which enables us to learn and speak any language from birth. A programme which can construct an unlimited number of grammatically correct sentences out of a finite list of pronounceable words.

To demonstrate this Noam Chomsky deliberately composed a nonsense sentence:

> Colourless green ideas sleep furiously.

The sentence doesn't make sense but the grammar can't be faulted. Similarly Lewis Carroll's *Jabberwocky*, which includes invented words, is doubly meaningless in that it looks and sounds meaningful:

> Twas brillig, and the slithy toves
> Did gyre and gimble in the wabe:
> All mimsy were the borogoves,
> And the mome raths outgrabe.

Of course what may look like nonsense to one person might mean something to someone else:

> Sofúr thu svid thitt
> Svartur i áugum
> Far i fulan pytt
> Fullan af dráugum.

According to poet W.H. Auden, and I take his word, this is an Icelandic lullaby which roughly translates:

> Sleep, you
> black-eyed pig.
> Fall into a deep pit
> of ghosts.

Being threatened at such an early age may account for the crime figures in Iceland being the world's lowest, as well as their suicide rate being the highest.

The printer, in setting Auden's poem *Journey to Iceland*, inadvertently altered *'And the poets have names for the sea,'* to *'And the ports have names for the sea'*. The mistake seemed to Auden more suggestive so he kept it. Artistic originality, even at this late hour, can depend on error. **[SEE P44]**.

'*It is a property of man to be capable of learning grammar'*, observed Aristotle anticipating the theories put forward by Noam Chomsky, and other experts knowledgeable in such matters. Indeed languages are no more than a cultural veneer overlaying a universal grammatical structure which is part of our nature. As Eliza Doolittle complained to Henry Higgins, *'I don't want to talk grammar. I want to talk like the lady in the flower shop.'*

Rather than read novels Austrian writer Alfred Polgar (1920s) preferred to read grammars. I'd put that on a par with reading car-maintenance manuals but for him grammars, at least so says writer Peter Conrad, possessed all *'the sleek, stylish, modernistic virtues, like the cool surfaces and aerodynamic curves of Art Deco ornament'*. Like the Eiffel Tower which dispensed with cladding, grammar is *'the basic frame of thought, with grooves, clamps, cross beams, and bolts'*.[1]

Perhaps we are also mind-mapped with visual grammars?

It is only through our instinctive and shared expressions of inner feelings that we are able to share thoughts and sensations with others. Just as a structuring of noise can create music, so the composition of a painting can create a comprehensive work of art rather than a meaningless colourful mess. Well that's the thought behind my suggestion – although when put down in words I confess it doesn't seem to hold up too well. Anyway Wassily Kandinsky and Paul Klee both wrote extensively that specific arrangements of colour and forms and marks convey specific moods and emotions. **[SEE P270]**.

Our deep-seated response to rhythms and harmonies is such that even if we don't understand other visual languages, we can still gain an instinctive pleasure from their configurations. For instance, the visual incantations depicted in a Navaho sand design or the stories embodied in Aborigine bark painting. **[SEE P287]**.

Brillig means four o'clock in the afternoon – the time when you begin *broiling* things for dinner. *Slithy* means 'lithe and slimy' … You see it's like a portmanteau – there are two meanings packed up into one word. *Toves* are something like badgers – they're something like lizards – and they're something like corkscrews. To *gyre* is to go round and round like a gyroscope. To *gimble* is to make holes like a gimlet. The *wabe* is the grass-plot round a sun-dial. *Mimsy* is 'flimsy and miserable' (there's another portmanteau for you). And a *borogove* is a thin shabby-looking bird with its feathers sticking out all round – something like a live mop. A *rath* is a sort of green pig; but *mome* I'm not certain about. I think it's short for 'from home' – meaning that they've lost their way, you know. *Outgrabing* is something between bellowing and whistling, with a kind of sneeze in the middle.

1. Peter Conrad. *Modern Times Modern Places*. Thames & Hudson (London 1998)

HELLO

About 100,000 years ago there was a dramatic jump in the quality of stone tools. This may also have been the moment when gasps, grunts and groans flowered into language. When man began to communicate thoughts and ideas.

Some people thought there was an original language which Adam spoke with Eve, and which after the destruction of the Tower of Babel, fragmented into the five to six thousand languages spoken around the world today. Babel, incidentally, has no connection with babble. Psammetichos, a ruler of ancient Egypt, believed this biblical language was inherent and had two children raised by shepherds who were under instructions never to speak to them. The hope was that the children might begin to use the lost words. They didn't. Among others who carried out the same experiment were Akbar Khan, Charles IV of France and James I of Scotland. All the children grew up unable to say anything whatsoever. Despite the lack of evidence medieval scholars concluded that the language of Adam was Hebrew.

Many years ago, drawing under the colonnades in Bologna, I gradually became aware of two attractive ladies engaged in conversation. Imagination took wing. They were, I became convinced, talking about intimate affairs. One was to leave the key of her apartment under the mat so the other could consummate an assignation. My pencil wobbled. Slowly my elementary grasp of the language asserted itself. They were complaining about the cost of radicchio.

I am deeply envious of those who speak several languages.

Dante was undecided whether to write the *Divine Comedy* in Italian, French or Provençal. Sir Richard Burton, explorer, soldier, writer and linguist, mastered 29 languages. On top of that he translated the 17 volumes of the *Arabian Nights* and (not surprisingly as I've read his biography) *The Perfumed Garden* and the *Kama Sutra*. And Cleopatra, Plutarch informs us, was fluent in Egyptian, Greek, Latin, Macedonian, Hebrew, Arabic, Ethiopian, Syrian, as well as the languages of the Medes and Parthians. Mind you I've also read that Cardinal Mezzofanti, polyglot and sometime curator of the Vatican Library, spoke 186 languages and 72 dialects. I don't believe a word of it. Such claims bring to mind

Dorothy Parker's fictional lady who spoke 18 languages but couldn't say 'no' in any of them.

Euskera, spoken by Basques, is the oldest living language in Europe. And in southern China, an extraordinary secret language only spoken and understood by women has been discovered. It even has its own unique script. The language, Nu Shu, is fading away as women become emancipated from rural life.

Then there are languages within languages. Strine, cockney, street slang, the argot of sodalities, professional jargons, the clicks of Hottentots, the Silbo whistle language of Canary Island mountain shepherds, and the Romany of gypsies who communicate across the world singing secret verses down the telephone.

Languages are also charged with symbolic values. For reasons known only to himself, Charles V of Germany spoke French to men, Italian to women, German to horses and Spanish to God. In Japan men use a different mode of speech from women and each social class has its own particular pronunciation. When the Japanese Emperor spoke over the radio to announce the end of the war in 1945, the general public (unaccustomed to being addressed by a descendant of the sun) could hardly understand what he was saying. Encapsulated in communication protocol you can end up talking to yourself.

Canadian legislation dictates that public information is in English and French. At the end of a supper in a Japanese restaurant in Toronto I was presented with a Chinese fortune cookie. I read the

Vous hériterez d'un peu d'argent ou de terre.

You will inherit some money or a small piece of land.

message in French on one side of the slip, and English on the other – not in Chinese which would be product–appropriate, nor in Japanese which would be restaurant–appropriate.

The purpose of language is to convey ideas and information from one head to another. Not so easy when in English/American one drives on a parkway and parks in a driveway, plays at a recital and recites in a play. Paradoxically, what is not said [allusion, implication, innuendo] is as relevant as that which is. A process of understanding similar to the encounter between two psychoanalysts who meet on the street. When one says, 'Good morning', the other immediately thinks, 'I wonder what he means by that?'

Reuters (1995): In Furu-awa, a tiny village on the border between Cameroon and Nigeria, an 87-year-old woman croons to herself in Bikya, a language she alone understands. She often cries. All those she once knew are dead. There is no one she can talk to in the language she learnt from her parents, and there is no one left to teach.

vernissage

The Bible is translated
into 2,000 languages.
These are the world's
major languages[1] and
the number of people
who speak them:

Chinese 700,000,000
English 350,000,000
Hindustani 200,000,000
Russian 200,000,000
Spanish 160,000,000
German 100,000,000
Japanese 100,000,000
Arabic 90,000,000
Bengali 90,000,000
Portuguese 85,000,000
Malay 80,000,000
French 80,000,000
Italian 65,000,000

1. *The Last Whole Earth Catalogue.* Portola Institute (USA 1971)

John Fowles   'I adore language, and especially English with its incomparable richness. I think of that richness less as a doomed attempt to impose order on chaos than as an attempt to magnify reality.'

picturespeak

New Guinea has the highest concentration of different languages in the world. A thousand different languages crammed into an area only slightly larger than Texas with each as different from the other as English is from Chinese.[1] More than a thousand languages are spoken in Africa alone and a quarter of those in the Cameroon. To get around this the locals speak *Cameroonian pidgin*, which borrows from them all. *Pidgin* bridges languages by playing with word and image. Papua New Guinea is famous for *Pidgin English*, which is a remarkable hybrid of colonial English vocabulary and Melanesian grammar that refers to the Prince of Wales, for instance, as *number one pikanini belong Mrs Queen*, and in which a submarine is a *bottom-bottom wata waka*, and a carpenter's saw a *pull 'im he come, push 'im he go*. In *Chinese pidgin* a three-masted steamship was a *thlee piecee bamboo, two piecee puff puff, walk along inside, no can see*. As *lingua franca* it works well. Artificial languages lack vividness as they don't bring pictures to mind. For instance *Volapuk*, brainchild of Johann Schleyer (1831-1912), was so grey and complex that the first *Congress of Volapukists* was the last. *Esperanto* did rather better. Invented by Ludwig Zamenhof and introduced through his book *Lingo Internacia* (1887) authored under the pseudonym of *Doktoro Esperanto* – Doctor Hopeful. A Russian Jew brought up in Poland, he spoke Russian at home, at synagogue worshipped in Hebrew, spoke Yiddish to relatives and Polish to the villagers, and studied Greek and Latin at school. Anyway in Esperanto a helicopter is *helikoptero* while in *Papuan pidgin* it's *Mixmaster him belong Jesus Christ*. I know which I prefer. By the way the ancient Greeks called peoples who couldn't speak Greek – *Barbarians*. They spoke in strange sounds, hence their *Bar Bar* theory.

Illustration. Keith Haring   1. Jared Diamond. *Guns, Germs and Steel*. Jonathan Cape (London 1997)

bow-wow theory: that language originated in imitations of natural sounds of birds, dogs and suchlike.

ta-ta theory: that language originated from body language – wagging the tongue to say bye-bye to echo waving the hand.

yo-he-ho theory: that language originated out of physical efforts which were accompanied by rhythmical grunts and groans.

la-la theory: that language originated in chants, song and play.

pooh-pooh theory: that language originated in instinctive noises and interjections which gradually acquired a meaning.

ding-dong theory: that language originated out of the correspondences between different objects and the various noises they make.

Question : Do you speak Esperanto ? **Answer :** Like a native !

'The limits of my language mean the limits of my world.'

Ludwig Wittgenstein

In 1820 the mathematician Carl Friedrich Gauss suggested communicating with other planets by creating a gigantic Pythagorean triangle in the Siberian forests. He assumed any extraterrestrial capable of building a telescope would know the theorem. The lines were to be made by cutting ten-mile-wide swathes through the forests, and the resulting triangle and squares were to be made into vast fields. Visibility would be naturally enhanced. In summer the yellow wheat would contrast with the green trees and in winter the snow would show up against the dark forests. His idea wasn't taken up. Actually the only two man-made creations visible from outer space are the Great Wall of China (built around 214 BC and 1500 miles long), * and the Japanese fishing fleet who pour megawatts of light into the sea to attract squid. [SEE P374].

Actually, the chance of making contact by sending a message into outer space is equivalent to putting a note in a bottle and throwing it into the ocean, except that in this case the distance is inconceivably vaster. By analogy if the entire Solar System were contained in a room in San Francisco the nearest star would be in Tokyo. The first serious attempt to communicate with extraterrestrial intelligence occurred on 3 March 1972 when Pioneer 10 was launched to become the first man-made object to leave the Solar System.

Scientist Carl Sagan, realizing the opportunity, managed to persuade NASA to let him put a message on the spacecraft. Working against a tight schedule he met with astronomer Frank Drake to decide the contents. In a few hours they concocted the information and the artwork was drawn up by Sagan's wife. The message is etched on a six-by-nine-inch gold-anodized aluminium plaque, and as the rate of erosion in interstellar space is negligible it should remain intact for hundreds of millions of years … the longest expected lifetime of any man-made artefact.[1]

Carl Sagan confesses that his message (see opposite) is not the optimum conceivable for such a grand purpose but asserts the only form of communication we could possibly share with intelligence out there is science. However, accepting that science has limitations when it comes to describing human beings, he also includes representational images. The figures were not shown holding hands in case it implied they represented a single organism. After all the ancient Greeks, unfamiliar with domesticated horses, had assumed the marauding mounted Scythians were weird beasts and called them Centaurs. Social conventions and physical attributes were also fed into the design. A raised hand was intended to show greetings, the bent arm to infer flexibility and opposing thumbs to indicate grasping. The woman lacks a line, therefore sex – Sagan suspected NASA might censor the message at the last minute. Here is mankind trying to communicate to an unknown and probably superior intelligence and some bureaucrat doesn't want them to know women have vaginas.

What, I wonder, will the extra-terrestrial intelligences who encounter the message make of this visual vocabulary? Even if the digital codes could be deciphered the outerspacer would also have to interpret the imagery, and could be left with some odd deductions. Assuming the figures were identified as living things they could be construed as linear dimensionless creatures. No indication of volume by light or shade distinguishes us from the rest of the numerical and diagrammatic data. With the actual flying object in front of him the extraterrestrial might recognize its silhouette at the bottom of the diagram, but since this is shown smaller than the man's hand, might conclude humans are very large indeed.

Scientific language may be universal but without shared experience a pictorial one is not.

* Emperor Qin Shi Huang ordered The Great Wall of China to be built, ordered all books written before his reign to be burnt, and authors still living – to be killed. He had a terracotta army of 8000 men made to guard his tomb [SEE P435], created a single Chinese script, rationalized weights and measures, instituted a single currency and gave his name to the nation. Qin is pronounced Chin.

1. Carl Sagan. *The Cosmic Connection*. Anchor Press (New York 1973)   2. Steven Pinker. *How The Mind Works*. Penguin (London 1997)

Galactic Graphics. According to the *International Herald Tribune* only one in ten scientists were able to work out the message. *Scientific American* took an academic line and speculated that extraterrestrials might not have our optical sensitivity to wavelengths and therefore might be unable to even see it. Less practical criticisms included a correspondent who complained that the Space Agency spread *filth beyond our solar system.* The *Philadelphia Inquirer* reproduced the design but removed the woman's nipples and the man's sexual apparatus while the *Chicago Sun Times* concentrated on airbrushing out his genitalia. The *Catholic Review* criticized the design because *it includes everything but God* and went on to suggest that instead of a nude couple it would have been better to have shown something meaningful *like a pair of praying hands.* NASA thought the message a good idea but decided to play it safer on *Voyager,* which followed *Pioneer 10,* by just sending salutations. They popped a gold-plated copper record into the missile with greetings in some sixty languages. These are a few of them. Burma: *Are you well?* Indonesia: *Good night, ladies and gentlemen.* Turkey: *Dear Turkish-speaking friends, may the honours of the morning be on your heads.* China: *Friends of space, how are you? Have you eaten yet? Come and visit us if you have time.* Nigeria: *As you probably know my country is situated on the west coast of the continent of Africa.* In addition the recording included the sound of whale language, a twelve-minute sound essay made up of a baby's cry, a kiss, and an EEG record of the meditations of a woman in love, and ninety minutes of music sampled from the world's idioms: Mexican mariachi, Peruvian panpipes, Indian raga, a Navaho night chant, a Pygmy girl's initiation song, a Japanese shakuhachi piece, Bach, Beethoven, Mozart, Stravinsky, Louis Armstrong, and Chuck Berry singing *Johnny B$_2$ Goode.* The disk also bore a message of peace from our species to the cosmos recited by the then secretary-general of the United Nations – Kurt Waldheim. Years later it was discovered that Waldheim had spent World War II in a unit that deported the Jewish population of Salonika to Nazi death camps. *This mordant joke on us will circle the centre of the Milky Way galaxy forever.* If outerspace intelligence ever receives these messages they will correctly assume that the earth is inhabited by morons and lunatics. It is calculated that Voyager will take 90,000 years to reach the outer limits of the Galaxy.

'If you wish to converse with me, define your terms.' *Voltaire*

'Language is a virus from outer space.' *William Burroughs*

'The astronauts! ... Rotarians in outer space.' *Gore Vidal*

'Graphic design is a language not a message.' *Tibor Kalman*

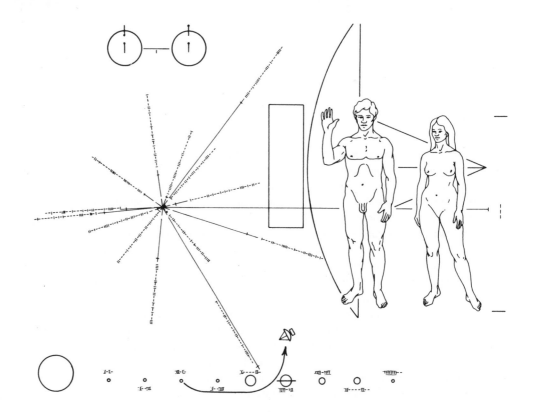

The drawing on the plaque aboard the *Pioneer 10* spacecraft.

Squid Speak. Squid talk to one another by changing their shape, colour and pattern. And giraffes (who can be heard fifty miles away), elephants and alligators, and blue whales, have infrasonic intercourse. Bees talk to each other through choreography. The honeybee flies around foraging, returns to the hive and dances a complex pattern – in darkness – to describe the direction and distance where food can be found. The other bees then take off to gather it up. The mysterious language of the gerbil has recently been translated by a scientist who has found sophisticated skills in the whistles and drumbeats used to warn of snakes and foxes. Vervet monkeys rely on different calls for different dangers. For a leopard they give one kind of call and the others take to the trees; if they see a python they make a different call and stand on their hind legs and look down; if it's an eagle they make yet another call and run for cover. If they spot an eagle when it is too late to run, they make the call for another danger – the potential victim, responding accordingly, might still stand a chance.

a bird does not **SING** *because it has an answer – it sings because it has a* **SONG**

Gibbons, the ones with long arms, are known for their haunting songs. The cadences, timbres, frequencies and amplitudes articulating territorial ownership and conveying messages or warnings can be heard a kilometre away. Each humpback whale has its own song. These can last for more than half an hour and always follow the same melody. The notes are eerie with deep basso groans and with almost inaudibly high soprano squeaks which alternate with repetitive squeals that suddenly rise or fall in pitch. Whale songs have repeating phrases that follow a structured grammar. Whales not only learn the complex language, but remember it from season to season. No one knows why. Perhaps they like singing.

'Through the chryselectric green with goatstep, ramshorns curled, sharp of eye, satyrs. Their musk precedes them, armpit and honeysuckle, quince flower descant upon a rackle of billy pizzle. Tuscan tan with the visages of Italic gods, their pentathletic torsos flow with bestial grace into dappled haunches. Stag tails frisking up from the holybone wag above the flat of narrow butts ... They can chatter with the squirrels, using squirrel words among themselves to bound their peripatesis. For time they use the vocabulary of the grey wolf, for elegy and boast the nicker and whinny of the horse, for familiar discourse a patois of birdsong, fox bark, goat bleat, and the siffle and mump of their cousins the deer.'

'The indri, largest of all surviving lemurs, is also the most spectacularly peculiar. Its neck is long, its limbs are lanky, its eyes glow yellow brown in a gawky black jackal-like face. Its ears are smallish and round, like a koala's. Although the dark-and-light pattern of its body fur suggests a giant panda, its shape is more gracile and humanoid ... The song of the indri is an unearthly sound. It carries through the forest for more than a mile. It rings in the air back at the Hotel-Buffet de la Gare. It has been said to be one of the loudest noises made by any living creature. It's a sliding howl, eerie but beautiful, like a cross between the call of a humpback whale and a saxophone riff by Charlie Parker.'

GUY DAVENPORT
Eclogues

DAVID QUAMMEN
The Song of the Dodo

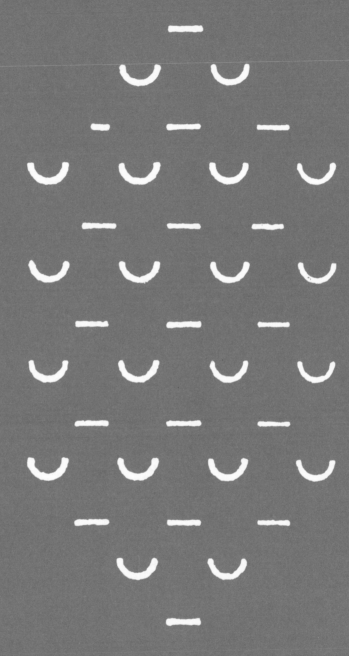

CHRISTIAN MORGENSTERN
Fisches Nachtgesang
[*Fishes' Nightsong*]

The whale moves in a sea of sound :

Shrimps snap, plankton seethes,

Fish croad, gulp, drum their air-bladders,

And are scrutinized by echo-location,

A light massage of sound

Touching the skin.

The small, toothed whales use high frequencies :

Finely tuned and focused sound-beams,

Intense salvoes of bouncing clicks, a thousand a second,

With which a hair, as thin as half a millimetre, can be detected;

Penetrating probes,

With which they can scan the contents of a colleague's stomach,

Follow the flow of their blood,

Take the full measure of an approaching brain.

From two cerebral cavities in their melon-shaped heads,

They can transmit two sonic probes, as if talking in stereo,

And send them in any direction at the same time:

One ahead, one behind, one above, one below...

Lengthening the sound-waves, shortening them, heightening them,

Until their acoustic switchboard receives the intelligence required.

Spoken to in English,

The smallest cetacean, the dolphin,

Will rise to the surface,

Alter its vocal frequencies to suit the measures of human speech,

Pitch its voice to the same level as that of human sounds

When travelling through air — an unfamiliar medium —

Adjust the elastic lips of its blow-hole,

And then, after courteously waiting for silence,

Produce a vibrato imitation of human language:

Words, phrases, sentences ...

Heathcote Williams *Whale Nation*. Jonathan Cape (London 1988)

Seeing Voices[1]

There have been many kinds of handsign languages. Some invented for secrecy (Druids), some to transcend language barriers (Red Indian, Mayan, Aborigine), some by monastic orders with vows of silence, and some by the deaf or dumb. These gesture systems range from simple transliterations of spoken languages to those which are languages in themselves like American Sign Language (ASL).

ASL is commonly called **Sign**.

Sign has its own poetry and songs. There are **Sign** story-tellers, **Sign** actors, **Sign** playwrights, and of course **Sign** bores.

In Martha's Vineyard, an island off Nantucket, the community was founded 250 years ago by a group of deaf settlers from Kent, a county in the south of England. Everyone, including those who weren't deaf, used **Sign**. The last deaf member died in 1952 but the elderly still use **Sign** when it suits them, or tourists are around. As Oliver Sachs explains, *'They would chat in* **Sign** *(it was much better than spoken language in many ways: for communicating across a distance, for instance, from one fishing boat to another, or for gossiping in church), debate in* **Sign***, teach in* **Sign***, think and dream in* **Sign***.'*

Sign is not a substitute for speech but an altogether different method of communication. The closest comparison is the cinema, when the camera sequence cuts from a middle view to a close-up, to a distant shot, to a close up, to flashback and flashforward. *Encyclopaedia Britannica (14th edn.)* puts it this way: Communicating by gestures is much more than *'a species of picture writing in the air'*. [SEE P466].

EROTIC
SURREALIST
HANDSIGNS

1 ACCOST
2 BURGLE
3 CUNNILINGUATE
4 DEFLOWER
5 ENSNARE
6 FUCK
7 GALLIVANT
8 HARASS
9 IRRUMATE
10 JISMIFY
11 KINK
12 LESBIANIZE
13 MASTURBATE
14 NIDIFY
15 OCCULT
16 PEDICATE
17 QUENCH
18 REAM
19 SYPHILIZE
20 TUP
21 URTICATE
22 VIOLATE
23 WAGGLE
24 XIPHIOIDIFY
25 YONINIZE
26 ZOOGONIZE
27 RECOMMENCE

1. Oliver Sachs. *Seeing Voices*. Picador (London 1991)

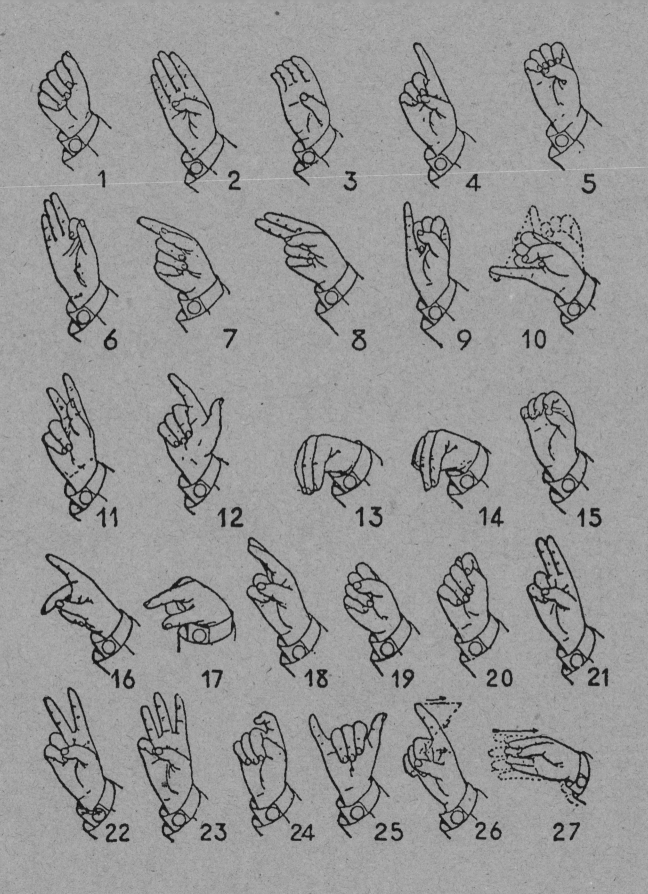

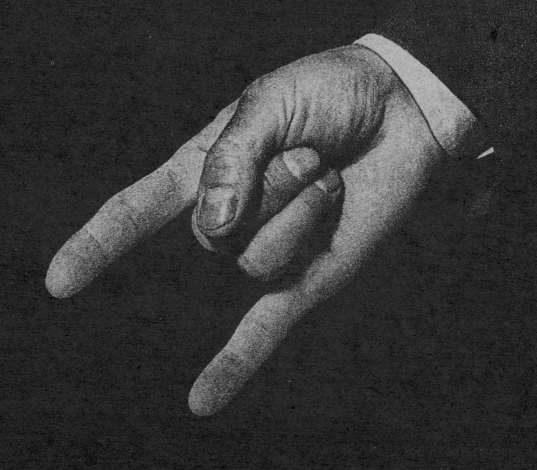

The Italian gesture known as *LA CORNA* (the horn) wards off a curse or the evil eye in much the same way as touching wood hopefully averts a disaster.

George Orwell   'All art is propaganda; on the other hand, not all propaganda is art.'

They said,
'You have a blue guitar,
You do not play things
as they are.'

The man replied,
'Things as they are
Are changed
upon the blue guitar.'

The Man with the Blue Guitar. Wallace Stevens's poetic meditation on a Picasso painting

Advertisement. From an in-flight magazine

Rhetoric, the art of persuasion, influences reason and emotion through particular associations for particular audiences in particular situations. In advertising rhetoric is all. After all, as it has been famously described, advertising is the science of arresting human intelligence long enough to separate it from money. If the advertisement doesn't stimulate or provoke desires it isn't likely to persuade anyone to do or buy anything. As the adage has it: *'Doing business without advertising is like winking at a woman in the dark.'* In other words, although you know what you're doing, nobody else does.

The ill-conceived advertisement can also backfire. A classy French perfume company discovered to its horror that the cheap end of the market thought of *their* scent when asked which brand they preferred. Further research revealed that so-called working-class women weren't keen on jazz. From then on the company only played jazz in television and radio commercials.

I was looking at a television discussion panel addressing the issues of waste, money, persuasion, coercion, and so forth in the techniques employed by commercial supermarket packaging. One of the audience kept banging on about manufacturers spending more on container than contents, the need to return to plain paper bags, and so on. The argument is regularly aired. Personally I was more entertained by the way he'd packaged himself: a claret coloured shirt, olive green corduroy jacket, blue jeans and white running shoes.

Every morning (during the 1950s) advertising doyen David Ogilvy (Ogilvy & Mather) used to pass a beggar in Central Park who had a sign round his neck which said BLIND . One morning Ogilvy stopped, took it off the man's neck, and wrote: IT IS SPRING AND I AM BLIND . And hung it back. On his way home he was pleased to notice that the vagrant had a full cap.

Prosaic information can also be rhetorical. Two examples come to mind: When Dorothy Parker was a young struggling writer working out of a small publisher's office in New York, she was so lonely that she lettered MEN on her door. A sandal, once worn by a prostitute in ancient Athens, had a message studded on the sole which imprinted an invitation in the dust – FOLLOW ME. Less entertainingly the huge signs on skyscrapers in Hong Kong are stationary as they aren't permitted to flicker or flash to avoid confusing aircraft which land close by. For the same reason signs in Nathan Road advertising BOOBY TRAPS, STRIP SHOWS and LIVE SEX are also static. There is something depressing about LIVE SEX which doesn't pulsate, flash, glitter, or even twinkle.

Then there is political rhetoric which, wrote Orwell, '... *is designed to make lies sound truthful and murder respectable, and to give an appearance of solidity to pure wind.'* And diplospeak, which like pretentious art catalogues, speaks volumes to make others believe that you believe what you don't believe. Diplomats [to the mannerism born] are expected to think twice before saying nothing. In this world chameleon and weasel words are useful. A chameleon word changes tone to conform to the prejudices of the other party, a weasel word sucks the meaning out of the words to which it is attached.

'It is not enough to conquer;' said Voltaire; *'one must know how to seduce.'*

OVER
STATED
UNDER

Rhetoric is an essential component of visual language. For instance the *Chanel No. 5* pack, dressed with thin black edging and restrained typography, projects classy [superior] understatement …

… fragrance rather than smell.

Detergent packs use a surplus of visual arm-waving and typographic exhortation to be distinctly unsophisticated and deliberately commonplace.

Both approaches are carefully tailored.

In 1936 a Copenhagen haberdasher hung excess inventory around his shop to create a spectacular display. It caught the imagination of the local press: 'By the time the harassed policeman had convinced the storekeeper that his coats must come down', read the newspaper caption, 'they had all been sold!'

It's not *what* you say but *how* you say it. Something the advertising profession calls *tone of voice* …

the bait must suit the fish not the angler.

N°5

CHANEL

PARIS

PARFUM

'Everybody in advertising is blonde, beautiful, families are happy, cars are never in traffic, everything is shiny, food looks like it's incredibly tasteful. I ask myself, "How stupid are we? How come the world is going one direction and advertising is going in a completely different direction?"'

OLIVIERO TOSCANI

'If you keep shouting, you are not making communication any better. You only remove talking and whispering from the system. I find our society a bit noisy. I just would like to contribute a little silence.'

BRUNO MONGUZZI

'The codfish lays a thousand eggs
The homely hen lays one
The codfish never cackles
To tell you what she's done
And so we scorn the codfish
While the humble hen we prize
Which only goes to show you
That it pays to advertise.'

ANON

'Catalogues, posters, advertisements of all sorts … contain the poetry of our epoch.' *Guillaume Apollinaire*

'News is what somebody somewhere wants to suppress. Everything else is advertising.' *Lord Northcliffe*

'Advertising is the rattling of a stick inside a swill bucket.' *George Orwell*

'Advertising is persuasion, graphic design is information.' *James Cross*

'Advertising and business are also elements of poetry.' *Tristan Tzara*

Design. Coco Chanel c.1925

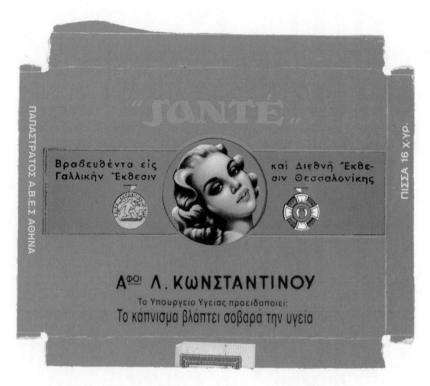

SANTÉ is a Greek cigarette pack reassuringly called HEALTH (oxymoron), in French (chic).
The two medallions are endorsements (approval). The graphic image implies the smokers
are young (desirable) and beautiful (blonde) and with the tilt of the head (alluring), very
– *la Jeunesse dorée* (trendy).

KELLY'S DIRECTORIES listed every person at every number of every street in every town. They also listed every trade, profession and service. I found these two on a dusty bookshelf in a local hotel. I stole them for graphic posterity – here they are …

'Historians and archaeologists will discover that the advertisements of our time are the richest and most faithful reflections that any society ever made of its entire range of activities.'
Marshall McLuhan

'**Eloquence,** *n*. A method of convincing fools. The art is commonly presented under the visible aspect of a bald-headed little man gesticulating above a glass of water.' (*The Devil's Dictionary*)

WILLIAM BLAKE

TIGER, TIGER WITH REFULGENT CONFLAGRATION

IN THE NOCTURNAL AFFORESTATION,

KINDLY PROVIDE DETAILS REGARDING

NATURE OF SUPERNATURAL DEITY

RESPONSIBLE FOR YOUR DESIGN AND TECHNOLOGY

A BUREAUCRAT

The fierce dog appears on an ancient Roman mosaic at the entrance to the HOUSE OF THE TRAGIC POET in the ruins of Pompeii. The Latin inscription *CAVE CANEM* translates into BEWARE OF THE DOG. The oldest directional road sign in Britain (1680) is a wooden post near Tewkesbury in Gloucestershire known as the TEDDINGTON HANDS – and here is a contemporary New York City traffic sign.

DON'T EVEN THINK OF PARKING HERE

DEPT OF TRANSPORTATION

BURMA-SHAVE signs are a part of American advertising folklore. Born in the Depression, they lasted until the early 1960s. The advertisements were on four to six boards nailed on poles positioned a hundred feet apart along the verges of country roads. Each board carried part of a droll slogan. *'During my college years,'* recalls one nostalgic motorist, *'we drove every September from Oysterville, Washington, to Redlands, California … returning every June … The one assured and unalloyed pleasure on those trips were the* BURMA-SHAVE *signs.'*[1] There was never any question of drivers and passengers not reading them. The signs were specifically aimed at Mom, Pop and kids, travelling along at thirty to forty miles an hour. Humour in advertising during the Depression was as scarce as a trace element. Burma-Shave were the exception. Their success was engagement, as to figure out the message you had to participate.

There was remonstration:

SLOW DOWN, PA | SAKES ALIVE | MA | MISSED SIGNS FOUR | AND FIVE.

There was drama:

BEN | MET ANNA | MADE A HIT | NEGLECTED BEARD | BEN-ANNA SPLIT.

Or warning:

HE LIT A MATCH | TO CHECK GAS TANK | THAT'S WHY | THEY CALL HIM | SKINLESS FRANK.

Or philosophy:

IF HARMONY | IS WHAT YOU CRAVE | THEN GET | A TUBA | BURMA-SHAVE.

Or advice:

DON'T TAKE | A CURVE | AT 60 PER | WE HATE TO LOSE | A CUSTOMER.

Or trade:

MY JOB IS KEEPING | FACES CLEAN | AND NOBODY KNOWS | DE STUBBLE I'VE SEEN.

Or punning:

HER CHARIOT | RACED AT 80 PER | THEY HAULED AWAY | WHAT HAD | BEN HUR.

NOW CA

EVERYSHA

1. Willard R. Espy. *An Almanac of Words at Play*. Clarkson N. Potter (New York 1975)

BY USING

THAN BEFORE

SIX MORE MINUTES

AN SNORE

VER

9.2.1982 Newport, Wales: the indoor market
Three brown doors: one labelled GENTLEMEN, one
labelled LADIES, one labelled TROUT.
Ian Breakwell's Diary. 1964-1985

Imagine strolling down a country road and coming across this sign, daubed in paint on a weather-beaten board. It expresses far more than the immediate message. It also says: 'I'm a farmer, my chickens run around freely, and the eggs were probably laid today.' It is evocative and appropriate . . .

FRE2H
FARM
EGGS

FREE FLYING LESSONS

... walking further along the road you come across another sign, equally crude

and daubed in paint on a weather-beaten board tacked on a leaning wood post.

It also says: **'you'd be out of your mind to even think about it.'**

five inflexions:

Those who sketch timidly
achieve nothing at all.
Only clear-cut illustration, verging on
caricature, makes any impact.
Do you imagine that Peter of Amiens
managed to drum up the First Crusade
simply by mentioning to a friend,
perhaps whilst picking strawberries,
that Christ's grave had fallen
into neglect and one ought
to provide a fence around it?

Theodor Fontane

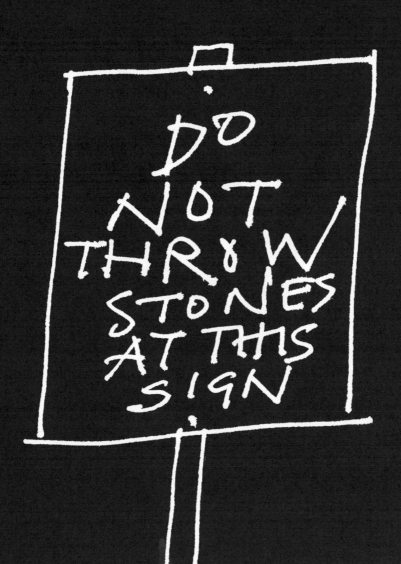

DO
NOT
THROW
STONES
AT THIS
SIGN

instructional

Sign. Displayed in the aircraft toilets of British Airways   **Poster.** By Fougasse. Issued by the British Government in the 1940s **[SEE** P497**]**

confrontational

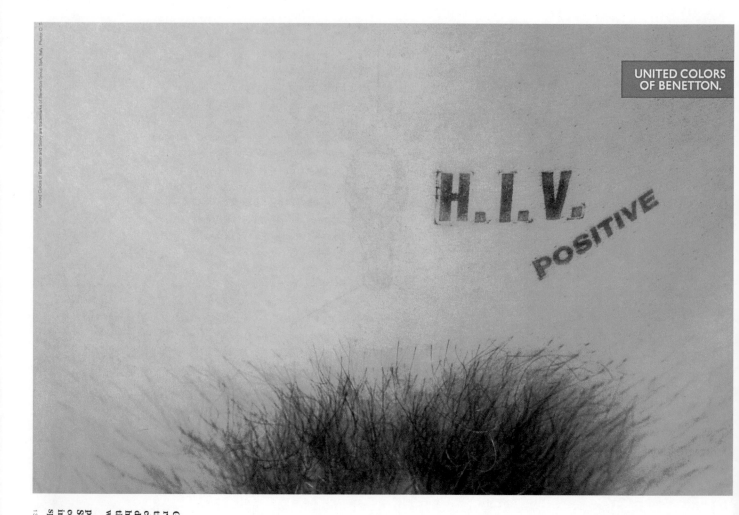

UNITED COLORS OF BENETTON.

H.I.V.
POSITIVE

Germany's highest court ruled yesterday that advertisements by the Italian clothes retailer Benetton displaying photos of human limbs stamped with the words "HIV Positive" were not indecent.

It upheld an appeal by the publisher of the magazine Stern against a 1995 lower court ruling, saying the ruling breached rules on free speech. *Reuters, Karlsruhe*

judgemental

Judgement Day
7946 0009

Poster. Benetton advertising campaign by Oliviero Toscani   **Card.** I found this card advertising a particular kind of personal service in a telephone box outside King's Cross station

THE
ARK
*DESIGNED
BY AN AMATEUR*

THE
TITANIC
DESIGNED
BY AN EXPERT

Asked whether he designed for pleasure or function, *Charles Eames* responded ...

… 'Who ever said pleasure wasn't functional?'

According to designer Bruce Archer's great aunt the catchy phrase **'the three Rs'** (reading, writing and 'rithmetic) was coined in the early nineteenth century by an illiterate member of Parliament speaking on an issue of education.[1] This phrase, the great aunt informed him, was a misquotation of an earlier aphorism: **Reading and writing, reckoning and figuring, wroughting and wrighting**. From **reading and writing** we get **LITERACY,** from **reckoning and figuring** comes **NUMERACY.** But we have no equivalent term for **wroughting and wrighting** – the creation and making of things. At one time back in the 1950s there was an effort to introduce the term **Technics** but the only word in current use is **Design** – spelt with a capital **D**. The habit of calling a finished product a **Design** is convenient but wrong. **Design** is what you do, not what you've done.

1. Bruce Archer in *The Guardian*, 1 March 1982

'No, Watson,' said Sherlock Holmes, 'this was not done by accident, but by design.' Design is what happens between conceiving an idea and fashioning the means to carry it out. Whether big stuff like painting a picture, making a movie, creating a commercial enterprise, or small stuff like rearranging the living room furniture. In short designing is what goes on in order to arrive at an intelligent equation between purpose and construction, thus converting a problem into an opportunity.

The British Design Council published fifty definitions of design. The most direct came from a ten-year-old who said: 'Design is important because if it were not designed it would not be made.' Surprisingly, a few people also earn their living by giving form to the amenities of life, in manufacture, communication and place. They call themselves designers. They are the blue-collar workers of the art world.

Whereas painters are concerned with solving their own problems the designer's role is to solve other people's problems. Actually that's an oversimplification, the real issue is the *elegance* of the solution which solves the problem. That is a personal challenge rather than a utilitarian discipline. A commitment rather than an involvement. A difference exemplified by ham and eggs, in which the pig is totally committed whereas the chicken is merely involved.

Designers derive their rewards from 'inner standards of excellence, from the intrinsic satisfaction of their tasks. They are committed to the task, not the job. To their standards, not their boss.'[1] So whereas most people divide their lives between time spent earning money and time spent spending it, designers generally lead a seamless existence in which work and play are synonymous. As Milanese designer Richard Sapper put it: 'I never work – all the time.'

1. Alvin Toffler. *Future Shock.* Pan (London 1970)
Illustration. Fougasse

The word design is meaningless, wrote a friend, the idea it covers is too vast and for most people inaccessible. It is really reverse entropy, or rather the opposite of that when entropy is the measure. I am afraid that, in the end, only philosophy and theology offer adequate terms to discuss the matter. *Ummm.* Vasari … [Design is] the animating principle of all creative processes. Herr Rosenthal … There is no design in a turbine, fifty per cent design in a teapot and a hundred per cent in a man's tie. Misha Black … an essential component which can no more be excluded from manufacture than stress calculations, production planning or public relations. Trevanian … a mental habit of seeing things simultaneously in their narrowest details and their broadest implications. Abraham Moles … to increase the legibility of the world. Arthur Pulos … a way to achieve a new ecology of the artificial environment. Ralph Caplan … the artful arrangement of materials or circumstances into a planned form. Kenji Ekuan … giving shape to man's dream. Buckminster Fuller … The opposite of design is chaos. Victor Papanek … the conscious effort to impose meaningful order. Roger Tallon … first and foremost an attitude. Jens Bernsen … translating a purpose into a physical form or tool. Leo Lionni … the power to command and hold attention, to create symbols, to clarify ideas. Wim Crouwel … pure form chosen to serve a particular function. Bruno Monguzzi … the instrument through which communication is accomplished. Stephen Jay Gould … expressed by correspondence between an organizer's form and an engineer's blueprint. Bruce Archer … a goal-directed problem-solving activity. Robert Brownjohn … concepts and ideas rather than abstractions and decorations. Art Kane … putting flesh on the spirit. László Moholy-Nagy … the integration of technological, social and economic requirements, biological necessities, and the psychophysical effects of materials, shape, colour, volume and space. Vernon Barber … the antithesis of accident. George Nelson … a process of relating everything to everything. Emilio Ambasz … to give poetic form to the pragmatic. Charles Handy … design is not just about survival and profitability, it is about making a difference for the better. Ettore Sottsass ... design is debating life. April Greiman ... seduce, shape, and perhaps more importantly, evoke emotional response. Jorge Frascara ... about the welfare of humanity. Stephen Bayley ... imposing meaning on the chaos of the market place. Isaac Asimov ... decision making, in the face of uncertainty, with high penalties for error. Le Corbusier ... good design is intelligence made visible. Saul Bass ... Design is thinking made visual. Tibor Kalman ... the difference between good design and great design is intelligence. Adrian Forty ... No design works unless it embodies ideas that are held in common by the people for whom the object is intended. Peter Gorb ... a plan to make something. Lionel Tiger ... If designers are highly etched people perhaps it is because they have a compound struggle – to create the function which they must then advertise themselves as being able to perform. Issey Miyake ... The designer is not an artist. If the clothes are not worn then the work is not finished. Hans Schleger ... It can give shape to thought and feeling as the glass does to wine. Eiko Ishioka ... There are no boundaries between artists and designers. Bruno Munari ... a planner with an aesthetic sense. Milton Glaser ... essentially a person who makes understandable, elements that are not as understandable without his participation. Buckminster Fuller ... an emerging synthesis of artist, inventor, mechanic, objective economist and evolutionary strategist. Ivan Chermayeff ... a borrower, co-ordinator, assimilator, juggler, and collector of material, knowledge and thought from the past and present. Ralph Caplan ... Engineers make things work; industrial designers make them workable. Lionel Tiger ... mere function is fine for armies but life is not altogether a war, industrial designers are the artists of our system and must, as it were, provide the spice as well as the nutrition. Giulio Carlo Argan ... those who forgo design accept being designed. Harry Bertoia ... The urge for good design is the same as the urge to go on living. The assumption is that somewhere, hidden, is a better way of doing things. Andre Toet ... Fuck design, let's dance.

Question

What's the difference between an interior decorator and an interior designer?

Answer

Only a degree or two.

JOURNALIST:

How did you
arrive upon
the image
of a toad
for work
or labour?

PHILIP LARKIN:

Sheer genius!

Marianne Moore
called poetry
an imaginary garden
inhabited with
real **toads**

Ralph Caplan
called design
a real garden
inhabited with
imaginary **toads**

…and suggested the designer's role
is to realize the toads.

MOST THINK OF DESIGN IN TERMS OF PUTTING LIPSTICK ON A GORILLA

POOR DESIGN IS MAKING SOMETHING WORTHLESS

Design is not merely manipulating forms and shapes, spaces and volumes, or playing with pen and paper, mouse and screen. Design is applied thought, a sensual activity as well as a cerebral exercise. As Ralph Caplan nostalgically recalled, the most elegant design solution of the 1950s was not a predictable classic : the moulded plywood chair, the Olivetti Lettera 22 typewriter, the Chapel at Ronchamp; it was the SIT-IN. *'Achieved'*, he writes, *'with a stunning economy of means, and a complete understanding of the function intended and the resources available … a form beautifully suited to its urgent task.'* Yet economy isn't always the criterion. The score for John Cage's *First Construction in Metal* called for a piano with a metal rod across the strings, tubular and sleigh bells, 12 oxen bells, eight cow bells, five thunder sheets, four brakedrums, four Turkish and four Chinese cymbals, three Japanese temple gongs, four muted and one suspended gong, four muted anvils and

GOOD DESIGN IS MAKING SOMETHING INTELLIGIBLE AND MEMORABLE

a tam-tam. This concoction, one critic thought, sounded like *'an ill-assorted collection of poorly-matching parts forming a distressing whole'*. Graphic, product and fashion design are merely some of the spheres inhabited by specialists with a particular bent and skill. Few turn their abilities to a variety of purposes. Notable exceptions include Brunelleschi who designed the dome of Florence Cathedral [**SEE** P146] as well as devising a scheme to defeat Lucca by changing the course of the River Serchio. Michelangelo designed the fortifications of Florence, the bridge over the Arno [**SEE** P146], the ceiling of the Sistine Chapel, the uniforms for Vatican Swiss Guards. Leonardo painted the Mona Lisa [**SEE** P283] and designed canals and arsenals for the Duke of Milan. John Logie Baird thought up the super-insulated undersock, mango jam and television. And Oberlandesbaudirektor Schinkel (Supreme Director of Public Buildings) designed palaces, churches, museums,

GREAT DESIGN IS MAKING SOMETHING MEMORABLE AND MEANINGFUL

theatres, bridges, warehouses, stoves, vases, beds, tables and chairs. His bronze and marble tables could give you a hernia just looking at them, but he also produced an elegant birchwood cane chair you could lift with one finger. Then there was Buckminster Fuller who designed dymaxion domes, an automobile, container ships, airplanes, and a lot more besides. Modestly he described himself as '… engineer, poet, architect, inventor, mathematician, cartographer, philosopher, cosmogonist, comprehensive designer and choreographer'. He also gave his name to a carbon particle – a Buckminsterfullerene – shown below. *'Failure in design is honourable,'* he noted, but, *'in science and engineering a mark of incompetence, and in politics and finance ruinous.'* And what is good design ? André Breton knew : *'The solution best adapted to necessity, but very superior to it.'* I go with that.

EXCEPTIONAL DESIGN IS MAKING SOMETHING MEANINGFUL AND WORTHWHILE*

A designer has to have the hide of a rhinoceros, the neck of a giraffe, the memory of an elephant and the persistence of a woodpecker.

'In my experience if you have to keep the lavatory door shut by extending your left leg, it's modern architecture.'

Nancy Banks Smith

'Architecture, probably more than any other form of art, should be considered as three-dimensional philosophy.'

Berthold Lubetkin

'Architecture is fantasy made of precisions.'

Gio Ponti

'We shape our buildings; thereafter they shape us.'

Winston Churchill

'Architecture is to masonry what poetry is to literature.'

Anon

'Never invest your money in anything that eats or needs repainting.'

Billy Rose

'Most modern buildings hate people.'

Joseph Rykwert

'A house is a machine for living in.'

Le Corbusier

'There are three arts – painting, music and ornamental pastry-making; of the last, architecture is a sub-division.'

A pastry cook

'Architecture is, and always will be concerned, roughly speaking, with carefully balancing horizontal things on top of vertical things.'

Reyner Banham

'I do not believe architecture should speak too much. It should remain silent and let nature in the guise of sunlight and wind speak.'

Tadao Ando

'From the sound of stone comes the silence of space.'

Richard England

'The history of architecture is the history of the world.'

Vincent Scully

'All architecture is great after sunset.'

G.K. Chesterton

'Music, perspective, architecture, etc, Embroider time, embroider space.'

Joseph Joubert

'One who drafts a plan of your house, and plans a draft of your money.'

Ambrose Bierce

'No architecture is so haughty as that which is simple.'

John Ruskin

Photograph. Fisherman's shack, Stavros beach, Crete

Designing is not capricious arrangement.

Freedom of expression is not anarchy.

Understanding the nature of new materials is not an exercise in novelty.

Good design is innovative

Functional form is not streamlining.

Gives a product utility

Order, discipline and proportion are not a Greek monopoly.

Is aesthetic

Simplicity is not nudity.

Makes a product easy to understand

'Space' does not mean empty space, nor is 'space articulation' the arbitrary placement of things in a void.

Is unobtrusive

Sensitivity is not fussiness nor is it preciousness.

Is honest

Glass bricks do not a modern house make.

Is long-lived

Lower-case letters and sans serif do not make modern typography.

Is consistent down to the smallest detail

Montage is not synthesized confusion.

Protects the environment

Cropping and bleeding are not the prerogative of a Bluebeard.

Good design is as little design as possible.

Texture is not exclusively a physical experience.

Paul Rand   **Dieter Rams**

Note. A marketing manager, resentful at being told by the Chairman that he had to see me, made his position clear. 'I know nothing about design,' he said, 'furthermore, I don't want anything to do with it.' He was kitted out in a chalk stripe brown suit, a distressed patterned tie, wore spectacles the colour of stewed glue, sat behind a tacky reproduction antique desk, and worked in a room to match. I believed him and left.

James Souttar: 'The surface of design may change according to fashion and device, but a human heart lies constantly within. For whether an idea is given form through earth pigments on the wall of a cave, sooty inks in a vaulted scriptorium, chunks of lead in a Venetian print shop, or bits and bytes on a Mac, that form is founded on enduring principles of emotion and understanding.'

Milton Glaser: 'The problem of abstract art when applied to graphic design, is that it eliminates the deepest and most useful means of communication, which are, in fact, the ones contained in simple images: birds, fishes, fruits, the sky. The images that are well known by everybody are those that have the power to evoke and communicate. Abstract art offers our work very useful elements, such as compounds; nevertheless, I would never compare them to the force that can be found in the shapes that we are all capable of recognizing.'

Anders Knutsen (President, Bang & Olufsen)**:** 'Design is a language. A way to tell a story. A story about a company or a story about a specific product ... Design is an emotional language. People do not buy based on reason or common sense, only. People feel for a product. And based on their feelings they decide whether it meets their expectations or not.'

Michael Bierut: '... we become designers because at some point in our lives we draw a picture, or combine words and images, or visualize an idea, and experience what might be called the thrill of creation – something didn't exist; now it does, and I made it happen.'

Misha Black: 'The job of the industrial designer is to produce useful and agreeable objects, but he can, at the least, make them express the living vigorous aspects of that society and not vacuously mirror its lowly common denominators.'

Lester Beall: 'The way a man lives is essential to the work he produces, the two cannot be separated.'

Ralph Caplan: 'If more designers had bad backs, we would have more good chairs.'

Zuzana Licko: 'The integration of previously isolated disciplines makes computer-aided design a seamless continuum of activity similar to that experienced by children. In fact, computer technology has advanced the state of graphic art by such a quantum leap into the future that it has brought the designer back to the most primitive of graphic ideas and methods. This return to our primeval ideas allows us to reconsider the basic assumptions made in the creative design process, bringing excitement and creativity to aspects of design that have been forgotten since the days of letterpress.'

Stephen Bayley: 'Design is about a quest for standards, a way of imposing meaning on the chaos of the market place, of adding value to eyesight and grey cells as much as the bottom line. Good designers want to change ugly and inappropriate objects, signs and environments. They want to make their clients more beautiful, their customers more happy, themselves more satisfied. But equally, good designers also recognize when something does not need fixing: Frascati's Aldobrandini Gardens, to take an example ... '

Alastair Reid (written in 1960)**:** 'Dear design – if we dare leave the word in simple type, uncoloured, unphotographed, undressed – is still in its brawling infancy, which means that, as it approaches the difficult years of its adolescence, we may expect to see words running visually wild – aeroplanes writing SMOKE in the sky, ties which say TIE all over themselves, legions of children forming the word OOOH on a mile-long chocolate bar, photographed from a helicopter, and eventually, at design's coming-out party, a great multicoloured firework display which goes off and blurts the word FIREWORKS into the night.'

Ginger: He's a product designer, who once shoved a prototype of a foodmixer into my hand. 'What do you think?' he enthusiastically asked. I thought the colour tepid and the form banal, but took a moment, toying around in my head, to find a diplomatic response. Unable to contain himself he impatiently exclaimed, 'It's too light, not heavy enough in the hand. Don't you agree?' Gratefully I did. Ginger was right. What you feel about things depends on where you're coming from.

A.G. Fronzoni: 'Design must not be understood as a simple professional activity, but it is primarily a way of life, a way of relating oneself to life, and a choice of behaviour. A design's most profound meaning is not so much that of building a house, but primarily building ourselves. And I also tell these young people that the design of their existence is the commitment which must be their main preoccupation; this commitment has to be continuous and total, not transitory and relative.'

Form versus function: James McNeill Whistler, after dining with friends, was descending the stairs to leave when he staggered and almost fell headlong. 'Who,' he demanded, designed the staircase?' 'Norman Shaw,' replied his host. 'Damned teetotaller!' was the outraged response.

Body Count: The term 'parting shot' is derived from the Parthian tactic of pretending to retreat by riding away, and then turning in the saddle to zap the unsuspecting pursuers with arrows. George Nelson: 'In 53 BC, Marcus Cassius, Roman proconsul of Syria, invaded Parthia with 40,000 men and the general idea of extending the Empire as far as India. The result was total disaster, largely because of the design of the Parthian bow, a weapon built like a laminated spring, with such range and power that the Roman legions were helpless against it. The body count, if you will excuse the expression, was 20,000 dead and 10,000 prisoners, not because the Parthians had a better general – but because they had a better designer.'

MAKESHIFT SHELTERS
Federal Office of Civil Defence, Switzerland

This book explains in comprehensive terms the technical specifications necessary for erecting temporary or makeshift shelters such as would, in the opinion of Swiss experts, be suitable in the event of a nuclear accident or attack.

Hardback   ISBN 0 863040 28 4   £14.95

'I like work –
it fascinates me –
I can sit and look
at it for hours.'

JEROME K. JEROME

Gold mining consists of shifting three tons of rubbish for each ounce of gold extracted.

Cerebral Acrobatics. Trying to explain how to ride a bicycle is notoriously difficult; the same distance lies between experience and theory in describing the design process. To my mind defining design as problem solving smacks more of routine procedures than creative thinking. What really motivates designers is the pleasure of playing around with problems. That's a private game, so if you ask a designer how they came up with an idea, you'll probably hear what they think you expect to hear. [They are too embarrassed to confess they've enjoyed mucking around with whatever it is.] Anything from 'it just popped up in the head' to 'levitating by reversing polarities like a llama'. Design is what happens between the thought and the action. I try to sum up the situation, back in edgeways, cut against the bias, and cast around for ideas on which to hang further ideas. It's an intuitive process involving search, discovery, recognition, evaluation, rejection or development. There are no specific rules or recipes. One might slip through a sequence of actions in seconds or sweat through step by step. Start backwards, move randomly from one point to another, or do what surfers call 'hang ten' – get your toes into the board and ride the waves. However, there are some essential conditions. A capacity for cerebral acrobatics so the mind can juggle while freewheeling around the possibilities. A mind-set which has the credulity of a child, the dedication of an evangelist and the spadework of a navvy. Above all a motivation to keep on trying and being prepared to kiss a lot of frogs before finding a prince. All of which is dedicated to one end. To achieve that 'condensation of sensations' which, Matisse said, 'constitutes a picture'.

If you can't ride two horses at the same time you shouldn't be in the circus.

'... for me banana leaves and boxes are the same thing.' Ettore Sottsass

The Peeling Onion Strategy. **A method of exposing hidden potentials by peeling the subject apart, layer by layer. Italo Calvino introduces this strategy in a story in which Marco Polo challenges Kubla Khan to look beyond treating his empire as an abstract chessboard. He points out that in addition to the individual values of the pawns and castles, there is the delicate carving of the ivory pieces and the subtle texture of the wooden board itself. Each square of the pattern contains a unique trace of a previous condition: the fibres indicating it was cut from a tree in a year of drought; the hint of a knot suggesting it was planted in the spring, the faint ring signifying the tree's age. The original plank from which it had been cut identifies the kind of forest – ebony or mahogany – where the tree grew, and the colour and resins indicate the rivers which brought the logs down from the hills of the imperial kingdom. Peeling reveals and informs.**

A Hungarian Recipe [**How to make an omelette: First … steal a chicken, then …].** **Frogmen of the mind, as Marshall McLuhan called motivational researchers, are regarded with grave suspicion in alarmist literature. However, their activities could be considered an aspect of ergonomics; the emotional relationship between man and product. Big in the 1950s, consumer psychology has long since gone into decline although merchandising still echoes with theories such as 'the average gaze of the average consumer glancing along a shelf in a supermarket rests on each pack for less than 0.3 seconds.' For that fleeting moment the pack has to attract attention and plant a deep desire in the shopper's psyche. Naturally commercial enterprises are interested in maximizing this opportunity. One of my first jobs was working in a studio run by a brilliant Hungarian. He always tested and presented new pack designs through a set of contraptions controlled with knobs. One was a large glass-fronted box which held packs of milk, beans, cereals, and was used to demonstrate degrees of legibility under different lighting conditions. For example, illuminating with fluorescents changed some colours and eliminated others – bad news in retail environments. Another box subjected packs to stroboscopic effects – now you see it, blink and then you don't. Another revolved packs to show branding at oblique and acute angles. All of this was directed towards maximizing presence in the 0.3 seconds. As presentation techniques they worked a treat and I don't remember a client ever turning down a proposal. Actually, when the old boy wasn't looking, we would pick the design we preferred and adjust the knobs to suit. Oscar Wilde provided the studio motto: 'It's only shallow people who don't judge by appearances.' Anyway to avoid losing the game why not change the rules?**

McDonald's Corollary to Murphy's Law. **In any given set of circumstances, the proper course of action is determined by subsequent events.** [SEE P152].

Note. For some design is an unreliable form of art while research is a scientific fact. I had a client who enthusiastically received the design of a logotype, but insisted on undertaking extensive consumer research to reassure himself. I thought it a waste of time and money. Had he heard about the Hollywood studio which was considering making a movie of a particular play? He hadn't. Well they picked on a typical community — say Colombus, Ohio — and went around asking people if they would like to see a movie about murder and incest. Apparently they wouldn't. They made Hamlet anyway. My client still did his consumer survey.

Blue skies & GREY BOXES

Basically there are two kinds of designer:

Helicopters and VENDING MACHINES.

The helicopters fly around the landscape

zooming in to investigate, backing off to get a better panoramic view.

On the other hand VENDING MACHINES tend to be INERT

until someone shoves money in the slot.

They then produce a lot of buzzing, WHIRRING and clanking,

until out pops a PRODUCT.

It is invariably the same as the previous one, and will be the same as the next.

The only difference is the next is usually staler.

I borrowed this analogy from the late Jay Doblin. I hope he doesn't mind.

'... if you want the rainbow, you gotta put up with the rain.'   Dolly Parton

If you're in a hole don't keep digging – look around. Then get the bits and pieces into some kind of order so as to point up the problem. Sometimes it comes easy, other times it's like confining jelly with a rubber band. Anyway, once achieved, the next move is to head off along the most promising route. The solution may become evident or you can end up in an exasperating period of hiatus when, despite trying this and that, the answer remains elusive. Hopefully the germ of an idea eventually peeps through, but before leaping on it with relief let it incubate for a while. Here the mind works on the idea in some mysterious way. Either the potential evaporates, in which case you have to start all over again, or it emerges [said Henry James] with 'a firm iridescent surface, and a notable increase in weight'. Designing looks easy if you don't know how, difficult if you do.

The art of thinking by jumping

PETER MAYLE

In the bad old days, corporate commitment to design largely consisted of lip service and the occasional new logotype. Public awareness was correspondingly low, with a general feeling that 'design' was something of an élitist vice, available from Scandinavian furniture makers or excitable men from Milan with access to unlimited quantities of free-form plastic. The designer was left to work in relative peace and anonymity, undisturbed by the pressures and criticisms that accompany widespread popular interest.

The extent of how much things have changed can be seen in a number of different areas. Designers now work on the product as well as the packaging, on the boardroom as well as the notepaper, on retail outlets and subway stations as well as labels and calendars. The influence of design has made shops and shopping more pleasant, books more attractive, chairs more comfortable, and thousands of everyday items better to look at and more efficient to use. The commercial value of good design has even been recognized on the stock market. In just about every sense of the phrase, design has gone public.

This may be good news for most of us, but it poses a terrible problem for those whose mission in life is to comment and explain. There is a seemingly irresistible temptation nowadays to analyse and define and pigeonhole any subject which makes a dent in public consciousness. We are told what makes a good film, a fine painting, a sensible diet, a prudent investment. The pundits are everywhere, taking their chosen subjects to pieces and rearranging them tidily so that they can be understood by that mythical figure with a thirst for simple explanation, the man in the street.

Unfortunately, a good design defies simple explanations, because it is often something that hasn't been done before. Trying to explain that is like commenting on a meal that hasn't been cooked.

You can, it's true, be more or less sure of your ground on the practical side of design – the clarity of one sign system versus another, for example – but that doesn't take into account the matter of the personality of a design. Typefaces, colours, images, shapes and materials can be used in limitless combinations which will provoke different reactions from different people. One man's Eames is another man's Bauhaus. What I like, you may not. It can be as personal and dismissive as that. So what constitutes good design is likely to escape a neat definition - certainly for as long as there are good designers who prefer to grow their own new ideas

Pentagram. *Ideas on Design*. Faber & Faber (London 1986)

rather than copy existing solutions and thus contribute to establishing fixed standards.

And that, in fact, leads to a more interesting question: what makes a good designer?

Above everything else, it should be a respect for function. We have all suffered from beautiful jugs that don't pour cleanly, handsome offices that are hell to work in, graphically imposing slabs of text that are almost unreadable. Designers who produce striking ideas that don't work are not good designers. This seems obvious, but it is being ignored every day. Take a look at the current crop of new products and new buildings and you will find, with depressing ease, examples of function coming a poor second, and 'design' coming an even worse first.

It is the ability to do the job in a totally appropriate way that makes a good designer, and that requires an unusual combination of apparently opposing characteristics. The first is logic, which assesses the problem and accepts the rules which have to govern the solutions. But you can be as logical as you like and still produce a dreary design. What separates humdrum work from brilliant work is the second characteristic – not normally given much freedom by logical people – and that is intuition.

Intuition, derived from knowledge, experience and God knows what else, is the unpredictable human element that saves us from a world designed by computers. It encourages the mind to jump away from the expected, and helps to produce ideas that are surprises as well as solutions. And there it might end, veiled in a certain amount of professional mystery, except that someone will inevitably back the designer into a corner and say, 'What made you think of doing it like *that*?'

Quite often there won't be a precise answer. If good designers have anything in common, it is that they all seem to be equipped with a subconscious sponge, capable of absorbing a wide and unrelated range of stimuli to be tucked away at the back of the mind for future use. A builder's yard or a factory are as likely to provide a fruitful scrap of inspiration as a book on Islamic calligraphy or a visit to the Louvre. But how did that scrap become part of a design solution? Logic? Intuition? Lateral rationalization? Maybe thinking by jumping is as close a description as we can get, particularly since designers spend most of their working lives hopping back and forth between different contexts and dimensions and periods in time.

[SEE P140]

Bespoking

Paul Rand, doyen of graphic design, records[1] how he thought through an advertisement for an agency pitching for the RCA account. The first decision was to take a page in *The New York Times* to catch the eye of the chairman of the corporation. The problem was what should the message be.

'The more I analysed the problem the more I became convinced that General Sarnoff (Chairman RCA) was the key. I knew that while a million eyes might see that copy of The Times, the only eyes that mattered were his. I knew that his career in radio had begun as a wireless operator with Marconi, and somewhere I had heard that his proudest moment was when he was one of the first to pick up the distress call from the Titanic. This brought me to the Morse code. The letters SOS might have made an arresting headline in code, but I didn't think RCA or the agency would appreciate the connotations. It was then that I decided to try RCA in code. My dictionary provided the symbols of the International code, and I knew I had the foundation of an idea ... I noted that the dot and dash of the last letter in my headline became a perfect exclamation mark when it was turned on end. It was only later that I realized that the A in advertising related to the symbol. Sarnoff must have seen it as there was a call later that morning to set up a meeting.'

[SEE P400]

1. Paul Rand. *Thoughts on Design*. Wittenborn (New York 1947)

To the executives and management of the Radio Corporation of America:

Messrs. Alexander, Anderson, Baker, Buck, Cannon, Carter, Coe, Coffin, Dunlop, Elliot, Engstrom, Folsom, Gorin, Folliffe, Kayes,

Marek, Mills, Odorizzi, Orth, Sacks, Brig. Gen. Sarnoff, Saxon, Seidel, Teegarten, Tuft, Watts, Weaver, Werner, Williams

Gentlemen: An important message intended expressly for your eyes is now on its way to each of you by special messenger.

William H. Weintraub & Company, Inc.   *Advertising*   *488 Madison Avenue, New York*

Not all so-called creative occupations conform to the same patterns of procedure.

The complexities facing an actor, for example, differ in execution and timeframe from those of a painter or an architect, cook, designer or music maker.

Advertising writer:

Immersion
Contemplation
Diversion
Revelation

David Bernstein

Fashion designer:

'I try one way of doing something, and then I try another, to see if that works. But even when I've done that I try its opposite, to see if that works.'

Vivienne Westwood

Choreographer:

'I prefer to drop a simple, single idea into my brain and let it rummage around for several months … two or three weeks before I begin to choreograph, I attempt to cast up the result of this Rorschach process. Then I like to choreograph swiftly and within a short span of time; I feel that in this out-pouring I keep the channels of my subject open.'

Alwin Nikolais

Poster artist:

'I pick up a book. I lay it down. I look out of the window. I stare at a blank wall, I move about … gaze at a blank piece of paper … paint in some kind of lettering … make it larger – smaller – slanting – heavy – light … make drawings of the object – in outline, with shadow and colours, large and then small … within the dimensions I have now set myself …'

McKnight Kauffer

Traveller:

'One can only really travel if one lets oneself go completely, and takes what every place brings without trying to turn it into a private pattern.'

Dame Freya Stark

Philosopher:

Michael Ignatieff writing on Isaiah Berlin: 'His lectures always involved compulsive over-preparation, endless refining from sixty pages to thirty, then to ten, and finally to single-headings on a single piece of paper, which were ignored when he entered the seance-like state of performance.'

Isaiah Berlin

Athlete:

'Listen – when the gun goes I run like hell.'

Linford Christie

Natural philosopher:

'I keep the subject constantly before me, and wait till the first dawnings open little by little into the full and clear light.'

Sir Isaac Newton

Writer:

'… the larger part of the labour of an author in composing his work is critical labour; the labour of sifting, combining, constructing, expunging, correcting, testing …'

T.S. Eliot

Civil engineer:

'… I'm a bit like a hound following a fox; I'm following something really close to the ground and I can't actually see where it's going. I've got my nose to the ground to make sure I'm following it properly.'

Peter Rice

Theatre director:

'An actor must continually check through his line of action to make sure he has the right activity, order, logic, colour, contrast and that all these elements contribute to the projection of the super-objective.'

Konstantin Stanislavsky

Movie director :

'My films are made on paper,' explained Hitchcock. For him the creative core was the mapping out of a film. Transcripts, outlines, treatments, and complex storyboards showing every shift of the camera.

Alfred Hitchcock

Actor :

'Acting is hard and gun metal. Crying just makes your mascara run, emoting is bunk.'

Anthony Hopkins

Painter :

'In order to paint my pictures, I need to remain for several days in the same state of mind, and I do not find this in any atmosphere but that of the Côte d'Azur.'

Henri Matisse

Architect :

'Always design a thing by considering it in its next context – a chair in a room, a room in a house, a house in an environment, and environment in a city plan.'

Eliel Saarinen

Automobile designer :

'Mr Giugiaro, he say that he have been in this business more than twenty years and he still have to accept suggestions from people who know nothing about design.'

Giorgio Giugiaro's translator

Composer :

'With me composition bears all the symptoms of serious illness: insomnia, fever, loss of appetite. After three days of that there emerged a song to words by Mallarmé.'

Maurice Ravel

Advertising director :

'You take one fact, turn it this way and that, look at it in different lights, and feel for the meaning of it. You bring two facts together and see how they fit. What you are seeking is the relationship, a synthesis where everything will come together in a neat combination, like a jig-saw puzzle ... In fact, it is almost like *listening* for the meaning instead of *looking* for it.'

James Webb Young

Physicist :

'Some people just sit at their desks and stare at a sheet of paper; others pace around. I personally like to lie flat on my back, with eyes closed. A scientist who is working really hard may look very much like one who is taking a little nap ...'

David Ruelle

Graphic designer :

'When I start to work on a job, first I wash my hands with soap. Then I sharpen ten or more pencils with a cutter-knife. This is a sort of ceremony aimed at putting the ideas I have into shape.'

Shigeo Fukuda

Snooker champion :

Before taking a shot Higgins says he *reads the table*. He registers the layout, observes the opponent's frame of mind, weighs the score, predicts strategies, recalls errors, calculates risks – probably would loosen his collar if he wasn't such a smart dresser – and only then takes the shot.

Hurricane Higgins

Political cartoonist :

'... I mostly form the idea in my mind. I don't prompt myself by looking at things. I just think around the subject.'

Peter Brookes

Poet :

Journalist: 'Can you describe the genesis and working-out of a poem based on an image that most people would simply pass by?'

Philip Larkin: '... I can't understand these chaps who go round American universities explaining how they write poems: it's like going round explaining how you sleep with your wife.'

Philip Larkin

designing and making

'There are five identifiable
stages in the sequence of
designing and making.'

Patrick Nuttgens

First, there is the identification,
discovery or recognition of needs.
This is finding out what the problem
is and what the designer has to do.

That sounds simple but is in fact
often elusive.

There is, for one thing, often a
considerable difference between
what people think they need and
what they may actually need:
between what they want and what
they need. But even if that sounds
patronizing, the technology of a
particular area often throws up
different realities from what was
at first envisaged.

Indeed the entire problem may need
to be redefined. The identification
of needs does not mean persuading
people, as the consumer society
relentlessly does, of new needs
and creating a profusion of them;
it means identifying genuine
existing needs.

Second, there is the collection of
information, the assembly of facts.

That is fairly straightforward,
ranging from everything known
about the artefact or similar
artefacts to the techniques and
technology appropriate to the
problem.

This is an exercise in history –
the history of the identifiable
immediate past.

Fifth is realization, which is self-explanatory, except to say that the first realization of the idea is the point at which a lot of disadvantages may appear as the thing takes shape, and works or ·fails.

Third is the analysis of those needs and facts – the drawn out, difficult and demanding intellectual exercise of putting all the aspects together, eliminating the irrelevant or unworkable, thinking out alternatives and reaching an understanding of what the problem really is.

This is the stage that calls for analytical thought. It includes the moment, or extended time, when the mind grapples with the whole of the problem, its demands and its possible means. When it comes to terms with them, discards, chooses, tries out, throws away, draws, makes experiments, thinks and thinks again; and sometimes emerges with an idea.

Fourth is that idea. In most fields of design, an idea, whether for a building, artefact or machine or process, is the new potential thing which exists, or will exist, to bring together and make into one the needs, techniques, demands and means.

It is a totality.

And it is the moment in the making of a thing when it potentially has a name – to describe and define the new totality. From that moment it can never really cease to exist.

If it fails or is seriously impaired, it may drive one back to further thought and analysis and may involve discarding the original idea and the formulation of a new one.

It is followed by implementation which involves production and the energy of other people.

STEP BY STEP

James Webb Young, one of the old school of American advertising, joined J. Walter Thompson in 1912 and retired in 1928. [SEE P424]. He wrote a slim volume on techniques for generating new ideas which became a bestseller and is still in print.[1] His premise was that one proceeded from problem to solution in four distinct steps.

Here is an extract from his book :

> 'And here again, is the way it happened in the discovery of the half-tone printing process, as told by Mr Ives, the inventor of it :
>
> "While operating my photostereotype process in Ithaca I studied the problem of half-tone process (*First step*). I went to bed one night in a state of brainfag over the problem (*end of second and beginning of third step*) and the instant that I woke in the morning (*end of third step*) saw before me, apparently projected on the ceiling, the completely worked-out process and equipment in operation (*fourth step*)."
>
> This is the way ideas come: after you have stopped straining for them, and have passed through a period of rest and relaxation for the search.
>
> Thus the story about Sir Isaac Newton and his discovery of the law of gravitation is probably not the whole truth. You will remember that when a lady asked the famous scientist how he came to make the discovery he is said to have replied, "By constantly thinking about it."
>
> It was by constantly thinking about it that he made the discovery possible. But I suspect that if we knew the full history of the case we should find that the actual solution came while he was out taking a walk in the country.' [SEE P140].

The photograph is a self-portrait by Frederic Eugene Ives, taken in the 1890s. It is reproduced in the half-tone printing process which he invented. Every time you look at a picture in a newspaper, magazine, book, poster, street hoarding, junk mail, sales leaflet, brochure, annual report, or almost any other piece of printed material – thank Mr Ives.

1. James Webb Young. *A Technique for Producing Ideas.* NTC Business Books (Chicago 1975)

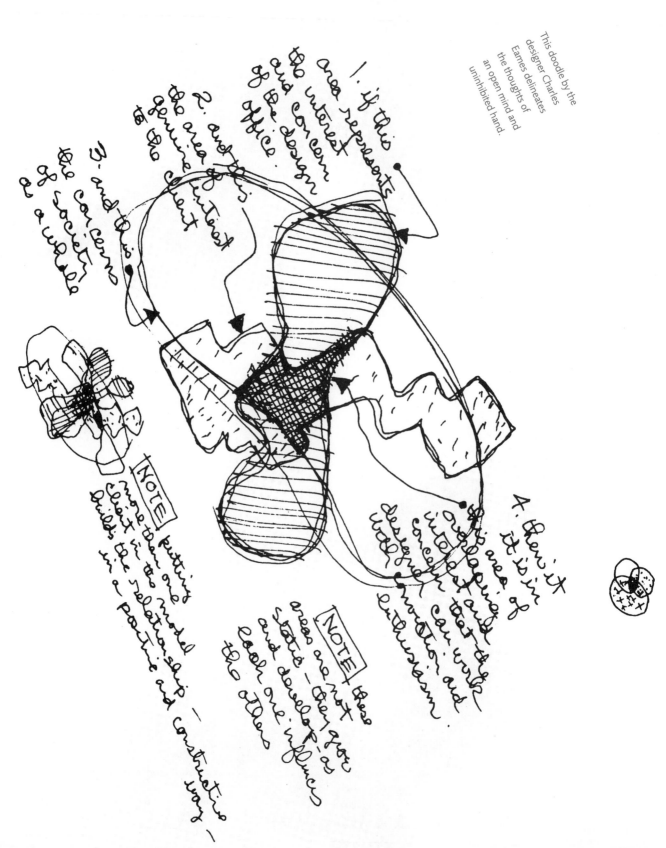

THE FIVE
STRATEGIC ARTS

THE SITUATION GIVES RISE
TO MEASUREMENTS

MEASUREMENTS GIVE RISE
TO ESTIMATES

ESTIMATES GIVE RISE
TO ANALYSIS

ANALYSIS GIVES RISE
TO BALANCING

BALANCE GIVES RISE
TO TRIUMPH.

Sun Tzu

THE EGYPTIAN HOURS

HOUR OF WATCHING

HOUR OF THE BROKEN PATTERN

HOUR OF THE FRAGMENTS

HOUR OF THE CLUE

HOUR OF THE SEAL

HOUR OF THE SHROUD

HOUR OF THE GARLAND

THE SIX PHASES

ENTHUSIASM

DISILLUSIONMENT

PANIC

SEARCH
FOR THE GUILTY

PUNISHMENT OF
THE INNOCENT

PRAISE FOR THE
NON-PARTICIPANTS

GAMEFORM OF SHIBUMI

FUSEKI
The opening stage of a game
when the entire board
is taken into account.

SABAKI
An attempt to dispose
of a troublesome situation
in a quick and flexible way.

SEKI
A neutral position in which
neither has the advantage.

UTTEGAE
A sacrifice play, a gambit.

SHICHO
A running attack.

TSURU NO SUGOMORI
A graceful manoeuvre
in which the enemy stones
are captured.

Trevanian. *Shibumi*. Panther Books (London 1979)

'OF COURSE, IF YOU WERE BORN ON THE
ELEPHANT'S BACK, YOU WOULD QUICKLY
LEARN TO SEE THE LIE OF THE LAND.'
HINDU APHORISM

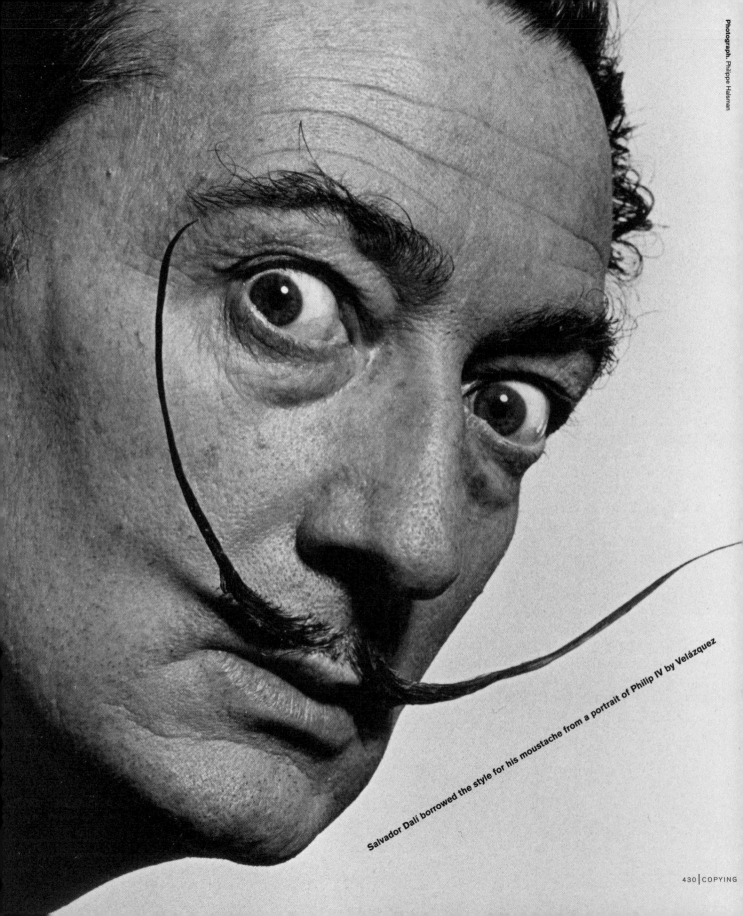

Photograph, Philippe Halsman

Salvador Dalí borrowed the style for his moustache from a portrait of Philip IV by Velázquez

Many a scarecrow serves as a roost for the enlightened crow.

My wife has always liked Modigliani. A big birthday was coming up so I thought I'd give *The Seated Nude* which hangs in the Courtauld Institute in London. It is currently worth several million dollars.

The *Royal Academy Magazine* carried an advertisement by an artist claiming he could make facsimile copies of any painting, providing he had access to good visual reference. I called him up. We agreed on £300, including materials.

The copy is illustrated opposite alongside the original.

Assuming the only tangible difference is one of price, why is one considered better than the other? Perhaps, because just as an original sound can produce an echo, an echo can't produce an original sound?

*In 1959 songwriter Joni Mitchell watched the legendary 'Garden of Allah', a Los Angeles landmark where movie stars lived in the 1930s, being torn down and recorded her feelings in: *'They paved Paradise and put up a parking lot.'*

Continuity. Antiquities were Freud's secret passion. When he fled to London he brought his collection (and couch) and placed everything in the same position as they had been in Vienna.[1] He kept his habits and before starting work each morning would stroke a marble baboon and greet a statue of a Chinese sage. Nostalgia is a powerful sentiment and continuity with the past provides reassurance.

Mimicry. Edward Lear was outraged when a new hotel blocked the view from his villa in San Remo. He moved out and built another – identical to the original – because he didn't want to confuse Foss, his cat. Russian silent movie star Alla Nazimova designed her swimming pool in the 'Garden of Allah' in the shape of the Black Sea.* More ambitiously Yassar Arafat so he confided during a television programme, adjusts and folds his *kafir* into the shape of Palestine. More happily orchids simulate the charms of female bees so successfully that male bees prefer them to the real thing.

Copying can also provide status on the cheap. Why else imitate ivory with plastic or gold with gilt? Saddam Hussein is rebuilding Babylon by bulldozing the ancient remains and building a brash new version in bright yellow brick. The President of Gabon spent £100 million on building a replica of St Peter's, Rome. He even got the Pope to pay a visit and give it his blessing to boost congregation figures. In Gabon only one in ten is Catholic. America is particularly partial to new antiquities. Nashville, Tennessee, has a full-size replica of the Parthenon. The locals think there's a copy in Greece. 'In Las Vegas,' records Peter Conrad, 'an Egyptian pyramid, a palace vaguely belonging to Caesar and a turreted castle which might have housed King Arthur's knights grow side by side, like a colony of genetically-boosted, air-conditioned fungi.'[2]

However, mimicry isn't necessarily tacky. An idea born in one context, and applied to another, can create something else. Although birdsong and woodwind work on different principles the parallels remain striking. When Sibelius wanted to summon up the call of the crane he used the clarinet. 'Capability' Brown landscaped the grounds of Blenheim Palace according to the battle lines of Waterloo. William van Alen designed the Chrysler Building (1931) with the vocabulary of the motor age: friezes of hubcaps and wheels, gargantuan winged chrome radiator ornaments, and a stainless-steel finial. The classic Chrysler Airflow (1934) was characterized by its 'waterfall' radiator. In

Jerusalem the dome of the Shrine of the Book, which houses the Dead Sea Scrolls, is modelled on the lids of the jars in which the scrolls lay hidden for 1,900 years.

Doppelgänging. Fawaz-al-Emari was enrolled as Saddam's double when the previous stand-in was assassinated. Facial similarity was enhanced by plastic surgeons in Yugoslavia and his vocal chords doctored in Baghdad. Fawaz appeared in motorcades, on parade grounds, swimming in the Tigris. When not on show he was shut up out of sight.

Latif Uahia wasn't keen to be the double of Uday, Saddam's monstrous scion, so was tortured until he agreed. Teeth were reorganized, a cleft carved in his chin, and hours spent watching videos of Uday walking, dancing, driving, talking, drinking and lighting cigarettes. He was sent to the front in the Gulf War but Uday collected the medals. After surviving nine assassination attempts Latif took off and ironically just missed being killed by Uday himself while escaping to Kurdistan in 1992.

Peter Shapallo spent half his life being Enver Hoxha, Albania's unsavoury dictator. A country dentist, he was taken to Tirana in the 1960s. His wife and two daughters, the surgeon who fixed his face, the tailor and the hairdresser who perfected the transformation, were all murdered to preserve the illusion of the illusion. When Hoxha died Shapallo sought refuge in the German Embassy – they thought he was a ghost. Once safe he disfigured himself in a attempt to be singular again. He at least wanted to die as himself. Of course it could be that the villain himself masqueraded as his double, and that it was the double who died. There's an explanation why an exact likeness is called a 'spitting image' but I can't remember what it is.

Then there was Liberace who employed a cosmetic surgeon to fix up his young boyfriend (Liberace's, not the surgeon's), to make him look as he (Liberace, not the surgeon) was as a young man. [SEE P314].

Borrowing. More entertainingly than Liberace's endeavour, David Bowie based his persona of Ziggy Stardust on a Vince Taylor – an American musician obsessed with aliens who spent much of his life in mental institutions, and ended up as an aircraft maintenance worker at Geneva airport.

Imitation. '… the crowning exhibit of the Palace's entire collection is', declares *Umberto Eco*, 'undoubtedly, the *Venus de Milo*. There we see her in all her pristine splendour, leaning gracefully against an

1. *Sigmund Freud and Art*. Thames & Hudson (London 1989)   2. Peter Conrad. *Modern Times Modern Places*. Thames & Hudson (London 1988)

'One moment you're the best thing since sliced bread, the next moment you're the bread and everybody's taking a slice.' *Steve Davis* (Snooker player)

THE great-grandson of the Eiffel Tower's designer yesterday turned off the lights of Paris's most famous monument — as the Eiffel Tower in Paris, Las Vegas, lit up for the first time.

Crowds filled the Las Vegas Strip to see the giant screens, which relayed live the moment when Xavier Larnoudie-Eiffel flicked a symbolic switch thousands of miles away in Paris. At the same time, fireworks exploded around the 510ft Las Vegas replica, the centre-piece of the new $785 million Paris resort — the fourth mega-resort to open in 11 months.

The exterior of Paris features intricate re-creations of famous Paris landmarks, including the Paris Opera House, the Arc de Triomphe and the Louvre. Inside, there are 2,800 slot machines, and video games with symbols fitting the French theme.

The Guardian, 1 September 1999

Painting(s). Modigliani. *The Seated Nude*

Ionian column of a classical temple with both arms now intact and her life-like colouring and gestures fully restored! Just as the original model would have stood before the original classical artist. As the accompanying inscription boasts: HERE IS *VENUS DE MILO* BROUGHT TO LIFE AS SHE WAS IN THE TIME WHEN SHE POSED FOR THE UNKNOWN SCULPTOR IN GREECE SOME TWO HUNDRED YEARS BC. And to highlight the claim that this reconstruction, made possible by the most advanced techniques of laser reproduction and holography, is far more "real" than the artwork it imitates, we are also presented with a small but exact copy of the one-armed, lustre-less and time-worn statue as it appears in the Louvre of Paris. Make no mistake about it, the Palace of Living Arts proclaims, the life-like reconstruction before your eyes is far more authentic than the classical original. Our imitations have now become so perfect it could be that they leave no more room for imagination.'

Counterfeiting. J.S.G. Boggs paints dollar notes. Authorities in America, Britain and other countries have closed his exhibitions, confiscated his artworks and taken him to court. Despite these setbacks he still sells handmade money for real money. What really gets up his nose is why the authorities give him aggro, while the public buy his stuff. He has a point.

In 1987 Boggs was brought to trial by the Bank of England accused of 'reproducing' pound notes. 'These are reproductions,' Boggs insisted passionately from the witness box, thrusting a fistful of pound notes into the air; 'these, by contrast,' he continued, fanning out his own drawings, 'are originals!'

I like the paradox that the official currency printers to the American government charge them 2.5 cents (price at time of writing) for each printed bill regardless of whether the denomination is $5, $10 or $20. Here, at the very fiscal centre, the value of the note is irrelevant in the commercial transaction.

Boggs is smarter. He sells his currency for a higher price than the denomination illustrated on the artwork. In lean times he compromises and has an arrangement with a restaurant where he pays with artworks the same price as the bill. Mind you he once settled a restaurant bill with a genuine $100 note, and the waiter returned with a drawing of his change. Boggs raises fundamental questions – what precisely is it that we value. Art or money? How do we value one in terms of the other? How do we place a value on anything? And how is it that we continue to credit the legitimacy of anything as fake and insubstantial as paper money?

Copying. Back in 1832, when Charles Babbage invented a mechanical calculator, a contemporary wrote: 'the wondrous pulp and fibre of the brain has been substituted by brass and iron; he has taught wheelwork to think.' Today this has been superseded by gigabyte robots. Hopefully they will be benevolent. As Nabokov put it, 'the good of mankind might have been sufficiently contagious to infect metal. In which case they may keep us around as pets.' And there is the map imagined by Jorge Luis Borges which was so large and detailed that it covered the real territory it purported to describe.

Masquerade. American artist Cindy Sherman makes masquerade photographic self-portraits. She put herself into the American myth in a series of photographs called *Untitled Film Stills*. In these she features as characters from films we've never seen, but feel we have: perhaps part of a story written in advance. [SEE P276].

Plagiarism. A writer was mortified to discover that he'd written a sentence which had also been written by George Bernard Shaw. Until, one day, he saw the same sentence in a book by Jonathan Swift.

In the back of our mind we often have a forgotten memory of something we once saw, only to have it emerge years later as an original thought. A different condition to plagiarism which works on the assumption that a slice from a cut loaf won't be missed.

Rodin was prolific and produced works from 'Paperweight to Large Economy Size', as Robert Hughes phrased it. Rodin never actually carved but modelled in plaster. Assistants did the hard work. When he died they carried on carving from his models until the art market became flooded. Eventually the courts put a stop to this dubious practice and gave responsibility for authentication to a museum. One sculpture authenticated was of the wife of the President of Chile. In fact only the head was by Rodin, the bust was of someone else and the cluster of flowers created by an assistant.

In 1985 a Greek statue was acquired by the Getty Museum for seven million dollars. Evidence now suggests it was one of those knocked off by Rodin's craftsmen. The Museum can't decide whether the statue is genuine or fake, whether it's worth seven million dollars or nothing, whether it's a creative masterpiece or a piece of junk. How can something be worth millions or nothing?

Technology now allows copy without error. We live in the age of the simulacrum.

I found the *collage* shown opposite on a market stall. The price, after haggling, was $200. Thoughts jostled through my head: was it genuine, stolen, a copy, or maybe a pass-off? The frame was cheap. The artwork had no provenance. It was drizzling.

Bringing all factors into focus clarified the issue. It couldn't be a facsimile because replicating identical ephemera would be impossible. Mimicking was feasible but why bother? The financial return, after the stallholder had taken his cut, would have been derisory.

I took it to a reputable art dealer's gallery. They told me that if it's a genuine Kurt Schwitters it's worth about $50,000. If it isn't – bin it.

[SEE PP112&211]

MIMESIS, the Oxford English Dictionary maintains, is 'a figure of speech whereby the words or actions of another are imitated'. Personally I prefer the idea that it means the representation of things as they were through things they were not.

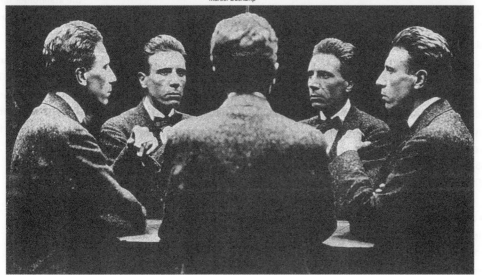

Marcel Duchamp

Henri-Pierre Roché

[SEE P.486]

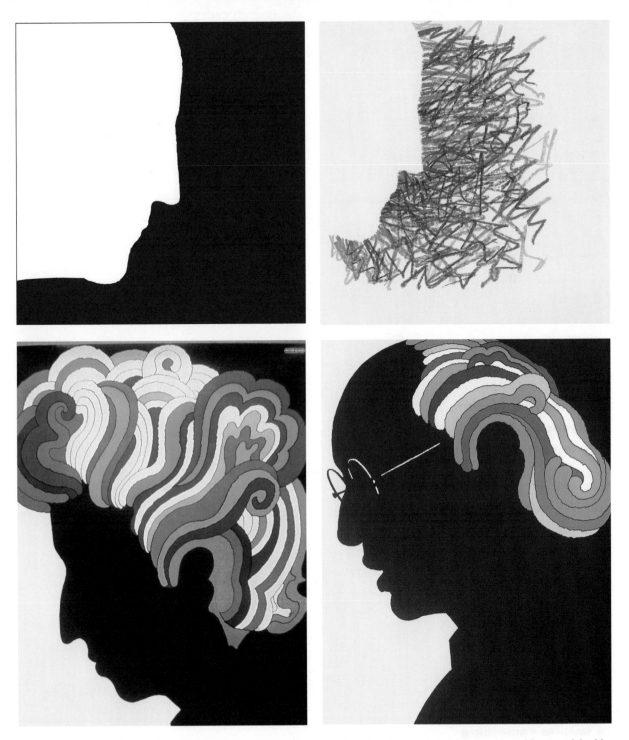

The instinctive way to learn is through imitation. As children most of us draw from imagination; then, gaining confidence and fired by curiosity, by copying out of comics and suchlike. Milton Glaser has made an art of borrowing. His famous concert poster (below left) converts Duchamp's silhouette (top left) into Bob Dylan. Some years later Woody Pirtle converted Bob Dylan into Glaser (below right). The version (top right) with coloured scribbles borrows Duchamp for a magazine article profiling personalities. I had always thought that the original Duchamp profile was a black and white silhouette, but actually it is also a copy. I saw the original in a Paris artshow – it was cut out of white paper and stuck on beige card.

T.S. Eliot

Lionel Trilling

John Updike

Igor Stravinsky

Philip Johnson

Pablo Picasso

'... exact imitation,
item for item, cannot
reproduce nature,
only equivalents can.

Milton Glaser

It is not by
making volcanoes that
sulphur is produced.
Retorts are better.

Michael Caine

Sir Joshua Reynolds

Nature is not
reconstituted by
imitating animal cries
or natural noises,
but by writing
pastoral symphonies.

Louis Armstrong

Frederic Goudy

Marcus Aurelius

To imitate something
is merely to stuff it.'

Amédée Ozenfant

Virgil

'Immature poets imitate; mature poets steal.'

'Immature artists imitate; mature artists steal.'

'My purpose in reading has ever secretly been not to come and judge but to come and steal.'

'A good composer does not imitate; he steals.'

'… what makes Mies such a great influence is that he is so easy to copy.'

'Copy anyone but never copy yourself.'

'If one's work is not imitated, one's work is not understood …'

'I only steal from the best people.'

'He who resolves never to ransack any mind but his own … will be obliged to imitate himself.'

'A lotta cats copy the Mona Lisa, but people still line up to see the original.'

'The old boys stole most of our good ideas.'

'To refrain from imitation is the best revenge.'

'Do not trust the horse, Trojans.'

It is said that Picasso first met the bulky Gertrude Stein

when she was sparring with her bantamweight partner

Alice, in their Paris apartment. An encounter which

inspired his series of lumbering nudes. An unlikely story,

but then influences are often unusual. Surprisingly,

at least to me, Alexander Rodchenko was an admirer of

Aubrey Beardsley. Kurt Schwitters said he owed his

fascination with printed ephemera to Jan Tschichold. Saul

Steinberg wrote that he was influenced by Egyptian

paintings, latrine drawing, insane art, children's drawings,

embroidery and Paul Klee. 'My time was late Cubism, late

Bauhaus', he reminisced, 'our clouds came straight out of

Arp, complete with a hole in the middle; even our trees

were influenced by the mania for the kidney shape.' Arthur

Rimbaud liked 'senseless paintings, entablatures of

doorways, backgrounds, the backcloths at fairs,

signboards, popular colour prints'. Film director Fred

Zinneman (*High Noon*) was influenced by Matthew Brady's

Civil War photographs. Toulouse-Lautrec borrowed from

Japanese woodcuts, Picasso from ethnic sculpture, and

Picabia based many of his drawings on diagrams from

Brewer's Motor Car Construction and Carburation in Theory

and Practice. Alexander Calder is said to have cut his

sculptural teeth making toys for The Gould Manufacturing

Company. Carl André, destined to be remembered for his

bricks, was influenced by the Pennsylvania Railroad

Company. At one time he had worked on the railway

and was intrigued to see how the engineers utilized

standardized interchangeable units. Salvador Dalí declared

the railway station at Perpignan the centre of the

universe. Irving Penn reckoned that 'all designers, all

photographers and all art directors whether they know it

or not are students of Alexey Brodovitch.' And Matisse,

the radio has just informed me, was a skilled violinist and

admirer of Wagner, while sci-fi writer Douglas Adams

confessed he was profoundly influenced by his mother's

readings of *Winnie the Pooh.* And I wonder if Buster Keaton

was influenced by Houdini — who was his godfather?

Note. I have an American friend [Nancy] who does a great impersonation of Katharine Hepburn doing an impersonation of Ethel Merman. Impersonations run in her family. Her aunt, she told me, so liked the effect of shadows thrown by her living room lights that she painted them on the wall.

Akira Kurosawa appropriated 'the grammar of the Western'. In 1961 he remade *Shane* as *Yojimbo*, changing a gunman to a *samurai* and backdating the nineteenth-century West to medieval Japan. In 1964 Sergio Leone took *Yojimbo* as the pretext for the first of his Spaghetti Westerns, *A Fistful of Dollars*. A link from America to Italy and Spain, and on to Japan, where he made the film. The grammar remained the same but generated a new vocabulary.

Daedalus was persuaded by Pasiphaë, Queen of Crete, to make a hollow wooden cow which would be sufficiently realistic to deceive a white bull for whom she had a passionate affection. Once finished she eagerly entered the model and to her pleasure the bull was deceived. When she bore a monster, Daedalus was called upon again, this time to design a labyrinth to house it. He also did this so effectively he found it difficult to make his way back out.

China's most extraordinary archaeological site is a vast man-made hill four times the size of Egypt's largest pyramid. 2,000 years old, it houses Qin Shi Huang, the first Emperor of China who took a replica of his empire with him. A miniature reproduction of palaces, pavilions, landscapes, rivers and seas of mercury. The imperial army of 8,000 life-size terracotta warriors and 300 horses. Each soldier's face is different, suggesting they were sculpted from life, right down to the studs on shoes and scarves which prevented armour rubbing their skin.

The Cargo Cult. During the last World War the Americans had flown in supplies to a South Pacific island and the locals, hoping the same would happen again, constructed their version of an airport. They cleared tracks through the forest and made a wooden hut for a man to sit in. Pieces of wood represent his headphones and sticks of bamboo poke out like antennas. He is the controller. They light fires along the edge of the track and wait for something to happen – but it doesn't. It looks the same; but isn't. Equally improbably they also thought Agatha Christie would be their queen.

In 1925 Louis Mountbatten was recalled from the Mediterranean fleet and converted his Mayfair bedroom into an exact reproduction of his ship's cabin. The walls were painted gloss white enamel, fixed with pipes and ducts, fitted with domed sidelights, regulation bunk, cupboards, folding washstand and two brass portholes with *trompe l'oeil* views of Valletta harbour which changed from day to moonlight at the turn of a switch. In front of this backdrop were models of the fleet which twinkled Morse signals. Sound effects hummed soothingly like a ship's engines.

Osbert Sitwell got extremely cross with Michael Arlen when he wrote *The Green Hat*, a best-seller which brought in enough money for him to buy a yellow Rolls Royce (maybe you recollect the film?). Sitwell maintained that Arlen had plagiarized his short story about a plagiarist – *The Machine Breaks Down*.

A man woke up and found that he'd been robbed. More disconcerting was the realization that everything had been replaced by an exact replica. Unnerved by this weird situation he called his neighbour. The neighbour, looking at him rather carefully, asked, 'Do I know you?'

In 1912 Oscar Kokoschka began an affair with Alma Mahler. When they broke up he had a full-size replica made of her complete in every anatomical detail, by a lady in Stuttgart with the unhappy name of Hermine Moos. He took his Alma out for supper, and taxi rides around town. In *Self-Portrait With Doll*, Kokoschka, wearing a wistful expression, indicates his frustration and despair. One night in Dresden, after drinking, he flung Alma into a garbage truck. Alma certainly symbolized something. She'd been pursued by Max Burckhardt, Gustav Klimt and Alexander von Zemlinsky. Her first husband was Gustav Mahler, her second Walter Gropius, her third Franz Werfel.

When Byron finished his tempestuous affair with Lady Caroline Lamb, she ceremoniously burnt his letters at a mock funeral attended by local village girls dressed in white. It was only a gesture. The letters were fake. She kept the originals.

Three other impersonations come to mind: a parrot which resided in the bar of the Beirut Hotel Commodore during the troubles used to frighten new arrivals with an imitation whistle of an arriving mortar. A hotel in Tokyo which when you set the alarm, awakes you by piping birdsong out of the window casements. And the blood in the shower scene in Hitchcock's film *Psycho*, which was chocolate sauce. At least so Saul Bass told me.

Salvador Dalí, inspired by Mae West's red lips, designed them as a sofa for the eccentric Edward James. [see p259]. James modelled his bedroom on the catafalque prepared for the burial of Nelson. The corner-posts of the canopied bed were carved as palm trees, and the dark green silk draperies trimmed with massive bullion fringing. The walls were hung with shimmering silver net, and curtains of mesh like medieval chain-mail concealed the radiators.

Glenn Brown is an artist who does 'Appropriations' – art jargon for copying. He will tackle the impasto of a painting by Frank Auerbach and re-render it flat, as a cool, hyper-smooth photo-realist copy replicating glistening highlights using tiny brushes. Gavin Turk replicates Andy Warhol self-portraits done with camouflage by photographing himself using the same kind of pattern. Another Turk replication is a life-size fibreglass figure of himself dressed like Sid Vicious posed like Warhol's famous photo of Elvis Presley holding a gun.

Anouska Hempel, asked how she came up with the design style of her London hotel, The Hempel, a virtual world of white and little else: 'I saw the buildings and the garden square and the possibilities were so endless,' she explained. 'I was inspired by pyramids, igloos, the desert, the Great Wall of China, Indian palaces, Bali, the inside of a shoe box ... light dancing through the leaves of trees in my garden, sitting in a puddle and staring upwards, a ship's funnel, the swish of crisp white cotton ... The space and height, though, were the most important things right from the beginning ... pure space, pure altitude, pure fantasy, huge surprises.'

Henry Ward Beecher

'Words are pegs to hang ideas on.'

ZAUM WAS A WORD INVENTED BY RUSSIAN FUTURISTS IN 1912 TO DEMONSTRATE THAT A WORD CAN BE GIVEN ANY MEANING. ZAUM, THEY CLAIMED, WASN'T MEANT TO MEAN ANYTHING.

AT LEAST THAT'S WHAT **THEY SAID** — IF **YOU** SEE WHAT **I MEAN**.

'WE ALL **KNOW** WHAT LIGHT IS; BUT IT IS NOT EASY TO **TELL** WHAT LIGHT IS.' DR JOHNSON [**SEE** P252]

The other day I passed Mrs O'Keefe's shop around the corner from where I live. Outside there was a placard offering *Speciality Handmade Sausages* and *Award Winning Black Pudding*. I turned the words over in my mind. What, I wondered, is capable of being called a *Speciality Sausage?* And come to that, what amazing ingredient constitutes an *Award Winning Black Pudding?* Probably not what I thought! Here are some other observations I've noted down. Bangkok dry cleaner: **Drop your pants here for best results.** Bangkok temple: **It is forbidden to enter a woman even a foreigner if dressed as a man.** Swiss restaurant: **Our wines leave you nothing to hope for.** Acapulco hotel: **The manager has personally passed all the water served here.** Tokyo bar: **Special cocktails for ladies with nuts.** Oslo bar: **Ladies are requested not to have children in the bar.** Moscow hotel: **If this is your first visit to the Soviet Union, you are welcome to it.** Paris hotel: **Please leave your values at the desk.** Austrian hotel: **Please do not perambulate the corridors in the hours of repose in the boots of ascension.** Athens hotel: **Visitors are expected to complain at the office between the hours of 9 a.m. and 11 a.m. daily.** Bucharest hotel: **The lift is being fixed for the next day. During that time we regret you will be unbearable.** Japanese hotel: **You are invited to take advantage of the chambermaid.** Peking hotel: **Prostitution, whoredom, gambling, drug taking, drug dealing and anything obscene are fobiden (sic).** Soviet Weekly: **There will be a Moscow exhibition of arts by 15,000 Soviet Republic painters and sculptors. These were executed over the last two years.** Budapest Zoo: **Do not feed the animals. If you have any suitable food, give it to the guard on duty.** Hong Kong dentist: **Teeth extracted by the latest Methodists.** Copenhagen airline office: **We take your bags and send them in all directions.** Of course it is easy to poke fun at foreigners' colloquial mistakes so here are some headlines from British newspapers. **'Stiff opposition expected to casketless funeral plan'. 'Drunk gets nine months in violin case'. 'Iraqi head seeks arms'.**

'Spoken words,' wrote Aristotle, *'are symbols of mental experience.'* And *'written words are the symbols of spoken words.'*

Words are so irrevocably stamped into our psyche they mislead us into thinking that what they are and what they symbolize, are one and the same. We know the word *dog* doesn't bite, but can be momentarily baffled when asked where our lap went when we stand up, or our fist when we open our hand.

Günter Grass said words nail down meanings whereas pictures only provide an approximate description. Certainly there is always the possibility of a mismatch between sign and meaning. When Wittgenstein lay dying the doctor's wife baked him a birthday cake decorated with 'Many Happy Returns'. He thanked her, then asked if she'd thought of the implications. She hadn't. And burst into tears.

Misunderstandings also arise when idiom gets in a twist: One of designer John McConnell's first commissions was a catalogue. The client was pleased with the layouts and John, aware that putting one's name on a job was a step towards establishing a reputation, asked if he could have a credit. The client turned white. *'How much?'* he asked.

A young Swiss designer came to work in London. The first evening he went out for dinner. He ordered fried potatoes and a *'bloody'* steak – direct translations are always tricky. The waiter blinked, wrote down the order, and returned ten minutes later. *'Here'*, he said, *'is your bloody steak'*, *'and here'*, slamming them down, *'are your fucking chips.'*

Speech has two aspects: the word itself and the pronunciation of the word. An oft-quoted example being the Chinese term *shi* which has 73 different meanings according to how it's pronounced. William Paley, walking along the beach at Santa Monica with Samuel Goldwyn, noticed a flock of birds circling overhead. *'Look at those gulls'*, he exclaimed, nudging Goldwyn. Goldwyn peered skyward, looked puzzled, and asked, *'How do you know they're not boys?'* How indeed. Looking through a menu in Tokyo I was bewildered to see a *'grass of wine'*. Then I got it, recollecting a Japanese designer telling me over supper the previous evening how much he'd *'roved lome'*.

Pronunciation is also an aspect of identity. In an effort to acquire a classy accent Mobster Bugsy Siegel strenuously attempted to eliminate his strident Brooklyn-Jewish accent by tirelessly incanting, *'Twenty dwarves took turns doing handstands on the carpet.'* Mercifully he was terminated before he achieved his ambition.

The last word goes to playwright Dennis Potter. *'The trouble with words',* he wickedly asides, *'is that you never know whose mouths they've been in.'*

Image. Japanese T-shirt. Courtesy Redstone Press

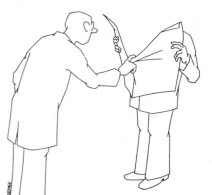

WORDS ARE LABELS attached to ideas. The thing is this: if you know the meaning behind a word it can be employed more effectively – much as a wine with a good **pedigree** invariably carries a better flavour. **Pedigree** is derived from *pie de grue*, Old French for a crane's foot. It also describes the branching of a business hierarchy or genealogical lineage, diagrams which resemble the wrinkles of the bird's claw.[1] Origins of words often yield surprises. I usually jot them down on a piece of paper – which I then lose. Here are a few I haven't: **Pupil** [eye – not student] comes from *pupilla* [Latin: doll], the small image which the Romans saw of themselves reflected in each other's eyes. **Fornicate** derives from *fornix* [Latin: arch] and as the colonnades of ancient Rome were frequented by prostitutes – to *fornicari* was to you know what.[2] *Choublac* is Creole for hibiscus, which [so I've read] was used by buccaneers to polish their boots as the sap generated a shiny sheen. **Trumpery** is a corruption of *trompe l'oeil*, an art term for mimicking reality. **Tawdry** is a contraction of St Audrey, a district in medieval London where they sold cheap clothes. **Rotten Row** in Hyde Park owes its name to the *Route du Roi*. **Sauntering** itinerants in the Middle Ages begged saying they were on their way to *La Sainte Terre* – the Holy Land. **A square meal** persists from the days when naval officers were served meals on a square wooden tray. This had a raised lip called the fiddle to prevent the plate slipping off in heavy seas – **'on the fiddle'** meant you got more on your plate than your due. **Porcelain** is circuitously derived from the sheen of cowry shells. At one time a common currency in Africa, shells were called *porce* as they looked like a sow's genitals. The **avocado** got its name from the Aztec for testicle, *ahuacatl*. Meanings can mean something else – it's quite unnerving. No wonder Max Ernst invented an alchemical product – **phallustrade** – a mischievous verbal collage of phallus, balustrade and autostrada. Lewis Carroll invented **chortle** by fusing chuckle and snort. Napoleon, the story goes, once stopped at an inn and was served coarse dark bread. Accustomed to the fine baguettes of Paris he ungraciously sneered, *'C'est pain pour Nicole'* [Nicole was his horse] which pronounced in English is **pumpernickel**. This fanciful suggestion by a language maven is less convincing than the view that it's colloquial German for a farting goblin. More

Note. In the corridor of a train in Sweden I noticed DRAG, a sign lettered on the swing door between the carriages. I mentally put a bet on the likelihood of the door on the other side of the door being labelled SHOVE. I opened the door and took a peek ... it said SKJUT.

Illustration. Miroslav Barták   1. Janet Whitent. *Book of Exotic Words.* Penguin (London 1996)   2. *A Browser's Dictionary.* Harper and Row (New York 1980)

"When I choose a word... it means just what I choose it to mean... neither more nor less."

Humpty Dumpty

In his biography,
David Ogilvy,
founder of
advertising agency
Ogilvy & Mather,
doyen of Madison
Avenue in the
1950s, creator of
the black eye-patch-
Hathaway-shirt-man,
Schweppes' character
Commander Whitehead,
and presenter of the
notion that at 60
miles an hour the
loudest noise in a
Rolls-Royce comes
from the electric
clock, lists his
favourite words.

Here they are:

abcedary
akimbo
chiaroscuro
diapason
egregious
epoptic
fandango
fardel
fubsy
fugleman
galumph
gravamen
hegira
hobbledehoy
hoyden
janizariat
jibber jabber
lallygag
nubile
panjandrum
pedicular
phantasmagoria
ragamuffin
rigadoons
rodomontade
roustabout
sodbuster
tatterdemalion
thimblerig
ukase
virago
wallydraigle

happily someone has suggested the word **poetry** has its roots in Aramaic (the language spoken by Christ) and expresses the sound of water flowing over pebbles.[1] In the fairy story *The Magic of Oz,* by pronouncing the word **PYRZOXGL** – correctly – one could magically turn oneself into any animal one desired. Shrew or pussy, werewolf or hush puppy, or whatever. Why, I wonder, are there so many **sh** and **gl** words for light? **Sh**immer, **sh**ine, **sh**one, **sh**een. **Gl**immer, **gl**int, **gl**eam, **gl**itter, **gl**isten, **gl**ow, **gl**ower. And so many **sl** words for unpleasantries like **sl**ink, **sl**udge, **sl**urp, **sl**um, **sl**eaze, **sl**ime. [SEE PP102&384]. Xavier Ducoro is an unlikely character in an improbable story[2] which takes place on a train on the London Underground. He has an obsession to turn Bakerloo Line stations into anagrams. He reassembles **Waterloo** into **a Wet Rolo** and **Woo later,** rearranges **Embankment** into **Met bank men,** and morphs **Charing Cross** from **Char crossing** to **Scotch in rags** to **Crash so ring C.** There are things that have names that I never knew had names. For instance the metal or plastic thing on the end of a shoelace is called an **aglet**. The indent at the bottom of a wine bottle is a **kick** or a **punt**. The wire contraption of a lampshade is a **harp**. The prongs of a fork are **tines**. Then there are words which other people know and I've never heard of. I took some books on holiday – just your run-of-the-mill-time-out-fodder – the kind of book you only read if you're wearing a seat belt or lying down. Anyway, after I was beach organized and had got into the first one, I hit a roadblock – **diegeses**. No dictionaries to hand on my desert island, so I noted it down. A few pages on, it happened again – **hermeneutics**. I wrote that down too. Then suddenly it got out of hand – **crepuscular, moidore, modadonic, muniments, syzygy, oleaginous, febrifuge, scilicet, descrials, onomastics, senescence, clerihews, exergues**. When I got back home I took down the *Shorter Oxford Dictionary* [3rd edition] to sort out what meant what. The first page which accidentally fell open announced **DILDO** on the top left corner of the page. Well I know what <u>that</u> means, but I still took a peek at the definition – I was gobsmacked. **DILDO**, the dictionary said, '*is a word used in the refrain of ballads*' or '*refers to a particular tree or shrub*'. **Words can't be trusted.**

1. Diane Ackerman. *A Natural History of the Senses.* Phoenix (London 1980)   2. Geoff Ryman. *253, The Journey of 253 Lifetimes.* Flamingo (London 1998)   3. David Ogilvy. *An Autobiography.* John Wiley & Sons (New York 1997)

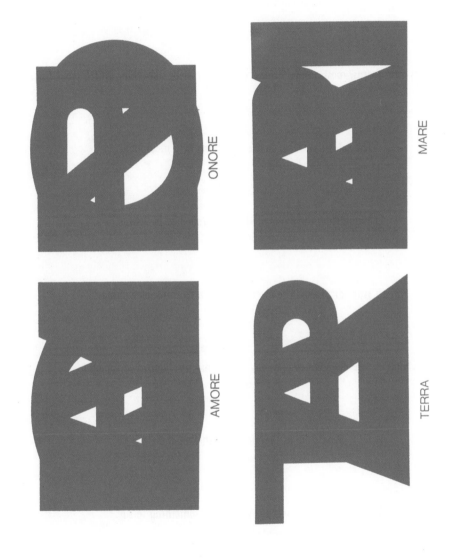

AMORE

ONORE

TERRA

MARE

When a word changes shape (by superimposing letters) it can change or lose meaning, but also acquire an unpredictable pictorial abstract quality.

'You can stroke people with words.'
F. SCOTT FITZGERALD

'Facts are like the individual letters, with their spikes and loops and thorns, that make up words.'
JOHN UPDIKE

'The paper burns, but the words fly away.'
BEN JOSEPH AKIBA

'When they hear words, most people think that there must be something worth pondering.'
GOETHE

'The coldest word was once a glowing new metaphor.'
THOMAS CARLYLE

'Thoughts die the moment they are embodied by words.'
ARTHUR SCHOPENHAUER

'Every word disappears the moment I begin to think over things.'
JACQUES HADAMARD

'Words … do not seem to play any role in my mechanism of thought.'
ALBERT EINSTEIN

'Words die as they bring forth thoughts.'
LEV VYGOTSKY

'Words are not just wind. Words have something to say.'
CHUANG TZU

'Designers have the last word with words.'
HERB LUBALIN

'I have devoted my life to poeting and paintry.'
KURT SCHWITTERS

The last word. The last entry in the twelve weighty volumes of the *Oxford English Dictionary*, which define 414,845 words, is the old Kentish word **zyxt** – the second person singular indicative present tense (in local argot) of the verb **to see.**

A connoisseur: A specialist who knows everything about something and nothing about anything.

A consultant: Someone who borrows your watch, and then charges you a fee to tell you the time.

Market research: By analogy a street lamp is for shedding light not for leaning on.

Presentation: *Canapés* are always served on toast; *hors d'oeuvres* appear by themselves.

Tradition: Something the middle-aged remember being taught 30 years ago.

Metaphysics: A restaurant where they give a 30-page menu and serve no food.

A proverb: A short sentence based on long experience.

A quotation: A starting-block for a hack in a hurry, a literary smoke signal between friends, or [as I prefer] a door to a new idea.

Weasel words: A weasel will make a small hole in an egg, suck out the insides, then place the egg back in the nest. Only when the egg is closely examined is it found to be hollow. Weasel words appear to say one thing when they say the opposite, or nothing at all.

The shortest pangram [contains all letters of the alphabet] is **Waltz, nymph, for quick jigs vex Bud.** The runner up is **Jackdaws love my big sphinx of quartz.** No one has managed to construct a pangram solely out of 26 letters without resorting to initials, proper names or mixing languages. This one gets near: **XV quick nymphs beg fjord waltz.** [SEE P346].

Sız Çekoslovakyalılaştıramadıklarımızdanmısınız? The longest word in Turkish translates as: 'Are you the one we tried to make into a Czechoslovakian, but couldn't succeed?' Equally tongue-tying is the longest word in English **Floccinaucinihilipilification** – the action of estimating as worthless. The only two words to contain all the vowels (a,e,i,o,u) in sequence are **abstemious** and **facetious.**

Marcel Duchamp: 'There is absolutely no chance for a word ever to express anything. As soon as we start putting our thoughts into words and sentences, everything goes wrong.'

Lawrence Durrell: 'Painting persuades by thrilling the mind and the optic nerve simultaneously, whereas words connote ... by their associative value. The spell they cast intends to master things – it lacks innocence. They are the instruments of Merlin or Faust. Painting is devoid of this kind of treachery – it is an innocent celebration of things, only seeking to inspirit and not coerce.'

Edward Lear: 'Gozo's coast scenery may truly be called pomskizillious and grophibberous.' [SEE P496].
A lost limerick by Lear has just been discovered and introduces a new nonsense word to join the lexicon of jumblies, pobbles, runcible spoons, and akonds of Swat. This is bombilious, a defunct adjective for humming like a bumble bee or as an editor of the *OED* reckons, a blend of bombast and bilious.

William Lutz: 'Doublespeak pretends to communicate but doesn't. It is language that makes the bad seem good, the negative appear positive, the unpleasant appear attractive. Doublespeak is language that avoids or shifts responsibility, language that is at variance with its real or purported meaning. It is language that conceals or prevents thought; rather than extending thought, doublespeak limits it.'

Robert Bresson: 'The things one can express with the hand, with the head, with the shoulders! How many useless and encumbering words then disappear!'

Alastair Reid: 'Words have a sound and shape, in addition to their meanings. Sometimes the sound is the meaning. Take a word like balloon and say it aloud, seven or eight times, you grow quite dizzy with it.'

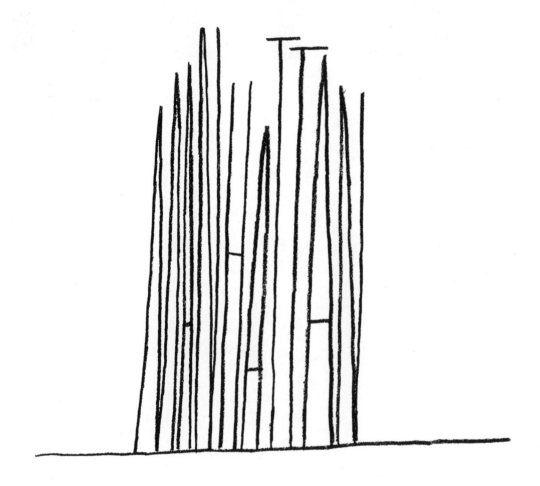

View driving in
from the Triboro bridge

Paul Valéry   'Seeing is forgetting the name of the thing one sees.'

'I see,' you said.

The uneasy relationship between verbal and visual was demonstrated in a painting by Jasper Johns in which the word 'red' was applied in yellow to label a blue patch. A proposition similar to the graphic statement shown here which is both correct and incorrect.

This ambiguity arises because visual symbols come in two kinds: pictorials which are recognizable and abstracts which have to be learnt. We perceive these through two independent cerebral systems; one recognizes images [say the PICTURE of a cross] while the other recognizes signs [say the WORD cross]. Both routes link in the brain and become synonymous with one another in the mind.

CROSS = +

Although word and picture can signify the same thing the effect they produce can be quite different. Writing 'Stars and Stripes' on a piece of cloth is not as effective as illustrating them. The words don't provoke the same emotional charge.

Having said that, if a person's mind-set is word-led, the effect will be biased: Bernard Shaw on first seeing the neon signs of Broadway commented that if he hadn't read them they would have been beautiful. And G.K. Chesterton, again on a first visit to Broadway, said it was an enchanted garden for anybody lucky enough to be unable to read. It's also a matter of era. Nowadays a large part of the contemporary art community from Jenny Holzer to Ed Ruscha find poetry in the verbal banality of advertising.

'The verbal and visual elements of modern communication are as indivisible as lyric and music in a song.'

George Lois

all my clothes have had other
people in them

Paola, age 7

Word Association. There is a game in which one word leads to another through association. For example a connection between sausage and brush might go: sausage – pork – pig – bristle – brush. Sometimes the thought for a graphic image arrives in a similar fashion. The image opposite figured on a poster aimed at stirring the conscience of people to contribute to a charity. It was prompted by the child's comment. Thus: poverty – second-hand clothes – laundry day – washing line – clothes peg – human figure. [SEE P439].

Sweet Hernia

Sweet Hernia on the heights of Plasticine
> *Sings to the nylon songs of Brassiere;*
The very aspirins listen, as they lean
> *Against the vitreous wind, to her sad air.*
I see the bloom of mayonnaise she holds
> *Colored like roof of far-away Shampoo*
Its asthma sweetens Earth! Oh, it enfolds
> *The alum land from Urine to Cachou!*
One last wild gusset, then she's lost in night …
> *And dusk the dandruff dims, and anthracite.*

Edward Blishen

Word Caricature. Walter de la Mare suggested that many essentially beautiful and evocative words have missed their vocation. *Linoleum,* for instance, might be a charming old Mediterranean seaport. Rossetti [or maybe Burne-Jones?] remarked that eighteenth-century art reminded him of a wet Sunday afternoon. I don't agree but I know what he meant. Words can conjure up mental images of things which would be less potent as pictures. Here are a few: The observation that Mick Jagger had child-bearing lips; that the Duchess of York reminded one of a bumper car in taffeta; that Arnold Schwarzenegger was a brown condom stuffed with walnuts, that a well-known bearded television personality looked like a rat peering through a lavatory brush. With a word caricature the mind can create its own pictorial image. [SEE P165].

IMAGING

Illustration. Tibor Kalman. *Lunch, Brunch, Supper* 1. Italo Calvino. *Six Memos for the Next Millennium*. Jonathan Cape (London 1992) 2. The *Sunday Times Magazine*, 30 April 2000

Italo Calvino: 'In devising a story, therefore, the first thing that comes to my mind is an image that for some reason strikes me as charged with meaning, even if I cannot formulate this meaning in discursive or conceptual terms. As soon as the image has become sufficiently clear in my mind, I set about developing it into a story; or better yet, it is the images themselves that develop their own implicit potentialities, the story they carry within them. Around each image others come into being, forming a field of analogies, symmetries, confrontations. Into the organization of this material, which is no longer purely visual but also conceptual, there now enters my deliberate intent to give order and sense to the development of the story; or rather, what I do is try to establish which meanings might be compatible with the overall design I wish to give the story and which meanings are not compatible, always leaving a certain margin of possible alternatives. At the same time, the writing, the verbal product, acquires increasing importance. I would say that from the moment I start putting black on white, what really matters is the written word, first as a search for an equivalent of the visual image, then as a coherent development of the initial stylistic direction. Finally, the written word little by little comes to dominate the field. From now on it will be the writing that guides the story toward the most felicitous verbal expression, and the visual imagination has no choice but to tag along.'[1] [SEE P165].

Alain de Botton: 'There is one writer/photographer at work today who seems to be properly exploiting the possibilities of integrating text and image. Sophie Calle, who is French, has published eight books to date, and each of them involves her in a documentary-type project of a most unusual sort. In one book, called simply *The Hotel*, Calle begins by explaining that she has long been fascinated by hotels and the lives that go on in them. So she took a job as a chambermaid in a small Paris hotel and over a number of days, took pictures of all the rooms when their occupants were away. In the accompanying text, she tries to work out who the occupants might be, based on the evidence they left around them – paperback, some jewellery, an apple, a linen suit and so on. The black-and-white pictures are fascinating; they offer a delightfully voyeuristic pleasure but they are sober too, suggesting fugitive hotel lives.'[2]

Contradiction

Although mixing up names, colours and shapes might seem nonsensical, the intention was to demonstrate the close relationship between word and picture by swapping elements, writing 'banana' on an 'orange shape', which was coloured 'apple green'. Of course bananas can be green and shapes of oranges mistaken for apples, but generally speaking preconceptions tell us what to see. We know lemons are yellow rather than pink.

[The illustration opposite is written in Italian. Arancia means orange, mela means apple – and I guess you can guess the rest.]

A shortfall in my technical skill suggested I search for images in nineteenth-century botanical prints, fruit wrappers, ends of cartons, old cookery books. Weekly visits to Portobello Road but nothing caught my eye. Eventually I decided the approach was to scissor out representative flat shapes and eliminate highlights or shadow.

The next move was to decide whether to spontaneously paint the shapes, to make careful outlines and then fill them in, to tear or cut them out of paper. Then there was the issue of colouring. Whether to use oils, acrylics, watercolours, pastels, chalk, gouache, dyes or inks.

Eventually I settled for careful scissoring and cheap coloured wrapping papers, which produced both forms and hues. Then there was the choice of background. Paper, card, board, masonite, canvas. And the texture of the material, the use of paste, gum, glue, rubber cement or adhesive spray. Making pictures is a hazardous occupation, much can go wrong.

This improbable rubberstamp of a contrived adhesive label demonstrates that verbal statements can be reinforced by visual contradictions.

Acknowledgement to René Magritte

Arancia

Pera

Banana

Mela

Limone

picture of a small place

Hugo Ball   **'The word and the image are one.'**

This commercial dog is his name.
A calligram is a graphic device which
combines thought, letters and picture. Calligrams have been
around a long time. For instance the Greek Simias (300 BC)
is probably better known for his picture-texts composed in the
shape of eggs, axes and wings, rather than the literary merit of
his poems .

Apollinaire composed his figurative poems less elaborately.
When he wrote *Il pleut* – the rain – he tore a page out of an
exercise book, casually jotted down words in descending lines
with red ink and got a printer to compose and proof it overnight.

Paradoxically, although his calligrams were conceived as images,
he was unconcerned with how they looked and his proof
notations only dealt with spelling, never with typeface or layout.
For a poet he was also unusually casual in his attitude towards
the reader. When an actress at a *soirée* was asked to read *Il
pleut* she dissolved into tears of frustration and the host hastily
had to transcribe it into horizontal lines.

The landscape being rained on by Apollinaire's *Il pleut* was
transcribed from the description of Luxembourg in *Pears
Cyclopedia*. Basically it states that the Grand Duchy is a small
place comprising mountains and valleys. As for the cat, she
speaks for herself.

The art of the calligram lies in its potential to communicate
several messages simultaneously.

```
      O        I
    am         my
    own        way
   of being  in
    view and yet
    invisible at
    once Hearing
     everything
      you see I
     see all of
    whatever you
    can have heard
    even inside the
    deep silences of
    black silhouettes
    like these images
    of furry surfaces
    darkly playing cat
   and mouse with your
   doubts about whether
   other minds can ever
   be drawn from hiding
   and made to be heard
   in inferred language
   I can speak only in
    your voice Are you
     done with my shadow
     That thread of dark
         word
          can
          all
          run
          out
          now
           and
            end
             our
             tale
```

Dog. The Spratts logo. Anon   **Cat.** John Hollander. *Kitty. Black domestic shorthair*

'Painting is silent poetry,

poetry is painting that speaks.'

Simonides of Ceos

**A rose is a rose is a rose, but
a box tree is not necessarily
a box tree. The illustration
opposite is of a box tree I
once saw in Rome.
The squarish picture and
name make sense if you're
an English speaker; however,
the name of this tree in
Italian, and other tongues,
happens to be different.
Thus if you don't know
the English term the
image is meaningless.**

Calligram. Marcel Béalu

'The physician
can bury
his mistakes,
but the architect
can only
advise his client
to plant vines.'

Frank Lloyd Wright

Diana Vreeland

'Pink is the navy blue of India.'

Portmanteaus and tropes. We *gather* our thoughts, *put* them into words, *convey* them to someone else who *gets* the message and *extracts* the meaning.[1] A metaphor is like a *portmanteau*, explained Humpty Dumpty, because there are two meanings packed into one. By using one way of saying two things, we can understand the unfamiliar by analogy with the familiar, convey the inexpressible by the expressible. Apparently the Apache Indian compares the human body with the corresponding parts of a car. Thus if an Apache is discussing a malfunction of the liver, only the context of the conversation would determine whether he needed hospitalization or his battery changed. Actually we all use figures of speech and tropes. A trope is a word used in a sense other than that which is proper to it. A body of water, a body of work, a body of men. The head of the household, head of the table, of an organization. The face of a clock, playing card or cliff. The foot of a mountain – we also foot the bill – the leg of a race, the eye of a needle, the brow of a hill. Cups have lips, combs and propositions have teeth, fixings have knuckles and joints. Even a book has a spine, a back, a body of text, headlines, footnotes and often a preface and appendix. Some are dog-eared. Body metaphors are everywhere: you hold a meeting, eye a babe, take things at face value, nose around the office, mouth lyrics, have teething troubles, neck in the back seat, arm the militia, shoulder a burden, elbow your way in, hand someone something, give someone the finger, knuckle under, thumb a lift, go belly up, have to stomach other people's complaints, rib a friend, toe the line. Comparisons can create a more vivid picture than a prosaic description. Here are three examples: In its domestic state the Gnu is said 'to resemble a horse, a buffalo and a stag, and in its wild condition a thunderbolt, an earthquake and a cyclone'. The *Oxford English Dictionary*

soberly describes it as a South African quadruped. A dance by Josephine Baker was described as 'a cross between a kangaroo, a cyclist, and a machine gun'. And a Turner painting, observed Mark Twain, looked 'like a ginger cat having a fit in a bowl of tomatoes'. Analogies make complex affairs more understandable by explaining them in metaphorical terms. If the nucleus of a human cell was magnified a thousand times it would be the size of a small aspirin, and the DNA wiring would stretch a mile. If the earth is compared to a calendar, it was born in January, life began during late November, and mankind only appeared at one minute to midnight on 31 December. Actually I prefer Mark Twain's version: 'If the *Eiffel Tower were now representing the world's age, the skin of paint on the pinnacle-knob at its summit would represent man's share of that age; and anybody would perceive that that skin was what the tower was built for.*' And my life, and yours, is merely a momentary glint of sunshine off that. Reviewing a De Kooning retrospective, a critic suggested the paintings were '*something like the experience of having sex with someone gorgeous in a bath filled with maple syrup and milk while eating a fried egg and bacon sandwich*'. A pity he wasn't more specific. Then there is the *Law of Unhelpful Comparisons.* This is when the attempt to make something comprehensible by comparing it with something else, does the opposite. The Greek newspaper *To Vima* reported that worldwide we consume about two billion eggs every day, enough, they wrote: '*to make an omelette the size of the island of Cyprus!*' And I've read that if you lined up all the cells of a polar bear in a row it would comfortably make the round trip from here to the moon and back.[2] Then there's Irina Dunn's comment that '*a woman needs a man like a fish needs a bicycle*'. You know of course that a glass of London tapwater might have passed through the Queen four times. All confirming Garcia Lorca's description of a metaphor as 'a leap that unites two worlds'.

Diane Ackerman: 'The word *face* probably came from the Latin *facere*, to make or shape. The etymology hints at artifice as a face is something we revise to fit the occasion ... In the English Midlands, I once heard a woman in her eighties refuse a second helping of cake by saying ... "Don't overface me." ... We face off, face the music, interface, lose face, do an about-face, face up to, fall flat on our faces, talk face to face. We regard the face of the clock or of a building, and remark how the face of the city has changed, and how life may vanish from the face of the earth. On the face of it, we are obsessed with faces.' [SEE P276].

Edward O. Wilson: 'Consider the technical language of the arts themselves. A plot first meant a physical site and building plan, then the stage director's plot or blocking plan, then the action or story blocked out. In the sixteenth century a frontispiece was a decorated front of a building, then the title page of a book ornamented with a figure, usually the allegorical representation of a building, and finally the illustrated page that precedes the title page. A stanza, which in Italian is a public room or resting place, has been appropriated in English to mean the roomlike set of four or more lines separated typographically from other similar sets.'

Ogden Nash: 'One thing that literature would be greatly the better for would be a more restricted employment by authors of simile and metaphor. Authors of all races, be they Greeks, Romans, Teutons or Celts, can't seem just to say anything is the thing it is, but have to go out of their way to say that it is like something else.'

Freud is an obvious butt for the punster. This portrait suggests that Freud looked at the world through a short-sighted pudendum.

   1. Steven Pinker. *The Language Instinct.* Penguin (London 1994)   2. Richard Dawkins. *River Out of Eden.* Phoenix (London 1995)

speed

The sketch of the back of a van was drawn by Alfred Hitchcock for an escape sequence in *The Lodger* (1926), one of his early films. His idea was that the heads of the driver and mate would be seen through the oval windows in the back doors. As the getaway van turned and swerved the heads, moving from side to side, would look as if the van had a face and was rolling its eyes.

'The negative is the score', said Ansel Adams 'but the print is the performance.' [SEE P360]. Demonstrated here by a metaphorical image of speed in this photograph by Man Ray of Francis Picabia hurtling along in his car.

It's impossible to imply movement in static images without resorting to visual metaphor. Velázquez anticipated photography by smudging the spokes of a spinning wheel in his painting entitled *Las Hilanderas* – the first blurred expression of movement, say art historians. Less optically literal in its rendering, and even more abstract, is Picasso's *Sleeper Turning*. This vaguely simultaneously indicates where she was and where she is.

A less obvious metaphor of speed is the BMW trademark. At one time the company made aeroplane engines, and corporate folklore reveals that the design was born when someone, looking along the fuselage from the cockpit, started the engine. The propellers started to turn, gave a rapid visual frisson, then overtook the eye and settled into the firmer pattern of a quadrant. You gain a similar static effect looking at the rapidly turning wheels of a car.

In Germany the emblem represents Bayerische Motoren Werke. In the hip black community BMWs are known as Black Man's Wagon (or Bob Marley and the Wailers) and in South Africa the letters are an invitation to Break My Windows.

'Memorandum: One cannot describe reality; only give metaphors that indicate it. All human modes of description (photographic, mathematical, and the rest, as well as literary) are metaphorical. Even the most precise scientific description of an object or movement is a tissue of metaphors.' John Fowles

Symbol [1910]   Symbol [1940]

a Francis Picabia en grand vitesse   man Ray Cannes 1924

'notice the convulsed orange inch of moon perching on this silver minute of evening.'   *ee cummings*

STROMBOLI

Make Believe

Prejudice, masquerading as common nonsense, precludes us from perceiving the irrational and persuades us to be affronted by the rational. Most see no connection between Meret Oppenheim's surrealist cup and saucer covered in fur and an umbrella stand made out of an elephant's foot. The first considered to be a piece of art and the other an object commonly encountered in the homes of retired colonials. My auntie had one (umbrella stand). [SEE P243].

'Extra Virgin' says the label on a bottle of olive oil. Oxymorons [*oxys* = sharp, *moros* = dull] are metaphors which make contradictory analogies. Jumbo shrimps, pretty ugly, paper tigers, military intelligence, and good grief, there are even genuine imitations [SEE P243] and plastic glasses. Visual oxymorons follow the same tack with plastic flowers, rubber ducks and stone angels. The aeroplane opposite is a symbol for an eccentric who builds solar-powered inflatable aeroplanes in his garage. An oxymoron delivered by an incongruous marriage between aerospace technology and calligraphic skill.

Numbly gazing at a boring television interview with the Chairman of the Association of British Newspaper Editors, I saw this representative of literary interface respond to a critical confrontation by saying: 'Don't wipe us off yet [why not, I thought] by a long chalk.' Then there are listemes which are idiomatic phrases which convey meaning but are meaningless. I think that's oxymoronic. Anyway they have to be learnt since they can't be deduced, and furthermore, they are untranslatable. Try putting 'kick the bucket' or 'spill the beans' into French.

'A metaphor always works both ways ... like a two-way street.' *Claude Lévi-Strauss*

'A newly invented metaphor assists thought by evoking a visual image.' *George Orwell*

'A good metaphor implies an intuitive perception of the similarity in the dissimilar.' *Aristotle*

'My work has become a simple metaphor of life. A figure walking down his road, making his mark.' *Richard Long*

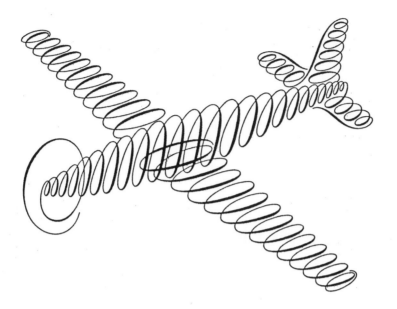

'A NOVEMBER STILLNESS WAS SETTLING LIKE A DEADLY OXYMORON ON THE APRIL LANDSCAPE'

Illustrations. Meret Oppenheim. *Breakfast in Fur. 1938.* John McConnell. *Aeroplane.* **Quote.** Donna Tartt

camel country

A liger is the offspring of a lion and a tiger. They've crossed a goat with a sheep and call it a geep or a shoat. The ancient Greeks called the strange African animal with a long neck and spotted body a camelopard – assuming the giraffe was conceived by a camel and a leopard. [SEE P49]. A journalist wrote that he only remembered useless things, such as the fact that camels can't walk backwards. I never knew that. It stuck in my mind. Once, when in camel country, I took the opportunity to check it out – he's wrong – they can. Camels get stick because they aren't perceived correctly. For instance the difference between the camel proper and, so to speak, the camel improper, is usually more than just being exhibited smirking and breaking wind. For comedians a camel is a horse with an air lock, although genetically it is more like a cow than a horse. For entrepreneurs a camel is a horse designed by a committee, although a committee is incapable of coming up with anything so perfectly designed to perform so effectively under such difficult conditions. Considering their background, and despite its attributes, the thought of using a camel to symbolize a brand of tobacco is somewhat obtuse. Still there's more to a camel than meets the needle's eye. The Arabs, I am informed, have ninety-nine names for God but only the camel knows the hundredth name. That accounts for its supercilious demeanour but nevertheless despite this insight the camel doesn't receive a single mention in *The Koran*. Elephants suffer the same shortfall, some considering them merely an inflated mouse built to government specifications. [SEE P28].

TURKISH & AMERICAN
BLEND

Note. I met a gentleman called Tom Hearn. He told me that during the 1930s his dad was an officer in the Camel Corps stationed in Egypt. For some reason the Camel Corps used the same military ranks as the Turkish army. His rank was Hearn Bey. If you're not a man of Kent, or a Londoner — forget it! [SEE P493].

Marcel Duchamp used this Tom Swiftie [SEE P457], to point out it takes time to judge the worth of a piece of work.

Arthur Koestler   'A pun is two strings of thought tied with an acoustic knot.'

Puns are words with the same sounds but different meanings. Some say a pun is the lowest form of wit, others that wit is the best form of pun. Here are two classics of the genre.

Lord Curzon, on hearing that the monks of Mount Athos were violating their cows, suggested they were sent a Papal Bull. And Dorothy Parker's observation that if all the girls attending the Yale Prom were laid end to end she wouldn't have been surprised.

A particular kind of visual pun is the rebus, a composition in which pictures represent words and things by sounds. Picture punning was a useful device in illiterate medieval times when it was often used to communicate identities. One such picture pun was the emblem of Thomas Beckington, Bishop of Bath and Wells, which was a beacon surmounting a tun (a barrel). Another appeared in the Arms of the City of Oxford and portrayed a red ox crossing a white ford, a motif later adapted by William Morris as the symbol for his car, the Morris Oxford, which was manufactured in Oxford. [SEE P507].

Rizla, the famous French brand of cigarette papers, owes its contemporary trademark to a similar adaptation. The La Croix family established a paper mill in 1799 and manufactured rice paper which became known as *Riz La Croix*. The step from this early brand name to their current logotype is not difficult to figure out.

The rebus opposite was the image for a 1960s poster on the theme of PEACE. [SEE P473]. The design plays on the fortune teller's symbol for death – the ACE of SPADES.

PE ?

Design. Robert Brownjohn

a
stinky pinky
and
some
Tom Swifties

Tenuous visual correspondences between words and pictures include **oxymorons, rebuses, palindromes, tropes, acronyms, anagrams, lipograms, macronics, onomatopoeia, nonce-words, stinky pinkies** and **Tom Swifties**. You won't find the last two in standard dictionaries. They were coined, I think, by Willard R. Espy, American language maven.[1]

In visual parlance **Tom Swifties** demonstrate what they state. The collage which tells you it is a collage [opposite] and the B A L A N C E S which balance – overleaf. This collage – typographic connoisseurs will notice – starts with the abbreviation for Company, incorporates a date from a Chinese calendar, and concludes with a portion from an Indian newspaper's masthead.

A **stinky pinky**, is 'a noun modified by an alliterative rhyming adjective'. A **Lazy Lucy** is a revolving tray in the middle of a table which allows whatever is being served to be turned to whoever needs serving. Shapes can rhyme as well as sounds. This logotype design by Herb Lubalin typographically converts letter to womb and ampersand to embryo. I hesitate to label this a **stinky pinky,** but that's what it is.

A **Tom Swiftie**, is a phrase in which a verb or adverb supplies the pun. For instance, '*Thank God I remembered to take my umbrella,*' he drily observed. The smudge breezily echoes a puff of wind to create a pictorial **Tom Swiftie**. Inclined letters help emphasize the proposition.

Rebus comes from Latin, *non verbis sed rebus*, meaning, '*not by words but by things*'. A **rebus** is a puzzle in which letters, syllables or words are replaced by visual images such as symbols and pictures. The same sort of association can be made with names. 'Chalky' White, 'Dicky' Bird and 'Dusty' Miller readily lend themselves to visual interpretation. So does this insignia of Dutch designer Piet Zwart (Peter Black).

A **pun** plays on the different meanings attached to one word. They're the sort of word that you figure out only to discover you have to figure out what you have figured out. Saul Bass didn't sign his name but rubberstamped a **punning** chimerical image instead.

An **anagram** is changing the order of the letters forming a word or phrase, to create another: for instance *total abstainers* can be happily re-arranged to *sit not at ale bars*. This one is a typographic version for a lady named Eva. The upside-down-lower-case ə approximates the shape of the right-way-up-lower-case a.

An **anonym** is a name written backwards. The concept is not as pointless as it may seem. A M B U L A N C E is sometimes reversed on the vehicle, so that drivers can get the message in their rear-view mirror. [SEE P247].

1. Willard R. Espy. *An Almanac of Words at Play*. Charles N. Potter (New York 1975)

六　月　JUN 198

Co. 11 AGE

WED 星期

Get ready fo

年　初工口　十六夏至

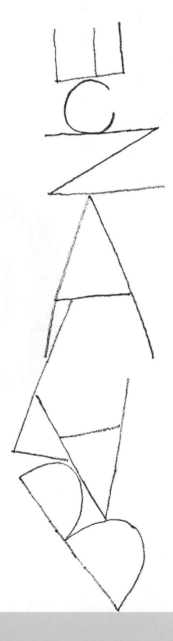

Crime is only
a lefthanded
form of human
endeavour

... as Louis Calhern said (as Alonzo Emmerich) in *The Asphalt Jungle*

GAUCHE

Over lunch Rodolfo Bonetto, a Milanese designer, was telling me that if he had to make a choice between two ways of doing something he invariably chose the wrong one. He wondered aloud whether this was because he was **left-handed**, and meanwhile he absent-mindedly ate the roll on my side plate.

For some reason those who confuse **left** with **right** don't have the same problem between top or bottom. Gravity rules. In most societies up to ten per cent of people are **left-handed**. It's probably always been that way. Most stone tools were shaped for the **right-handed** and prehistoric handprints in a cave at Castillo (Spain) reveal that out of seventeen impressions thirteen are of the **left** hand and only four of the **right**. You need your **right** hand to stencil your **left**.

Despite being a minority, **left-handers** are dominant in certain activities. When they recruit astronauts the shortlist always has more **left-handed** people. **Left-handers** abound in the visual arts perhaps because the **right** half of the brain is concerned with spatial affairs. Mind you a check around thirty designers at a London design studio revealed only two **left-handers**. I can't figure out whether that's **all right** or not.

The Semitic inventors of writing wrote **right** to **left**, which is still the custom in the Middle East, but I haven't come across an explanation of why in the West we ended up writing **left** to **right**. Whatever the reason, different cultures have a bias towards one direction or the other, although in some instances the balance is more equal. For example, when half the population in Britain clasp their hands together they fold the **left** thumb above the **right**, the other half do it the other way. And when it comes to handedness, the Negritos in the Andaman Islands are an exception as they are ambidextrous. Mind you, although they can blink they find it difficult to wink.

'Not being a political thinker,' wrote Philip Larkin, 'I suppose I identify the **Right** with certain virtues and the **Left** with certain vices.' So do most of us : **my rights, being right, legal rights, right ideas, right of way. Dexter**, the Latin for **right**, is still reflected in the advantages of being **dextrous** and **adroit**. **Left-footed** implies clumsiness, and there is no **Bill of Lefts**. The Latin for **left** is **sinister**. A word which is also associated with undesirable connotations. We even go **right ahead** or get **left behind**. As a lyric delivered by Elvis Presley goes : **'I'm left, you're right, she's gone.'** Speaking for myself I'm right-handed but don't like to be **left out**. On the other hand my left-handed daughter pointed out to me that if the right side of the brain controls the left side of the body, then only left-handed people are in their **right mind**.

Right hand — left hand

From Mr Tim Hembry.

Sir, I would be interested to hear from anyone who could explain to me a query I have had for some time now. It is to do with the terms "right-handed" and "left-handed" in referring to batsmen in cricket, I myself being a "left-handed" batsman.

One is called "left-handed" if one has his front foot (right), one shoulder (right), and the top hand, which is supposed to be the one which does the work, is also the right hand.

It only seems sensible to me for a "left-handed" batsman in fact to be called "right-handed" and vice-versa. It also seems sensible that if one is right-handed normally for writing, etc, one should be taught to but "left-handed" as one's right arm is stronger and would be the "top hand".

Therefore if one is "left-handed" normally one should bat "right-handed", again for the same reason and surely this would help one to play over the ball and keep it down. As yet no one has been able to explain to me the reason for this phraseology. Is this because there is no logical answer?

Yours sincerely,
TIM HEMBRY,
41 Hartington Court,
Lansdowne Way,
Stockwell, SW8.

Ferniehirst Castle, home to the left-handed Kerr family for 500 years, has an anti-clockwise main staircase so that swordsmen had an advantage. Border families fought endless feuds with savage enthusiasm and the Kerrs were no exception.[1]

So well the Kerrs their left-hands ply,
The dead and dying round them lie,
The castle gained, the battle won,
Revenge and slaughter are begun.

Andrew Kerr, founder of the dynasty in 1457, taught his sons and manservants (who by custom took the family name) to wield sword and axe with their left hands. They in turn taught their sons and eventually left-handedness and family name became synonymous.

But the Kerrs were aye the deadliest foes
That e'er to Englishmen were known,
For they were all bred left-handed men,
And fence against them there was none.[2]

To check out this legendary characteristic doctors in Britain and America were asked (1974) to note the handedness of their patients called Kerr or Carr. The results revealed that 29.5 per cent were left-handed – or ambidextrous – so if you are a Kerr or Carr your chances of being left-handed are threefold more than anyone else's.

Left-handers have always been treated with suspicion and referred to as **kerr-handed**, **cack-handed**, **corry-fisted**, **cawry fistit**, **dolly-pawed**, or **cuddy wifter**. A **south paw** may have the advantage in sports like cricket or tennis but a left-hander can't be a polo player.

Left-handers are lucky they aren't snails. Snails which have a spiral which curls to the left can't mate with those that have one which curls to the right. And I guess you know that when Saint Patrick brought christianity to the Emerald Isle he asked all those snakes who wished to stay — to raise their right hand.

Left hand, right hand

From Colonel J. Lloyd-Jones

Sir, Tim Hembry's query (June 11) on left and right-handedness applies equally to golf.

The right-handed golfer (so-called) uses the left hand predominantly in controlling the club. Thus, if one can persuade a true left-hander who wishes to take up golf to approach the game in a right-handed manner, his stronger left arm and hand will give him a significant advantage over the naturally right-handed, or vice versa!

Left-handed golf is rather more expensive!

Yours sincerely,
JOHN LLOYD-JONES,
(Past chairman, Army Golf Club),
White Lodge,
Wentworth Crescent,
Ash Vale,
Aldershot,
Hampshire.
June 11.

Newsclips. *The Times*, 11 and 12 June 1982

ADROIT

1. Stanly Coren. *The Left-hander Syndrome*. Murray (London 1993)   2. Walter Laidlaw. *The Reprisal*

ASYMMETRIC PREFERENCES. I read about an experiment in which a photographer took pictures of two subjects.[1] A symmetrical scene with a tree in the middle of the frame; an asymmetrical scene with a car positioned on one side of the picture travelling left to right. They probably looked something like these sketches.

 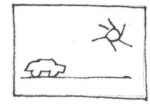

Each of the two photographs was then printed two ways: In the way they were actually photographed and in reverse. That is to say with the image flipped left to right.

 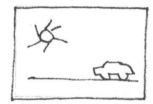

The original and reversed photographs of the tree were then shown to an audience who were asked to choose which they preferred. Not surprisingly, the choice between the two was roughly equal.

However, when shown the original and reversed pictures of the car 75 per cent favoured the version with the car travelling left to right. Perhaps we are so used to reading and writing left to right that most of us feel more at ease looking at things that way. The same pair of photographs were then shown to an extremely orthodox Jewish community who only read Hebrew. The choice between the trees was again predictably even, but when it came to the cars almost all of them selected the one travelling right to left. How we read and write influences our view of the world.

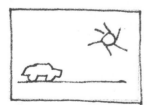 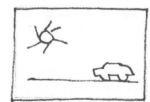

   1. Martin Gardner. *The Ambidextrous Universe.* Penguin (Harmondsworth 1970)

 [SEE next page]

I FELT A

IN MY

AS IF M

HAD

I TRIED TO

SEAM B

BUT COU

MAKE T

THE THOU

I STROVE

UNTO THE TH

BUT SEQUE

OUTO

LIKE BALLS U

EMILY

'Johnnie Walker, symbol of one of
the most famous whisky brands,
is performing a sharp about turn.
Hitherto the striding figure, 'born
1820 and still going strong', has
paced from right to left. But the
brand owners, United Distillers
and Vintners, fear that it makes
Johnnie look as if he is walking
back into the past. From the new
year, the figure will be reversed
so that he steps left to right –
heading for a bright new future.'

[*The Times,* 27 December 1999]

[**SEE** previous page]

CLEAVAGE
Y MIND
Y BRAIN
SPLIT,
MATCH IT,
Y SEAM,
ULD NOT
HEM FIT,
GHT BEHIND
TO JOIN
OUGHT BEFORE,
NCE RAVELLED
F REACH
PON A FLOOR.

DICKINSON

Stripes on British ties run diagonally top right to bottom left (as you view them) and they are the sartorial equivalent of heraldic bars on a shield. If you were a bastard the direction was reversed and known as a bar *sinister* (Latin: left). American ties run down top left to bottom right, not because of dubious parentage but because their cutters work with the material face down. British cutters work with the fabric face up. The British (High Right) and American style (Reverse Bias) are a handy indication of those entitled to wear particular ties and those who simply like the colours. [SEE P506].

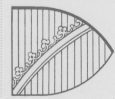

Women button up right over left because popular fashion was influenced by the times when upper-class ladies were dressed by maidservants. It's easier for a right-handed person to dress someone else facing them. Men buttoned left over right as they dressed themselves – with their right hand – and, as some wag pointed out, could unbutton their trousers in a hurry.

There is an account in Plato's *Symposium* of hermaphrodites (or androgynes). Zeus split the hermaphrodites in half, the legend goes, so they are all halves wandering around seeking the half they lost. Each is both. The fundamental basis of love.

Some brain-damaged unfortunates were taken to the *Piazza del Duomo* in Milan and asked to describe the scene. They were able to identify everything in the right half of their field of vision, but none in the left. From the opposite end they were able to describe the right half, that's to say the left side they couldn't see from the other end. They were condemned to only see the right half of everything.

The Automobile Association says that left-handed traffic is the result of a papal declaration by Pope Boniface VIII in the 14th century. This advised pilgrims heading to Rome to travel 'sword to sword' to protect themselves against attack.

'Why are twice as many left shoes as right washed ashore in Holland, while the opposite is true for Scottish beaches?' Steve Jones, *Almost like a Whale*, page 320.

The Greek Olympics (circa 776BC) were run anti-clockwise although for some odd reason, the first modern Olympics (1896) were run clockwise. Nowadays athletics run 'left hand inside', one explanation being that most athletes (and horses) have stronger right legs. Perhaps the reason fairground carousels head off anti-clockwise. Of course if you're a clock – you also run anti-clockwise. Imagine you *are* a clock, looking out. For you time runs backwards across your face.

Author Patrick O'Brian took his readers on epic sea voyages. His own history was even more turbulent and when he died it emerged he wasn't who he said he was. Perhaps this accounts for his habit of writing his manuscripts using his right hand for the first page and his left for the next, and so on. Maybe he never let the left hand know what the right hand was doing.

Design writer Steven Heller interviewing Seymour Chwast, American designer and illustrator:

Heller – You treat your right hand like a second child and your left hand like royalty. Does your right hand serve any useful purpose?

Chwast – Well, yes. I use my right hand to hold my head up at the correct distance from my drawing table. I couldn't work any other way.

I've undertaken personal research on hydraulics, and am able to confirm that in Australia the water goes down the washbasin hole anti-clockwise. In England, or more specifically in Notting Hill Gate where I live, it goes clockwise. I once adjourned to the lavatory on a flight back from Sydney precisely at the moment when it crossed the Equator, filled the basin, and pulled the plug. The water seemed to be sucked straight down. I suspect the equipment was having me on – particularly since I've now learnt that the bubbles in a glass of Guinness go down, not up.

tfel eht ot daer ot

Everyone knows whether they are right-handed, or left-handed. Few know whether they are right- or left-eyed.

Do you?

If you don't know, stretch out an arm, either will do, and point with a finger to a distant corner of the room – keep both eyes open.

Staying in this position close one eye, then the other. In one case your eye will match whatever you're pointing at in the corner, in the other your finger will be pointing way off the mark.

If you're on target, that's your leading eye.

If you're right-eyed you probably see the above figure as a rabbit, if you're left-eyed you probably plump for a bird.

Illustration. This is the original image with appeared in *Die Fliegenden Blätter*. Popular science books generally reproduce bastardized versions.

Nasrudin,
the mullah,
was sitting
with a friend
as dusk fell.

'Light
a candle',
the friend said,
'there is one
just by your
left side.'

'How
can I tell
my right
from my left
in the dark,
you fool?'
said the mullah.

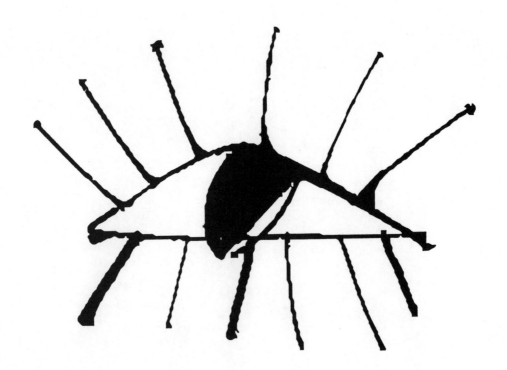

Navaho proverb

'Many tongues – one eye.'

ROCK WRITING

Rock Writing,[1] as it is called by Native Americans, is a sophisticated system of pictograms based on metaphors and handsigns. It is quite different from conventional writing.

The location and position of inscribed rocks indicate the direction in which the messages are to be read. Top to bottom, for example, or left to right. The humps, holes and cracks in the stone, the use of paint or charcoal, whether signs are scratched, chiselled, abraded or rubbed are all significant. Then there are the details within the pictograms.

One ubiquitous motif variously looks like a sheep, goat or deer. Actually it isn't any of these but a generic animal with body language. The body might be square, rectangular, or semicircular. The legs, straight or bent, long or short, have feet pointing forwards or backwards. The horns are curved, angled, of different lengths, wide apart, close together, or not shown at all. The animal might be fat or thin, have two heads, three legs, face left or right, be upside down or incomplete … nuances which signify something.

Some are obvious. A pictogram placed vertically means travelling uphill, hind legs placed towards the centre of the body signify the end of a journey, feet pointing in one direction and the body in the other means there and back – or a change of mind. Other meanings are less apparent.

The principles apply to other creatures. A bird could represent an overview of an event, while flying away means just that, and alighting indicates a safe place. Strutting signifies showing off; tilting forward indicates waiting. Secondary information is expressed through size and shape of body, length of neck and beak, angle of wings, number of feathers, or the direction of track marks.

Once one knows what lies behind the signs one doesn't look at them in the same way.

1. LaVan Martineau. *The Rocks Begin to Speak*. KC Publications (Las Vegas 1973)

The partial deciphering of *Rock Writing* (it finally died out in the nineteenth century) has exposed a mind-bender. How could it be that the versatile sheep/goat/deer inhabited prehistoric sites around the world? Does this imply that in remote antiquity there might have been a universal language of handsigns?

When American LaVan Martineau put his expert *Rock Writing* experience to deciphering ancient pictograms at Cemmo in Italy, he discovered that he could broadly understand what they depicted. His interpretation goes into considerable detail but in essence reveals they record the events of a prehistoric battle. Think about it – a modern American (half American Indian too) reading an account by a prehistoric European *rock writer* drawn up some four thousand years ago. That all seems fanciful but Martineau offers an explanation.

There is a natural human instinct to use the same shapes to denote the same things. Stick figures are just as likely to be found doodled on a businessman's notepad as on a cave wall.

However, many prehistoric signs have absolutely no visual relationship to people or objects, and their common appearance in different far-flung places suggests they are unlikely to have been invented independently. Martineau maintains that these ancient pictograms were born out of handsigns – a shared *lingua franca*. His thesis is that American Indians from different tribes with different languages – which between them differ as widely as English does from Chinese or Bantu[1] – were able to communicate through a common sign language, and its visual expression in *Rock Writing*. The same could have applied to early man. Thus *Rock Writing* remained relatively unchanged for thousands of years.

[SEE P397]

a neolithic battle

   1. F. David Peat. *Blackfoot Physics*. Fourth Estate (London 1994)

Dear Sir :

In 1876, on the American frontier, Capt. W. P. Clark of the 2nd Cavalry was placed in command of 300 Indian scouts. He was amazed to find that his scouts communicated easily by sign, although speaking vastly different languages – Pawnee, Shoshone, Arapaho, Cheyenne, Crow and Sioux. Intrigued, Clark asked to learn the language, and did. After subsequent contact with other tribes, Clark concluded that signing was a basic language known among virtually all American Indians, enabling them to live and function in close harmony, sharing their cultures and, to some degree, their religions.

In 1881 he was ordered to visit many tribes and prepare a dictionary. The result was published in 1885. Then as now, little attention was paid to Clark's pioneering study. But Isabel Crawford, a Baptist missionary sent in 1893 to live among the Cheyenne at Elk Creek (in what is now western Oklahoma), obtained a copy. Deafened by quinine at 16, she used the book to learn the Indian sign language. She then moved, alone, onto the Kiowa-Comanche-Apache reservation. Using sign, she taught the Kiowa farming, gardening, canning and cooking, and gave her 'Jesus talks,' as well.

Leonard Sanders
Fort Worth

Greek epigram : 'A poem is a speaking picture, a picture is a silent poem.'

Native Americans recorded annual events like floods, snow, meteors, epidemics, ceremonies on an animal hide. These records were called *Winter Counts.* Ruth Beebe Hill, who lived with the *Dakotah*, noted down this comment made by a tribal artist while he was drawing : '… all *Dakotah* hunt thoughts by way of pictures … **pressing the essence of a thought into a hide** … drawings are a string that ties memory to the truth.'[1]

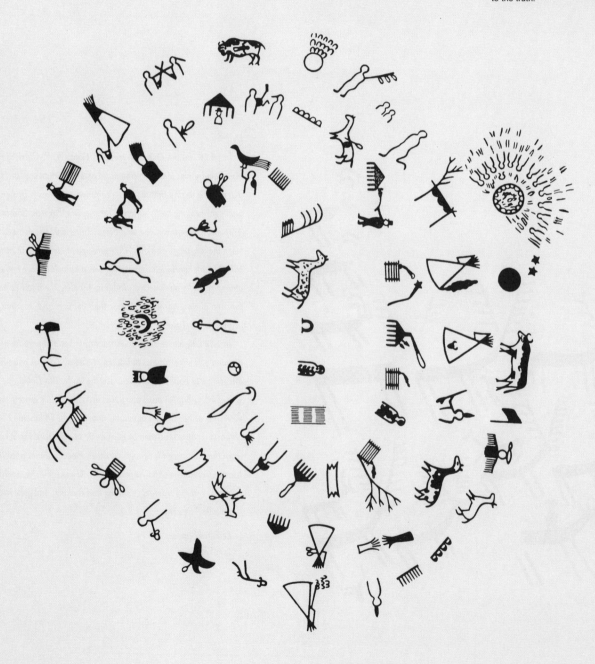

1. Ruth Beebe Hill. *Hanta Yo.* Futura Books (London 1980)

Arno Schmidt : 'Signs are cold expressions for a warm set of facts.'

POLICE VERY ACTIVE

POLICE INATTENTIVE

MAN WITH GUN

STOP HERE

TELL A PITIFUL STORY

DAMP PLACE

DANGER POLICE

EVERYTHING OK

FEROCIOUS DOG

WOMAN

DOG

WATCH OUT

MAN

VERY GOOD

FREINDLY

BE AT EASE

DANGER

NOBODY

GOOD PLACE FOR BEGGING

Marks used by tramps in Italy to convey useful information to each other

'THIS ART

WHICH SPEAKS TO THE EYE,

'WHENCE DID THE WOND'ROUS MYSTIC ART ARISE

WHICH PAINTS FOR THE SIGHT

OF PAINTING SPEECH, AND SPEAKING TO THE EYES?

WHAT SOUND EXPRESSES TO

THAT WE, BY TRACING MAGIC LINES ARE TAUGHT

THE MIND THROUGH THE

HOW TO EMBODY, AND TO COLOUR THOUGHT?'

MEDIUM OF THE EAR,

WILLIAM MASSEY

WHICH IS AS FIXED AS

THE VOICE IS FUGITIVE.'

COMTE DE GUEBLIN

Gnomic observation   Writing is the knife and fork of the mind.

scry:

SCRY is a word which encompasses gaze, discover, and cry out with pleasure. Or, as the *Oxford English Dictionary* yawningly defines it: 'to perceive something with an exclamation'. Dr Dee was occultist, astrologer, mathematician, sorcerer, alchemist, inventor, typographer, and secret agent. In this last capacity he was sent to Cracow by Queen Elizabeth to spy on the Spanish. I can't imagine why Poland was relevant but it was. While there he disseminated misinformation by forecasting that storms in the Channel would destroy the Armada. They did. Ironically, he had also invented the 'paradoxical' compass which eliminated navigational errors. Meanwhile gazing into his SCRYING GLASS (crystal ball) Dr Dee saw radiant colours, iridescent patterns of light, images of rivers, mountains, stars and rainbows, all magically becoming transformed into letters. The alphabet of angels, no less. Divine messages from heaven. He was also convinced the messages were sent in reverse order as normal transmission was destructive.[1] [SEE P243]. Dee also believed that joining up stars revealed the origin of Hebrew letters, a speculation as improbable as the thought that letter shapes were derived from the curl of the tongue in pronunciation, or that Hebrew is Welsh written and spoken backwards. Celestial writing is still with us in today's newspaper horoscope.

brick libraries:

The earliest system of writing emerged in the Middle East six thousand years ago. Known as *cuneiform* [*cuneus* = wedge; *forma* = shape] it predated Egyptian *hieroglyphics* and Chinese *ideograms* by a few hundred years. From birth to demise *cuneiform* spanned three thousand years – about a third longer than the entire history of the Western alphabet to date. *Cuneiform* anticipated the computer: the stylus was the keyboard, the tablet the monitor. The stylus was a reed with a point for scratching lines at one end, and a wedge for stamping at the other. *Cuneiform* could create hundreds of combinations and characters. This one means 'to drink'.

The technique was to hold a damp clay tablet in one hand and write the characters in rows with the other. Tablets were easy to transport and store. They tabulate the first records to enshrine ideas and beliefs and Babylonian laws which took mankind beyond blood feud and personal retribution. Laws which included judgements on slaves, property, sale, lease, barter, gift, marriage and divorce. Loans to the hungry were free, loans to business charged at 30 % interest. Legal casuistry is no modern innovation, nor are the principles underlying most new technologies.

futharc:

Runes, also known by the undignified name of *Futharc*, emerged in Scandinavia and Northern Europe during the third century (BC). *Runes* are associated with secrecy, sorcery and alchemy. The very word means 'to whisper'.

The letters had mystical correspondences with trees as did *Beth-Luis-Nion* – an Irish variation of the script. *Beth* seems ubiquitous in alphabetworld. [SEE P172]. By the sixteenth century *runes* had died out although a few characters persisted – notably in:

Ye Olde Englishe Tea Shoppe

Ye is *Runic* for *th* [*the*], the rest is phoney *Olde Englishe*. James Joyce used *runes* to title the eighteen chapters of *Ulysses*, and Robert Graves exhaustively describes their attendant meanings, associations and mythologies in *The White Goddess*. The Nazis adopted the *runic* S as a symbol for the ⚡ *Shutzstaffel*.

ogma Sunface:

This Celtic deity is credited with inventing *Ogham*, a script of short lines which stem off or cross longer lines. You wouldn't think one could do much with that, but like the point and wedge of *Cuneiform*, or the plus and minus of digital electronics, it could. With rare exceptions *Ogham* only appears on stones in the coastal areas of the British Isles.

The lines come in groups of five which some think reflect the Druids' secret hand signals. It has also been claimed that they appear on African prehistoric rock paintings. Scholars are not convinced. Rock paintings are much older. Credo Mutwa is a Zulu diviner in possession of an ancient slate, a *Rosetta Stone* so to speak, except that his displays Egyptian *hieroglyphics*, early Arabic, and *Ogham*, keyed in columns.[2] Using his slate Credo Mutwa translated an *Ogham* inscription next to a prehistoric painting of a giraffe into early

Arabic as RZRF – adding vowels (necessary in early writings) it reads *Rai ZaRaFa* : 'behold the giraffe!' In Arabic '*Zarafa*' also means 'charming'. Conveniently the word passed into English. At another ancient site is a drawing of a zebra accompanied by an inscription which translates as *Zeb DaBba* – 'painted ass'. Sounded cobblers to me but then I came across a reference in a medieval Arabic manuscript that refers to a script called *Ogham*. So if the Zulu is right how did this script jump across the ancient world? Many early African artefacts have scratched marks which resemble *Ogham*. Maybe some trade route carried the script north, much as early Greeks traded with Cornish tin miners. More probably *Ogham* was no more than an extension of notching sticks to record sheep and goats.

oracle bones:

The turtle, the world's longest-living creature, was considered by the Chinese to be a repository of eternal truths. To gain access to this knowledge, turtle shells were heated over a fire until they produced cracks. A Shaman would divine these just as the witch doctor did with entrails or the gypsy with tea leaves. Buried and forgotten for over 3,000 years, the comparatively recent discovery of 'oracle bones' gives an unadulterated glimpse into the distant past. Early man, at least early Chinaman, believed that shells and bones carried messages from supernatural spirits. Perhaps it all began as imagined by Rudyard Kipling, writing about Taffy, a young Stone-Age girl who explains how she invented marks through resemblance – 'this one looks like a tree, that one a person'. This is what must have happened when fissures were transcribed into pictograms, and they in turn into ideograms. The most complex early Chinese ideogram had 64 brush-strokes and, appropriately, meant 'talkative'. Today the most complex characters only have 36. This one, appropriately, means 'sniffle'.

glyphs:

In 1945 Russian troops rampaged through Berlin. Among them was a young soldier who personally liberated an extremely rare Mayan codex. A codex is an early document. Virtually all Mayan writings had been destroyed by the *Conquistadores* and only survived through carvings on buildings. First discovered in the jungle cities of Guatemala and Mexico they proved obdurate to decipher and fact and fantasy has been so blended that only specialists can

tell which is which. The script reveals a culture obsessed with warfare, dynastic rivalries, torture, sacrifices and ritual blood-letting. One of the places devoted to this task, so I've read, is – surprise, surprise – Novosibirsk, in Russia.

This glyph is of a complicated set of dates. I find the glyphs both comical and menacing. However, the images do convey an aura of concentrated information – much as the squashed automobile condensed into a neat block expresses a density of different parts. An apt analogy, since to make any sense of a glyph or automobile, requires an understanding of the culture which produced them. Today's carburettor would have nonplussed yesterday's Mayan. The Maya mapped the skies yet the concept of the wheel eluded them; they comprehended the notion of eternity but didn't progress from corbel to arch, they invented zero and counted in millions but never knew how to weigh a sack of corn, they had herbal medicines but murdered on a genocidal scale. Invented a script 2000 years ago, calculated a calendar 500 years before the birth of Christ, forecast the eclipse of the sun on 26 February 1998 and dates of other celestial events well into the next century. They predicted the destruction of the universe on 23 December 2012.

talking stones:

Inventing a new alphabet doesn't carry the same inhibitions as adapting an old one. In the 1820s Cherokee Chief Sequoyah, impressed by white man's writing, designed an alphabet. Taking the letters he cannibalized them to make new ones adding curlicues and flourishes, and allocating them phonetic sounds. The Cherokee [who called white man's books 'talking leaves'] called Sequoyah's typographic font 'talking stones'.

A thought : Here is an illiterate Native American in the early nineteenth century, appropriating Roman letters, which had been adopted from the ancient Greeks, who had in turn copied them from a rudimentary Phoenician script developed from pictograms used in ancient Sumer, which had originated in an even more ancient Egypt – long, long before the dynasties of Pharaohs.

rosetta stone:

Hieroglyphs died out 400 years after the birth of Christ and their meaning was soon forgotten. In 1799 a black basalt slab inscribed with Egyptian hieroglyphics, Arabic script and ancient Greek was found by Napoleon's troops in Egypt at Rosetta. The first step towards decipherment happened when it was noticed that the name Ptolemy appeared in the hieroglyphs (sacred [and secret]) and the other two scripts at similar intervals. In hieroglyphics a *cartouche* (a loop of rope) enclosed royal names. The word *cartouche* was coined by the French soldiers. The ovals enclosing hieroglyphs within an inscription reminded them of the cartridges (*cartouches*) in their guns. In ancient Egypt the ankh ♀ adopted by hippies and Flower Power in the 1960s once represented a sandal. Anyway it graduated to represent 'life' and form a component of Tut*ankh*amun's name. This is the *cartouche* …

By cross-referencing the three inscriptions the rest was eventually deciphered. Nowadays the Rosetta stone resides in the British Museum.

These miscellanea give some idea of the rich history behind scripts. To find out more, read on :

David Diringer. *Writing*
Thames and Hudson (London 1962)

David Diringer. *The Alphabet* (2 Vols)
Hutchinson (London 1968)

Etiemble. *The Written Word*
Prentice-Hall International (London 1961)

John Foley. *The Guinness Encyclopedia of Signs & Symbols*. Guinness Publishing (Enfield 1993)

Wayne Senner. (ed.) *The Origins of Writing*
University of Nebraska Press (Nebraska 1989)

Johanna Drucker. *The Alphabetic Labyrinth*
Thames and Hudson (London 1995)

James Hutchinson. *Letters*
The Herbert Press (London 1983)

Nigel Pennick. *The Secret Lore of Runes and Other Alphabets*. Rider (London 1991)

Andrew Robinson. *The Story of Writing*
Thames & Hudson (London 1995)

1. Peter Ackroyd. *The House of Doctor Dee*. Penguin (London 1994)   2. Lyall Watson. *Lightning Bird*. Simon & Schuster (New York 1982)

Early man could read long before he could write. A desert explorer, I think Wilfred Thesiger, described how an illiterate Bedouin examining camel tracks in the sand and crumbling dry droppings between his fingers concluded: 'They were Awamir. There were six. They have raided the Hunuba on the southern coast and taken three of their camels. They have come here from Sahma and watered at Maghshin. They passed here ten days ago.'

During the cultural journey from tracking to scripting humans have developed many ingenious ways of recording thoughts and transferring messages. Tribes in north China would dispatch a chicken liver, three pieces of chicken fat and a chilli wrapped in red paper. The recipients immediately understood that war was declared.

Other communications are less messy. The Incas used an elaborate arrangement of strings (quipus) of different lengths, thicknesses and colours, knotted at intervals to signify something or other. African tribes would thread cowrie shells in different combinations and sizes, back to back, front to front, and pointing in various directions. When a member of the Yoruba tribe of Nigeria sent six sea shells to his beloved it meant, 'I fancy you.' Eight sent back in reply meant, 'I'll leave the door open.' The Iroquoi in North America were more visually inclined and elaborately stitched tiny shells and beads to compose pictorial messages on belts (wampum).

Writing in 1718 from Constantinople Lady Mary Wortley Montagu described a Turkish love letter, '... comprising a pearl, a jonquil, a rose, pieces of soap and coal, a match and a carnation'. All signified amorous thoughts. Lady Mary went on to explain that in Turkey 'there is no colour, no flower, no weed, no fruit, herb, pebble or feather that has not a verse belonging to it.'

Less agreeably, I had a friend who split from his wife in acrimonious circumstances. She later sent him a birthday present – his photograph stuck to the centre of a dartboard and three darts. Altogether a more vituperative communication than could have been achieved by words. As Apollinaire said: 'One can paint with pipes, stamps, postcards or playing cards, candlesticks, waxed cloth, collars, painted paper, newspapers.' The same applies to making messages.

This is a diagram
of a sad love letter
from a Youkaghir
girl in Siberia.

The original was
constructed out
of feathers and
birchbark sometime
during the 1890s.

It translates as :

'You are far away, you
love a Russian woman
who stands in my way;
there will be children,
you will have joy and a
family. I will always
think of you even if
another man loves me.'

God knows how it
was deciphered but
you have to take
experts on trust.

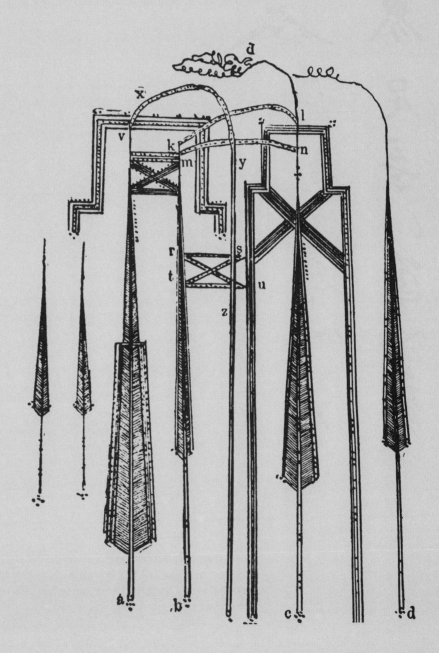

These charmingly illustrated correspondences between ideogram and picture are no more than a whimsical notion from the pen of Chiang Yee.[1] Nevertheless they capture the essence of characterization.

1. Jèrome Peignot. *Typoésie.* Imprimerie Nationale Édtions (Paris 1993)

'Writing is closer to thinking than speaking.'
Joseph Joubert

Prehistoric marks had magical meanings, were of social significance, indicated ownership, were *aides-mémoires*, or merely idle doodlings.

They were not writing.

Writing is a graphic counterpart of speech in which signs represent sounds.

The first step towards this began when rudimentary sketches of things developed into simple designed marks.

These are **Pictograms.**

The second step was when these marks became agreed signs for an abstract value. A circle used to represent the sun for instance.

These are **Ideograms.**

The third step was when ideograms became visually independent of things and ideas, and solely represented sounds.

These are **Phonograms.**

Phonograms come in two sorts :

those which represent syllables (fa-mi-ly)
and
those which represent basic sounds (f-a-m-i-l-y).

The second sort are **Letters.**

The illustration on the right roughly shows sequence from pot to Chinese ideogram for pot. The Latin alphabet developed in much the same way except the ideogram mutated into a letter. [**SEE** P173]. Of course it wasn't that simplistic. Early scripts were a mixture of marks, some inherited, some borrowed, some invented. [**SEE** P172].

For the picky-minded :

Hieroglyphs (sacred signs) are a particular form of **Pictogram** exclusive to ancient Egypt. **Pictograms** are called **Petroglyphs** when carved and **Petrograms** when painted. **Logograms** are metaphorical signs such as a jagged stroke of lightning to represent electricity.

OBJECT

SKETCH

PICTOGRAM

IDEOGRAM

Illustration. Philip B. Meggs. *A History of Graphic Design.* Allen Lane (London 1983)

picture punning

Before the discovery of picture punning <u>the spoken word and written sign were completely unrelated</u> and totally separate ways of communication. That's a difficult concept to grasp. And that's because <u>the two have become synonymous</u> in our minds.

Hieroglyphs, invented in Egypt some five thousand years ago, were punning pictograms in that the sounds of the names of the objects depicted formed spoken words.

Abstract thoughts which couldn't be directly illustrated by one picture were conveyed either by adding marks, or by combining pictures. For example (in English) the picture of a *bee* and a *leaf* would yield the spoken word *belief*.

More complex ideas were expressed through analogy and metaphor. Water was represented by a wavy line, the sun by a circle and a dot. Additional marks could indicate whether something was female or male, singular or plural and so on.

Picture punning was the root of all written languages. This message says:

Commenting on Egyptian hieroglyphs Roman historian Diodorus Siculus wrote: '... their writing does not express the intended idea by a combination of syllables ... but by the outward appearance of what has been copied and by the metaphorical meaning ... So the hawk symbolizes for them everything which happens quickly. And the idea is transferred, through the appropriate metaphorical transfer, to all swift things ...'

signs for things, sounds, thoughts

(rō^uz)

rose

Eric Gill

'Letters are signs for sounds.'

ROMAN INSCRIPTIONS WERE

CARVED IN CAPITAL LETTERS

INTO STONE. THE EFFECT OF

THE LIGHT AND SHADE WAS

ENHANCED BY RAIN WHICH

WASHED DOWN THE VERTICAL

STROKES AND THE DIRT WHICH

COLLECTED ALONG THE

HORIZONTALS. AS AN EARLY

SCRIBE ELOQUENTLY PUT IT,

THE BEAUTY OF THE LAPIDARY

LETTER RESIDES IN A PRINCIPLE

AS SIMPLE AS IT IS INSPIRED:

A STROKE OF SHADE

A FLASH OF LIGHT.

Photograph. Nicholas Biddulph. Carved 'square capitals'. Trajan Forum, Rome, 2nd century

The Яussian alphabet developed from *Cyrillic*, a set of Greek letters supposedly designed by St Cyril, which emigrated eastwards, and in which odd characters still prefer to face the direction of Oriental scripts – that is to the left.

'Letters are legible. If some things are not legible, then they are not letters. Illegible letters do not exist. Illegibility does not exist.'
Peter Mertens

'I just think of a letter and mark around it.'
Frederic Goudy

'I have come to the conclusion that if Euclid, the prince of geometry, returned to this world of ours, he would find that the curves of the letters could never be constructed by means of circles made with compasses.'
Giovanni Cresci,
(*Vatican scribe*)

'Letters are things, not pictures of things.'
Eric Gill

'There are letters, I believe, which are specially meant for poets, or even for multinationals. And there are letters you would only use to write dirty words.'
Coes de Jong

'Concepts are communicated by conventional words. By letters they are designed.'
El Lissitzky

'the shape of the white and the black

in characters fascinates me

the white inside a letter

and the white around

or between letters

in particular with the egyptian faces

where the serif embraces the white

between the type.'

Willem Sandberg

'You have to give a letter of the alphabet the dignity it deserves. This becomes clear when you don't know the language. Think of Arabic, or Chinese. It is beautiful by itself, an art apart.'

Franco Maria Ricci

'Letters are symbols which turn matter into spirit.'

Alphonse de Lamartine

'The graphic signs called letters are so completely blended with the stream of written thought that their presence therein is as unperceived as the ticking of a clock in the measurement of time.'

W.A. Dwiggens

'Geometry can produce legible letters, but art alone makes them beautiful.'

Paul Standard

'A typeface that sometimes is described as having character is often merely bizarre, eccentric, nostalgic, or simply buckeye.'

Paul Rand

'The making of letters … was to me what a song is to the singer, a picture to the painter, a shout to the elated, or a sign to the depressed.'

Rudolph Koch

'With its twenty-four signs this literature is appropriately termed letters.'

Stéphane Mallarmé

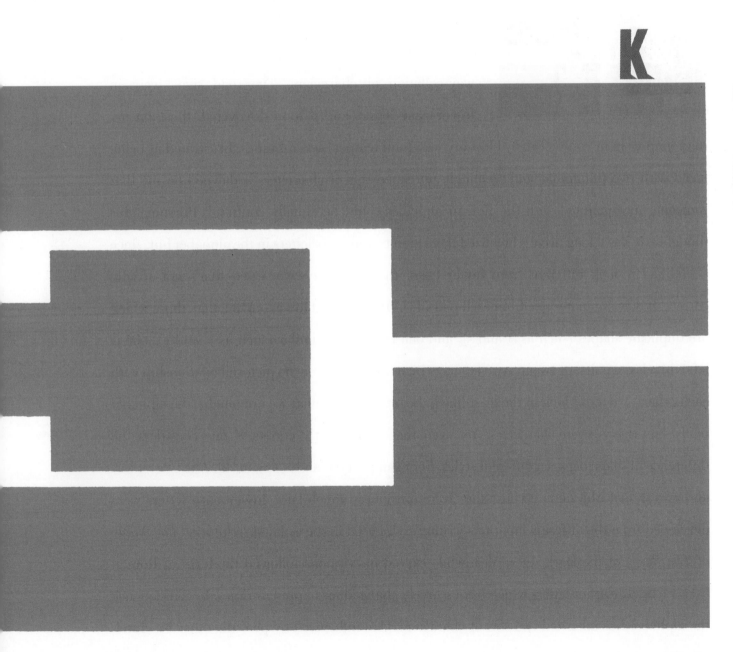

This letter is from a typeface called Egyptian Expanded

Letter K. Designed by Tom Geismar

the 37 letters

Driving south through Greece from Patras to Kythira was rather difficult. The Greek alphabet is an-every-which-way-collation of characters. The road signs were in **lower-case** letters and, I soon discovered, those on my road map were in CAPITALS. I lost my way (and temper) several times. Frustrated at being faced with two unfamiliar and seemingly unrelated sets of characters it dawned on me that someone unacquainted with the Roman alphabet could be equally confused. Pursuing this thought – it was a long drive – I realized there aren't twenty-six letters in the alphabet but, since CAPITALS look different from **lower-case**, there are fifty-two. Even that's not strictly correct. If one eliminates one from each pair of CAPITAL and **lower-case** letters those which are duplicate shapes (such as S and s), and one from those similar (such as Y and y), one is left with eleven pairs, or twenty-two letters, which bear absolutely no pictorial relationship with each other. A doesn't look in the least like a. So, contrary to what we are taught, the alphabet really has thirty-seven characters. Yet even that's not strictly correct if one considers the difference in shape between different styles. For example an a and *a*, or g and *g*. The V W X Y Z and **vwxyz** look the same because they were introduced much later. **lower-case** letters were developed from the differing laborious writing styles used in the isolated scriptoria (*The Name of The Rose*) of the Dark Ages. Meanwhile carved inscriptions followed the form of Roman CAPITALS, elegant letters which have scarcely changed up to present times. In consequence the alphabet has inherited two sets of characters. One influenced by pen, the other by chisel.

the 52 letters

A B C D E F G
a b c d e f g
H I J K L M N
h i j k l m n
O P Q R S T U
o p q r s t u
V W X Y Z
v w x y z

'there are no capitals in speech, why
should there be in writing?'
max bill

'AS LOWER CASE IS A NECESSARY EVIL
WHICH WE SHOULD DO WELL TO SUBORDINATE
SINCE WE CANNOT SUPPRESS IT,
IT SHOULD BE AVOIDED WHEN IT IS
AT ITS LEAST RATIONAL AND LEAST
ATTRACTIVE – IN LARGER SIZES.'
STANLEY MORISON

'wHy ShOuLd We PrInT wItH tWo aLpHaBeTs?
BOtH lArGe AnD sMaLl sIgNs
aRe NoT nEcEsSaRy
To iNdIcAtE a SiNgLe SoUnD.'
hErBeRt BaYeR

the 26 letters

'one cannot *speak* a capital letter,' complained architect adolf loos [in the 1920s] referring to one aim of the modern movement which was to reduce the alphabet to 26 specific single letters. everyone who was anyone in the visual arts at the time had a go at drawing what they thought the alphabet should look like. and they've been at it ever since.

with the same aim, in the 1950s, american designer bradbury thompson proposed to eliminate those letters with strokes which stick up – as with the d. and down – as with p. from the remaining pairs of capitals and lower-case characters [see previous page] he picked the one he thought looked best – for example preferring the positive stance of R to the less assertive demeanour of r. he then made the letters uniform in height, except for some odd reason the j …

a B C D e
F G H I J K
L m n O P
Q R S T U
V W X Y Z

bradbury thompson titled and spelt his revised alphabet :

aLPHABET 26

however, as you see from the first letter of the above title he couldn't shake off the notion of capitalizing. the american poet ee cummings didn't compromise and always insisted his name and writings only appeared in lower-case. a practice i've followed whenever i have quoted him in this book. [SEE P452].

the fact is the odd-looking letters of the alphabet [SEE P172] are so deeply ingrained in our nature that they tenaciously resist change. nevertheless the computer age has drastically altered traditional communication techniques. in turn these are influencing the shapes and forms of letters. goodbye quill — hello silicon.

Red = CAPITALS. Blue = lower-case. Grey = Characters which look the same in capitals and lower-case

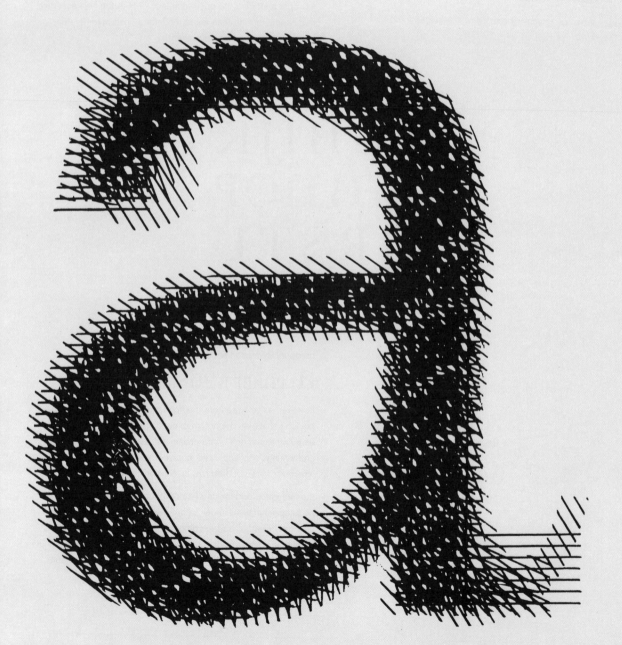

Illustration. Adrian Frutiger

John Baskerville rendered the O in his eponymous typeface as a perfect circle – in acknowledgement of his apprenticeship to a gunmaker.

Degas was fascinated by letters and said he knew of nothing more perfect than the four words 'Typographie de Firmin-Didot' which were displayed above a printer's shop in Paris. You can still see them today, high up on a wall in the Rue Jacob, on the left bank. I always pay them a visit when I'm there.

Although legend attributes the origin of italics to the handwriting of Petrarch their shaping depended more on technique than fancy. Another story is that in 1501 (or thereabouts) Aldus Manutius introduced a type that would get more words to the page to produce cheaper editions. He was also Italian so the style was called *italics*. Burmese script is rounded because, written on palm leaves, straight strokes would have cut the fabric. Chinese ideograms are composed of strokes and flicks as they were rendered by brush. Western capitals are angular because they were chiselled in stone, lower-case letters fluid as they were written with a quill.

Form follows technology.

The invention of printing imposed its own constraints. Although cut in wood or cast in metal, the new movable typefaces followed traditional styles. Today the computer is both tool and material. At first electronic engineers tried to combine modular shapes with traditional letter styles. The offspring of this miscegenation was a cast of clumpy awkward characters. In an attempt to reconcile this mismatch Adrian Frutiger,[1] typeface designer, did an exercise on what makes a letter a letter. Just as a sculptor makes an armature to support his model of malleable clay, so Frutiger began inside out by superimposing variations of the same letter in different typefaces. The illustration opposite shows eight 'a's of popular typefaces reproduced in different linear screens superimposed one over the other. The overlapping creates density.

This pattern revealed the armature of the character – the 'a'-ness of the 'a'. [SEE P489]. Working from this Frutiger translated the essence into an electronic module. 'The nucleus of the character is like the pure tone in music', he enthused, 'while the outer form provides the sound.'

ARMATURE

1. Adrian Frutiger. *Type Sign Symbol*. ABC Edition (Zurich 1979)

Lattice Letters

In 1692 King Louis of France commissioned the design of the ideal alphabet. I'm not clear whether he had a tidy mind or a desire to monopolize the printed word ...

probably both.

His designers came up with a square – a square with ambition. The square was divided into a grid of 64 units subdivided into 2,300 tiny squares. The aim was to create a uniform standard set of letters. The alphabet was set out on this lattice so that enlarged or reduced the letters would be proportionately constant.

It was a striving for perfection, an idealistic aspiration, and a smart business move.

Although the alphabet, named *Romain du Roi*, anticipated the computer pixel by using a module of squares to structure letters, it still kept the traditional shapes of thick and thin strokes to render them.

The grid is employed to preserve the handmade form of letters, in contrast to the gridfonts shown opposite. Here the grid is used to create letters rather than preserve them.

Romain du Roi was engraved on copper plates for exclusive use by the *Imprimerie Royale*. Use by anybody else constituted a capital offence and a visit to the *guillotine*. Nowadays for such copyright a commercial corporation would give a right arm ... probably yours.

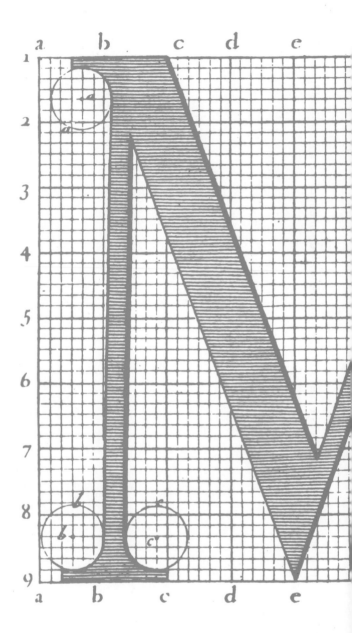

... speaking of earlier fonts, typographer Frederic Goudy said : 'The old fellows stole all of our best ideas.'

Gridfonts

In the 1970s Douglas Hofstadter (of Pulitzer Prize winning *Gödel, Escher, Bach*) wrote of the 'Letter Spirit' domain.[1] A region in which mysterious factors endow typefaces with personalities. Where the essence which distinguishes one letter from another becomes distilled to reveal how one 'a' becomes another 'a', or when an 'a' ceases being an 'a' – and loses its personality.

When, as he succinctly expressed it : **'... a sense of essence, in essence, is, in a sense, the essence of sense, in effect.'**

To explore the territory of the 'Letter Spirit' domain Hofstadter came up with *gridfonts*. These are letters constructed on simple matrices, like the one illustrated here, to create numerous versions of letters. In this case 'a'.

'I simply boiled away,' he writes, *'at what I considered to be less interesting aspects of letterforms – I boiled and boiled – until I was left with what might be called the "conceptual skeletons" of letterforms. That is what "gridfonts" are about ... There are a huge number of them, and their variety is astounding.'*

To give some idea of the potential – even using the most basic of grids – this particular version can generate at least 88 different 'a's. [SEE P272].

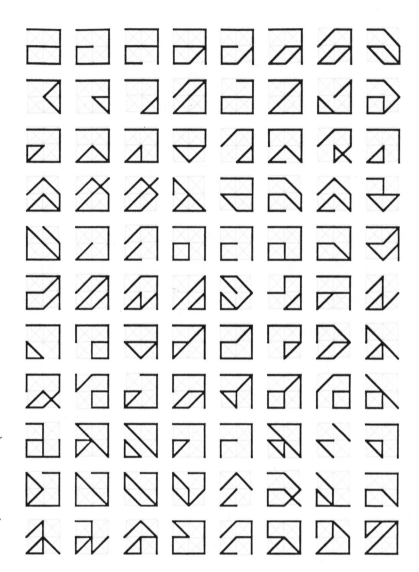

1. Douglas Hofstadter. *Metamagical Themas*. Penguin (Harmondsworth 1986)

the ghoti factor

I'm not surprised that Benjamin Franklin wrote a *Proposal for a Reformed Alphabet* since his other half signed her letters: *Your a feck shonet wife*. Matthew Arnold, Alfred Tennyson, Brigham Young, Mark Twain, and many others before and since, have advocated relating sign to sound. One nineteenth-century reformer suggested that potato should be spelt goughphtheightteeau: 'g as p, as in the last letters of hiccough [pronounced hiccup]; ough for o, as in dough; phth for t, as in phthisis [he was a doctor]; eigh for a as in neighbour; tte for t as in gazette; and eau as in beau.' And Bernard Shaw along the same lines gleefully suggested that fish should be spelt ghoti. The gh as in tough, o as in women [he pronounced it wimen] and the ti as in nation. Shaw bequeathed £500 for developing a 'typically British alphabet with phonetic characters which could be pronounced as close as possible to a gramophone recording of the voice of King George V'. The executors held a competition and chose a font submitted by [appropriately named] Mr Kingsley Read. His typeface made its debut in a special edition of Shaw's *Androcles and the Lion* published by Penguin. To help the reader the left-hand pages had the 'new' alphabet while the facing pages the 'familiar' alphabet – designed by Edward Johnston. The introduction was by James Pitman of shorthand fame. The proposal didn't catch on. No wonder, can you imagine having to learn all those squiggles? The dictionary not only tells us what a word means but also how to pronounce it indicated by weird letters enclosed in brackets. For example : **Speech** (spītʃ). The page opposite is the same text as this page, but typeset in a pronunciation font. To misquote eminent typographer Walter Tracy: *Type designers – like writers – are not the only ones to confuse the nature of speech with its representation.*

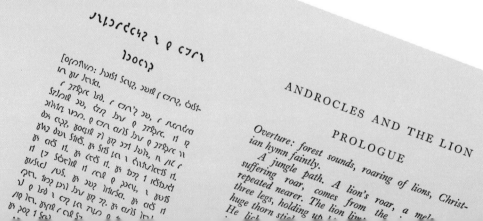

Your a feck shonet wife.

Speech (spītʃ),

Type designers — like writers — are not the only ones to confuse the nature of speech with its representation.

[ˈωɥ ɪ đɪđ γσ ˜š γʔ]

ZIPF'S LAW states that the more frequently
FORMULATED BY G.K. ZIPF, A PROFESSOR OF PSYCHOLINGUISTICS
an expression is used the more likely it will be replaced
by a shorter equivalent. For instance **ad**(vertisement),
photo(graph), **dipso**(maniac), or initials such as **NATO** (North
Atlantic Treaty Organization), **SPAM** (shoulder, pork, ham, or
was it Specially Pressed American Meats?). If the initials form a
word like **ASH** (Action on Smoking and Health) that's really
smart. The ultimate is when word devolves into motif. The signs
for **multiplication** and **minus** originated in ancient Egypt. The
X from the hieroglyph for stirring a pot.[1] The — from a
hieroglyph of outspread arms ﹏ (meaning 'who knows', or
NOT). The **+** was coined by Robert Recorde[2] in 1557 and I have
absolutely no idea where the ÷ comes from. In 1862 wondering
about sales after writing *Les Misérables*, Victor Hugo sent a note
to his publisher with the mark **?** The publisher responded **!** An
exclamation at fabulous sales. 'The nature of the **question-
mark** is questionable,' suggested Saul Steinberg. 'You always
wonder how come the upper part of the question-mark is always
passively following the ball, whereas the top half of an
exclamation point is so rigid, so arrogant and egotistical.'
Perhaps the **?** is merely a tired **!** …**?** [SEE P90]. Actually the mark
of interrogation derives from *quaestio* (Latin for 'question')
which was often abbreviated by imposing the first letter over the
last $\frac{q}{o}$ [thus **?**]. Similarly the exclamation *Io* (Latin for 'joy') was
often abbreviated as $\frac{I}{o}$ [thus **!**]. The origins of @ appears in early
documents as an abbreviation for **amphora**, the pot that,
because it usually contained olive oil, gave rise to a mark
(meaning 'at the price of') which represented a unit of currency.

This ancient symbol was still in use hundreds of years later on
typewriters and adding machines, and recently in computer
technology to signify 'at', without which no **e**-mail will
ever arrive. The origin of the **$** is controversial. One view has it
representing the two pillars of Hercules (Rock of Gibraltar and
peak of Jebel Muza) with a scroll saying *non plus ultra* (the end
of the line). Another version cites the **doubloon**, a Spanish coin
of large value often cut into **pieces of eight**. An expression
which still survives with the American **bit**. Each **piece** was
stamped with **8** and **||** (double) signifying it had been cut from a
doubloon. Over time the **8** became surprinted with the **||**
to become **$**. The probable derivation is even more convoluted.
A silver coin struck in 1519 in the German village of
Joachimsthal became known as a **thaler,** or **dahler.**[3]
Emigrants to the New World fixed the value of their **dahlers**,
or **dollars**, on the conquistadores' **peso**. The abbreviation for
peso was p[s] . The marks below illustrate the morph of **peso** to
dollar. **Zipf's Law** is also revealed in medieval manuscripts
where scarcity and cost of parchment encouraged the custom.
The invention of the **ampersand** (**&**) also known as **Ampussy
and**, **Curly and**, **Round and**, **Short and**, is attributed to
Marcus Tullius Tiro (Cicero's secretary). The character **&** is a
combination of the letters **et** (Latin for 'and'). **Et cetera** ('and so
on') was abbreviated to **etc**, or **&c**, or **&c**, – the **&** a simplified
version of **&**. Early alphabet books were often captioned **'and
per se &'** to indicate **&** was a sign, not a letter. And children
when learning the alphabet chanted '… x, y, z, **and per se and**',
– which became garbled into **'ampersand'.**

1672   1768   1778   1778   1796

1. Richard Gregory. *Odd Perceptions*. Routledge (New York 1993)   2. Georges Jean. *Signs, Symbols & Ciphers*. Thames & Hudson (London 1998)   3. Karl Menninger. *A Cultural History of Numbers*. MIT Press (Cambridge 1977)

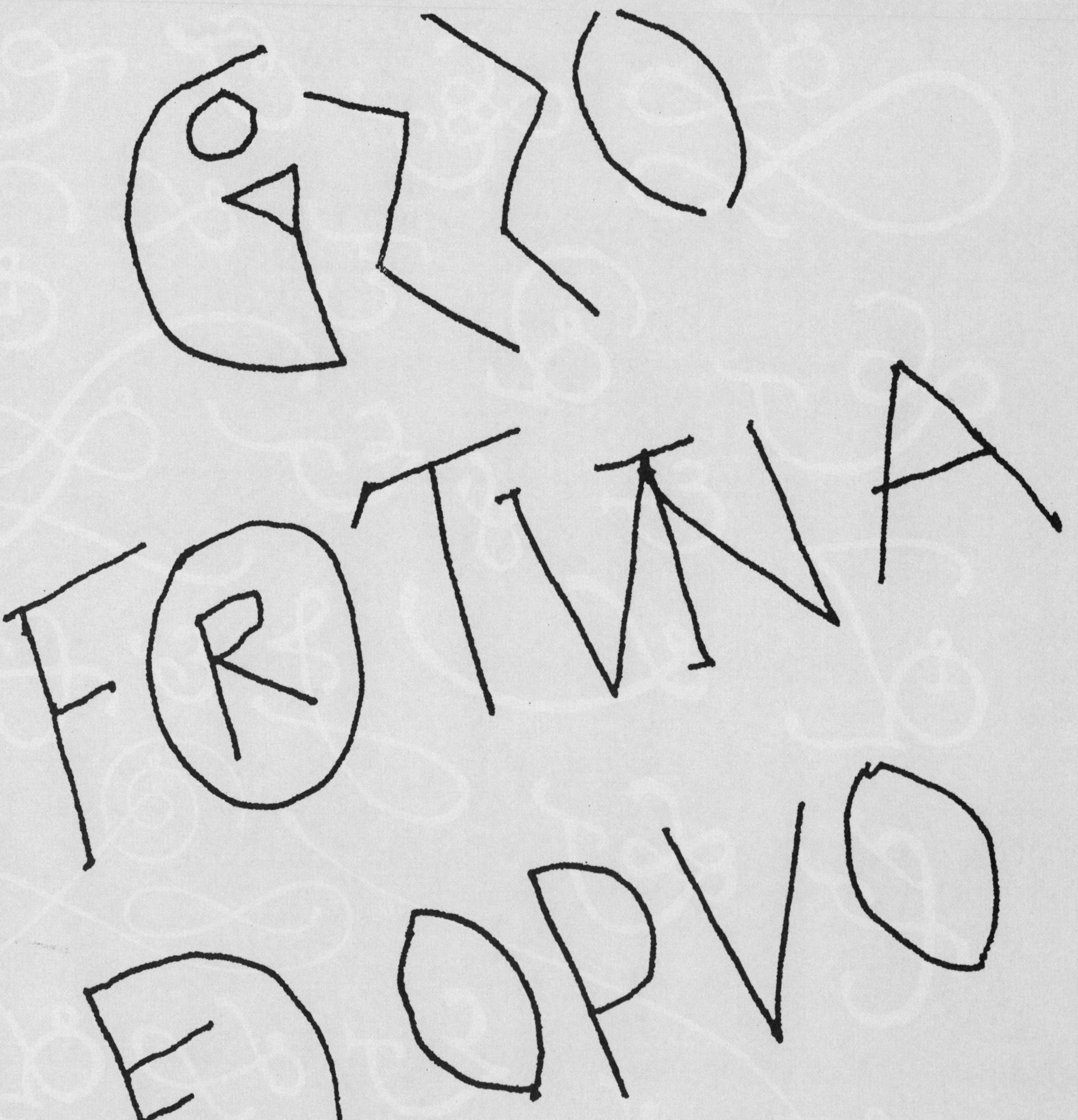

hindsight on foresight

The inscription below was carved in the first century AD on a tomb in the ancient city of Ephesus in Turkey. The craftsman got into deep trouble on the first line – note the last letter. And, even though decreasing the size of letters on successive lines, he didn't do much better on the third and fourth lines either. Actually he only got his act together by the seventh line, and then overcompensated by ending up too soon. Each letter is elegantly rendered and he had an eye for detail but fell short in spatial planning and execution.

Two thousand years later and we haven't lernt anyfing. The door is around the corner from where I live.

The words shown left were roughly copied from an inscription on a stone slab in the museum at Rabat on Gozo. The slabs were carved in 1579 with a dedication to the local hero, a soldier. Ignoring the conventions of lettering the carver either misjudged the available space by making the letters too large or, and I think this more likely since the designs look so considered, opted for large letters and contrived the graphic abbreviations. The art of the deliberate mistake. GOZZO (Gozo in modern spelling) is an island off Malta. FORTUNA is Latin for fortune. DEOPUO the name of the soldier.

[A FORGET-ME-NOT]

Tony Hancock   'Did Beethoven look like a musician? No, of course she didn't.'

In 1902 the great French detective Alfonse Bertillon was able to arrest a murderer when, for the first time, fingerprints were legally accepted as an irrefutable statement of identity. The one shown here is mine. This cliché has been converted into a metaphor [SEE P450] as it is not an imprint of my thumb but a copy drawn, line by line, in pencil. A matter of drawing one's own identity.

Description by author Anne Enright of a picture of Henrietta Lacks on the internet. A woman looks down at the camera: hands on hips, smiling, as if to say: is this the way you want me? It is a confident, intimate picture. She has a strong chin, her hair is in a Victory Roll, she is wearing a short fitted jacket and is standing in front of a brick wall. When Henrietta Lacks died of cervical cancer in 1951, cells from her body were taken for research by Johns Hopkins University. Apparently they proved vital in development of the polio vaccine and in testing the effects of nuclear radiation. Their ability to multiply was spectacularly successful. Almost too successful since they have the tendency to contaminate other cell cultures causing problems in research laboratories all over the world. Indeed in terms of bio-mass there is said to be more of her now than when she was breathing, walking and talking. Scientists call Henrietta's cells the HeLa Line. They are nurtured in a solution of placenta and hen bone marrow. Placentas aren't considered to be part of mother or child, and apparently hospitals sell them on to laboratories and the cosmetic industry. In the 1960s a test compared 17 cultures of ostensibly different tissue types and found that they were all HeLa. The American Type Culture Collection, a cell bank I imagine, tested its store of human cells and found that out of their 34 cell lines, 24 were HeLa. In 1972 the Russians supplied American scientists with six different cancer cells from different parts of the Soviet Union – all turned out to be HeLa.[1] When in the 1970s her family learnt that bits of their mother were still living – and in several places at once – they were understandably shocked. I guess the issue is this: at what point are you not you?

1. Abridged from an article by Anne Enright. *London Review of Books*, 13 April 2000

OUR IDENTITY IS A TRICKY BUSINESS. HUMAN CELLS ARE CONSTANTLY BEING RENEWED AND THOSE WHICH NOW CONSTITUTE OUR PERSONA ARE QUITE DIFFERENT FROM THOSE OF TEN YEARS AGO. THUS THE CELLS OF OUR BODY ARE A GREAT DEAL YOUNGER THAN WE ARE. SO ALTHOUGH WE THINK WE'RE THE SAME PERSON, IT COULD BE AN ILLUSION TO WHICH WE ARE ATTACHED THROUGH HABIT.

Note. An evening at the theatre. It occurred to me that there is something weird about someone wanting to be someone else. And even more so about someone sitting down for a couple of hours to look at someone they don't know, pretending to be someone else, talking to someone who is also pretending to be someone else. A dialogue, furthermore, invented by somebody who imagined they were pretending to be each of these in turn.

Excuse me. Who did you say you were?'

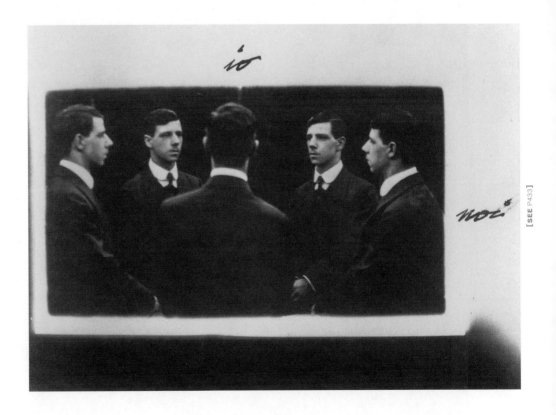

[SEE P433]

Photomontage. Umberto Boccioni. *Io Noi Boccioni* (c.1907/10)

picture of a pessimist

An image extrapolated from an abandoned cardboard transit carton. Interpretation: Umbrella forever open awaiting rain. Tautological arrow representing constant need for reassurance. Always gets the broken glass.

bumps and lumps

In the nineteenth century many people considered the head a topology of attributes. The head was divided into 150 areas which conveyed traits such as love of pets and the desire to see ancient places.

Scientist Alfred Russel Wallace believed in phrenology, as did poet Walt Whitman and novelist George Eliot. She even had her head shaved twice to gain better analysis of her bumps. Sculptor Thomas Crawford's bust of Beethoven at the New England Conservatory of Music has a prominent bump on the forehead indicating musicality. One art critic even managed to persuade the authorities to open Raphael's tomb so that he could make plaster casts of the master's skull so they could be analysed.

'At 50', said George Orwell, 'everyone has the face he deserves.'

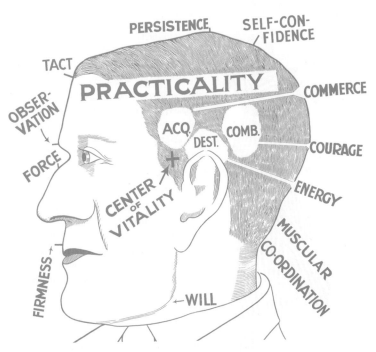

A fairground phrenological chart

kharakter

'Talent is developed in quiet places. Character in the full current of life.' *Goethe*

The word character (Gk. kharakter) originally meant an engraving tool, and by extension the impression or mark made by that tool, and by further extension the features and qualities associated with the mark.

Individuals have character and so do groups of people. Both have structure, form, features, behaviour and personality. Groups which evolve a shared culture acquire a corporate identity and *esprit de corps*. To express this they invent signals which indicate hierarchical differences within a uniform appearance: tribal scars, royal regalia, ecclesiastical garb, military insignia.

Political, social and religious authorities have always understood the purpose and need for such trappings, but commercial organizations were rather late to embrace the notion of corporate identity: the outward expression of an inner state or the outward statement of an inner commitment.

One of the first commercial applications was pioneered by a manufacturer of light bulbs. Peter Behrens, painter, designer and architect, was the mind and hand behind the style of AEG. Among those he employed to achieve the company ambition were Mies Van der Rohe, Walter Gropius and Le Corbusier. In spite of his prolific achievements Behrens wasn't popular – Gropius called him 'an artist on the make', and he was accused by his peers of ingratiating himself with the Third Reich. [SEE P350].

The blurb on the book jacket of the *Handbook on German Military Forces*[1] says: '… exhaustively detailed, the handbook examines German military personnel from the lowest levels to the High Command. It describes the Wehrmacht's administrative structure, unit organization, field tactics, fortification and defence systems, weapons, other equipment, uniforms and insignia.' A reasonable synopsis of the ingredients required to create a typical corporate identity for a commercial organization.

Of course participants and outsiders need to recognize the signals and emblems, otherwise you are into confusion. In the 1940s Alexander Woollcott, leaving a Manhattan restaurant, asked the resplendent uniformed figure by the door to call a taxi. The gentleman angrily spluttered that he wasn't the doorman but an admiral in the Navy. Nonplussed, Woollcott asked him to summon a battleship.

Many businesses confuse identity with image. Identity is composed of the signals which help you recognize a person or organization, whereas the image is the impression you have of that person or organization, and your reaction to this once you've recognized them. Image is more important because it's no good being easily recognized if you give a bad impression. On the other hand if you trade on your image then you have to be readily recognized. Nobody actually needs a sticky carbonated drink, which is why Coca Cola spent $600 million in 1992 to make sure that you remembered not only who they are, but how they want to be perceived – young, trendy etc.

Oscar Wilde said only shallow people don't judge by appearances and Aristotle Onassis took his word for it. He began his career flogging newspapers on the streets of Manhattan and noticed that really rich people were always suntanned, all year round, and behind the ears too. To be successful it helps to look successful. The opposite attitude to that of the actuary who feels he doesn't have enough personality to be an accountant. Then there are people who are so translucent they have to pass through the same place twice to leave a shadow.

You probably remember from Peter Pan that a shadow belongs to a person as much as their face. No two are ever the same. Furthermore, they change according to dress, location, season, and time of day. The one opposite belongs to Sarah who helped me put this book together. The clue to deciphering this adumbrated portrayal lies in the shape of two shoes which reveal her standing facing to the right, at the top of the shadow.

'A photograph is not only an image … it is also a trace, something directly stencilled off the real, like a footprint or a death mask.' *Susan Sontag*

A Kodak girl. The corporate uniform for female employees was a black and white striped dress, as shown in this illustration for a company advertisement (c1913).

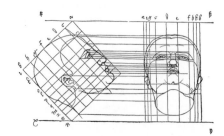

1. Stephen E. Ambrose. *Handbook on German Military Forces*. Louisiana State University Press (Baton Rouge & London 1990)   **Shadow projection.** Dupain [de Montesson]

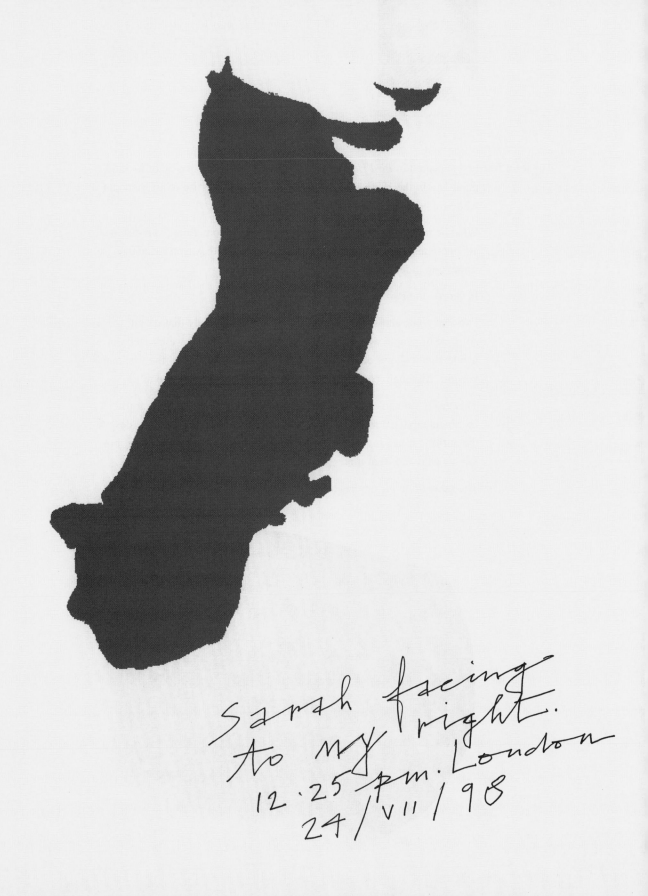

Sarah facing
to my right.
12·25 pm. London
24/VII/98

The term Jizz first appeared in *Bird Haunts and Nature Memories,* a classic of its kind published in the 1920s. One article featured the expertise of an Irishman who said he could name birds at a glance by their Jizz.

What he meant was that if you see somebody, or something, at a distance, although unable to distinguish face, features or clothes, you recognize something indefinable.

In short – their Jizz.

I've also come across another definition of Jizz. Namely that it's an attribute of people who have got themselves so mentally well sorted out inside, that it shows on the outside. A nice idea, but I prefer the Irishman's version. Although, come to think about it, maybe it's the same thing.

This grotty tin-can, squashed flat and considerably distressed by traffic, lay abandoned in a road. I picked it up and kept it. Why? Because despite the attrition it has Jizz. I can hardly read the name or read the shape, but I know who and what it is.

The same principle applies to the living logo opposite.

'Species' comes from the Latin *specere*, 'to look at'. For birdwatchers, or Twitchers as they call themselves, the thrill lies in spotting and distinguishing between the glaucous gull, great black-headed, Mediterranean, laughing, Franklin's little, Sabine's, Bonaparte's, black-headed, slender-billed, ring-billed, common, herring, Thayers', yellow-legged, Iceland, lesser black-backed, greater black-backed, Ross's and ivory gulls.

'Watching sport in company can be much like watching birds in company,' writes sports journalist Simon Barnes who compares it with a Twitchers' coven. You start convincing each other of small details about the players and their performance … 'That bill's just too long for a skylark, isn't it? Oh certainly. And that wasn't a crest was it? Just the wind ruffling the head-feathers. And before you know it, you have turned a skylark into a pectoral sandpiper and you're sending the report to the rarities committee. It's called Stringing in the trade. And let me tell you, Team Hobbit brought us as merry an afternoon of Stringing as I can remember since someone told me an immature fish eagle was definitely a palmnut vulture.'[1]

Drawing. Fernand Léger. *Charlot cubiste*

'No writer long remains incognito.'

E.B. WHITE

*Note. Orton G. [Brother] King, a retired American gentleman,
has a turtle sanctuary on an island [Bequia] in the Grenadines.
He collects the eggs before the predators move in and looks after
the new-born. When they can look after themselves he takes
them to the beach on a moonlit night – this is an important
factor – and puts them down at the water's edge. This is so they
can follow their instincts to paddle towards the light reflected off
the sea from the moon. If it's overcast they head off in the reverse
direction towards the lights of a new swanky leisure resort and
end up as turtle soup. 'I put them down', Brother King confided
to me, 'so they imprint themselves in the sand.' I looked
perplexed. 'They imprint their identity,' he explained patiently,
'so they know where to come back and lay their eggs.' I got it.
He paused. 'And then,' he triumphantly declared, 'it happens
all over again.' Sticking a finger in my chest, 'And that's why,'
he said vehemently, pressing home his enthusiasm, 'I believe in
God, and not evolution.' I humbly nodded in agreement. After
all BELIEF leaves alternative views dead in the water.*

Someone was taking a walk in the park when
Someone-else stopped him and said: 'Excuse me, can
I ask you some questions?' **Someone** hesitated, but
then agreed. 'Well first of all', said **Someone-else**, 'who
are you?' 'Aah', responded **Someone**, 'you ask the most
difficult question first.'

Italo Calvino: 'Who are we, who is each one of us,
if not a *combinatoria* of experiences, information,
books we have read, things imagined? Each life is an
encyclopedia, a library, an inventory of objects, a
series of styles, and everything can be constantly
shuffled and reordered in every way conceivable.'

A pipe – says the old
advertising axiom –
improved a man's image
by presenting a confident,
trustworthy and
authoritative individual.

Incognito: During the reign of communist Premier Ceaucescu [for economic reasons] the Romanian secret police were issued cheap suits of identical make.

Robert Hughes: 'Victor Hugo is the only writer to have a stone mark his place of conception. His parents' epochal embrace took place in a forest 900 metres up on the flank of Mount Donon, overlooking the Rhineland, in May 1801, though it's typical of Hugo's own mythomania that in adult life he claimed it happened 900 metres higher still, and on Mont Blanc.'

Stand in: Woody Allen asked Luis Buñuel to play himself in a short appearance in the movie *Annie Hall*. For some reason Buñuel couldn't accept – Marshall McLuhan stood in for him instead.

Teamwork: There were four people: Everybody, Somebody, Anybody and Nobody. An important job had to be done. Everybody was asked to do it. Everybody was sure Somebody would do it. Anybody could have done it, but Nobody did it. Somebody got angry about that, because it was Everybody's job. Everybody thought Anybody could do it but Nobody realized that Everybody wouldn't do it. It ended up that Everybody blamed Somebody when Nobody did what Anybody could have done.

Corporate identity: Wally Olins: 'Real corporate identity is about behaviour as much as appearance, and certainly about reality, as much as symbolism. Whenever behaviour and appearance are linked, real corporate identity emerges. The need for a new corporate identity most often manifests itself when a country, or for that matter any organization, is in a volatile state, when its management has changed, when it wants to expand, move in new directions – or alter its structure, when it wants or needs to demonstrate a new sense of direction to the various groups of people among whom it lives.'

A folk tale: A stranger walked through a village wearing a hat. It was painted red on one side, white on the other, green in front and black behind. Later that evening the villagers were sitting around discussing the stranger. One who had been working in a field to the west of the village described him in one way, another who had been in a field opposite vehemently disagreed, while another who had followed the stranger into the village called both of them liars. The argument heated up. They began to fight.

Gestalt: You meet someone you haven't seen for a while. They look different but you can't work out why. They've changed the colour of their hair, or grown a moustache. A small thing, but small things can produce different effects. The reason is that we view people as a whole and each component is inextricably affected by every other part. If one bit changes, then the whole changes.

Veiled threat: The Kenyan Government has allowed Muslim women to wear their veils in photographs for new national identity cards. The women had threatened to boycott the scheme if they were obliged to be portrayed without them. *The Nation*.

Likeness: They say the shape of an African elephant's ear is the shape of Africa, and that an Indian elephant's ear is the shape of India. They also say that different people look like different animals, and that people end up looking like their dogs. It's true, I know, I'm acquainted with someone who has a pet llama.

Princess Langwidere (languid air): The wicked witch in L. Frank Baum's book *Return to Oz* had a collection of thirty beautiful heads and selected a different one each morning.

Charades: We think that we navigate life through free will. But when one reads about twins who have been separated at birth and are reunited in middle age only to discover that in many respects they have become the same person, leads one to the unthinkable. It suggests that life is predetermined and identity stamped on us from conception. And that all we do is live out the script written in our genes.

An incident: Anthony Trollope, a civil servant in the Post Office and famous novelist, was in America on postal matters. A straight-laced middle-class Victorian married man, he was fascinated by the lifestyle of polygamist Brigham Young, leader of the Mormon Church. Passing through Salt Lake City he called to pay his respects. Brigham Young opened the door, Trollope introduced himself, Young said he'd never heard of him, and assuming he was an itinerant slammed the door in his face.

Rem Koolhaas: 'I woke up as the sun was reddening; and that was the one distinct time in my life, the strangest moment of all, when I didn't know who I was – I was far away from home, haunted and tired with travel, in a cheap hotel room I'd never seen, hearing the hiss of steam outside, and the creak of the old wood of the hotel, and footsteps upstairs, and all the sad sounds, and I looked at the cracked high ceiling and really didn't know who I was for about fifteen strange seconds. I wasn't; I was just somebody else, some stranger, and my whole life was a haunted life, the life of a ghost.'

Reuters: *Algemeen Dagblad*, Amsterdam. Police arrested a Nigerian and found he had 186 false papers: 29 Nigerian passports, 30 British passports, 74 Dutch work permits, 12 British driving licences, 18 birth or death certificates, two British student cards, an international driving licence and 20 forged cheques. Police said they were not yet certain who he was.

Drawing. Bob Gill

Photograph. Susan Lipper. Untitled image from TRIP. Dewi Lewis Publishing (Manchester 2000)

Karen Blixen

'… a child is made known to itself by its name.'

pocari sweat

Writer *Graham Greene* liked to play practical jokes. One favourite was to look up a *Greene* in the telephone directory, call them up, and then proceed to verbally abuse the other party for their moral turpitude. They couldn't deny they were *Mr Greene* but only weakly respond they weren't *that Mr Greene*.

There are four traditional kinds of English surname. Patronymics such as *Harrison* and matronymics such as *Maude*, trade names such as *Fletcher*, place names like *Crosby* and nicknames like *Hillman*. A recent survey in Britain revealed that 20 per cent had names of the first kind, 15 per cent of the second, 10 per cent of the third and 5 per cent of the last. Names in order of commonness are *Smith, Jones, Williams, Brown, Taylor, Davies, Evans, Thomas, Roberts* and *Johnson*. The uncommonest is the one and only *Leone Sextus Denys Oswolf Fraduati Tollemache-Tollemache-de-Orellana-Plantagenet-Tollemache-Tollemache*.

The town of *Watford* has plenty of girls called *Florence* but I bet that there isn't one in *Florence* called *Watford*. Names influence perceptions of who and what you are. The penniless James Joyce married Nora Barnacle. 'She will not leave me in a hurry with a name like that,' he wrote happily. *Salvador Dalí* was snidely referred to by his anagram *Avida Dollars*. Sir Winston Churchill once effectively put down a Member of Parliament called *Bossom* by remarking he was neither one nor the other, and the *Prince of Wales* is hardly likely to respond to being called *Chuck*.

Hollywood realized that glamour could be enhanced by a change of name. *Judge Learned Hand* (!) granted permission for *Shmuel Gelbfisz* (who called himself *Samuel Goldfish*) to legally change to *Samuel Goldwyn*. *Goldwyn* was created by combining the names of *Goldfish* and *Selwyn*, a fellow director. On the same glamour principle Louis B. Mayer got Hedwig Eva Maria Kiesler to change to Hedy Lamarr as he thought Kiesler sounded too much like Yiddish slang for buttocks. [SEE P384]. Other famous stars such as *Bill Pratt, Kappelhof, Leach, Derek Gentron Gaspart Ulric van den Bogaerde* and *Micklewhite* also took other names.[*] *Maurice Micklewhite* called himself *Michael Scott*, a suitable name, he felt, for a

493

[*] Boris Karloff, Doris Day, Cary Grant, Dirk Bogarde, Michael Caine

young man aspiring to be a young actor. In a phone box in Leicester Square talking to his agent, he heard that there was an audition, but couldn't apply as his stage name was apparently shared with another actor. He had, his agent said, to think of another name – immediately. Looking out of the phone box he saw the cinema opposite was showing *Caine Mutiny*. And in the Warhol menagerie there were *Ingrid Superstar* and *Ultra Violet*.

A fellow art student called *Bill Board* had aspirations to be a poster artist and changed his name to *Marcus Cornelius*. He thought it better suited to his talents and future fame. It was and it wasn't. Designer *Hans Schleger* began his career as an immigrant in Chicago during the 1920s. A German Jew with no money, no commissions and no obvious prospects he took the soubriquet *Zero*. In 1990 the Design Museum in London had a retrospective exhibition of his work. Marcel Duchamp invented an *alter ego* who signed artworks and wrote letters. She was *Rrose Sélavy* (*c'est la vie*). T.E. *Lawrence* tried to submerge his personality in the persona of *Aircraftman Shaw No. 3388171*. Not with much success, as *Noël Coward* demonstrated when he wrote him a letter starting *Dear 3388171, may I call you 338?* Incidentally Noël got his name by being born during the christmas period in 1899. Then there's that old *Ronnie Barker* joke: 'Have you seen Fellini's 8 ½ ?' To which the reply was, 'No, but it's only a rumour.'

By contrast advertising agencies, like law firms, are addicted to their own names. Instead of calling themselves *Ace Advertising* they are *Still Price Twiry Court D'Sousa*, or *Citron Haligman & Bedcarre*. Two weeks of that and the switchboard gets a speech impediment. The painter *Diego María Concepción Juan Nepomuceno Estanislao de la Rivera y Barrientos Acosta y Rodríguez* recognized the problem and settled for *Diego Rivera*. *Hokusai* opted for mood rather than simplicity, and chose a name according to how he felt. During his life he changed it at least thirty times.

Self-esteem wasn't the strong point of a young man I saw interviewed on television who revealed his nickname was *Gravy*. When the interviewer asked why, he replied it was because his mates said he'd go with anything. Then there was *Keats*, who dying at the age of 25 in Rome asked that his gravestone should merely carry the epitaph: 'Here lies one whose name was writ in water.'

The *nomenclator* was the Roman slave who announced the names of arriving guests. Nowadays new products are introduced by advertising, and their names concocted from the computer, laboratory and launching pad. Marketing experts like to invest products with secret ingredients suggestive of technological prowess and X – from X-ray perhaps – carries a charge of technical know-how well beyond the experience of the average consumer. It's no coincidence we have *Xerox, Timex, Rolex, Amex, Pyrex* and *Exxon*. Perhaps it's also the reason why the chairman of the *London Rubber Company*, pondering over a name for his new product while on a train from London to Southend in 1929, is reputed to have startled fellow passengers by suddenly leaping to his feet exclaiming: '*Durex! That's the name!*' The official line is that the name is a combination of DUR – ability, and EX – cellence, but I think that's hindsight. Condoms are known as Trojans in the US and in the schmutter trade as 'Menswear for Women'.

During the 1940s the *Du Pont* Corporation were ready to launch a revolutionary new man-made fibre. They had tentatively settled on the acronym *DUPROH* (*Du Pont Pulls Rabbit Out of Hat*) but felt it lacked the ring of technical achievement. The people at the advertising agency were instructed to put their heads together and a call went out to company employees to see what they could come up with. One executive, flying from New York to London and settled into his first dry martini, decided to devote the journey to the problem. After considerable concentration, he gave up, opened his briefcase to review impending business meetings, and suddenly – the story goes – he got it. The airline tag tied on the handle.[1]

Walking down a street in Milan I passed the inexpensive clothing store called *Coin* and remarked to my Italian companion that I thought the name brilliant. She looked puzzled. 'Well, it's small change,' I said, 'it's appropriate,

A lady, sitting next to Raymond Loewy at dinner, struck up a conversation.

'Why,' she asked, 'Did you put two Xs in Exxon?'

'Why ask?' he asked.

'Because,' she said, 'I couldn't help noticing.'

'Well', he responded, 'that's the answer.'

1. James Burke. *Connections*. Macmillan (London 1978)

short and memorable.' She laughed, 'Don't be silly, I think in English you spell it *Cohen*.'

Once upon a time if your name was *Ford* your company was called *Ford*. Mr *Lemon Hart* imported rum, Mr *Birdseye* invented custard (and patented 250 other inventions), Mr *Boot* was a chemist and Mr *Cessna* sold planes. Mr *Scratcherd*, yeoman stock I assume, has his own business in a van on the Yorkshire moors – the sign declares BRIAN'S CAFE – no doubt he felt *Scratcherd* lacked appeal. If you didn't use your own name you usually decided on something like *General Electric*, or invented or borrowed a name. *Odeon* cinemas, the company says, was coined from the slogan '*Oscar Deutsch Entertains Our Nation*', and *Esso* was derived from S.O. – the initials of *Standard Oil*.

Borrowed names sometimes yield surprises. *Polystyrene*, *Polyvinyl* and *Polyethylene* were not three Greek shepherds but the result of modern alchemy. *Betty Crocker* was the boss's secretary. *Maxwell House* a hotel in Nashville with a reputation for good coffee. *Ayn Rand*, author of *The Fountainhead*, was born *Alisa Rosenbaum*. She took her Christian name from a favourite Finnish author and her surname from her *Remington Rand* typewriter. The *Mercedes* automobile owes its name to *Mercedes Jellinek*, the daughter of a company executive. *Giacomo Balla*, the Italian futurist painter, was so fascinated by speed that he even called one of his daughters propellor (*Elica*). As you might have predicted art director *Art Black* named his son *Matt*, and designer *Tibor Kalman* called his daughter *Lulu Bodoni* and his son *Alex Onomatopoeia*. [SEE P102].

Sometimes choice of name is random. *Eliza Marchpane*, born in Stepney in 1760, became a famous courtesan and travelled the courts of Europe with her aristocratic lovers. When in Vienna, apart from probably seducing *Mozart*, she developed a passion for a sweetmeat made of sugar and crushed almonds. Returning to London she adopted the title of *Marquise de Marzipan*, became the mistress of *Prince Mwawalele Akimbo* [of arms akimbo], and the *Prince Regent*. She died peacefully, in Brighton. *The Minnesota Mining and Manufacturing Company* called its product *Scotch* after

accused of being mean with the adhesive. *L. Frank Baum*, author of *The Land of Oz*, took the title from the letters O – Z on a filing cabinet, and similarly *George Lucas*, at a loss as to what to call his android in *Star Wars*, noticed the code R2-D2 on a box containing soundtrack from the film *American Graffiti*. *Dorothy Parker* mischievously called her parrot *Onan* because it spilled seed on the ground. But why the chief of an African tribe called himself *Oxford University Press* is difficult to fathom, although I can guess why some of the girls were named *Frigidaire*.

In the early nineteenth century Polish Jews were obliged by the authorities to acquire surnames. Previously they named themselves, as everyone else, after their father. The name had to be paid for and the name given depended on the amount of money they could afford. The rich bought names like *Goldberg* (gold mountain – no less), the poor such names as *Einstein* (one stone). The totally impoverished ended up with derisory labels like *Wanzenknicker* (bug-squasher). [SEE P507].

Naming is powerful as it can give a status independent of function. When *Veronese* got into trouble with the Inquisition over his painting of *The Last Supper*, he was ordered to repaint elements they thought blasphemous, within a month and at his own expense. It was a large canvas. He thought of a simpler remedy and merely changed the title. Apparently that satisfied them.[1] In 1939 auteur *Luís Buñuel* was down and out in Hollywood working on a film about the Spanish Civil War while *Dalí* was rich and living it up in New York. *Buñuel* wrote to *Dalí*, who had embraced *Franco's* policies with enthusiasm, and asked for a loan. 'I haven't yet forgotten,' replied *Dalí*, 'that you did not include my name on the screen credits of *Un Chien Andalou*.' And refused. [SEE P69].

A name is as much a part of the product as the design or the engineering. And for automobiles, as a *Ford* executive commented, 'It's gotta be catchy, memorable and meaningful.' *Mustang* was, *Edsel* (Son of Henry) wasn't. Poetess *Marianne Moore* had been commissioned to think up a poetic name for the new *Ford* and came up with *Ford*

1. Mary McCarthy. *Venice Observed*. Heinemann (London 1961)

Fabergé, Utopian Turtletop and *Mongoose Civique.* Faced with that lot *Ford* chose *Edsel* — serve 'em right. Paradoxically, the Japanese aren't too fussed about meanings as long as they like the sound. However, I doubt *Nissan* had much luck with their *Leopard J. Ferie* or *Pantry-boy.* Perhaps I'm wrong. *Mazda* managed to sell *Scrums, Bongo Friendee* and *Honda Lettuces*; I hope that one meets a *Volkswagen Rabbit.* A name should match the expectation otherwise a grubby pub called *The White Swan* will surely become known as *The Mucky Duck.*

Apart from having the right ring a name must also mean the right thing. In Portugese *Nescafé* implies 'not coffee', *Cona* and *Foden* are obscene. On the other hand the Portuguese manage to market tuna fish under the label *Atum Bom.* Other blunders include a Finnish motor product called *Super Piss,* the Italian yoghurt *Mukk,* a French soft drink called *Pschitt,* a Turkish chocolate biscuit called *Bum,* Swedish toilet rolls named *Krapp* and the German brand *Happy End.* Then there are *Richard Branson's* shingles. He built a palatial house on a small Caribbean island. I've heard, I haven't been there, that the wood shingles cladding the place are stamped with the gnomic slogan *Fuck Brazil,* the trade name of a timber merchant from that country.

In the global village one can no longer simply invent a cute name, adopt an exotic foreign word, or pick something out of the Ankara telephone directory. Nowadays potential brand names are run through computers to identify those already registered and to check multi-lingual meanings. However, even that's not foolproof. Recently at a hotel in Tokyo I rang room service for some mineral water. The waiter arrived with a tray of glasses, canapes, ice, and a bottle of mineral water. The label announced it was called *Pocari Sweat.* I went down to the bar and had a gin and tonic instead.

Note. In Japan it is mandatory to have a business card printed in Japanese and English – hotels provide an overnight service. To transcribe foreign names into ideograms requires matching the sound of the name to a Japanese character with a similar sound. As an ideogram represents a thing or a thought in addition to a sound, the chance of the translation coming up something fetching like Noble Tiger or Fragrant Blossom, is against all odds. It probably translates as something nonsensical – or possibly extremely rude. Mindful of being introduced around Tokyo with a wildly comical name I thought it prudent to check mine out. Nothing too awful it seems. But when presented alongside a Westerner, I always look to see if I can detect a faint smile in the face of the Japanese host.

My name according to Ikko Tanaka San

阿ア   Phonetic sound for A

蘭ラン   Phonetic sound for LAN
Meaning ORCHID

府フ   Phonetic sound for FU
(no L in Japanese)
Meaning PREFECTURE

烈レッ   Phonetic sound for LE
Meaning ENERGETIC

茶チャ   Phonetic sound for CHA
Meaning TEA

Eponyms. Everyone knows that the Earl of **Sandwich** couldn't bear to leave the card table and had his meal between slices of bread. Here are some eponyms you may not recollect. Admiral Vernon wore a coat of a rough fabric called grogram and became known as **Old Grog**. His nickname is still with us because of his attempts to instil sobriety in the Navy by diluting the sailors' rum ration. Despite this anti-social measure Vernon, by all accounts, was greatly loved and one of his officers, Lawrence Washington (half-brother of George), named his Virginia plantation **Mount Vernon** in his honour. Ludwig **Doberman**, a tax collector in Germany in the 1880s, developed a fierce breed of dogs to protect him while collecting taxes. Some origins can be accurately attributed but I've heard that Domenico **Comma** (1264-1316) invented the punctuation mark, that Matthias **Easel** was an indifferent painter with a talent for carpentry, that Sir Samuel **Hoarding** erected screens for public advertising alongside the new railway lines, that E.C. **Booze** was an illicit distiller, and that Sir Oswald **Binge** was infamous for the scale and duration of his drinking bouts. Subaltern **Snooker** played billiards so badly that his name became synonymous with ending up in an impossible position (one definition of snooker is chess with balls). Henry **Stipple** was an American artist who painted in dots.[1] The solid portrait was named after the artist Etienne de **Silhouette**. Lazlo **Biro** invented the ballpoint pen. Then there were Mrs Amelia **Bloomer** and Jules **Léotard** the trapeze artiste. A German cartographer, for reasons best known to himself, translated the first name of transatlantic voyager **Amerigo** Vespucci into Latin and called the new land **America**. Anyway, one expert Basil Cottle disagrees with this version. He maintains that **America** was derived from the Welsh name **Ap Menric**. And that a descendant of Richard (some say John) **Amerik**, a customs official in Bristol and investor in Cabot's [aka Giovanni Caboto] voyage of 1498 is really the source.[2] Anyway Vespucci had another claim to fame – he was brother of Simonetta Vespucci, the model for Venus in the famous painting by Botticelli. Well you can't believe everything you read but some of it must be true.

1. James Cochrane. *Stipple, Wink and Gusset.* Random Century (London 1992)   **2.** James Michener. *Caribbean.* Secker & Warburg (London 1989)

M. HENRI KISTEMACKERS

Reverse eponymics is the study of
people who look like their names.
I think that Mr Kistemackers qualifies.

496

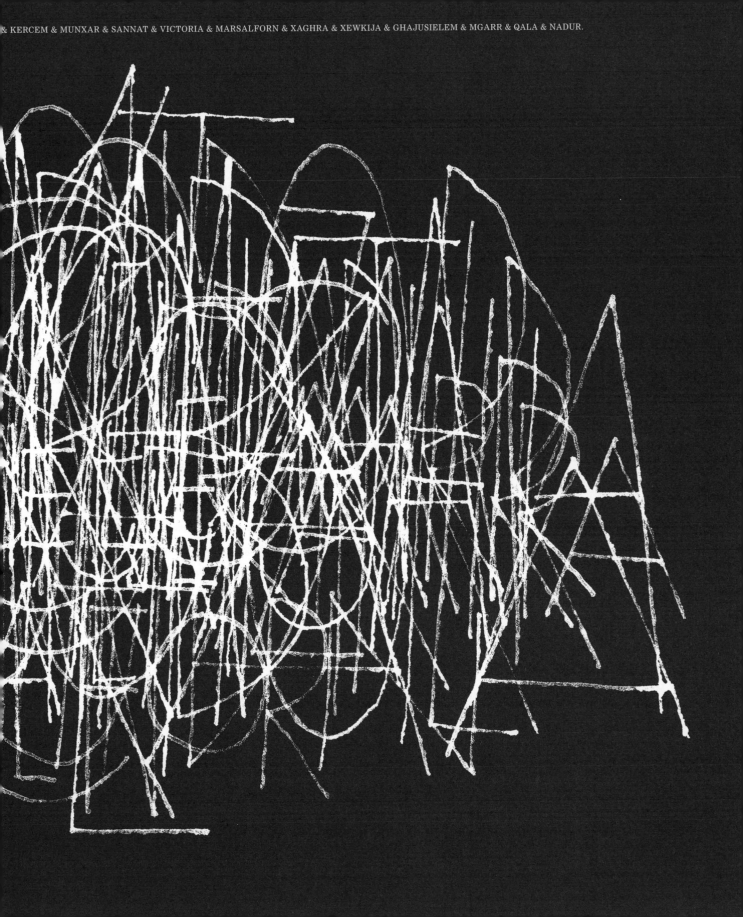

Name calling

Bill Bryson : 'There is almost no area of British life that isn't touched with a kind of genius for names. Just look at the names of the prisons. You could sit me down with a limitless supply of blank paper and a pen and command me to come up with a more cherishably ridiculous name for a prison and in a lifetime I couldn't improve on **Wormwood Scrubs** or **Strangeways**. Even the common names of wildflowers – **Stitchwort, Lady's Bedstraw, Blue Fleabane, Feverfew** – have an inescapable enchantment about them. But nowhere, of course, are the British more gifted than with place names. There are some 30,000 place names in Britain, a good half of them, I would guess, notable or arresting in some way. There are villages without number whose very names summon forth an image of lazy summer afternoons and butterflies darting in meadows: **Winterbourne Abbas, Weston Lullingfields, Theddlethorpe All Saints, Little Missenden.** There are villages that seem to hide some ancient and possibly dark secret: **Husbands Bosworth, Rime Intrinseca, Whiteladies Aston.** There are villages that sound like toilet cleansers (**Potto, Sanahole, Durno**) and villages that sound like skin complaints (**Scabcleuch, Whiterashes, Scurlage, Sockburn**). In a brief trawl through any gazetteer you can find fertilizers (**Hastigrow**), shoe deodorizers (**Powfoot**), breath fresheners (**Minto**), dog food (**Whelpo**) and even a Scottish spot remover (**Sootywells**). You can find villages that have an attitude problem (**Seething, Mockbeggar, Wrangle**) and villages of strange phenomena (**Meathop, Wigtwizzle, Blubberhouses**). And there are villages almost without number that are just endearingly inane – **Prittlewell, Little Rollright, Chew Magna, Titsey, Woodstock Slop, Lickey End, Stragglethorpe, Yonder Bognie, Nether Wallop** and the unbeatable **Thornton-le-Beans.** (Bury me there!) You have only to cast a glance across a map or lose yourself in an index to see that you are in a place of infinite possibility. Some parts of the country seem to specialize in certain themes. Kent has a peculiar fondness for foodstuffs: **Ham, Sandwich, Rye**. Dorset goes in for characters in a Barbara Cartland Novel: **Bradford Peverell, Compton Valence, Langton Herring, Wootton Fitzpaine**. Lincolnshire likes you to think it's a little off its head: **Thimbleby Langton, Tumby Woodside, Snarford, Fishtoft Drove, Sots Hole** and the truly arresting **Sitall in the Street**. It's notable how often these places cluster together. In one compact area south of Cambridge, for instance, you can find **Blo Norton, Rickinghall Inferior, Hellions Bumpstead, Ugley** and (a personal favourite) **Shellow Bowells**. I had an impulse to go there now, to sniff out **Shellow Bowells**, as it were, and find what makes **Norton Blo** and **Rickinghall Inferior**.'[1]

Notes & Queries. *The Guardian*, 22 July 1998

1. Bill Bryson. *Notes from a Small Island*. Black Swan (London 1995)
Photographs. Harry Pearce

E.M. Küpper = **Theo van Doesburg**

Domenikos Theotocopoulos = **El Greco**

Gyula Halász = **Brassaï**

Charles-Edouard Jeanneret = **Le Corbusier**

Isidore Ducasse = **Comte de Lautréamont**

Adolphe Jean-Marie Mouron = **Cassandre**

Helmuth Hertzfelde = **John Heartfield**

Jacopo Robusti = **Tintoretto**

Giovanni da Fiesole = **Fra Angelico**

Romain de Tirtoff = **Erté**

Hans Schleger = **Zero**

Leonardo of Pisa = **Fibonacci**

Johann Gänsefleisch = **Johannes Gutenberg**

Endre Friedmann = **Robert Capa**

Emmanuel Radnitsky = **Man Ray**

Piero Kardeen = **Pierre Cardin**

Edward Muggeridge = **Eadweard Muybridge**

Moissey Segal = **Marc Chagall**

Wilhelm Apollinaris de Kostrowitzky = **Guillaume Apollinaire**

Balthasar Klossowski de Rola = **Balthus**

Robert Clark = **Robert Indiana**

William Nicholson & James Pryde = **Beggarstaff Brothers**

Elio Romano Ervitz-Romano = **Elliott Erwitt**

William Berkeley Enos = **Busby Berkeley**

Paolo Caliari = **Veronese**

Kenneth Bird = **Fougasse**

A *fougasse* is a primitive mortar made
by digging a deep hole and packing
it with gunpowder, rocks, and anything
else handy to decimate the enemy.
Kenneth Bird was a cartoonist. [**SEE** P409].

O FE dear, what XTC

I MN8 when U IC!

Once KT 1 me with her I's;

2 LN I O countless sighs.

T'was MLE while over Cs

Now all 3 R nonNTTs,

4 U XL them all U C

U suit me FE 2 a T.

Louise J. Walker

Avant-garde musician, composer, poet and writer John Cage records that while composing these prose celebrations he thought he was writing acrostics. Until someone pointed out that the highlighted letters occur in the middle of a word so they should be called mesostics. These mesostics were dedicated to MARCEL DUCHAMP.[1] [SEE P503].

since other **M**en

mA**k**e

aR**t**,

he **C**annot.

tim**E**

is vaL**u**able.

a utility a**M**ong

sw**A**llows

is thei**R**

musi**C**.

th**E**y produce it mid-air

to avoid co**L**liding.

More

th**A**n

nou**R**ishment,

eating's a so**C**ial occasion.

h**E**

ate very **L**ittle.

Me ?

i sleep e**A**sily

unde**R**

any a**C**oustic condition.

as h**E** said:

Lullaby.

getting ol**D**?

then give **U**p. or

Continue.

go **H**ome.

ch**A**nge

your **M**ind.

still com**P**osing?

questions i **M**ight

h**A**ve

lea**R**ned

to ask **C**an

no long**E**r

receive rep**L**ies.

when we **D**ecided to go to the falls,

he said he wo**U**ldn't go with us.

in **C**adaques too

He

Always stayed

at ho**M**e

when we went to swim and **P**lay chess on the beach.

finally he telephone**D**.

it had been hard to **U**nderstand

what had **C**aused

Him

not to **A**ppear.

he said there were **M**any things

we should have the o**P**portunity to discuss.

let **M**e

h**A**ve

you**R** baggage

i will **C**arry it for you.

no n**E**ed

i'm wearing a **L**ot of it.

(Last homage to Marcel Duchamp)

1. John Cage. *M. Writings '67–'72*. Calder Boyars (London 1973)

In the opening chapter of *The Man Who Was Thursday* G.K. Chesterton explains that passengers on the London Underground look glum because '... after they have passed Sloane Square they know that the next station must be Victoria, and nothing but Victoria. Oh, their wild rapture! Oh, their eyes like stars and their souls again in Eden, if the next station were unaccountably Baker Street!' [SEE P440].

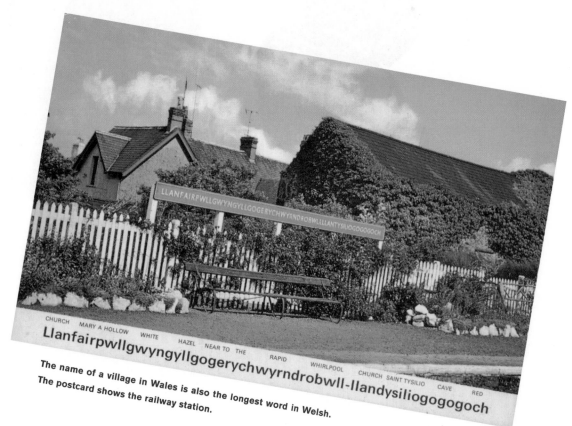

The name of a village in Wales is also the longest word in Welsh. The postcard shows the railway station.

Brussels sprouts

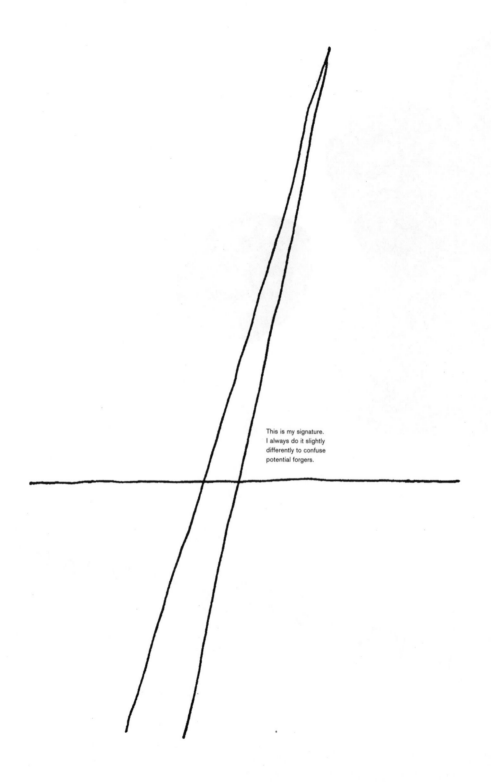

This is my signature.
I always do it slightly
differently to confuse
potential forgers.

Hancocks

For some inexplicable reason the Panama hat is made in Ecuador and the best quality is called a *Monte Cristo*. You know it's special (apart from the price) as it's signed by the craftsman inside the crown. If you're not convinced with this endorsement hold it up to the light. The more rings the better the material, the longer in the making, the more skilled the craftsman, the classier the hat, the bigger the hole in your pocket.

An advertisement by Rolls-Royce states that when Dennis Jones has built a radiator he neatly engraves his initials on the back 'like an artist signing a painting'. No idle comparison as every radiator is constructed by hand and eye. As Dennis explains: 'Measuring instruments would be of no real help, because there isn't a single straight line or flat surface on the radiator. Perfectly flat surfaces tend to retain light and appear dished, so to create the illusion of rectilinearity every line of the radiator has to be slightly bowed.' The same principle behind the optical adjustments employed by Callicrates when he designed the Parthenon. [SEE P278].

Stradivarius signed all his violins and Rembrandt all his paintings. Although in Rembrandt's case he sometimes also signed apprentices' canvases to generate sales. Today that's discouraged. Han van Meegeren, who knocked off Vermeers and others, signed who he wasn't and ended up in jail. Conversely Michelangelo only signed one of his works – the *Pietà* in St Peter's – all of which suggests that we put more value on the signature than on the object endorsed.

In early days, desperate for work in New York, I applied for a job with Raymond Loewy. After a long wait in the reception I became transfixed by a circular white clock hanging on the wall. It was without numbers but to compensate had a gold knob stuck on the end of the hour hand. I knew I was in the wrong place and hastily left. Emerging into the street I saw his 1957 Studebaker parked right outside on 5th Avenue. It had a discreet gold inscription on the door which stated: *Designed by Raymond Loewy*. I didn't like his clock but admired his style. We met many years later over breakfast. At least I had the breakfast and he had a dry Martini – a man in his eighties doesn't eat that much.

I'd bought a copy of his book which he kindly signed. Now someone has stolen – or indefinitely borrowed – my book. Since it's readily available I assume the signature must have been the attraction rather than the book. If the culprit reads this please return it.

Art by proxy. It's a rare signature which bears much relation to an individual's writing style. The very act of penning one's name seems to unleash secret passions expressed through tortured loops and whirls, staccato strokes and lines, jabbed dots and theatrical flourishes. Anyway I ask friends who visit my home to sign a large white canvas [opposite]. I think of it as a signature painting. At first I envisaged rapidly arriving at a knitted abstract pattern like a Fair Isle sweater but years, and years, and years later, new friends still find spaces. When I run out of friends I'll sign it off in the top right corner.

Provenance by stealth. Vasari tells of Michelangelo going to look at his *Pietà* and finding a crowd from Lombardy admiring it. Apparently one of them asked who'd made it, and was told 'Gobbo from Milan'. Michelangelo kept quiet. That night he returned with chisels, locked himself in, lit a lamp, and chipped out: MICHELANGELUS BUONARROTUS FIORENTINUS FACIEBAT [Michelangelo Buonarroti the Florentine made this].

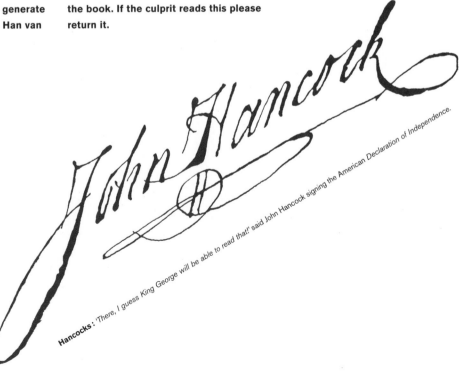

Hancocks: 'There, I guess King George will be able to read that!' said John Hancock signing the American Declaration of Independence.

Unlimited editions   and a   one-off

6 cm = 300,000 DM

Signing an old door at the Venice Biennale Marcel Duchamp turned it into a work of art. The renovators repainting it after the exhibition turned it back into an old door. A signature can be more valuable than whatever it endorses. A phenomenon underlined by Robert Rauschenberg when he erased a pastel by Willem de Kooning, signed the phantom image, and then sold it. And Duchamp who, among others, signed blank cheques and then sold them for cash.

Salvador Dalí took the principle a stage further when he discovered he could earn $40 in advance for signing blank sheets of paper for future limited editions. With one aide sliding the paper under his pencil and another pulling it away, he managed to sign one sheet every two seconds. That generates $72,000 an hour. He is said to have signed some 350,000 sheets. Along the way thousands of signed sheets fell into the wrong hands and the art market is now inundated by fake prints bearing genuine signatures.

The difficulty of distinguishing the genuine from the counterfeit is compounded as his signature would change 'depending on who came into the room or what music he was playing'. At the last count he had 678 different styles of signing his name.

When Dalí learnt that art dealers were making fast bucks with his signature he tried to recall the printing plates on the excuse he needed them to clad the urinals in his museum at Figueres. Paradoxically the dealers' art world isn't bothered about how things look, but in the veracity of the signature which authenticates provenance. Since the current article exhibited is a replica of the original, and the signature a pseudonym, the Grimm brothers' fable about the Emperor's clothes comes to mind.

March 27, 1975.

Dear Friends,
   As you know, profits for 1974 were very large, and few shareholders have ever received such a dividend. All the same, I have a feeling that we must renew ourselves. We can't go on haggling over unmanageable and sentimental rubbish like paintings and sculptures.
   Why not concentrate on the most important part of a work of art, THE SIGNATURE? I have therefore invented PRATT-MULLER'S SUPERELASTIC SIGNATURES! The owner of such a SIGNATURE has unlimited possibilities of STRETCHING THE SIGNATURE to whatever value he likes. Precious stones are all very well, but elastic they are not.
   With best art wishes

Arnold Forel Pratt-Müller

for example SALVADOR DALI ⫸➔

180 cm = 9,000,000 DM

Letters and signatures. Arnold Forel Pratt-Müller aka Carl Fredrik Reuterswärd

Duchamp's Fountain   and   Brian Eno's Leak :

'The attempts to keep art special become increasingly bizarre. This was a theme of a talk I gave at the Museum of Modern Art in New York as part of the HIGH ART/LOW ART exhibition.

Looking round the show during the day, I noticed that Duchamp's Fountain – a men's urinal basin which he signed and exhibited in 1917 as the first 'readymade' – was part of the show. I had previously seen the same piece in London and at the Biennale of São Paolo.

I asked someone what they thought the likely insurance premium would be for transporting this thing to New York and looking after it. A figure of $30,000 was mentioned. I don't know if this is reliable, but it is certainly credible. What interested me was why, given the attitude with which Duchamp claimed he'd made the work – in his words, "complete aesthetic indifference" – it was necessary to cart precisely this urinal and no other round the globe. It struck me as a complete confusion of understanding: Duchamp had explicitly been saying, "I can call any old urinal – or anything else for that matter – a piece of art", and yet curators acted as though only this particular urinal was A Work Of Art. If that wasn't the case, then why not exhibit any urinal – obtained at much lower cost from the plumber's on the corner?

Well, these important considerations aside, I've always wanted to urinate on that piece of art, to leave my small mark on art history. I thought this might be my last chance – for each time it was shown it was more heavily defended. At MOMA it was being shown behind glass, in a large display case. There was, however, a narrow slit between the two front sheets of glass. It was about three-sixteenths of an inch wide.

I went to the plumber's on the corner and obtained a couple of feet of clear plastic tubing of that thickness, along with a similar length of galvanized wire. Back in my hotel room, I inserted the wire down the tubing to stiffen it. Then I urinated into the sink and, using the tube as a pipette, managed to fill it with urine. I then inserted the whole apparatus down my trouser-leg and returned to the museum, keeping my thumb over the top end to ensure that the urine stayed in the tube.

At the museum, I positioned myself before the display case, concentrating intensely on its contents. There was a guard standing behind me and about 12 feet away. I opened my fly and slipped out the tube, feeding it carefully through the slot in the glass. It was a perfect fit, and slid in quite easily until its end was poised above the famous john. I released by thumb, and a small but distinct trickle of my urine splashed on to the work of art.

That evening I used this incident, illustrated with several diagrams showing from all angles exactly how it had been achieved, as the basis of my talk. Since decommodification was one of the buzzwords of the day, I described my action as re-commode-ification.'[1]

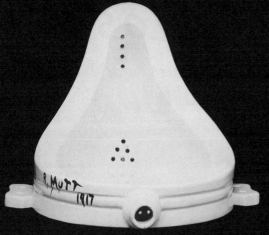

1. Brian Eno. *A Year with Swollen Appendices.* Faber & Faber (London 1996)

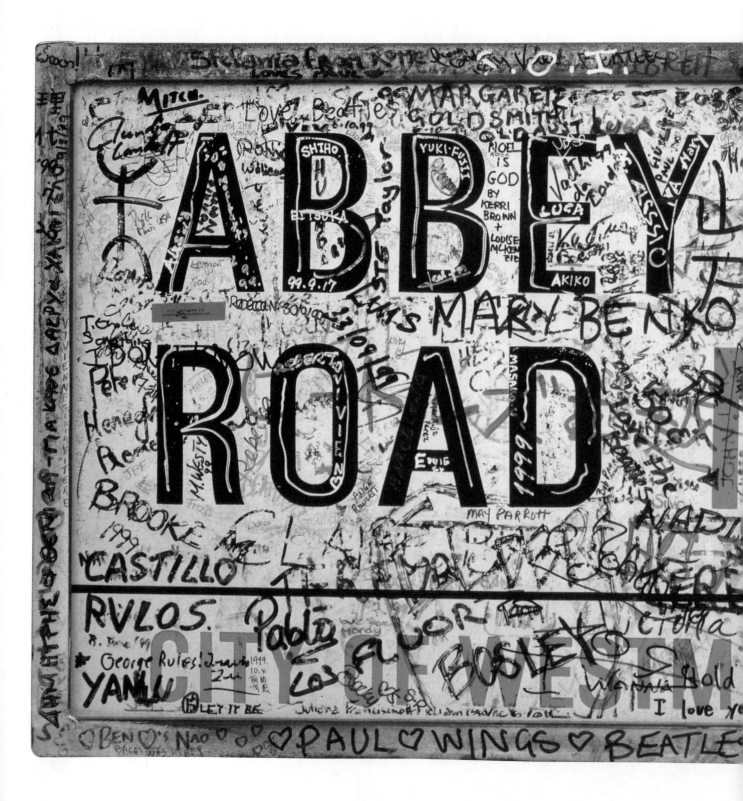

In 1841 a survey revealed that half the women and a third of men in England were able to sign the electoral register with their names. In the past few could sign their name, let alone write a letter, and this menial task was done by scribes. As the signature began to assume legal status it was important that it should deter counterfeiters. One Turkish scribe not only elaborately penned the name of his Sultan but, to confirm authenticity, also incorporated his own signature among the flourishes.

Conserving antiquity

From Mr G. de la Bédoyère

Sir, There are graffiti, and there are graffiti on archaeological sites (letters, October 10).

On the base of one of the Colossi of Memnon, across the Nile from Luxor, is the scratched announcement: *Camilius, hora prima semis'audivi Memnoni.* It means, "At half-past the first hour I, Camilius, have heard the Memnon", a reference to the noise the cracked colossus made daily when the rising sun warmed it. Camilius was, I believe, an early second-century governor of the province of Egypt. The noise ceased when the statue was repaired many years later.

Personally, I was captivated. If Camilius was a vandal he had an eye for the moment, and I am pleased to have shared it with him.

Yours faithfully,
G. de la BEDOYERE,
20 Eltham Park Gardens,
Eltham, SE9.
October 10.

Today you can hardly do anything without signing for it. Actually signing has become a virus and graphic hooligans sign everything in sight. 'I have put my name', said Super Kool, 'all over the place. There ain't nowhere I go I can't see it. I sometimes go on Sunday to Seventh Avenue 86th Street station and just spend the whole day watching my name go by.' These graphic entrepreneurs are as proud of their signatures as any corporation of its logotype.

Despite vandalism, graffiti has a visually poetic quality. 'You're standing there in the station, everything is grey and gloomy', said Claes Oldenburg, talking about the Manhattan subway system, 'and all of a sudden a train slides in like a big bouquet from Latin America.' However, as Tom Wolfe mischievously suggested, for most people graffiti is only art when it's in the next town. Or in a gallery – as Keith Haring and Jean-Michel Basquiat later exploited.

These earmarks on cattle in Madagascar display the maternal lineage on the left ear and the paternal on the right.

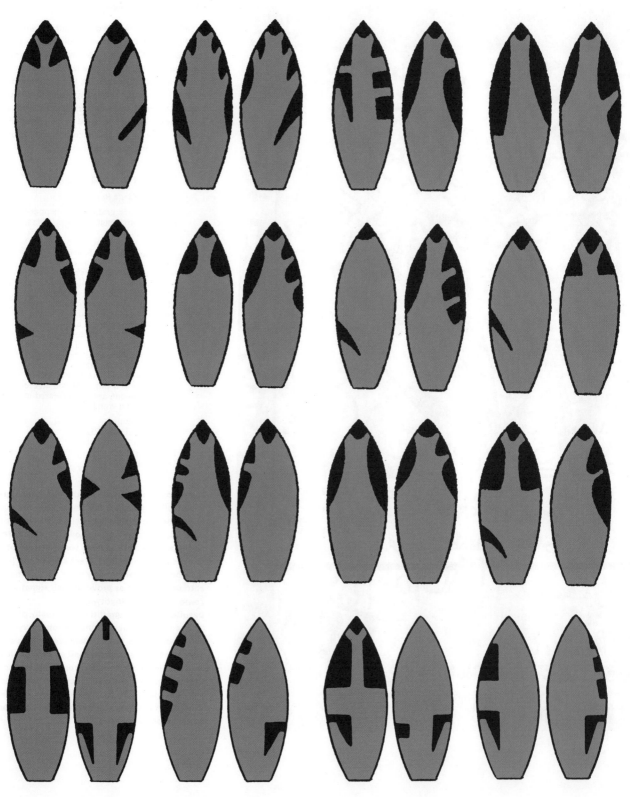

Oxford English Dictionary

Insignia : Marks or tokens indicative of anything.

emblazoned on a flag or shield the BAR SINISTER declares you are a bastard

[SEE P460]

genealogy

Our inner ear bones have developed from those of our jaws when we were ancient fish. As embryos we still show vestiges of tail and gills. We are living fossils carrying a heritage within us that goes back to the beginning of humanity and far beyond that.

Nonetheless our recollection of the past is pathetic. Few even know the names of their four pairs of great grandparents or even of their grandparents. I don't either – I find that sad.

Heraldry is an expression of this past.

Obviously a classy genealogy is more desirable than a dubious one. The more illustrious ancestors you can muster the greater the implications of wealth, social importance and personal grandeur.

The catch is that there is only a one in eight possibility of inheriting a gene from a great grandparent, you don't have to be a genius to figure out that one set of genes is rapidly diluted, or more accurately phrased, recombined, every generation. Furthermore, it so happens that you probably share an ancestor who lived a couple of hundred years ago with the next-door neighbour. Sorry, but that's how it is.

And if one unravelled a family line all the way back to the time of Christ, and counted up the forebears – each of us would probably have had as many direct ancestors as there were people living in the world at that time. [1] We *are* a family of man. [SEE P8].

1. Colin Tudge. *The Engineer in the Garden*. Jonathan Cape (London 1993)

Dorothy Parker once worked for the senior editor on *Vanity Fair* who was called Mr Crowninshield. With a name like that he should have been President. *Heraldry* provided the faceless world of armoured knights with a visual symbology which identified individual, family, status and alliances.

🦁 🦁 🦁

Blazon is the language of *heraldry*. If you don't know the grammar and vocabulary you can make a frightful mistake. The protocol is formidable and the syntax extensive. The identity was *blazoned* on a shield by *ordering* the main areas of division known as *chief, fess, base, dexter, sinister, pale,* and *marshalling* the colours (*tinctures*) and devices (*charges*) within them. Because of confined space, the areas (*ordinaries*) often had to be further divided (*quartered*) and the *charges* stuck on top of each other (*impaled*). The borders separating *ordinaries* could be *embattled, dancetted, nebulé* or *raguly,* just four of the many articulated variations the line or partition could take. *Charges* such as unicorns, leopards, birds and lions could be *rampant, couchant, guardant, salient,* and so on, in up to fifty different postures. These are just a few of the graphic nuances. The *coat of arms* of the Temple-Nugent-Bridges-Chandos-Grenville family (alas extant) managed to incorporate 719 *quarterings* displaying the family's extensive genetic links. The shield of the Lloyds of Stockton illustrated opposite has a paltry 323.[1]

🦁 🦁 🦁

Coats of arms were usually created in one of two ways. The first was by displaying devices which took the fancy of the originator, or something with which they were associated. For instance a crown for a royal family. The second was by *canting* arms. These make a visual pun on the family name or place. For instance, Oxford was represented by an ox crossing a ford. Canting could also work in reverse whereby the name of the family or person was derived from the *coat of arms*. In 1526 the King of Denmark obliged the nobility to adopt a surname. [SEE P493]. To be called Eric the Red wasn't enough, you had to be Eric Somebody. The Rosenkranz family are so called because they took their name from the rose wreath (*Rosenkranz*) displayed on their shield.[2]

🦁 🦁 🦁

Rules of *armory* are governed by *The College of Arms*, also known as *Heralds' College*, which was founded in 1484 to appoint *Heralds*, or *Officers of Arms*, as ambassadors and officials at jousting tournaments. Today the College consists of three *Kings of Arms*: *Clarenceux, Garter Principal, Norroy and Ulster.* Six *Heralds*: *Windsor, York, Somerset, Lancaster, Chester, Richmond.* And four *Pursuivants*: *Rouge Dragon, Portcullis, Bluemantle* and *Rouge Gold.* I'm not clear what they do but it's important. And more pleasurable to the ear and uplifting of the spirit than being an anodyne marketing manager, sales director, chief executive or head of personnel.

1. A.C. Fox-Davies. *A Complete Guide to Heraldry.* Orbis (London 1985)   2. Per Mollerup. *Marks of Excellence.* Phaidon (London 1996)

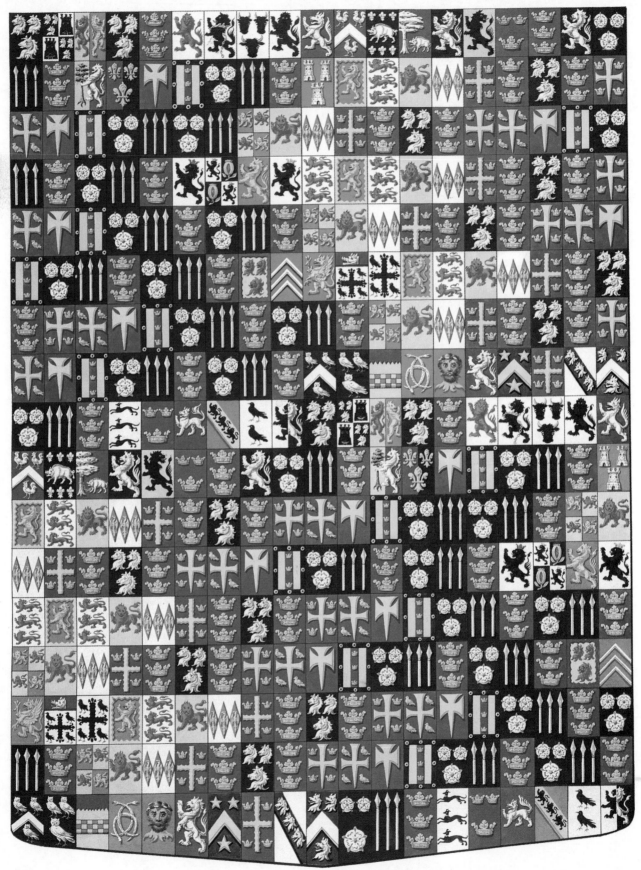

The custom of inheriting insignia through marriage led to the 323 separate quarterings on the coat of arms of the Lloyds of Stockton. These go back to the ninth century, or earlier, and are a vivid document of inbreeding. The three simplistic shields shown opposite are known as rogue coats of arms and were found scratched on the walls of a dungeon in Lucerne, Switzerland.

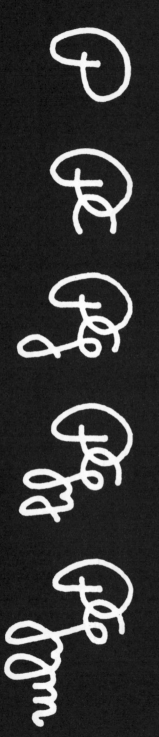

Cadency. Cadency marks denote seniority within families and distinguish one family branch from another. In English heraldry there are nine charges which display the male line. First son has a three-pronged device, the second a crescent, the third a star – and so on. Cadency in folk heraldry has a more immediate logic as seen by these Mexican cattle brands. The 𝒟 represents Don Miguel, father of the family. I know it looks like a P but it's a D. Then the first son Carlos added 𝒞. Followed by Luis, the second, who added 𝓵. The 𝒿 is for José the third, and 𝓜 for Mario the fourth.

Cachet. Heraldic paraphernalia implies both 'provenance' and 'class'; thus Harrods and other tradesmen ostentatiously display coats of arms declaring themselves supplier 'by appointment' to royal families. Those who can't make the claim but fancy the connection, resort to 'cachet' heraldry. This is an art form more dependent on the febrile imaginations of graphic designers and advertising art directors, than on the rules of armory. For instance the badge of Alpha Romeo [number one lover] combines elements from the heraldic identities of Württemberg, Milan, Stuttgart and Cologne. Cachet heraldry is not only a Western conceit. Suntory, a Japanese Corporation and the world's largest private brewer, incongruously not only sports a coat of arms but also has a Latin motto. This, an executive once proudly informed me, was '*in vino velitas*'. However, being represented by this heraldic device in the rough and tumble of the proletarian market was considered inappropriate, so they commissioned designer Tak Igarashi to come up with a commercial emblem. His solution was elegant and ingenious. He morphed the oriental ideogram of the corporate name step by step into the adopted Western coat of arms. A visual synthesis of East and West, old and new, traditional and modern. The middle point of the morph provided the Suntory emblem.

SQUARING THE CIRCLE

Stonemasons. Like other medieval craftsmen, masons fiercely guarded their skills and formed fraternities. Each lodge developed peculiar rites and rituals, and the members recognized each other through particular postures, special handshakes and secret signs. They also employed a private heraldry which operated through a Mother Diagram. This was a geometric pattern exclusive to each lodge and the basis of each individual's mark. The examples shown here are from the cathedral of St Stephen in Vienna.

Freemasons. '*n*. An order with secret rites, grotesque ceremonies and fantastic costumes, which, originating in the reign of Charles II, among working artisans of London, has been joined successively by the dead of past centuries in unbroken retrogression until now it embraces all the generations of man on either side of Adam and is drumming up distinguished recruits among the pre-Creational inhabitants of Chaos and the Formless Void. The order was founded at different times by Charlemagne, Julius Caesar, Cyrus, Solomon, Zoroaster, Confucius, Thothmes, and Buddha. Its emblems and symbols have been found in the Catacombs of Paris and Rome, on the stones of the Parthenon and the Chinese Great Wall, among the temples of Karnak and Palmyra and in the Egyptian Pyramids – always by a Freemason'.[1]

Benchmark

Bishop mark

Brandmark

Cadency mark

Certification mark

Orb mark

Chatter mark

Earmark

Flummox mark

Freezemark

Hallmark

King's mark

Kite mark

Mason mark

Mintmark

Plimsoll mark

Postmark

Punctuation mark

Scratch mark

Swan-mark

Service mark

Touchmark

Trademark

Watermark

Woolmark

1. Ambrose Bierce. *The Devil's Dictionary*. Penguin (Harmondsworth 1971)

M O T H E R   D I A G R A M S

B R A N D A R T . The Broad Arrow – ⋀ – variously called the Imperial Brand or King's Mark, was first used to brand and identify the English horses during the Hundred Years War and is still used to mark British Army equipment.[1] ⋀ The ancient Greeks cut the feet off captive silversmiths to prevent them running away, a mutilation which also signified the slave's trade. Equally effective was the practice of earmarking, and branding, and the Tsarists stamped a large red diamond right in the middle of criminals' backs. Butchery and indelibility have finality in presentation. ⋀ Sisyphus, it is said, engraved his monogram inside the hooves of his cattle. In the Wild West branding developed into a sophisticated cataloguing of identification and provenance. It was rigorously enforced by hanging offenders. Texan rancher Samuel Maverick (1803-70) declined to brand, either through indolence or to claim unmarked steers as his own. He was an exception. ⋀ Cattle brands, often a visual pun on the name of the ranch, were designed with initials or graphic devices. The brand illustrated opposite is a witty amalgamation of two similar shapes into one whimsical image. Although simple – you can't be too subtle with a red-hot branding iron – such marks were geometrically sophisticated in order to confound rustlers and unscrupulous ranchers. In the American Civil War, the Union Army branded deserters with a large letter D one and a half inches high on their bum or cheek – the regulations were quite specific on this point. ⋀ Bernadotte, a soldier of fortune in Napoleon's army who eventually acceded to the throne of Sweden, ironically achieved this in spite of the tattoo on his arm which said, '*Death to the Kings*'. An embellishment acquired in his revolutionary youth. ⋀ The trick of branding is to avoid creating devices which can be easily altered, for instance letters like **C** which can be converted into **O**. In *Ulysses* James Joyce has someone change a sign which said *POST NO BILLS* into *POST 110 PILLS*, and school maintenance manuals in Manhattan include instructions on how to use a magic marker to convert aerosol graffiti – such as *FUCK* – into something more respectable like *BOOK*. ⋀ If the art of branding is to create marks difficult to alter, the art of clandestine communications may involve the opposite principle. From *Our Time* by John Le Carré: 'I passed the sidedoor a second time, looking not at the chalkmark but in the direction indicated by the tail of the *L*. *L* for Larry. *L* for Larry's tradecraft in the days when he and Checheyev exchanged their secret materials by way of letterboxes and safety signals. In parks. In pub lavatories. In parking lots. In Kew Gardens. *L* for "I have filled the deadletter box," signed Larry. The *L* converted to a *C* for "I have emptied it," signed *CC*. Back and forth, not once but more like fifty times in the four years of their collaboration: microfilm for you; money and orders for me; money and orders for you; microfilm for me.' ⋀

1. Per Mollerup. *Marks of Excellence*. Phaidon (London 1996)

SITTING HEART LAZY B RANCH

It was the Chinese who came up with the brilliant scam of giving a worthless piece of paper a value it didn't have. And then persuading other people that that's what the paper was worth. Marco Polo in China: 'All these sheets of paper bear the seal of His Majesty, without which they are worthless. They are produced with as much ceremony as if they were made of pure gold or silver, for a number of specially appointed officers subscribe their names on each note, each one affixing his seal.'

Ootje Oxenaar is the designer of the exuberant Dutch banknotes, a visual delight of dazzling patterns and flamboyant colours. Jam-packed with arcane insignia, typographic devices, symbolic images and *moiré* patterns. And a few surprises as well. Hidden in the watermark of the 250 guilder note is his pet rabbit, and imprinted in the flowing locks of Spinoza on the 1000 Guilder note lies his thumb print. Also concealed in the background is a tiny green spot which viewed through a red filter reveals yet another rabbit, this one peering out of a hole. Less subversively he also signs his name on the edge of these artworks. [SEE P501].

I learnt all this at a lecture. Seated behind me was a Japanese delegate who I thought might have missed the subtleties exhibited in the slides, so I passed him all my Dutch currency. What I didn't know was that fake samples had already been distributed for this very purpose. My Japanese friend took my real notes to be these, inspected them and passed them on to the next row, who passed them on to the next, and so on to the next. The lecture ended. I was guilderless. It took three days to track them down. I retrieved most of them – at least I think they were mine.

Inserting personal marks is forbidden by most authorities. In the 1980s the US Treasury discovered that unauthorized markings had been secretly etched into the postage stamps. An engraver had etched his name in the grass of a stamp honouring First World War veterans; a Star of David lay hidden in a stamp celebrating the centenary of Yeshiva University. The engraver, incidentally, had also threatened to blow up the Holocaust Memorial Museum in Washington. Another mischief-maker, more appealingly, inserted his name into a stamp (1986) celebrating stamp collecting! They all got into big trouble.

During the Second World War the Germans produced a series of British stamps hoping to screw up the postal service. The forger, however, couldn't resist topping the crown above George VI's head with a Star of David, and subtly constructing the 'D', representing pence, from a hammer and sickle. Conceits which gave the game away. Whimsies which distinguished fake from genuine.

Such things may seem juvenile but I disagree. Anything which can insinuate a sliver of individuality into a morass of beaurocratic systematization deserves a secret smile.

CUKLY STREKI	YULCK SKRETI	KUCLY SKITER	UKLYC TESKIR	YKUCL ESKIRT
YLUCK SIKTRE	LUCYK RISKET	UCLYK KRISTE	CLUKY SKETRI	LUKYC TRISKE
CLYKU RESTIK	KLUCY SEKTRI	LYKUC SKRITE	ULCYK KISTER	YLCUK STERIK
KYCUL KERSTI	LYCUK TRIESK	UCYLK TISKER	YLKUC RETSIK	CYLUK STIREK
LKUCY SKETIR	KYCLU RITESK	LCUKY EKIRTS	CYKLU IKSTRE	KYLCU EIRTSK
YLUCK ISTKRE	ULKYC RIESKT	YCLUK KISTRE	KYLUC TRESKI	YKCUL RISTEK
YUKCL SKERTI	UKCLY ETSKIR	CLYUK IRKEST	UCKYL TRIKES	LUCKY STRIKE

Groucho Marx   'I never forget a face, but I'll make an exception in your case.'

A trademark
is a symbol of
a corporation.

It is not
a sign
of quality …

It is
a sign
of the quality.

PAUL RAND

 Coca-Cola was concocted by pharmacist John Pemberton who also lettered the name. Another source says that it was a copy of the book-keeper's signature. Either way it's the best-known, even if not the best-looking, signature in the world. [SEE P519]. Mr Samuelson of the Root Glass Company came up with the distinctive bottle shape so that customers would know they'd grabbed the right thing when they felt for it during the night. At least that's the story. Raymond Loewy declared the curvaceous bottle 'the most perfectly designed package in use today'.

 His Master's Voice was the title of a picture painted by Francis Barraud in the late 1880s. He submitted it to the Royal Academy annual summer exhibition but it was rejected. Surprising really, I thought they'd accept almost anything. He then tried to sell it to the manufacturer of the phonograph. They turned him down. Barraud then substituted an up-to-date gramophone for the phonograph. The Gramophone Company liked it, bought it for £100, and paid him a £250 annuity for its use as a trademark. It subsequently came to represent HMV, and later, RCA. The dog, affectionately known as Nipper, was born in 1884 and died in 1895. It says so on a wall plaque where it lived in Eden Street, Kingston, a suburb of London. [SEE P84].

 Nobody is sure where the tubby bird came from. One version has it revealed to Allen Lane during a brainstorming session with his brothers in the bathroom. Another has the brothers trying to cross a dolphin with an albatross. Apparently not happily – their secretary said it looked like a penguin. The brothers agreed and summoned a junior employee, Edward Young, gave him sixpence, and sent him off to Regent's Park Zoo. He returned with a sketch which became both name and colophon. The penguin shown here was redrawn by Jan Tschichold in the late 1940s. When Terry Waite was a hostage in Lebanon in the 1980s and wanted something decent to read, he drew a picture of a bird in an oval and asked his captors to find a book with one on the spine.

Bibendum, the inflated character of Michelin, was inspired by a heap of old tyres noticed by Edouard Michelin and drawn by poster artist O'Galop in 1898. Shell derived both name and symbol from the days when they imported exotic sea shells. The original poster campaigns for Guinness were the joint product of thriller writer and medievalist Dorothy L. Sayers, and portrait painter John Gilroy. The zoo-keeper is a self-portrait. Mr Gilroy also painted Colman's mustard-seed man, the striding Johnnie Walker [SEE P462], Skippers Sardines' sou'westered fisherman, and the odious plump Virol child who was an illustration of his son. The stout baby in a painting by Sir Joshua Reynolds of Hercules throttling a snake was copied by a Victorian advertiser to promote something called Woodward's Gripe Water. Cassandre designed the monogram of Yves St Laurent and Piet Mondrian one (1961) of the myriad marks registered by 3M since 1906.

Gottlieb Daimler bought a postcard of Deutz, his home-town, drew a star in the sky and sent it to his wife. When his sons needed a trademark, they remembered papa's postcard, and chose a three-pointed star to represent land, sea and air. The automobile industry has almost as many logo stories as marques. The double chevron of Citroen was derived from the intermeshed teeth of the gears. [SEE P516]. Volvo ['I roll'] are backed by a Swedish ball bearing company and the mark is based on the cartographic sign for iron. Chevrolet's parallelogram was copied from a hotel wallpaper which caught the eye of the head of General Motors. The mascot for Jaguar was dreamt up in 1936 by the head of their public relations department, and drawn by a commercial artist at *Autocar* magazine. The story goes that Rolls-Royce displayed their initials in red until Sir Henry Royce died, then changed them to black. Not true.

'One of the deepest mysteries to me is our logo' wrote Jean-Louis Gassée, a former Vice-President of Apple Computer (quoted in *So Far – The First Ten Years of a Vision*) – 'the symbol of lust and knowledge, bitten into, all crossed with the colours of the rainbow in the wrong order. You couldn't dream of a more appropriate logo: lust, knowledge, hope and anarchy.' Legend has it that the company was conceived by Steve Jobs and Stephen Wozniak in a garage in California on April Fools' Day 1976. Jobs was eating an apple at the time. Depicted in a deliberately expensive six-colour glory, the apple (with its visual pun on 'byte') was designed in 1977 by Regis McKenna.

The splodgy star on the cap of the Meisterstuck No. 149 – the pride of Mont Blanc fountain pens – symbolically represents the mountain surrounded by the six valleys. Well that's what they say. The height of Mont Blanc is 4810 metres which is recorded on the nib in case you forget. The Mont Blanc is considered a very classy piece of equipment by connoisseurs: they clip it in the outside jacket pocket, rather than inside.

LOGOBILITY

Tom Wolfe : '… These abstract logos, which a company … is supposed to put on everything from memo pads to the side of its 50-storey building, make absolutely no impact – conscious or unconscious – upon its customers or the general public, except insofar as they create a feeling of vagueness or confusion. I'm talking about the prevailing mode of *abstract* logos. Pictorial logos or written logos are a different story. Random House (the little house), Alfred Knopf (the borzoi dog), the old Socony-Vacuum flying red horse, or the written logos of Coca-Cola or Hertz – they stick in the mind and create the desired effect of instant recognition ("identity"). Abstract logos are a dead loss in that respect, and yet millions continue to be poured into the design of them. Why? Because the conversion to a total-design abstract logo formation somehow makes it possible for the head of the corporation to tell himself : "I'm modern, up to date, with it, a man of the future. I've streamlined this old baby."'[1]

'What's the difference between a trademark and a logo?' asks and replies design consultant Stephen Bayley, 'not much really, except that a trademark is a logo that went to art school.'

Obviously this one didn't.

I like the thought that a trademark feels obliged to inform one that that's what it is. And furthermore to spell out what it represents. 'My friend you should use Frazers Axle Grease,' says the guy on the right. 'That is just what I shall do after this.' responds the other guy.

A sophisticated marketing system doesn't favour idiosyncratic emblems. Among the victims of visual laundering I affectionately recollect a host of commercial characters – the winged pegasus of Mobil, the growling lion of MGM, Bombadier Billy Wells banging his gong. What has taken their place are sleek abstract gismos, more distinguished by similarity than individuality.

Commercial marks are like people. Some are reasonably well put together but lack personality, others are dull or aggressive, or pompous, or unpleasant. Occasionally one encounters an interesting character.

To be effective a trademark should fulfil criteria : utilitarian values of being relevant, appropriate and practical; intangible qualities of being memorable, attractive and distinctive; and that visual tweak which creates a unique personality.

As legibility is to words, so logobility is to trademarks. Logobility is the capacity of a name to lend itself to a unique typographic conversion.

The word logo, itself, has logobility, as revealed by Swiss designer Niklaus Troxler.

The Volkswagen symbol is a good work-a-day example of logobility, designed in 1937 or thereabouts by F.X. Reimspeiss, engineer of the Beetle's engine. The geometry plays on the similar angles of the V (Volks) and W (Wagen) to combine them into a single composite whole.

Sometimes a logotype has to work a bit harder.

MICHÆL

A brand name MICHAEL could be personalized by typographic ligature – a single character made up of two letters.

MICHĒLE

And MICHÈLE, a brand of lingerie and cosmetics, could, by the creation of an accent by deft graphic surgery, imply a French personality.

no-sag

This odd logotype was designed by Alexander Girard for the No-Sag Spring Company in the 1940s. The letters suggest the stubborn characteristics of a steel wire mattress, but by so emphatically portraying the negative it could plant a seed of doubt in the mind of the customer which may not have existed previously.

Although the designer creates the mark, it is only the organization which it represents that can give it meaning. The trademark of Chanel, as Paul Rand pointed out, 'only smells as good as the perfume it stands for'.

Or as Stefan Sagmeister put it – 'Trademarks are to corporations what glasses are to wine : they will influence ever so slightly how you will perceive their content. However, at the end of the day it will be the quality of the wine that will determine your opinion.'

1. AIGA Congress. *New York*, 17 July 1972

LEGIBILITY

Many people are puzzled as to what makes a good, bad or indifferent logotype. Here are some views from the standpoint of the eminent typographer Jan Tschichold.[2] They were written in the 1950s which is why they sound a bit quaint. They are 'specimens' from what he called 'a horror chamber of contemporary lettering'.

Englebert: Swollen, tortured lower case letters. Unnatural connection between E and t. Ugly g, such as a pretentious, uncultured person might write it. The crossbar of t is too high. Very poor.

Richard: One of the many examples of the foolish desire to connect the first and last letters of a name by means of a contrived line that is meant to be 'organic'. In this case it is the D which is rendered almost illegible as a result.

??ahmann: This should read 'W.Rahmann'. The tail of the R is stiff and too heavy at the end. W and R cannot be merged like this, since the W becomes most unclear. The curve of the R is much too large and seems forced. The lower case letters are mediocre.

Vespa: No feeling for form. The letters are incredibly bad. The insipid line under the word is of no help. Graphologists say that underlining of one's own name means either that the writer fears not to be taken seriously or that he wants to show off.

?aub: Should read as 'Laub'. Very poor Fraktur letters. The L is unclear because the main stroke has been misused to support the rest of the letters. The b is ill conceived and topheavy. The upper strokes of the u and the end strokes of the a and u are too long.

Candidad: Should read 'Candida'. But the first d looks like an a because of its crippled ascender. The white i-dot on the loop looks like a mistake. Although the C is not good, its beginning flourish is genuine. The tail end of the a is too forced. It is a poor attempt at symmetrical design. Symmetrical word images are particularly hard to read.

Armstrong: This A, bad enough as it is, does not lend itself to this kind of elongated stroke. Outmoded, rhythmically poor letters.

Hoover: The crossbar of the H is too low so that the H is not readily recognized. No one, not even a person who writes an H like this, would draw out the crossbar that far to load it with the rest of the letters. These lower case letters are typical of the bloated stiffness of 'modern' logotypes.

Pirelli: The main part of the P is so absurdly elongated that the word becomes almost incomprehensible.

Note. For the typophile the Pirelli logotype is the Elephant Man of Logoworld. However, the distortion grabs attention, a major factor of recognition, and thus is memorable. Recognition and memorability are essential values in commercial visual currency. A nice piece of typography may be welcome but can be irrelevant.

2. Jan Tschichold. *Treasury of Alphabets and Lettering.* Lund Humphries (London 1992)

The marks of the top
1,000 companies in
America can roughly be
categorized as follows :

35 per cent are purely
typographic such as
Kellogg's.

27 per cent are initials
such as IBM.

14 per cent integrate
typography with a graphic
such as Sun.

13 per cent are pictorial
like Shell.

11 per cent are abstract
like Chase Manhattan.

If the client moans and sighs,

make his logo twice the size.

If he still should prove refractory,

show a picture of his factory.

Only in the gravest cases,

should you show your client's faces.

The German Bible Society
commissioned Kurt
Weidemann to design
them a typeface.

He called it Biblica.

It was then marketed
commercially under the
name ITC Weidemann.

The advertising ditty is
printed in that typeface.

The blood and bandages of the medieval surgeon-barber gave the world the striped barber's pole. **Photograph.** Walker Evans. New Orleans 1935

Roland Barthes[1] asserted that the Citroën symbol *'was proceeding from the category of propulsion to that of spontaneous motion, from that of the engine to that of the orgasm.'* When you've got used to that proposition you mightn't be surprised to learn that he also likened the famous Citroën DS model to both Gothic cathedrals and Christ's seamless robe, at the same time disparagingly describing it as *'the very essence of petit-bourgeois advancement'*. This is semioticspeak, but the associations less imaginative people make with symbols can be equally bizarre and even less favourable. The CND* symbol, designed by Gerald Holtom, was derived from the semaphore signal for *'N'* and *'D'*. Well, that's what I always thought, until I read that someone reckons it was based on the typographic insignia of Hitler's 3rd Panzer division. However, it's not the lunatic fringe which are surprising, it's the pressure groups. What is currently termed *'politically correct'*, could on occasion be rephrased *'morally enfeebled'*. What's so offensive about golliwogs? They are a jolly caricature and no more racially

offensive than a podgy John Bull or a spindly Uncle Sam. Nevertheless Robertson's, the British jam company, thought it prudent to drop their golliwog trademark – at least in the United States – and to avoid hassles. So did the publishers of Enid Blyton's children's books who replaced their golliwogs with gnomes. No pressure group from that quarter.

* Campaign for Nuclear Disarmament

1. Roland Barthes. *Mythologies*. Jonathan Cape (London 1972)

Saudia is the national airline of Saudi Arabia and by implication flies the flag of Islam. Muslims are notoriously sensitive about religious symbolism and it only needed someone to pedantically – or mischievously – point out that the white space between the letters S and A formed a cross, for the authorities to order (1981) that the design be changed instantly. If you squint very hard you might spot the cause of the bother.

saudia

with the subliminal cross

saudia

the amended design

The livery of **Swissair** is a white cross on a red ground, and the airline came up against this problem on their Middle East routes. On asking them how they negotiated their way through this situation they sent me this statement: 'through diplomatic channels … it was proven that the logo is a national symbol and cannot be altered or removed from our aeroplanes and offices. We simply do not do business with those who object.'

Procter and Gamble originally sported a logo of 13 stars to symbolize the American colonies. The man in the moon was added when the mark was registered in 1882. One hundred years later in 1982 the company, by now the largest advertiser in the United States, began receiving complaints in that their trademark did not illustrate the man in the moon but a ram and the number 666, both cited in the Book of Revelation as signs of the anti-Christ. Personally I can't see how even a vivid imagination could conjure up a ram, and seeing unholy digits would require an obsessive fantasy. Nevertheless rumours crossed the Atlantic to England and papers were circulated at Baptist meetings with the gnomic suggestion that 'Satan is creeping into your kitchen.' Ironically, the company had always been particularly strait-laced and its first brand name (IVORY SOAP) was even selected from the Bible – from the 45th Psalm. God is next to cleanliness and all that. However, business is business and P&G considered it expedient to stop labelling products with their symbol.

Tutankhamun was buried 3300 years ago with some three dozen jars of wine labelled with vintner, vineyard and year of bottling. Roman bricks were frequently stamped with motifs representing manufacturer, quarry, brickyard, builder, consul and emperor. A pedigree as distinguished as any contemporary vintage wine. The reason was not pride but control. Soapmakers in ancient Rome were fined for selling unbranded soap, and medieval Flemish tapestry workers could have a hand cut off for failing to mark their work. Trademarks have always been a serious business.

The first American trademark was granted in 1870 to the Averill Paint Company – an eagle on a rock (labelled chemistry) holding a can of paint with a claw and brush with its beak. In the background the town complete with factory, river, steamboat, and ringing slogan: *'economical/beautiful/durable'*. The oldest American trademark which is still in use belongs to Samson Cords (1884). The first British trademark [1875] is held by brewers Messrs Bass & Co. A red triangle famous enough to appear among the bottles in a corner of Manet's painting *A Bar at the Folies Bergère.* And one which is still going strong.

The criteria for ownership of product or idea with protection against being copied are more or less the same the world over. In the United States: 'any word, name, symbol or device, or any combination thereof adopted and used by a manufacturer or merchant to identify his goods and distinguish them from those manufactured and sold by others.' In Britain: 'any sign capable of being represented graphically which is capable of distinguishing goods or services of one undertaking from those of other undertakings.' However, registration of three-dimensional things was less clear. In Britain the distinctive shape of the Coca-Cola bottle could not be registered as it was judged functional, whereas the radiator of Rolls-Royce was adjudged to be symbolic and could be registered. New Trade Mark Acts passed in the 1990s now encompass registration for all sorts of things including smells and sounds.

This famous painting has been reversed and in my opinion outflanks copyright as it is not the

same picture as the original, even though you know it's been reversed. Possibly it's a scene

seen by someone looking out of the mirror depicted in the painting. Anyway despite the

reversal left to right and back to front the Bass triangle remains a triangle.

Painting. Image flipped left to right. Edouard Manet. *A Bar at the Folies Bergère*

You can't register descriptive, laudatory, generic or geographical names. Things like 'computer', or pass-offs like 'computa'. You can register an invented name (Kodak), a family name (Hoover) or combination names (Lea and Perrins), a foreign word (Persil, parsley in French), or incongruous names like Harp for beer or Virgin for an airline. Providing, that is, no one else registered it first. You cannot register someone's face, as the charity found out to their chagrin after the death of Princess Diana when they tried to stop tacky souvenir merchandising.

To qualify for registration a device has to look different from marks previously registered. This is tricky. The legal profession thinks in words not pictures and so decisions are based on what a mark looks like, not on how it looks. Justice is represented by a blindfolded lady holding a pair of scales – in these cases blindfolded is the salient factor, not the scales.

The doctrine of intellectual property, the ownership of ideas, is comparatively new. In the convention of his age Handel appropriated and refashioned works by others as his own, but today anyone who writes a tune that shares ten consecutive notes with an existing melody has to give a percentage of their royalties to the original composer.

Back in 1965 changes in international law required trade names to be re-registered. A certain Robert Aries, an expert in commercial poker, and quick to spot an opportunity, appeared one afternoon at the trademark office in Monaco. He registered the names of ICI, St Michael, Celanese, Revlon, de Beers, and some two hundred others. This cost him the equivalent of a dollar apiece. The companies then found out, to their fury, that to continue trading they had to buy their names backs. His big scam was in 1972 when he anticipated Standard Oil's brand name might be changed from Esso to Exxon. He registered Exxon in France which automatically gave him copyright in 22 countries. How much he consequently levered out of Exxon is a guess, but a million dollars is a low estimate. 'We had a lot of fun with that one', laughed Aries, 'we dined in some beautiful restaurants.'[1]

Charles Sykes

The Spirit of Ecstasy, the winged lady of Rolls-Royce which is mounted over the grille, was modelled in 1911 by Eleanor Thornton, a secretary in the company. The sculpture was copyrighted from all angles as a precaution against anyone making replicas facing sideways, backwards or upside down. As three-dimensional objects weren't registrable at the time they registered the photographs instead.

René Lacoste, French tennis star, earned the nickname '*le crocodile*' for winning a crocodile-skin suitcase in a bet. '*A friend drew a crocodile*,' he said, '*and I had it embroidered on the blazer I wore on the courts*.' His polo shirts were launched in 1933 and are probably the first example of sportswear as fashion.

Henry Steiner lives and works in Hong Kong, and took the photograph of this neon sign: '*I believe this is the only non-verbal sign illuminating the waterfront*,' he says. A local garment manufacturer registered this mark in Hong Kong before the famous heretofore mentioned French brand of knitted polo shirts, which also sports an amphibious reptile, albeit facing right. Although the French company owned their emblem they were enjoined from selling in the territory until the owner of the pictured brand struck a deal with his erstwhile competitor allowing both of the embroidered saurians to be marketed in harmony.

1. Profile by Marjorie Wallace. *Sunday Times*, 8 June 1980. **Photograph.** Henry Steiner

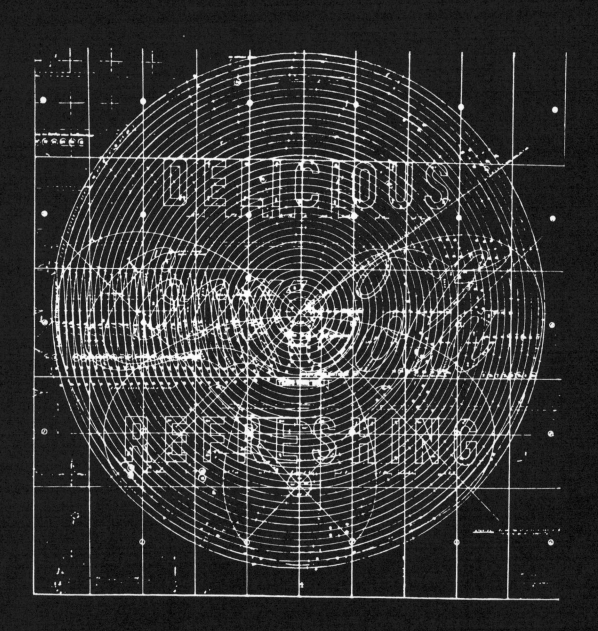

Anti-monopoly. Trademarks, patents, copyrights and intellectual property can be bought, sold, leased and mortgaged. Indeed they can be of more value than the tangible assets which appear on the Annual Report's balance sheet. In 1988 Rank Hovis McDougall, one of Britain's largest companies at the time, decided to list its brand names as assets. At a stroke the balance sheet increased from £250 million to £928 million. The brands had more value than the products and factories that made them. The value of **Coca-Cola**'s logo was estimated by subtracting the company assets from the capitalization: the calculation revealed that the logo was worth $13 billion. Not surprisingly, corporations are nervous of losing rights to names or brands but the danger isn't from pirates, but language. The problem arises when the brand name becomes the general name of the thing or activity – like **hoover**. That is to say when brand names appear printed in lower-case letters without a capital. This is the fatal moment when they legally pass from being names of things, to descriptions of what those things did or do. Thus passing into everyday language and thus becoming public property. This happened to **cellophane** when the courts judged it to be the name of the material rather than the brand. The result meant Du Pont lost exclusive rights to the brand name. Other casualties include **aspirin, escalator, kerosene, lanolin, zipper, yo-yo, linoleum, thermos, milk of magnesia** and **shredded wheat**. Even **Monopoly** lost its monopoly. In 1982, after 47 years and 85 million sales, the law ruled that Parker Brothers who owned the game must share the name. The successful action was brought by economics professor Ralph Anspach, who had invented **Anti-monopoly**, a game in which trust-busters seek to break up the multinationals.

This template was issued by Coca Cola to ensure display signs followed the correct proportions of the registered mark. Deviations could give rise to claims by competitors that the logo was not unique, therefore not exclusive, and in consequence public property and freely available for use by anyone.

'Journalists only have to print the word coke, xerox or something similar, without a capital letter, to cause a small explosion and the arrival of a guided missive urging you to respect the trademark which has been fully registered against idiots like you. Does coca-cola have teams of readers scanning the public prints for mistakes? It sometimes seems to – unless the coke people are alerted by a central body of all-purpose spies. This once irked me enough to print a list in *Punch* magazine of fifty trade names, all with lower-case letters and all with new meanings. paraquat, for instance, I defined as a small tropical bird. quink, I revealed was the noise made by a paraquat. I sat back and waited for fifty furious letters. All I got was a polite request from a journal of trademarks for permission to reprint the piece.'

Miles Kington

the logotype business The *Guardian*[1] newspaper reports that a logotype is more than a fancy way of writing your name: 'It is just 10cm wide, barely enough for a decent company logo. But this modest portion of Michael Schumacher's baseball cap yesterday became one of the most expensive pieces of real estate in sports advertising when a German company [DVAG] paid the Formula One star more than £5m for the privilege of squeezing its badge on to it for three years.'

In 1999 DVAG [a boring name – they should hide it, not advertise it] joined Marlboro, Shell, Bridgestone and Federal Express in Ferrari's Formula One sponsorship portfolio. I assume DVAG have a decent logotype to grace the space, otherwise they're wasting a lot of money. 'There's nothing to worry about there,' a company spokeswomen replied when questioned on this point, 'We're quite sure everyone will be able to read it.' Well, I would think so. But will they remember it?

In addition to lodging the name in the mind a logotype can become synonymous with the image with which it is associated. Glamour, sophistication, *machismo* or whatever. Our brand choices say a great deal about us as individuals, promising authenticity and reliability, offering technological empowerment or a luxurious lifestyle. [SEE P328]. Are you more Gucci than Nike? Few companies take advantage of this commercial potential, but those that do guard their logos fiercely.

Protecting the reputation of brands from shoddy imitations is gleefully described by trademark agents as a jungle. These days the visitor's impression of the Far East isn't palm trees, pink gin and sunsets, but wall-to-wall imitation *Gucci* bags, *Cartier* watches, and *Dunhill* lighters. The third world strikes back. Actually it's lucrative for everyone: the companies being ripped off generate revenue through successful legal action, there is quick money for shady operators, and kudos on the cheap for customers. *Cartier* even acquired free worldwide publicity by covering a Paris street with imitation watches and trundling over them with a steamroller.

It sort of all began in the 1920s when farmers began to wear *International Harvester* caps and truck drivers sported *Peterbilt* belt buckles. The first product to be licensed was probably the Mickey Mouse watch launched in 1933. The *Lacoste* crocodile was probably the first trademark to actually become a worldwide cult symbol. [SEE PP335, 518].

Symbols are open to hijack. In the 1980s *Mercedes* fell victim to fans of a rock group who adopted the symbol as a fashion accessory. The company had to run an emergency service for outraged car owners who had had badges stolen. And less amusingly, a certain Carl Marcus (wrote the *Herald Tribune*), fumbling for the keys to his *Rolls* in Beverly Hills, felt the cold steel of a gun against his head. A voice behind him announced: 'It's *Rolex* time, mother.' He handed it over. At the time a *Rolex* could cost anything from $1,000 for the utility stainless steel version to telephone numbers for one smothered in diamonds. As a *Rolex* executive commented, our product is 'the symbol for the *nouveau riche*. They're big, they're chunky, and from Afghanistan to Zaire everyone knows *Rolex* – it's one of the best-known words in the world.' He's right, street value is based on *cachet* more than price.

'A trademark printed on a raw egg yolk by a no-contact, no-pressure printing technique,' prophesied Marshall McLuhan in the 1960s, 'Imagine the possibilities to which this device will give birth!'

An American financier told me that his hobbies were his polo ponies and three Harley-Davidsons. You have to mix in the right sort of company to get this kind of information.
He then went on to confide that the last time he'd been in London he visited a smart shop in Jermyn Street where they stitch monograms on slippers.
He ordered a pair to be embroidered with the Harley-Davidson symbol. He'd brought the badge with him and, handing it over, said, 'Bet you don't get many requests for this one.' 'No, we don't', replied the man behind the counter courteously, 'only had a couple this month.'

1. Alan Henry, *The Guardian*, 16 November 1999

Would you pay £5 million for this patch?

Written by a bereaved Italian lady, this letter has a thick black border which, custom dictated, diminished each successive year. Writing in both directions to save paper was also common in Victorian England. Judging from the date on the envelope's postmark it persisted in Italy rather longer.

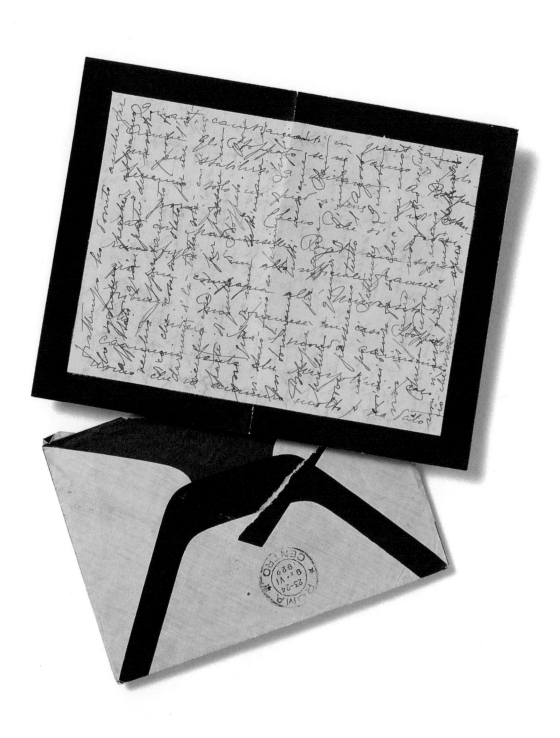

Plato   'Writing is the geometry of the soul.'

Roland Barthes: 'Writing is not only a technical process; it is also a joyous physical experience.'

'Ts'ang Kie cried during the night: he really had something to cry about.' [Ts'ang Kie, legendary inventor of writing]

Victorian advertising slogan: 'They came as a boon and a blessing to men. The Pickwick, the Owl, and the Waverley Pen.'

Paul Steinberg: 'I draw because the essence of a good piece of writing is precision. Drawing is a very precise mode of expression.'

The moving finger writes;   and having writ,

A talisman can be protective, preventive, evocative, curative. Taoist drawings are a secret writing which influences supernatural forces, or looked at in another way, diagrams the cartography of superstition. The calligraphic gesture illustrated here establishes contact with the Spirits of Earth and Wind through the Spirits of the Five Chinese Emperors – at least, at the moment of rendering. If you have need of their assistance you write, then burn the paper in front of the altar and mutter an incantation of eight words. I don't know which words, but maybe they're not important. Anyway there you go.

Moves on: nor all thy piety   nor wit

Among primitive peoples it seemed miraculous that a dead person could speak from the past. Not surprisingly writing was endowed with magical powers. One cunning Aramaic incantation was written on the inside of a bowl as a spiral and kept outside the house as protection against evil spirits. The spirits read until they reached the centre – here they were trapped as they couldn't read backwards. Ancient Egyptians wrapped their corpses in texts to help them through to the next world. One ancient Greek amulet optimistically carried an inscription: 'Flee Gout, Perseus is chasing you!' Siamese tattooed themselves with words to make them bulletproof. Tibetans wouldn't destroy paper which carried writing.

Shall lure it back to cancel   half a line,

Even today the Berber medicine-man writes a potion in a bowl, fills it with water and then gives it to the sick. And the power conferred by the written word still holds sway in Leicester:[1] 'Thousands of Muslims are travelling to a terrace house in the back streets of Leicester to see what is claimed to be a miraculous *aubergine*.' I am quoting from an article in *The Guardian* newspaper, 'Farida Kassam asks visitors to take off their shoes as a mark of respect for the sliced vegetable, exhibited in a bowl of white vinegar in her front room. Beside it is a plate bearing the inscription YAH-ALLAH in Arabic, meaning Allah is everywhere. Mrs Kassam, aged thirty, proudly points out that the unusual seed pattern inside the aubergine appears to match the Arabic writing. The discovery has fulfilled the faithful and confounded the curious, who have flocked to inspect the evidence. A magnifying glass has thoughtfully been provided. Mrs Kassam said: "It is a miracle. This has happened to an ordinary family, that is why I am very proud of it. Allah never forgets anybody. We will preserve the aubergine as long as we can and then bury it in holy ground."'

Nor all thy tears wash out   a word of it.

Such manifestations are not exclusive to Taoists and Muslims. Catholics also tend to find HAIL MARY written in weird places. [SEE P208].

Omar Khayyám. *Rubaiyat*   1. *The Guardian*, 28 March 1990